Lecture Notes in Computer Science 4186

Commenced Publication in 1973
Founding and Former Series Editors:
Gerhard Goos, Juris Hartmanis, and Jan van Leeuwen

T0189814

Chris Jesshope   Colin Egan (Eds.)

Advances in Computer Systems Architecture

11th Asia-Pacific Conference, ACSAC 2006
Shanghai, China, September 6-8, 2006
Proceedings

Springer

Volume Editors

Chris Jesshope
University of Amsterdam, Informatics Institute, School of Computer Science
Kruislaan 403, 1098 SJ Amsterdam, The Netherlands
E-mail: jesshope@science.uva.nl

Colin Egan
University of Hertfordshire, School of Computer Science
College Lane, Hatfield, Hertfordshire AL10 9AB, UK
E-mail: c.egan@herts.ac.uk

Library of Congress Control Number: 2006931938

CR Subject Classification (1998): B.2, B.4, B.5, C.2, C.1, D.4

LNCS Sublibrary: SL 1 – Theoretical Computer Science and General Issues

ISSN   0302-9743
ISBN-10   3-540-40056-7 Springer Berlin Heidelberg New York
ISBN-13   978-3-540-40056-1 Springer Berlin Heidelberg New York

Springer is a part of Springer Science+Business Media

springer.com

© Springer-Verlag Berlin Heidelberg 2006

Typesetting: Camera-ready by author, data conversion by Scientific Publishing Services, Chennai, India
Printed on acid-free paper   SPIN: 11859802   06/3142   5 4 3 2 1 0

Preface

On behalf of all of the people involved in the program selection, the program committee members as well as numerous other reviewers, we are both relieved and pleased to present you with the proceedings of the 2006 Asia-Pacific Computer Systems Architecture Conference (ACSAC 2006), which is being hosted in Shanghai on September 6–8, 2006.

This is the 11th in a series of conferences, which started life in Australia, as the computer architecture component of the Australian Computer Science Week. In 1999 it ventured away from its roots for the first time, and the fourth Australasian Computer Architecture Conference was held in the beautiful city of Sails (Auckland, New Zealand). Perhaps it was because of a lack of any other computer architecture conference in Asia or just the attraction of traveling to the Southern Hemisphere but the conference became increasingly international during the subsequent three years and also changed its name to include Computer Systems Architecture, reflecting more the scope of the conference, which embraces both architectural and systems issues. In 2003, the conference again ventured offshore to reflect its constituency and since then has been held in Japan in the beautiful city of Aizu-Wakamatsu, followed by Beijing and Singapore. This year it again returns to China and next year will move to Korea for the first time, where it will be organized by the Korea University.

To understand the scope and constituency of the conference, papers have been submitted from China, Taiwan, Korea, Japan, Australia, the UK, the Netherlands, Brazil, the USA, Norway, Sweden, Iran, Cyprus, India and Romania with the majority of papers coming from the Asia-Pacific region. The scope of the conference can be gleaned by looking at the diversity of submissions, which include papers on processor and network design, reconfigurable computing and operating systems, including both low-level design issues in hardware and systems as well as papers describing large and significant computer-based infrastructure projects. In keeping with the trends in this field, many of the papers that reflect the changing nature of computing systems and the constraints that the industry is working under. For example, there are many papers that reflect the move to concurrency on chip in multi-core devices, and many more are concerned with the significant problems industry will face with stricter budgets in power dissipation.

In addition to the submitted papers we have three keynote presentations. These presentations reflect the changing aspects of our industry as described above. Guang R. Gao, who is the Distinguished Professor of Electrical and Computer Engineering at Delaware University, will give a presentation on his work in programming chip multiprocessors and other highly concurrent systems. Gao's research is closely linked to IBM's recently announced cell processor, and he is developing compilers that enable thousands of processors to work together smoothly and efficiently by dividing various tasks among them. This work is conducted through the Computer Architecture and Parallel Systems Laboratory (CAPSL). Our second keynote speaker is from Europe and represents a key company in the embedded computer systems area. Vladimir Vasekin is a Russian Computer Scientist who was recruited by ARM Ltd. in 2003. He started his career working in the Kronos Research Group at Novosibirsk University, developing the first 32-bit Russian workstations. While at ARM he has been involved in extensions to the ARM V6 architecture as well as in optimizing power dissipation in systems on chip. Our final invited speaker is Alex Shafarenko, who is professor of Software Engineering at the University of Hertfordshire in the UK and coordinator of the Compiler Technology and Computer Architecture Research Group (CTCA). Shafarenko is undertaking pioneering work in strongly-typed languages for coordinating concurrency in an asynchronous distributed environment.

Finally we would like to thank all of those who worked hard to make ACSAC 2006 a success this year. This includes all of the authors for submitting their work and the program committee and reviewers, without whose significant effort in producing reviews by our deadlines, we would have been unable to put this conference program together. Finally we thank the other General Chairs, Minglu Li of Shanghai Jiao Tong University and Minyi Guo from the University of Aizu for their effort in managing the conference arrangements and last and by no means least, Feilong Tang, also from Shanghai Jiao Tong University, who was in charge of local arrangements.

June 2006   Chris Jesshope
                                                                Colin Egan

Organization

General Chairs

Chris Jesshope   University of Amsterdam, Netherlands
Minglu Li   Shanghai Jia Tong University, China
Minyi Guo   University of Aizu, Japan

Program Chair

Colin Egan   University of Hertfordshire, UK

Local Arrangements Chair

Feilong Tang   Shanghai Jia Tong University, China

Program Committee

Vijayan Asari   Old Dominion University, Norfolk, VA, USA
Lim Hock Beng   National University of Singapore
Sangyeun Cho   University of Pittsburgh, USA
Lynn Choi   Korea University Seoul, South Korea
Bruce Christianson   University of Hertfordshire, UK
Oliver Diessel   University of New South Wales, Australia
Colin Egan   University of Hertfordshire, UK
Skevos Evripidou   University of Cyprus, Cyprus
Michael Freeman   University of York, UK
Guang G. Gao   CAPSL, University of Delaware, USA
Jean-Luc Gaudiot   University of California, Irvine, USA
Alex Gontmakher   Technion, Israel
Minyi Guo   Aizu University, Japan
Gernot Heiser   National ICT, Australia
Wei-Chung Hsu   University of Minnesota, Twin-Cities, USA
Chris Jesshope   University of Amsterdam, Netherlands
Hong Jiang   University of Nebraska-Lincoln, USA
Jeremy Jones   Trinity College, Dublin, Ireland
Norman P. Jouppi   Hewlett Packard, USA
Feipei Lai   National Technological University, Walden, USA
Minglu Li   Shanghai Jiao Tong University, China
Philip Machanick   University of Queensland, Australia
Worawan Marurngsith   Thammasat University, Bangkok, Thailand
Henk Muller   University of Bristol, UK
Sukumar Nandi   Indian Institute of Technology Guwahati, India
Tin-Fook Ngai   Intel China Research Center, China

Amos Omondi   Yonsei University, Seoul, South Korea
L M Patnaik   Indian Institute of Science, Bangalore, India
Andy Pimentel   University of Amsterdam, Netherlands
Ronald Pose   Monash University, Australia
Stanislav G. Sedukhin   The University of Aizu, Japan
Won Shim   SNUT, South Korea
Mark Smotherman   Clemson University, USA
K. Sridharan   Indian Institute of Technology Madras, India
Paul Stravers   Philips Research, Netherlands
Feilong Tang   Shanghai Jiao Tong University, China
Rajeev Thakur   Argonne National Laboratory, USA
Mateo Valero   Technical University of Catalonia, Spain
Stamatis Vassiliadis   University of Delft, Netherlands
Lucian N. Vintan   "Lucian Blaga" University of Sibiu, Romania
Tanya Vladimirova   University of Surrey, UK
Wong Weng Fai   National University of Singapore, Singapore
Chengyong Wu   Chinese Academy of Sciences, China
Jingling Xue   University of New England, Armidale, Australia
Pen-Chung Yew   University of Minnesota, Twin-Cities, USA

Co-reviewers

Ahmed Zekri   Manvi Agarwal
Andrei Terechko   Marc Daumas
Antonia Zhai   Marios Mavronicolas
Arun Arvind   Michael Hicks
Cees de Laat   Murali Vilayannur
Costas Kyriacou   Patrick (Boggle) Quick
Daniel Rolls   Pavlos Moraitis
Dmitry Cheresiz   Pedro Trancoso
Herman ter Horst   Peter Tische
Huiyang Zhou   Rajkumar Kettimuthu
Hyunjin Lee   Ramón Beivide
James A. Malcolm   Renato Hentschke
Jason Holdsworth   Rob Latham
Jason McGuiness   Sam Lang
Jinpyo Kim   Sanghoon Lee
Joe Ryan   Shaoshan Liu
Kanad Chakraborty   Thomas Bernard
Kim Marshall   Toshiaki Miyazaki
Kyueun Yi   Venkatesan Packirisamy
Lei Jin   Won Woo Ro
Lian Li   Yuichi Okuyama
Long Chen   Zhi-Li Zhang
Lotfi Mhamdi

Table of Contents

The Era of Multi-core Chips -A Fresh Look on Software Challenges

Guang R. Gao

Endowed Distinguished Professor
Dept. of Electrical and Computer Engineering
University of Delaware
ggao@capsl.udel.edu

Abstract. In the past few months, the world has witnessed the impressive pace that the microprocessor chip vendors' switching to multi-core chip technology. However, this is preventing steep software challenges – both in the migration of application software and in the adaptation of system software.

In this talk, we discuss the challenges as well as opportunities facing software technology in the era of the emerging multi-core chips. We review the software effort failures and lessons learned during the booming years on parallel computing – in the 80s and early 90s, and analyze the issues and challenges today when we are once more trying to explore large-scale parallelism on multi-core chips and systems. We then predict major technology innovations that should be made in order to assure a success this time.

This talk will begin with a discussion based on our own experience on working with fine-grain multithreading from execution/architecture models, system software technology, and relevant application software studies in the past decade. We then outline our recent experience in working on software issues for the next generation multi-core chip architectures. We will present a case study on a mapping of OpenMP on two representative classes of future multi-core architecture models. We discuss several fundamental performance issues facing system software designers.

C. Jesshope and C. Egan (Eds.): ACSAC 2006, LNCS 4186, p. 1, 2006.
© Springer-Verlag Berlin Heidelberg 2006

Streaming Networks for Coordinating Data-Parallel Programs (Position Statement)

Alex Shafarenko

Compiler Technology and Computer Architecture Group, University of Hertfordshire,
United Kingdom
A.Shafarenko@herts.ac.uk

Abstract. A new coordination language for distributed data-parallel programs is presented, call SNet. The intention of SNet is to introduce advanced structuring techniques into a coordination language: stream processing and various forms of subtyping. The talk will present the organisation of SNet, its major type inferencing algorithms and will briefly discuss the current state of implementation and possible applications.

Process concurrency is difficult to deal with in the framework of a programming language. If properly integrated into the language semantics, it complicates and often completely destroys the properties that enable the kind of profound optimisations that make compilation of computational programs so efficient. One solution to this problem, which is the solution that this talk will present, is the use of so-called coordination languages. A coordination language uses a readily-available computation language as a basis, and extends it with a certain communication/synchronisation mechanism thus allowing a distributed program to be written in a purely extensional manner. The first coordination language proposed was Linda[Gel85, GC92], which extended C with a few primitives that looked like function calls and could even be implemented directly as such. However an advanced implementation of Linda would involve program analysis and transformation in order to optimise communication and synchronisation patterns beyond the obvious semantics of the primitives. Further coordination languages have been proposed, many on them extensional in the same way, some not; for the state of the art, see a survey in [PA98] and the latest Coordination conference [JP05].

The emphasis of coordination languages is usually on event management, while the data aspect of distributed computations is not ordinarily focused on. This has a disadvantage in that the structuring aspect, software reuse and component technology are not primary goals of coordination. It is our contention that structuring is key in making coordination-based distributed programming practically useful. In this talk we describe several structuring solutions, which have been laid in the foundation of the coordination language SNet. The language was introduced as a concept in [Sha03]; the complete definition, including semantics and the type system, is available as a technical report [Sha06].

The approach proposed in SNet is based on streaming networks. The application as a whole is represented as a set of self-contained components, called

C. Jesshope and C. Egan (Eds.): ACSAC 2006, LNCS 4186, pp. 2–5, 2006.
© Springer-Verlag Berlin Heidelberg 2006

"boxes" (SNetis not extensional) written in a data-parallel language. SNet deals with boxes by combining them into networks which can be encapsulated as further boxes. The structuring instruments used are as follows:

- Streams. Instead of arbitrary communication, data is packaged into typed variant records that flow in a sequence from their producer to a single consumer.
- Single-Input, Single-Output(SISO) box and network configuration. Multiple connections are, of course, possible and necessary. The unique feature of SNet is that the multiplicity of connection is handled by SNet combinators so that a box sees a single stream of records coming in. The records are properly attributed to their sources by using types (which include algebraic types, or tagged, disjoint unions). Similarly, the production of a single stream of typed records by a box does not preclude the output separation into several streams according to the type outside the box perimeter.
- Network construction using structural combinators. The network is presented as an expression in the algebra of four major combinators (and a small variety of ancillary constructs): serial (pipelined) composition, parallel composition, infinite serial replication (closure) and infinite parallel replication (called index splitter, as the input is split between the replicas according to an "index" contained in data records). We will show that this small nomenclature of tools is sufficient to construct an arbitrary streaming network.
- Record subtyping. Data streams consist of flat records, whose fields are drawn from a linear hierarchy of array subtypes[Sha02, SS04]. The records as wholes are subtyped since the boxes accept records with extra fields and allow the producer to supply fewer variants than the consumer has the ability to recognise.
- Flow inheritance. Due to subtyping, the boxes may receive more fields in a record than they recognise. In such circumstances flow inheritance causes the extra fields to be saved and then appended to all output records produced in response to a given input one[1]. Flow inheritance enables very flexible pipelining since, on the one hand, a component does not need to be aware of the exact composition of data records that it receives as long as it receives sufficient fields for the processing it is supposed to do; and on the other, the extra data are not lost but passed further down the pipeline that the components may be connected by.
- Record synchronizers. These are similar to I-structures known from dataflow programming. SNet synchronisers are typed SISO boxes that expect two records of certain types and produce a joint record. No other synchronisation mechanism exists in SNet, and no synchronisation capability is required of the user-defined boxes.
- The concept of network feedback in the form of a closure operator. This connects replicas of a box in a (conceptually) infinite chain, with the input

---

[1] This is a conceptual view; in practice the data fields are routed directly to their consumers, thanks to the complete inferability of type in SNet.

data flowing to the head of the chain and the output data being extracted on the basis of fixed-point recognition. The main innovation here is the proposal of a type-defined fixed point (using flow inheritance as a statically recognisable mechanism), and the provision of an efficient type-inference algorithm. As a result, SNet has no named channels (in fact, no explicit channels at all) and the whole network can be defined as a single expression in a certain combinator algebra.

The talk will address the following issues. We will first give an overview of stream processing pointing out the history of early advances [Kah74, AW77, HCRP91], the semantic theory [BS01] and the recent languages [Mic02]. Then the concepts of SNet will be introduced, focusing in turn on: overall organisation and combinators, type system and inference algorithms, concurrency and synchronisation, and the binding for a box language. Finally a sketch of a complete application in the area of plasma simulation using the particle-in-cell method will be provided.

Work is currently underway to implement SNet as a coordination language for a large EU-sponsored Integrated Project named "EATHER" [Pro], which is part of the Framework VI Advanced Computing Architecture Initiative. University of Hertfordshire is coordinating the software side of the project; if time permits, the talk will touch upon the progress achieved to date.

References

[AW77]   E. A. Ashcroft and W. W. Wadge. Lucid, a nonprocedural language with iteration. *Communications of the ACM*, 20(7):519–526, 1977.

[BS01]   M Broy and G Stefanescu. The algebra of stream processing functions. *Theoretical Computer Science*, (258):99–129, 2001.

[GC92]   D Gelernter and N Carriero. Coordination languages and their significance. *Communications of the ACM*, 35(2):96–107, Feb. 1992.

[Gel85]   David Gelernter. Generative communication in linda. *ACM Trans Program. Lang Syst.*, 1(7):80–112, 1985.

[HCRP91]   N. Halbwachs, P. Caspi, P. Raymond, and D. Pilaud. The synchronous data-flow programming language LUSTRE. *Proceedings of the IEEE*, 79(9):1305–1320, September 1991.

[JP05]   Jean-Marie Jacquet and Gian Pietro Picco, editors. *Coordination Models and Languages. 7th International Conference, COORDINATION 2005, Namur, Belgium, April 20-23, 2005*, volume 3454 of *Proceedings Series: Lecture Notes in Computer Science, Vol. 3454 Jacquet, Jean-Marie; Picco, Gian Pietro (Eds.) 2005, X, 299 p., Softcover Lecture Notes in Computer Science*. Springer Verlag, 2005.

[Kah74]   G Kahn. The semantics of a simple language for parallel programming. In L Rosenfeld, editor, *Information Processing 74, Proc. IFIP Congress 74. August 5-10, Stockholm, Sweden*, pages 471–475. North-Holland, 1974.

[Mic02]   Michael I. Gordon et al. A stream compiler for communication-exposed architectures. In *Proceedings of the Tenth International Conference on Architectural Support for Programming Languages and Operating Systems, San Jose, CA. October 2002*, 2002.

[PA98]   G A Papadopoulos and F Arbab. Coordination models and languages. In
          Advances in Computers, volume 46. Academic Press, 1998.
[Pro]   The AETHER Project. http://aetherist.free.fr/Joomla/index.php.
[Sha02]   Alex Shafarenko. Coercion as homomorphism: type inference in a system
          with subtyping and overloading. In *PPDP '02: Proceedings of the 4th
          ACM SIGPLAN international conference on Principles and practice of
          declarative programming*, pages 14–25, 2002.
[Sha03]   Alex Shafarenko. Stream processing on the grid: an array stream trans-
          forming language. In *SNPD*, pages 268–276, 2003.
[Sha06]   Alex Shafarenko. Snet: definition and the main algorithms. Technical
          report, Department of Computer Science, 2006.
[SS04]   Alex Shafarenko and Sven-Bodo Scholz. General homomorphic overload-
          ing. In *Implemntation and Application of Functional Languages. 16th
          International Workshop, IFL 2004, Lübeck, Germany, September 2004.
          Revised Selected Papers.*, LNCS'3474, pages 195–210. Springer Verlag,
          2004.

Implementations of Square-Root and Exponential Functions for Large FPGAs

Mariusz Bajger[1] and Amos R. Omondi[2]

[1] School of Informatics and Engineering
Flinders University, Bedford Park, SA 5042, Australia
[2] School of Electrical and Electronic Engineering
Yonsei University, Seoul, Korea
Mariusz.Bajger@flinders.edu.au, amos@yonsei.ac.kr

Abstract. This paper discusses low-error, high-speed evaluation of two elementary functions: square-root (which is required in IEEE-754 standard on computer arithmetic) and exponential (which is common in scientific calculations). The basis of the proposed implementations is piecewise-linear interpolation but with the constants chosen in a way that minimizes relative error. We show that by placing certain constraints on the errors at three points within each interpolation interval, relative errors are greatly reduced. The implementation-targets are large FPGAs that have in-built multipliers, adders, and distributed memory.

1 Introduction

Many techniques exist for evaluating elementary functions: polynomial approximations, CORDIC algorithms, rational approximations, table-driven methods, and so forth [1], [2]. For hardware implementation, accuracy, performance and cost are all important. The latter two mean that many of the better techniques that have been developed in numerical analysis (and implemented in software) are not suitable for hardware implementation. CORDIC is perhaps the most studied technique for hardware implementation. Its primary merits are that the same hardware can be used for several functions, but, because of its iterative nature, its performance is rather poor. High-order polynomial approximations can give low-error implementations, but are generally not suitable for hardware implementation, because of the number of arithmetic operations (multiplications and additions) that must be performed for each value; either much hardware must be used, or performance be compromised. And a similar remark applies to pure table-driven methods, unless the tables are quite small: large tables will be both slow and costly. The practical implication of these constraints is that many of the better techniques that have been developed in numerical analysis, and which are easily implemented in software, are not suitable for hardware implementation.

C. Jesshope and C. Egan (Eds.): ACSAC 2006, LNCS 4186, pp. 6–23, 2006.

Given trends in technology, it is apparent that at present the best technique for hardware function-evaluation is a combination of low-order polynomials and small look-up tables. This is the case for both ASIC and FPGA technologies, especially for the latter, in which current large devices (such as the Xilinx Virtex [5], [6]) are equipped with substantial amounts of distributed memory as well as many arithmetic units (notably mulipliers and adders).[1] The combination of low-order polynomials (primarily linear ones) is not new – the main challenges has always been one of how to choose the best interpolation points and how to ensure that look-up tables remain small.

For most elementary functions, interpolation with uniformly-sized intervals (i.e. uniformly-spaced abscissae) is not ideal. Nevertheless, for hardware implementation, the need to quickly map arguments onto the appropriate intervals dictates the use of such intervals. With this choice and linear interpolation, the critical issue then becomes that of what function-value to associate with each interval. The most common choice has been to arbitrarily select the value at the midpoint of the interval — that is, if $x \in [L, U]$, then $f(x) = f((L+U)/2)$ — or to choose a value that minimizes absolute errors.[2] Neither is particularly good: as we shall show, even with a fixed number of intervals, the best function-value for an interval is generally not the midpoint. And, depending on the "curvature" of the function at hand, relative error may be more critical than absolute error. For the functions we consider, the effect of a given value of absolute error is not constant or linear, and therefore the relative error is more critical than the absolute error.

The rest of the paper is organized as follows. Section 2 gives a brief overview of the Xilinx Virtex-4 FPGA. Section 3 outlines the general approach that we use in the function approximation, and the next two sections, the main parts of the paper, corespond to each of the two functions. Section 5 is a discussion of the results we obtained. And Section 6 is a concluding summary.

2   Xilinx Virtex-4 FPGA

As indicated above, our primary target is large FPGAs. The structure of such devices makes them particularly well suited to low-order polynomial approximations: the devices have in-built (and reasonably wide) adders and multipliers, as well as relatively large amounts of memory. Moreover, the arrangement of the arithmetic units is eminently suited to the multiply-then-add sequence that is required in polynomial approximations. In this section, we shall briefly give the details of a current FPGA device, the Xilinx Virtex-4, that is typical of such state-of-the-art FPGA devices. We also indicate how its structure is well-suited to piecewise-linear interpolation.

---

[1] This is validated by a recent study of FPGA implementations of various techniques [3].

[2] Following [4], we use *absolute error* to refer to the difference between the exact value and its approximation; that is, it is not the absolute value of that difference.

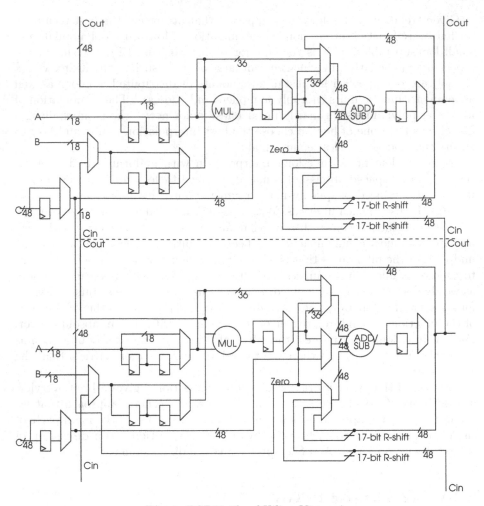

Fig. 1. DSP48 tile of Xilinx Virtex-4

The Virtex-4 is actually a family of devices with many common features but with variations in speed, logic-capacity, and so forth. A Virtex-4 device consists of an array of up to 192×116 *tiles* (in generic FPGA terms, two tiles form a CLB), up to 1392 Kb of *Distributed-RAM*, up to 9936 Kb of *Block-RAM* (arranged in 18-Kb blocks), up to 2 PowerPC 405 processors, up to 512 *Xtreme DSP slices* for arithmetic, several Input/Ouput blocks, and so forth [18, 19]. There are currently 17 devices in the family:

- eight LX devices, optimized for logic intensive applications;
- three SX devices, optimized for embedded applications; and
- six FX devices, optimized for digital-signal-processing applications.

Table 1 gives the parameters for typical members (the largest) of each class. Observe that many neural-network computations are DSP-like, and, therefore, the FX class may be taken as the ideal target.

Table 1. Xilinx Virtex-4 devices

Device	Logic Slices	Distr. RAM (Kb)	XDSP Slices	Block RAM (Kb)	Power PC
XC4VLX200	89,088	1,392	96	6,048	0
XC4VSX55	24,576	384	512	5,760	0
XC4VFX140	63,168	987	192	9,936	2

A tile is made of two Xtreme DSP48 slices that together consist of eight function-generators (configured as 4-bit lookup tables capable of realizing any four-input boolean function), eight flip-flops, two fast carry-chains, 64 bits of Distributed-RAM, and 64-bits of shift register. There are two types of slices: SLICEM, which consists of logic, Distributed RAM, and shift registers, and SLICEL, which consists of logic only. Figure 3 shows the basic elements of a tile. (For ease of visual presentation, we have not shown the memory elements.) Since the approximation scheme we use is based on linear interpolation, Distributed RAM is not suitable for the storage of the required constants, unless there is only a small number of such constants and they are of low precision. Block RAM should therefore be used for such storage.

Blocks of the Block-RAM are true dual-ported and are reconfigurable to various widths and depths (from $16K \times 1$ to 512×36); this memory lies outside the slices but operates at the same high speed. Distributed RAM is located inside the slices and is nominally single-port but can be configured for dual-port operation. The PowerPC processor core is of 32-bit Harvard architecture, implemented as a 5-stage pipeline. The significance of this last unit is in relation to the serial parts of even highly parallel applications — one cannot live by parallelism alone. The maximum clock rate for all of the units above is 500 MHz.

Arithmetic functions in the Virtex-4 fall into one of two main categories: arithmetic within a tile and arithmetic within a collection of slices; the latter is necessary for high-precision computations. All the slices together make up what is called the *XtremeDSP*. DSP48 slices are optimized for multipliy, add, and mutiply-add operations. There are 512 DSP48 slices in the largest Virtex-4 device, organized in two-slice tiles (Figure 1). Each slice consists primarily of an 18-bit×18-bit multiplier (with sign-extension of the result to 48 bits), a 48-bit adder/subtractor, multiplexers, registers, and so forth. Given the importance of inner-product computations, it is the XtremeDSP that is here most crucial for neural-network applications. With 512 DSP48 slices operating at a peak rate of 500 MHz, a maximum performance of 256 Giga-MACs (multiply-accumulate operations) per second is possible. (As an aside, observe that this is well beyond anything that has so far been offered by way of a custom ASIC neurocomputer.)

The scheme we describe below is based on piecewise linear interpolation; that is, the basic approximation function is $\widehat{f} = c_1 + c_2 x$, for some constants c_1 and c_2. So the structure of Figure 1 is naturally suitable. Also, while it might appear that for low-precision outputs, and given the relatively large amounts of memory in the Virtex-4, a pure table-lookup approach might be better, that is not so: That might be an important consideration in ASIC technology, because it eliminates the need for a multiplier and an adder, but there is no advantage gained if these arithmetic units are already available. We shall below return briefly to this point.

3   Basic Approach

The general approach we take is as follows. Let $I = [L, U]$ be a real interval with $L < U$ and let $f : I \rightarrow \mathbf{R}$ be a function to be approximated (where $\mathbf{R}$ denotes the set of real numbers). Suppose that $\widehat{f} : I \rightarrow \mathbf{R}$ is a linear function — that is, $\widehat{f}(x) = c_1 + c_2 x$, for some constants c_1 and c_2 — that approximates f. Our objective is to investigate the relative-error function

$$\varepsilon(x) = \frac{f(x) - \widehat{f}(x)}{f(x)}, \quad x \in I, \tag{1}$$

and to find c_1 and c_2 such that $\varepsilon(x)$ is small. One way to obtain reasonably good values for c_1, c_2 is to impose the condition

$$f(L) = \widehat{f}(L), \quad f(U) = \widehat{f}(U) \tag{C}$$

to calculate c_1 and c_2. As we shall show, a much better result can be obtained using the "improved" condition

$$|\varepsilon(L)| = |\varepsilon(U)| = |\varepsilon(x_{stat})|, \tag{IC}$$

where x_{stat} (stationary point) is the value of x for which $\varepsilon(x)$ has a local extremum.

An example of the use of this technique to approximate reciprocals can be found in [2], the approximation of the reciprocal function. (The second and third columns of Tables 1 and 2 show the differences between the direct reduction of the relative error, i.e. our approach, and reduction of the relative error via reduction in the absolute error.) We will study each of the three functions seperately and in each case show that, compared with the results from using the condition (C), the improved condition (IC) yields a massive 50% reduction in the magnitude of the relative error. In each case we shall also give the analytical formulae for the constants c_1 and c_2.

It is well-known that by using more than two data points one can get better approximation; that is, by subdividing the main interval for interpolation into several subintervals and keeping to a minimum the error on each of the subintervals yields to a better accuracy of approximation for the given function.

Since for computer-hardware implementations it is convenient that the number of data points be a power of two, we will assume that the interval $I = [L, U]$ is divided into 2^k intervals: $[L, L + \Delta/2^k)$, $[L + \Delta/2^k, L + 2\Delta/2^k]$, ..., $[L + (2^k - 1)\Delta/2^k, U]$, where Δ denotes the difference $U - L$. Then, given an argument, x, the interval into which it falls can be located readily by using, as an address, the k most significant bits of the binary representation of x. The proposed hardware implementation therefore has the high-level organization shown in Fig. 2. The two look-up tables (ROMs, or RAMs in the case of FPGAs) hold the constants c_1 and c_2 for each interval.

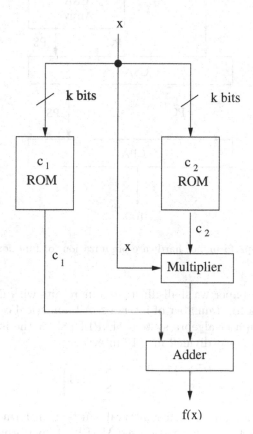

Fig. 2. Hardware organization for function evaluation

For a high-speed implementation, the actual structure may differ in several ways. Consider for example the Multiplier-Adder pair. Taken individually, the adder must be a carry-propagate adder (CPA); and the multiplier, if it is of high performance will consist of an array of carry-save adders (CSAs) with a final CPA to assimilate the partial-sum/partial-carry (PC/PS) output of the CSAs.

Now, the multiplier-CPA may be replaced with two CSAs, to yield much higher performance. Therefore, in a high speed implementation the actual structure would have the form shown in Fig. 3. It should be noted, though, that this new oraganization may not be the best one for the sort of FPGAs that we envisage, because the in-built structure of FPGAs impose certain constraints.

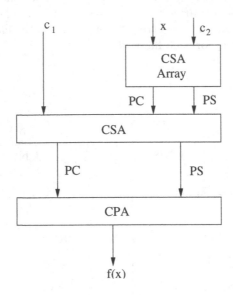

Fig. 3. High-performance hardware organization for function evaluation

Throughout the paper we shall illustrate our results with detailed numerical data obtained for a fixed number of intervals. All numerical computations, were done with the computer algebra system MAPLE [8] for the interval $I = [0.5, 1]$ and $k = 4$; that is, I was divided into 16 intervals:

$$\left[\frac{1}{2}, \frac{17}{32}, \frac{9}{16}, \frac{19}{32}, \frac{5}{8}, \dots, 1 \right].$$

(Note that evaluation on any other interval can be transformed into evaluation on the interval $[0.5, 1]$.) We have also used MAPLE to perform many of complex symbolic computations required throughout the paper.

Floating-point calculations in MAPLE are carried out in finite precision, with intermediate results rounded to a precision that is specified by MAPLE constant *Digits*. This constant controls the number of digits MAPLE uses for calculations. Thus, generally, the higher the *Digits* value is, the higher accuracy of the obtainable results, with roundoff errors as small as possible. We set *Digits* value to 35 for numerical computations. Numerical results will be presented using standard decimal scientific notation.

4   The Square-Root Function

Let $f : I \rightarrow \mathbf{R}$, $f(x) = \sqrt{x}$, and $\widehat{f} : I \rightarrow \mathbf{R}$, $\widehat{f}(x) = c_1 + c_2 x$, where c_1, c_2 are constants. By condition (C) we get the system

$$\begin{cases} c_1 + c_2 L = \sqrt{L}, \\ c_1 + c_2 U = \sqrt{U}, \end{cases}$$

which has the solution

$$c_1 = \frac{-U\sqrt{L} + \sqrt{U}L}{-U + L},$$

$$c_2 = \frac{-\sqrt{U} + \sqrt{L}}{-U + L}.$$

Hence, $\widehat{f}$ may be written as

$$\widehat{f}(x) = \frac{-U\sqrt{L} + \sqrt{U}L - x\left(\sqrt{U} - \sqrt{L}\right)}{-U + L}, \quad x \in I.$$

Substituting the above into (1) and simplifying, we obtain the formula for the relative error on the interval $I = [L, U]$:

$$\varepsilon(x) = 1 + \frac{U\sqrt{L} - \sqrt{U}L + x\left(\sqrt{U} - \sqrt{L}\right)}{(-U + L)\sqrt{x}},$$

of which the first derivative with respect to x is

$$\varepsilon'(x) = \frac{x\sqrt{U} - x\sqrt{L} - U\sqrt{L} + \sqrt{U}L}{2x^{3/2}(-U + L)}.$$

By solving the equation $\varepsilon'(x) = 0$, we get the unique stationary point

$$x_{stat} = \sqrt{UL}.$$

If we now take the second derivative of the error function

$$\varepsilon''(x) = \frac{x\sqrt{U} - x\sqrt{L} - 3U\sqrt{L} + 3\sqrt{U}L}{4x^{5/2}(-U + L)},$$

substitute x_{stat} into this formula, and simplify, we obtain

$$\varepsilon''(x_{stat}) = \frac{U\sqrt{L} - \sqrt{U}L}{2(-U + L)LU\sqrt{\sqrt{UL}}}.$$

Since $U > L$, the second derivative is negative at x_{stat}, which means that the relative error has a maximum value at this point. Moreover, by condition (C), ε vanishes at the end points of I, so it is in fact an absolute maximum. With this extremum value for the error function, it makes sense to consider an (IC)-type of condition, in which we equalize errors at the end-point and the error at the point of maximum-error amplitude.

For the 16-interval example, application of the condition (C) gives the results shown in Fig. 4, of the approximation plots together with the corresponding graph of the error function.

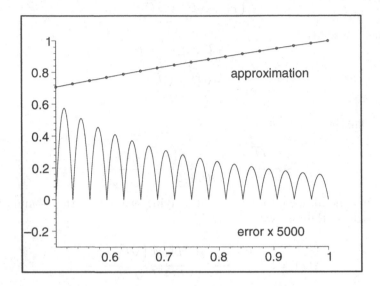

Fig. 4. Piecewise-linear approximation of the square-root function

Note, that the maximum value for error occurs on the first interval and is

$$\varepsilon_{max} = 1.148435e - 04, \tag{2}$$

which corresponds, approximately, to 0.57 on our (magnified) graph. We will later compare this number with the corresponding value obtained using our improved approximation.

We next derive an improved error-formula based on the condition (IC). The first equation in condition (IC) gives

$$\frac{\sqrt{U} - c_1 - c_2 U}{\sqrt{U}} = \frac{\sqrt{L} - c_1 - c_2 L}{\sqrt{L}},$$

whence

$$c_2 = \frac{c1\left(\sqrt{L} - \sqrt{U}\right)}{-\sqrt{L}U + \sqrt{U}L} = \frac{c_1}{\sqrt{UL}}. \tag{3}$$

Consequently, by (1), we get

$$\varepsilon(x) = 1 - \frac{c_1}{\sqrt{x}} - \frac{c_1\sqrt{x}}{\sqrt{UL}} \tag{4}$$

and, taking the first and second derivative,

$$\varepsilon'(x) = \frac{c_1\left(\sqrt{UL} - x\right)}{2x^{3/2}\sqrt{UL}} \quad \text{and} \quad \varepsilon''(x) = \frac{c_1\left(x - 3\sqrt{UL}\right)}{4x^{5/2}\sqrt{UL}},$$

for $x \in I$. Solving $\varepsilon'(x) = 0$, gives $x_{stat} = \sqrt{UL}$, and substituting x_{stat} into the second derivative formula yields

$$\varepsilon''(x_{stat}) = \frac{-c_1}{2UL\sqrt{\sqrt{UL}}}.$$

Since c_1 is positive ($f(0) > 0$ and f is increasing), from the last equation, we may infer that the second derivative is negative at x_{stat}, which means that the error attains maximum at this point. It is a simple matter to check that it is in fact an absolute maximum. By (1), we may now write

$$\varepsilon(x_{stat}) = 1 - \frac{c_1}{\sqrt{x_{stat}}} - \frac{c_1\sqrt{x_{stat}}}{\sqrt{UL}} = 1 - \frac{2c_1}{\sqrt{x_{stat}}}, \qquad (5)$$

since $x_{stat} = \sqrt{UL}$.

Observe that from condition (IC), we have

$$\varepsilon(L) = -\varepsilon(x_{stat}).$$

That is, by (4) and (5),

$$1 - \frac{c_1}{\sqrt{L}} - \frac{c_1}{\sqrt{U}} = -1 + \frac{2c_1}{\sqrt{x_{stat}}},$$

whence

$$c_1 = \frac{2x_{stat}}{2\sqrt{x_{stat}} + \sqrt{U} + \sqrt{L}},$$

and, by (3),

$$c_2 = \frac{2}{2\sqrt{x_{stat}} + \sqrt{U} + \sqrt{L}}.$$

Therefore

$$\widehat{f}(x) = \frac{2(x_{stat} + x)}{2\sqrt{x_{stat}} + \sqrt{U} + \sqrt{L}}, \quad x \in I.$$

Finally, (1) gives the following improved formula for the relative error on interval I

$$\varepsilon(x) = 1 - \frac{\sqrt{x_{stat} + x}}{\left(2\sqrt{x_{stat}} + \sqrt{U} + \sqrt{L}\right)\sqrt{x}}.$$

Figure 5 gives the graphs for the new approximation and the corresponding relative error on the sixteen intervals.

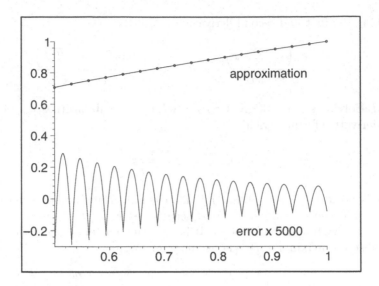

Fig. 5. Improved piecewise-linear approximation of the square-root function

The maximum value for relative error is now

$$\varepsilon_{max} = 5.742506e - 05,$$

which corresponds approximately to 0.29 on the "magnified" graph. MAPLE ensures us that this value is in fact the global maximum of the error-magnitude. (We omit the tedious and rather long, but elementary, proof of this fact for the general case). In fact, the maximum magnitude for the left-end is $5.74249902e - 05$, and for the right-end it is $5.74245863e - 05$.

To conclude the section, we compare the current maximum value to our previous error estimation given by (2). An easy computation shows that the magnitude of the maximum relative-error decreased by 50.00279 percent. There is one further additional point that should be noted regarding the new approximation: observe that in Fig. 4 all the errors are of the same sign, i.e. positive. This means that in a sequence of square-root evaluations, the total error will be cumulative. On the other hand, in Fig. 5 there are changes of sign, which means that there will be some cancellation. Note that this is precisely the reason why in the mandated rounding method in IEEE-754 (i.e. round-to-nearest), boundary cases are alternately rounded up or down, according to the least significant bit of the number being rounded.

5   The Exponential Function

In this section we consider $f : I \to \mathbf{R}$, where $f(x) = e^x$ and, as in the preceding section, we will look for a linear function $\widehat{f} : I \to \mathbf{R}$, where $\widehat{f}(x) = c_1 + c_2 x$, such that $\varepsilon(x)$, given by (1), is small.

We begin by an analysis based on a natural assumption expressed by condition (C): the error should vanish at both end-points of the considered interval. This is expressed by the following pair of equations, with c_1, c_2 as unknown variables

$$\begin{cases} c_1 + c_2 L = e^L, \\ c_1 + c_2 U = e^U. \end{cases}$$

A routine algebraic calculation gives

$$c_1 = \frac{-Ue^L + e^U L}{-U + L} \quad \text{and} \quad c_2 = \frac{-e^U + e^L}{-U + L}.$$

Now, the function $\widehat{f}$ may be expressed as

$$\widehat{f}(x) = \frac{-Ue^L + e^U L - xe^U + xe^L}{-U + L}, \quad x \in I,$$

and the relative error on I is then

$$\varepsilon(x) = \frac{\left(-e^x U + e^x L + Ue^L - e^U L + xe^U - xe^L\right) e^{-x}}{-U + L}.$$

Differentiating $\varepsilon(x)$ twice, with respect to x, gives

$$\varepsilon'(x) = \frac{e^{-x} \left(e^U - e^L - Ue^L + e^U L - xe^U + xe^L\right)}{-U + L}, \quad x \in I,$$

and

$$\varepsilon''(x) = \frac{e^{-x} \left(-Ue^L + e^U L - xe^U + xe^L\right)}{-U + L}, \quad x \in I.$$

Solving $\varepsilon'(x) = 0$, we find that the only stationary point is

$$x_{stat} = \frac{-e^U + e^L + Ue^L - e^U L}{-e^U + e^L}.$$

To check for local extremum, we investigate the sign of the second derivative at this point. Performing elementary algebraic computations, we derive the formula

$$\varepsilon''(x_{stat}) = \frac{e^\alpha \left(-e^U + e^L\right)}{-U + L},$$

where, for simplicity of notation, we have used α to denote the value

$$\frac{-e^U + e^L + Ue^L - e^U L}{-e^U + e^L}. \tag{6}$$

Since e^α is positive and the exponential is an increasing function, we may infer that $\varepsilon''(x_{stat})$ is positive, which means that the magnitude of the relative error has a maximum at this point. It suggests, as in the case of square-root function, that a better error approximation can be obtained if we try to bound the error at this point. Figure 6 shows the approximation and the corresponding relative-error for the 16-interval case. The maximum amplitude of the error is

$$\varepsilon_{max} = 1.220761e - 04 \tag{7}$$

which translates approximately to 0.61 on our "magnified" graph.

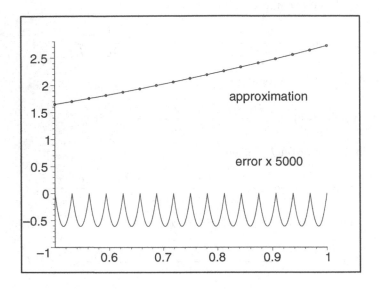

Fig. 6. Piecewise-linear approximation of the exponential function

We next show that condition (IC) yields a much better error approximation. The following equality, which follows immediately from (6), will be useful in the sequel

$$1 - \alpha = \frac{-e^L U + e^U L}{e^L - e^U}. \tag{8}$$

Observe that the relative error is now

$$\varepsilon(x) = \frac{e^x - c_1 - c_2 x}{e^x}, \qquad x \in I. \tag{9}$$

Comparing $\varepsilon(L)$ and $\varepsilon(U)$ gives

$$\frac{e^U - c_1 - c_2 U}{e^U} = \frac{e^L - c_1 - c_2 L}{e^L}.$$

Hence, using (6),

$$c_2 = \frac{c_1 \left(e^L - e^U\right)}{-e^L U + e^U L} = \frac{c_1}{1 - \alpha}. \tag{10}$$

Substituting for c_2 into (9) we obtain

$$\varepsilon(x) = \frac{e^x - c_1 - \frac{c_1}{1-\alpha}x}{e^x}, \qquad x \in I, \tag{11}$$

and differentiation with respect to x yields

$$\varepsilon'(x) = c_1 e^{-x}\left[1 - \frac{1}{1-\alpha}(1-x)\right] = c_1 e^{-x}\left[\frac{x-\alpha}{1-\alpha}\right], \qquad x \in I. \tag{12}$$

Thus, $\varepsilon'(x) = 0$ iff $x = \alpha$ (since $e^{-x} > 0$ and $c_1 > 0$); that is, α is the only stationary point for ε.

We now need to check the sign of the second derivative at this point in order to ensure that it is a local extremum. Let us take the second derivative of the error function and apply (8):

$$\varepsilon''(x) = \frac{c_1}{1-\alpha}\left[-e^{-x}x + e^{-x} + \alpha e^{-x}\right] = \frac{c_1 e^{-x}}{1-\alpha}(-x+1+\alpha), \qquad x \in I.$$

Hence

$$\varepsilon''(\alpha) = c_1 \frac{e^{-\alpha}}{1-\alpha}.$$

This clearly shows that the second derivative is positive at this point, and, therefore, that α is a local minimum for ε.

We now turn to (11), which gives

$$\varepsilon(\alpha) = \frac{e^\alpha - c_1 - \frac{c_1\alpha}{1-\alpha}}{e^\alpha},$$

$$\varepsilon(L) = \frac{e^L - c_1 - \frac{c_1}{1-\alpha}L}{e^L}.$$

From condition (IC), we have, in particular, $\varepsilon(L) = -\varepsilon(\alpha)$; that is,

$$\frac{e^\alpha - c_1 - \frac{c_1\alpha}{1-\alpha}}{e^\alpha} = \frac{-e^L + c_1 + \frac{c_1}{1-\alpha}L}{e^L}.$$

Whence, by (8),

$$c_1 = \frac{2e^\alpha(1-\alpha)\left(-e^U + e^L\right)}{-e^U + e^L - e^\alpha(U-L)},$$

and by (10),

$$c_2 = \frac{2e^\alpha\left(-e^U + e^L\right)}{-e^U + e^L - e^\alpha(U-L)}.$$

We are now in a position to produce the final error formula:

$$\varepsilon(\alpha) = \frac{e^x - c_1 - c_2 x}{e^x} = 1 - \left[\frac{2e^\alpha(1-\alpha)\beta}{\beta - e^\alpha(U-L)} + \frac{2e^\alpha\beta}{\beta - e^\alpha(U-L)}x\right]e^{-x}$$

$$= \left[1 - \frac{2e^\alpha\beta(1-\alpha+x)}{\beta - e^\alpha(U-L)}\right]e^{-x} = e^{-x} - \frac{2e^\alpha\beta(1-\alpha+x)e^{-x}}{\beta - e^\alpha(U-L)}, \qquad x \in I,$$

where $\beta = -e^U + e^L$ and α is given by (6).

For the 16-interval case, Fig. 7 shows the graphs for the improved approximation and the relative-error function.

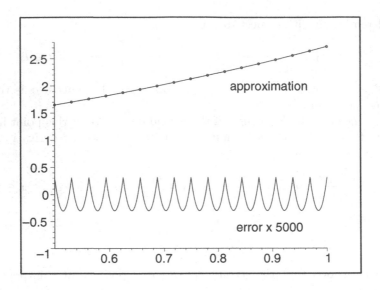

Fig. 7. Improved piecewise-linear approximation of the exponentialfunction

The maximum amplitude of the error is

$$\varepsilon_{max} = 6.103433e - 05$$

which translates approximately to 0.3 on our graph. A comparison of this result with (7) finding that the reduction of the maximum error magnitude is 50.00968 percent. And similar remarks to those made at the end of the last section apply equally here.

6   Comparison of Errors

In this section we will compare the average and maximum errors for the discussed two approximation schemas: the one based on condition (C) and the other using the improved condition (IC). Following [7], we define average error as follows. For function $f : I = [L, U] \rightarrow \mathbf{R}$ approximated by $\widehat{f} : I \rightarrow \mathbf{R}$ the average absolute error is the average value of $\left| f(u) - \widehat{f}(u) \right|$ for u uniformly sampled on N points in the interval I. That is,

$$\text{Average Absolute Error} = \frac{\sum_{i=0}^{N-1} \left| f(u_i) - \widehat{f}(u_i) \right|}{N},$$

where $u_i = L + i * \Delta$, and $\Delta = \frac{U-L}{N}$. Similarly, we define the average relative error over the interval I:

$$\text{Average Relative Error} = \frac{\sum_{i=0}^{N-1} \frac{|f(u_i) - \widehat{f}(u_i)|}{f(u_i)}}{N}.$$

Let us also also remind ourselves the definition of the L-infinity norm on the interval I:

$$\text{Maximum Absolute Error} = \max_{u \in I} \left| f(u) - \widehat{f}(u) \right|.$$

Analogously, for the relative error, we will use

$$\text{Maximum Relative Error} = \max_{u \in I} \frac{\left| f(u) - \widehat{f}(u) \right|}{f(u)}.$$

We will use the above definitions to compare the two approximation techniques.

As we have already seen in previous sections the improved schema yields approximately 50 percent maximum error reduction for each of the considered functions. In the sequel we present data showing that error reduction of similar magnitude also happens for the average errors for each of those functions. We also investigate the influence on relative and absolute error of rounding $c1$, $c2$ to k bits, where k is choosen based on most common applications of a given function. Since for functions $\sqrt{x}$ and $\exp(x)$, $k = 16$, $k = 32$ and $k = 64$ are most important we treat these cases separately. All error values are obtained for the interval $I = [0.5, 1]$ with $N = 2^{10}$ uniformly sampled points. The precision used in an an actual implementation will, naturally, depend on the particular device employed. For example, given the size of the mutipliers and adders in the Xilinx Virtex-4, 16-bit precision would be ideal.

Table 2 presents results based on condition (C), and Table 3 shows the corresponding values for the improved condition (IC) for $\sqrt{x}$ and $\exp(x)$.

7   Conclusion

The paper shows the use of piecewise-linear interpolation to provide relative error evaluation for certain important elementary functions. Applications to high-performance hardware implementation is also discussed. The square-root function, which is part of the IEEE standard for floating-point arithmetic on all computers is investigated first. Then, the exponential function, which is commonly used in numerical computations, is treated.

In each case we demonstrate that it is possible to find a low-error linear approximation, which can be relatively easily implemented in hardware, resulting in a low-error, high-performance implementation of these mathematical functions.

Table 2. Absolute and relative errors for condition (C)

		c_1, c_2	$\sqrt{u}$	$\exp(u)$
		exact	3.369593e-05	1.740368e-04
	average	16 bits	3.281906e-05	1.751525e-04
		32 bits	3.369593e-05	1.740368e-04
absolute		64 bits	3.369593e-05	1.740368e-04
error		exact	8.245153e-05	3.266860e-04
	maximum	16 bits	7.397733e-05	3.369909e-04
		32 bits	8.245153e-05	3.266861e-04
		64 bits	8.245153e-05	3.266860e-04
		exact	4.066859e-05	8.136299e-05
	average	16 bits	3.962489e-05	8.172013e-05
		32 bits	4.066859e-05	8.136299e-05
relative		64 bits	4.066859e-05	8.136299e-05
error		exact	1.148435e-04	1.220761e-04
	maximum	16 bits	1.030403e-04	1.266475e-04
		32 bits	1.148435e-04	1.220762e-04
		64 bits	1.148435e-04	1.220761e-04

Table 3. Absolute and relative errors for condition (IC)

		c_1, c_2	$\sqrt{u}$	$\exp(u)$
		exact	1.541342e-05	7.960265e-05
	average	16 bits	1.534050e-05	7.934758e-05
		32 bits	1.541342e-05	7.960264e-05
absolute		64 bits	1.541342e-05	7.960265e-05
error		exact	4.185535e-05	1.659085e-04
	maximum	16 bits	4.298745e-05	1.717649e-04
		32 bits	4.185525e-05	1.659085e-04
		64 bits	4.185535e-05	1.659085e-04
		exact	1.860786e-05	3.722859e-05
	average	16 bits	1.857589e-05	3.706073e-05
		32 bits	1.860787e-05	3.722858e-05
relative		64 bits	1.860786e-05	3.722859e-05
error		exact	5.742506e-05	6.103433e-05
	maximum	16 bits	5.987699e-05	6.531079e-05
		32 bits	5.742520e-05	6.103440e-05
		64 bits	5.742506e-05	6.103433e-05

References

[1] Muller, J.M.: Elementary Functions: Algorithms and Implementation. Birkhauser, Boston, USA, 1997.

[2] Omondi, A.R.: Computer Arithmetic Systems: Algorithms, Architecture, and Implementations. Prentice-Hall, UK, 1994.

[3] Mencer, O, Luk, W.: Parameterized high throughput function evaluation for FPGAs. Journal of VLSI Signal Processing **36** (2004) 17–25.

[4] Pizer, S.M., Wallace, V.L.: To compute numerically: concepts and strategies. Little, Brown, Boston, USA, 1983.

[5] Xilinx. 2004. Virtex-4 User Guide.

[6] Xilinx. 2004. XtremeDSP Design Considerations: User Guide.

[7] Massayuki Ito, Naofumi Takagi, Shuzo Yajima: Efficient Initial Approximation for Multiplicative Division and Square Root by a Multiplication with Operand Modification. IEEE Trans. Computers 46(4): 495-498 (1997)

[8] Waterloo Maple Inc.: Maple 8 Programming Guide, 2002.

Using Branch Prediction Information for Near-Optimal I-Cache Leakage

Sung Woo Chung[1,*] and Kevin Skadron[2]

[1] Division of Computer and Communication Engineering, Korea University,
Seoul 136-713, Korea
swchung@korea.ac.kr
[2] Department of Computer Science, University of Virginia
Charlottesville 22904, USA
skadron@cs.virginia.edu

Abstract. This paper describes a new on-demand wakeup prediction policy for instruction cache leakage control that achieves better leakage savings than prior policies, and avoids the performance overheads of prior policies. The proposed policy reduces leakage energy by more than 92% with only less than 0.3% performance overhead on average. The key to this new on-demand policy is to use branch prediction information for the wakeup prediction. In the proposed policy, inserting an extra stage for wakeup between branch prediction and fetch, allows the branch predictor to be also used as a wakeup predictor without any additional hardware. Thus, the extra stage hides the wakeup penalty, not affecting branch prediction accuracy. Though extra pipeline stages typically add to branch misprediction penalty, in this case, the extra wakeup stage on the normal fetch path can be overlapped with misprediction recovery. With such consistently accurate wakeup prediction, all cache lines except the next expected cache line are in the leakage saving mode, minimizing leakage energy.

Keywords: Instruction Cache, Low Power, Leakage, Drowsy Cache, Branch Prediction.

1 Introduction

As process technology scales down, leakage energy accounts for a significant part of total energy. The International Technology Roadmap for Semiconductor [23] predicts that by the 70nm technology, leakage may constitute as much as 50% of total energy dissipation. In particular, the leakage energy for on-chip caches is crucial, since they comprise a large portion of chip area. For instance, 30% of the Alpha 21264 and 60% of the StrongARM are devoted to cache and memory structures [13]. However, cache size can not be decreased to reduce leakage power since cache size is directly related to the performance.

There have been four major circuit techniques to reduce leakage energy dynamically: ABB (Adaptive-reverse Body Biasing) MTCMOS [16], DRG (Data-Retention Gated-ground) [1], Gated-Vdd [17], and DVS for Vdd (which is also called drowsy cache) [3]. In the ABB MTCMOS technique, threshold voltage is dynamically

---

* Corresponding Author.

C. Jesshope and C. Egan (Eds.): ACSAC 2006, LNCS 4186, pp. 24–37, 2006.

changed but the wakeup penalty between the active mode and the leakage saving mode is long, which makes it difficult for use in L1 caches [4]. DRG retains the data while reducing leakage by gating ground and using remaining leakage to retain cell contents, but the wakeup penalty is long. Thus, this technique may be inappropriate for timing critical caches such as an L1 cache, even if it is effective for less timing critical caches such as L2 [10]. The gated-Vdd technique reduces the leakage power by breaking the connection from the supply voltage (Vdd) or ground (the difference compared to DRG is that a larger sleep transistor is used and cell contents are not preserved) when the cell is put to sleep. While this technique dramatically reduces the leakage, its main disadvantage is that it does not preserve the state of the data in the sleep mode [4]. When the line is needed after it has been put into the leakage saving mode, the line must be refetched from a lower-level memory, which leads not only to additional dynamic energy consumption but also to performance degradation. To prevent these costs, conservative prediction policies should be employed [5][20][21]. Gated-Vdd may, however, be suitable for some L1 data caches where re-fetch penalty is short [12]. Another leakage saving technique is to lower the supply voltage. In this technique, data is not lost when the cache line is in the leakage saving mode (called "drowsy" mode). In the drowsy mode, data is retained, although it can not be accessed for read or write operation. Fortunately, most cache lines are unused for long periods due to temporal locality. Thus, by putting infrequently used cache lines into drowsy mode and keeping frequently accessed cache lines in the active mode, much leakage power is reduced without significant performance degradation. Please note that there is a wakeup penalty to restore the voltage level of the Vdd from the drowsy mode into the active mode. However, the wakeup penalty is expected to be one cycle in 70nm process technology [3]. There has been concern that drowsy cache is more susceptible to soft errors than conventional caches [10]. Fortunately, instructions are read-only and must be protected by parity even in the absence of drowsy techniques. In the infrequent cases when an error is detected, the instruction only has to be refetched.

Among the above four techniques, drowsy technique is most suitable for L1 instruction caches, since it retains data and has short wakeup penalty. In order to prevent (or hide) the wakeup penalty of the drowsy cache, many prediction policies have been proposed. The easiest policy is "no prediction": to place all the cache lines into the drowsy mode periodically and restore the voltage level of Vdd of accessed cache lines, suffering the wakeup penalty. It performs well with data caches because they have high temporal locality, leading to little performance loss, and out-of-order processors can often tolerate extra latency from waking up lines [3]. For instruction caches, however, this "no prediction" technique does not perform well, because any wakeup penalty that stalls fetching directly impacts the performance. Many prediction policies have been proposed for instruction caches. (Details will be explained in the next section). None of them has simultaneously shown consistent leakage energy reduction with negligible performance degradation. In this paper, we propose a new *on-demand* wakeup prediction policy for an instruction cache. By on-demand, we mean that *only currently necessary cache line(s) needs to be awake*. This technique takes advantage of the fact that we can accurately predict the next cache line by using the branch predictor. Thus, the wakeup prediction accuracy capitalizes on branch predictors that have already proven to be very accurate [14]. A further advantage compared to previous policies is that the proposed policy does not require an additional predictor. To utilize the branch predictor for wakeup prediction, we can allow a pipeline stage between branch prediction and instruction cache fetch. Allowing the branch predictor to be accessed one cycle earlier permits the branch prediction outcome to be used for wakeup, without harming branch prediction accuracy or requiring additional wakeup prediction hardware. Please note that this approach does not suffer the traditional branch-misprediction overhead of inserting extra stage in the pipeline. On a branch misprediction, the extra wakeup stage is overlapped with misprediction recovery. For further details, see Section 3.

This work focuses on use of drowsy cache (actually super-drowsy cache [9], explained in Section 2) for the leakage saving circuit technique. In this paper, we distinguish the wakeup prediction *policy* from the leakage saving *circuit technique*. The wakeup prediction policy predicts which cache line will be woken up, while the leakage saving circuit technique is the mechanism for putting lines to sleep and waking them up, independent of the prediction policy.

2 Background

Kim et.al proposed a refinement of the drowsy technique, called *super-drowsy cache* [9]. A single-Vdd cache line voltage controller with Schmitt trigger inverter replaces multiple supply voltage sources in order to alleviate interconnect routing space. In addition, the on-demand gated bitline precharge technique [19] is employed to reduce the bitline leakage. We apply our prediction policy to the super-drowsy cache because it is the most advanced circuit technique for instruction cache leakage control as far as we know.

The success of the drowsy-style cache depends on how accurately the next cache line can be predicted and woken up. Especially for an instruction cache, accuracy is crucial since the accuracy directly affects performance degradation. A simple policy is *noaccess* [3]: This uses per-line access history and puts all the unused lines into drowsy mode periodically. For more accurate wakeup prediction, two prediction policies were proposed for a drowsy instruction cache [8] – *NSPB* (Next Subcache Prediction Buffer) and *NSPCT* (Next Subcache Predictor in Cache Tags). Additional storage is required to predict the next subbank (not a cache line) using NSPB, whereas cache tags are extended to provide the subbank predictor in NSPCT. Therefore, NSPCT requires less hardware overhead but is comparable to NSPB in accuracy (performance loss is 0.79%). However, leakage reduction is weak [8] due to large sub-bank turn-on energy. Zhang et.al. proposed the *Loop* policy [21] where all cache lines are put into the drowsy mode after each loop was executed. This bears some similarity to the *DHS* (Dynamic HotSpot Based Leakage Management) policy, which was proposed in [5]. DHS makes use of the branch target buffer (BTB), since branch behavior is an important factor in shaping the instruction access behavior. In the DHS policy, the global turn-off (drowsy) signal is issued when a new loop-based hotspot is detected. Thus this policy can lower the supply voltage of unused cache lines before the update window expires by detecting that execution will remain in a new loop-based hotspot. The *DHS-PA* (DHS-Per Access) policy employs a Just-In-Time-Activation (JITA) strategy on top of the DHS policy [5]. The JITA strategy is to wake up the next sequential line, exploiting the sequential nature of code. However, this is not successful when a taken branch is encountered. The *DHS-Bank-PA* policy [5] issues the global turn-off signal at fixed periods, when the execution shifts to a new bank, or when a new loop hotspot is detected. It attempts to identify both spatial and temporal locality changes. It also employs hotspot detection to protect active cache lines and the JITA policy for predictive cache line wakeup. As shown in [5], although the DHS-Bank-PA reduced leakage energy significantly, performance degradation is severe.

The super-drowsy cache deploys the noaccess-JITA policy with as large as a 32K-cycle update window size for next cache line prediction to achieve high accuracy [9]. The noaccess-JITA puts only lines that have not been accessed during a fixed time period into drowsy mode and activates the first sequential cache line. The super-drowsy cache also deploys an additional *NTSBP* (Next Target Sub-Bank Predictor) that predicts next sub-bank to be bitline precharged in advance, since the on-demand gated precharge incurs extra penalty to enable an inactive sub-bank, and this can result in significant execution time increase. The noaccess-JITA/NTSBP with 32K cycle update window size is a leakage energy reduction policy with the most accurate wakeup prediction but with modest leakage energy reduction. However, the accuracy of the noaccess-JITA/NTSBP is so dependent on program behavior, especially locality, that the accuracy of no-access-JITA/NTSBP is poor in some applications.

3 Novel Wakeup Prediction Policy: Utilizing Branch Prediction Information

In previous wakeup prediction policies, additional predictors are required in order to wake up a cache line, and accessed cache lines remain active for a fixed time period. Accordingly, the accuracy of the previous policies is highly dependent on the locality. As shown in Figure 1(a), the additional predictors, such as JITA [5], NSPB [8],

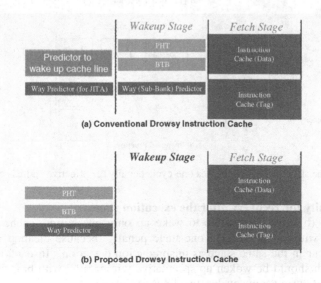

Fig. 1. Pipeline stage comparison

NSPCT [8] and NTSBP [9], are accessed before looking up the branch predictor in order to hide the wakeup penalty. However, the accuracy of additional predictors was not satisfactory. For near-optimal leakage energy reduction and performance, we propose a new wakeup prediction policy which enables on-demand wakeup. In the proposed policy, as shown in Figure 1(b), the branch predictor, consisting of Prediction History Table (PHT) and Branch Target Buffer (BTB), is accessed one cycle earlier than in conventional policies.

There are two architectural options in branch resolution. When a branch turns out to be mispredicted in the execution stage, some time is usually required to clean up mis-speculated state and generate the next address (Figure 2(a)), but depending on exactly where during the branch-resolution cycle the misprediction is detected, it may be possible to complete this without any extra overhead (Figure 3(a)). Requiring at least one cycle for cleanup and fetch-address generation, as shown in Figure 2 (a), appears to be common [22].

- **Additional penalty for recovery after the execution stage**

As shown in Figure 2 (b), after the execution/branch-resolution stage of the instructtion *n*, cleanup, effective address calculation, and wakeup occur simultaneously. Thus there is always only one active cache line.

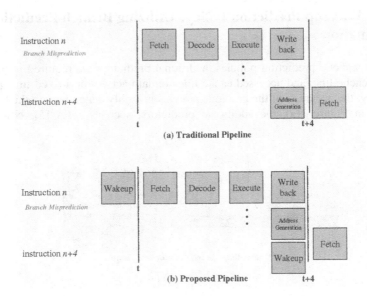

Fig. 2. Pipeline structure (when there is one-cycle penalty for effective address calculation)

- **No penalty for recovery after the execution stage**

In Figure 3 (b), it is impossible to wake up only one correct cache line after a misprediction without incurring a one-stage penalty, because cleanup and address generation occur in the same stage as misprediction detection. Instead, the potential alternative path should be woken up speculatively in parallel with branch resolution. This means that during some cycles, two lines are awake.

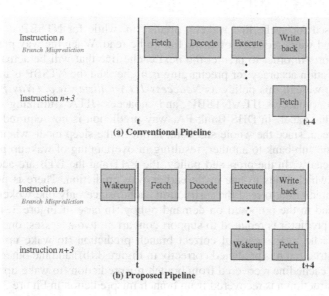

Fig. 3. Pipeline structure (when there is no penalty for effective address calculation)

It is possible to determine the alternative path in parallel with branch resolution. For predicted-taken branches, the not-taken path must be woken up and the branch address itself (usually carried with the instruction) can be used. For predicted not-taken branches, the taken target is needed. This can either be carried with the instruction or reside in some dedicated storage. This capability must exist anyway in current microprocessors because every taken branch in flight must be able to check whether the target address obtained from the BTB is correct or not. Note that the taken target is available at branch-prediction time regardless of predicted direction, because the direction predictor and target predictor are usually consulted in parallel.

In both options of Figure 2 and Figure 3, there is no penalty when there is no branch misprediction. In case of branch target misprediction, the penalty is inevitable. However, there is only one case that we can not hide the penalty in case of branch direction misprediction. Since the stored cache line address woken up is not that of (mispredicted branch instruction address + 4), but the mispredicted branch instruction address itself, there is a penalty when the resolved branch instruction is at the end of the cache line and the correct next instruction is sequential. It is possible to make use of the instruction address +4, but it requires extra adder or storage for the instruction address + 4. Even though this cost may be minor, in this paper we do not use an extra adder or extra storage, since the probability that a mispredicted instruction is at the end of the cache line is rare.

In the proposed policy, only one cache line (or two cache lines in Figure 3) expected to be accessed exists in the active mode and all the other cache lines are in the drowsy mode. For a set-associative cache, only one way should woken up to save the energy. We adopt a way predictor [18] that employs MRU (Most Recently Used) bit and integrates a way predictor and a BTB for high accuracy, which is known as one of the most accurate way predictors. In the noaccess-JITA/NTSBP, the way predictor is used for cache line wakeup prediction, while for NTSBP it is used for precharging and way prediction of cache line to be read. When the way predictor can have 2-read ports in order to predict the next cache line that will be actually read as well, the prediction accuracy for precharging is higher and the NTSBP is unnecessary (In this paper, we call this policy as *Noaccess-JITA utilizing w.p. (Way Predictor)*). Both options (noaccess-JITA/NTSBP and noaccess-JITA (utilizing w.p.) are evaluated in this paper. In DHS-Bank-PA, way prediction is not required in case of actual cache read, since the whole sub-bank is put in the sleep mode when execution jumps from one sub-bank to another, resulting in overlapping of wakeup penalty and precharging penalty. In the proposed policy, the PHT and the BTB are accessed one cycle earlier, which leads to one cycle earlier way prediction. There is no need for another way prediction to read the instruction cache, since only one woken up cache line can be read in the proposed on-demand policy. In case of Figure 3, however, a two-port way predictor is required to support concurrent two accesses: one is to wake up the next cache line in case of correct branch prediction (to wake up instruction n+3, when instruction n is predicted correctly in Figure 3 (b)) and the other is to wake up a probable cache line recovered from branch misprediction (to wake up instruction n+3, when instruction n is recovered from branch misprediction in Figure 3 (b)).

4   Experimental Methodology

We extended Simplescalar 3.0 [2] to evaluate energy and performance. The processor parameters model a high-performance microprocessor similar to Alpha 21264 [7], as shown in Table 1. The power/energy parameters are based on the 70nm/1.0V

Table 1. Architecture/circuit parameters

Processor Parameters	
Branch Predictor	Gshare/4K, 1024-entry 4-way BTB
L1 I-Cache	32 KB, 4 way, 32B blocks, 1 cycle latency, 4KB sub-bank size
L1 D-Cache	32 KB, 4 ways, 32B blocks, 1 cycle latency
Power/Energy Parameters	
Process Technology	70 nm
Threshold Voltage	0.2 V
Supply Voltage	1.0 V (active mode), 0.25 V (drowsy mode)
Leakage Power/Bit in Active Mode w /o Gated Precharging (1 cycle)	0.0778 µW
Leakage Power/Bit in Active Mode w / Gated Precharging (1 cycle)	0.0647 µW
Leakage Power/Bit in Drowsy Mode w/o Gated Precharging (1 cycle)	0.0167 µW
Leakage Power/Bit in Drowsy Mode w/ Gated Precharging (1 cycle)	0.00387 µW
Turn-on (drowsy to active) Energy/Bit	115fJ
Turn-on (drowsy to active) Latency	1 cycle
Clock Cycle Time	12 * FO4 (395ps)

technology [9]. We use all integer and floating point applications from the SPEC2000 benchmark suite [24]. Each benchmark is first fast-forwarded half a billion instructions and then simulated the next half a billion instructions.

We selected three previous prediction policies (noaccess-JITA/NTSBP, noaccess-JITA (utilizing w.p.), and DHS-Bank-PA, described in Section 2 and Section 3) for comparison. We use same details of the policies as proposed in [5][9]. The noaccess-JITA/NTSBP has a 32 K cycle update window to periodically update mode of each cache line. Although execution moves from one sub-bank to another sub-bank, the precharge circuits of the previous sub-bank remain on for 16 cycles to prevent the misprediction of sub-bank. After 16 cycles, the bitline of the sub-bank is isolated. The DHS-Bank-PA has 2 K cycle update window and its hotness threshold is 16.

5 Experimental Methodology

This section presents our simulation results and compares the proposed policy to other policies. We analyze each policy's energy reduction and execution time increases.

5.1 Drowsy Fraction and Gated Bitline Precharging Fraction

Figure 4 shows the drowsy fraction in the 4-way set-associative cache. Since the update window size of the noaccess-JITA/NTSBP is as large as 32K, the drowsy

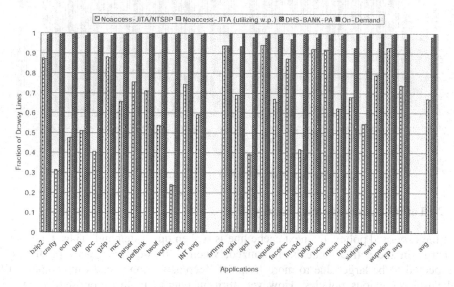

Fig. 4. Average drowsy fraction in instruction cache

fraction is 66.9%, on average. In the DHS-Bank-PA, the drowsy fraction is 98.2%, on average. The reason is that the update window size is as small as 2K and additionally cache lines are put into the drowsy mode when a new hotspot is detected. In the proposed on-demand policy, only one (or two in the proposed policy of Figure 3) cache line is in the active mode and the others are in the drowsy mode, resulting in 99.9% (or 99.8% in the proposed policy of Figure 3) drowsy fraction, on average. There is little difference between the noaccess-JITA/NTSBP and the noaccess-JITA (utilizing w.p.), since the NTSBP and the 2-read port way predictor are not related to the drowsy fraction but related to the precharging fraction.

Figure 5 shows the fraction of isolated bitines in the 4-way set associative cache. In case of bitline precharging prediction, there is no energy penalty but there is one cycle timing penalty when mispredicted. In the noaccess-JITA/NTSBP, on average 75.7% of the sub-banks are bitline gated. The fraction is relatively small, because a sub-bank should be remained bitline precharged for 16 cycles to prevent bitline precharging mispredictions when execution moves to another sub-bank. However, the noaccess-JITA (utilizing w.p.) always has 87.5% since way predictor is used for subbank prediction. In the other two techniques, only one sub-bank is bitline percharged. Thus, the portion of gated bitline precharging is always 87.5% (1 sub-bank/8 sub-banks).

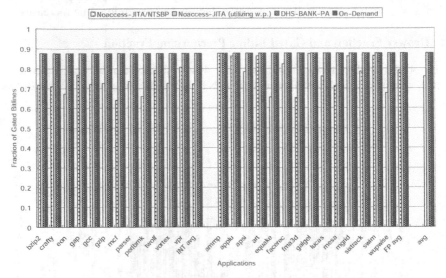

Fig. 5. Average isolated bitline fraction in instruction cache

5.2 Total Leakage-Related Energy

In the proposed policy, the next cache line is woken up on-demand. Thus, the leakage energy in the active mode is minimized, whereas turn-on energy by prediction is expected to be larger due to more frequent sleep/activation round-trips compared to the other previous policies. However, turn-on energy in the proposed policy still accounts for a small portion of total leakage-related energy. Figure 6 shows normalized leakage-related energy to the base model. The base model does not use any leakage-saving policy but it has the way predictor. Average leakage-related energy reduction is 68.1%, 69.8%, 90.4%, 92.5%, 92.2%, and 92.6% in the noaccess-JITA/NTSBP, noaccess-JITA (utilizing w.p.), DHS-Bank-PA, on-demand of Figure 2, on-demand of Figure 3, and optimal policies, respectively.

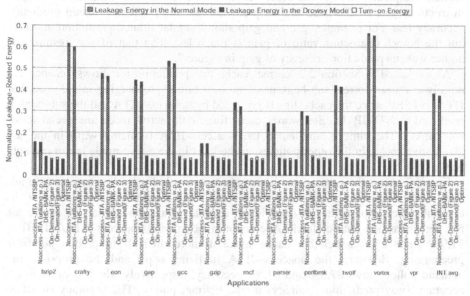

(a) SPEC2000 INT applications

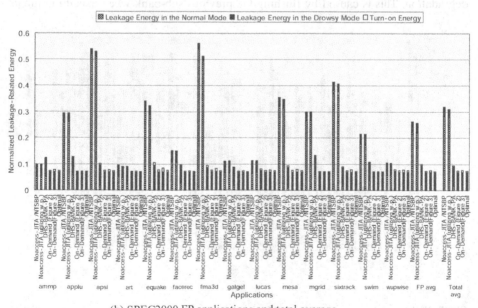

(b) SPEC2000 FP applications and total average

Fig. 6. Normalized leakage-related energy

5.3 Wakeup Prediction Accuracy

On average, the branch prediction accuracy is 94.3% and the branch instruction ratio is 8.7% for SPEC applications. Recall that wakeup misprediction is mainly caused by branch misprediction by incorrect target address. As the number of branch instructions gets smaller, the branch prediction accuracy affects wakeup prediction accuracy less. For example, gcc and gzip shows similar branch prediction accuracy but the branch instruction ratio of gzip is much less than that of gcc, resulting in higher wakeup prediction accuracy of gzip in Figure 7.

As explained in Section 2.2, correct cache line prediction for drowsy cache does not always mean correct sub-bank prediction for bitline precharging in the noaccess-JITA/ NTSBP, since the cache line is predicted by noaccess-JITA and the sub-bank is predicted by NTSBP (In other words, cache lines in the active mode are spread across sub-banks). The same is applied to the noaccess-JITA (utilizing w.p.) in the set-associative cache. In the other policies, cache lines in the active mode are in one sub-bank.

Figure 7 shows the wakeup prediction accuracy, including bitline precharging and way prediction accuracy in the 4-way set-associative cache. The accuracy of the optimal policy implies the way prediction accuracy. Please note that the results are not per instruction but per fetch. Average accuracy of the noaccess-JITA/NTSBP is 71.9% since a set-associative cache make it more difficult to predict sub-bank precharging. However, the noaccess-JITA (utilizing w.p.) and the proposed on-demand policy shows 87.3% and 87.6% accuracy, respectively which is close to the accuracy (way prediction accuracy) of the optimal policy. The accuracy of DHS-Bank-PA is as low as 57.6%, on average, which might result in severe performance degradation. This is caused by flushing the previous sub-bank when execution jumps

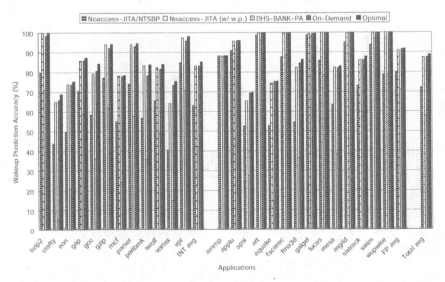

Fig. 7. Wakeup prediction accuracy per fetch, Including bitline precharging and way prediction accuracy

from one sub-bank to another, since the sub-bank hoppings are much more frequent in a set-associative cache.

5.4 Execution Time

Even one percent increase of execution time leads to substantial increase of the total processor energy, which might counterbalance the reduced L1 instruction cache leakage. Thus, it is crucial to maintain execution time close to the base model. We only show the proposed policy of Figure 2, since there is negligible difference from that of Figure 3.

When a wakeup misprediction (including precharging misprediction and way misprediction) and an instruction cache miss occur at the same time, the wakeup penalty is hidden by the cache miss penalty. Thus, the wakeup prediction accuracy is related to the execution time but this is not always exactly proportional.

Figure 8 shows the execution time normalized to the base model in the 4-way set-associative cache. The increases of execution time are 2.09%, 0.15%, 5.36%, and 0.27% for noaccess-JITA/NTSBP, noaccess-JITA (utilizing w.p.), DHS-Bank-PA, and the proposed on-demand policy. Though the noaccess-JITA/NTSBP increases the execution time by inaccurate next sub-bank prediction, the noaccess-JITA (utilizing w.p.) does not since it utilizes the 2-read port way predictor which is more accurate than the NTSBP. In equake, The DHS-Bank-PA degrades the performance as much as 30.1%, which is too severe to be tolerated.

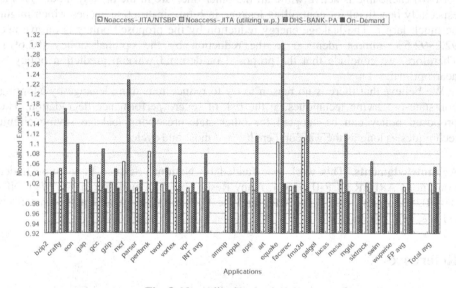

Fig. 8. Normalized execution time

5.5 Comparison of Hardware Overhead

For a wakeup prediction policy, hardware overhead is inevitable in additional to the DVS control circuitry. We compare the hardware overhead of each policy. In the noaccess-JITA/NTSBP, one bit per cache line is required in order to detect whether the cache line is accessed or not in the fixed time period. In addition, the NTSBP has 1K entries (3 bits/entry). The noaccess-JITA (utilizing w.p.) requires one bit per cache line same as the noaccess-JITA. In addition, it needs the 2-read port way predictor for bitline precharging (sub-bank) prediction. In the DHS-Bank-PA, one bit per cache line is also required to store the access history. Additionally, ten bits (half for the target basic block counter and the other half for the fall-through basic block counter) are required to locate a hotspot [5]. Since the BTB has 1024 entries, the total storage overhead is 10K. For the proposed policy, only a small register (ex. 10 bit for our 1024-entry cache) is needed to record the most recently accessed cache line.

6 Conclusions

In this paper, we propose an on-demand wakeup prediction policy using the branch prediction information. Our goal is not only less energy consumption but also consistent near-optimal performance. The noaccess-JITA/NTSBP and the noaccess-JITA (w/ w.p.) show competitive performance consistently but their energy consumption is more than four times of the proposed policy, on average. The DHS-Bank-PA reduces leakage-related energy significantly but it increases the execution time by more than 10% in many cases. In several cases, the increase is more than 20%. The proposed policy degrades the performance by only 0.27%, on average, and 2.1% for the worst case. At the same time, leakage energy is almost eliminated since only one (or two) cache line is active while all the other lines are in the drowsy mode. This is especially beneficial for controlling leakage in future instruction caches which might be much larger. The leakage energy reduction by the proposed policy is on average 92.2~92.5%, almost identical to the reduction by the optimal policy (92.6%). Therefore, we conclude that the proposed on-demand wakeup prediction policy is near-optimal.

We believe that there is no reason to try to reduce remaining leakage by adopting non-state-preserving techniques, at the risk of severe performance degradation. The proposed policy can be adopted for other state-preserving leakage saving circuit techniques as long as the wakeup penalty is at most one cycle.

Acknowledgments. This work was funded by National Science Foundation under grant no. CAREER CCR-0133634, Army Research Office under grant no. W911NF-04-1-0288, a grant from Intel MRL and the IT National Scholarship Program from IITA & MIC, Korea.

References

1. A. Agarwal, L. Hai, and K. Roy. A Single-Vt Low-Leakage Gated-Ground Cache for Deep Submicron. IEEE Journal of Solid-State Circuits. Vol. 38, Feb, 2003, pp. 319-328.
2. T. Austin, E. Larson, and D. Ernst. Simplescalar: An Infrastructure for Computer System Modeling. IEEE Computer Magazine. vol. 35, 2002, pp. 59-67.
3. K. Flautner, N. S. Kim, S. Martin, D. Blaauw, T. Mudge. Drowsy Caches : Simple Techniques for Reducing Leakage Power. Proc. of Int. Symp. on Computer Architecture, 2002, pp. 148-157.

4. F. Hamzaoglu, Y. Ye, A. Keshavarzi, K. Zhang, S. Narendra, S. Borkar, M. Stan, and V. De. Analysis of Dual-VT SRAM cells with Full-Swing Single-Ended Bit Line Sensing for On-Chip Cache. IEEE Transaction on VLSI Systems, vol. 10, April 2002, pp. 91-95.
5. J. S. Hu, A. Nadgir, N. Vijaykrishnan, M. J. Irwin, M. Kandemir. Exploiting Program Hotspots and Code Sequentiality for Instruction Caches Leakage Management. Proc. of Int. Symp. on Low Power Electronics and Design, 2003, pp. 593-601.
6. S. Kaxiras, Z. Hu, and M. Martonosi. Cache decay: Exploiting generational behavior to reduce cache leakage power. Proc. of Int. Symp. on Computer Architecture, 2001, pp 240-251.
7. R. Kessler. The Alpha 21264 Microprocessor. IEEE Micro Magazine. 1999, pp.24-36.
8. N. S. Kim, K Flautner, D. Blaauw, and T. Mudge. Circuit and Microarchitectural Techniques for Reducing Cache Leakage Power. IEEE Transaction on VLSI Systems, vol.12, no. 2, Feb. 2004, pp 167-184.
9. N. S. Kim, K. Flautner, D. Blaauw, T. Mudge. Single-Vdd and Single-Vt Super-Drowsy Techniques for Low-Leakage High-Performance Instruction Caches, Proc. of Int. Symp. on Low Power Electronics and Design, 2004, pp.54-57.
10. L. Li, V. Degalahal, N. Vojaykrishnan, M. Kandemir, and M. J. Irwin. Soft Error and Energy Consumption Interactions: A Data Cache Perspective. Proc. of Int. Symp. on Low Power Electronics and Design, 2004, pp. 132-137.
11. L. Li, I. Kadayif, Y-F. Tsai, N. Vijaykrishnan, M. Kandemir, M. J. Irwin and A. Sivasubramaniam. Leakage Energy Management in Cache Hierarchies. Proc. of Int. Conf. on Parallel Architectures and Compilation Techniques, 2002, pp.131-140.
12. Y. Li, D. Parikh, Y. Zhang, K. Sankaranarayanan, M. Stan, and K. Skadron. State-Preserving vs. Non-State-Preserving Leakage Control in Caches. Proc. of the Design Automation and Test in Europe Conference. 2004, pp. 22-27.
13. S. Manne, A. Klauser, and D. Grunwald, Pipeline Gating : Speculation Control for Energy Reduction. Proc. of Int. Symp. on Computer Architecture, 1998, pp.132-141.
14. S. McFaring. Combining Branch Predictors. Technical Note TN-36. DEC June 1993.
15. K. Nii et. al. A Low Power SRAM Using Auto-Backgate-Controlled MT-CMOS. Proc. of Int. Symp. on Low Power Electronics and Design, 1998, pp. 293-298.
16. M. Powell, S.-H. Yang, B. Falsafi, K. Roy, and T. N. Vijaykumar. Gated-Vdd : A circuit technique to reduce leakage in deep-submicron cache memories. Proc. of Int. Symp. on Low Power Electronics and Design, 2000, pp 90-95.
17. G. Reinman and B. Calder. Using a Serial Cache for Energy Efficient Instruction Fetching. Journal of Systems Architecture. vol. 50 , issue 11, 2004, pp.675-685.
18. S. Yang and B. Falsafi. Near-Optimal Precharging in High-Performance Nanoscale CMOS Caches. Proc. of Int. Symp. on Microarchitecture, 2003.
19. S. Yang, M. Powell, B. Falsafi, K. Roy, and T. Vijaykumar. An Integrated Circuit/ Architecture Approach to Reducing Leakage in Deep-Submicron High-Performance I-Caches. Proc. of Int. Symp. on High-Performance Computer Architecture, 2001, pp.147-157.
20. W. Zhang, J. Hu, V. Degalahal, M. Kandemir, N. Vijaykrishnan, and M. J. Irwin. Compiler-Directed Instruction Cache Leakage Optimization. Proc. of Int. Symp. on Microarchitecture, 2002, pp.208-218.
21. ARM. ARM 1136 Technical Reference Manual. Available in http://www.arm.com
22. ITRS (International Technology Roadmap for Semiconductor). Available in http://public.itrs.net.
23. Standard Performance Evaluation Corp.. Available in http://www.specbench.org.

Scientific Computing Applications on the Imagine Stream Processor[*]

Jing Du, Xuejun Yang, Guibin Wang, and Fujiang Ao

School of Computer, National University of Defense Technology, Changsha 410073, China
jdstarry@yahoo.com.cn

Abstract. The Imagine processor is designed to address the processor-memory gap through streaming technology. Good performance of most media applications has been demonstrated on Imagine. However the research whether scientific computing applications are suited for Imagine is open. In this paper, we studied some key issues of scientific computing applications mapping to Imagine, and present the experimental results of some representative scientific computing applications on the ISIM simulation of Imagine. By evaluating the experimental results, we isolate the set of scientific computing application characteristics well suited for Imagine architecture, analyze the performance potentiality of scientific computing applications on Imagine compared with common processor and explore the optimizations of scientific stream program.

Keywords: scientific computing application, Imagine, stream, three level parallelism, multinest.

1 Introduction

Scientific computing applications widely used to solve large computation problems are pervasive and computationally demanding. These applications require very high arithmetic rates on the order of billions of operations per second. But the performance of these applications is restricted by both the latency and bandwidth of memory accessing [1][2]. Scientific computing applications often exhibit large degrees of data parallelism, and as such maybe present great potential opportunities for stream architectures [3][4], such as Imagine architecture [4]. Imagine is a programmable stream processor aiming at media applications [5], which contains 48 arithmetic units, and a unique three level memory hierarchy designed to keep the functional units saturated during stream processing [6][7]. With powerful supports of the architecture, Imagine can exploit the parallelism and the locality of a stream program, and achieve high computational density and efficiency [8]. In this paper, we describe and evaluate the implementation of mapping scientific computing applications to stream programs formed of data streams and kernels that consume and produce data streams on the Imagine stream architecture, and compare our results on a cycle-accurate simulation of Imagine. The purpose of our work is to exploit the salient features of these unique scientific computing applications, isolate the set of application characteristics best

---

[*] This work was supported by the National High Technology Development 863 Program of China under Grant No. 2004AA1Z2210.

C. Jesshope and C. Egan (Eds.): ACSAC 2006, LNCS 4186, pp. 38–51, 2006.

suited for the stream architecture by evaluating the experimental results, and explore the optimizations of scientific stream program.

2   The Imagine Stream Processing System

2.1   Imagine Architecture

The Imagine architecture developed at Stanford University is a single-chip stream processor that operates on sequences of data records called streams, supporting the stream programming system. It is designed for computationally intensive applications like media applications characterized by high data parallelism and producer-consumer locality with little global data reuse [6][7]. The Imagine processor consists of 48-ALUs arranged as 8 SIMD clusters and three level memory hierarchy to ensure the data locality and keep hundreds of arithmetic units efficiently fed with data. Several local register files (LRFs), directly feed those arithmetic units inside the clusters with their operands. A 128 KB stream register file (SRF) reads data from off-chip DRAM through a memory system interface and sequentially feeds the clusters [8][9]. Fig. 1 diagrams the Imagine stream architecture. One key aspect of Imagine is the concept of producer-consumer locality, where data is circulated between the SRF and arithmetic clusters, thereby avoiding expensive off-chip memory access overhead [10]. Based on the foregoing architecture supports, Imagine can efficiently exploit data parallelism along three levels: instruction-level parallelism (ILP), data-level parallelism (DLP), and task-level parallelism (TLP).

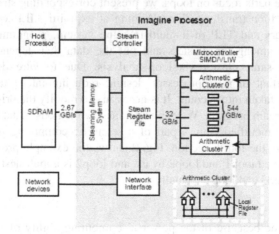

Fig. 1. The Imagine stream architecture

2.2   Imagine Programming Model

The programming model of Imagine is described in two languages: the stream level and the kernel level [11][12][13][14]. A stream level program is written in StreamC language, which is derived from C++ language. A kernel level program of the clusters is written in KernelC language, which is C-like expression syntax. The StreamC program executed for the host thread represents the data communication between the kernels that perform computations. However, programmers must consider the stream organization and communication using this explicit stream model, increasing the programming complexity [15]. So the optimization for stream programming is important to achieve significant performance improvements on the Imagine architecture. The fine stream program can explore ILP, DLP and TLP to maximize performance, as it processes individual elements from streams in parallel.

3 Implementation of Scientific Computing Stream Applications

Imagine system promises to solve many computationally intensive problems much faster than their traditional counterparts. Scientific computing applications contain a great lot of loops possessing a high degree of instruction, data and task level parallelism that can be exploited by decomposing the scientific computing task into smaller subtasks, which are mapped into different computational elements, distributing the scientific stream to different processors. However, because a stream program is more complex than an equivalent sequential program, to realize this increase in speed some challenges must be overcome first [12].

3.1 Stream Level

The key tasks of stream level are partitioning kernels and organizing input streams. Since parallelizable parts focus on loops, we present corresponding streaming method based on different loop transformations. Aiming at exploiting ILP within a cluster, DLP among clusters and TLP of a multi-Imagine system, programmers distribute parallelizable data among the clusters and put the data that dependence can't be eliminated on the same cluster via loop analysis. Due to wire delay becoming increasingly important in microprocessor design, reducing inter-cluster communication must also be taken into account. It is necessary to modify the original algorithm when we write a stream program. We explicate our key methods in detail according to an example that is modified from a part of a scientific computing program named Capao introduced in the fourth section. Fig. 2 shows the example program including two main loops named loop1 and loop2 by us, and loop2 is a multinest with two inner loops labeled as loop3 and loop4 specially.

3.1.1 Multinest
In order to make the best use of the powerful computing ability of Imagine, kernel must process suitable granularity. Computationally intensive operations centre on multinest loops. It is a simple method to look upon each inner loop as a separate kernel. But this partition method brings memory access overhead due to replacing microcode frequently, and causes so much lower repeatable use ratio of SRF as to

```
1    alfa[0] = 0;
2    alfa[1] = b/c;
3    for (i=2;i<511;i++)            ⎫
4        alfa[i]=b/(c-a*alfa[i-1]); ⎬ loop1
                                     ⎭
5    alfa[511]=0;
6    beta[0]=0;
7    for (j=1;j<511;j++)
8    {                                          ⎫
9        for (i=1;i<511;i++)                    |
10        ⌈{                                     |
11         |      f=t[i][j+1]-t[i][j];           |
12  loop3⎨      beta[i]= (f+beta[i-1])/alfa[i-1];|
13         ⌊}                                    ⎬ loop2
14       w[511][j]=0;                            |
15        ⌈for (i=510;i>0;i--)                   |
16  loop4⎨   w[i][j]=alfa[i]*w[i+1][j]+beta[i];  |
17       w[0][j]=0;                              |
18   }                                          ⎭
```

Fig. 2. Example program

make memory access become bottleneck. So that multinest loop is mapped into a big kernel results in better execution time than several small kernels. Because having more operations in one kernel gives more opportunities to parallel the operations and generates more compact schedules with better resource utilization. There are two key steps to partition multinest loops into kernel codes on Imagine.

- Loop combination

Combine the inner loops without array dependence by instruction scheduling. This way can increase the computing scale within kernels, and reduce the number of single instructions outside the inner loops.

- Loop splitting

If inner loops can't be combined, then consider splitting the multinest loop. In this way, the computing amount of outer loops can be involved in kernels, and accordingly parallelism of kernel level program can be improved. This method relates to array saving creating array copies. We can add one dimension based on original array to save the results of previous loops. It is a way that bartering space overhead for efficiency. For example, loop3 and loop4 in Fig. 2 exist array dependence. Hence we split the big multinest loop2 into two two-nest loops. The computing scale of kernels is increased from 510 to 510*510. For loop splitting, the dimension degree of array beta is increased to save the results of loop3, and prepare the input data for loop4. Fig. 3 shows loop2 is divided to two new multinest named loop3' and loop4' according to the dimension variety of array beta.

```
for (j=1;j<511;j++)
    for (i=1;i<511;i++)
    {
        f=t[i][j+1]-t[i][j];                    } loop3'
        beta[i][j]=(f+beta[i-1][j])/alfa[i-1];
    }
for (j=1;j<511;j++)
{
    w[511][j]=0;
    for (i=510;i>0;i--)                         } loop4'
        w[i][j]=alfa[i]*w[i+1][j]+beta[i][j];
    w[0][j]=0;
}
```

Fig. 3. Loop splitting

3.1.2 Coupled Dependent Loop

It is difficult that single loop existing data coupled dependence is parallelized. So expanding one dimension based on the original array within multinest to exploit parallelism on the new dimension is an optional means. Then we can choose multi-form methods of stream organization, aiming at exploiting parallelism among clusters and making full use of LRF according to the LRF capacity. For instance, in Fig. 2, the array beta in the twelfth row of the example code is expanded into two-dimension array. The new dimension direction j exists data coupled dependence, but there is independence between new columns. The coupled dependent code is as follows.

```
beta[i][j] = (f + a * beta[i-1][j] ) / alfa[i-1].
```

For making full use of arithmetic units per cluster, we must avoid assigning the coupled dependent data to different clusters. Doing everything possible to place the coupled dependent data within a cluster can reduce the influence of wire delay, and improve parallelism on Imagine. There are two ways to solve this problem.

- Combine the coupled dependent record into a big record according to the capacity of LRF. Then make the big records form a new input stream. The implementation of this method is complex in some sort, but comprehended easily. We emphasize that the infilling of new records may flush the LRF. So the dependent records are loaded into LRF as successively as possible. At the same time, we must claim attention to save the array boundary of big record. Because the record may be as large as the capacity of LRF. When next record coming, we must save the previous record as the input data of the next operation to avoid record losing. Fig. 4 presents the stream organization of this method on Imagine with 8 clusters.

- Compared with the foregoing way, the second method is easy to implement, because the records of stream are not altered. We place the dependent record onto a cluster by a special index stream. Same as the foregoing method, every eight columns are treated as a group. The index stream is formed successively by row of independent records in a group. Each column of records is assigned onto a cluster. Fig. 5 presents the stream organization of this method.

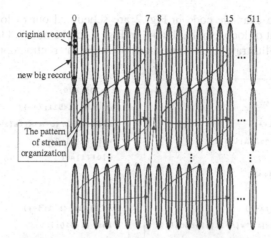

Fig. 4. The first method of coupled dependent loop mapping on Imagine

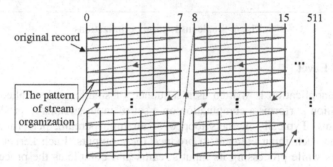

Fig. 5. The second method of coupled dependent loop mapping on Imagine

3.1.3 Single Instruction

If there are a great deal of single instructions in original program, whether they are within loops or not, the partition of kernel is influenced, and the kernel granularity can't be suitable. To solve the problem, we present two optimization methods.

- Loop expending

In order to increase the computing scale of kernels and avoid using index stream that causes DRAM reordered overhead, some single instructions need to be expanded into appropriate loops. Then we can either use successive basic stream as input data or provide uniform loop variable for multinest combination. For instance, the second instruction of the example code in Fig. 2 is expanded into loop1.

- Instruction scheduling

When above factors are satisfied, on the premise of accuracy being ensured, this method may reduce the number of write times to the same record, and prepare for combining single instruction operations. For example, the fourteenth and seventeenth instructions of the example code in Fig. 2 are scheduled out of loop2 to lessen the computing amount of loop4 so that loop4' in Fig. 3 can be mapped to stream program obviously. Fig. 6 illustrates the two methods of single instruction optimization.

```
alfa[0] = 0;
alfa[1] = b/c;
for (i=2;i<511;i++)
  alfa[i]=b/(c-a*alfa[i-1]);
...
for (j=1;j<511;j++){
  w[511][j]=0;
  for (i=510;i>0;i--)
    w[i][j]=alfa[i]*w[i+1][j]+beta[i];
  w[0][j]=0;
}
```

```
alfa[0] = 0;
for (i=1;i<511;i++){
  alfa[i]=b/(c-a*alfa[i-1]);
  w[511][i]=0;
  w[0][i]=0;
}
...
for (j=1;j<511;j++)
  for (i=510;i>0;i--)
    w[i][j]=alfa[i]*w[i+1][j]+beta[i];
```

Fig. 6. Single instruction optimizations

3.2 Kernel Level

An Imagine application is written as a sequence of smaller tasks, called kernels. A kernel operation performs a computation on a set of input streams to produce a set of output streams. Typically, kernels loop over an input stream, performing identical operations on each input element to produce their outputs. Each kernel runs on all eight clusters while processing its input streams and completes the processing of its input streams before the next kernel begins. In this way, producer-consumer locality is exploited by consuming the result of one kernel as soon as it is produced. As an example, Fig. 7 shows how the program in Fig. 2 is mapped to streams and kernels. In the event where inter-cluster communication is required, each cluster has a cluster id tag that can be used to identify the cluster and send/receive data to/from the right cluster. In order to expand the scale of kernel, a long stream is generally as input data. When computing data are not in native register, additional inter-cluster communications are required to transfer the data to the right cluster. And since all applications are not perfectly data parallel, many kernels require data reordering to place the data on the right clusters.

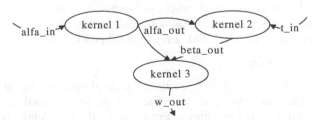

Fig. 7. Example program mapping to stream program model

4 Experimental Results and Analysis

We implement some scientific computing applications on ISIM that is a cycle-accurate simulator of Imagine [14], including 171.Swim in SPEC2000 and Capao.

4.1 Application Analysis

Swim is a weather prediction program for comparing the performance of current supercomputers. Fig. 8 shows data flow chart of Swim. Its main computing amount focuses on a loop of calculating fourteen arrays with 513*513 size. The data amount of Swim is large, but the computing operations are few correspondingly. The array access pattern presented in Fig. 9 is irregular.

Capao is an application on the field of optics. Its computing amount is very huge. According to its result of serial version, 65.49% of time overhead comes from subroutine dfft, and 13.36% comes from subroutine transp. So we just consider mapping the two subroutines to stream program so that improve performance of the whole application. The subroutine dfft possesses small computing amount and fine computation intensiveness. We implement two version of dfft. One that applies butterfly algorithm is called DFFTN in this section, and another formulized without any optimization is called DFFT. The computing amount is exponent distinction between DFFTN and DFFT. It is time-consuming on general scalar processors that DFFTN performs bit reverse operation. Imagine supports this operation on hardware level, so the performance of DFFTN may be increased. The experiment on DFFT purposes certifying powerful computing ability of Imagine.

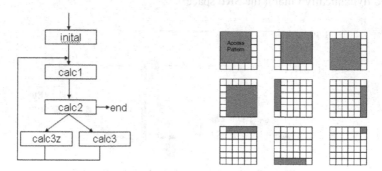

Fig. 8. The data flow chart of Swim   **Fig. 9.** Accessing pattern of Swim

4.2 Experimental Results

For comparison purpose, actual measurements of performance were taken using a general scalar processor system. Table 1 illustrates the result of a rough comparison between the performance of Imagine and the general scalar processor. It is obvious that Imagine provides high speedup of computationally intensive applications such as DFFTN, DFFT and Transp compared with general processor system in terms of number of cycles, due to the simple control logic and parallel processing ability of many arithmetic units. And compared with highly sensitive to memory latency of general processor, these applications can hide latency to achieve good performance. But for data intensive applications such as Swim, the speedup is low due to irregular access pattern so that memory access latency can't be hided.

Table 1. Comparison of different implementation for the scientific applications

	DFFTN	Swim	DFFT	Transp
Cycles (StreamC& KernelC)	52335	6689051178	1620615	9287445
Cycles (C code)	3705560	132895126660	28093910	158444624

Fig. 10 shows the three level bandwidth hierarchy of these applications. The LRF to memory bandwidth ratio are over 33:1, 70:1 and 592:1 across DFFTN, Transp and DFFT, due to the abundant memory access of these three applications focusing on LRF. So they can achieve good performance on Imagine with relatively low memory bandwidth for exposing a large register set with two levels of hierarchy to the compiler enables considerable locality to be captured that is not captured by a conventional cache. While the streams of Swim are very long, which can't be partitioned due to dependence, causing low locality of SRF and LRF. Notice that the bandwidth of LRF is much lower than that of SRF, because a mass of index streams derived dynamically inhabit the SRF space.

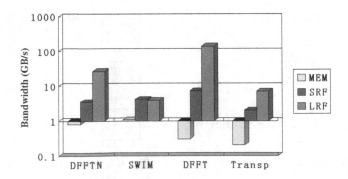

Fig. 10. Bandwidth hierarchy of applications

Table 2 presents the computation rate of these applications measured in the number of operations executed per second. Imagine achieves 16 GOPS ALU performance on media applications and sustains between 2% and 31% of the peak performance on these applications. On DFFT, Imagine averages 10 arithmetic operations per cycle across all the clusters for an aggregate rate of 5 GOPS. This high computation rate indicates that the stream programming system delivers high computational density on the DFFT application. But for Swim, the computing time is 13%~38% of the whole run time. The great mass of work is to wait for result of memory accessing leading to inefficient performance.

Table 2. Computation rate of applications

	DFFTN	Swim	DFFT	Transp
Cycle	52335	6733615303	1620615	9287515
Ops	209920	3409274134	16248880	8359056
GOPs	2.0	0.25	5.0	0.45

Fig. 11 shows the size of the computation kernel, as well as the number of arithmetic operations per memory access. Imagine's stream model requires large number of arithmetic operations per memory access to effectively use the underlying hardware. We can observe that Transp has enough bandwidth to sustain one operation per memory access, while DFFT and DFFTN that are computationally intensive applications require high computation per memory access to amortize off-chip memory bandwidth. Swim characterized by irregular data access results in low computation per memory access, and the SRF is not used effectively since there is bad producer-consumer locality in this example. In conclusion, Swim is not well suited for the Imagine architecture. The performance is limited by memory bandwidth due to the relatively low computation per memory access.

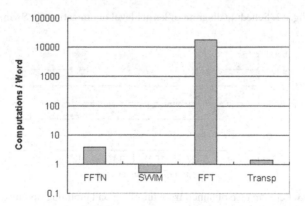

Fig. 11. Computational intensity of applications

4.3 Optimization

Aiming at solving the inefficiency problem of Swim, we apply some optimizations on the application. There are two levels of stream program optimized method.

4.3.1 Kernel Level Optimization

Computation is the bottleneck in the unoptimizable version of our stream programs not for saturation of the ALUs but for their poor utilization. The Imagine software environment allows for automatic code optimizations such as loop unrolling and software pipelining [12]. At the kernel level, the programmer can instruct the compiler to unroll/pipeline by simple compiler directives for program optimization. Then the loop in the cluster is unrolled and pipelined in order to achieve higher arithmetic intensity. The left part of Fig. 12 shows that the VLIW schedule of the unoptimizable code is quite sparse. The optimized schedule shown in the right part of Fig. 12 is dense. Fig. 13 presents that the computation time is reduced according to unrolling and piplining of diverse times on identical program. We can conclude that unrolling four times is a critical point. Unrolling too many times increase loading overhead of the microcode with enlarging code amount.

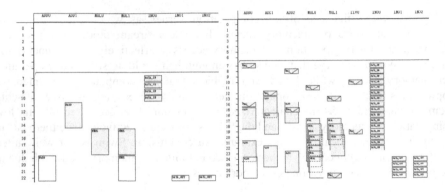

Fig. 12. Schedule diagram of kernel level optimization for Swim

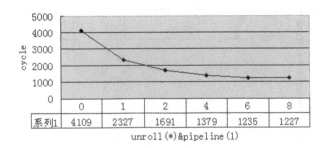

Fig. 13. Performance obtained from unrolling and piplining optimizations

4.3.2 Stream Level Optimization

By exploiting kernel level optimization, the total execution time reduces. Based on the most perfect optimization in kernel, we adjust the input stream length to observe the performance variety. Fig. 14 shows that it gives more improvements with shorter input stream, and longer stream results in worse speedup. Specially, when the length longer than 512*4, performance is reduced sharply due to appearance of double-buffer. Optimization is invalid when the stream length greater than 512*32, because the optimization increases microcode loading overhead with enlarging code amount.

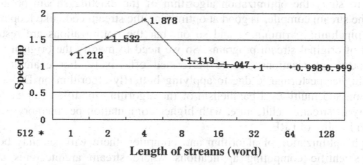

Fig. 14. Speedup obtained from varying stream length

Above analyses show that the organization of stream, especially the partition of long stream, influences on program performance deeply. To eliminate this bottleneck, it is necessary to reduce data transmission between memory and SRF so that the locality of SRF is enhanced. There are two optimizations of stream level accordingly, stripmining and Software pipelining.

The input streams of most applications are too large to fit the SRF directly. To solve this problem, stripmining is brought forward to process a great deal of input stream into small portions that fit in the SRF. Then the small input portions are applied to produce small portions of the final output that fit in the SRF. This optimization is important to achieve good performance [16].

Software pipelining divides a loop into sections so that the execution of one section in an iteration can be overlapped with execution of another section of another iteration. This optimization is implemented for exploiting producer-consumer locality and effectively hiding memory access overhead.

5   Conclusion and Future Work

In this paper, we explain the method of scientific computing applications mapping to stream programs, and present the experimental results. Partial programs fit for stream application, such as DFFT and DFFTN. For analyzing whether scientific computing applications are suited for stream architecture, we come up for discussion.

Three level parallelisms and two level data localities of Imagine architecture make the performance of scientific computing stream programs improve possibly. And the memory operations and computation overlapping can be propitious to cover the memory delay and implement optimizations, with the goal of keeping all the units busy at all times. Scientific computing applications often exhibit large degrees of data parallelism, and as such may be good candidates for SIMD stream applications. But comparing scientific computing applications with media applications, the former has irregular data organization, multiform data accessing pattern, new compiling problems caused by large computing scale, much higher precision in calculation, and bandwidth in great demand. It is difficult to suit for the stream architecture completely. For the reason of making full use of the supports of stream architecture and exploiting the potentiality of scientific computing programs mapping to Imagine, we need to study the optimization algorithm of the existing stream programs. At present, the stream compiler is good at optimizing the stream code like loop unrolling, software pipelining, stripmining and so on, but the optimizations are restricted to algorithm of original stream programs. So we need to modify the original algorithm so that these optimizations can be performed effectively. For example, DFFTN achieves higher performance due to applying butterfly algorithm on DFFT. Stream organization and multi-level parallelism of the algorithm modified can exploit more potentiality of stream architecture, with higher computation per memory access and better data locality of LRF.

Through optimization of algorithm and compiler, there will certainly be a large class of scientific computing applications where stream architectures are more effective. Since there exists a lot of data parallelism in such applications, and the overhead of loading and changing kernels is amortized by large stream sizes [16][17][18]. Also, the memory operations and computation can overlap in order to hide the time spent in memory accesses, with large kernel of scientific computing stream programs. Furthermore, the amount of arithmetic units are enough to exploit data parallelism effectively, and memory accessing focuses on LRF and SRF mostly after optimizations to take advantage of consumer-producer locality so that make more efficient use of the memory bandwidth hierarchy. Powerful computational ability of stream architecture is emerged to sustain a high computation rate.

Future plans include exploiting common programming model to improve coding efficiency, due to existing program model exposing so many controls to programmers. Also, it is significant to construct a scientific computing kernel library that is valuable on algorithm design and shifting much of the complexity to the development of stream applications. This approach lowers the barrier to developer participation and can simplify collaborations among research teams by allowing each group to focus on their interests and expertise.

Acknowledgements. We gratefully thank the Stanford Imagine team for the use of their compilers and simulators and their generous help. We specifically thank lab 620 of School of Computer Science in National University of Defense Technology for helpful discussions and comments on this work. We also acknowledge the reviewers for their insightful comments. This work was supported by the National High Technology Development 863 Program of China under Grant No. 2004AA1Z2210.

References

1. W. A. Wulf, S. A. McKee. Hitting the memory wall: implications of the obvious. Computer Architecture News, 1995. 23(1): 20-24.
2. D. Burger, J. Goodman, A. Kagi. Memory bandwidth limitations of future micro-processors. In Proceedings of the 23rd International Symposium on Computer Architecture, Philadelphia, PA, 1996.78-89.

3. Saman Amarasinghe, William. Stream Architectures. In PACT 2003, September 27, 2003.
4. B. Khailany et al. Imagine: Media processing with streams. IEEE Micro, 21(2): 35–46,March 2001.
5. Ujval J. Kapasi, Scott Rixner, William J. Dally, Brucek Khailany, Jung Ho Ahn, Peter Mattson and John D.Owens. Programmable Stream Processors. *IEEE Computer,* pages 54-62, August , 2003.
6. Brucek Khailany, William J. Dally, Andrew Chang, Ujval J. Kapasi, Jinyung Namkoong, and Brian Towles. VLSI design and verification of the Imagine processor. In Proceedings of the IEEE International Conference on Computer Design, pages 289–296, September 2002.
7. Brucek Khailany. The VLSI Implementation and Evaluation of Area-and Energy-Effcient Streaming Media Processors. Ph.D. thesis, Stanford University, 2003.
8. Ujval J. Kapasi, William J. Dally, et al. The Imagine Stream Processor. In Processings of the 2002 International Conference on Computer Design, 2002.
9. Nuwan S. Jayasena. Memory Hierarchy Design for Stream Computing. Ph.D. thesis, Stanford University, 2005.
10. Scott Rixner, William Dally, Ujval J. Kapasi, Brucek Khailany, Abelardo Lopez-Lagunas, Peter Mattson and John D.Owens. Media processing applications on Imagine media processor. In Proceedings of the 2002 International Conference on Computer design,2002.
11. Peter Mattson et al. Imagine Programming System Developer's Guide. http:// cva. stanford.edu, 2002.
12. Peter Raymond Mattson. A Programming System for the Imagine Media Processor. Dept. of Electrical Engineering. Ph.D. thesis, Stanford University, 2002.
13. Saman Amarasinghe et al. Stream Languages and Programming Models. In PACT 2003, September 27, 2003.
14. Abhishek Das, Peter Mattson, et al. Imagine Programming System User's Guide 2.0. June 2004.
15. Ola Johnsson, Magnus Stenemo, Zain ul-Abdin. Programming & Implementation of Streaming Applications. Master's thesis, Computer and Electrical Engineering Halmstad University, 2005.
16. Jinwoo Suh, Eun-Gyu Kim, Stephen P. Crago, Lakshmi Srinivasan, and Matthew C. French. A Performance Analysis of PIM, Stream Processing, and Tiled Processing on Memory-Intensive Signal Processing Kernels. In ISCA03, 2003.
17. Mattan Erez,Jung Ho Ahn, Ankit Garg, William J.Dallyet et al. Analysis and Performance Results of a Molecular Modeling Application on Merrimac. In SC'04, Pittsburg, Pennsylvania, USA, November 6-12, 2004.
18. Jung Ho Ahn, William J. Dally, et al. Evaluating the Imagine Stream Architecture. In ISCA2004, 2004.

Enhancing Last-Level Cache Performance by Block Bypassing and Early Miss Determination*

Haakon Dybdahl[1] and Per Stenström[2]

[1] Dept. of Computer and Information Science,Norwegian University of Science and Technology, N-7491 Trondheim, Norway
dybdahl@idi.ntnu.no
[2] Dept. of Computer Engineering, Dept. of Computer Engineering, Chalmers University of Technology, S-412 96 Goteborg, Sweden
per@ce.chalmers.se

Abstract. While bypassing algorithms have been applied to the first-level cache, we study for the first time their effectiveness for the last-level caches for which miss penalties are significantly higher and where algorithm complexity is not constrained by the speed of the pipeline. Our algorithm monitors the reuse behavior of blocks that are touched by delinquent loads and re-classify them on-the-fly. Blocks classified as bypassed are only installed in the level-1 cache. We leverage the algorithm to early send out a miss request for loads expected to request blocks classified to be bypassed. Such requests are sent to memory directly without tag checks at intermediary levels in the cache hierarchy. Overall, we find that we can robustly reduce the miss rate by 23% and improve IPC with 14% on average for memory bound SPEC2000 applications without degrading performance of the other SPEC2000 applications.

1 Introduction

As the speedgap between processor and memory has increased, the cache memory hierarchies have become deeper and the last-level caches (typically L2 or L3) have become bigger. Unfortunately, continuing along this route yields diminishing returns on investments because cache hit rate improves quite modestly with cache size and adding more levels increases the penalty taken when a request misses at all levels. Thus, it is important to study techniques that increase the utilization of deep cache memory hierarchies and that reduce the miss penalty.

One source of poor resource utilization is blocks with streaming behavior. Typically, there are multiple accesses to such blocks just after the miss. After this initial burst of accesses, the reuse distance is typically very long. When such blocks are installed in the cache, they may trigger replacement of blocks with a shorter reuse distance, thereby increasing the miss rate. One approach to reduce the detrimental effect of such blocks is to *bypass* them, rather than installing them. Several techniques to predict blocks subject to bypassing have

---

* This work is partly sponsored by the HiPEAC Network of Excellence funded by EU under FP6.

C. Jesshope and C. Egan (Eds.): ACSAC 2006, LNCS 4186, pp. 52–66, 2006.

been studied in the past. They typically fall into two broad categories – static [4, 15] and dynamic [15, 7, 10, 6, 9, 13, 8, 16, 5]. In the static approach, either blocks touched by specific memory instructions in the program are bypassed, or the compiler partitions memory blocks that should be bypassed into special address space regions that are bypassed. In the dynamic approach, bypassing is based on the past behavior of an instruction or a block which guides future decisions whether to bypass or not. Statistics are stored in special data structures which guide bypassing decisions. Blocks predicted to have a reuse distance longer than their lifetime in the cache will be bypassed. To exploit the spatial locality of the initial burst of accesses, most approaches assume that they are installed in a special buffer that is significantly smaller than the cache. A misprediction can increase the miss rate: If the block is reused after it has been replaced from the special buffer but before it would have been replaced in the cache, the bypass operation results in a miss that would have been avoided without bypassing. While published prediction techniques have achieved high prediction coverage, they sometimes increase the miss rate due to low accuracy which leads to inconsistent performance gains.

While previous attempts using bypassing were applied to first-level caches, we study in this paper block bypassing algorithms for last-level caches. They have a much higher potential than for the first-level cache for several reasons. First, the first-level cache is heavily constrained by the speed of the pipeline. Hence, cache management algorithms must be simple. Second, the latency of first-level cache misses that hit in subsequent levels does not incur much penalty because it can be often successfully hidden by the latency tolerance capability of multiple-issue out-of-order cores of moderate issue rate. Third, bypassing has much higher potential at the lower levels as the miss penalty is significantly higher. On the contrary, mispredictions are also much more costly making algorithm robustness a key issue. However, assuming a two-level cache hierarchy, which forms the base for our experiments, our overall strategy is to bypass blocks at the second level but always install them at the first level. As a result, as long as the reuse distance for incorrectly predicted bypassed blocks is smaller than the size of the level-1 cache, there will be no penalty for mispredictions.

Previous studies [12, 1] have shown that a few load instructions are responsible for most of the cache misses, called *delinquent loads*. Our approach is to base the prediction of which blocks to be bypassed by detecting such loads and record them at run-time. However, we validate the correctness of the prediction and change it by also monitoring whether we erroneously bypass a block with a reuse distance shorter than the L2 cache but longer than the L1 cache by monitoring the reuse at the L2 cache. While this basic approach uses some of the components from the dynamic scheme proposed by Tyson et al. [15], we found that the Tyson scheme increased the miss rate for many of the applications. We identified several useful extensions that eventually offered more consistent performance improvements. For example, by storing tags for bypasses we can identify when bypasses are done incorrectly and stop bypassing for the involved instruction.

Another disadvantage of using deeper memory hierarchies addressed in the paper, is the increased miss penalty for the requests that miss at all levels. If one could determine that a miss will not be satisfied at any level without doing tag checks at all levels, the miss penalty can be reduced quite significantly. We also present results for a simple early miss determination approach that leverages our bypassing algorithm. If the instruction that causes the L1 miss is predicted to bring a bypassed block into the cache, it is likely that it will not be found at any level. We then send this request speculatively to the memory, potentially reducing the miss penalty.

We evaluated our algorithm using 23 applications from SPEC2000 on a simulation model based on SimpleScalar V3 modeling a 4-issue out-of-order core. On average we improved the L2 miss rate by 23% as compared to the upper-bound achieved by an oracle algorithm which is 34%. The infrastructure needed to monitor access behavior is quite small – the storage area of the cache is increased with less than 7%. We found that our early miss determination scheme could correctly predict that the block is not available for 27% of the cases with only 1% of the accesses incorrectly predicted as misses on average. Overall, the bypassing algorithm together with the early miss determination scheme improved the IPC by 14% for the memory bound applications. The algorithm is robust and for the non-memory-bound applications the average IPC is slightly improved in contrast to Tyson's scheme [15] where most of the applications suffer.

Our baseline architecture and the Tyson algorithm are presented in the next section. Sections 3 to 5 present the new schemes including our bypassing algorithm, an oracle algorithm and our early miss determination algorithm. Experimental methodology and our evaluation are found in Sections 6 and 7. We relate our findings to prior work in Section 8 and conclude in Section 9.

2   The Tyson Scheme for Dynamic Bypassing

Two schemes for dynamic bypassing of memory accesses for the L1 cache were described and evaluated by Tyson et al. in [15]. Only one of them, called *improved dynamic bypassing scheme*, improved the performance and therefore we do not consider the other scheme. We call this scheme the *Tyson scheme*. The principle of this scheme is that a few instructions load data that pollute the cache. These instructions shall not store data in cache – data is bypassed to the processor. This increases the hit rate for the other instructions and for the total system. Another advantage is that when bypassing data only a single word is read from main memory and hence the memory bandwidth usage is reduced.

2.1   Structures

A table associates a counter with each instruction that is a candidate for bypassing as shown in Fig. 1(a). Instructions are identified by their static memory address (*inst*). The cache blocks are extended with the *fetched by* field which refers to an entry in the instruction table, see Fig. 1(b).

Instruction	Counter
inst a	2
inst c	3
...	...

(a) The instruction table

Index	Tag	Cache line	Fetched by inst
0	tag a	..	inst a
1	tag c	..	inst c
....	...	..	..

(b) The extended cache structure

Fig. 1. The structures for Tyson Scheme

2.2 Algorithm

The Tyson scheme uses the following events:

1. *Cache miss.* The instruction (*inst*) that triggers a cache miss is inserted into the instruction table with a zero counter if it is not already present. For instructions that are already present, the counter is incremented. In Fig. 1(a), if instruction $inst_a$ is requesting a non-existing cache block, $inst_a$'s counter is increased from two to three.
2. *Cache hit.* The instruction (*inst*) that caused the cache hit is looked up in the instruction table and its counter is decremented. The instruction referred to by the *fetched by* field is also looked up in the instruction table, and if present its counter is decremented. For example if instruction $inst_x$ requests the cache block with index 1, which was fetched by $inst_c$, the counter of $inst_c$ is decremented from value three to value two, see Fig. 1.
3. *Bypassing.* A bypass is performed when an instruction causes a cache miss and the instruction is found in the instruction table with its counter equal or greater than a preset threshold value. Instead of loading a cache line, only a single word is fetched from main memory and it is not stored in L1 cache.

The threshold value for bypassing and the maximum value for the counter in our evaluation of the Tyson scheme later in the paper is set to three.

2.3 Discussion

The processor is able to load a single word of eight bytes in the Tyson scheme, and this is said to be four times more efficient than loading a cache line that consists of four words. This is not true for today's systems with wide data buses, interleaved main memory banks, pipelined memory accesses and burst transfer options. Incorrect or very aggressive bypassing of cache lines in the Tyson scheme have a limited impact since the latency of bypassing a cache line, i.e., fetching a single word, is less than loading a cache line (in their model). In [15] it was found that the memory bandwidth requirements was reduced by more than 20% for integer applications which is not surprising as most of the integer application do not benefit from prefetching of longer cache lines. It was found that the cache hit ratio was increased by up to 26% for some floating point benchmark applications, and for some cache configuration the cache hit ratio was increased by 2-3% on average. Unfortunately, the performance was found to be unstable across the benchmarks and the median performance is a degradation of the cache hit rate.

Using Tyson's scheme in an L2 setting increases the aggressiveness by which blocks are bypassed. Instructions with three consecutive cache misses trigger bypassing if the fetched cache lines are not re-accessed in L2 between the execution of each of these instructions. Data is more likely to be re-accessed in the L1 cache than in L2 cache since the L1 cache filters out some of the hits in the L2 cache. This makes Tyson's algorithm more aggressive in bypassing the L2 cache than in its original setting in the L1 cache and creates a serious disadvantage.

In general, out-of-order execution processors tolerate memory latency to some extent, which makes L1 misses that hit in L2 less serious. However, misses caused by incorrect bypassing in the last level cache (L2 in our experiments) is expected to stall the processor for a significantly longer time. Consequently, a more sophisticated heuristic is needed to control the bypassing of the L2 cache. The accuracy of the bypassing heuristics then becomes crucial.

3   New Scheme for Bypassing

Our proposed scheme increases the precision of the bypassing using a feedback loop in which the correctness of its decisions is used as inputs to the heuristics controlling the algorithm. In addition to keeping the tag for the present cache line, each cache block contains the tag for the other cache line that would have been present if the previous fetch was bypassed/not bypassed. Detection of eviction of cache blocks that are not accessed is used to determine if instructions should be bypassed. All this information is used for the feedback loop to enable or disable bypassing for each instruction which results in robust performance.

3.1   Structures

Like in the Tyson scheme, instructions that cause cache misses are inserted in a table as shown in Fig. 1(a). Instructions are identified by their static memory address (*inst*). The cache block is extended with new fields as shown in Fig. 2. The *fetched by* field contains the instruction (*inst*) that fetched the cache line.

Index	Tag	Cache line	Fetched by inst.	Used	Shadow inst.	Shadow tag	Shadow status
0	tag a	..	inst a	FALSE	instb	tag b	bypassed
1	tag c	..	inst c	TRUE	instd	tag d	replaced
....	...	..	....	...	..	..	..

Fig. 2. The cache structure is extended to include data used for the heuristics

The *used* field is used to detect cache blocks that are replaced without being accessed, an indication that the cache line should have been bypassed. It is reset when the cache line is replaced, and set on a cache hit. The *shadow instruction* is set to the instruction (*inst*) that caused the replacement or that was bypassed. For a replaced cache line the *shadow tag* is updated with the tag of the replaced cache block, and for bypassed cache lines the *shadow tag* is updated with the value of the tag of the block that is bypassed. *shadow status* indicates if the last request was bypassed or caused a replacement.

3.2 Algorithm

The events that trigger actions in the new scheme are the following:

1. *Cache miss.* An instruction that triggers a cache miss is inserted into the instruction table with a zero counter if it is not already present. The counter is incremented for the instruction. For example, if instruction $inst_a$ is requesting a non-existing cache block, its counter is increased (Fig. 1(a)). The *shadow tag* is updated with the tag of the data that was in the cache block, the *shadow instruction* with the instruction that caused the miss and the *shadow status* is set to "replace".

2. *Cache hit.* The counter for an instruction that triggers a cache hit is decreased if present in the instruction table. If the instruction referred to by the *fetched by* field in the cache block is in the instruction table, its counter is also decreased. Finally, the field *fetched by* is cleared. This means that fetching data for other instructions is only used once by the heuristic. For example if instruction $inst_x$ requests a cache block with index 1 which was fetched by $inst_c$, its counter is decreased from value three to two, see Fig. 2.

3. *Cache hit caused by bypassing.* A cache hit is said to be caused by bypassing when the cache block contains information about bypasses for that cache block. The counter for the instruction referred to by the *shadow instruction* is increased if the instruction is present in the instruction table. If not, it is inserted. Finally the shadow information is cleared which means that this event is only used once. For example if data with tag_a in index 0 is requested, the $inst_b$ will be inserted into the instruction table.

4. *Cache miss caused by bypassing.* A cache miss is said to be caused by bypassing when the tag of the requested data is found in the *shadow tag* and the *shadow status* indicates bypassing. The counter for the instruction that caused the bypassing is decreased in the instruction table, if present. For example if the data with tag_b is requested in index 0, the counter for $inst_b$ is decreased if the instruction was in the instruction table.

5. *Cache miss caused by not bypassing.* A cache miss is said to be caused by *not* bypassing when the requested tag matches the *shadow tag* and the *status bit* indicates that the shadow data reflects a replacement. The counter for the instruction that replaced the cache block is increased. If the instruction is not present in the table, the instruction is inserted. For example if data with tag_d is requested with index 1, the counter for $inst_c$ is increased.

6. *Data replaced without being used.* This happens when an instruction loads a cache block that is not accessed before it is overwritten. The counter of the instruction that fetched the data is increased, if present. For example if the first cache block is replaced, the counter for $inst_a$ is increased.

7. *Bypassing.* A bypass is triggered by a cache miss and requires that the counter for the instructions that caused the cache miss is above a threshold

limit. The cache block is loaded from main memory and into the L1 cache without being stored in the L2 cache. The *shadow tag* is updated with the tag of the data that is bypassed, the *shadow instruction* with the instruction that caused the miss and the *shadow status* is set to "bypass".

Each event can increase or decrease the value of the counter with different values, see Fig. 3, and different levels of threshold and maximum value of the counter can be used.

		Tyson	New Scheme	Shadow	Replace	Equal	Tyson II
1	Cache miss	1	1	0	0	1	2
2	Cache hit	-1	-2	0	0	-1	-3
3	Cache hit caused by bypassing	0	3	1	0	1	0
4	Cache miss caused by bypassing	0	1	1	0	1	0
5	Cache miss caused by not bypassing	0	-1	-1	0	-1	0
6	Data replaced without being used	0	1	0	1	1	0
7	Bypassing threshold/max counter value	3	9	3	3	3	6

Fig. 3. Different configurations for the heuristics for bypassing

3.3   Discussion

The shadow data is used to monitor the consequences of bypasses and replacements. Different applications benefit from different parameter settings. However, as we will see, the described algorithm with the new scheme (see Fig. 3) works well across different benchmarks and for different cache sizes.

Structures for storing the data shown in Figures 1(a) and 2 are assumed to be implemented in hardware. The instruction table is limited in size and all simulations are done with a size of 32 elements. The resources needed are therefore small in comparison to the ones needed for an L2 cache. The extension of the cache block to include information for the heuristics will however require more hardware. The number of bits needed to store a cache block for a conventional architecture and the new scheme are shown in Fig. 4. The *shadow tag* is of the same size as the tag for the cache block. Given a system with 8-GByte physical memory (33 bits) and a 1-MByte 4-way set associative cache 6 bits are used to address the byte within the cache line and 12 bits are used to index the cache block which leaves $33 - 6 - 12 = 15$ bits for the tag. There are two references to two instructions in the instruction table, i.e. the fields *fetched by instruction* and *shadow instruction*. These contain the address for the instruction in memory. The address of the instruction is used as a key and is 33 bits. By changing the algorithm slightly so that instructions are only placed in the instruction table on cache misses, these two fields only need to point to an instruction in the instruction table and it is not necessary to store the whole address of the instruction. This modification does not incur any measurable performance degradation. However, when these address fields only point to the instruction table, there is no way of detecting when the instructions in the table are replaced. Therefore the instruction address should be hashed and stored in the cache block to discover when instructions are replaced. This results in 5 bits for pointing into the

Field	Tag	Cache Line Data	LRU data	Fetched by inst.	Used	Shadow inst.	Shadow tag	Shadow status	Total
Conv. architecture	15	512	2	0	0	0	0	0	529
New Scheme	15	512	2	33	1	33	15	1	612
Instruction pointers	15	512	2	9	1	9	15	1	564

Fig. 4. The number of bits used for storing a cache block for a computer with 8 GBytes memory (33 bits) and a 1 MByte 4-way set associative cache

instruction table, and let us assume 4 bits for hashing the instruction address. The total increase in number of bits of storage is less than 7% for the cache block with pointers as shown to the right in the table.

Bypassing breaks the *inclusion*; blocks in L1 cache are not guaranteed to exist in the L2 cache. The L1 cache must be accessed to get the latest values by memory coherence schemes. However, this is no different from conventional caches with delayed write back schemes. Directory coherence protocols can be used to know what data that are loaded in L1.

4   Oracle Bypassing Algorithm

In this section, we derive an algorithm to assess how optimally our scheme can avoid misses by bypassing blocks in the cache. Optimal algorithms depend on the problem space, e.g. deciding which cache block that should be replaced. In this case the trace of memory accesses can be analyzed and blocks are installed in the cache if the reuse distance is shorter than the reuse distance for the block that is replaced [3,14]. However, we are not considering the replacement policy for the cache. We are interested in the optimal algorithm for deciding whether to bypass cache blocks combined with the standard least recently used (LRU) policy. This makes the optimal algorithm more complex, it can not just look at the reuse distance to decide upon bypassing or not.

We have made a new algorithm that requires only a single run of the benchmark and is optimal for direct-mapped caches and set-associative caches with random replacement policies. The algorithm is based on the idea to postpone the decision regarding bypassing until it is known whether it reduces the cache miss rate or not. For an instruction that causes a miss, the algorithm maintains the cache state for the two possible outcomes: bypassing versus not bypassing. That is, each cache block is extended dynamically to keep track of data for both outcomes. On a hit to the cache block it is known which requests that should have been bypassed and which should be replaced, and the simulation will only consider one of the alternatives for the rest of the simulation. Consider the following example. Several requests that map to the same cache block appear in the following order: a, b, c, and a. Without bypassing, b will replace a, c will replace b and then a will replace c, i.e. only cache misses. With optimal bypassing b and c are bypassed, and the last a will become a hit instead of a miss. Our oracle algorithm will extend the cache structure dynamically to contain first a, then a and b, and then a, b and c. In the end when a is requested again, it sees that by bypassing b and c, a hit is generated for a, and the decision about bypassing is done. The extra data stored can be deleted at this point. An application without any hits will build up a large data structure, but only linear to the number of instructions. Set-associative caches with LRU algorithms are more complex. Storing information about both decisions doubles the storage requirement for each missed block. One way to reduce the storage requirements is to change the replacement policy. For each bypass we change the LRU cache block to become the recently used in the same way as a replacement of the cache blocks does, i.e. bypass and replacement change the LRU stack in the same way. A decision to bypass or not only regards one element in the cache and only one additional element need to be stored for each miss. Again, the data structure needed is linear in the number of instructions (in case of only misses).

The result is an oracle algorithm with a cache with an LRU replacement policy that is not LRU when accesses are bypassed. This tends to underestimate the performance gains of bypassing and hence reduces the upper bound. With this caveat, the oracle algorithm is nevertheless used to assess if there is a potential for using bypassing, and whether there is room for improvement.

5   Early Miss Determination

A problem with deep hierarchies is that the miss penalty is increased for each level added. By predicting early on whether a request will miss at all levels, and accessing main memory in parallel with tag checks at the intermediary level, the miss penalty is expected to be reduced substantially [11].

If the data is found in the cache, the data from cache is used. However, we assume that there is no way of removing the ongoing memory access to main memory system. Miss-prediction will thus increase the memory bandwidth usage and can stall other memory accesses. We look at using the heuristic for bypassing data in the new scheme to early determine cache misses and launch a memory access. Instructions that are in the instruction table and with maximum counter value are considered to miss in the L2 cache. An oracle scheme for early miss determination would manage to predict all cache misses.

6   Methodology

Simulation is used to study the efficiency of the two schemes for bypassing memory accesses for the L2 cache, the oracle algorithm, and early miss determination scheme. The *sim-cache* model is used for studying cache miss rates and the execution model is single-issue in-order. No timing information is included in these simulations. The *sim-outorder* model used for studying IPC improvements is a clock-cycle level out-of-order execution model with non-blocking caches. The models are part of SimpleScalar version 3 [2]. These models are extended to simulate memory congestion, the different bypass schemes, the oracle algorithm, and the early miss determination scheme. A logical sketch of the simulated system is shown in Fig. 5.

Fig. 5. The simulated single processor core with the memory hierarchy

Parameter	Value
RUU size	128 instructions
LSQ size	64 instructions
Fetch queue size	4 instructions
Fetch, Decode, Issue and Commit width	4 instructions/cycle
Functional Units	4 INT ALUs, 4 FP ALUs, 1 INT Multiply/Divide, 1 FP Multiply/Divide
Branch Predictor	Combined, Bimodal 4K table, 2-Level 1K table, 10-bit history table, 4K Chooser
BTB	512-entry, 4 way
Mispredict Penalty	7 cycles
L1 Instruction/Data Cache	32K, 4-way (LRU), 64 B Blocks, 1 cycle latency
L2 Cache	Unified, 1 M, 4-way (LRU), 64 B Blocks, 24 cycles latency
Main Memory	200 cycles first chunk, 10 cycles inter chunk, 4 independent subbanks
I-TLB/D-TLB	128-entry, fully associative, 30 cycles miss penalty

Fig. 6. Micro-architectural parameters

The baseline for the simulator is shown in Fig. 6. Data and instruction look-aside buffers (DTLB and ITLB) are not simulated in the *sim-cache* model. We assume that the hit and miss latency for the L2 cache are equal.

The size of the instruction table is 32 for all experiments. The original Tyson scheme used a branch predictor like table for the L1 cache. This means that our implementation of Tyson is slightly different, and the reason is that we are bypassing the L2 cache.

SPEC2000 applications were used as benchmarks with the reference data sets. Each simulation is forwarded one billion instructions and then simulated for two billion instructions.

7 Evaluation

7.1 L2 Cache Misses Reduction

There are two groups of applications that are of interest: (a) memory bound applications that should obtain increased speedup and reduced cache miss rate for L2 cache and (b) non-memory-bound applications. The last group will not receive much benefit, but should not be slowed down or suffer from an increased cache miss rate. The reduction of the L2 cache miss rate is shown for the Tyson scheme, the new scheme, and the Oracle algorithm for SPEC2000 applications in Fig. 7. For the 1-MByte configurations and the memory bound applications (*art*, *mcf* and *ammp*) all schemes reduce the average miss rate. However, for the rest of the applications Tyson's scheme increases the miss rate by average 43%. The scheme is aggressive and therefore is only suitable for applications that benefit from bypassing. The new scheme is more robust and only increases the miss rate with average 2%. Compared to the Oracle scheme 68% of the possible misses are removed for the memory bound application and the new scheme, which means that the scheme is working well but there is still room for improvement.

Spec benchmark	# of L2 accesses	256k L2				1 MByte L2			
		Convent. Miss rate	Reductions of miss rate in %			Convent. Miss rate	Reductions of miss rate in %		
			Tyson	New Sch.	Oracle		Tyson	New Sch.	Oracle
art	308461787	0.826	3	9	15	0.603	58	47	67
mcf	265670845	0.616	-44	-5	1	0.599	-13	-3	5
ammp	132534118	0.920	5	7	8	0.845	27	25	29
average	235555583	0.787	-12	4	8	0.682	24	23	34
swim	77712825	0.591	-17	-2	0	0.590	-20	-2	0
applu	63107223	0.667	0	0	1	0.666	0	0	2
gcc	59690438	0.153	13	16	40	0.037	-19	2	23
lucas	51951704	0.862	-7	3	15	0.843	-16	3	14
facerec	36104376	0.657	-34	5	15	0.360	-69	-7	1
apsi	34560805	0.435	-9	4	18	0.206	-60	0	0
mgrid	31808765	0.760	-14	2	15	0.478	-53	-1	0
parser	24836151	0.349	-76	-5	11	0.165	-111	-18	7
galgel	20719227	0.880	4	13	24	0.352	-61	50	75
bzi2p	17548828	0.384	-33	-6	9	0.175	-27	3	14
crafty	16956861	0.065	-24	-2	21	0.007	-2	0	15
gzip	15660311	0.072	-3	4	19	0.039	-13	-6	1
gap	9244337	0.505	-78	0	0	0.499	-78	0	0
wupwise	8914610	0.679	-33	0	6	0.628	-44	-7	2
fma	8064048	0.000	0	-36	0	0.000	2	-37	0
equake	2758253	0.028	-84	-1	0	0.028	-84	-1	0
eon	2293674	0.000	0	-13	0	0.000	0	-13	0
perlbmk	799811	0.285	-146	-2	16	0.239	-132	-5	5
average	26818458	0.410	-30	-1	12	0.295	-43	-2	9

Fig. 7. Reduction of cache miss rate for different bypass schemes for two sizes of L2

For the 256-KByte configuration Tyson scheme does not work even for the memory bound application. The new scheme reduces the miss rate by 4% while the Oracle scheme obtains an 8% reduction.

7.2 Early Miss Determination

The results for using the proposed scheme for early miss determination is shown in Fig. 8. Each bar in the graph consists of four parts. The top part, which is black, is the amount of the L2 cache accesses that are predicted as misses incorrectly. These increase the memory bandwidth usage by a modest 1%. 27% of the memory accesses with cache misses are correctly predicted as misses. The advantage of the early miss determination depends on the latency of cache misses in the L2 cache. This miss latency increases with the size of the cache.

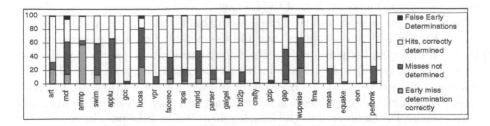

Fig. 8. Memory accesses to the L2 cache divided into four groups

7.3   Memory Bandwidth Reduction

The reduction of the memory bandwidth usage is shown in Fig. 9. The total number of accesses is decreased for both the new scheme and also when the new scheme is combined with early miss determination. Tyson's scheme reduces the number of accesses well for the *MCF* application even though it increases the miss rate for the same application. This is because Tyson's scheme reduces the number of write-backs by 48% for the L2 cache. By comparison the new scheme only reduces the number of write-backs by 8%.

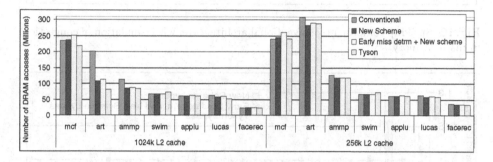

Fig. 9. The number of DRAM accesses (sum of L2 misses and L2 write-backs) executed for the different applications in the SPEC2000 benchmark

7.4   Instructions Per Clock Cycle (IPC)

We have studied the IPC for two different configurations, with and without main memory congestion. Four memory banks are used for simulation with congestions. These are interleaved so that one cache line fits into one bank. Each bank can handle only one read or write access at any time, which means that the entire system is capable of handling up to four read/write accesses simultaneously. There is no writeback buffer for the main memory, but L1 and L2 have writeback buffers. The model without congestion uses unlimited size writeback buffers to main memory and an unlimited number of parallel read operations can be executed simultaneously. Simulation with congestion is shown in Fig. 10 and no congestion in Fig. 11. These figures represent the speedup compared to the IPC of the conventional architecture which is shown in Fig. 12. We see two important observations: The first is that the performance for the memory bound applications is improved significantly. However, for the Tyson scheme the performance is decreased for non-memory bound application. For *galgel*, the simulation with congestion results in an IPC degradation of 22% and for the non-congestion simulation the IPC is degraded by 10%. There are three applications that are memory-bound: *ammp*, *art* and *mcf*. With memory congestion modeled, Tyson's scheme is able to increase the IPC quite well. This is not true when not using congestion because the bandwidth consumed by write-backs of dirty cache blocks then does not have any impact. Tyson's scheme bypasses

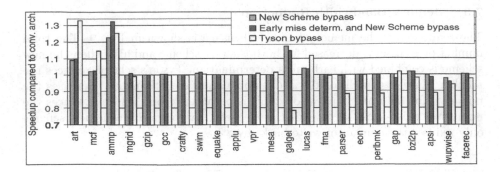

Fig. 10. Speedup compared to conventional architecture, with simulation of congestion in main memory

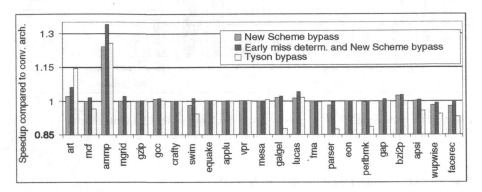

Fig. 11. Speedup compared to conventional architecture, with no simulation of congestion in main memory

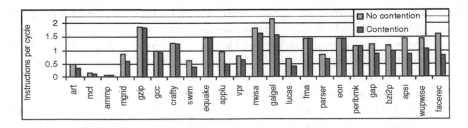

Fig. 12. IPC with and without simulation of congestion to main memory

write-backs from dirty L1 cache blocks well. Overall, the combination of bypassing and early miss determination can improve IPC with up of up to 34%. For applications with many incorrect early determinations (see Fig. 8) the IPC can be degraded.

7.5   The Heuristics

In the description of the algorithm used by the new scheme, the counter was added/subtracted with different values for different events. Different configurations for the heuristic is shown in Fig. 3. In the *shadow* configuration only the shadow events are enabled. This is learning by considering what could have been in the cache line if the bypass decision was inversed. In some sense this is learning by history and mistakes. In the *Replace* configuration bypassing is done when an instruction fetches a cache block which is replaced without having any cache hits. The configuration is aggressive since there are no negative numbers in the configuration. The *Equal* configuration increases/decreases the counter with the value one for all events. The *Tyson II* is the Tyson algorithm tweaked a little bit to become less aggressive. The different configurations from Fig. 3 are evaluated in Fig. 13. Even though the new scheme has overall good performance, tuning the heuristic differently for each application has a potential for improving the performance further.

	Tyson	New Scheme	Shadow	Replace	Equal	Tyson II	Conventional
ammp	1	3	10	7	8	0	37
apsi	82	0	0	22	42	18	0
art	0	26	46	4	7	33	140
bzi2p	54	0	23	226	26	7	3
crafty	17	1	29	562	13	3	0
facerec	75	7	9	74	70	36	0
galgel	231	24	0	203	22	7	147
gcc	24	1	0	2	11	4	3
gzip	17	7	1	0	14	10	1
lucas	11	3	0	6	17	9	5
mcf	14	3	12	34	9	8	0
mesa	13	1	0	0	2	3	0
mgrid	52	1	2	12	45	21	0
parser	124	18	20	100	67	35	0
swim	17	1	0	8	14	28	0

Fig. 13. The numbers show the increase in cache miss ratio compared to the best configuration. The best configurations are grayed and have value zero

8   Related Work

Bypassing can reduce conflict misses by using a bypass buffer in parallel with a direct mapped cache [7, 10, 6]. However, direct mapped caches are not used in state-of-the-art high performance microprocessors and reduce the potential for these techniques.

9   Conclusion

This work is the first to explore the gains of bypassing for last-level caches. The potential for improvement is higher compared to bypassing L1 cache because the latency of an L2 miss is much higher than an L1 miss seen from the processor. A new scheme for bypassing is presented based on a feedback loop. This improves the performance in terms of cache miss ratio and IPC to the same level as simpler schemes for memory bound applications, but it does not degrade the performance for non-memory bound applications which is the case for earlier schemes. We include early miss determination which further improves performance by predicting misses in the cache simply by using the heuristics for the bypassing scheme. This reduces the latency time for memory accesses at the cost of a small increase in bandwidth usage. The final contribution is our establishment of an upper-bound of miss-rate reduction in last-level caches by devising an oracle algorithm. Even though this algorithm is not fully optimal, it shows that there is room for improvements and more research is needed.

References

1. S. G. Abraham, R. A. Sugumar, D. Windheiser, B. R. Rau, and R. Gupta. Predictability of load/store instruction latencies. In *MICRO 26*, 1993.
2. T. Austin, E. Larson, and D. Ernst. SimpleScalar: an infrastructure for computer system modeling. IEEE Computer, Vol. 35, Issue2, 2002.
3. L. Belady. A study of replacement algorithms for a virtual-storage computer. IBM Systems Journal, 5(2):78-101, 1966.
4. Chi-Hung Chi and Henry Dietz. Improving cache performance by selective cache bypass. *Annual Hawaii International Conference on System Sciences*, 1989.
5. J. Jalminger and P. Stenstrom. A cache block reuse prediction scheme. *Microprocessors and Microsystems, V28*, pages 373–385, 2004.
6. L.K John and A. Subramanian. Design and performance evaluation of a cache assist to implement selective caching. *Proc. of Intl. Conf. on Comp. Design*, 1997.
7. T.L. Johnson, D.A. Connors, M.C. Merten, and W.-M.W Hwu. Run-time cache bypassing. *IEEE Transactions on Computers, V48 I12*, pages 1338–1354, 1999.
8. M. Kampe, P. Stenström, and M. Dubois. Self-correcting LRU replacement policies. In *CF '04: Proc. of the 1st conf. on Computing frontiers*, 2004.
9. M. Karlsson and E. Hagersten. Timestamp-based selective cache allocation. *High Performance Memory Systems, Springer-Verlag*, 2003.
10. Scott McFarling. Cache replacement with dynamic exclusion. In *ISCA '92*, pages 191–200. ACM Press, 1992.
11. G. Memik, G. Reinman, and W. H. Mangione-Smith. Just say no: Benefits of early cache miss determination. In *HPCA*, 2003.
12. V.-M. Panait, A. Sasturkar, and W.-F. Wong. Static identification of delinquent loads. In *int. symp. on Code generation and optimization*, 2004.
13. J. A. Rivers, E. S. Tam, G. S. Tyson, E. S. Davidson, and M. Farrens. Utilizing reuse information in data cache management. In *ICS*, 1998.
14. R. A. Sugumar and S. G. Abraham. Efficient simulation of caches under optimal replacement with applications to miss characterization. In *Joint International Conference on Measurement and modeling of computer systems*, 1993.
15. G. Tyson, M. Farrens, J. Matthews, and A. R. Pleszkun. A modified approach to cache management. *MICRO*, 1995.
16. Wayne A. Wong and Jean-Loup Baer. Modified LRU policies for improving second-level cache behavior. *HPCA*, 2000.

A Study of the Performance Potential for Dynamic Instruction Hints Selection

Rao Fu[1], Jiwei Lu[2], Antonia Zhai[1], and Wei-Chung Hsu[1]

[1] Department of Computer Science and Engineering
University of Minnesota
{rfu, zhai, hsu@cs.umn.edu}
[2] Scalable Systems Group
Sun Microsystems Inc.
jiwei.lu@sun.com

Abstract. Instruction hints have become an important way to communicate compile-time information to the hardware. They can be generated by the compiler and the post-link optimizer to reduce cache misses,
improve branch prediction and minimize other performance bottlenecks.
This paper discusses different instruction hints available on modern
processor architectures and shows the potential performance impact on
many benchmark programs. Some hints can be effectively selected at
compile time with profile feedback. However, since the same program
executable can behave differently on various inputs and performance
bottlenecks may change on different micro-architectures, significant performance opportunities can be exploited by selecting instruction hints
dynamically.

1   Introduction

Cache misses and branch mispredictions have become the major bottlenecks of
modern microprocessors. Attacking such performance issues has been a challenge for both hardware designers and software developers. Many modern architectures, including RISC, VLIW and EPIC, have paid much attention to the
effective cooperation between the compiler and the hardware to achieve highly
efficient execution. For instance, new instructions such as data and instruction
cache prefetch have been introduced and they have been effectively used by the
compiler and post-link optimizers (including runtime optimizers) to reduce cache
miss penalties. Besides introducing new instructions, recent architectures also
use *instruction hints* as another way to facilitate the communication between
the compiler and the hardware. Unlike adding new instructions, using hints does
not compromise binary compatibility. Instruction hints use a small number of
available bits in the instruction encoding to allow programmers, compilers and
other software tools to convey suggestions to the hardware. Since they are defined as hints, they do not pose correctness issues. Their presence can be simply
ignored if the underlying micro-architecture does not support the needed feature.

C. Jesshope and C. Egan (Eds.): ACSAC 2006, LNCS 4186, pp. 67–80, 2006.

Instruction hints are often used in architecture extensions and new architectures to expose new hardware features to software via some reserved bits.

Judiciously selecting the instruction hints can have very significant performance impact on applications. The selection of instruction hints relies on information such as working set, access patterns and effective memory latencies, which are not generally available at the compile time. Although profile-guided optimization (also known as profile-based or profile-directed optimization) can assist the selection process by using profile information collected via training runs, applications can behave differently on various inputs, and the profile collected from the training input may not be representative for the actual run. Furthermore, the runtime behavior of a program can change even within one run (i.e. execution phase changes). Although we have seen encouraging results from static hint selection, we believe there are significant performance potentials to be exploited with dynamic hint selection.

Dynamic binary optimizers [6][7] can monitor the execution of a program and perform the cost-effective optimization based on observed hot spots and respective performance bottlenecks. Dynamic hint selection requires relatively small amount of code analysis and binary modification and can be a good candidate for dynamic optimization. However, the extension of current dynamic binary optimization frameworks and the enhancement of current microprocessors are needed to support comprehensive dynamic hint selection.

The paper makes the following contributions,

- We show the performance impact of several architecture hints using the SPEC2000 CPU programs.
- We show the potential of using correct architecture hints over what have been done statically by the compiler.
- We discuss the limitations and difficulties associated with static hint selection.
- We discuss the current limitation on the hardware performance monitoring capability for exploiting dynamic hint selection.

The rest of the paper is organized as follows. Section 2 will provide a survey of instruction hints available on the mainstream architectures. Section 3 shows the performance impact of several instruction hints. In section 4, we discuss the selection of hints by some production compilers, the effectiveness of such selection, and the limitations. In section 5, we discuss the upside potential of selecting such hints at runtime, and the constraints and challenges for the dynamic optimizers. Related work is highlighted in section 6. Section 7 contains the conclusion and future work.

2   Instruction Hints

Most instruction hints are targeting at the two major performance bottlenecks, cache misses and branch mis-predictions. They can be divided into three main categories, branch prediction hints to improve branch prediction, memory locality hints to improve both data and instruction cache performance, strong/weak prefetch hints to improve the effectiveness of the data prefetch instructions.

2.1 Branch Prediction Hints

Many architectures use one or two bits in the conditional branches as a hint for static branch prediction. Itanium [14] uses one bit to indicate whether prediction resources should be allocated for the branch and the other bit to indicate the direction. Similarly Power4 [8] uses two previously reserved bits in conditional branch instructions for software branch prediction. Hardware branch prediction can be overridden by software branch prediction on Power4. One bit is used for that purpose while the other bit indicates the direction. PA-RISC 2.0 [15][17] does not have the luxury of one available bit but it defines the *branch prediction convention* to achieve the same effect. If the register numbers of the two operands in a conditional branch is in increasing order, the backward branch is predicted taken and the forward branch is predicted not taken; otherwise the branch is predicted the other direction. Compared with using a dedicated hint bit, this approach adds complexity to the instruction decoding.

Many microprocessors uses a return address stack to predict the target of a procedure return. When a procedure call is executed, the address of the next instruction is pushed onto the stack. The stack will be popped during the execution of a procedure return and the instruction fetching will start from the popped address. But in architectures such as Alpha [1], PowerPC [12] and PA-RISC [11][15], there are no dedicated instructions for procedure call and return. In Alpha [1], hints are introduced to push and pop procedure return addresses. PA-RISC 2.0 [15] and Power4 [8] adopted the same approach.

2.2 Memory Locality Hints

Memory locality hints are designed to achieve better cache performance by improving the allocation and replacement policy or initiating hardware prefetching. The temporal locality hints are used to indicate whether the data will be reused to help the hardware decide whether to allocate the data in a higher cache level. The temporal locality hints can be applied to all memory instructions including load, store and data prefetching. HP PA-RISC 1.1 architecture [11] defines a 2-bit cache control field, *cc*, which provides a hint to the processor on how to allocate data in the cache hierarchy. On PA-7200 [16], the processor will not allocate the cache line on the off-chip cache if the *cc* is specified to indicate poor temporal locality. The cache control field is also included in the prefetch instruction introduced in PA-RISC 2.0 [15].

Five variants of prefetch are defined in Sparc V9 [18], *read many, read once, write many, write once* and *prefetch page*[1]. The *once* and *many* hints are used

---

[1] *prefetch page* has not been implemented in any existing Sparc v9 microprocessors.

to indicate the temporal locality. UltraSparc III [20] implements a small prefetch cache (2KB) which can be accessed in parallel with the L1 data cache for
floating-point loads. The *once/many* hint specifies whether the data should be
brought into P-cache. However, no temporal hints are available for other memory
instructions.

Itanium [14] provides locality control with finer granularity. Four completer
(*t1, nt1, nt2* and *nta*) are used to specify whether the data has temporal locality
at a given cache level. These completers will affect how cache lines are allocated
in the cache hierarchy and whether the LRU bit should be updated. Using *t1*
will cause the data to be allocated at all cache levels while using *nt1* suggests
the data not to be allocated at L1. The Itanium 2 processor does not have a non-
temporal buffer and L2 is used for that purpose. *nt2* accesses are still allocated
in L2 but the LRU bit will not updated and thus the line has a high probability
to be replaced. *nta* completer further causes the line not to be allocated in L3.
Only *lfetch* instructions can use all four possible completers and the completers
for different memory instructions may have different meanings.

Instruction references exhibit good sequential locality. Many microprocessors implement hardware prefetcher to sequentially prefetch instruction cache
lines. Itanium [14] introduces the *sequential prefetch hint* to initiate instruction prefetching. The *sequential prefetch hint* on branches indicates how many
cache lines the processor should prefetch starting at the branch target. On Itanium 2 [13], a branch with the *many* completer initiates the hardware streaming
prefetching and the prefetch engine will continuously issue prefetch requests for
subsequent instruction cache lines till a stop condition[2] happens.

2.3   Weak/Strong Prefetch Hints

The effectiveness of prefetching can be affected by whether micro-architecture
implementations allow a prefetch to continue if it triggers a data TLB miss or
there is not enough resource to handle the prefetch request. The UltraSparc
IV+ processor [21] implements two more variants of prefetch instructions in addition to the five flavors defined in Sparc V9 [18]. Weak prefetches are dropped
if the target address translation misses the TLB, while strong prefetches will
generate software traps and be re-issued after the TLB entries are filled. The
prefetch requests are tracked by an eight-entry prefetch queue. A strong prefetch
will not be dropped even if the prefetch queue is full when it is issued and the
pipeline will stall until one of the outstanding prefetches completes. The PCM
(P-Cache Mode) in DCU (Data Cache Unit) control register provides further
control on the behavior of weak prefetches under a prefetch queue full event.
When the bit is on, a weak prefetch will also be recirculated if the prefetch
queue is full.

On Itanium [14], a TLB miss will not necessarily generate a fault since it implements hardware page walker to reduce the latency of a TLB miss. If a lookup

---

[2] A stop condition can be a branch misprediction, the execution of an taken branch
or the execution of a special instruction explicitly indicating the stop condition.

fails in both levels of the DTLB, hardware page walker can be triggered to resolve the miss by searching the page table. Slightly different with strong prefetch on UltraSparc IV+, *fault* completer is used to indicate whether a fault raised by an *lfetch* instruction should be handled by the processor. If the hardware page walker fails, only *lfetch.fault* will raise a software fault. Unlike UltraSparc IV+ [21], there is no dedicated resource for tracking data prefetching requests on Itanium. They share the same resource with the other memory requests. An *lfetch* instruction will not be dropped if there is not enough resource to handle it. Instead it will wait for the resource to be available.

3 Performance Impact of Instruction Hints

Though the instruction hints do not affect the correctness of a program's execution, they can have great impact on program performance. This section uses several instruction hints to show the compiler can improve program performance by judiciously using the available hints.

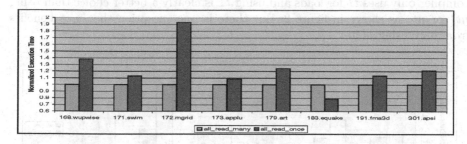

Fig. 1. Performance comparison of prefetch variants with different locality hints on UltraSparc III Cu for SPEC CPU2000 [19]. All binaries are compiled with the base option including PBO using Sun Studio 11 compiler and the data are collected on Sun Blade 1000. The execution time is normalized using the binaries generated by the compiler as the bases. The first bars are all 1 since the compiler only generates *many* hints.

Figure 1 shows the comparison of using two different locality hints for data prefetching on UltraSparc III Cu. By using the *read many* hint, the prefetched data are brought into both P-cache and L2 cache while the data are only brought to P-cache for *read once*. The compiler only generates *read many* hint for prefetches intended for data reads. Although only using the *read many* hint gives better performance in most cases, for 183.equake, only using *read once* actually has a 27% speedup.

The comparison of using different locality hints for load on Itanium 2 is shown in figure 2. For every possible completer allowed, we convert all loads into that single flavor and compare the performance with the binaries generated by the compiler. Two separate graphs are shown for SPEC CINT2000 and CFP2000

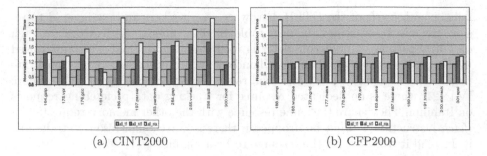

(a) CINT2000   (b) CFP2000

Fig. 2. Performance comparison of load variants with different locality hints on Itanium 2. All binaries are compiled with the base option including PBO using Intel C/C++ Compiler 9.0 and the data are collected on HP zx6000. The execution time is normalized using the binaries generated by the compiler as the bases. The first bars are all 1 since the compiler only generates *t1* hints.

[19] since *t1* and *nt1* have different meanings for floating point loads [3]. Intel compiler only uses *t1* for loads and using *t1* is clearly a better choice than using *nt1* or *nta* as shown in figure 2. But there is one exception that *mcf* benefits from only using *ld.nta*.

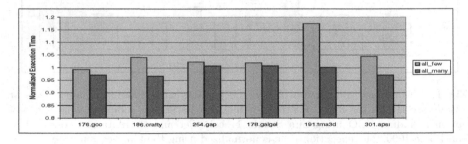

Fig. 3. Performance impact of streaming prefetch hint on Itanium 2. The same environment as specified in figure 2 is used for data collection.

The performance impact of streaming prefetch hint on Itanium 2 is shown in figure 3. The *many* completer is clearly preferable than the *few* completer. On three occasions (*gcc*, *crafty* and *apsi*), triggering streaming prefetches on every branch delivers better performance. Only using *few* completers can slow down a program as much as 17% in the case of *fma3d*.

Figure 4 shows the comparison for weak and strong prefetches on UltraSparc IV+. Again we show two extreme cases by converting all prefetches into weak or strong versions. In general, the compiler chooses strong versions for the majority

---

[3] For floating point loads, data are not allocated in L1 even *t1* is used and LRU bit is not updated for *nt1*.

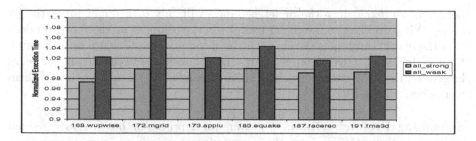

Fig. 4. Performance comparison of weak/strong prefetches on UltraSparc IV+. The data are collected on a Sun Fire E4900 sever and all binaries are compiled with the latest Sun Studio compiler [22] with the base option including PBO. The execution time is normalized using the binaries generated by the compiler as the bases.

of the prefetches and it yields better performance for six programs compared with only using the weak versions. Only using strong prefetches provides even slightly better performance overall. For *168.wupwise*, 3% speedup can be obtained by only using strong prefetches.

4   Static Selection of Instruction Hints

As shown in section 3, prudently using instruction hints can significantly improve program performance. In this section, we discuss the issues involved in static selection of these hints, including the branch prediction hints, instruction prefetching hints, data cache locality hints and weak/strong prefetch hints. We also show limitations of static selection using case studies for several benchmark programs.

4.1   Issues in Static Selection

Locality Hints for Data Prefetching. The cache hierarchies in modern processors are increasingly more complex. The cache hierarchy in the Itanium 2 has three levels of on-chip caches. They are non-blocking and can handle cache miss requests out-of-order. Therefore, it is difficult to estimate the precise cost of an *lfetch* instruction. In general, *lfetch* instructions with *t1* completers are more expensive than those with *nt* completers while *lfetch* instructions with *nt* completers (*nt1*, *nt2*, and *nta*) have similar costs.

On Itanium 2, every memory request that cannot be satisfied by L1D will be sent to L2 and must be scheduled within a 32-entry queue called OzQ. If the OzQ is full, the L1D pipeline must stall and it in turn causes the main pipeline to stall. Bank conflicts and multiple misses to the same cache line can increase the lifetime of the entries in the OzQ. An *lfetch* can be expensive if it cause either case to happen. Placing one of the *nt* completers mitigates those effects and reduces the cost of an *lfetch*. However, using the *nt* completer reduces the benefit of an *lfetch* since the prefetched data will only be brought up to the L2 cache. When deciding to use the *t1* completer, the compiler needs to be confident that the benefit outweighs the cost. The Intel compiler tends to use *nt* more often than *t1* for SPEC CINT2000 programs. But choosing between *t1* and *nt* relies largely on the application's working set as discussed in 4.2 and neither of them works best all the time.

Streaming Prefetch Hints. The Itanium 2 processor has a relative small instruction cache (16K), from the perspective that it has a very strong issue bandwidth (up to 6 instructions can be issued per cycle). Overly aggressive streaming prefeching can cause instruction cache pollution and have negative impact on the pipeline front-end. The benefit of streaming prefetching can be determined by whether the lines brought into the L1I are used in the near future. A good indicator will be the number of instructions between the branch target to the first statically predicted taken branch. ISpike [4] defines this as *span* and uses a size of 128 bytes as a threshold to trigger streaming prefetching.

Intel compiler is rather conservative in selecting *many* completers. On average only one out of four branches uses the *many* completer for SPEC CPU2000 programs even we compile all programs with high optimization level (O3) and profile based optimization. Three programs (*gcc, crafty* and *apsi*) benefit as much as 4.5% from only using *many* completers as show in figure 3. All three programs have large instruction footprints and streaming prefetch can reduce the stalls when the pipeline front-end is unable to supply new instructions to the back-end.

Weak/Strong Prefetch Hints. As shown in section 3, strong prefetch can provide additional benefits over weak prefetchs on UltraSparc IV+, but a strong prefetch could be more expensive than a weak one. Firstly, a strong prefetch must wait when the prefetch queue is full while a weak prefetch can be simply dropped in this case. Secondly, a TLB miss triggered by a strong prefetch must be handled. The compiler must carefully use strong prefetches and make sure the performance gain from the prefetches is higher than the additional cost. The weak prefetches can be made "stronger" on UltraSparc IV+ by setting the PCM bit to 1 so that they will not get dropped when the prefetch queue is full. With the PCM bit set on, the difference between weak and strong prefetches becomes smaller, which makes it easier to select strong prefetch as the default. However, we have observed that setting the PCM bit on does not always yield better performance since programs may spend a significant portion of execution on waiting for available entries in the prefetch queue. The stall can be avoidable by providing flexible control over the PCM bit and relying on the compiler to more intelligently select the more suitable prefetch variants.

4.2   Limitations of Static Selection

As shown in section 3, though overall the compilers do well in selecting instruction hints, there are cases the compilers still leave significant performance opportunities on the table. This is evident when we blindly convert all instruction hints into one flavor. Static selection of instruction hints is also limited by lacking knowledge of a program's runtime behavior.

```
while (node) {
    ...
    temp = node;
    node = node->child;
}
```

```
(p17)  adds r46=40,r37
        ...
(p17)  ld8 r36=[r46]
        ...
(p17)  cmp.eq p0,p16=r36,r0
        ...
(p16)  br.wtop.dptk.few
```

(a) C code   (b) assembly code

Fig. 5. Code snippet from 181.mcf

Ambiguous Memory Access. The static analysis can be hindered by some programming language features. Figure 5 shows a code snippet from function *refresh_potential* in SPEC CINT2000 benchmark *181.mcf*. The loop is software pipelined but no prefetch instructions are generated by the compiler. The *ld8* instruction which tries to access *node* → *child* is delinquent and the program stalls on the *cmp* instructions. Since the data loaded by *ld8* are not reused, changing its completer to *nta* can reduce its latency without increasing the number of cache misses. The program can be sped up by 8.7% after this simple change. However, it is unlikely that the compiler can determine whether the data are reused with the presence of intensive dynamic memory objects and frequent pointer references.

```
void daxpy(double *x, int ix, double *y, int iy, int a, int n)
{
    int i;

    for (i = 0; i < n; i++)
        y[i * iy] += a * x[i * ix];
}
```

Fig. 6. DAXPY loop

Memory Access Pattern. The behavior of a program can change dramatically with different memory access patterns. Figure 6 shows a typical DAXPY loop with the strides for both arrays passed as the parameters. The Sun Studio compiler generates one strong prefetch for each array on UltraSparc IV+. As seen in the figure 7, the benefit of using weak prefetches is decreasing as the stride gets larger. When the memory stride (1024 for the arrays) is equal to

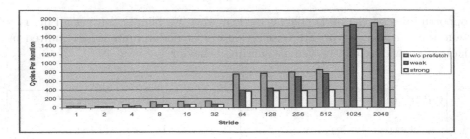

Fig. 7. Average cycles per iteration for DAXPY loop for different array stride (ix and iy.

the page size (8KB), we can see a sharp increase on average cycles spent on each iteration because of the TLB pressure. Using weak prefetches cannot provide better performance since most of the prefethes will cause TLB misses and get dropped. Strong prefetches clearly outperform weak prefetches for the large strides. But when the stride is no larger than 512 bytes (64 for ix and iy), using strong prefetches is hardly better than using weak prefetches. If the PCM bit is set to be off, weak prefetches may be more profitable for smaller strides because of their lower costs.

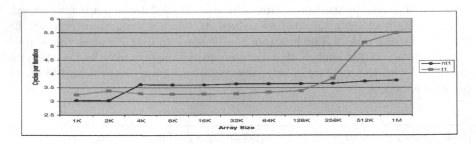

Fig. 8. Average cycles per iteration for IAXPY loop

Working Set Size. The runtime behavior of a program can largely rely on its working set. A static hint is unlikely to provide good performance across different working sets. To show the effect of $t1$ completer, we change the DAXPY loop in figure 6 to IAXPY (i.e., both x and y are changed to integer arrays and the strides are fixed to be 1). The Intel C compiler generates a software-pipelined loop for IAXPY and one prefetch is included to prefetch both array x and y alternatively. Figure 8 shows the average cycles per iteration for the IAXPY on an Itanium 2 machine for two cases when the temporal completer of the prefetch is $nt1$ or $t1$. When the working set of the loop is bigger than the size of L1D (16K) and but less than the size of L2 (256KB), using $t1$ gives better performance. But if the size of array exceeds the size of L2, $nt1$ will provide better performance and the performance gap is increasing as the work set increases.

5   Dynamically Selecting Instruction Hints

Static selection of instruction hints is limited by the lack of knowledge of program's runtime behavior and a static hint cannot adapt to behavior changes at runtime. Two ways can be used to select instruction hints dynamically. The first approach uses the compiler to generate multiple copies of an instruction with all possible hints, and have check instructions to select the desirable one based on the runtime performance information. The second approach is to use a dynamic binary optimizer, such ADORE [6], to adjust the hint bits at runtime.

5.1   Generating Multiple Copies

Compiler can generate multiple copies of an instruction with different hints and the corresponding code to select the hints at runtime as discussed in [2][3]. The selection can be based on the calculation on various runtime parameters (working set, stride and etc.). This scheme has two disadvantages which make it impractical. Firstly, it is known to cause severe code expansion since the compiler has to generate extra instructions to select the instruction with the wanted hint. Secondly, the cost of the additional calculations can offset the performance gain of using the right hints.

5.2   Adjusting Instruction Hints Using Dynamic Binary Optimizers

Using compiler to generate multiple copy of an instruction with different hints causes code expansion and has high runtime overhead. This approach has another limitation since the compiler can only generate the instruction hints with the knowledge of the target architecture. A binary compiled for an older micro-architecture cannot benefit from the additional instruction hints available on the newer micro-architecture. Recompilation is one possible solution but the source code for the legacy binaries may not be available.

A dynamic binary optimizer can monitor a program's performance during the execution of the program. It can identify program hot spots as well as pin down the performance bottlenecks. Based on the observed performance bottleneck and hot spots, the dynamic optimizer can perform the most needed optimizations, and deploy the optimized code by patching the binary. It has been shown to effectively address runtime performance bottlenecks such as data cache misses. Compared with generating multiple copies at the compile time, using dynamic binary optimizers to adjust instruction hints can have very low overhead and adapt to different target micro-architectures and computing environments.

Compared with other optimizations currently implemented in dynamic binary optimizers, dynamically adjusting the instruction hints is less expensive. Optimizations such as partial dead code elimination requires flow analysis of the binary. Those optimizations also need to be carefully applied since they can change the architecture state and cause imprecise exceptions. Most optimizations require some free registers and acquiring them from the binary at runtime is very challenging. For dynamically adjusting instruction hints, if sufficient information can be obtained from hardware, the optimization only needs to patch one or two bits for some instructions. Trace formation and register acquisition, two of the most difficult tasks in dynamic optimizers, can be avoided.

However, similar to other runtime optimizations, dynamic hint selection needs proper support from software and hardware. The lack of appropriate performance counter information related to the instruction hints may limit the effectiveness of hint selection. Furthermore, the lack of comprehensive control flow information may also limit the code region where hint selection can be applied.

Hardware Support. Dynamic binary optimizers rely on the runtime performance monitoring features provided by recent architectures. Itanium 2 provides more than 400 different counters and advanced monitoring features such as Branch Trace Buffer (BTB) and Event Address Registers (EAR). Those features are very useful in the design of a dynamic binary optimizer. However, they are still insufficient for dynamically adjusting instruction hints. For example, to select the memory locality hints, *nta*, no temporal locality at all cache levels, requires cache reuse information. We need to know if the cache line referenced by one memory operation is not going to be reused, or the line may be replaced before it is used again. Current hardware performance counters do not provide this type of details. Furthermore, it is important that the cache line reuse information should be associated with the PC address of the memory instruction. One naïve hardware implementation is to tag the cache line with the full address of the instruction which requests the line. This may be too expensive to be practical. So using partial address (e.g. lower bits) may be a good compromise. A few bits like the LRU bits can also be added to track whether the line has been used recently.

Software Support. Data cache prefetching is the major optimization performed in current dynamic binary optimizers such as ADORE/Itanium [6] and ADORE/Sparc [7]. Therefore the trace selection and formation in these two systems focus on loops which are the best candidates for data cache prefetching. Dynamically adjusting instruction hints requires different type of traces. The effect of changing some instruction hints such as the temporal hints may not be visible immediately. For example, adjusting the temporal hints for a loop may not improve the performance of itself but the performance of another loop next to it. In such cases, we need a larger scope such as a complex loop nest in the trace selection in order to effectively apply hint selection. Secondly, self monitoring and dynamically undoing and redoing the optimization become critical. For example, the dynamic optimizer may initiate some hint selection to a loop, and monitor what performance change it may have. If the performance degrade in the monitored region, the optimizer should undo the selected hints.

6   Related Work

Even though there are quite a few instruction hints available on recent architectures, very limited research has been done to evaluate their performance impacts and no one has tried to select instruction hints using dynamic binary optimizers.

Memory Locality Hint: Wang et al. [10] propose to add an *evict-me* bit to each cache line, which indicates a cache line is a good candidate for replacement. Compilers set this bit for memory instructions based on locality analysis. Their study shows that using the evict-me algorithm in both L1 and L2 caches can improve the performance of a set of scientific programs over LRU policy by increasing the cache hit rate. Yang [5] et al. has a detailed study on the compiler algorithms to generate cache hints. Beyles and D'Hollander [2][3] proposes a compiler framework using reuse distance profile to generate temporal hints for memory instructions. Their study is based on the temporal completers available on Itanium architecture [14] and they used a physical Itanium server for their experiment. They also propose to use prediction or extending the format of the memory instructions to support dynamic cache hint for an individual access.

Weak/Strong Prefetch: Song et al. [9] briefly describe the weak and strong prefetch on UltraSparc VI+ [21]. They only use strong prefetches in the statically generated helper thread by the compiler and they claim the benefit of helper thread will be greatly reduced if prefetches are dropped on TLB misses. In [7], Lu et al. evaluate the performance impact of using strong prefetches in their dynamic helper threaded prefetching on UltraSparc IV+ [21]. Even though they conclude using strong prefetches in the helper thread code is generally a preferable strategy, they also find cases when weak prefetches yield better performance.

Sequential Prefetch Hint: Luk et al. [4] study the performance potential of streaming prefetching on Itanium [14] using a post-link optimizer (Ispike). They find streaming prefetching helps a little for SPEC CPU2000 Int [19] programs but they observe larger speedup on a commercial database application with a much bigger code footprint.

7   Conclusions and Future Work

Modern processors have increasingly relied on using hints associated with instructions to pass performance related information from software to hardware. We have shown the use of such hints could have significant performance impact on recent Itanium and Sparc processors. The statically hint selection by the compiler cannot address the performance opportunities created by dynamic program behavior changes and has room for improvement. With appropriate software and hardware support, we believe a dynamic optimizer can make more effective use of instruction hints for future systems.

Our future work will focus on the software and hardware support for dynamic selecting instruction hints. We want to enhance the current dynamic binary

optimizer to handle more complex trace types other than loops. We also plan
to improve the self-monitoring ability and add support for undoing and redoing
optimizations. Finally we would like to have more detailed study and evaluation
for possible hardware support to assist future dynamic selection of instruction
hints.

Acknowledgment This work is partly supported by grant EIA-0220021 and
grants from Intel and Sun Microsystems. The authors want to thank Abhinav
Das and Jinpyo Kim for their suggestions and help. We also thank all of the
anonymous reviewers for their valuable comments.

References

1. Alpha architecture handbook, Oct 1998.
2. K. Beyls and E. D'Hollander. Compile-time cache hint generationfor epic architectures. In *EPIC-2*, Nov 2002.
3. K. Beyls and E. H. D'Hollander. Generating cache hints for improved program efficiency. *J. Syst. Archit.*, 51(4):223–250, 2005.
4. C. K. Luk et al. Ispike: a post-link optimizer for the intel®itanium®architecture. In *CGO 2004*, pages 15–26, 2004.
5. H. Yang et al. Compiler-assisted cache replacement: Problem formulation and performance evaluation. *Lecture Notes in Computer Science*, 2958:77–92, 2004.
6. J. Lu et al. Design and implementation of a lightweight dynamic optimization system. *JLPT*, 6(1), 2004.
7. J. Lu et al. Dynamic helper threaded prefetching on the sun ultrasparc cmp processor. In *MICRO '05*, pages 93–104, 2005.
8. J. M. Tendler et al. Power4 system microarchitecture, Oct 2001.
9. Y. Song et al. Design and implementation of a compiler framework for helper threading on multi-core processors. In *PACT '05*, pages 99–109, 2005.
10. Z. Want et al. Using the compiler to improve cache replacement decisions. In *PACT '02*, pages 199–208, 2002.
11. Hewlett-Packard Company. *PA-RISC 1.1 Architecture and Instruction Set Reference Manual*, 3rd edition, Feb 1994.
12. IBM. *PowerPC User Instruction Set Architecture*, Sep 2003.
13. Intel Corp. *Intel®Itanium®2 Processor Reference Manual for Software Development and Optimization*, May 2004.
14. Intel Corp. *Intel®IA-64 Architecture Software Developer's Manual*, Jan 2006.
15. Gerry Kane. *PA-RISC 2.0 Architecture*. Prentice Hall, 1995.
16. G. et al. Kurpanek. Pa7200: a pa-risc processor with integrated high performance mp bus interface. In *Compcon Spring '94, Digest of Papers*, pages 375–382, 1994.
17. R. Lee and J. Huck. 64-bit and multimedia extensions in the pa-risc 2.0 architecture. In *Compcon '96*, pages 152–160, Feb 1996.
18. SPARC International, Inc. *The SPARC Architecture Manual Version 9*, 1994.
19. Standard Performance Evaluation Corp., http://www.spec.org/cpu2000.
20. Sun Microsystems Inc. *UltraSPARC®III Processor User's Manual*, Jan 2004.
21. Sun Microsystems Inc. *UltraSPARC®IV+ Processor User's Manual Supplement*, Oct 2005.
22. Sun Studio Compilers and Tools, http://developers.sun.com/prodtech/cc/-index.jsp.

Reorganizing UNIX for Reliability

Jorrit N. Herder, Herbert Bos, Ben Gras,
Philip Homburg, and Andrew S. Tanenbaum

Computer Science Dept., Vrije Universiteit Amsterdam
De Boelelaan 1081a, 1081 HV Amsterdam, The Netherlands

Abstract. In this paper, we discuss the architecture of a modular
UNIX-compatible operating system, MINIX 3, that provides reliability beyond that of most other systems. With nearly the entire operating
system running as a set of user-mode servers and drivers atop a minimal
kernel, the system is fully compartmentalized.

By moving most of the code to unprivileged user-mode processes and
restricting the powers of each one, we gain proper fault isolation and
limit the damage bugs can do. Moreover, the system has been designed
to survive and automatically recover from failures in critical modules,
such as device drivers, transparent to applications and without user intervention.

We used this new design to develop a highly reliable, open-source,
POSIX-conformant member of the UNIX family. The resulting system
is freely available and has been downloaded over 75,000 times since its
release.

1 Introduction

Operating systems are expected to function flawlessly, but, unfortunately, most
of today's operating systems fail all too often. As discussed in Sec. 2, many
problems stem from the monolithic design that underlies commodity systems.
All operating system functionality, for example, runs in kernel mode without
proper fault isolation, so that any bug can potentially trash the entire system.

Like other groups [1,2,3,4], we believe that reducing the operating system
kernel and running drivers and other core components in user mode helps to
minimize the damage that may be caused by bugs in such code. However, our
system explores an extreme position in the design space of UNIX-like systems,
with almost the entire operating system running as a collection of independent,
tightly restricted, user-mode processes. This structure, combined with several
explicit mechanisms for transparent recovery from crashes and other failures,
results in a highly reliable, multiserver operating system that still looks and
feels like UNIX.

To the best of our knowledge, we are the first to explore such an extreme
decomposition of the operating system that is designed for reliability, while providing reasonable performance. Quite a few ideas and technologies have been
around for a long time, but were often abandoned for performance reasons. We
believe that the time has come to reconsider the choices that were made in
common operating system design.

C. Jesshope and C. Egan (Eds.): ACSAC 2006, LNCS 4186, pp. 81–94, 2006.

1.1 Contribution

The contribution of this work is the design and implementation of an operating system that takes the multiserver concept to its logical conclusion in order to provide a dependable computing platform. The concrete goal of this research is to build a UNIX-like operating system that can transparently survive crashes of critical components, such as device drivers.

As we mentioned earlier, the answer that we came up with is to break the system into manageable units and rigidly control the power of each unit. The ultimate goal is that a fatal bug in, say, a device driver should not crash the operating system; instead, a local failure should be detected and the failing component should be automatically and transparently replaced by a fresh copy without affecting user processes.

To achieve this goal, our system provides: simple, yet efficient and reliable IPC; disentangling of interrupt handling from user-mode device drivers; separation of policies and mechanisms; flexible, run-time operating system configuration; decoupling of servers and drivers through a publish-subscribe system; and error detection and transparent recovery for common driver failures. We will discuss these features in more detail in the rest of the paper.

While microkernels, user-mode device drivers, multiserver operating systems, fault tolerance, etc. are not new, no one has put all pieces together. We believe that we are the first to realize a fully modular, POSIX-conformant operating system that is designed to be highly reliable. The system has been released (with all the source code available under the Berkeley license) and over 75,000 people have downloaded it so far, as discussed later.

1.2 Paper Outline

We first survey related work and show how operating system structures have evolved over time (Sec. 2). Then we proceed with an architectural discussion of the kernel and the user-mode servers and drivers on top of it (Sec. 3). We review the system's main reliability features (Sec. 4) and briefly discuss its performance (Sec. 5). Finally, we draw conclusions (Sec. 6) and mention how the system can be obtained (Sec. 7).

2 Related Work

This section gives an overview of the design space that has monolithic systems at one extreme and ours at the other. We briefly discuss starting with the shortcomings of monolithic systems and ways to retrofit reliability. Then we survey increasingly modular designs that we believe will help to make future operating systems more reliable.

It is sometimes said that virtual machines and exokernels provide sufficient isolation and modularity for making a system safe. However, these technologies provide an interface to an operating system, but do not represent a complete system by themselves. The operating system on top of a virtual machine, exokernel, or the bare hardware can have any of the structures discussed below.

2.1 Retrofitting Reliability in Legacy Systems

Monolithic kernels provide rich and powerful abstractions. All operating system services are provided by a single program that runs in kernel mode. A simplified example, vanilla Linux, is given in Fig. 1(a). While the kernel may be partitioned into domains, there are no protection barriers enforced between the components.

Monolithic designs have some inherent reliability problems. All operating system code, for example, runs at the highest privilege level without proper fault isolation, so that any bug can potentially trash the entire system. With millions of lines of executable code (LOC) and reported error rates up to sixteen or 75 bugs per 1000 LOC [5,6], monolithic systems are prone to bugs. Running untrusted, third-party code in the kernel also diminishes the system's reliability, as evidenced by the fact that the error rate in device drivers is 3 to 7 times higher than in other code [7] and 85% of all Windows crashes are caused by drivers [8].

An important project to improve the reliability of commodity systems such as Linux is Nooks [8,9]. Nooks keeps device drivers in the kernel but transparently encloses them in a kind of lightweight *protective wrapper* so that driver bugs cannot propagate to other parts of the operating system. All traffic between the driver and the rest of the kernel is inspected by the reliability layer.

Another project uses *virtual machines* to isolate device drivers from the rest of the system [2]. When a driver is called, it is run on a different virtual machine than the main system so that a crash or other fault does not pollute the main system. In addition to isolation, this technique enables unmodified reuse of device drivers when experimenting with new operating systems.

A recent project ran Linux device drivers in user mode with small changes to the Linux kernel [3]. This work shows that drivers can be isolated in separate user-mode processes without significant performance degradation.

While isolating device drivers helps to improve the reliability of legacy operating systems, we believe a proper, fully modular design from scratch gives better results. This includes encapsulating *all* operating system components (e.g., file system, memory manager) in independent, user-mode processes.

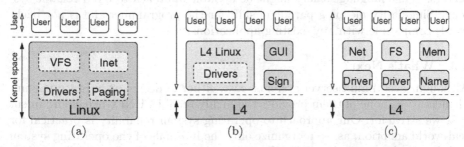

Fig. 1. Three increasingly modular designs of the Linux operating system: (a) Vanilla Linux (widely deployed); (b) L^{4}Linux and specialized components (working prototype); and (c) envisioned structure of SawMill Linux (abandoned project)

2.2   Architecting New Modular Designs

In modular designs, the operating system is split into a set of cooperating servers. Untrusted code such as third-party device drivers can be run in independent user-mode modules to prevent faults from spreading. In principle, modular designs have great potential to increase reliability as each module can be tightly confined according to the principle of least authority [10].

One approach is running the operating system in a single user-mode server on top of a microkernel, for example, L^4Linux on top of L4 [11]. This structure can be combined with specialized components as in DROPS [1] and Perseus [12], which is illustrated in Fig. 1(b). While the specialized components run in isolation, a single bug can still crash Linux and take down all legacy applications.

Some commercial systems like Symbian OS and QNX [13] are also based on multiserver designs, but do not use such an extreme decomposition of the operating system as we do. In Symbian OS, for example, only the file server and the networking and telephony stacks are hosted in user-mode servers, while the QNX kernel still contains process management and other functions which could have been isolated in separate user-mode processes.

SawMill Linux [14] would have been a more sophisticated approach to split the operating system into pieces and run each one in its own protection domain, as illustrated in Fig. 1(c). Unfortunately, the project was abruptly terminated in 2001 when many of the principals left IBM Research, and the only outcome was a rudimentary, unfinished prototype.

The GNU Hurd is a collection of servers that serves as a replacement for the UNIX kernel. The goal of this project is similar to ours, but the distribution of functionality over various servers is different. The current status seems to be that the multiserver system did not work as intended on top of either Mach or L4, and the project is currently seeking another microkernel.

A recent multiserver system developed by Microsoft Research is Singularity [4]. In contrast to other systems, Singularity uses language protection and bypasses the hardware protection offered by the MMU. The system can be characterized as a microkernel running a set of verifiably safe, software-isolated servers. While language safety might be a viable approach to build reliable systems, Singularity means a paradigm shift for the programmer and is not backwards compatible with any existing applications.

2.3   What's Next?

Although several multiserver systems exist, either in design or in prototype implementation, none of them provides the highly reliable, UNIX-like environment that we strive for. Our approach to operating system reliability is practical for real-world adoption, as we reorganize only the internals of the operating system and do not change the interface offered to applications. Users can still run their favorite software, but now without rebooting their computer every now and then.

In the rest of this paper, we present a new, highly reliable, open-source, POSIX-conformant multiserver operating system that is freely available for download, and has been widely tested.

3   Our Multiserver Architecture

In our design, called MINIX 3, the operating system runs as a set of user-mode servers and drivers on top of a tiny kernel, as illustrated in Fig. 2. The kernel is responsible for low-level and privileged operations such as programming the CPU and MMU, interrupt handling, and IPC, and contains two tasks (SYS and CLOCK) to support the user-mode parts of the operating system.

The simplest servers provide file system (FS), process management (PM), and memory management (MM) functionality. The data store (DS) is a small database server with publish-subscribe functionality. Finally, the reincarnation server (RS) keeps track of all servers and drivers and can transparently repair the system when certain failures occur.

Each component in our design is a small, well-defined entity with limited responsibility and power, as in the original UNIX philosophy. The kernel consists of under 4000 lines of executable code (LoC) and the sizes of the servers approximately range from 1000 to 3000 LoC per server, which makes them easy to understand and maintain. The small size also might make it practical to verify the code either manually or using formal verification tools.

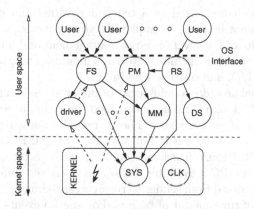

Fig. 2. The core components of the full multiserver operating system, and some typical IPC paths. Top-down IPC is blocking, whereas bottom-up IPC is nonblocking.

Before we continue with the discussion of the core components, we illustrate how our multiserver operating system actually works. Although the POSIX API is implemented by multiple servers, system calls are transparently targeted to the right server by the system libraries. Four examples are given below:

(1) An application that wants to create a child process calls the fork() library function, which sends a request message to the process manager (PM). PM verifies that a process slot is available, asks the memory manager (MM) to allocate memory, and instructs the kernel (SYS) to create a copy of the process. Finally, PM sends the reply and the library function returns. All message passing is hidden to the application.

(2) A read() or write() call to do disk I/O is sent to FS. If the requested block is in the buffer cache, FS asks the kernel (SYS) to copy it to the user. Otherwise it sends a message to the disk driver asking it to retrieve the block from disk. The driver sets an alarm, commands the disk controller through an I/O request to the kernel (SYS), and awaits the hardware interrupt or timeout notification.

(3) Additional servers and drivers can be started on the fly by requesting them from the reincarnation server (RS). RS then forks a new process, sets the process' privileges at the kernel (SYS), and, finally, executes the given path in the child process (not shown in the figure). Information about the new system process is published in the data store (DS), which allows parts of the operating system to subscribe to updates in the system's configuration.

(4) Although not a system call, it is interesting to see what happens if a user or system process causes a fatal exception, for example, due to an invalid pointer. In this event, the kernel's exception handler notifies PM, which transforms the exception into a signal or kills the process when no handler is registered. Recovery from failures in servers and drivers is handled by RS and is discussed below.

3.1   The Kernel

The kernel can be characterized as a true microkernel and provides low-level operations that cannot be done by unprivileged user-mode processes. First, the kernel is responsible for low-level resource management and interaction with the hardware. For example, this includes interrupt handling, programming the CPU and MMU, device I/O, and process scheduling.

Second, the kernel provides a reliable set of interprocess communication (IPC) primitives. Our IPC design eliminates the need for dynamic resource allocation, both in the kernel and in user space. The standard request-reply sequence uses a rendezvous. If the destination is not waiting, the IPC_REQUEST blocks the sender until the IPC_REPLY has been sent. Similarly, a receiver is blocked on IPC_SELECT when no IPC is available. Messages are never buffered in the kernel, but always directly copied from sender to receiver, speeding up IPC and eliminating the possibility of running out of buffers. For special events, the IPC_NOTIFY primitive can be used to send nonblocking notification messages. Notifications are not susceptible to resource exhaustion either, since at most one bit per event is saved in a bitmap that is statically declared as part of the process table.

Third, the kernel maintains several lists and bitmaps to restrict the powers of all system processes. As discussed in Sec. 4, the restriction include IPC primitives that can be used, possible IPC destinations, kernel calls available, I/O ports, IRQ lines, and memory regions. The policies are set by a trusted user-space server (RS), and enforced by the kernel at run time. Each process has its own policy, allowing for fine-grained control of privileges in the system.

Fourth, two independently scheduled processes, SYS and CLOCK, are part of the kernel to support the rest of the operating system. These processes are called tasks to distinguish them from the user-mode servers. Although the tasks are in kernel address space and run in kernel mode, they are treated in the same manner as any other user processes.

System Task (SYS). SYS is the interface to the kernel for all user-mode servers and drivers that require low-level kernel-mode operations. All kernel calls in the system library are transformed into a request message that is sent to SYS, which handles the request if the caller is authorized and sends a reply. SYS never takes initiative by itself, but is always blocked waiting for a new work.

The kernel calls handled by SYS can be grouped into several categories, including process management, memory management, copying data between processes, device I/O and interrupt management, access to kernel data structures, and clock services. Some typical examples of kernel calls were already mentioned in the scenarios above: SYS_DEVIO to do device I/O, SYS_VIRCOPY to copy data using virtual addressing, SYS_SETALARM to schedule an alarm, and SYS_PRIVCTL to set a process' privileges.

Clock Task (CLOCK). CLOCK is responsible for accounting for CPU usage, scheduling another process when a process' quantum expires, managing watchdog timers, and interacting with the hardware clock. When the system starts up, CLOCK programs the hardware clock's frequency and registers an interrupt handler that is run on every clock tick. The interrupt handler only increments a process' CPU usage and decrements the scheduling quantum. If a new process must be scheduled or an alarm is due, a notification is sent to CLOCK to do the real work at the task level.

Although CLOCK has no direct interface from user space, its services can be accessed through the kernel calls handled by SYS. The most important call is SYS_SETALARM that allows system processes to schedule a *synchronous alarm* that causes a 'timeout' notification upon expiration. Since both tasks are in the kernel, SYS can directly call CLOCK's functions.

3.2   The User-Space Servers

On top of the kernel, we have implemented a POSIX-conformant multiserver operating system. All servers and drivers run as independent user-mode processes and are highly restricted in what they can do, just like ordinary user applications. The servers and drivers can cooperate using the kernel's IPC primitives to provide the functionality of an ordinary UNIX operating system. Below we will discuss the core operating system servers shown in Fig. 2 in detail.

Process Manager (PM). Together with FS, PM implements the POSIX interface that is available to application programs. PM is responsible for process management such as creating and removing processes, assigning process IDs and priorities, and controlling the flow of execution. Furthermore, PM maintains relations between processes, such as process groups and parent-child blood lines. The latter, for example, has consequences for signaling the parent of exiting processes and accounting of CPU time.

PM is also responsible for POSIX signal handling. When a signal is to be delivered, by default, PM either ignores it or kills the process. Ordinary user processes can register a signal handler to catch signals. In this case, PM interrupts pending system calls, and puts a signal frame on the stack of the process to run the handler. This approach is not suitable for system processes, however, as it interferes with IPC. Therefore, we implemented an extension to the POSIX sigaction() call so that system processes can request PM to transform signals into notification messages. Since event notification messages have the highest priority of all message types, signals are delivered promptly.

Although the kernel provides the low-level mechanisms, for example, to set up the CPU registers, PM implements all process management policies. As far as the kernel is concerned all processes are similar; all it does is schedule the highest-priority ready process. The higher-level process management provided by PM is responsible for the UNIX look and feel of our system.

Memory Manager (MM). To facilitate ports to different architectures, we use a hardware-independent, segmented memory model. Each process has a text segment, which can be shared with processes that execute the same program, and a stack and data segment. System processes can be granted access to additional memory segments, such as the video memory or the RAM disk memory. In addition, they are allowed to request chunks of free memory.

The text segment of all processes has read-only protection and the stack and data segments are not executable, which makes buffer overrun vulnerabilities harder to exploit by viruses and worms, since injected code cannot be executed directly. Other memory protection mechanisms are discussed in Sec. 4.

Although the kernel is responsible for hiding the hardware-dependent details such as programming the MMU, MM does the actual memory management. MM maintains a list of free memory regions, and can allocate or release memory segments for other system services. Currently MM is integrated into PM, but work is in progress to split it out and offer virtual memory capabilities.

File Server (FS). FS manages the file system. It is an ordinary file server that handles standard POSIX calls such as open(), read(), and write(). More advanced functionality supported includes symbolic links and the select() system call. For performance reasons, file system blocks are buffered in FS' buffer cache. To maintain file system consistency, however, crucial file system data structures use write-through semantics, and the cache is periodically written to disk.

Currently, our system offers only one file system—our own native file system—but work is in progress to transform FS into a virtual file system server (VFS) that supports multiple, different file system servers. Both VFS and each file server will be run as an isolated, user-mode process. The file system underneath each mount point will be served by a separate file server so that a file server failure can affect only a subtree of the virtual file system.

Since device drivers can be dynamically loaded in our system, each file server maintains a mapping of major numbers onto specific drivers. As discussed below, changes in the configuration are broadcast through a publish-subscribe system. This mechanism decouples the file servers and the drivers they depend on.

Reincarnation Server (RS). RS is the central component responsible for managing all operating system servers and drivers. While PM is responsible for general process management, RS deals with only privileged processes: servers and drivers. It acts as a guardian and ensures liveness of the operating system. Administration of system processes also is done through RS. A utility program, service, provides the user with a convenient interface to RS. It allows the administrator to start and stop system services and (re)set the policy script that is run on certain events, including driver crashes.

Fault detection and recovery works as follows. During system initialization RS adopts all processes in the boot image as its children. System processes that are started later, also become children of RS. This ensures immediate *crash detection*, because PM raises a SIGCHLD signal that is delivered to RS when a system process exits. In addition, RS can check the liveness of the system. If the policy says so, RS does a periodic status check, and expects a reply in the next period. Failure to respond will cause the process to be killed. The status requests and the consequent replies are sent using a nonblocking event notification.

Whenever a problem is detected, RS can replace the malfunctioning component with a fresh copy, but the precise actions taken can be different for each server and each driver. The associated policy (shell) script could restart the failed component, enter the failure in a system log, backup the core image of the failed component for later inspection, send an e-mail to a remote system administrator, or other things. If crashes reoccur, a binary exponential back-off protocol could be used to prevent bogging down the system with repeated recoveries. More details about the recovery process are given in Sec. 4.

Data Store (DS). DS is a small database server with publish-subscribe functionality. It serves two purposes. First, system processes can use it to store some data privately. This redundancy is useful in the light of fault tolerance. A restarting system service, for example, can request state that it lost when it crashed. Such data is not publicly accessible, but only to the process that stored it.

Second, the publish-subscribe mechanism is the glue between operating system components. It provides a flexible interaction mechanism and elegantly reduces dependencies by decoupling producers and consumers. A producer can publish data with an associated identifier. A consumer can subscribe to selected events by specifying the identifiers or regular expressions it is interested in. Whenever a piece of data is updated DS automatically broadcasts notifications to all dependent components.

Among other things, DS is used as a *naming service*. Because every process has a unique IPC endpoint that is automatically generated by the kernel, system processes cannot easily find each other. Therefore, we introduced stable identifiers that consist of a natural language name plus an optional number. The identifiers are globally known. Whenever a system process is (re)started RS publishes its identifier and the associated IPC endpoint at DS for future lookup by other system services.

Device Drivers. All operating systems hide the raw hardware under a layer of device drivers. To get started and prove that our principles work in practice, we have implemented drivers for ATA, S-ATA, floppy, and RAM disks, keyboards, displays, audio, printers, serial line, various Ethernet cards, etc.

Although device drivers can be very challenging, technically, they are not very interesting in the operating system design space. What is important, though, is that each of ours runs as an independent user-mode process to prevent faults from spreading and make it easy to replace failing driver without a reboot.

We are aware that not all bugs can be cured by restarting a failed driver, but since the bugs that make it past driver testing tend to be timing bugs or memory leaks rather than algorithmic bugs, a restart often does the job. Moreover, our system can take other measures as well, such as pinpointing the driver that is responsible for the failure and notifying a remote administrator.

4   Reliability

One of the strengths of our system is that it moves device drivers and other operating system functionality out of the kernel into unprivileged user-mode processes and introduces protection barriers between all modules. This strong compartmentalization improves the system's reliability in various ways [15,16]. Faults are properly isolated and the system can often gracefully recover by restarting the failed component rather than rebooting the entire computer.

4.1   Fault Isolation

The kernel and MMU hardware ensure that processes are fully isolated. Each server and driver is encapsulated in a private address space that is protected by the MMU hardware. Illegal access attempts are caught, just like for user applications. Processes can exchange data in a controlled way by using the kernel's virtual copy construct. Copying is possible only with a capability-like descriptor—created by the other party—that grants access to a precisely specified memory region. This prevents memory corruption, even in the light of malicious processes.

The user-mode operating system components do not run with superuser privileges. Instead, they are given an unprivileged user and group ID to restrict file system access and POSIX calls. In addition, each user, server, and driver process has a restriction policy, according to the principle of least authority [10]. The policies are set by RS and the kernel enforces them at run time.

Driver access to I/O ports and IRQ lines are assigned when they are started. In this way, if, say, the printer driver tries to write to the disk's I/O ports, the kernel will deny the access. Stopping rogue DMA is not possible with current hardware, but as soon as an I/O MMU is added, we can prevent that, too. A temporary solution that is possible in our system is to deny access to the DMA controller and, instead, have a trusted server to mediate any DMA attempts.

Furthermore, we tightly restrict the IPC and kernel call capabilities of each process. For each user, server, and driver process we specify which IPC primitives it may use, which IPC endpoints are allowed, and which kernel calls it can make, depending on their needs. Ordinary applications, for example, cannot request kernel services at all, but need to contact the POSIX servers instead.

4.2 Fault Resilience

While we do not claim that our system is free of bugs, in many cases we can recover from crashes due to programming errors or attempts to exploit vulnerabilities, transparent to applications and without user intervention. As discussed in Sec. 3, the RS server executes a policy script when it detects a failure and can automatically replace a failed system process with a fresh copy.

Next to RS, DS is an integral part of our design for fault tolerance. Its publish-subscribe mechanism makes it very suitable to inform other processes of changes in the operating system. For example, FS subscribes to the identifier for the disk drivers. When a driver crashes and RS registers a new one, DS notifies FS about the event; FS then can take further action to recover from the failure.

Different recovery strategies are used depending on the kind of driver that fails [15]. When a block device driver failure is detected, the file server can recover transparently by retrying the I/O operation that failed. For character devices, the file server pushes errors to user space, but transparent recovery sometimes is also possible. A print job, for example, can be reissued by the print spooler system. Finally, for Ethernet drivers, transparent recovery is possible when a reliable transport protocol, such as TCP, is used. In this case, the network server (not discussed here) can retransmit lost packets.

The underlying assumption of our approach is that failures are transient and that restarting a component allows to fix the problem. The *fault set* that RS deals with are internal errors, timing failures, aging bugs, and attack failures. Internal errors mean that a system process encounters an exception and panics or gets killed, for example, because it dereferences an invalid pointer. Timing failures are caused by specific configuration or unexpected hardware timing issues. Aging bugs are implementation problems that cause a component to fail over time, for example, when it runs out of buffers due to memory leaks. Finally, attack failures are caused by malicious code, such as variations on the 'ping-of-death.'

Byzantine failures and logical errors where a server or driver perfectly adheres to the specified system behavior but fails to perform the actual request are excluded. For example, consider a printer driver that accepts a print job and confirms that the printout was successfully done, but, in fact, prints garbage. Such bugs are virtually impossible to catch in any system.

In principle, RS guards both servers and drivers, but our system currently is mainly designed to deal with device driver failures. If one of the core servers discussed in the previous section crashes, recovery is not (yet) possible and the system will be hampered. For example, a crash of PM or FS that together implement the POSIX interface will directly affect application programs. However, given that typically about 70% of the operating system consists of device drivers and that they have error rates 3 to 7 times higher than ordinary code [7], we have tackled an important class of problems with our design.

5   Performance

Modular systems have been criticized for decades because of alleged performance problems. Modern multiserver systems, however, have proven that competitive performance can be realized [3,11]. We have done extensive measurements of our system (on a 2.2 GHz Athlon), showing that the performance overhead compared to the base system with in-kernel drivers is limited to 5–10% [17].

The simplest system call, getpid(), takes 1.011 microseconds, which includes passing two messages and two context switches. Rebuilding the full system, which is a heavily disk bound job, has an overhead of 7% compared to the base system with in-kernel device drivers. Jobs with mixed computing and I/O, such as sorting, sedding, grepping, prepping, and uuencoding a 64-MB file have overheads of 4%, 6%, 1%, 9%, and 8%, respectively. The system can build the kernel and all user-mode servers and drivers in the boot image within 6 sec. In that time it performs 112 compilations and 11 links (about 50 msec per compilation). The overhead on disk transfer times of user-mode disk drivers is shown in Fig 3(a). Fast Ethernet easily runs at full speed, and initial tests show that we can also drive gigabit Ethernet at full speed from a user-mode driver. Finally, the time from exiting the multiboot monitor to the login prompt is under 5 sec.

We have also measured the performance overhead of our recovery mechanisms by simulating repeated crashes of the Ethernet driver during a transfer of a 512-MB file from the Internet with crash intervals ranging from 1 to 15 sec. The results are shown in Fig. 3(b). The transfer successfully completed in all cases, with a throughput degradation ranging from 25% to only 1%. The mean recovery time was 0.36 sec. This recovery time is due to the TCP retransmission timeout; restarting the failed driver takes only a few milliseconds.

It has to be noted that the overhead of the many new security checks is not related to the multiserver design per se and will be visible in any system. Furthermore, we did not yet do any performance optimizations. Careful analysis and removal of bottlenecks may bring the performance.

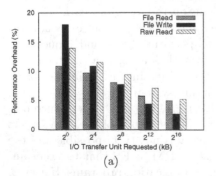

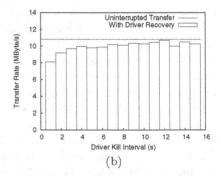

(a)   (b)

Fig. 3. Performance measurements: (a) Overhead of our user-mode disk driver compared to the in-kernel driver of the base system. (b) Throughput while repeatedly killing the Ethernet driver during a 512-MB transfer with various time intervals.

6 Conclusions

Our main contribution in the research presented in this paper is that we have actually built a highly reliable, UNIX-compatible multiserver operating system with a performance loss of only 5% to 10%. We have discussed the design and implementation of a useful and stable prototype that currently runs over 400 standard UNIX applications, including the X Window System, two C compilers, many editors, a complete TCP/IP stack that supports BSD sockets, and all the standard shell, file, text manipulation, and other UNIX utilities.

To achieve high reliability we have reorganized the monolithic design that is common to many UNIX operating systems. Our design consists of a small kernel running the entire operating system as a collection of independent, isolated, user-mode processes. The kernel implements only the minimal mechanisms, such as interrupt handling, IPC, policy enforcement, and contains two kernel tasks (SYS and CLOCK) to support the user-mode operating system parts. The core servers are the process manager (PM), memory manager (MM), file server (FS), reincarnation server (RS), and data store (DS). The size of the kernel and the core servers ranges from about 1000 to 4000 lines of code.

Our multiserver architecture realizes a highly reliable operating system. We moved most operating system code to unprivileged user-mode processes that are encapsulated in a private address space protected by the MMU hardware. Each user, server, and driver process has a restriction policy to limit their powers to an absolute minimum. By fully compartmentalizing the operating system's device drivers, we were able to reduce the size of the TCB by over two orders of magnitude. We do not claim we have removed all the bugs, but the system is fault tolerant, and can withstand and often recover from common failures.

Given the low costs for this increase in operating system reliability and the fact that we were able to maintain the look and feel of an ordinary UNIX system, we believe that our reorganization of UNIX is practical for real-life adoption.

7 Availability

The system is called MINIX 3 because we started with MINIX 2 as a base and then modified it very heavily. It is free, open-source software, available via the Internet. You can download MINIX 3 from the official homepage at: http://www.minix3.org/, which also contains the source code, documentation, news, contributed software packages, and more. Over 75,000 people have downloaded the CD-ROM image since the release (October 2005) resulting in a large and growing user community that communicates using the USENET newgroup *comp.os.minix*. MINIX 3 is actively being developed, and your help and feedback are much appreciated.

Acknowledgments

This work was supported by Netherlands Organization for Scientific Research (NWO) under grant 612-060-420.

References

1. Härtig, H., Baumgartl, R., Borriss, M., Hamann, C.J., Hohmuth, M., Mehnert, F., Reuther, L., Schonberg, S., Wolter, J.: DROPS-OS Support for Distributed Multimedia Applications. In: Proc. 8th ACM SIGOPS Eur. Workshop. (1998) 203–209
2. LeVasseur, J., Uhlig, V., Stoess, J., Gotz, S.: Unmodified Device Driver Reuse and Improved System Dependability via Virtual Machines. In: Proc. 6th Symp. on Operating Systems Design and Implementation. (2004) 17–30
3. Leslie, B., Chubb, P., Fitzroy-Dale, N., Gotz, S., Gray, C., Macpherson, L., Daniel Potts, Y.T.S., Elphinstone, K., Heiser, G.: User-Level Device Drivers: Achieved Performance. Journal of Computer Science and Technology 20(5) (2005)
4. Hunt, G.C., Larus, J.R., Abadi, M., Aiken, M., Barham, P., Fahndrich, M., Hawblitzel, C., Hodson, O., Levi, S., Murphy, N., Steensgaard, B., Tarditi, D., Wobber, T., Zill, B.: An Overview of the Singularity Project. Technical Report MSR-TR-2005-135, Microsoft Research (2005)
5. Basili, V., Perricone, B.: Software Errors and Complexity: An Empirical Investigation. Comm. of the ACM (1984) 42–52
6. T.J. Ostrand and E.J. Weyuker: The Distribution of Faults in a Large Industrial Software System. In: Proc. of the 2002 ACM SIGSOFT Int'l Symp. on Software Testing and Analysis, ACM (2002) 55–64
7. Chou, A., Yang, J., Chelf, B., Hallem, S., Engler, D.: An Empirical Study of Operating System Errors. In: Proc. 18th ACM Symp. on Operating System Principles. (2001) 73–88
8. Swift, M., Bershad, B., Levy, H.: Improving the Reliability of Commodity Operating Systems. ACM Trans. on Computer Systems 23(1) (2005) 77–110
9. Swift, M., Annamalai, M., Bershad, B., Levy, H.: Recovering Device Drivers. In: Proc. 6th Symp. on Operating Systems Design and Implementation. (2004) 1–15
10. Saltzer, J., Schroeder, M.: The Protection of Information in Computer Systems. Proceedings of the IEEE 63(9) (1975)
11. Härtig, H., Hohmuth, M., Liedtke, J., Schönberg, S., Wolter, J.: The Performance of -Kernel-Based Systems. In: Proc. 6th Symp. on Operating Systems Design and Implementation. (1997) 66–77
12. Pfitzmann, B., Stüble, C.: Perseus: A Quick Open-source Path to Secure Signatures. In: 2nd Workshop on Microkernel-based Systems. (2001)
13. Hildebrand, D.: An Architectural Overview of QNX. In: Proc. USENIX Workshop in Microkernels and Other Kernel Architectures. (1992) 113–126
14. Gefflaut, A., Jaeger, T., Park, Y., Liedtke, J., Elphinstone, K., Uhlig, V., Tidswell, J., Deller, L., Reuther, L.: The SawMill Multiserver Approach. In: ACM SIGOPS European Workshop. (2000) 109–114
15. Herder, J.N., Bos, H., Gras, B., Homburg, P., Tanenbaum, A.S.: MINIX 3: A Highly Reliable, Self-Repairing Operating System. ACM SIGOPS Operating System Review 40(3) (2006)
16. Tanenbaum, A.S., Herder, J.N., Bos, H.: Can We Make Operating Systems Reliable and Secure? IEEE Computer 39(5) (2006) 44–51
17. Herder, J.N., Bos, H., Tanenbaum, A.S.: A Lightweight Method for Building Reliable Operating Systems Despite Unreliable Device Drivers. In: Technical Report IR-CS-018 [www.cs.vu.nl/~jnherder/ir-cs-018.pdf], Vrije Universiteit (2006)

Critical-Task Anticipation Scheduling Algorithm for Heterogeneous and Grid Computing

Ching-Hsien Hsu[1], Ming-Yuan Own[1], and Kuan-Ching Li[2]

[1] Dept. of Computer Science and Information Engr. Chung Hua University, Taiwan
chh@chu.edu.tw
[2] Dept. of Computer Science and Information Engr. Providence University, Taiwan
kuancli@pu.edu.tw

Abstract. The problem of scheduling a weighted directed acyclic graph (DAG) to a set of heterogeneous processors to minimize the completion time has been recently studied. The NP-completeness of the problem has instigated researchers to propose different heuristic algorithms. In this paper, we present an efficient Critical-task Anticipation (*CA*) scheduling algorithm for heterogeneous computing systems. The *CA* scheduling algorithm introduces a new task prioritizing scheme that based on urgency and importance of tasks to obtain better schedule length compared to the Heterogeneous Earliest Finish Time algorithm. To evaluate the performance of the proposed algorithm, we have developed a simulator that contains a parametric graph generator for generating weighted directed acyclic graphs with various characteristics. We have implemented the *CA* algorithm along with the *HEFT* scheduling algorithm on the simulator. The *CA* algorithm is shown to be effective in terms of speedup and easy to implement.

1 Introduction

The demand for powerful computing to solve a large application has emerged in recent years. Some parallel architecture, such as multiple computers, or multiple processor system, that employ numerous processors interconnected by high-speed network to achieve superior performance than use a single computer. Because the diverse quality among that processors (computers) or some special requirement, like exclusive function, memory access speed, or the customize I/O devices, etc.; the tasks have distinct execution time on different processors (computers) and it named hetero-geneous computing system.

The purpose of such system is to drive processors cooperate to get the application (an application consists of tasks) done quickly. Therefore, one of the key factors is how to schedule individual task among processors to minimize execution time or maximize processor utilization and so on. The primary scheduling methods can be classified into two categories: dynamic scheduling and static scheduling. In dynamic algorithm, it executes redistribution of tasks between processors during run-time, expect to balance computational load, and reduce processor's idle time. On the contrary, in static algorithm, it assigns tasks to processors at the compile time, attempt to minimize the entire completion time, and satisfy the precedence of tasks [6, 14]. When the

C. Jesshope and C. Egan (Eds.): ACSAC 2006, LNCS 4186, pp. 95 – 108, 2006.

information of an application which predict tasks execution time, the message size of communication among tasks, and tasks dependences are known a priori at the compile-time, it called static model [6, 14], thus, schedule analysis must be done before run time.

A Direct Acyclic Graph (DAG) [2] is used for modeling parallel applications which consists of several independent tasks. The nodes of DAG correspond to tasks and the edges of which indicate the precedence constraints between tasks. In addition, the weight of an edge represents communication cost among tasks. Each node is given a computation cost and it is represented by a computation costs matrix. Figure 1 depicts an example of DAG and the computation cost matrix. Moreover, we consider that each task can be executed on a single processor only and tasks are non-preemptable. A task n_j is a successor (predecessor) of task n_i if there exists an edge from n_i to n_j (from j to i) in the graph. The task has precedence constraint, that is, only if the predecessor n_i completes its execution and then its successor n_j receives the *messages* from n_i, the successor n_j can start its execution.

The scheduling problem has been widely researched in heterogeneous system where the computational ability of processors is different and the processors communicate over an underlying network. Many researchers had proposed articles on the subject. The scheduling problem in general is proved to be NP-complete, so the desire of optimal scheduling can lead to higher scheduling overhead. The negative result motivates the requirement for heuristic approaches to solve the scheduling problem. A comprehensive survey about static scheduling algorithms is given in [14]. The authors of [14] have shown that the heuristic-based algorithms can be classified into a variety of categories, such as clustering algorithms, duplication-based algorithms, and list-scheduling algorithms.

The keynote of clustering algorithms is a mapping of the tasks onto n clusters. Each task in a cluster must execute in the same processor. A nonlinear clustering is that at least one cluster contains two independent tasks, otherwise it called linear clustering. It iterates clustering steps while no improvements in the scheduling length can be obtained. The requirement of unbound processors was a disadvantage and it causes the algorithm to work badly in practice [3, 16]. With the auxiliary of some cluster merge steps, the problem was solved [7, 8], although the approach is expensive.

The duplication-based algorithms [1, 9, 11] are another different skills. Those algorithms utilize the duplicate technique which duplicates some critical tasks (i.e. the parent tasks) on the same or another processor so that reduce the communication cost. When duplication of the execution of tasks occurs in processors, it will result in an increase in the space complexity since data must be duplicated too.

The list-scheduling algorithms [10, 13, 14, 15] divided the approach into two independent parts, list phase and processor-selection phase. In the first part, list phase, they used heuristic method to give the task a priority and then according as the priority, make an arrangement for the task set. In the second part, processor-selection phase, they used the result of the first part to select the most suitable processor for the task assignment. Our Critical-task Anticipation (*CA*) algorithm belongs to this classi-fication. This typical method is superior to the others because it is easier to practice, lower complexity, and good performance.

In this paper, our proposed algorithm uses the following scheduling system model. There are P fully connected heterogeneous processors in the system. The processors communicate over an underlying communication network which is contention-free. The main intent of this problem is to minimize the schedule length (schedule length also called *makespan*).   Our proposed algorithm takes advantage of some graph attributes used by heterogeneous earliest-finish-time (*HEFT*) algorithm [14], and furthermore we came up with a novel idea to improve the performance. In the *HEFT* algorithm, it detects the critical path length of a given node. To do so, it uses *critical score*, i.e., as the name implies, an accumulative value that are computed recursively travels along the graph upward, starting from the exit node. In the literature, the authors exhibited the brilliant performance as compared with the Dynamic Level Scheduling Algorithm [13], the Levelized-Min Time Algorithm [5], and the Mapping Heuristic Algorithm [12]. Our algorithm is similar to the *HEFT* algorithm, except that we use a critical-task anticipation skill.   We add a simple modification to make significant improvements in schedule length as well as speedup of the application.

The rest of this paper is organized as follows: Section 2 introduces the scheduling system and problem formulation.   Section 3 presents the definitions used in our proposed algorithm. In section 4, we discuss details of the *CA* scheduling algorithm and give a simple comparison to the *HEFT* algorithm. Section 5 shows the simulation results. Finally, in Section 6, some concluding remarks are made.

2 Preliminaries

2.1 Heterogeneous Scheduling System

As mentioned in section 1, the heterogeneous computing architecture is a set of heterogeneous processors $P = \{p_k: k = 1: p\}$ connected in a fully connected topology, where $p = |P|$. We also assume that:

1) There is no network contention between any arbitrary processors.
2) Computation and communication can be worked simultaneously because of the separated I/O.
3) Tasks are non-preemptable. In other words, once a task is assigned to a processor, it starts execution and finishes to its completion.
4) After accomplish the task's execution, the task have to send operational result to all immediate successor of it instantly.

W is an $n \times p$ matrix in which $w_{i,j}$ indicates estimated computation time to execute task n_i on processor p_j. The mean value of task n_i is calculated as follow:

$$\overline{w_i} = \sum_{j=1}^{p} w_{i,j} / p \qquad (1)$$

The communication cost depends on the size of message and communication latency of processors.   A $p \times p$ matrix T is structured to represent data transfer rate among processors.   Latency of processors is given in a p-dimensional vector V.   The communication cost of transferring data from task n_i (execute on processor p_m) to task n_j (execute on processor p_n) is denoted by $c_{i,j}$ and can be calculated by the following equation

$$c_{i,j} = V_m + \frac{Message_{i,j}}{T_{m,n}}, \qquad (2)$$

Where:

V_m is the latency of processor p_m,

$Message_{i,j}$ is the size of message from task n_i to task n_j,

$T_{m,n}$ is data transfer rate from processor p_m to processor p_n.

In static scheduling model, it is usually to use the mean value of communication cost to simplify the presentation in a given DAG (as shown in Fig. 1). The mean value of communication cost between tasks n_i and n_j can be formulated by the following equation,

$$\overline{c_{i,j}} = \overline{V} + \frac{Message_{i,j}}{\overline{T}}. \qquad (3)$$

Where:

$\overline{V}$ is the average latency of processors.

$\overline{T}$ is the average transfer rate.

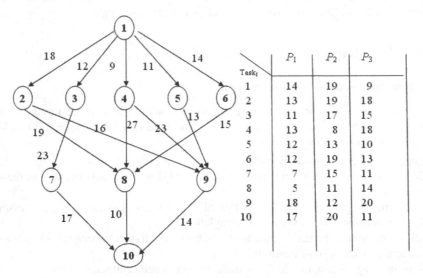

Fig. 1. An example of Direct Acyclic Graph (DAG) and the computation cost matrix

2.2 Problem Formulation

The application can be represented by a Directed Acyclic Graph (DAG), $G = (V, E, C)$, where $V = \{n_j: j = 1: v\}$ is the set of nodes and $v = |V|$, $E = \{e_{i,j} = <n_i, n_j>\}$ is the set of communication edges and $e = |E|$; C is the set of edge communication costs. In the DAG model, each node indicates least indivisible unit, in other words, each node must be executed on a processor from beginning to end. Each edge $<n_i, n_j>$ is a direct arc on which n_i is the immediate predecessor and n_j is the immediate successor. There is precedence relationship between tasks, namely task n_j takes it's turn to prepare for starting execution after the n_i has finished it's execution and n_j receive the essential message from n_i. The weight of edge $<n_i, n_j>$ indicates the average communication cost between n_i and n_j.

The node without any inward edge is called *entry node* n_{entry}, and a node without any outward edge is called *exit node* n_{exit}. In general, it is supposed that the application has only one *entry node* and one *exit node*. If the actual application claims more than one *entry (exit) node*, we can accede a zero-cost fake *entry (exit) node* with zero-cost edge.

The goal of scheduling problem is minimizing the total execution time of the application. If there are more than one *exit tasks*, we consider that the latest completion task is the ending of the application. In other word, we want to shorten the schedule length as far as possible.

3 Definitions

The list scheduling algorithm is broadly distinguished into list phase and processor-selection phase. In this section, we give some definitions that will be used in both *CA* and *HEFT* algorithms.

3.1 Parameters for List Phase

Definition 1: In the list phase, the *Critical Score* of the task n_{exit} denoted by $CS(n_{exit})$ is defined as $CS(n_{exit}) = \overline{w_{exit}}$, where $\overline{w_{exit}}$ is the average computation cost of task n_{exit}.

Definition 2: $CS(n_i) = \overline{w_i} + \underset{n_j \in suc(n_i)}{Max} (\overline{c_{i,j}} + CS(n_j))$, where $\overline{w_i}$ is the average computation cost of task n_i, $\overline{c_{i,j}}$ is the average communication cost of edge $<n_i, n_j>$, and $suc(n_i)$ is the set of immediate successors of task n_i.

3.2 Parameters for Processor-Selection Phase

In the processor-selection phase, the algorithm exploits a partial schedule to meet the minimum schedule length. There is an intuitional idea to calculate the *finish time* (*FT*) of task n_j that will be executed on processor p_k, then we can select the minimum finish time from the calculated results and determine which processor is chosen to execute the task n_j. In such approach, each processor p_k will maintain a list of tasks, *task-list*(p_k), keeps the latest status of tasks correspond to the *EFT*(n_i, p_k), the earliest finish time of task n_i that is assigned on processor p_k.

Recall having been mentioned above that the application represented by DAG must satisfy the precedence relationship. Taking into account the sequence of tasks which are assigned on the processors, a task n_j can intend to execute on a processor p_k only if its all immediate predecessors send the essential messages to n_j and n_j successful receives all these messages. Thus, the latest message arrive time of node n_i on processor p_k, denoted by *LMAT*(n_j, p_k), is evaluated by the following equation,

$$LMAT(n_j, p_k) = \underset{n_i \in pred(n_j)}{Max} \left(EFT(n_i) + \overline{c_{i,j}} \right) \tag{4}$$

where *pred*(n_j) is the set of immediate predecessors of task n_j. Note that if tasks n_i and n_j are assigned to the same processor, $\overline{c_{i,j}}$ is assumed to be zero because it is negligible.

Definition 3: The n_{entry} has no inward arc, therefore for the task n_{entry}, $LMAT(n_{entry}, p_k) = 0$, for all $k = 1$ to p.

Definition 4: The _start time_ of task n_j executed on processor p_k is denoted as $ST(n_j, p_k)$. The determination of start time aims to search available time slot on processor p_k that is large enough to execute task n_j (i.e., length of time slot $> w_{j,k}$). Note that the search of available time slot is started from $LMAT(n_j, p_k)$.

Definition 5: The _finish time_ of task n_j completes its execution on processor p_k is denoted as $FT(n_j, p_k)$ and calculated by the following equation,

$$FT(n_j, p_k) = ST(n_j, p_k) + w_{j,k} \tag{5}$$

Definition 6: The _earliest finish time_ of task n_j completes its execution is denoted as $EFT(n_j)$ and determined by the following equation,

$$EFT(n_j) = \underset{p_k \in P}{Min} \{FT(n_j, p_k)\} \tag{6}$$

Definition 7: According to definition 6, if the _EFT_ of task n_j is determined upon task n_j executed on processor p_t, then the target processor of task n_j is denoted by $TP(n_j)$, and $TP(n_j) = p_t$.

4   The Proposed Scheduling Algorithm

In this section, we first present a new scheduling algorithm, the critical-task anticipation algorithm (outlined in Figure 2) which will be operated in the heterogeneous scheduling system. The proposed scheduling algorithm will be verified beneficial for the readers while we delineate a sequence of the algorithm and show some example scenarios. In the rest of this section, we will review the _HEFT_ algorithm which is the best known list-scheduling algorithm and provide some different viewpoint between both algorithms.

4.1   The Critical-Task Anticipation Scheduling Algorithm

The $CS(n_i)$ is known as the maximal summation of scores including the average computation cost and communication cost from task n_i to the exit task, that is, $CS(n_i)$ is the longest length of critical path. Therefore, the magnitude of the task's critical score is regarded as the decisive factor when we arrange the priority. In the _HEFT_ algorithm, it sorts the tasks in L by non-increasing order of critical scores. This method seems good intuitively that it provides suitable priorities for the tasks. In this study, we propose an improving scheduling heuristic, the critical-task anticipation scheduling algorithm (CA). The origin of the CA algorithm is owing to the following three observations.

Observation 1: The processors are heterogeneous, namely, there are variations in execution cost from processor to processor for each task. Different processor assignments for tasks result in a different computational cost. In that event, we always wish to give the task n_i which has large average computation cost higher priority. This can aid the task n_i to get chance to reduce the finish time.

Observation 2: Except for the *entry task*, each task has to receive the essential messages from its immediate predecessors. In other words, a task will be in waiting state when it does not collect complete message yet. For this reason, we emphasize the importance of the last arrival message such that the succeeding task (node) can start its execution earlier. Therefore, it is imperative to give the predecessor who sends the last arrival message higher priority. This can aid the task to get chance to advance the start time.

Observation 3: If a task n_i is inserted into the front of the scheduling-list, it occupies advantage position. Namely, n_i has higher probability to reduce its finish time. Consequently, the start time of $suc(n_i)$ can be advanced with higher probability.

According to the above observations, we have a different viewpoint on the importance of a key task, the *critical-task* is defined as following.

Definition 8: A task n_i is a critical-task of task n_j, denoted as $CT(n_j)$, iff n_i is not inserted into scheduling list L yet and $CS(n_i) = \underset{n_k \in pred(n_j)}{Max} (CS(n_k))$.

Our viewpoint differs from the majority of literatures in terms of task prioritizing. In most algorithms, their thought is to schedule high critical score task first (even the estimation of critical scores in these algorithms are different). In our approach, the *CA* algorithm prioritizes the task n_i according to the influence of task n_i, which effects the successors of n_i (Observation 2) and devotes to lead to an accelerated chain (Observation 1). In short, our scheme is not only prioritizing tasks by the importance (i.e., critical score) but also prioritizing tasks by the urgent among tasks.

Begin:
1. Input the information of DAG and matrix.
/* List Phase */
2. Construct an empty scheduling-list L which is FIFO.
3. Calculate $CS(n_i)$ for task n_i, $\forall n_i \in$ V.
4. Prioritize the tasks into L by CA procedure.
   //*CA* procedure is shown in figure 3.
   /* In the *HEFT* algorithm, tasks in L are sorted by
   non-increasing order according to critical
   scores */
/* Processor Selection Phase*/
5. **While** L is not empty **do**
6.   Remove task n_i from L.
7.   Compute $LMAT(n_i, p_k)$, $ST(n_i, p_k)$, $FT(n_i, p_k)$ for all $k = 1$ to p.
8.   Determine $EFT(n_i)$, $EST(n_i)$.
9.   Assign task n_i to processor $TP(n_i)$
10.   Modify the *task-list* $(TP(n_i))$.
11.**Endwhile**
End

Fig. 2. The Proposed Critical-Task Anticipation Algorithm

4.2 Details and Example

The procedure of Critical-task Anticipation is outlined in Fig. 3. It maintains the following data structures: a scheduling list L which is first-in first-out, an auxiliary stack S, a temporary container C and an array of Boolean called queue vector (QV). $QV[n_i]$ = true indicates that task n_i has queued into L. $QV[n_i]$ = false indicates that task n_i has not yet queued into L.

We now perform a running trace of the CA algorithm. Let's consider again the example shown in figure 1, which has ten tasks. These tasks will be executed on three fully-connected heterogeneous processors. According to this DAG, the *critical scores* of tasks can be evaluated by definitions 1 and 2. We proceed to the computation of critical scores from the n_{exit} by bottom-up fashion. For example, for the exit node n_{10}, the $CS(n_{10})=16$, and for node n_8, $CS(n_8)=10 + max(10 + CS(n_{10})) = 10 + max(26) = 36$. We start to examine the procedure of critical-task anticipation algorithm which is illustrated in Fig. 3. The step by step execution sequence is given below.

Initially, QV = [F, F, F, F, F, F, F, F, F, F], S is empty, L is empty, where F is *false* and T is *true*. The index is the serial number of the task, from 1 to 10.

1)   Push n_{10} on stack S. S = $[n_{10}]$.
2)   S is not empty, begin the while loop (Fig. 3, Line 5).
3)   Pop n_{10}, predecessors of task n_{10} are n_7, n_8, n_9. Since the condition of QV at line 7 isn't satisfied, it then goes to the next stage, searching $CT(n_{10})$ at line 11 and resulting C = $\{n_7, n_8, n_9\}$. Finally, S = $[n_9, n_7, n_8, n_{10}]$. Note that $CT(n_{10}) = n_9$, which is pushed on the top of S, and n_9 has the highest priority than the other tasks in stack S.
4)   Peek at n_9 (top of stack), then S = $[n_4, n_2, n_5, n_9, n_7, n_8, n_{10}]$ (after lines 11-20 in CA procedure are processed).
5)   Peek at n_4, then S = $[n_1, n_4, n_2, n_5, n_9, n_7, n_8, n_{10}]$.
6)   Peek at n_1, note that n_1 is entry node, so it follows lines 7~10, S = $[n_4, n_2, n_5, n_9, n_7, n_8, n_{10}]$, L = $[n_1]$ and set QV[n_1] = T.
7)   Peek at n_4, because $pred(n_4) = \{n_1\}$, we then check QV[n_1] and have QV[n_1] = T. This implies that $pred(n_4)$ are inserted into L. Therefore, S = $[n_2, n_5, n_9, n_7, n_8, n_{10}]$, L= $[n_1, n_4]$ and set QV[n_4] = T (Lines 7-10).
8)   Peek at n_2, S = $[n_5, n_9, n_7, n_8, n_{10}]$, L = $[n_1, n_4, n_2]$ and set QV[n_2] = T.
9)   Peek at n_5, S = $[n_9, n_7, n_8, n_{10}]$, L = $[n_1, n_4, n_2, n_5]$ and set QV[n_5] = T.
10)   Peek at n_9, $pred(n_9) = \{n_2, n_4, n_5\}$. Since QV = [T, T, F, T, T, F, F, F, F, F], the condition "all QV[n_i] are true, $n_i \in pred(n_j)$" at line 7 is satisfied. We then have S = $[n_7, n_8, n_{10}]$, L = $[n_1, n_4, n_2, n_5, n_9]$ and set QV[n_9] = T.
11)   Peek at n_7, then S = $[n_3, n_7, n_8, n_{10}]$.
12)   Peek at n_3, then S = $[n_7, n_8, n_{10}]$, L = $[n_1, n_4, n_2, n_5, n_9, n_3]$ and set QV[n_3] = T.
13)   We omit the rest process until only task n_{10} remains in stack S. When task n_{10} is popped, S becomes empty and L = $[n_1, n_4, n_2, n_5, n_9, n_3, n_7, n_6, n_8, n_{10}]$; the values of QV are all *true*. The list phase is done.

We continue the processor-selection phase by deploying tasks from list L in FIFO manner to suitable processor. According to L = $[n_1, n_4, n_2, n_5, n_9, n_3, n_7, n_6, n_8, n_{10}]$, at the beginning, task n_1 is assigned to processor p_3 because it produces the earliest finish time, i.e., $EFT(n_1) = 9$ and $TP(n_1) = p_3$. Then, n_4 is the next task to be removed from L. The $LMAT(n_4, p_1) = Max(EFT(n_1) + 9) = 18$, according to the partial schedule, the

$ST(n_4, p_1) = 18$ and $FT(n_4, p_1) = ST(n_4, p_1) + w_{4,1} = 18 + 13 = 31$. We have $FT(n_4, p_2) = 18 + 8 = 26$ and $FT(n_4, p_3) = 9 + 18 = 27$. Therefore, the $EFT(n_4) = $ Min $\{31, 26, 27\} = 26$ and $TP(n_4)$ is p_2 since p_2 is the best choice among the processors.

```
1. Procedure Critical-task Anticipation:
2.      Initially, construct an array of Boolean QV and a stack S.
3.      QV[n_j] = false, ∀ n_j∈ V.
4.      Push n_exit on top of S.
5.      While S is not empty do
6.          Peek task n_j on the top of S;
7.              If( all QV[n_i] are true, for all n_i∈ pred(n_j) or task n_j is n_entry)
8.                  Pop task n_j from top of S and put n_j into scheduling-list L;
9.                  QV[ n_j] = true;
10.         EndIf.
11.             Else     /* search the CT(n_j) */
12.                 For each task n_i, where n_i∈ pred(n_j) do
13.                     If(QV[n_i] = false)
14.                         Put CS(n_i) into container C;
15.                     Endif
16.                 EndFor
17.                 Push tasks pred(n_j) from C into S by non-decreasing order
                    according to their critical scores;
18                  Reset C to empty;
19.                 /* if there are 2+ tasks with same CS(n_i), task n_i is randomly
                    pushed into S. */
20.             EndElse
21. EndWhile
```

Fig. 3. The Critical-Task Anticipation Procedure

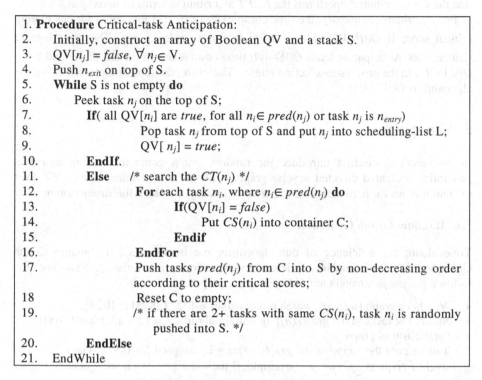

(a)

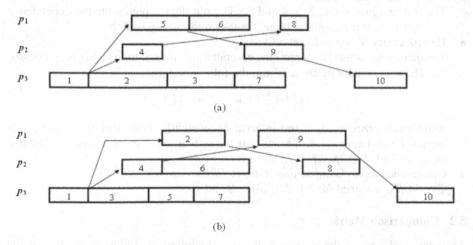

(b)

Fig. 4. Scheduling results for the DAG in Fig. 1 using (a) *CA* algorithm (makespan = 81) (b) *HEFT* algorithm (makespan = 92)

The scheduling result obtained by the *CA* algorithm for the DAG given in Fig. 1 is depicted in Fig. 4(a). On the other hand, the *HEFT* results L = [n_1, n_4, n_3, n_2, n_5, n_6, n_9, n_7, n_8, n_{10}] in the list phase and the scheduling result is given in Fig. 4(b) and it demonstrates that the *CA* algorithm outperforms the *HEFT* algorithm in terms of makespan.

For algorithm complexity, the time complexity of the *CA* algorithm for calculating critical score is $O(|P|+|E|)$, where $O(|P|)$ is for $\overline{w}_i$ calculation. The procedure of Critical-task Anticipation leads $O(|E|+|V|)$ time complexity in the list phase and takes $O(|E|\times|P|)$ in the processor-selection phase. Therefore, the time complexity of the *CA* algorithm is $O(|E|\times|P|)$.

5   Simulation

In this section, we first introduce the random graph generator, a simulator that generating weighted directed acyclic graphs with various characteristics. We then explain metrics for performance comparison. Finally, we show the simulation results.

5.1   Random Graph Generator

To evaluate the efficiency of our algorithm, we implemented a Random Graph Generator (RGG) to simulate applications with various characteristics. RGG uses the following input parameters to produce diverse graphs.

- Weight of graph (*weight*), which is a constant = {32, 128, 512, 1024}.
- Number of tasks in the graph (*n*). In our simulation, *n* = {20, 40, 60, 80, 100}.
- Parallelism of graph (*p*)
  It influences the shape of the graph. The *p* is assigned for 0.5, 1.0 and 2.0. The level of graph is $\lfloor \sqrt{v} / p \rfloor$. For example, if the value *p* = 2.0, it will generate higher parallelism graph and vice versa.
- Out degree of a task (*d*).
  The *d* is assigned for 1, 2, 3, 4 and 5. The out degree represents the dependence among tasks. If the degree is large, the task relationship is high.
- Heterogeneity of computation cost (*h*).
  This parameter is used to control the computation cost $w_{i,k}$ for a task n_i on processor p_k. The $w_{i,k}$ is randomly chosen from the following formula.

$$w_i \times \left(1 - \frac{h}{2}\right) \le w_{i,k} \le w_i \times \left(1 + \frac{h}{2}\right). \tag{7}$$

RGG randomizes w_i from the interval [1, *weight*]. Note that if the *weight* is assigned with larger value, it represents the estimation of great precision. The *h* is assigned for 0.1, 0.25, 0.5, 0.75 and 1.0.
- Communication to Computation Ratio (*CCR*).
  The *CCR* is assigned for 0.1, 0.5, 1.0, 2.0 and 10.0.

5.2   Comparison Metrics

As mentioned earlier, the objective of our scheduling algorithm is to shorten the completion time of an application. Several comparative metrics are given below:

- Makespan
  The *makespan* (also known as schedule length) is defined as

$$makespan = \max(EFT(n_i), \text{ for all } i = 1 \sim n \tag{8}$$

- Speedup
  The speedup is defined as

$$Speedup = \frac{\min_{P_j \in P}\{\sum_{n_i \in V} w_{i,j}\}}{makespan} \tag{9}$$

The numerator is the minimal accumulated sum of computation cost of tasks which are assigned on one processor. The meaning of Speedup is comparison between sequential execution time and parallel execution time.

- Percentage of Quality of Schedules (PQS)
  The percentage of the *CA* algorithm produces better, equal and worse quality of schedules compared to the *HEFT* algorithm.

5.3 Simulation Results

In [14], *HEFT* demonstrated superior performance to other scheduling techniques, the Dynamic Level Scheduling Algorithm [13], the Levelized-Min Time Algorithm [5], and the Mapping Heuristic Algorithm [12]. Upon this reason, in this simulation, our emphasis is on the performance comparison with *HEFT*. The first simulation aims to demonstrate the merit of the *CA* algorithm by showing the quality of schedules using the RGG. Figures 5 and 6 show the simulations make use of the parameters which generate 1875 different DAGs. The *CA* scheduling algorithm provides superior performance for 70% ~ 80% test samples. Fig. 5 (a) shows the effect of setting different *weight* = {32, 128, 512, 1024}. This result shows that PQS does not changed largely by varying the *weight*. Therefore, it is interesting to discover the effect on different number of processors. Fig. 5 (b) shows that the *CA* algorithm performs very well when the number of processor becomes large.

weight	32	128	512	1024
CA Better:	74.61%	73.22%	72.42%	73.13%
Equal:	0.21%	0.05%	0.05%	0.05%
CA Worse:	25.18%	26.73%	27.53%	26.82%

Processors	5	6	7	8
Better:	77.41%	80.45%	82.56%	85.46%
Equal:	0.10%	0.00%	0.16%	0.10%
Worse:	22.49%	19.55%	17.28%	14.44%

(a)   (b)

Fig. 5. PQS (a) *CA* compared with *HEFT* (3 processors) (b) *CA* compared with *HEFT* (*weight* = 128)

Figures 6 present the simulation results in terms of speedup by varying *n, p, d, CCR* and *h*, respectively. The effect of number of task is shown in Fig. 6 (a). For both algorithms, while the simulation has small number of processors, the speedup is placid. However, when we adapt processors to eight, it is apparent that speedup increased

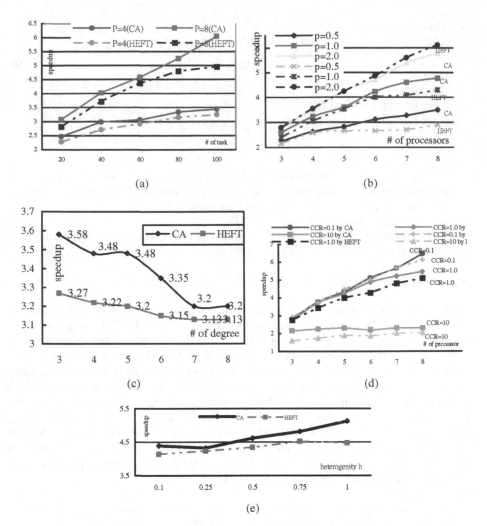

Fig. 6. Performance comparison of the *CA* and the *HEFT* algorithms (a) speedup comparison with different number of tasks (*n*) (b) speedup comparison with different degree of parallelism (*p*) (c) speedup comparison with different out-degree of tasks (*d*) (d) speedup comparison with different *CCR* (e) speedup comparison with different heterogeneity of computation cost (*h*)

significantly, especially in the situation of large number of task. Compare with the *HEFT* algorithm, the improvement rate of the *CA* algorithm in terms of average speedup is about 7% at processor = 4 and 11% at processor = 8; the Improvement Rate (IR_{CA}) is estimated by the following equation:

$$IR_{CA} = \frac{\sum speedup~(CA) - \sum speedup~(HEFT~)}{\sum speedup~(HEFT~)} \tag{10}$$

Fig. 6 (b) helps in investigating the sensitivity of task parallelization. It is noticed that, when p is large, the graphs are tending parallelism. As shown in Fig. 6 (b), the *CA* algorithm favors linear graphs ($p=0.5$), also outperforms the *HEFT* algorithm in general graphs too ($p=1.0$), but is defeated in high parallelism graphs ($p=2.0$). Fig. 6 (c) gives the observation about the dependence relationship among tasks by fixing number of processors at 5. Although the speedups of both algorithms are stable, the *CA* algorithm outperforms the *HEFT* in most cases. In Fig. 6(d), the impact of communication on speedup is plotted for various value of *CCR*. We vary *CCR* by 0.1, 1.0 and 10. It is noted that an increase in *CCR* decreases the speedup rapidly. For example, speedup offered by the *CCR*=0.1 used *CA* at processor = 8 is 6.45 and *CCR* =10.0 used *CA* at processor =8 is only 2.2. This is due to the fact that when the communication is higher than computation, the behavior of migration of tasks is not useful. Beside, when the *CCR* is large, there is still poor performance even if the numbers of processors are added. Namely, there is no benefit of increase of processors when communication is the bottleneck. Fig. 6 (e) shows the effect of heterogeneity (h) by fixed number of processor =8. From Fig. 6 (e), we observe that the speedup increases with increasing h in both algorithms. As the result of simulation, we consider the *CA* algorithm achieves significant performance improvement in majority part.

6 Conclusion

In this paper, we proposed a new scheduling heuristic, the critical-task anticipation (*CA*) algorithm for heterogeneous computing systems. The *CA* scheduling algorithm is a list scheduling heuristic and has a simple structure and low complexity.

For performance evaluation, we compared *CA* with *HEFT* scheduling algorithm. The experimental results showed that *CA* is in most cases equal or superior to *HEFT* due to a more appropriate task prioritizing. Graphs with medium and high *CCR* were always best scheduled by *CA*. In the case of low *CCR*, the *CA* algorithm delivered comparable results to the *HEFT* algorithm. Overall speaking, from the simulation, the performance of the *CA* algorithm has been observed to fit most *DAG*.

References

1. R. Bajaj and D. P. Agrawal, "Improving Scheduling of Tasks in a Heterogeneous Environment," *IEEE Transactions on Parallel and Distributed Systems,* vol. 15, no. 2, pp. 107-118, 2004.
2. S. Behrooz, M. Wang, and G. Pathak, "Analysis and Evaluation of Heuristic Methods for Static Task Scheduling," *Journal Parallel and Distributed Computing,* vol. 10, pp. 222-232, 1990.
3. A. Gerasoulis and T. Yang," On the Granularity and Clustering of Directed Acyclic Task Graphs," *IEEE Transactions on Parallel and Distributed Systems,* vol.4, no.6, pp. 686-701, 1993.
4. T. Hagras and J. Janecek, " A High Performance, Low Complexity Algorithm for Compile-Time Task Scheduling in Heterogeneous Systems," *IEEE Proc. IPDPS*, 2004.

5. M. Iverson, F. Ozguner, and G. Follen, "Parallelizing Existing Applications in a Distributed Heterogeneous Environment," *Proc. Heterogeneous Computing Workshop,* pp. 93-100, 1995.
6. Y. Kwok and I. Ahmed, "Benchmarking the Task Graph Scheduling Algorithms," *Proc. IPPS/SPDP,* 1998.
7. J. Liou and M. A. Palis, "A Comparison of General Approaches to Multiprocessor Scheduling," *Proc. Int'l. Parallel Processing Symposium,* pp. 152-156, 1997.
8. S. S. Pande, D. P. Agrawal, and J. Mauney, "A Scalable Scheduling Method for Functional Parallelism on Distributed Memory Multiprocessors," *IEEE Transactions on Parallel and Distributed Systems,* vol. 6, no. 4, pp. 388-399, 1995.
9. C.I. Park and T.Y. Choe, "An Optimal Scheduling Algorithm Based on Task Duplication," *IEEE Transactions on Computers,* vol. 51, no. 4, pp. 444-448, 2002.
10. A. Radulescu and A. van Gemund, "Fast and effective task scheduling in heterogeneous systems," *Heterogeneous Computing Workshop, 2000,* pp. 229-238, May, 2000.
11. S. Ranaweera and D. P. Agrawal, "A Task Duplication Based Scheduling Algorithm for Heterogeneous Systems," *IEEE Proceedings of IPDPS,* pp. 445-450, 2000.
12. H. Rewini and T. G. Lewis, "Scheduling Parallel Program Tasks onto Arbitrary Target Machines," *Journal of Parallel and Distributed Computing,* vol. 9, pp. 138-153, 1990.
13. G. C. Sih and E. A. Lee, "A Compile Time Scheduling Heuristic for Interconnection - Constrained Heterogeneous Processors Architectures," *IEEE Transactions on Parallel and Distributed Systems,* vol. 4, no. 2, pp. 175-187, 1992.
14. H. Topcuoglu, S. Hariri, and W. Min-You, "Performance-Effective and Low-Complexity Task Scheduling for Heterogeneous Computing," *IEEE Transactions on Parallel and Distributed Systems,* vol.13, no. 3, pp. 260-274, 2002.
15. M. Wu and D. Gajski, "Hypertool: A Programming Aid for Message-Passing System," *IEEE Trans. Parallel and Distributed Systems,* vol. 1, no. 3, pp.330-343, 1990.
16. T. Yang and A. Gerasoulis, "DSC:Scheduling Parallel Tasks on an Unbounded Number of Processors," *IEEE Tran. on Parallel and Distributed Systems,* vol. 5, no.9, pp. 951-967, 1994.

Processor Directed Dynamic Page Policy

Dandan Huan[1,2], Zusong Li[1,2], Weiwu Hu[1], and Zhiyong Liu[1]

[1] Institute of Computing Technology, Chinese Academy of Sciences,
100080 Beijing, China
[2] Graduate School of the Chinese Academy of Sciences,
100039 Beijing, China
{hdd, lisoon, hww}@ict.ac.cn

Abstract. The widening gap between today's processor and memory performance makes memory subsystem design an increasingly important part of computer design. Processor directed dynamic page policy is proposed by investigating the memory access patterns of applications. Processor directed dynamic page policy changes page mode adaptively in accordance with the directions of processor. It combines the advantages of close page policy and open page policy. The processor directed dynamic page policy is based on future memory access behavior. Compared with the direction information of existing dynamic page policies which is based on the history of memory access behavior, the direction information of processor directed dynamic page policy is more accurate. Furthermore, memory access requests of processor are scheduled based on the page policy to increase the page hit rate and reduce page conflict miss rate. The performance of SPEC CPU2000 benchmarks is improved significantly. The IPC is improved by 7.1%, 5.9% and 3.4% on average compared with close page policy, open page policy and conventional dynamic page policy, respectively.

Keywords: Godson-2, Memory Control Policy, Dynamic Page Policy, Open Page, Close Page.

1 Introduction

With the processor-memory performance gap continuing to grow, the performance of memory access becomes the major bottleneck of the performance improvement for modern microprocessors [1]. It becomes a hot spot of research activities to propose new memory control policies in order that processor-memory gap will be decreased [2].

Several optimization techniques of memory control system to reduce DRAM access latency have been developed [3], [4]. These techniques are based on open page policy, which enables the accessed row active. In open page policy, if the next access to the same bank goes to the same page, that is page hit, only column access is necessary. One major bottleneck limiting open page policy comes from page conflict misses. Page conflict misses occur in the row buffer, when a sequence of requests on different pages goes to the same bank. Compared with a page hit, a page conflict miss may cause additional DRAM precharge latency. Frequent page conflict misses will significantly increase access latency and degrade overall performance. The latency of open page policy is even longer than that of close page policy, when page conflict

C. Jesshope and C. Egan (Eds.): ACSAC 2006, LNCS 4186, pp. 109–122, 2006.
© Springer-Verlag Berlin Heidelberg 2006

miss rate is high. Dynamic page policies effectively reduce DRAM access latency by changing page mode dynamically [5], [6]. The page mode is changed from open page mode to close page mode, when the memory access result is speculated to page conflict miss.

Based on investigations of memory access behavior, through experimentations of SPEC CPU2000 benchmarks running on Godson-2 processor, a novel dynamic page policy that can improve performance of memory system significantly, called processor directed dynamic page policy is proposed and evaluated in this paper. The Godson project [7] is the first attempt to design high performance general-purpose microprocessors in China. Godson-2 processor [8] is a 4-issue superscalar, 9-stage superpipeline microprocessor, which implements the 64 bit instruction set. Processor directed dynamic page policy combines the advantages of close page policy and open page policy. The direction information of processor directed dynamic page policy is based on future memory access behavior. Compared with the direction information of existing dynamic page policies which is based on the history of memory access behavior, the direction information of processor directed dynamic page policy is more accurate. Memory access requests of processor are scheduled based on the page policy to increase the page hit rate and reduce page conflict miss rate. The hardware cost of the processor directed dynamic page policy is trivial. We evaluate the performance of various page policies for SPEC CPU2000 benchmarks [9] and STREAM benchmarks [10]. It is shown that processor directed dynamic page policy dramatically increases the page hit rate and reduces page conflict miss rate. The memory access latency is reduced by 18.52% and 19.64% compared with close page policy and open page policy respectively. The IPC is improved by 7.1%, 5.9% and 3.4% on average compared with close page policy, open page policy and conventional dynamic page policy, respectively. The memory bandwidth is improved by 15% and 21% on average compared with close page policy and open page policy respectively.

The remainder of the paper is organized as follows. Section 2 describes related work on page policy. Section 3 analyzes the memory access patterns of applications. Section 4 proposes processor directed dynamic page policy. Section 5 evaluates the performance of processor directed dynamic page policy for SPEC CPU2000 benchmarks and STREAM benchmarks, after introducing our experimental environment. Finally, conclusions and directions for future work are given in section 6.

2 Related Work

An access to DRAM consists of row access, column access and precharge. The lowest order bits in memory access address are column address, the next bits are bank address, and the highest order bits are row address. During row access, a row is activated, namely a row of data containing the desired data is loaded into the row buffer according to its row address. The data in the row buffer is also called a page of data. Concurrent accesses to multiple interleaved memory banks are supported in modern computer systems, where each bank has a row buffer holding a page of data. During column access, the data is read or written according to its column address. The page can be either open or closed after column access determined by memory page mode control policy. Memory page mode control policy is simply called page policy. In open page policy, the DRAM precharge operation is not performed and the row maintains active state. If the next access is page hit, only column access is necessary. However, if the next access is page conflict miss, the DRAM precharge will not start until the next request arrives. The close page policy allows the precharge operation to begin immediately after the current column access completes. Both open page policy and close page policy have their advantages and limitations, mainly depends on the memory access patterns of applications. If the page hit rate is high, open page policy is more beneficial than close page policy, and vice versa.

Figure 1 shows state transition and timing for DRAM read operation in close page policy. In Figure 1, CL (CAS* Latency) denotes the latency from column access start to the first data return. tRCD (RAS* to CAS*) denotes the latency from row access to column access. tRP (RAS* Precharge) denotes the latency from precharge to row access. The values of CL, tRCD and tRP depend on the clock frequency of system bus and the clock frequency of DRAM. The CL, tRCD and tRP are usually 2 cycles, 3 cycles, and 2 cycles. In close page policy, because the DRAM is in an idle state (Idle), activate row (ACT, Activate Row), read (RD, Read), and precharge (PRE, Precharge) operations are performed when DRAM is accessed. The latency of read operation is from row access to desired data return. Hence, the latency of read operation includes the cycles of activate row and read, that is Latency = tRCD + CL = 3 + 2 = 5 cycles.

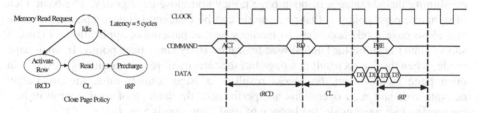

Fig. 1. State transition and timing diagram for DRAM read operation in close page policy

Figure 2 shows state transition and timing for DRAM read operation in open page policy. In open page policy, row buffers in each of the banks of the DRAM can work as a cache memory with large block size because the DRAM is in row active state (Row Active) after accessed. The latency of DRAM access is non-uniform according to page hits and page conflict misses. When the access result is a page hit, memory access latency is reduced because precharge and activate row operations are eliminated. As a result, the latency of read operation only includes the cycles of read, and the DRAM operating latency is Latency = CL = 2 cycles. When the access result is a page miss, the latency of read operation includes the cycles of precharge, activate row and read, that is Latency = tRP + tRCD + CL = 2 + 3 + 2 = 7 cycles. The latency of read operation is two cycles longer than the latency in close page policy because the extra precharge operation is needed. If the page miss rate is high, open page policy is negative than close page policy.

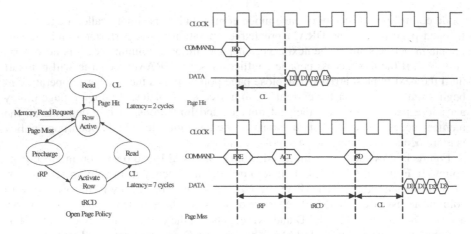

Fig. 2. State transition and timing diagram for DRAM read operation in open page policy

Most DRAM systems nowadays have multiple banks so that multiple row buffers on different banks can maintain row active state simultaneously. However, DRAM row buffer conflicts occur when a sequence of requests on different rows goes to the same memory bank in open page policy, causing much higher memory access latency than requests to the same row or to different banks. Dynamic page policy is aims at combining the advantages of open page policy and close page policy. The basic idea of dynamic page policy is that page mode can be changed between open page mode and close page mode according to memory access patterns of applications. Figure 3 shows state transition for DRAM read operation in dynamic page policy. In open page mode, when the access result is a page hit, the latency of read operation is 2 cycles. In open page mode, when the access result is a page conflict miss, the precharge, activate row and read operations are performed, the latency of read operation is 7 cycles. In close page mode, the latency of read operation is 5 cycles.

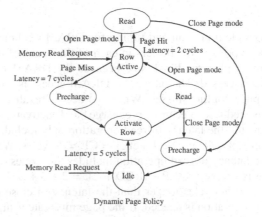

Fig. 3. State transition diagram for DRAM read operation in dynamic page policy

Miura proposed a dynamic page policy, called dynamic SDRAM mode control scheme [5], which changes page mode between open page and close page based on the history of memory access behavior. If there are several successive misses in open page mode, the dynamic page policy changes the page mode from open page to close page after column access completes. The memory controller of Alpha 21174 [6] also implements dynamic page policy based on the history of memory access behavior.

The essential direction information of page change in existing dynamic page policies is the future memory access patterns speculated by the history of memory access behavior. The perfect dynamic page policy is directed by real memory access behavior in the future. On the other hand, the memory access requests of processor are not scheduled based on the page policy in existing dynamic page policies. Thus access locality is not exploited effectively for reusing the data in the row buffer. Furthermore, the existing dynamic page policies do not take the page mode change occasion into account. Most memory controllers nowadays maintain multiple requests from processor in its queue, and send the requests to DRAM device in the order determined by the memory access scheduling scheme. Suppose there are multiple requests in the queue of memory controller and the existing dynamic page policies perform precharge operation for changing to close page mode according to the history of memory access, precharge operation will delay the process of successive memory requests.

3 Analysis of Memory Access

This section analyzes the memory access locality of SPEC CPU2000. Figure 4 shows the proportion of page hits and page misses in open page policy. The average page hit rate of SPEC CPU2000 is 49.7%, which is almost equal to average page miss rate. However, page hit rates are distinct in different programs. The page hit rates of gcc, mcf, parser, eon, perlbmk, wupwise, vortex, twolf, applu, mesa, art and ammp programs are higher than their page miss rates respectively. Especially, the page hit rates of wupwise and ammp programs are up to 90%. The page hit rates of gzip, vpr, crafy, gap, bzip2, swim, mgrid, equake, sixtrack and apsi programs are lower than their page miss rates respectively. Especially, the page hit rate of swim program is only 6.4%. Open page policy will take negative effect on these programs whose page hit rates are low.

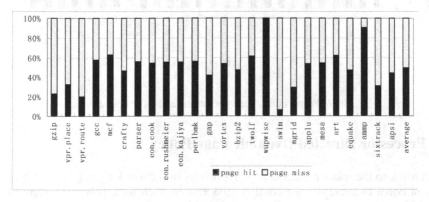

Fig. 4. Proportion of page hits and page misses

Figure 5 shows the times of memory access during each thousand instructions executed. The average times of memory access is 14. The times of memory access affects the efficiency of memory access optimization. In this paper, we implement processor directed dynamic page policy, and evaluate performance for mcf, parser, perlbmk, gap, vortex, swim, mgrid, applu, art, equake, ammp and apsi programs in SPEC CPU2000 benchmarks. These programs are memory access intensive. Memory access optimization plays major role to improve performance of processor.

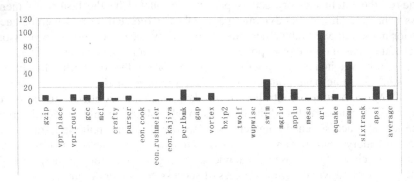

Fig. 5. Times of memory access during each thousand instructions executed

Figure 6 shows proportion of read operations (memread_count) and write operations (memwrite_count) in all memory access operations. It indicates that the proportion of read operations is 76.7%. The times of read operations are more than the times of write operations clearly. The write operations have little effects on page hit rate. Hence, page policy only need to optimize read operations. The latency of memory access is usually the latency of read operation.

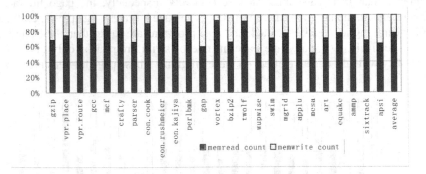

Fig. 6. Proportion of read operations and write operations

4   Processor Directed Dynamic Page Policy

According to the memory access analysis results in section 3, average page hit rate is almost equal to average page conflict miss rate in open page policy. Dynamic page policy can change page mode from open page to close page and from close page to open page dynamically based on the row buffer locality of the applications. Therefore, dynamic page policy is prior to fixed page policy. In this paper, we propose a novel dynamic page policy, called processor directed dynamic page policy, by analyzing the limitations of existing page policies. Processor directed dynamic page policy compares the future memory access row address with last access row address of the same bank. If the result is that no bank arise page hit, and a bank arises page conflict miss, then the bank arising page conflict miss is directed to adopt close page mode. The direction information that includes adopting close page mode and the corresponding conflict bank address is sent to memory controller from processor. Furthermore, processor schedules memory access requests and the request whose row address equals to last access address of the same bank has high priority to send memory access operation. When memory controller has no memory access request to send to DRAM device, it changes page mode according to the direction of processor. Memory controller sends precharge command and bank address to DRAM device for changing to close page mode.

Processor directed dynamic page policy includes processor directed scheme, memory access scheduling scheme and page mode control scheme. We describe these schemes and the advantages of processor directed dynamic page policy in detail.

4.1 Processor Directed Scheme

Control logic of processor directed scheme is shown in Figure 7. The processor maintains a bank access history table, which saves bank address and last access row

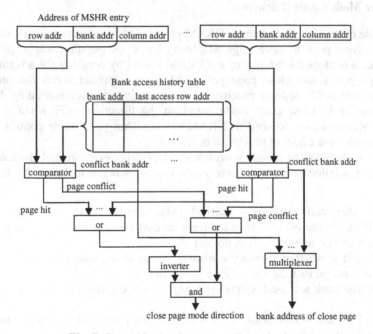

Fig. 7. Control logic of processor directed scheme

address of each bank. The future memory access requests are in MSHR (miss state handle register) [11] of the processor. Processor directed scheme compares row address (row addr) and bank address (bank addr) in each MSHR entry with bank address (bank addr) and last access row address (last access row addr) in each bank access history table entry. If the result is that no bank arise page hit (page hit), and a bank arises page conflict miss (page conflict), then the bank arising page conflict miss is directed to adopt close page mode. The direction information that includes adopting close page mode (close page mode direction) and the corresponding conflict bank address (bank address of close page) is sent to memory controller from processor. Compared with the direction information based on the history of memory access in existing dynamic page policies, the direction information of processor directed dynamic page policy is more accurate.

4.2 Memory Access Scheduling Scheme

MSHR schedules memory access requests according to the criterion of page hit priority. The request whose row address equals to last access address of the same bank has high priority to send memory access operation. If memory controller has multiple requests in its queue, it also schedules multiple requests to send to DRAM device according to the criterion of page hit priority. Thus memory access requests of processor are scheduled based on the page policy to increase the page hit rate and reduce page conflict miss rate.

4.3 Page Mode Control Scheme

Page mode control scheme changes DRAM page mode from open page to close page and from close page to open page adaptively based on the direction of processor. Therefore, it reduces the latency of the DRAM access by combing the advantages of open page policy and close page policy. Memory controller sends the precharge command and bank address precharged for changing the corresponding bank of DRAM device to close page mode based on the direction, only when it has no memory access request to send to DRAM device. Thus page mode control scheme avoids the negative effect of precharge operation.

Figure 8 shows page mode control scheme of processor directed dynamic page policy. The detailed process of page mode control scheme includes the following steps.

Step 1: After read operation is finished, judge whether page mode control enable bit is 0. If the enable bit is 0, then the bank accessed adopts close page mode and is precharged, and go to Step 5. Else, do Step 2.

Step 2: Judge whether memory controller has read requests to process. If it has requests to process, then do Step 3. Else, go to Step 4.

Step 3: The bank accessed adopts open page mode. Continue to process successive requests.

Step 4: The bank of processor directed adopts close page mode and is precharged.

Step 5: Process ends.

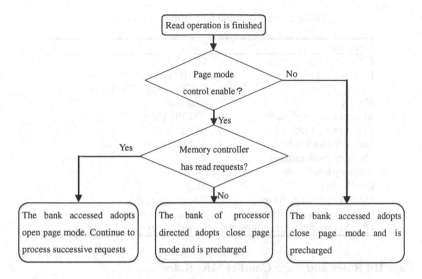

Fig. 8. Page mode control scheme

4.4 Advantages of Processor Directed Dynamic Page Policy

Compared with existing page policies, processor directed dynamic page policy has the following advantages: (1) Processor directed dynamic page policy combines the advantages of open page policy and close page policy. It can change page mode dynamically according to row buffer locality characteristics of applications. (2) The direction information of processor directed dynamic page policy is based on future memory access behavior. Compared with the direction information which is based on the history of memory access behavior in existing dynamic memory page control policies, the direction information of processor directed dynamic page policy is more accurate. (3) Memory access requests are scheduled based on the page policy to increase the page hit rate and reduce page conflict miss rate. (4) Only when memory controller has no memory access request to send to DRAM device, it changes page mode according to the direction of processor. It avoids the negative effect of precharge operation to successive memory access.

5 Performance Evaluation

5.1 Experimental Environment

Performance evaluation is based on simulations. We developed our own cycle-by-cycle simulator based on Godson-2 processor to build the processor prototype and make performance analysis. Table 1 shows the architectural parameters of simulation. The memory system contains 4 memory banks. The row buffer size of each bank is 8K Byte. Our experiments show that the simulator can match the real CPU chip quite well. The error range is within 5%. We use SPEC2000 benchmarks [9] and STREAM benchmarks [10] as workloads.

Table 1. Architectural parameters of simulation

Parameter	Value
CPU clock rate	800 MHz
L1 inst Cache	64KB, 4-way, 32B block
L1 data Cache	64KB, 4-way, 32B block
MSHR	8 entries
System bus overhead	20 CPU clock
System bus width	64 bits
Memory clock rate	133 MHz
Memory bank number	4
Memory bus width	64 bits
Row buffer size	8KB
DRAM precharge latency	2 memory cycles
DRAM row access latency	3 memory cycles
DRAM column access latency	2 memory cycles

5.2   Page Hit Rates and Page Conflict Miss Rates

Figure 9 compares page hit rates in open page policy (page hit rate base) and that in processor directed dynamic page policy (page hit rate control) of SPEC CPU2000 benchmark programs. The experimental results indicate that average page hit rate of

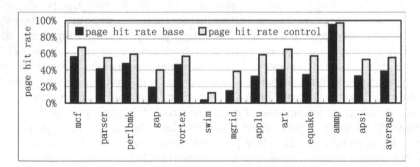

Fig. 9. Comparison of page hit rates

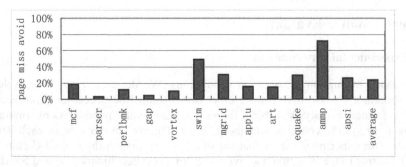

Fig. 10. Proportion of page conflict misses avoided

memory access intensive programs of SPEC CPU2000 is increased from 38.6% to 55% by memory access scheduling scheme combined with page policy.

Figure 10 presents the proportion of page conflict misses avoided by adopting processor directed dynamic page policy. The results show that on average 24.5% page conflict misses are avoided effectively due to changing page mode from open page to close page adaptively directed by processor.

5.3 Comparison of Memory Access Latency

We estimate the average read operation latency of DRAM in open page policy, close page policy and processor directed dynamic page policy. The average read operation latency of DRAM is defined as

$$\text{Latency} = P_{\text{open\_hit}} \times L_{\text{open\_hit}} + P_{\text{open\_miss}} \times L_{\text{open\_miss}} + P_{\text{close}} \times L_{\text{close}} \quad (1)$$

$$P_{\text{open\_hit}} + P_{\text{open\_miss}} + P_{\text{close}} = 1 \quad (2)$$

Where $P_{\text{open\_hit}}$ is the page hit rate in open page mode. As shown in Figure 9, $P_{\text{open\_hit}} = 55\%$ in processor directed dynamic page policy. $P_{\text{open\_miss}}$ is the page miss rate in open page mode. As shown in Figure 9 and Figure 10, $P_{\text{open\_miss}} = 1 - 38.6\% - 24.5\% = 36.9\%$ in processor directed dynamic page policy. P_{close} is the proportion of close page mode. By Definition 2, $P_{\text{close}} = 1 - P_{\text{open\_hit}} - P_{\text{open\_miss}} = 1 - 55\% - 36.9\% = 8.1\%$ in processor directed dynamic page policy. $L_{\text{open\_hit}}$ is the page hit latency in open page mode. As shown in Figure 2, $L_{\text{open\_hit}} = CL = 2$ memory cycles. $L_{\text{open\_miss}}$ is the page miss latency in open page mode. As shown in Figure 2, $L_{\text{open\_miss}} = tRP + tRCD + CL = 7$ memory cycles. L_{close} is the latency in close page mode. As shown in Figure 1, $L_{\text{close}} = tRCD + CL = 5$ memory cycles.

By Definition 1, $L_{\text{page\_control}} = 55\% \times 2 + 36.9\% \times 7 + 8.1\% \times 5 = 4.074$ memory cycles in processor directed dynamic page policy. By Definition 1, $L_{\text{close\_page}} = 1 \times 5 = 5$ memory cycles in close page policy. Compared with close page policy, processor directed dynamic page policy reduces memory access latency by $(L_{\text{close\_page}} - L_{\text{page\_control}}) / L_{\text{close\_page}} = (5 - 4.074) / 5 = 18.52\%$. By Definition 1, $L_{\text{open page}} = 38.6\% \times 2 + (1 - 38.6\%) \times 7 = 5.07$ memory cycles in open page policy. Compared with open page policy, processor directed dynamic page policy reduces memory access latency by $(L_{\text{open\_page}} - L_{\text{page\_control}}) / L_{\text{open\_page}} = (5.07 - 4.074) / 5.07 = 19.64\%$. The memory access latency analysis results indicate that the latency of open page policy is even longer than that of close page policy. However, processor directed dynamic page policy can reduce memory access latency significantly by changing page mode from open page to close page for avoiding most page conflict misses and changing page mode from close page to open page for page hits.

5.4 Comparison of Memory Bandwidth

Figure 11 compares memory bandwidth of STREAM benchmarks in open page policy (open_page), close page policy (close_page) and processor directed dynamic page policy (page_control). Experimental results indicate that the memory bandwidth of STREAM benchmarks is improved efficiently by adopting processor directed

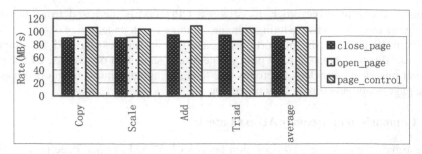

Fig. 11. Comparison of memory bandwidth

dynamic page policy. The bandwidth is improved by 15% and 21% on average compared with close page policy and open page policy respectively.

5.5 Comparison of IPC

Figure 12 compares the IPC (instruction per cycle) of SPEC CPU2000 benchmark programs in close page policy (close_page), open page policy (open_page), dynamic page policy proposed by Miura (dynamic_page), processor directed dynamic page policy proposed in this paper (page_control), and the page policy combining processor directed dynamic page policy with Miura's page policy (dyn_con_page). Experimental results show that the IPC of processor directed dynamic page policy is improved by 7.1%, 5.9% and 3.4% on average compared with close page policy, open page policy and conventional dynamic page policy, respectively. Especially for ammp program and art program, the IPC is improved significantly.

As shown in Figure 12, only for ammp program whose page hit rate is up to 90.3%, the IPC of open page policy approximates to the IPC of processor directed dynamic page policy. Otherwise, the IPC of processor directed dynamic page policy is higher than open page policy. For swim program and mgrid program, the IPC of open page policy is dramatically lower than the IPC of close page policy due to their low page hit rates. However, the performance of processor directed dynamic page policy is improved due to its adaptive page change policy. The IPC of dynamic page

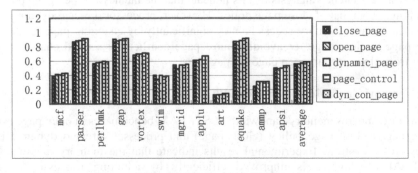

Fig. 12. Comparison of IPC

policy proposed by Miura is also higher than the IPC of open page policy and close page policy. However, processor directed dynamic page policy is prior to Miura's policy due to its more accurate direction information.

When memory access requests are not intensive and there are no future requests in MSHR, processor directed dynamic page policy has no information to direct page mode. Thus open page mode is adopted by default. In this case, the dynamic page policy proposed by Miura has history information to direct page mode. We implement the page policy combining processor directed dynamic page policy with Miura's page policy and evaluate its performance. A memory access history table is maintained in memory controller. If processor has no future request in MSHR to direct page mode, memory access history is used to direct page mode as Miura's policy. The experimental results are shown in Figure 12. The results indicate that the IPC of the page policy combining processor directed dynamic page policy with Miura's page policy is improved by 7.5% compared with close page policy. The speedup of processor directed dynamic page policy is approximately to the page policy combining processor directed dynamic page policy with Miura's page policy. The locality of row buffer is low, when there is no future memory access in MSHR. Therefore, the direction information based on memory access history is not accurate in this case. Additional hardware overhead of the page policy combining processor directed dynamic page policy with Miura's page policy does not bring performance improvement. In summary, processor directed dynamic page policy proposed in this paper can direct page mode change effectively and improves performance significantly.

6 Conclusions

In this paper, we propose processor directed dynamic page policy by investigating memory access address spatial locality characteristics of applications. Our experimental results show that average page hit rate is increased from 38.6% to 55%. The memory access latency is reduced by 18.52% and 19.64% compared with close page policy and open page policy respectively. In terms of overall performance, the IPC is improved by 7.1%, 5.9% and 3.4% on average compared with close page policy, open page policy and conventional dynamic page policy, respectively. The memory bandwidth is improved by 15% and 21% on average compared with close page policy and open page policy respectively. Our future work includes the study of dynamic page policy and memory access scheduling scheme which adapt to SMT and CMP processors.

Acknowledgments. We would appreciate the anonymous reviewers for their advices. Our work is supported by the National Natural Foundation of China for Distinguished Young Scholars under Grant No.60325205; Knowledge Innovation Project of the Institute of Computing Technology, Chinese Academy of Sciences under Grant No.20056240; the National High-Tech Research and Development (863) Plan of China under Grant Nos. 2002AA110010, 2005AA110010 and 2005AA119020; The Basic Research Foundation of the Institute of Computing Technology, Chinese Academy of Sciences under Grant No.20056020; Knowledge Innovation Program of

Chinese Academy of Sciences under Grant No.KGCX2-109; The National Basic Research (973) Program of China under Grant No. 2005CB321601.

References

1. W. Wulf and S. McKee. Hitting the Memory Wall: Implications of the Obvious. ACM Computer Architecture News. 1995, 23(1): 20–24.
2. Wei-fen Lin, Steven K. Reinhardt, and Doug Burger. Reducing DRAM Latencies with an Integrated Memory Hierarchy Design. Proceedings of the Seventh International Symposium on High Performance Computer Architecture (HPCA'01). January 2001. 301–312.
3. Y. Kanno, et al.. A DRAM System for Consistently Reducing CPU Wait Cycles. 1999 Symposium on VLSI Circuits Digest of Technical Papers. 1999. 131–132.
4. T. Watanabe, et al., Access Optimizer to Overcome the Future Walls of Embedded DRAMs in the Era of Systems on Silicon. 1999 ISSCC Digest of Technical Papers. 370–371.
5. Seiji Miura, Kazushige Ayukawa, Takao Watanabe. A Dynamic-SDRAM-mode-control Scheme for Low-power Systems with a 32-bit RISC CPU. ISLPED 2001. 358–363.
6. Reinhard C. Schumann. Design of the 21174 Memory Controller for DIGITAL Personal Workstations. Digital Technical Journal. 1997, 9(2): 57–70.
7. Weiwu Hu, Zhimin Tang. Microarchitecture design of the Godson-1 processor. Chinese Journal of Computers. April 2003, 26(4): 385–396 (in Chinese).
8. Weiwu Hu, Fuxin Zhang, and Zusong Li. Microarchitecture of the Godson-2 Processor. Journal of Computer Science and Technology. March 2005, 20(2): 243–249.
9. Standard Performance Evaluation Corp. SPEC CPU2000 Documentation. http://www.spec.org/ osg/cpu2000/docs. 2000.
10. John D. McCalpin. STREAM: Sustainable Memory Bandwidth in High Performance Computers. http://www.cs.virginia.edu/stream/.
11. D. Kroft. Lockup-free Instruction Fetch/Prefetch Cache Organization. Proceedings of the 8th annual symposium on Computer Architecture (ISCA'81). May 1981: 81–87.

Static WCET Analysis Based Compiler-Directed DVS Energy Optimization in Real-Time Applications[*]

Yi Huizhan, Chen Juan, and Yang Xuejun

Section 620, School of Computer, National University of Defense Technology,
Changsha, 410073, Hunan, P.R. China
{huizhanyi, juanchen, xjyang}@nudt.edu.cn

Abstract. Compiler-directed dynamic voltage scaling (DVS) is one of the effective low-power techniques for real-time applications. Using the technique, compiler inserts voltage scaling points into a real-time application, and supply voltage and clock frequency are adjusted to the relationship between the remaining time and the remaining workload at each voltage scaling point. In this paper, based on the *WCET* (the worst case execution time) analysis tool *HEPTANE* and the performance/power simulator *Sim-Panalyzer*, we present a DVS-enabled simulation environment *RTLPower* (**Real**-**T**ime **L**ow **P**ower), which integrates static *WCET* estimation, performance/power simulation, automatically inserting the DVS code into a real-time application, and profile-guided energy optimization. By simulations of some benchmark applications, we prove that the DVS technique and the profile-guided optimization technique significantly reduce energy consumption.

Keywords: Real-time, Low-power, WCET, Compiler.

1 Introduction

In the recent years, embedded systems for mobile computing, such as mobile phone and PDA, are developing rapidly, and a crucial parameter of mobile systems is the continued time of energy supply. Although the performance in the integrated circuits (ICs) has been increasing rapidly in recent years [1], battery techniques are developed very slowly [2] and it is of significant importance for battery-powered mobile systems to utilize more effective low-power techniques.

Many novel low-power techniques in circuit, logic, architecture and software levels, in order of increasing abstraction, have been proposed to reduce energy consumption. Dynamic voltage scaling (DVS) [3], [4] is one of the low-power techniques in architecture level, and it is widely used in embedded systems for mobile computing and desktop systems. Real-time dynamic voltage scaling dynamically reduces supply voltage to the lowest possible extent that ensures a proper operation when the required performance is lower than the maximum performance. Since the dynamic energy consumption, the dominant energy consumption in ICs, is in direct

---

[*] Supported by the National High Technology Development 863 Program of China under Grant No. 2004AA1Z2210 and Server OS Kernel under Grant No. 2002AA1Z2101.

C. Jesshope and C. Egan (Eds.): ACSAC 2006, LNCS 4186, pp. 123–136, 2006.

proportion to the square of supply voltage V, it is possible for DVS to significantly reduce energy consumption.

The voltage scheduling in a single task called an intra-task dynamic voltage scaling (IntraDVS) [7] is proposed. IntraDVS assisted by compiler automatically inserts voltage scaling points into a real-time task and divides the task into some execution sections, and then supply voltage is adjusted to the relationship between the remaining time and the remaining workload.

It is crucial for IntraDVS to properly place voltage scaling points in a real-time application, and the configuration of voltage scaling points significantly affects energy consumption. A good configuration could save more energy; however, due to voltage scaling overhead, the improper one could waste much energy. For the past few years, much work has been published on compiler-directed real-time dynamic voltage scaling [5], [6], [7], [8], [9], [10], [11], [12], [13], and the algorithms have utilized two kinds of configurations of voltage scaling points. The first is to make use of fixed-length voltage scaling sections, the whole execution of a task is divided into some equal subintervals and the voltage adjustment is made at the beginning of each subinterval [6] [11]. The second is a heuristic method, the condition and loop structure in real-time applications often bring about the workload variation and energy consumption can be reduced enormously if voltage scaling points are put at the end of the structures [7] [13]. Yi, et al proved that the heuristic configuration is the optimal one when not considering the voltage scaling overhead [14]. At the same time they presented a profile-guided optimizing configuration methodology, and using some synthetic applications, they proved that the methodology significantly reduces energy consumption. But they have not explained how to realize the method, and no experimental results of real benchmark applications are given. Another problem of the past works is not integrating with the WCET analysis tightly, but for real-time applications, it is a key to give the time estimate method in detail.

In this paper, based on the *WCET* (the worst case execution time) analysis tool *HEPTANE* and the performance/power simulator *Sim-Panalyzer*, we present a DVS-enabled simulation environment *RTLPower*, which integrates static *WCET* estimation, performance/power simulation, automatically inserting the DVS code into a real application, and profile-guided energy optimization. By simulations of some real benchmark applications, we prove that the DVS technique and the profile-guided optimization technique significantly reduce energy consumption.

The rest of this paper is organized as follows. In Section 2, we list the related terms of compiler-directed dynamic voltage scaling. In Section 3, we give the inserting method of DVS code. In Section 4, we present the profile-guided energy optimization method. In Section 5, we show by experiments that the DVS technique and the profile-guided optimization technique significantly reduce energy consumption. Finally, we give the conclusions.

2   Related Terms

A real-time task has strict timing constraint and must finish before its deadline (d), missing the deadline might lead to a catastrophic result. Real-time dynamic voltage scaling guarantees a correct operation of a real-time task and dynamically reduces supply voltage and clock frequency to the lowest possible extent in the execution course. Therefore, for real-time applications, the worst-case execution time (*wcet*) or the worst-case execution cycle (*wcec*) must be estimated in advance [19] to ensure that the timing constraint is met, that is, the worst-case execution time must be less than or equal to the deadline. If the *wcet* is less than the deadline, we can proportionally reduce clock frequency beforehand. Consequently, the *wcet* is equal to the deadline *d* and the obtained initial frequency is f_{static}, that is, $d=wcec/f_{static}$. This is the starting point of dynamic voltage scaling in this paper. Current DVS-enabled systems only can change the clock frequency on some discrete levels [15], [16], [17], and therefore we assume that the clock frequency can change on some discrete levels between consecutive interval [f_{min}, f_{max}].

IntraDVS divides the whole execution cycle of a task into n sections, and the worst-case execution cycle and the actual execution cycle of each section are denoted by wc_i and ac_i for $i = 1,...,n$, respectively. It is obvious that $0 \leq ac_i \leq wc_i$ for $i = 1,...,n$, and $wcec = \sum_{l=1}^{n} wc_l$. The reduced worst-case execution cycle of the ith point is denoted by $rwec_i$ for $i = 1,...,n+1$, and we have $rwec_i = \sum_{l=i}^{n} wc_l$ for $i = 1,...,n$, $rwec_{n+1} = 0$.

At the beginning of each section, supply voltage (V_i for $i = 1,...,n$) and clock frequency (f_i for $i = 1,...,n$) are adjusted to the relationship between the remaining time and the remaining workload, and the lowest supply voltage and clock frequency are utilized within timing constraint. The proportional voltage scaling sets the frequency of the ith section to

$$f_i = rwec_i / (d - \sum_{l=1}^{i-1} t_l)$$

where t_l denotes the actual execution time of the lth section. In the above formula, the new clock frequency at the beginning of the ith section is set to the quotient of the reduced worst-case execution cycle divided by the reduced time, which can guarantee that the task can finish before its deadline at any time.

The formula $f \propto (V - V_T)^2 / V$ defines the relationship between clock frequency and supply voltage of CMOS, where V_T denotes the threshold voltage of CMOS. The execution time t_i of each section can be computed by

$$t_i = ac_i / f_i$$

Finally, dynamic voltage scaling have some energy overhead and time overhead, which are closely related to the initial voltage V_{DD1}, the final voltage V_{DD2}, and the switch capacitance C. Burd, et al [18] present the formula of energy overhead

$$E = (1 - \eta) \cdot C \cdot \left| V_{DD2}^2 - V_{DD1}^2 \right|$$

and the formula of time overhead

$$t_{TRAN} = \frac{2 \cdot C}{I_{max}} \cdot \left| V_{DD2} - V_{DD1} \right|$$

In this paper, we let $\eta = 0.9$ (the typical value) and $C = 5pF$. The time overhead is fixed as 200 cycles for 100Mhz frequency variation.

3 Inserting Method of DVS Code

Based on the *WCET* analysis tool *HEPTANE* [20], we present an automatically inserting method of DVS code. For a real application program, it includes condition structures, loop structures, and function calls, besides the sequential codes. Our method can insert into any location of an application program. At each voltage scaling point, we need three parameters: the reduced worst case execution cycle ($rwec_i$), the deadline (d), and the current time (ct). The deadline is defined before hand, and the current time can be obtained dynamically from the simulation system. The modified simulation system *Sim-Panalyzer* can accumulate the actual execution time, and convey the time information to real-time applications by some predefined memory port. Therefore, if $rwec_i$ is known, we can set the supply voltage and clock frequency of each voltage scaling point. Furthermore, in order to make it possible to optimize the insertion of voltage scaling points, we make each point executed by a prediction *insert_or_not[i]*. Therefore, at each point, the DVS pseudo-code is illustrated at Fig. 1. The function *getcurrenttime* obtains the current actual execution time from the simulation environment. The function *setnewfrequency* sets new system execution frequency, and based on the remaining time and the remaining workload, the function computes new frequency and sets the nearest discrete voltage/frequency level that guarantees the real-time execution. Both functions are realized by embedded assemble language, which is supported by GCC compiler. Based on the different cases, *computecurrentRWEC* can correctly give the reduced worst case execution cycle.

```
1 if (insert_or_not[i]) {
2     getcurrenttime(ct);
3     computecurrentRWEC(rwec_i);
4     nf = rwec_i / (d-ct-overhead);
5     setnewfrequency(nf);
6 }
```

Fig. 1. The pseudo-code of DVS at each point

The time estimation process of the *WCET* analysis tool *HEPTANE* is as follows:

1. Based on the source code of an application, a syntax tree is produced, which corresponds to the source code structure.

2. From the syntax tree, a context tree is formed, which corresponds to the execution process of the application. At the same time, some labels are inserted in the syntax tree, which are used to mark the basic block (no branch structure). The resultant syntax tree is used to output the modified source code.

3. The modified source code is compiled using GCC compiler, and the assemble file and binary file are produced. Using the specific architecture information (such as cache size, pipeline stage), the worst case execution time of each basic block is estimated.

4. Using the context tree and the time information of basic blocks, the worst-case execution time of the whole application is accumulated by depth-firstly traversing the context tree.

Based on the time estimation process of *HEPTANE*, we select inserting the DVS code in the syntax tree of the source code. By traversing the syntax tree, we mark the location for all the DVS points. When outputting the modified source code, the DVS code is inserted into the source code automatically. Therefore, the final time estimation includes the execution time of the DVS code (not DVS overhead), and the safe real-time DVS program is produced.

Next, we present how to correctly get the value of $rwec_i$ for the different cases. For the code without loops and function calls, it is simple to make use of *HEPTANE* to estimate the worst case execution cycle of each point. For the voltage scaling points inserted into loops, the $rwec_i$ of each iteration is different. Similarly, for the voltage scaling point inserted into function calls, the different call sites of the function have the different $rwec_i$. Since it is possible for our inserting method to insert a point into any place, we must solve the problem due to loops and function calls.

Loop1::for(i1...)	_index1 ⋯ _indexN = 0
Loop2::for(i2...)	Loop1::for(i1...)
	Loop2::for(i2...)
LoopN::for(iN...)	
Votage scaling point	LoopN::for(iN...)
LoopN end	Votage scaling point
	_indexN++
Loop2 end	LoopN end
Loop1 end	_indexN =0
	Loop2 end
	_index2 =0
	_index1++
	Loop1 end
	_index1 = 0

Fig. 2. The pseudo-code of instrumented code for loops

3.1 Compute the $rwec_i$ of Voltage Scaling Points Inserted into Loops

For the voltage scaling points inserted into loops, the $rwec_i$ of each iteration has the different value, which is closely related to the specific iteration. We give the $rwec_i$ by the parametric method:

$$rwec_i = rwec_{base_i} + \sum_{j=0}^{n} (loop^{j}_{max\_iteration_i} - loop^{j}_{cur\_iteration_i} - 1) \cdot wcec^{j}_{loop_i}$$

where $rwec_{base_i}$ is the reduced worst case execution cycle for last iterations of all loop levels including the voltage scaling point, $wcec^{j}_{loop_i}$ is the worst case execution cycle of the jth loop level, $loop^{j}_{max\_iteration_i}$ is the maximum iteration number of the jth loop level, $loop^{j}_{cur\_iteration_i}$ is the current iteration number of the jth loop level. Here, we specify the compute method of $rwec_i$ when there are no function calls.

Using the *HEPTANE* tool, we can obtain $loop^j_{max\_iteration_i}$ from the loop annotation, whereas $loop^j_{cur\_iteration_i}$ need add some instrumented code. Based on the syntax tree of the source code, we insert the instrumented code to get $loop^j_{cur\_iteration_i}$, as is shown in Fig. 2. At the beginning of the loop, the indexes of the corresponding loop levels are initiated to zero. When getting into a more deep loop level, the corresponding index is incremented; on the contrary, when getting out of a loop level, the index is cleared to zero. The instrumented code is directly inserted into the syntax tree, and when outputting the modified source code, the result includes the instrumented code.

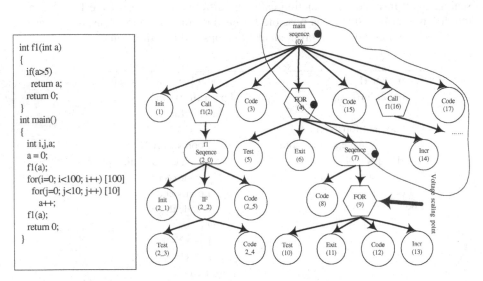

```
int f1(int a)
{
    if(a>5)
        return a;
    return 0;
}
int main()
{
    int i,j,a;
    a = 0;
    f1(a);
    for(i=0; i<100; i++) [100]
        for(j=0; j<10; j++) [10]
            a++;
    f1(a);
    return 0;
}
```

Fig. 3. A source code and the corresponding context tree for time estimation

We can estimate $wcec^j_{loop_i}$ directly using *HEPTANE* tool, but cannot directly get $rwec_{base_i}$ from *HEPTANE*. In order to compute $rwec_{base_i}$, we modified the *HEPTANE* tool, and estimate time by pruning the context tree of *HEPTANE*. The source code and the corresponding context tree for time estimation are shown in Fig. 3. The source code is a typical program except including some annotations of the maximum number of loop iterations. The context tree is an expanded syntax tree, and it consists of all execution instances of the functions. Suppose For(9) is selected as an voltage scaling point, then only the nodes surrounded by the free curve have contribution to the $rwec_{base_i}$, the nodes marked by the black dots only need to estimate the time of their partial sub-nodes. From the voltage scaling point, we search the parent node, prune the sibling node before current node, and maintain the current node and the sibling node after current node. For loop node, only a single iteration is considered. Finally, we estimate the worst case execution cycle of the reduced context tree from bottom to top, which is equal to $rwec_{base_i}$.

3.2 Compute the $rwec_i$ of Voltage Scaling Points Inserted into Function Calls

If the voltage scaling points are inserted into function calls, the $rwec_i$ is different for each instance of a function call. We add the hint information of function calls to estimate the $rwec_i$:

$$rwec_i = rwec_{func_i} + rwec_{loop_i}$$

$$rwec_{loop_i} = rwec_{base_i} + \sum_{j=0}^{n} (loop^j_{max\_iteration_i} - loop^j_{cur\_iteration_i} - 1) \cdot wcec^j_{loop_i}$$

where $wcec^j_{loop_i}$, $loop^j_{max\_iteration_i}$, and $loop^j_{cur\_iteration_i}$ have the same meanings as before, $rwec_{base_i}$ is the reduced worst case execution cycle between current voltage scaling point and the end of the function, $rwec_{func_i}$ is the reduced worst case execution cycle of the end of current instance of the function call. For the different instances of function call, $rwec_{base_i}$ could have the different value, and we simply use the maximum $rwec_{base_i}$ for all instances. Using the $rwec_{func_i}$, we can differ one instance from the others.

f1()	f1(float rwec)
{	{
voltage scaling point	voltage scaling point
}	}
f2()	f2(float rwec)
{	{
f1()	rwec1 = rwec+rwec_a;
f1()	f1(rwec1)
}	rwec2 = rwec+rwec_b;
	f1(rwec2)
	}

Fig. 4. The pseudo-code of instrumented code for function calls

As before, we need insert the instrumented code, and an example is shown in Fig. 4. The function $f1$ includes a voltage scaling point, we add a parameter for the function $f1$, which represent the $rwec_{func_i}$ for the function $f1$. When the function $f1$ is called, we can know the reduced worst case execution cycle at the end of the current instance of the function $f1$. Similarly, the function $f2$ includes the call instance of the function $f1$, and then it also needs an additional parameter to represent the reduced worst case execution cycle at the end of the instance of the function $f2$. At the same time, we make use of *HEPTANE* to estimate the worst case execution cycle $rwec\_a$ between the end of the first instance of the function $f1$ and the end of the function $f2$, and the worst case execution cycle $rwec\_b$ between the end of the second instance of the function $f1$ and the end of the function $f2$. As a result, we can compute the $rwec_{func_i}$ for two instances of the function $f1$, which are transferred to the voltage scaling point by the function parameter. Besides the voltage scaling points, some other points such as *rwec_a* and *rwec_b* also need estimate the reduced worst case execution cycle, and we call them assistant voltage scaling points.

For each voltage scaling point, we find out the function including the point in the syntax tree. Then, we search for the syntax tree and find out all the call sites of the function. The call sites are the assistant voltage scaling points. Combining all the voltage scaling points with the assistant voltage scaling points, we continue to find out more assistant voltage scaling points till the number of the voltage scaling points is not changed. For the different kinds of voltage scaling points, we insert the corresponding code and correctly compute the $rwec_i$. The pseudo-code algorithm of searching for voltage scaling points is shown in Fig. 5.

Input:

list_dvspoint represents a list of all initial voltage scaling

points (the end of the uncertain loop and the beginning of each

condition path)

1 while(the size of list_dvspoint is changed)
2   while(list_dvspoint is not empty)
3   get a dvs point
4   search for the function *f* including the dvs point
5   search for all the call sites of *f*, insert into a call site list
      list_callpoint
6   combine list_callpoint with list_dvspoint, get an updated
    list_dvspoint
7 for(each point in the list_dvspoint)
8   if(dvs point)
9   output the *RWEC* computing code
      and the voltage scaling code
10   else if(assistant dvs point)
11   output the *RWEC* computing code, add the function
      parameter and the parameter of function call

Fig. 5. The pseudo-code algorithm of searching for voltage scaling points

4   Profile-Guided Energy Optimization

When not considering the voltage scaling overhead, the optimal configuration minimizing the energy consumption inserts voltage scaling points at the end of the uncertain loop (for example, "while" in C language) and the beginning of each condition path (for example, if-then-else and "switch" in C language). We realize the inserting method, search for the syntax tree, and insert voltage scaling points into the end of each uncertain loop and the beginning of each path of the condition structure.

When considering the voltage scaling overhead, the inserting method are not the optimal. Yi, et al [14] have presented an analytical energy model, and based on the energy model, they give an optimizing method, which deleted overmany voltage scaling points from the initial set of voltage scaling points. The optimizing method considers each time voltage adjustment as a voltage scaling point, and attempts to maintain the optimal voltage adjustment. For a real application program, voltage scaling points can be inserted into any place, each voltage scaling points can correspond to multiple instances. For example, as shown in Fig. 2, a voltage scaling point is inserted into a loop, and any iteration of the loop has made voltage adjustment. For the voltage scaling point included in Fig. 4, each instance of the function $f1$ corresponds to one voltage adjustment. It is not simple problem to delete voltage adjustment of an application.

Generally speaking, a voltage scaling point corresponds to an inserting location. For example, for the voltage scaling point included by $f1$ in Fig. 4, we consider it as a voltage scaling point. When we delete the voltage scaling point, we really delete two times voltage adjustment corresponding to two instance of the function $f1$. It is obvious that the voltage scaling point definition can lead to the ineffective optimization, and the main problem comes from the voltage scaling points inserted into loops. For example, for the voltage scaling point in Fig. 2, it is possible that it corresponds to a large number of voltage adjustment, and as a result, its deletion leads to ineffective voltage scaling placement. Therefore, we need give special meaning for the points inserted into loops.

```
1 if (insert_or_not[i] && indexj mod stride == 0) {
2      getcurrenttime(ct);
3      computecurrentRWEC(rwec_i);
4      nf = rwec_i / (d-ct-overhead);
5      setnewfrequency(nf);
6 }
```

Fig. 6. The modified pseudo-code of DVS inserted into loops

We consider the point inserted into loops as multiple voltage scaling points and need to be deleted in some sequence. Taking into account a modified DVS pseudo-code as shown in Fig. 6, we add a prediction (*indexj* mod *stride*), where *indexj* is the index of the *j*th loop level, *stride* is the stride length, and mod represents the modulus operator. We can delete a voltage scaling point by clearing *insert_or_not[i]* to zero. For the voltage scaling points inserted into loops, we also can delete some voltage adjustment by setting *indexj* and *stride* to the different value. Therefore, we divide the original optimizing methods [14] into two steps: optimizing the points inserted into loops and globally optimizing the points inserted into the application. At the first step, we delete the voltage adjustment by the order that firstly, *stride* is equal to 2^n and n changes from small to large value, where n belongs to positive integer and 2^n is less than the maximum iteration number of the *j*th loop level, then *indexj* changes from more deep loop level to more exterior loop level. Actually, the process of deleting voltage points is increasing the voltage scaling granularity, from more fine adjustment to more coarse, and balances the energy saving with voltage scaling overhead. At the second step, we consider each inserting location as a voltage scaling point, and delete the voltage scaling point by setting *insert_or_not[i]* into zero. The detailed optimizing step is shown in Fig. 7. All the profile-guided time statistics are from *HEPTANE* tool.

First Step:	Second Step:
Input: the execution pattern of each loop in the most frequent execution case.	Input: the output from the first step.
Output: a configuration of voltage scaling points inserted into the loop.	Output: a configuration of voltage scaling points.
1 An initial optimal configuration without considering voltage scaling overhead.	1 Compute the energy consumption with n points by using the analytical model from [14]
2 Compute the energy consumption by using the analytical model from [14]	2 Compute the energy consumption with one point deleted (n-1).
3 Compute the energy consumption with *stride* incremented or *indexj* being more exterior loop level.	3 Compute the difference of the energy consumption between step 2 and step 1, and find out the minimum.
4 Compare the energy consumption for step 2 and step 3.	4 If the minimum is larger than zero, stop!
5 If step 2 has smaller energy consumption, stop!	5 Or else use the configuration with the minimum as the new configuration, update n (-1).
6 Or else repeat the steps from 2 to 6.	6 repeat the steps from 2 to 5.

Fig. 7. The improved optimizing method

5   The Experiment Environment and Results

We realize an experiment environment named *RTLPower* (Real-Time Low Power), which integrates static time estimation, cycle-accurate performance/power simulation, dynamic voltage scaling, and energy optimization. The front end is the modified *HEPTANE WCET* analysis tool [20], and the back end is the modified *Sim-Panalyzer* performance/power simulator [21]. The whole environment is based on the *StrongARM* architecture, as shown in Fig. 8. The gray regions are the modified or added modules. The front end of *RTLPower* receives the configuration information and C source code file with the annotation [20], the configuration information and source code file build the syntax tree of the application, and the code modification module modifies the source code by manipulating the syntax tree. The modified syntax tree is translated into context tree that is used to time estimation in *HEPTANE* tool. Using *HEPTANE* we estimate the worst case execution cycle of the application, the worst case execution cycle of all the loops, and the reduced worst case execution cycle of all the inserting points. The estimated time information is returned to the code modification module, and is used to create the complete syntax tree and output the DVS-enabled source code file. Integrated with the profile-guided optimization, we get the modified source code file and the final executable binary file.

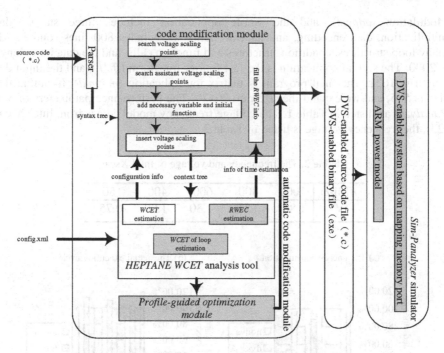

Fig. 8. *RTLPower* experimental envioment

Table 1. The performance parameters of *Sim-Panalyzer*

Fetch width	1	Decode width	1
Issue width	1	Commit width	1
RUU size	2	Lsq size	2
Int ALU	1	Int MUL	1
Flt ALU	1	Flt MUL	1
Mem Port	1	In-order issue	true
L1 data cache	16 sets, 32 bytes block, 32 ways, 1 cycle latency		
L1 inst cache	16 sets, 32 bytes block, 32 ways, 1 cycle latency		
TLB	32 sets, 4096 bytes page size, 32 ways, 30 cycles miss latency		

The back end of *RTLPower* cycle-accurately simulates the binary program and makes dynamic voltage scaling. It outputs time statistics, power statistics.

We use three typical applications of SNU-RT benchmark [22] from Real-Time Research Group, Seoul National University to analyze the realization and optimization of DVS. One of the applications is Adaptive Differential Pulse Code

Modulation (*adpcm*), and the whole application includes three stages: data initialization, data encoding, and data decoding. It includes 800 lines source code, many loop structures, condition structures and function calls, and the data input length is 2000. The second application is the fast fourier transform (*fft1k*), and the input data length is 1024. The final program is matrix multiplication (*matmul*). Its initial data size is 5x5, and we expand the size into 20x20. The performance parameters of *Sim-Panalyzer* are listed in Table 1. The voltage/frequency model comes from Intel Xscale [23], the frequency/voltage is listed in Table 2.

Table 2. The frequency and voltage of Intel Xscale

f(Mhz)	1000	800	600	400	150
V(V)	1.80	1.60	1.30	1.00	0.75

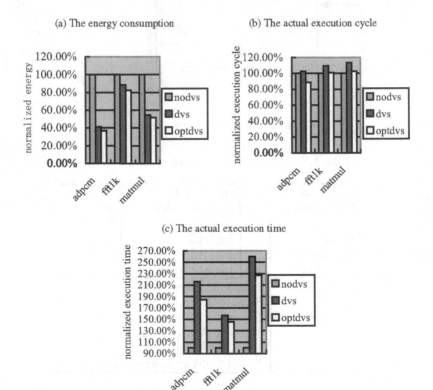

Fig. 9. The statistics of experimental results

We presents the experiment results in Fig. 9, where nodvs indicates the results of no voltage adjustment, dvs is the results with voltage adjustment, and optdvs is the results after profile-guided optimization. All the results are normalized to the maximum. The energy consumption without dvs and after voltage adjustment are shown in Fig. 9(a), we can save 10%~60% energy consumption. After the profile-guided optimization, we further save 3%~6% energy consumption. In Fig. 9(b), we show the actual execution cycle, which indicates the incremented computation quantity. Generally speaking, dynamic voltage scaling leads to less computation quantity increment. For the application *adpcm*, after profile-guided optimization, fewer cycles are used, and we analyze that the result attributes to cache effect. Dynamic voltage scaling reduces energy consumption by slowing the execution and decreasing supply voltage, and in Fig. 9(c) we show the effect. The actual execution times are prolonged by 50~150%, and after optimization, both the execution cycle and time are reduced.

6 Conclusions

Based on the *WCET* (the worst case execution time) analysis tool *HEPTANE* and the performance/power simulator *Sim-Panalyzer*, we present a DVS-enabled simulation environment *RTLPower*, which integrates static WCET estimation, performance/power simulation, automatically inserting the DVS code into a real application, and profile-guided energy optimization. By simulations of some real applications, we prove that the DVS technique and the profile-guided optimization technique significantly reduce energy consumption.

References

1. ITRS, "International Technology Roadmap for Semiconductors 2003 Edition," Can get from http://public.itrs.net
2. Kanishka Lahiri, "Battery-Driven System Design: A New Frontier in Low Power Design, " ASP-DAC/VLSI Design 2002, January 07 - 11, 2002, Bangalore, India.
3. T. Burd, T. Pering, A. Stratakos, and R. Brodersen, "A Dynamic Voltage Scaled Microprocess- or System," in Proc. of IEEE International Solid-State Circuits Conference, 2000, pp. 294 295.
4. C.M. Krishna, Yann-Hang Lee, "Voltage-Clock-Scaling Adaptive Scheduling Techniques for Low Power in Hard Real-Time Systems," IEEE TRANSACTIONS ON COMPUTERS, December 2003 (Vol. 52, No. 12).
5. Daniel Mosse, H. Aydin, B.R. Childers, R. Melhem, "Compiler-Assisted Dynamic Power-Aware Scheduling for Real-Time Applications," Workshop on Compilers and Operating Systems for Low-Power (COLP'00), Philadelphia, PA, October 2000.
6. S. Lee and T. Sakurai, "Run-Time Voltage Hopping for Low-Power Real-Time Systems," in Proc. of Design Automation Conference, 2000, pp. 806–809.
7. Dongkun Shin, Seongsoo Lee, Jihong Kim, "Intra-Task Voltage Scheduling for Low-Energy Hard Real-Time Applications," In IEEE Design & Test of Computers, Mar. 2001.
8. H.Saputra, M. Kandemir, N.Vijaykrishnan, M.J.Irwin, J.S. Hu, C-H.Hsu, U.Kremer, "Energy-Conscious Compilation Based on Voltage Scaling," In ACM SIGPLAN Joint Conference on Languages, Compilers, and Tools for Embedded Systems and Software and Compilers for Embedded Systems , June 2002.
9. Flavius Gruian, "Hard Real-Time Scheduling for Low-Energy Using Stochastic Data and DVS Processors," In Proceedings of the International Symposium on Low-Power Electronics and Design ISLPED'01 (Huntington Beach, CA, Aug. 2001).

10. Ana Azevedo, Ilya Issenin, Radu Cornea, "Profile-based Dynamic Voltage Scheduling Using Program Checkpoints," In Proceeding of Design, Automation and Test in Europe Conference (DATE), March 2002.
11. Nevine AbouGhazaleh, Daniel Mosse, B.R. Childers, R. Melhem, Matthew Craven, "Collaborative Operating System and Compiler Power Management for Real-Time Applications," in Proc. of The Real-time Technology and Application Symposium, RTAS, Toronto, Canada (May 2003).
12. Chung-Hsing Hsu, Ulrich Kremer, "The Design, Implementation, and Evaluation of a Compiler Algorithm for CPU Energy Reduction," in Proceedings of the ACM SIGPLAN 2003 conference on Programming language design and implementation, pp. 38--48, June 2003.
13. Dongkun Shin and Jihong Kim, "Look-ahead Intra-Task Voltage Scheduling Using Data Flow Information," In Proc. ISOCC, pp. 148-151, Oct. 2004.
14. Huizhan Yi and Xuejun Yang, "Optimizing the Configuration of Dynamic Voltage Scaling Points in Real-Time Applications," In Proc. of PATMOS 2005, Sep 22-25,2005.
15. M. Fleischmann, "Crusoe Power Management: Reducing the Operating Power with LongRun," in Proc. of HotChips 12 Symposium, 2000.
16. Intel, Inc., "The Intel(R) XScale(TM) Microarchitecture Technical Summary," 2000.
17. AMD, Inc., "AMD PowerNow Technology," 2000.
18. Thomas D.Burd, Robert W.Brodersen, "Design Issue for Dynamic Voltage Scaling ," in Proc. of the 2000 international symposium on low power electronics and design, Rapallo, Italy, pages: 9-14.
19. Peter Puscher, Alan Burns, "A Review of Worst-Case Execution-Time Analysis (Editorial)," Kluwer Academic Pubilishers, September 24, 1999.
20. Antoine Colin, Isabelle Puaut, "Worst Case Execution Time Analysis for a Processor with Branch Prediction," Real-Time System, 2000, vol 18(2/3): 249-274.
21. Nam Sung Kim, Todd Austin, Trevor Mudge, "Challenges for Architectural Level Power Modeling," Book Chapter from Power Aware Computing, 2001.
22. SNU Real-Time Benchmarks. Get from http://archi.snu.ac.kr/realtime/benchmark/.
23. Dakai Zhu, Daniel Mosse and Rami Melhem, "Power Aware Scheduling for AND/OR Graphs in Real-Time Systems," IEEE Trans. On Parallel and Distributed Systems, vol. 15, no.9, pp.849-864, 2004.

A Study on Transformation of Self-similar Processes with Arbitrary Marginal Distributions

Hae-Duck J. Jeong[1] and Jong-Suk R. Lee[2]

[1] School of Information Science, Korean Bible University
Seoul, South Korea
joshua@bible.ac.kr
[2] Grid Technology Research Department, Supercomputing Centre
Korea Institute of Science and Technology Information
Daejeon, South Korea
jsruthlee@kisti.re.kr

Abstract. Stochastic discrete-event simulation studies of communication networks often require a mechanism to transform self-similar processes with normal marginal distributions into self-similar processes with arbitrary marginal distributions. The problem of generating a self-similar process of a given marginal distribution and an autocorrelation structure is difficult and has not been fully solved. Our results presented in this paper provide clear experimental evidence that the autocorrelation function of the input process is not preserved in the output process generated by the inverse cumulative distribution function (ICDF) transformation, where the output process has an infinite variance. On the other hand, it preserves autocorrelation functions of the input process where the output marginal distributions (exponential, gamma, Pareto with $\alpha = 20.0$, uniform and Weibull) have finite variances, and the ICDF transformation is applied to long-range dependent self-similar processes with normal marginal distributions.

Keywords: Self-similar process, Arbitrary marginal distribution, Autocorrelation function, Inverse cumulative distribution function, Stochastic simulation.

1 Introduction

Stochastic simulation studies of communication networks often require the generation of random variables, or stochastic processes, characterized by different probability distributions. We have investigated generation of self-similar sequences with a normal marginal distribution. We can obtain sequences of numbers from normal distributions with different mean values and variances by applying such standard transformations as shifting and rescaling/normalization. In practical simulation studies, however, generation of self-similar processes of several different non-normal marginal probability distributions might be required. The most common method of transforming realizations of one random variable into realizations of another random variable is based on the inverse cumulative

C. Jesshope and C. Egan (Eds.): ACSAC 2006, LNCS 4186, pp. 137–146, 2006.

distribution function (ICDF) [1]. This method and its application in transformations of self-similar processes are discussed in [2] and [3] in detail.

The theory of transformations of strictly second-order self-similar processes has not been fully developed. In this paper, we investigate how well ACFs of the input process are preserved when transforming self-similar processes with normal distributions into processes with arbitrary marginal distributions. We look at applications of the ICDF transformation[1] to the generation of long-range dependent (LRD) sequences governed by non-normal marginal distributions from LRD sequences of normal marginal distributions.

For studying the properties of the ICDF transformation in the context of self-similar processes we investigate its properties when it is applied to the exact self-similar process, taking the self-similar fractional Gaussian noise (FGN) process as the references [2], [8], [9], [10]. This FGN process was generated by the *Durbin-Levinson* algorithm, described in [11] and [2]. We consider output processes with different marginal probability distributions (exponential, gamma, Pareto, uniform and Weibull), with finite and infinite variances, and compare autocorrelation functions (ACFs) of output processes with those characterizing input self-similar FGN processes. Our findings are summarized in Section 4.

2   Generation of LRD Self-similar Processes with Arbitrary Marginal Distributions

Simulation studies of communication networks require a mechanism to transform self-similar processes into processes with arbitrary marginal distributions [12], [13], [10]. In this paper, we investigate preservation of ACFs in output processes with different marginal distributions when transforming exact self-similar FGN processes into self-similar processes with five different marginal distributions (exponential, gamma, Pareto, uniform and Weibull), with finite and infinite variances, using the ICDF transformation.

2.1   The Methods of the ICDF Transformation

The ICDF transformation is based on the observation that given any random variable X_i with a cumulative distribution function (CDF) $F(x)$, the random variable $u = F(x)$ is independent and uniformly distributed between 0 and 1. Therefore, x can be obtained by generating uniform realizations and calculating $x = F^{-1}(u)$ [1].

We assume that a process $\mathbf{X}$ is a Gaussian process with zero mean, variance of one and a given autocorrelation function (ACF) $\{\rho_k\}$. Let $F_X(x)$ be its marginal CDF and $F_Y(y)$ be a marginal CDF of the process $\mathbf{Y}$. The process $\mathbf{Y}$ with the desired marginal CDF $F_Y(y)$ can be generated by the ICDF transformation from

---

[1] The TES (Transform-Expand-Sample) process [4], [5] and the ARTA (Autoregressive-to-Anything) process [6], [7] can be used the generation of correlated sequences.

the process **X**. Following the ICDF transformation, when transforming a random variable X_i into a random variable Y_i, we use the formula:

$$F_X(x) = F_Y(y), \tag{1}$$

Thus:

$$y = F_Y^{-1}(F_X(x)) \tag{2}$$

hence the method is called the ICDF transformation.

Here we consider five marginal distributions of output processes that are frequently used in simulation practice: exponential, gamma, Pareto, uniform and Weibull distributions. While exponential, gamma, Pareto with $\alpha > 2$, uniform and Weibull distributions have a finite variance, Pareto distribution with $\alpha \leq 2$ has an infinite variance. For detailed discussions of five marginal distributions, see [2], [3], [1].

2.2 Effects of Transformation

In simulation studies of such stochastic dynamic processes as those that occur in communication networks one needs to decide both their marginal probability distributions and autocorrelation structures. The problem of generating a strictly and/or second-order self-similar process of a given marginal distribution and an autocorrelation structure is difficult and has not been fully solved. No existing procedure is entirely satisfactory in terms of mathematical rigor, computational efficiency, accuracy of approximation, and precise and concise parameterization [14].

Applications of the transformation in Equation (2) to transformations of correlated processes have been studied by several researchers [15], [2], [9], [4]. In general, as proved by Beran (see [16], pp. 67-73), a transformation $y = G(x)$ applied to a strictly and/or second-order LRD self-similar sequence of numbers $\{x_1, x_2, \ldots\}$ does not preserve LRD properties in the output sequence $\{y_1, y_2, \ldots\}$. However, as proved in [15], if in (2):

- $F_X(\cdot)$ represents normal distribution,
- $\{x_1, x_2, \ldots\}$ is an LRD self-similar sequence,
- the transformation $G^2(x)$ is integrable, i.e.,

$$\int_{-\infty}^{+\infty} G^2(x) dF_X(x) < \infty, \quad \text{and} \tag{3}$$

- $E(XY) \neq 0$,

then the output sequence $\{y_1, y_2, \ldots\}$ is asymptotically self-similar, with the same coefficient H as the sequence $\{x_1, x_2, \ldots\}$.

Related issues have been investigated. Wise et al. [17] and Liu and Munson [18] showed that, following the transformation of marginal distribution, the transformation of ordinary ACF can be characterized when the input process is normal. They also indicated other processes for which this could be applied. Huang et al. [15] demonstrated that, if the process **X** is self-similar and has a normal marginal distribution, under general conditions, the output process **Y** is an asymptotically self-similar process with the same Hurst parameter ($\frac{1}{2} < H < 1$); for proof of the invariance of the Hurst parameter H, see [15]. Geist and Westall [19] demonstrated that arrival processes, obtained by the FFT (Fast Fourier Transform) method proposed by Paxson [10], have ACFs that are consistent with LRD. However, it has not been fully developed to generate self-similar processes with arbitrary marginal distributions from self-similar processes with (normal) marginal distributions and autocorrelation structures [14], [19].

3   Numerical Results

The numerical results of this section are used to investigate how well ACFs of the original Gaussian processes are preserved when they are converted into processes with non-normal marginal distributions. For each of $H = 0.6$, 0.7, 0.8 and 0.9, 100 exact self-similar sample sequences of 32,768 (2^{15}) numbers starting from different random seeds are used.

The following five different marginal distributions are investigated: the exponential distribution with $\lambda = 0.9$; the uniform distribution with $a = 0$ and $b = 1$; the gamma distribution with $\alpha = 2$ and $\beta = 1$; the Pareto distributions with $\alpha = 1.2$, 1.4, 1.6, 1.8 (i.e., infinite variance) and 20.0 (i.e., finite variance); and the Weibull distribution with $\alpha = 2$ and $\beta = 1$.

3.1   Analysis of Autocorrelation Functions

Preservation of H in output processes with marginal probability distributions and finite variances, which we showed in [3], are accompanied by preservation of ACFs in all these cases as well; for $H = 0.6$, 0.7, 0.8 and 0.9, see Figures 1 – 4. The output ACFs that significantly differ from the input ACFs of the exact FGN process are associated with Pareto distributions with infinite variances (i.e., $\alpha = 1.2$, 1.4, 1.6, 1.8).

ACFs curves of LRD self-similar processes decay slowly and hyperbolically rather than exponentially as H values increase. For example, Figure 4 (a) shows ACFs for the exact self-similar FGN process, and five approximately self-similar processes with exponential, gamma, Pareto ($\alpha = 1.2$), uniform and Weibull marginal distributions for a range of lags. The ACF curve obtained from the Pareto marginal distribution with $\alpha = 1.2$ and $H = 0.6393$ lies lower than other ACF curves with $H > 0.88$. In contrast, the ACF curve of a Poisson process assumes value one at lag equals 0, and zero otherwise. We considered here a Poisson process with $\lambda = 0.9$.

Note that all ACFs of marginal probability distributions with finite variances differ from the input ACFs by no more than 4% (Lower and upper dotted lines in Figures 1 – 5 are ± 4% apart from the input ACFs.). In all cases of output processes with Pareto distributions with infinite variances, the differences between their ACFs and the ACF of input FGN process are substantial. Thus, there is clear experimental evidence that ACF of the input process is not preserved in the output process generated by transformation (2), where the output

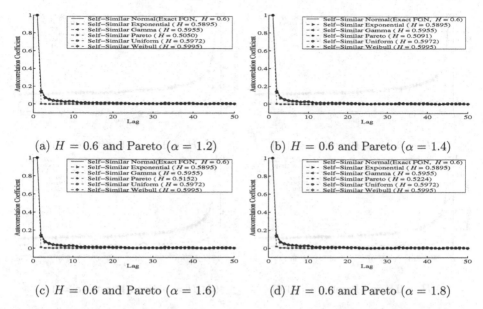

(a) $H = 0.6$ and Pareto ($\alpha = 1.2$)   (b) $H = 0.6$ and Pareto ($\alpha = 1.4$)

(c) $H = 0.6$ and Pareto ($\alpha = 1.6$)   (d) $H = 0.6$ and Pareto ($\alpha = 1.8$)

Fig. 1. Autocorrelation functions for the exact self-similar FGN process, five exponential, gamma, Pareto ($\alpha = 1.2, 1.4, 1.6$ and 1.8), uniform and Weibull marginal distributions in autocorrelation lags between 1 and 50 for $H = 0.6$. The output processes preserve LRD properties, except the Pareto marginal distribution with $\alpha = 1.2, 1.4, 1.6$ and 1.8.

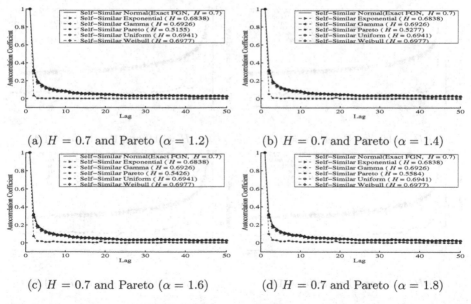

(a) $H = 0.7$ and Pareto ($\alpha = 1.2$)   (b) $H = 0.7$ and Pareto ($\alpha = 1.4$)

(c) $H = 0.7$ and Pareto ($\alpha = 1.6$)   (d) $H = 0.7$ and Pareto ($\alpha = 1.8$)

Fig. 2. Autocorrelation functions for the exact self-similar FGN process, five exponential, gamma, Pareto ($\alpha = 1.2, 1.4, 1.6$ and 1.8), uniform and Weibull marginal distributions in autocorrelation lags between 1 and 50 for $H = 0.7$. The output processes preserve LRD properties, except the Pareto marginal distribution with $\alpha = 1.2, 1.4, 1.6$ and 1.8.

142   H.-D.J. Jeong and J.-S.R. Lee

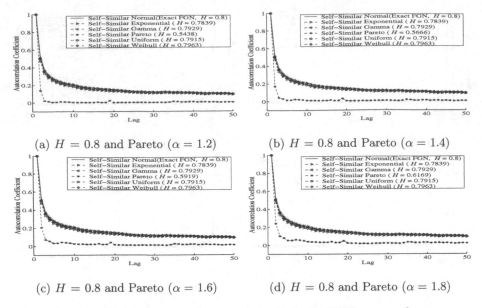

(a) $H = 0.8$ and Pareto $(\alpha = 1.2)$ (b) $H = 0.8$ and Pareto $(\alpha = 1.4)$

(c) $H = 0.8$ and Pareto $(\alpha = 1.6)$ (d) $H = 0.8$ and Pareto $(\alpha = 1.8)$

Fig. 3. Autocorrelation functions for the exact self-similar FGN process, five exponential, gamma, Pareto $(\alpha = 1.2, 1.4, 1.6$ and $1.8)$, uniform and Weibull marginal distributions in autocorrelation lags between 1 and 50 for $H = 0.8$. The output processes preserve LRD properties, except the Pareto marginal distribution with $\alpha = 1.2, 1.4, 1.6$ and 1.8.

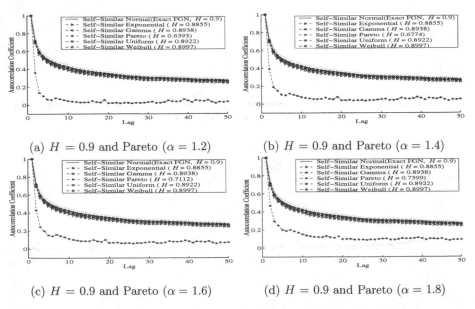

(a) $H = 0.9$ and Pareto $(\alpha = 1.2)$ (b) $H = 0.9$ and Pareto $(\alpha = 1.4)$

(c) $H = 0.9$ and Pareto $(\alpha = 1.6)$ (d) $H = 0.9$ and Pareto $(\alpha = 1.8)$

Fig. 4. Autocorrelation functions for the exact self-similar FGN process, five exponential, gamma, Pareto $(\alpha = 1.2, 1.4, 1.6$ and $1.8)$, uniform and Weibull marginal distributions in autocorrelation lags between 1 and 50 for $H = 0.9$. The output processes preserve LRD properties, except the Pareto marginal distribution with $\alpha = 1.2, 1.4, 1.6$ and 1.8.

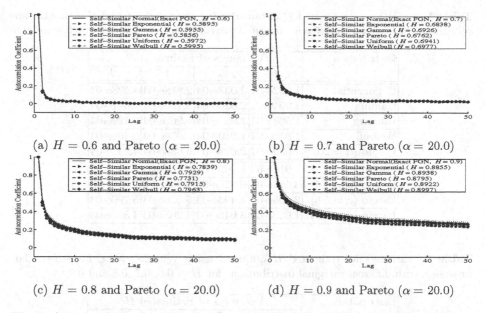

(a) $H = 0.6$ and Pareto ($\alpha = 20.0$)   (b) $H = 0.7$ and Pareto ($\alpha = 20.0$)

(c) $H = 0.8$ and Pareto ($\alpha = 20.0$)   (d) $H = 0.9$ and Pareto ($\alpha = 20.0$)

Fig. 5. Autocorrelation functions for the exact self-similar FGN process, five exponential, gamma, Pareto ($\alpha = 20.0$), uniform and Weibull marginal distributions in autocorrelation lags between 1 and 50 for $H = 0.6, 0.7, 0.8$ and 0.9. The output processes preserve LRD properties.

process has an infinite variance. However, for $\alpha = 20.0$ (i.e., in the case of a finite variance) and $H = 0.6, 0.7, 0.8$ and 0.9, Figure 5 shows the effects of transforming ACFs from the original exact FGN process using the ICDF transformation. Our results in Figure 5 show that ACFs of the input process are preserved in the output process.

Thus, for $H = 0.6, 0.7, 0.8$ and 0.9, and autocorrelation lags between 1 and 50, this is evidence of the preservation of the original ACF after the ICDF transformation is applied, except where the Pareto marginal distribution with $\alpha = 1.2, 1.4, 1.6$ and 1.8.

3.2   Analysis of Variances for Estimated H

Tables $1 - 2$ show variances for estimated H obtained using the wavelet-based H estimator and Whittle's MLE[2] for the exact self-similar FGN process with different marginal distributions for $H = 0.6, 0.7, 0.8$ and 0.9. Estimated variances for the output processes with five different marginal distributions were slightly higher than the original, but those with the Pareto marginal distribution with $\alpha = 1.2, 1.4, 1.6$ and 1.8 had the highest variances. All variances gradually increased as the H value increased.

---

[2] Our results have shown that the wavelet-based H estimator and Whittle's MLE are the least biased of the H estimation techniques. For more detailed discussions, see [2].

Table 1. Variances for estimated H obtained using the wavelet-based H estimator for self-similar processes with different marginal distributions for $H = 0.6, 0.7, 0.8$ and 0.9

Distribution	Variances of Estimated H			
	.6	.7	.8	.9
Exponential	1.662e-04	2.033e-04	2.878e-04	4.528e-04
Gamma	1.994e-04	2.025e-04	2.156e-04	2.641e-04
Uniform	1.993e-04	1.992e-04	1.962e-04	2.129e-04
Weibull	1.812e-04	1.910e-04	2.076e-04	2.366e-04
Pareto ($\alpha = 20.0$)	1.689e-04	2.098e-04	3.088e-04	4.982e-04
Pareto ($\alpha = 1.2$)	5.016e-03	1.002e-02	9.702e-03	9.155e-03
Pareto ($\alpha = 1.4$)	3.515e-03	6.633e-03	7.135e-03	7.376e-03
Pareto ($\alpha = 1.6$)	2.405e-03	4.490e-03	5.526e-03	5.790e-03
Pareto ($\alpha = 1.8$)	1.622e-03	3.046e-03	4.263e-03	4.395e-03

Table 2. Variances for estimated H obtained using Whittle's MLE for self-similar processes with different marginal distributions for $H = 0.6, 0.7, 0.8$ and 0.9

Distribution	Variances of Estimated H			
	.6	.7	.8	.9
Exponential	1.270e-05	1.544e-05	2.005e-05	3.084e-05
Gamma	1.158e-05	1.292e-05	1.450e-05	1.664e-05
Uniform	1.152e-05	1.286e-05	1.433e-05	1.797e-05
Weibull	1.158e-05	1.245e-05	1.339e-05	1.550e-05
Pareto ($\alpha = 20.0$)	1.343e-05	1.763e-05	2.382e-05	4.041e-05
Pareto ($\alpha = 1.2$)	1.019e-04	2.582e-04	1.037e-03	5.067e-03
Pareto ($\alpha = 1.4$)	9.652e-05	3.678e-04	1.310e-03	4.985e-03
Pareto ($\alpha = 1.6$)	1.010e-04	4.626e-04	1.505e-03	4.404e-03
Pareto ($\alpha = 1.8$)	1.028e-04	5.084e-04	1.572e-03	3.665e-03

4   Conclusions

We investigated how well ACFs of the original processes were preserved when the self-similar processes were converted into suitable self-similar processes with five exponential, gamma, Pareto, uniform and Weibull marginal distributions. For the stochastic simulation of communication networks with self-similar tele-traffic we used the ICDF transformation to produce self-similar processes with five different marginal distributions. Our results presented in this paper provide clear experimental evidence that ACFs of the input process are not preserved in the output process generated by transformation (2) where the output process has an infinite variance. In other words, it preserves ACF of the input process where the output marginal distribution has a finite variance, and transformation (2) is applied to LRD self-similar processes with normal marginal distributions. In addition, estimated variances for the output processes with five different marginal distributions including Pareto marginal distribution with $\alpha = 20.0$ were slightly higher than the original, but those with the Pareto marginal distribution with $\alpha = 1.2$, 1.4, 1.6 and 1.8 had the highest variances.

Acknowledgements. The authors acknowledge Dr. Don McNickle and Dr. Krzysztof Pawlikowski for their valuable comments. The authors also wish to thank the financial support of Korea Institute of Science and Technology Information, Korea. This work was partially supported by the Korean Bible University's Research Grant.

References

1. Law, A., Kelton, W.: Simulation Modeling and Analysis. 2nd ed., McGraw-Hill, Inc., Singapore (1991)
2. Jeong, H.D.: Modelling of Self-Similar Teletraffic for Simulation. PhD thesis, Department of Computer Science, University of Canterbury (2002)
3. Jeong, H.D., Lee, J.S., Park, H.W.: Teletraffic Generation of Self-Similar Processes with Arbitrary Marginal Distributions for Simulation: Analysis of Hurst Parameters. In: Lecture Notes in Computer Science 3045 (Proceedings of International Conference on Computational Science and Its Applications (ICCSA2004)), Springer-Verlag (2004) 827–836
4. Melamed, B.: TES: a Class of Methods for Generating Autocorrelated Uniform Variates. ORSA Journal on Computing **3**(4) (1991) 317–329
5. Melamed, B., Hill, J.R.: A Survey of TES Modeling Applications. Simulation (1995) 353–370
6. Cario, M., Nelson, B.: Autoregressive to Anything: Time-Series Input Processes for Simulation. Operations Research Letters **19** (1996) 51–58
7. Cario, M., Nelson, B.: Numerical Methods for Fitting and Simulating Autoregressive-to-Anything Processes. INFORMS Journal on Computing **10**(1) (1998) 72–81
8. Jeong, H.D., McNickle, D., Pawlikowski, K.: Generation of Self-Similar Time Series for Simulation Studies of Telecommunication Networks. In: Proceedings of the First Western Pacific and Third Australia-Japan Workshop on Stochastic Models in Engineering, Technology and Management, Christchurch, New Zealand (1999) 221–230
9. Jeong, H.D., McNickle, D., Pawlikowski, K.: Generation of Self-Similar Processes for Simulation Studies of Telecommunication Networks. Mathematical and Computer Modelling **38**(11-13) (2003) 1249–1257
10. Paxson, V.: Fast, Approximate Synthesis of Fractional Gaussian Noise for Generating Self-Similar Network Traffic. Computer Communication Review, ACM SIGCOMM **27**(5) (1997) 5–18
11. Abry, P., Flandrin, P., Taqqu, M., D.Veitch: Self-Similarity and Long-Range Dependence Through the Wavelet Lens. In: Theory and Applications of Long-Range Dependence. Birkhäuser, Doukhan, Oppenheim, and Taqqu (eds), Boston, MA (2002) 527–556
12. Leroux, H., Hassan, M.: Generating Packet Inter-Arrival Times for FGN Arrival Processes. In: The 3rd New Zealand ATM and Broadband Workshop, Hamilton, New Zealand (1999) 1–10

13. Leroux, H., Hassan, M., Egudo, R.: On the Self-Similarity of Packet Inter-Arrival Times of Internet Traffic. In: The 3rd New Zealand ATM and Broadband Workshop, Hamilton, New Zealand (1999) 11–19
14. Geist, R., Westall, J.: Practical Aspects of Simulating Systems Having Arrival Processes with Long-Range Dependence. In: Proceedings of the 2000 Winter Simulation Conference, Orlando, Florida, USA, J.A. Joines, R.R. Barton, K. Kang, and P.A. Fishwick (eds.) (2000) 666–674
15. Huang, C., Devetsikiotis, M., Lambadaris, I., Kaye, A.: Modeling and Simulation of Self-Similar Variable Bit Rate Compressed Video: A Unified Approach. Computer Communication Review, Proceedings of ACM SIGCOMM'95 $25(4)$ (1995) 114–125
16. Beran, J.: Statistics for Long-Memory Processes. Chapman and Hall, New York (1994)
17. Wise, G., Traganitis, A., Thomas, J.: The Effect of a Memoryless Nonlinearity on the Spectrum of a Random Process. IEEE Transactions on Information Theory **IT-23**(1) (1977) 84–89
18. Liu, B., Munson, D.: Generation of a Random Sequence Having a Jointly Specified Marginal Distribution and Autocovariance. IEEE Transactions on Acoustics, Speech and Signal Processing **ASSP-30**(6) (1982) 973–983
19. Geist, R., Westall, J.: Correlational and Distributional Effects in Network Traffic Models. Performance Evaluation **44** (2001) 121–138

µTC – An Intermediate Language for Programming Chip Multiprocessors

Chris Jesshope

Institute for Informatics, University of Amsterdam, Kruislaan 403, 1098 SJ Amsterdam,
Netherlands
Jesshope@science uva.nl

Abstract. µTC is a language that has been designed for programming chip multiprocessors. Indeed, to be more specific, it has been developed to program chip multiprocessors based on arrays of microthreaded microprocessors as these processors directly implement the concepts introduced in the language. However, it is more general than that and is being used in other projects as an interface defining dynamic concurrency. Ideally, a program written in µTC is a dynamic, concurrent control structure over small sequences of code, which in the limit could be a few instructions each. µTC is being used as an intermediate language to capture concurrency from data-parallel languages such as single-assignment C, parallelising compilers for sequential languages such as C and concurrent composition languages, such as Snet. µTC's advantage over other approaches is that it allows an abstract representation of maximal concurrency in a schedule-independent form. Both Snet and µTC are being used in a European project called AETHER, in order to support all aspects of self-adaptive computation.

Keywords: Self-adaptive computing, concurrent languages, data-driven computation, programming chip multiprocessors.

1 Introduction

This paper describes language work originating in the *MicroGrid* project at the University of Amsterdam, which is designing chip multiprocessors based on the microthreaded model of concurrency [1]. It is also being adapted as a virtual system's architecture (SVM) for highly concurrent, self-adaptive systems in the European *AETHER* project. In the former, it represents a transparent view over the underlying hardware support for concurrency and in the latter it presents a pragmatic attempt to define the functionality of a virtual machine for system-level interfaces between self-adaptive network entities (SANEs). SANEs are the concurrent components that are dynamically manipulated to achieve the project's goals of self-adaptive computing.

The language defined in this paper provides the functional definition and concurrency of the virtual machine describing SANE components. Most of the scheduling and resource aspects of SVM are outside of the scope of this paper. However, as µTC directly captures the hardware implementation of microthreaded microprocessors it has an abstract view of resource issues in this context. More details including simulations chip-multiprocessors based on this model can be found in [2].

C. Jesshope and C. Egan (Eds.): ACSAC 2006, LNCS 4186, pp. 147–160, 2006.
© Springer-Verlag Berlin Heidelberg 2006

μTC is a rather profound but simple extension to the C language, allowing it to capture thread-based concurrency. μTC is capable of expressing static, heterogeneous concurrency and dynamic, homogeneous concurrency. It is similar in some aspects to OpenMP [3], however there are significant differences. One of the most significant differences is that the language assumes a synchronizing memory. This captures dependencies between threads allowing sequence to be transformed into concurrency, where any dependencies are managed transparently in a data-driven manner. The other major difference is that C is extended with executable constructs rather than being annotated with pragmas as in OpenMP. For example, families of threads are created as named entities within the language and can be referenced, for example in a control component for a given SANE. This difference is fundamental and provides the mechanism for dynamically manipulating SANEs (as families of threads) as required in self-adaptive systems. For example, an identified family of threads can be terminated, either with prejudice or in a controlled and orderly manner that allows pending synchronizations to complete, so that a concurrent program can be moved to new resources or have its behaviour modified.

μTC is based on the concept of microthreading [1], which includes synchronising memory and efficient, low-level scheduling. Our prior results [2] on microthreading show that very efficient implementations of these concepts are possible. In general, there is a range of scheduling options for μTC. On a microthreaded microprocessor, μTC programs are scheduled dynamically and the constructs introduced simply reflect instructions in the ISA. On conventional processors, some kind of static schedule will need to be generated by the μTC compiler or its run-time system, to remove the requirement for synchronising memory. For example, a sequential implementation of μTC exists, which executes threads in creation order with no interleaving. The philosophy adopted, captures maximal application concurrency and reflects the asynchrony and locality of communication that is found in chip multi-processors. The assumption is that the transformation from concurrent to sequential is trivial in principle, although difficult to define in the case of non-determinism in timing. However, the real goal is to execute μTC directly, which is indeed possible. Ideally, a program written in μTC is a dynamic concurrent structure over small sequences of code, which, in the limit, could be just a few instructions each.

2 Motivation and Background

Reference [4] provides a compelling argument for the elimination of non-determinacy in programming concurrent systems and claims that we are on the threshold of a potential disaster as multi-threaded code is migrated to chip multi-processors with non-deterministic scheduling. The same argument is made in [5], where similar issues are raised about programming state-of-the-art multiprocessor systems. These include the following real or perceived problems:

- the user has to parallelise existing serial code;
- explicitly threaded programs using a thread library are not portable;
- writing efficient multi-threaded programs requires intimate knowledge of the machine's architecture and micro-architecture.

Here the following solutions are adopted to these problems. Users do not normally parallelise applications but generate μTC from deterministic code, such as plain old C or Single-assignment C (SAC) [6] (a functional, data-parallel language). Moreover, concurrency in μTC is achieved in an abstract way that does not require reference to a thread-library, thus only the μTC compiler will need to have knowledge of the architecture or micro-architecture and any run-time support for a given target.

The main tools in the AETHER project will be compilers for conventional languages and for the configuration language Snet [7] all of which will target μTC, as well as various implementations of μTC to specific targets. Our own interest is the compilation of μTC to microthreaded binaries and their implementation in reconfigurable processor arrays to provide dynamic management of resources, e.g. see [8]. For this, gcc will be modified to compile μTC to schedule-invariant, microthreaded binary code. As the tool chain above is being developed, μTC will be used as a user programming language. The first implementation of μTC is a translation to C, using a rather trivial schedule that executes all threads in index sequence. Subsequent work will focus on the automatic parallelisation of C programs targeted to μTC, which together with the μTC compiler, will allow the execution on microthreaded binaries from legacy, sequential C code on our Microgrid simulator.

The remainder of this paper introduces the language and provides numerous examples to illustrate the semantics of the constructs and how they would be used in a number of different application scenarios.

3 Additions to C

Only a small number of constructs are added to C, along with the semantics of the synchronising memory, which is described in detail below. The constructs map onto low-level operations that provide the concurrency controls in a microthreaded ISA, see [1] and allow concurrent programs to be dynamically instanced and preempted, either gracefully or with a prejudice. Family identifiers provide the control over the concurrent sections. No other language to our knowledge provides such support for families of threads and this enables many of the dynamic aspects of SANEs.

μTC adds the following keywords to standard C. They can be used anywhere in a C program, subject to restrictions described in each keyword's description. They are:

create	Control construct used to create a family of microthreads;
thread	Type specifier to indicate the functions that define the microthreads;
shared	Type qualifier of variables shared between microthreads;
index	Type qualifier of the index variable of a family of microthreads;
sync	Construct that waits for the termination of a specified family;
break	Construct that terminates a family from one of its of threads;
kill	Construct that terminates a specified family externally;
squeeze	Construct that preempts the execution of a specified family so that it may be restarted without loss of state.

Before these constructs are defined in detail, a brief definition of the memory model used in implementing them must be given. It is assumed that there are two kinds of memory (analogous to registers and main memory in the sequential machine model).

They are a synchronising memory and a non-synchronising memory. The latter is shared main memory with no assumptions about access time. All inter-thread communication is performed in synchronising memory, which is assumed to be fast, on-chip and close to the processor. There are also restrictions on inter-thread communication that reflect the asynchrony and locality of on-chip communications. Synchronising memory is allocated dynamically to a thread on its creation and is released when that thread completes (or is forced to complete). It implements dataflow synchronisation and threads block on reading it. Thus if a thread attempts to read an undefined location in synchronising memory, it will not proceed beyond the statement that attempted to read the undefined variable.

Non-synchronising memory has relaxed consistency and is bulk synchronous with respect to a family of microthreads. This means that during the execution of a family of threads, threads may read from or write to a structure in synchronising memory but the state of the writes is not consistently defined until the whole family completes (or is forced to complete). This means that two concurrent threads in the same family cannot usefully share data via non-synchronising memory.

3.1 create

```
create(fid; start; limit; step; block) <named thread>|
                            <compound statement>;
```

The create construct defines a concurrent section as a family of microthreads over an index variable. Threads can be defined either by a compound statement or a named thread, which is similar to a function (see Section 3.2). create returns a unique family identifier, *fid*, to identify and control the family created and may be used anywhere within a C program, including from within another thread. create has the following components:

- *fid*: a variable from the creating context that receives the family identifier, that uniquely identifies the created family and can then be used to synchronise or terminate the family.
- *start:* an expression defining the start of the index sequence for the family of microthreads; it is evaluated when the create is executed (default: 0).
- *limit:* an expression defining the limit of the index sequence for the family of microthreads; it is evaluated when the create is executed (default: unlimited).
- *step:* an expression defining the step value between indices; it is evaluated when the create is executed (default: 1).
- *block:* an expression defining the maximum number of index values allocated per processor in a single allocation round; the expression is evaluated when the create is executed (default: maximum possible).

The triple (*start, limit, step*) defines an index sequence over the threads created and a unique value from this sequence is available to each thread. Any of these expressions may be omitted and an appropriate default value will be assumed. A blank *limit* statement causes an infinite number of threads to be created and in this case, thread creation will have to be terminated by a break, squeeze or kill. A blank *block* expression means that an implementation will allocate as many threads as there are resources available to do so.

The `create` construct creates threads in block-index order and dynamically allocates synchronising memory to each thread it creates (the memory is released when the thread completes). Variables in synchronising memory are initialised empty (i.e. they block a thread that attempts to read them). The exception is the thread index, which is initialised to the index value for the thread as defined by the triple above.

An arbitrary number of processors, *p* say, which can be defined at create time, may be used to execute the created threads and the implementation will distribute the threads over those processors in block-index order. Block-index order is where the first *block* index values are allocated to the first processor and so on, to each processor involved, so that *p*block* indices are created in a round of allocation over the *p* processors. This allows infinitely many threads to be defined and managed and is similar to k-bounded loops used in dataflow, i.e. it provides an artificial dependency limiting the use of resources and providing management over resource deadlock.

Two examples that create exactly the same family of threads are given in Table 1, together with the equivalent sequential code for reference.

Table 1. Creating families of threads with compound statements and named threads

Compound statement	Named thread	Sequential equivalent

```int a[10];```
```int fid, s=0;```
```...```
```create(fid; 0; 9)```
```   index int i;```
```   shared int s;```
```   s = s + a[i];```
```}```
```sync(fid);```
```...s...```
	```thread sint(shared int su```
	``` int array[])```
	```index int idx;```
	```sum = sum + array[idx];```
	```}```
	
	```int a[10];```
	```int fid, s = 0;```
	```...```
	```create(fid; 0; n-1)```
	``` sint(s, a[]```
	```sync(fid);```
	```... s ...```
		```int a[10];```
		```int fid, s=0;```
		```...```
		```for(i=0; i<10; i++)```
		``` s = s + a[i];```
		```}```
		```...s...```

Each thread in this homogeneous family contains its own copy of the shared variable s/sum, which defines a dependency chain through the family of threads, with each thread reading its neighbour's shared variable. For more detail on this see also the definition of `shared` in section 3.7.

A heterogeneous `create` makes use of a list of named threads. In the heterogeneous case, the compiler must know the index range statically. This form can be used to represent ILP in basic blocks or to manage MIMD concurrency at the application level. Again there can be `shared` variables that define dependency chains between the threads and these are declared in the argument list of the threads, must be common to all threads and bound to variables in the creating thread. An example is given in Table 2 below, along with the equivalent sequential code.

Table 2. Creating a heterogeneous family of threads.

Thread list	Sequential equivalent

```thread mt1(shared real sr){```
```   sr=b*b-sr;}```
 	
```thread mt2(shared real sr){```
```   r1=(sr-b)/2*a;```
```   r2=-(sr+b)/2*a;```
```   }```
```...```
```real a, b, c, sr, r1, r2; int fid;```
```create(fid;1;3)```
```   mt1(sr),sqrt(sr),mt2(sr);```
```sr=4*a*c```
```sync(fid)   /*r1, r2 now valid*/```
	```...```
	```real a, b, c, sr, r1, r2;```
	```sr=sqrt(b*b-4*a*c);```
	```r1=(sr-b)/2*a;```
	```r2=-(sr+b)/2*a;```

In this example, a single shared variable, `sr`, defines a dependency chain between the threads. Note that the built-in thread `sqrt` gets its parameter and passes its result via this shared variable. When created, each user-defined thread can proceed with some computation. Thread `mt1` can compute b^2 and `mt1` can compute 2a, while the main thread computes 4ac. Then the computation is constrained by the shared variable `sr`, which is passed from main to `mt1`, `mt1` to `sqrt` and `sqrt` to `mt2`. The result is written in two global variables in non-synchronising memory, which are defined only when the threads have been synchronised. The code in Table 2 is an example of explicitly programmed ILP.

3.2 thread

```
thread <name> (<argument list>){...}
```

The `thread` construct defines a C function as a thread in μTC. It can be used with `create` to generate instances of the function as dynamic threads and to match an argument list in the definition with a set of parameters from the creating environment. There are a number of differences between a function and a thread. Firstly, there is no return type (or it is assumed to be void), as threads do not return values other than by shared variables or writes to non-synchronising memory. A `break`, see Section 3.4, can also return a value to the creating thread that via the `sync` construct.

Threads cannot contain calls to functions but can create further subordinate threads, which are concurrent function calls, where the thread is triggered by writing values to its arguments and the creating environment waits on results using `sync`. Results are either defined by the local variable used to initialise a shared-variable dependency chain or can be written to non-synchronising memory, which is shared (both are used in the example in Table 2). There is no reason why C programs cannot be completely translated to threaded programs using threads instead of functions.

3.3 sync

```
sync(fid; return);
```

The sync construct is used to detect the termination of a concurrent section defined by a family of threads with identifier *fid*. It also returns a value to *return* in the definition above, which defaults to *maxint* if the family terminates normally. The construct blocks until the family specified by *fid* has completed and then completes its execution by setting the return value. sync returns a value that is set by a break construct, if one was executed, otherwise the return value defaults to *maxint*. A create and corresponding sync define a concurrent section, which includes both the creating thread as well as the family of created threads. Global memory written in a concurrent section cannot be reliably read by other threads in the same concurrent section, nor by another family, until the family writing global memory has been synchronised using the sync construct. Only one sync may be issued on a given family of threads and a sync in two concurrent threads on the same family may have unpredictable results.

3.4 break

```
break(result);
```

The break construct terminates a family of threads from within one of its threads. It stops any remaining thread creation and releases all synchronising memory, losing any synchronising state that the family may have had. It also allows the breaking thread to return a value to the creating environment by its parameter *result*.

An important issue in the implementation of break/sync is the guarantee that an outstanding synchronisation on a location in synchronising memory will not interfere with any subsequent use of that location, i.e. if it is subsequently allocated to another family of threads. For example, assume that a load from non-synchronising memory had been issued in a thread and a break released the target location in synchronising memory before the load was satisfied. The implementation of break/sync must ensure that any subsequent response from memory for that family will no longer update synchronising memory.

3.5 squeeze

```
squeeze(fid; return);
```

The squeeze construct is similar in operation to sync but is executed concurrently with the creating environment and is used to bring a family of threads identified by *fid* to a well-defined termination state. It stops any remaining thread creation and waits for any outstanding synchronisations to complete before returning the index value of the first thread not created to its *return* parameter. Like sync it blocks until the family of threads has terminated. The *return* is the concurrent program's equivalent of a program counter in a sequential program when pre-empting the program and enables the family to be restarted (perhaps on different resources) without loss of data. Note that termination of a thread requires the termination of any synchronised, subordinate threads within it and these subordinate families are not automatically squeezed. If a deep squeeze is required, it must be programmed, as it requires the building of a data structure of index values for all subordinate squeezed families. In practice this construct could be executed in any thread that has access to a family's *fid* and it is required to dynamically migrate SANE components.

Only one squeeze may be issued on a given family of threads and squeezing in two concurrent threads on the same family may have unpredictable results. An example of the use of squeeze is given below:

```
int fid1, fid2, resume;
...
create(fid1;1;1){   /*job wrapper*/
    shared int fid2;
    create(fid2)job(); /*job to be squeezed*/
    }
sync(fid1)
...
squeeze(fid2,resume)
```

In this example the job wrapper, family *fid1*, creates an infinite family of threads defined by a thread named *job* and returns the family identifier, *fid2*, back to the main thread, leaving the family detached, as *fid2* is never synchronised. This example shows how to obtain and use *fid2* to asynchronously terminate the family. Note that *fid2* becomes defined on the sync on family *fid1*. This code skeleton is an example of a SANE component having a control part and a functional part running side by side.

3.6 kill

```
Kill(fid);
```

The kill construct is similar in operation to squeeze and is also executed from a concurrent control thread but it is used to bring a concurrent section defined by *fid* to a forced termination, by stopping any thread creation and forcibly terminating any executing threads, i.e. all pending synchronisations are lost! The other difference is that kill does operate recursively, i.e. it kills not only the family of threads that is identified but also any subordinate families that have been created.

3.7 index/shared

```
index int i; shared real s;
```

The index and shared keywords are type modifiers used in μTC; index defines the thread sequence number and is set automatically by create and shared defines any variables in synchronising memory that are shared between threads in a family.

4 Memory Model

4.1 Synchronising Memory

The most important aspect of µTC code is the concept of synchronising memory. Each thread has a context of local, scalar variables dynamically allocated to it in synchronising memory, which are initialised to the *empty* state and which are garbage collected when the thread completes. These variables provide synchronisation with data from non-synchronising memory and also with other threads if the variables are declared as shared. Reading an empty variable in synchronising memory will block the thread reading it until the value has been set (it gets suspended and can no longer proceed until the data is available). Synchronising memory is dynamic and data created by threads must either be shared or written to non-synchronising memory before the thread terminates or it will be lost.

To communicate between threads in the same family, synchronising memory must be used and must be declared as shared. Sharing is deliberately restricted to reflect the locality of communication found in silicon systems. Each thread has one *neighbour* that can read its shared local values, which is defined as the next thread in index sequence in the create for that family. To initialise this chain of neighbours, the first thread reads a variable of the same name from the creating environment (not declared as shared) or in the case of a named thread; a binding is made to a variable in the creating environment. Following the termination of the family, a read to the variable in the creating environment will yield the value written to the shared variable from the last thread created. Dependency chains through a family of threads are therefore initialised and closed using variables from the creating thread.

The following example illustrates a potential problem with shared variables:

```
int *a, n, s = 0;
...
create(fid; 0; n-1){
    index int i; shared int s;
    s = s + 1;
    s = s * 2;
    a[i] = s;
}
```

Here, the shared variable s is written twice in each thread. The value obtained by a read from a neighbour is therefore non-deterministic. Dataflow synchronisation ensures s can not read until it is written but when written it can be read before or after the second write. The solution used in the µTC compiler is to enforce single assignment semantics for shared variables, introducing further local variables as required. A family will then give exactly the same results as if each thread were executed sequentially. The compiler must ensure that the first read of s is from the prior thread and that only the last write will synchronise with the following thread. All other uses of s must be local. The µTC compiler would therefore generate the equivalent of the following code in this example:

```
int *a, n, s = 0;
...
create(fid 0; n-1){
    index int i; shared int s; int t;
    t = s + 1;
    s = t * 2;
    a[i] = s;
    }
```

An example using non-local shared variables is given below. It implements a recurrence relation with dependencies from the neighbour and neighbour's neighbour. It computes Fibonacci numbers:

```
int i, fid, temp1, temp2, Fibonacci[10];
temp1=fibonacci[0]=0;
temp2=fibonacci[1]=1;
create(fid; 2; 9){
    index int i; shared int temp1, temp2;
    fibonacci[i] = temp1 + temp2;
    temp1 = temp2;
    temp2 = fibonacci[i];
    }
sync(fid);
```

More generally, a shared variable may pass data to an arbitrary thread in a family using deterministic choice within the thread index (this is data-routing).

4.2 Non-synchronising Memory

Non-synchronising memory has relaxed consistency during the execution of a family of threads and writes to this memory are only well defined only after the family of threads has completed (defined by the sync construct). Using non-synchronising memory, a thread may write to any declared variable that is in scope (normal C rules) or has been passed to it as a parameter. It is a requirement for deterministic execution, that each thread in a homogeneous family must write to a unique element of a data structure, which is selected by its index value, e.g. x[i], where i is the family's thread index. The range of i is defined by create. In heterogeneous families uniqueness must be guaranteed by the threads' code and can be to non-indexed variables. In either case, a read after a write to variables updated in a thread family cannot be safely be performed until a sync has been executed on the family of threads that performed the write.

When assigning to indexed variables, care must be taken with expressions other than the local index value, as reads and writes to the same element of an indexed structure can only be guaranteed to be consistent within the same thread or following the sync. An example is where different elements of an indexed data structure are required in a thread. Consider the following poorly defined μTC code fragment:

```
int a[10], fid, n=10;
create(fid; 0; n-2){
    index int i;
    a[i] = a[i] + a[i+1];
    }
```

This program does not give deterministic results as a[i+1] could be read by a thread either before or after its neighbour had updated a. A deterministic program i.e. one that guarantees the result expected from a sequential schedule requires the following transformation:

```
int a[10], shift_a[10], fid, n=10;
create(fid; 0; n-2){
    index int i;
    shift_a[i] = a[i+1];
    }
sync(fid);
create(fid;0; n-2){
    index int i;
    a[i] = a[i] + shift_a[i];
    }
```

In C, dependency chains may be defined through iterations spaces by indexed data structures, which if translated naively could also give non-determinism. For example:

```
int *sum, *a, fid, n = 10;
sum[0] = a[0];
create(fid; 1; n-1){
    index int i;
    sum[i] = a[i] + sum[i-1];
    }
```

Here, sum is a global array in non-synchronising memory indexed in each thread (it is not a local shared variable). Although the μTC compiler could allocate shared variables to implement this dependency chain, it would require the compiler to check that the index expression defined neighbours in the family of threads. Although this is trivial in the example above, it may not always be the case and run-time checks may be unavoidable in some code. To avoid this, shared variables in μTC must always be declared explicitly and the above example should be written as:

```
int *sum, *a, fid, n = 10, s;
sum[0] = s = a[0];
create(fid; 1; n-1){
    index int i; shared int s;
    sum[i]= s = a[i] + s;
    }
```

A more complex example is given below, which uses both thread index and global index expressions. It performs matrix-vector multiplication and is defined as a thread.

```
thread matvec(int *a, *x, *y, n){
    int fido;
    create(fido; 0; n)
        {
        index int i;
        int fidi, s = 0;
        create(fidi; 0; n; 1; 4){
            index int j
            shared int s;
            s = s + a[i][j]*x[j]
            }
        sync(fidi);
        y[i] = s;
        }
    sync(fido);
    }
```

This thread creates n^2 threads, where the n outer threads are independent and the n inner threads contain a dependency chain on s. In the inner family, the code uses both thread-index selection, using j, as well as global index selection, using i.

5 Resource Management

The use of the create's *block* parameter provides for management of resources on thread creation. There are two issues here, the placement of code on specific resources and the management of deadlock. The latter is illustrated in the example above. The block parameter in the outer create says that no more than 4 threads should be allocated to a processor at any time. This allows resources to be allocated to the inner threads. If the *block* parameter had not been used and n was such that the outer loop exceeded the resources available on one processor, then no inner family threads could have been created and no outer thread could have completed, hence deadlock!

In general it is possible to create families of threads that exceed the resources available for their creation and the use of *block* allows those resources to be spread through a chain of creates to avoid or resource deadlock or to minimise inefficiency in virtualising resources in the hardware.

The *block* parameter can also be used to create a thread in a particular processor. A modification of the code in Section 3.5 can be made that creates the detached job on a specific processor. For example on p processors the following code would load the detached job onto the jth processor.

```
int fid1, fid2, j;
...
create(fid1;1;p;1;1){  /*loader - p processors*/
    index int i; shared int fid2;
    if (i = j)create(fid2)job();
    }
sync(fid1) /*family fid2 loaded on processor j*/
}
```

6 Cost Models

μTC will require a different cost model for each target and that model must be embedded in the compiler for the target. However, no attempt should be made to schedule threads in the μTC language, as this is counter to its philosophy. If the cost model dictates, compilers for a given target will create schedules for execution, either statically, as in the case of translating μTC to C, or dynamically as in the case of a microthreaded pipeline. It is important therefore not to carry over a cost model from the world of conventional software threads when writing an application in μTC.

For a microthreaded target no scheduling is necessary as the constructs in μTC map onto binary instructions and even a family of single-instruction threads can be created and scheduled with little or no overhead. In fact threaded code will often show super-linear speedup on a microthreaded processor [2] as thread index management is implemented in hardware and does not require the increment and test instructions to be generated as a part of the thread code, would be the case if the thread were executed as a loop.

7 Conclusions

A language μTC has been defined and is currently being implemented using gcc targeting microthreaded chip-multiprocessors. Prior work has used hand-compiled code kernels to produce the results published in [2]. The analysis involved in developing this language has allowed us to extend the microthreading model to capture recursive concurrency and our CMP simulator has been updated to reflect the semantics captured by this. With a μTC compiler and this updated simulator it will be possible to be simulate much more significant benchmarks, as well as supporting work within the AETHER project.

The main difference between this and prior work is that μTC code is schedule invariant and based on the following assumptions:

- There is a synchronising memory, which is limited in size and which holds local scalar variables. This memory is used to synchronise between executing threads and between a thread and the shared non-synchronising memory.
- The latter is assumed to have arbitrary delay and to be bulk synchronous with respect to a given family of threads.
- Local synchronising memory is shared to provide communication between threads. This sharing however, is restricted to linear chains, which reflect the locality of communication in silicon.

N.b. the model could be generalised to provide planar local sharing, or indeed arbitrary communication between threads. However, the simplest model has been adopted until the necessity of generalising it further it can be shown.

We already have an interpreter for μTC, which creates a static sequential schedule from it in C, which can be compiled to any target and we are currently working on two compilers, one from μTC to microthreaded binaries and the other a parallelising compiler from C to μTC. Collaborators from Hertfordshire University are working on compilers from Snet and SAC to μTC.

Acknowledgements

I would like to acknowledge input in the form of discussions on µTC from Thomas Bernard, Konstantinos Bousias, Peter Knijnenburg and Mike Lankamp (University of Amsterdam) and Sven-bodo Scholz (University of Hertfordshire). Support for this research is gratefully acknowledged from NWO in funding the MicroGrids project and from the European Union in funding the AETHER project. Without their support, this work would not have been possible.

References

[1] Jesshope C. R. (2005) Microthreading – a model for distributed instruction-level concurrency, to be published, *Parallel processing Letters*, see: http:// staff. science. uva. nl/~jesshope/Papers/µ-thread.pdf.

[2] Bousias, K, Hasasneh N M and Jesshope C R (2006) Instruction-level parallelism through microthreading - a scalable Approach to chip multiprocessors, *Computer Journal*, **49** (2), pp 211-233.

[3] OpenMP (2005) *OpenMP Version 2.5 Specification*, (accessed 16/4/2006), http://www. openmp.org/drupal/mp-documents/draft_spec25.pdf.

[4] E A Lee (2006) The Problem With Threads, *IEEE Computer*, **36**, (5), May 2006, pp 33-42.

[5] X Tian, M Girkar , A Bik and H Saito (2005) Practical Compiler Techniques on Efficient Multithreaded Code Generation for OpenMP Programs, *The Computer Journal*, **48**(5), pp588-601.

[6] Sven-Bodo Scholz (2003) Single Assignment C - Efficient Support for High-Level Array Operations in a Functional Setting, *Journal of Functional Programming*, **13**, (6) pp1005-1059.

[7] A.Shafarenko (2006) *The principles and construction of SNet*, Internal report, Dept of Computer Science, University of Hertfordshire.

[8] Bousias, K. and Jesshope, C. R. (2005) The challenges of massive on-chip concurrency. *Tenth Asia-Pacific Computer Systems Architecture Conference*, Singapore, October 24-26. LNCS 3740, pp. 157-170. Springer-Verlag.

Functional Unit Chaining: A Runtime Adaptive Architecture for Reducing Bypass Delays

Lih Wen Koh and Oliver Diessel

School of Computer Science & Engineering,
The University of New South Wales, Sydney, Australia
Embedded, Real-Time, and Operating Systems (ERTOS) Program,
National ICT Australia*

Abstract. Bypass delays are expected to grow beyond 1ns as technology scales. These delays necessitate pipelining of bypass paths at processor frequencies above 1GHz and thus affect the performance of sequential code sequences. We propose dealing with these delays through a dynamic functional unit chaining approach. We study the performance benefits of a superscalar, out-of-order processor augmented with a two-by-two array of ALUs interconnected by a fast, partial bypass network. An online profiler guides the automatic configuration of the network to accelerate specific patterns of dependent instructions. A detailed study of benchmark simulations demonstrates these first steps towards mapping binaries to a small coarse-grained array at runtime can improve instruction throughput by over 18% and 25% when the microarchitecure includes bypass delays of one cycle and two cycles, respectively.

1 Introduction

The datapath of a microprocessor includes *bypass* (also known as forwarding) paths that route computed results among the register file, data cache and execution units. These bypass paths are typically routed in higher-level metal layers [10] with resistance and capacitance delays that increase with the scaling of feature size [2]. Thus, under continuous scaling of feature size and processor frequency, the performance of future processors is increasingly limited by the wire delays associated with bypassing for data-dependent sequences [9]. Several approaches have been suggested over the past decade to cope with this problem.

The best known approach focuses on reducing bypass latency through bypass hierarchy, as seen in clustered architectures [8,9] where each cluster contains a small number of functional units interconnected via a fast local bypass network. Data-dependent sequences are ideally steered into the same cluster to make use of the faster intra-cluster bypass.

Self-forwarding arithmetic & logic units (ALUs) with closed loop bypass were introduced in NetBurst [4] and Sassone's work in [12] to efficiently execute linear dependent chains. Sassone uses the self-forwarding ALUs to compute results for

---

* National ICT Australia is funded through the Australian Government's *Backing Australia's Ability* initiative, in part through the Australian Research Council.

C. Jesshope and C. Egan (Eds.): ACSAC 2006, LNCS 4186, pp. 161–174, 2006.

transient chains of sequences, where the intermediate results in the chain are only ever consumed once by the immediate successor instruction. Intermediate results are not forwarded after use but are simply discarded. The applicability of this approach is limited to situations where the transient rule is known to hold.

As an alternative approach, hardware/software partitioning speeds up execution by collapsing a sequence of operations into an atomic operation. This approach shortens the critical path of sequential operations and absorbs result bypasses into custom circuits. Typically, this is achieved by Application Specific Integrated Circuits (ASIC) co-processors in the embedded domain, whereas fine-grained units in the form of Field Programmable Gate Arrays (FPGA) are employed in reconfigurable microprocessors as configurable functional units in the datapath or as coprocessors attached to the memory or system bus. Traditionally, sequences that can be collapsed are identified at compile time. Runtime analysis has recently been introduced by Stitt *et. al.* [13] and Yehia *et. al.* [14] to support a more dynamic system. Nevertheless, FPGAs come with high synthesis and runtime reconfiguration costs.

In contrast to previous approaches, we propose the acceleration of program binaries through the mapping of data-dependent sequences to a small array of coarse-grained structures at runtime. We add to a superscalar, out-of-order processor an execution unit called the *chained* integer ALU (CIALU) which consists of a two-by-two array of closely-packed ALU cells (Fig. 1).

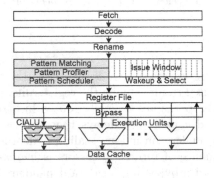

Fig. 1. A MIPS-like architecture (adapted from [9]) enhanced with a CIALU and modules (shown as grey blocks) to support runtime analysis of dataflow patterns

By reorganizing the floorplan and reorienting the ALU cells, we show that a fast, partial internal bypass network quickly routes results among the cells. Runtime analysis is a natural choice to make efficient use of the CIALU. An online profiler tracks the relative frequency of specific dataflow patterns over time to guide the CIALU configuration. Significant shifts in the profile history lead to reassessment of the configuration choice, providing a CIALU that adapts to various dataflow patterns over successive periods of execution.

Our results demonstrate that a partial internal bypass network is sufficient to handle the small set of data-dependent patterns commonly seen at runtime. In comparison to the full local bypass network in clustered architectures, the smaller size of our partial network results in lower capacitive loads and faster operations. Overheads associated with collapsing sequences and mapping them to FPGAs do not apply in our design, but some overheads incurred by runtime analysis remain. The runtime nature of our design achieves binary compatibility for pre-compiled code and offers performance benefits without exposing application developers to additional design complexity.

In Section 2, we provide an architectural overview of our design and a normalized model of typical integer ALUs that forms the basis of our timing characterization of the CIALU. We describe in Sect. 3 our experimental framework based on the SimpleScalar toolset [3]. Our results are presented in Sect. 4. We conclude with an assessment of our results and our plans for future work in Sect. 5.

2   Proposed Architecture

2.1   Supported Dataflow Patterns

Our CIALU is a two-by-two array of integer ALU cells tightly interconnected via an internal bypass network. Assuming a full internal bypass network, the CIALU structure supports execution for a variety of dataflow patterns. Figure 2 depicts some of these patterns as nodes and edges. Each node in the pattern may correspond to an instruction in the processor's issue queue and each directed edge represents dataflow between two nodes. A CIALU with a full internal bypass network can support indefinitely long patterns, where up to three outgoing edges for results forwarding are allowed for each node in the pattern. We use the term *branching pattern* to refer to a pattern with more than one incoming or outgoing edge for any of its nodes, such as patterns 2b, 2c and 3b. We note that pattern 1a simply represents up to four parallel operations with no data dependencies. In our experiments, we consider a small subset that covers all possible data-dependent patterns of up to four nodes. Our analysis of the benefits of accelerating patterns 2a, 2b, 2c, 2d, 2e, 3a, 3b and 4a is reported in Sect. 4.

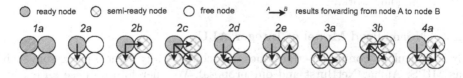

Fig. 2. An array of four integer ALUs with low-latency internal bypasses can support a variety of data-dependent patterns

2.2   Architecture Overview

The CIALU is an execution unit in the integer datapath of a superscalar, out-of-order processor. Figure 1 illustrates our model based on the MIPS architecture. We enhance the baseline model with a CIALU and three modules that support runtime analysis of dataflow patterns: the *pattern matching* circuit, the *pattern profiler* and the *pattern scheduler*.

Initially, the processor executes a binary just as normal. The pattern profiler monitors the integer issue queue entries for instances of the supported dataflow patterns. A pattern instance is detected when the pattern matching circuit is able to map one or more ready-to-execute instructions to some of the nodes of a particular pattern, and all other nodes of the pattern are semi-ready, i.e. waiting only on the results that will be forwarded by the ready instructions. A dataflow pattern is merely characterized by the relationship of data dependencies. Thus the actual operation (e.g. addition, subtraction or logical operation) of each pattern node may vary.

The profiler updates a count history to reflect the relative frequencies of each dataflow pattern over a period of execution. Based on the count history, the profiler selects a CIALU configuration that appears most beneficial for the next period. A CIALU configuration involves setting multiplexer select signals to internally route results among the ALU cells according to the interconnection required by the selected pattern mapping.

When the next instance of the selected mapping is matched, the pattern scheduler takes over the normal integer scheduler. Each instruction in the pattern instance is scheduled to the CIALU in the order enforced by data dependencies. If the CIALU is requested but not ready to accept new operations, scheduling is handed back to the normal integer scheduler. Execution of ready instructions then falls back onto the processor's fixed ALUs.

In our architecture model, the CIALU is able to replace some of the processors' fixed integer ALUs. Therefore, the number of register file ports need not increase. Currently, we are studying the integration of the runtime analysis modules into the processor's issue logic. The performance gains of our design may be partially offset by the overheads of these modules. In this paper, we assume negligible overheads for the runtime analysis modules and we measure the performance benefits of the CIALU to save bypass cycles for dataflow patterns with dependencies. A detailed characterization of the runtime overheads will be part of our on-going work.

2.3   Normalized Model of Integer ALUs

It is difficult to compare performance of architecturally diverse processors such as MIPS, Alpha, NetBurst and our proposal. We therefore propose an execution performance model in which delays of various architectures are normalized against clock ticks. Execution times therefore need to be compared on the basis of number of clock cycles and clock frequency.

Our normalized model of an integer ALU has the following characteristics: *computation latency*, C; *bypass latency*, B; and *issue latency* (or initiation rate),

R. In the case of the single-issue processor in Fig. 3(a), the bypass path feeds the ALU output back to its own input as well as routing the ALU output to the register file for result writeback. Normally, execution and forwarding (C + B) fits into a single processor clock cycle. As processor frequency increases, the ALU logic and/or the bypass path have to be pipelined to meet the requirement of the clock frequency. We expect the pipelined ALU will continue to have an initiation rate of one cycle, i.e. R = 1.

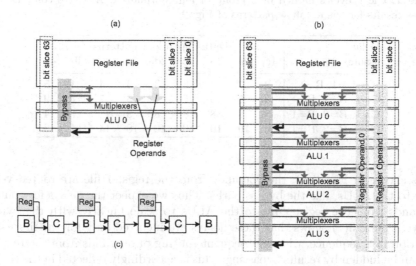

Fig. 3. Layout of the integer datapath for (a) a single-issue processor and (b) a multiple-issue processor. (c) shows the timeline of pattern 3a executed on a group of four normalized ALUs with parameters C=1, B=1 and R=1.

Figure 3(b) shows a typical bit-sliced, linear layout of a multiple-issue processor datapath with four integer ALUs. For a multiple-issue processor, the bypass paths span all ALUs. Similar to the single-issue case, (C + B) fits into a processor clock cycle at relatively low clock frequencies. However, as processor frequency increases, the ALU logic and/or the bypass path have to be pipelined.

While logic and local wires scale according to feature size, wires routed in higher metal levels grow slowly in speed relative to logic [5]. Authors have different opinions on whether the bypass paths for multi-issue ALUs are local wires routed in low-level metal layers [5] or more global wires routed in higher-level metal layers [10]. The assumption that bypass paths are local wires implies that C = B regardless of the scaling of feature size. On the other hand, although the bypass wires are unlikely to be routed in the topmost metal level as the global clock signal does, we lean towards the assumption that the bypass paths are routed in higher metal levels such that the values of B will grow relatively more quickly with respect to C, i.e. C < B. Nevertheless, we derive ALU timing models with values of C and B as shown in Table 1 to cover both design views. We also list in Table 1 the number of cycles needed for register access, execution and writeback/forwarding, for each of the dataflow patterns from Fig. 2, scheduled to a group of four ALUs. For example, Fig. 3(c) illustrates the execution timeline of pattern 3a on a group of four normalized ALUs with C=1, B=1 and R=1. The motivation behind our design is to eliminate the bypass delays found between the dependent computations.

Table 1. Clock cycles needed by a group of four normalized ALUs to compute and bypass results for the dataflow patterns of Fig. 2

Delay assumption	Data-dependent patterns								
	1a	2a	2b	2c	2d	2e	3a	3b	4a
C + B=1, R=1	2	3	3	3	3	3	4	4	5
C=1, B=1, R=1	3	5	5	5	5	5	7	7	9
C=1, B=2, R=1	5	8	8	8	8	8	11	11	14
C=2, B=2, R=1	6	10	10	10	10	10	14	14	18

As shown in Fig. 3(b), the operands from the register file are routed vertically to the ALUs, like the bypass paths. Thus we expect the delays for routing operands from the register file to the ALUs to scale linearly with the bypass delays. Figure 3(c) shows that these delays are incurred only for the first computation in a sequence, where subsequent routing of operands from the register file can be hidden by results bypassing. This is accordingly reflected in the timing calculations for Tables 1 and 2.

2.4   CIALU Model

Our CIALU model comprises a two-by-two array of cells, organized to optimize the internal bypass paths. The CIALU has the following characteristics: *computation latency* of each cell, C; *global bypass latency*, B; *internal bypass latency*, I and *issue latency* (or initiation rate), R. Each of the cells in the CIALU is a fully-fledged ALU, with similar latency scaling trends to the normalized ALU model described in Sect. 2.3. The *global bypass* paths of the CIALU are the usual paths that feed the cell results back to the register file, the cache and other functional units in the processor's datapath. We use the term *global bypass* here to differentiate from the *internal bypass* paths, which are shorter wires in lower level metals that route results between the cells in the CIALU.

The CIALU structure accelerates computation sequences where global bypass paths are normally in use. The tight internal bypass interconnect within the CIALU quickly feeds the cells with pending operands. The number of execution cycles for each dataflow pattern scheduled to a CIALU is listed in Table 2. The bracketed values show the savings in global bypass cycles over a typical multi-issue processor with four normalized ALUs of equivalent parameters, as assessed in Table 1. We note that an aggressive, four-cell CIALU has the same performance as a group of four normalized ALUs when executing instances of

Table 2. Timing model for a CIALU with an initiation rate of one clock cycle

Delay assumption	Data-dependent patterns							
	2a	2b	2c	2d	2e	3a	3b	4a
C=1, B=1, I=0	4 (1)	4 (1)	4 (1)	4 (1)	4 (1)	5 (2)	5 (2)	6 (3)
C=1, B=2, I=0	6 (2)	6 (2)	6 (2)	6 (2)	6 (2)	7 (4)	7 (4)	8 (6)
C=1, B=2, I=1	7 (1)	7 (1)	7 (1)	7 (1)	7 (1)	9 (2)	9 (2)	10 (3)
C=2, B=2, I=0	8 (2)	8 (2)	8 (2)	8 (2)	8 (2)	10 (4)	10 (4)	12 (6)
C=2, B=2, I=1	9 (1)	9 (1)	9 (1)	9 (1)	9 (1)	12 (2)	12 (2)	15 (3)

pattern 1a because there is no need to wait for results to be forwarded via the global bypass paths.

The internal and global bypass paths essentially form a bypass hierarchy, where I < B. For processors with B > 1, we consider two models: an aggressive CIALU model where the internal bypass delays are absorbed into the computation latency such that I=0; and a conservative model with I=1. Figures 4(a) and 4(b) illustrate the execution timelines of pattern 3a on each of these models.

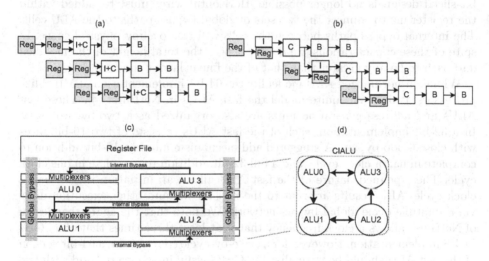

Fig. 4. Timeline for pattern 3a executed on (a) an aggressive CIALU model with C=1, B=2, I=0, R=1 and (b) on a conservative model with C=1, B=2, I=1, R=1. (c) shows the floorplan of the CIALU and (d) a high-level view of its internal bypass network.

Figure 4(c) shows the layout of our final CIALU design. The dataflow orientation of each ALU cell is chosen to minimize the internal bypass routing between the cells for the most prevalent patterns (2a, 2b, 2e, 3a and 4a) as indicated by our results in Sect. 4. For example, pattern 2e may be mapped as ALU0 → ALU1 and ALU2 → ALU3, whereas pattern 3a may be mapped as ALU0 → ALU1 and ALU1 → ALU2.

Our design essentially restricts the full bypass network to a partial interconnection network as shown in Fig. 4(d). This partial interconnection network allows the mapping of indefinitely long patterns, where up to two outgoing edges are allowed for each of the pattern nodes. As a result, patterns 2c and 3b cannot be efficiently executed on the CIALU. However, both are relatively infrequent and are simply extensions to pattern 2b. They can thus be scheduled without loss of performance as an instance of pattern 2b and an additional operation.

The set of supported dataflow patterns do not utilize all four of the CIALU cells simultaneously. Thus some of the cells in the CIALU may be idle in a particular clock cycle. Each of these free cells functions just like an integer ALU, and therefore may accept ready-to-execute integer operations. Furthermore, the CIALU's issue latency of one cycle allows the scheduling of a new pattern instance, if available, on a per cycle basis. Scheduling constraints may occur when there is a conflict of cell mappings for two pattern instances. For example, pattern 2e cannot be scheduled to the CIALU on the third execution cycle of pattern 3a due to a cell mapping conflict on ALU2. In this case, the scheduling of pattern 2e is delayed by a further cycle.

A two-dimensional organization of the ALU cells implies that a completely bit-sliced design is no longer possible. Horizontal wires must be added within the register file to connect the two sets of global bypass paths to the ALU cells. The internal bypass paths between the cells will also occupy physical space. In spite of these considerations, we do not expect the total height of the modified datapath to be any greater than that of the linear layout shown in Fig. 3(b).

While our normalized ALU model fits the 64-bit implementation of MIPS-like processors, it does not quite model the fast ALUs in NetBurst [4]. These fast ALUs and address generation units are also organized as a two-by-two array. In a 32-bit implementation, each of the fast ALUs consists of two 16-bit slices with closed-loop bypass. A staggered add mechanism allows a 16-bit addition to complete in half a clock cycle, and a full 32-bit addition to complete in one clock cycle. The pipelined nature of the fast ALU allows an initiation rate of half a clock cycle. ALU results are sent to the register file and other execution units via a multiple cycle global bypass network. We note that the aggressive design of NetBurst allows a clock frequency that is at least three times that of a 1GHz MIPS implementation. However, for a cycle-by-cycle comparison, a 64-bit version of the fast ALU should be normalized to $C=2$ (assuming staggered add with two 32-bit slices), an optimistic value of $B=2$, $I=0$ and $R=1$. The normalized fast ALUs are able to execute indefinitely long linear chains of dependent operations such as patterns 2a, 2e, 3a and 4a in the same time as the CIALU model listed in the fourth row of Table 2. However, the timing of the fourth row of Table 1 applies for the other branching patterns.

3   Experimental Setup

We use the cycle-accurate SimpleScalar [3] *out-of-order* simulator to evaluate the impact of varying processor configurations on the performance of our design.

Global bypass delays, B, are added as a parameter to the *out-of-order* simulator. The CIALU is also added as an integer functional unit, with a default issue latency of one cycle (R=1), a parametrizable computation latency, C, and a parametrizable internal bypass delay, I. We considered four-way and eight-way baseline and enhanced processor configurations in which the total number of ALUs corresponds to the issue width of the processor. Table 3 lists the non-default parameter settings of interest.

The mechanism of the pattern matching circuit, pattern profiler and scheduler are as described in Sect. 2.2. The modified simulator implements an architecture where the runtime analysis modules do not incur any overheads and the size of the profile window is set to one instruction. This setting allows us to measure the performance gains contributed by the ability of our CIALU to save bypass cycles for dependent patterns.

Table 3. Non-default processor configurations for *sim-outorder*

Parameters	4-way Baseline	4-way Enhanced	8-way Baseline	8-way Enhanced
Register Update Unit size	16	16	32	32
Load/Store Queue size	8	8	16	16
Number of ALUs	4	0	8	4
Number of CIALUs	0	1	0	1
Computation latency of an ALU	1/2	1/2	1/2	1/2
Computation latency of a CIALU	1/2	1/2	1/2	1/2
Global bypass delay	0/1/2	1/2	0/1/2	1/2
Internal bypass delay of a CIALU	n/a	0/1	n/a	0/1

We performed simulations for benchmarks selected from the SPEC2000 [1] and MediaBench [7] suites. We included program binaries we were able to compile for SimpleScalar's Portable Instruction Set Architecture (PISA) model. The input sets packaged with the MediaBench benchmarks were used to run the programs to completion. The SPEC2000 benchmarks were run using the MinneSPEC [6] inputs, favoured for their smaller sizes. All performance figures reported, unless otherwise stated, are averages of the results obtained over the applications in each benchmark set.

4   Results and Analysis

4.1   Prevalence of Dataflow Patterns at Runtime

In order to determine the prevalence of the dataflow patterns of interest, we disabled the runtime profiler and fixed the CIALU configuration for a particular pattern for the entire execution of a program. Pattern instances matched at runtime are scheduled to the CIALU. The processors' fixed ALUs (if any) and idle CIALU cells were used for the execution of parallel integer operations. For pattern 1a, our choice of parameters yields the same settings for both the baseline and enhanced processors. Thus, no performance gains are expected from pattern 1a.

From Table 4, we observe that linear chains of dependent sequences (patterns 2a, 2e, 3a and 4a) are most prevalent at runtime. For four-way processors, up to 45.92% of integer operations are scheduled as pattern 2a, achieving an Instructions Per Cycle (IPC) gain of 13.05%. Patterns 2b and 3b which involve results bypassing to two pending operations are less frequent, with a frequency of up to 7.62% and an IPC gain of 2.23%. Patterns 2c and 2d account for approximately 1% of integer instructions for four-way processors. Clearly, patterns 2c, 2d and even 3b do not contribute much to the overall performance benefits of the CIALU. While similar trends are observed for eight-way processors, the larger processor bandwidth allows more patterns to be mapped at runtime, achieving a slightly better performance speedup.

Table 4. Percentage of integer operations scheduled to the CIALU (*op2cialu*) and Instructions Per Cycle (IPC) gain (%) achieved by processors enhanced with a CIALU (C=1, B=1, I=0 and R=1) fixed to accelerate the given pattern for the entire execution of a program

Data-dependent patterns	MediaBench				SPEC2000			
	4-way		8-way		4-way		8-way	
	op2cialu	Gain	*op2cialu*	Gain	*op2cialu*	Gain	*op2cialu*	Gain
2a	45.92	13.05	55.18	14.11	35.64	8.71	41.24	9.21
2b	7.62	2.23	13.41	3.31	6.22	1.16	9.82	1.62
2c	0.92	0.23	2.37	0.23	1.09	0.24	4.54	0.59
2d	0.87	0.13	1.43	0.19	0.72	0.09	0.97	0.13
2e	14.67	3.07	32.56	6.80	12.86	3.78	21.88	5.16
3a	24.22	10.86	33.16	13.39	21.73	10.33	25.73	11.92
3b	3.69	1.62	9.15	3.90	2.68	0.74	5.25	2.01
4a	11.91	6.49	16.79	14.70	6.45	2.97	9.59	4.67

4.2   A Runtime Adaptive CIALU

Here we attempted to gain a sense of the benefit of a CIALU which is able to adapt its internal bypass paths to match dataflow patterns at runtime. Due to the profile window size of one instruction, more than one dataflow pattern may be matched in a given clock cycle. Thus, a simple greedy priority scheme was used. Priority was given to ready instances of patterns that offered the greatest savings of bypass cycles and then to those that used the highest number of cells in the CIALU. Thus, ready instances of pattern 4a were given precedence over patterns 3a, 2e, 2d, 2b, and 2a, in that order. Our CIALU design in Fig. 4(c) excludes patterns 2c and 3b due to the limitation of the partial internal bypass network. The results from Sect. 4.1 show that the low frequencies of patterns 2c and 3b allow us to reschedule both patterns as pattern 2b without loss of performance. The CIALU's issue latency of one cycle allows the scheduling of a new pattern instance on a per cycle basis, subject to the scheduling constraint discussed in Sect. 2.4.

Table 5 lists for each benchmark the IPC gains for a four-way enhanced processor. Similar to the CIALU with fixed configurations in Sect.4.1, instances of pattern 2a are most frequent in many of our benchmarks, followed by pattern 3a, 4a, 2e, 2b and 2d. However, slightly different trends are observed for the *epic* and *301.apsi* applications.

Table 5. IPC gains (%) and breakdown of pattern frequencies (%) for a four-way processor enhanced with a runtime adaptive CIALU (C=1, B=1, I=0, R=1)

Benchmarks	Gain	Data-dependent patterns					
		2a	2b	2d	2e	3a	4a
MediaBench							
adpcm.enc	21.45	16.57	0.31	1.56	12.21	12.42	15.56
adpcm.dec	16.73	14.54	0.47	0.00	12.12	22.00	5.27
epic.enc	2.74	20.65	0.15	0.02	2.50	4.62	0.25
epic.dec	5.68	13.35	1.81	0.02	7.74	8.59	0.67
g721.enc	18.80	24.27	2.84	0.14	9.87	10.65	7.62
g721.dec	16.53	22.55	3.29	0.28	10.13	9.58	7.59
jpeg.enc	24.00	14.42	1.07	0.76	9.67	19.56	7.52
jpeg.dec	29.04	11.69	0.52	0.02	4.39	19.51	18.31
mpeg2.enc	13.23	14.38	13.29	1.03	3.10	9.28	4.20
mpeg2.dec	15.23	14.98	0.87	0.01	1.64	14.84	13.74
pegwit.enc	27.01	10.47	3.58	1.11	5.02	17.87	16.43
pegwit.dec	26.32	11.64	3.11	0.37	4.83	18.46	15.22
average	18.06	15.79	2.61	0.44	6.93	13.95	9.36
SPEC2000							
171.swim	10.98	14.83	1.61	0.00	3.70	8.53	5.00
173.applu	18.42	17.70	1.29	0.05	3.38	16.76	15.95
176.gcc	7.18	12.29	2.84	1.24	3.46	7.91	3.85
181.mcf	5.12	13.73	3.02	0.01	1.62	5.31	9.62
188.ammp	3.14	17.47	4.13	0.13	3.48	3.96	1.91
197.parser	10.73	16.57	9.97	0.55	2.61	3.18	1.15
301.apsi	42.49	2.57	0.18	0.01	0.32	65.92	1.15
average	14.01	13.59	3.29	0.28	2.65	15.94	5.52

The *epic* benchmark recorded an unusually low percentage (<1%) of pattern 4a at runtime, in contrast to the average 11.92% for the other applications in MediaBench. Pattern 4a is the longest chain in the set of patterns we analyzed and instances of this pattern can potentially save the largest number of global bypass cycles. The low frequency of pattern 4a yields the low IPC gains of 2.74% and 5.68% for the *epic* encoder and decoder applications, respectively. As for *301.apsi*, 65.92% of operations scheduled to the CIALU belong to instances of pattern 3a, but less than 3% correspond to pattern 2a. The larger number of global bypass cycles saved by pattern 3a contributes to a large IPC gain of 42.49% for *301.apsi*.

4.3   Impact of Global Bypass Delays

Table 6 reports on the impact of global bypass delays on both baseline and enhanced processors. As we expect, IPC decreases as both register access delays and global bypass delays are increased from zero to two clock cycles. The decrease in IPC can be partly compensated for by the higher processor frequency possible with the pipelining of the ALUs and/or the global bypass paths. For ease of comparison, we report our results in terms of IPC.

We also observe that the additional instruction issue bandwidth provided by eight-way processors is insufficient to compensate for the loss of IPC caused by the gradual increase in the global bypass delays, due to the prevalence of dependent data patterns in the benchmark applications. For example, a baseline eight-way processor with ALUs of parameters C=1 and B=1 achieved an IPC of 1.1487, which is a slowdown of 30.9% compared to a baseline four-way processor with ALUs of parameters C=1 and B=0.

Table 6. IPC and IPC gains (%) for processors with different global bypass delays

Delay assumption	MediaBench				SPEC2000			
	4-way		8-way		4-way		8-way	
	IPC	Gain	IPC	Gain	IPC	Gain	IPC	Gain
Baseline								
C=1, B=0	1.6634	n/a	2.1778	n/a	1.2720	n/a	1.5408	n/a
C=1, B=1	0.8715	n/a	1.1487	n/a	0.7175	n/a	0.8875	n/a
C=1, B=2	0.5810	n/a	0.7646	n/a	0.5002	n/a	0.6197	n/a
C=2, B=2	0.5125	n/a	0.6812	n/a	0.4526	n/a	0.5616	n/a
Enhanced								
C=1, B=1, I=0	1.0083	18.06	1.3612	20.43	0.8206	14.01	1.0205	15.25
C=1, B=2, I=0	0.7160	25.77	0.9789	29.67	0.6006	20.59	0.7506	22.45
C=2, B=2, I=0	0.6211	23.18	0.8394	25.83	0.5339	18.49	0.6700	20.29

4.4   Impact of Internal Bypass Delays of the CIALU

The timing model of the CIALU (Table 2) shows that the aggressive model saves twice as many global bypass cycles as the conservative model. This is reflected in the performance reported in Table 7 which indicates that the IPC gains for the aggressive model are roughly doubled that of the conservative model. The results also indicate that our design benefits both four-way and eight-way processors, achieving IPC gains of up to 25.77% and 29.67%, respectively.

Table 7. IPC gains (%) for the aggressive and conservative CIALU models

Delay assumption	MediaBench		SPEC2000	
	4-way	8-way	4-way	8-way
C=1, B=2, I=0 *(aggressive)*	25.77	29.67	20.59	22.45
C=1, B=2, I=1 *(conservative)*	13.38	15.47	10.93	12.20
C=2, B=2, I=0 *(aggressive)*	23.18	25.83	18.49	20.29
C=2, B=2, I=1 *(conservative)*	12.12	13.91	10.03	11.05

5 Conclusion and Future Work

In this paper we studied the benefits of allowing the functional units of a modern microprocessor to reorganize themselves into connected structures to reduce delays in forwarding results to dependent operations. These delays are expected to increase to several clock cycles and substantially limit instruction throughput of superscalar architectures as process technology and clock periods continue to decrease. We proposed adding to a superscalar, dynamically scheduled processor a functional assembly we refer to as a chained functional unit (CIALU), a two-by-two array of fully-fledged integer ALUs with a fast, partial interconnection network. The network is configured to simultaneously bypass results between the ALUs with minimal delay. At high execution initiation rates, this structure allows long chains of linearly dependent operations and more complex branching dataflow patterns to be accelerated. The CIALU is dynamically configured for the dataflow pattern identified through runtime profiling of the executing binary. Over a defined number of subsequent cycles, instances of the configured pattern are sought out in the issue queue and mapped to the configured CIALU. During this period the dataflow patterns present in the queue are monitored to reassess the configuration choice and adapt to changes in the pattern distribution.

The diverse collection of existing architectures with disparate clock frequencies and computational output per cycle presented the problem of comparing the performance results of our proposal with these architectures. To overcome this problem, we proposed a normalized timing model that takes into account the number of clock cycles needed for register accesses, execution, results bypassing and writebacks. The model was then used to derive the relative execution performance of architectures such as MIPS, NetBurst and our proposed CIALU. We thereby laid the groundwork for a high fidelity SimpleScalar simulation of these architectures executing a variety of common benchmarks.

Our analysis of the results indicates that non-branching, linear chains of operations are by far the most prevalent dependent dataflow patterns found in the issue queue of pending instructions. These contributed most to speedups. We found that a four-way processor that has its four integer ALUs replaced by a CIALU with an internal forwarding delay of zero cycle and a global bypass delay of one cycle is capable of boosting the number of instructions executed per cycle by approximately 18% for MediaBench, and approximately 14% for the MinneSPEC inputs for SPEC2000. The improvements on these benchmarks rise towards 30% when an eight-way processor is enhanced and as bypass delays increase to two cycles. Unfortunately, the contribution to performance improvement due to branching dataflow patterns is relatively small. They accounted for less than 10% of the dataflow patterns accelerated by our system.

Our on-going work will include profiling entire loop bodies, deriving the dataflow graphs and mapping them at runtime to larger coarse-grained arrays. We are also interested to investigate how our results will vary for in-order, soft-core processors targetted to FPGAs for embedded applications.

References

1. CPU SPEC2000 Benchmarks. http://www.spec.org
2. International Technology Roadmap for Semiconductors. http://www.itrs.net
3. The SimpleScalar Toolset. http://www.simplescalar.com
4. G. Hinton, D. Sager, M. Upton, D. Boggs, D. Carmean, A. Kyker, and P. Roussel. The Microarchitecture of the Pentium 4 Processor. Intel Technology Journal Q1, 2001.
5. R. Ho, K. Mai, and M. Horowitz. The Future of Wires. In the Proceedings of the IEEE, April 2001, pp. 490-504.
6. A. J. KleinOsowski, and D. J. Lilja. MinneSPEC: A New SPEC Benchmark Workload for Simulation-Based Computer Architecture Research. Computer Architecture Letters, Volume 1, June 2002.
7. C. Lee, M. Potkonjak, and W. H. Mangione-Smith. MediaBench: A Tool for Evaluating and Synthesizing Multimedia and Communications Systems. International Symposium on Microarchitecture, 1997, pp. 330-335.
8. M. Matson, D. Bailey, S. Bell, L. Biro, S. Butler, J. Clouser, J. Farrell, M. Gowan, D. Priore, and K. Wilcox. Circuit Implementation of a 600MHz Superscalar RISC Microprocessor. International Conference on Computer Design, October 1998, pp. 104-110.
9. S. Palacharla, N. P. Jouppi, and J. E. Smith. Complexity-Effective Superscalar Processor. In Proceedings of the 24th Annual International Symposium on Computer Architecture (ISCA), 1997, pp. 206-218.
10. J. M. Rabaey, A. Chandrakasan, and B. Nikolic. Digital Integrated Circuits: A Design Perspective. Prentice-Hall, Second Edition, 2003.
11. P. G. Sassone, and D. S. Wills. Multi-cycle Broadcast Bypass: Too Readily Overlooked. In Proceedings of the Workshop on Complexity-Effective Design (WCED), May 2004.
12. P. G. Sassone, and D. S. Wills. Dynamic Strands: Collapsing Speculative Dependence Chains for Reducing Pipeline Communication. International Symposium on Microarchitecture (MICRO), 2004, pp. 717.
13. G. Stitt, R. Lysecky, and F. Vahid. Dynamic Hardware/Software Partitioning: A First Approach. Design Automation Conference (DAC), 2003, pp. 250-255.
14. S. Yehia, and O. Temam. From Sequences of Dependent Instructions to Functions: A Complexity-Effective Approach for Improving Performance without ILP or Speculation. International Symposium on Computer Architecture (ISCA), 2004, pp. 238-249.

Trace-Based Data Cache Leakage Reduction at Link Time

Lian Li[1,2] and Jingling Xue[1,2]

[1] Programming Languages and Compilers Group, School of Computer Science and
Engineering, University of New South Wales, Sydney, NSW 2052, Australia
[2] National ICT Australia

Abstract. This paper investigates the benefits of conducting leakage energy optimisations for data caches at link time for embedded applications. We introduce an improved algorithm for identifying and constructing the traces in a binary program and present a trace-based optimisation for reducing leakage energy in data caches. Our experimental results using Mediabench benchmarks show that good leakage energy savings can be achieved at the cost of some small performance and code size penalties. Furthermore, by varying the granularity of optimisation regions, which is a tunable parameter, embedded application programmers can make the tradeoffs between energy savings and these associated costs.

1 Introduction

Leakage power dissipation is estimated to be around 10-15% of the total power dissipation in high-speed processes [6] and this fraction is projected to be the dominant part of the chip power budget beyond the 0.1 micron feature sizes [2]. Leakage energy consumption in caches is particularly significant since they contain a significant fraction of the on-chip transistors in a microprocessor. It is projected that leakage will represent more than 70% of the energy consumed in caches if left unchecked for the 0.07 micron process [10]. Therefore, reducing leakage energy for caches is of practical importance in modern microprocessors.

In our earlier work [12], we introduced a trace-based, link-time compilation framework for embedded systems and reported its benefits in reducing leakage energy on functional units. In this work, we investigate the benefits of supporting leakage energy optimisations on data caches in such a framework. In particular, we present an improved algorithm for constructing the traces in a binary program. Based the traces thus generated, we introduce a trace-based optimisation for reducing leakage energy on data caches. We present experimental evaluations of our optimisation using Mediabench benchmarks.

Guided by some execution profiling information, the frequently executed paths in a binary program are identified and duplicated as single-entry traces. Separating frequently from infrequently executed paths (spanning both user and library functions) at link time enables the compiler to focus energy optimisations on the hot traces (i.e., spots) across the whole program. The traces are further connected to form the so-called optimisation regions, where their entries and exits are less frequently executed than what are inside. To reduce the leakage energy on a cache in an optimisation region, the

C. Jesshope and C. Egan (Eds.): ACSAC 2006, LNCS 4186, pp. 175–188, 2006.

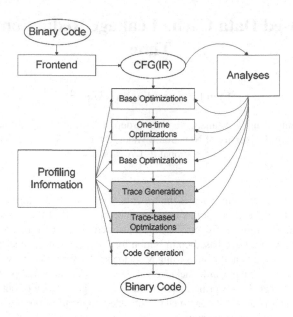

Fig. 1. A traced-based, link-time framework implemented in `alto` for the Alpha architecture

compiler invokes an appropriate architectural feature at the entries of the region to put the cache in an energy-saving mode and then restores the cache to its normal mode at its exits. Our experimental results using Mediabench programs show that significant leakage energy savings can be obtained at the cost of small execution time and code size increases. In addition, varying the granularity of optimisation regions makes it possible to make the tradeoffs between energy savings and these associated costs.

The rest of this paper is organised as follows. Section 2 introduces our trace-based methodology. In particular, we discuss an improved algorithm for identifying and constructing the traces in a binary program. Section 3 presents a traced-based optimisation for reducing leakage energy on caches. In Section 4, we evaluate this work with Mediabench benchmarks. Section 5 reviews the related work. Section 6 concludes the paper.

2   Trace-Based Methodology

Figure 1 depicts our trace-based framework for supporting energy-oriented optimisations on binaries. We have implemented it `alto`, a link-time optimiser for the Alpha architecture [15]. The two components we have added to `alto` are highlighted by the two boxes in gray. We refer to [12] for a description of the functionalities of all the components in the framework. Our framework supports static binary optimisations. The advantage is that no runtime system is needed. However, applications that use shared or runtime libraries cannot be handled. In addition, static binary translators such as `alto` [15] rely on the reallocation information from the linker to reconstruct a CFG from a binary file. So all relocatable addresses in the file must be identifiable.

```
1  #DEFINE BB_THRESHOLD = 5%
2  #DEFINE BB_MIN = the execution frequency of basic block bᵢ such that i
      is the largest satisfying: BB_THRESHOLD ⩾ (i/N) × 100(%), where
      b₁,...,b_N are the N basic blocks in the program sorted in the non-increasing
      order of their execution frequencies
3  #DEFINE BB_PROB = 50%

4  Boolean FUNCTION Hot(block)
5  return block.freq ⩾ BB_MIN × BB_PROB

6  PROCEDURE GenTrace()
7  Initialise headerlist with loop headers or
      function entry blocks h such that
           h.freq ⩾ BB_MIN
8  while headerlist is not empty
9      header = block h removed from headerlist such that h.freq is the largest (by
           favouring a tieing candidate that is a successor of a trace exit in order
           to create well-connected traces)
10     Identify the trace starting from header h
11     Duplicate the trace in the program
12     UpdateHeaderList(headerlist)

13 PROCEDURE UpdateHeaderList(headerlist)
14 Remove every block b from headerlist
      such that Hot(b) does not hold
15 for every successor block s of a trace exit
16     if s is not in a trace such that Hot(s) holds
17        Add s to headerlist
```

Fig. 2. A static trace generation algorithm

Let us present an improved algorithm of [12] for identifying and constructing the traces in a binary program. A *trace* is a frequently executed path in a binary program. Such a trace may cross function boundaries. The first (basic) block in a trace is called a *trace header*. A block in a trace is called a *trace exit* if it has one successor block that is not in a trace. Based on profiling information, the frequently executed paths in the CFG of a program are identified and duplicated as single-entry traces. Thus, a trace t_1 can only branch into a trace t_2, where t_1 and t_2 may be identical, via the trace header of t_2. Single-entry traces allow compiler optimisations to be easily applied. In [12], we presented an algorithm for constructing the traces in binaries. We give a high-level sketch of that algorithm in Figure 2 and describe three improvements we have made.

Our algorithm identifies and builds the hot traces in a program by making use of three profiling-related parameters, which are defined in lines 1 – 3. In fact, BB_THRESHOLD is introduced only to define BB_MIN, which, together with BB_PROB, are used explicitly in our algorithm. These three parameters serve the following purposes. Initially, our algorithm starts with loop headers or function entries b that are potential trace headers only when $b.freq \geqslant$ BB_MIN, where $b.freq$ is the (profiled) execution frequency of block b (line 7). When a trace grows, the blocks that join the trace become progressively non-larger in terms of their execution frequencies. However, every block that appears in a trace must be hot. A block b is *hot* if the predicate $Hot(b)$ defined in lines 4 – 5 evaluates to true, i.e., if $b.freq \geqslant$ BB_MIN $\times$ BB_PROB. In addition, a block b does not belong to a trace if its execution frequency has dropped below BB_PROB(%) of the execution frequency of the header of that trace.

BB_THRESHOLD is a tunable parameter introduced to define BB_MIN and is set to be 5% for Mediabench programs. Depending on the application domains under consideration, appropriate threshold values need to be empirically determined. Unlike [12], BB_MIN can vary from program to program, allowing the traces to be identified and constructed in a program-dependent manner. Once a trace header h is found (line 7), the **while** loop in line 8 grows the trace from h by adding more and more blocks to the trace. The trace always grows from its last block along its hottest outgoing edge (i.e., branch). Let s be the successor block along this edge. The trace is terminated if s is the pseudo block, a trace header or the exit block of the CFG for the program. The trace is also terminated if s is not hot (i.e., $Hot(s)$ does not hold) or $s.freq < b.freq \times$ BB_PROB (i.e., the execution frequency of s has dropped below BB_PROB (%) of that of the trace header b). In line 11, a trace that is identified in line 10 will be duplicated with the execution frequencies of all affected blocks and edges being updated appropriately.

In line 12, UpdateHeaderList is called to do two things. First, some blocks in *headerlist* that are no longer hot are removed (line 14). This can happen since part of its execution frequency may have been allocated to its duplicate in a hot trace. Second, in lines 15 – 17, the successor blocks s of every trace exit are examined. If s is not already in a trace, we add s to *headerlist* if it is hot, i.e., when $s.freq \geqslant$ BB_MIN $\times$ BB_PROB (even if $s.freq <$ BB_MIN may hold). Unlike [12], this ensures that both branches of an if statement are included in traces if both are parts of frequently executed paths.

We have also improved [12] by using a profile-guided devirtualisation technique to reduce the number of unknown indirect jumps in virtual call sites. In the case of a virtual call site, alto may represent all possible function invocations as unknown indirect jumps. Based on profiling information, our profile-guided devirtualisation pass devirtualises the hot functions invoked at each virtual call site by means of method test [4]. This involves replacing the indirect jump to a hot function by a direct jump guided by a test on the address of the function.

Our illustrating example is given in Figure 3(a). For a block identified by n_f, n denotes its block number and f its execution frequency. The number drawn on an edge (x, y) represents its execution frequency; the number is omitted if the edge is the only outgoing edge of x. In Figure 3(a), the edge $(7,12)$ introduced by alto serves to indicate that block 12 will be executed after the call made in block 7. The edges of this kind are ignored during trace generation. Running our algorithm over the example given in Figure 3(a) produces the modified CFG shown in Figure 3(b). There are a total of three traces generated. They are highlighted in gray boxes, where the trace D7-D8′-D9′-D11′-D12 crosses the boundaries of the two functions in the example.

In Figure 3(a), $(7, 8)$ is a call edge, which is part of the trace denoted by T_3. In this case, we rely on the procedure InlineCriticalPaths available in alto [15] to inline a frequently executed subgraph rooted at the entry block of the callee. Afterwards, our al-

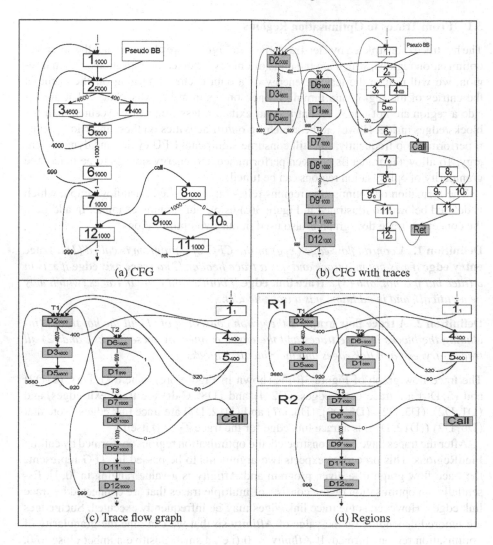

Fig. 3. An example CFG

gorithm will continue to grow the trace on the inlined subgraph as usual. In Figure 3(b), the blocks 7, 8, 9, 8', 9' and 11' are dead, which will eventually be removed.

3   Trace-Based Leakage Optimisation

In Section 3.1, we give an algorithm for clustering the traces into optimisation regions, the units of our energy-oriented optimisations. In Section 3.2, we describe the architectural features required for supporting our leakage optimisation. Section 3.3 presents our trace-based optimisation for reducing the data cache leakage energy.

3.1   From Traces to Optimisation Regions

The hot traces constructed by GenTrace given in Figure 2 are clustered into the so-called optimisation regions, which are the units of energy-oriented optimisations. Given a region, we will reduce the leakage energy of a data cache by turning off the cache at the entries of the region and turning it back on again at its exits. Since what are inside a region are hot traces, its entries and exits are less frequently executed than the blocks/edges inside. However, the switching on/off activities on these insertion points, if performed too frequently, can still consume significant CPU cycles and dynamic energy. To allow the tradeoffs between performance and energy savings to be made, the granularity of optimisation regions can be tuned.

The formation of optimisation regions relies on a so-called trace flow graph, which is defined below and illustrated in Figure 3(c) using our running example. In addition, the concept of trace flow graph is also used in our two optimisations.

Definition 1. *A control flow edge* (x, y) *in the CFG of a program is called (1) a* **trace entry edge** *if x is not in a trace and y is a trace header, (2) a* **trace exit edge** *if x is in a trace but y is not, and (3) a* **trace link edge** *if both x and y are in traces (which may be identical), and in addition, y is a trace header.*

Definition 2. *A* **trace flow graph** *is the graph consisting of (1) all the hot traces (including the blocks in these traces and the edges connecting these blocks), and (2) all trace entry, exit and link edges and their incident blocks.*

The trace flow graph of Figure 3(b) is shown in Figure 3(c), where $(1, D2)$, $(5, D2)$ and $(5, D6)$ are trace entry edges, $(D2, 4)$ and $(D8', \text{Call})$ are trace exit edges, and $(D1, D2)$, $(D5, D2)$, $(D5, D6)$, $(D6, D7)$ and $(D12, D7)$ are trace link edges. Note that $(D5, D2)$ $((D12, D7))$ is a trace link edge for the trace T_1 (T_3) itself.

After the traces have been constructed, the optimisation regions are formed by calling FindRegions. This procedure expects two arguments to be passed in: *TFG* represents the trace flow graph of a given program and *Affinity* is a value ranging in $[0, 1]$. Essentially, an optimisation region consists of multiple traces that are connected by trace link edges. However, some trace link edges may be infrequently executed. Such edges are ignored depending on the value of *Affinity* so that we can tune the granularity of optimisation regions formed. If *Affinity* $= 0$ (i.e., a small positive number close to 0, in practice), then all regions are singleton traces. Such a setting is the most aggressive in turning off unused or infrequently used hardware components (e.g., cache) in a region. If *Affinity* $= 1$, then every region is the largest possible with the largest number of directly connected traces. Such a setting aims at reducing the execution cycles and dynamic energy consumed by the power-aware instructions inserted. Varying the value of *Affinity* allows tradeoffs to be made between energy savings and performance.

Figure 3(d) depicts the two regions formed for the program shown in Figure 3(c) with *Affinity* $= 1/1.2$ under the assumption that BB_MIN $= 1000$.

3.2   Architecture Support

The leakage power of a CMOS circuit is directly proportional to the product of the power supply voltage (V_{DD}) and the leakage current in a CMOS transistor. Circuit

```
1  PROCEDURE FindRegions(TFG, Affinity)
2  Let L be the set of all trace link edges e in TFG such that e.freq < (1/Affinity − 1) * BB_MIN
3  TFG' = TFG with all edges in L removed
4  return (set of all connected subgraphs in TFG')
```

Fig. 4. An algorithm for forming regions

techniques such as power gating (SG), input vector control (IVC) and dynamic voltage scaling (DVS) [2,6] can reduce the leakage power by reducing the supply voltage and/or leakage current. To support our optimisations, we assume the availability of on and off instructions in the underlying instruction set architecture (ISA).

Following [19], we use the same state-preserving leakage control mechanism as proposed in [6], which can preserve the contents of a cache line when the line is put into a low leakage mode. Thus, the cache behaviour of a program is not affected.

The execution of an on (off) instruction causes all the cache lines in the cache to be placed in a normal (leakage-saving) state. Whenever a cache line is accessed, if it is in the leakage-saving state, the normal state will be restored first for the cache line before the access is executed. The execution of an on (off) instruction with respect to an cache line that is in the normal (leakage-saving) state has no effect on the leakage status of the cache line. The latencies and dynamic energy overheads of on/off instructions depend on the exact implementation mechanism.

3.3   Leakage Optimisation for Data Caches

Given an optimisation region, all the cache lines in the cache are "turned off", i.e., placed in the low-leakage mode at its entries and "turned on", i.e., placed in the normal mode at its exits. A cache line accessed in a region, once restated to the normal mode, will remain so until the region has been executed.

Figure 5 gives our algorithm, CacheOpt, for reducing the data cache leakage energy. In lines 3 and 4, we identify the traces and then form the optimisation regions. In line 5, we call InsertOnOffInsts to insert the required on/off instructions at the entries and exits of every optimisation region straightforwardly. In lines 8 − 9, we insert one single "off instruction" on every trace entry edge. In lines 10 − 11, we insert one single "on instruction" on every trace exit edge. In lines 12 − 14, we find every trace link edge (x, y) such that x and y are two distinct regions, in which case $x.region \neq y.region$. Every such an edge serves as a exit edge of the region x and an entry edge of the region y. Therefore, an "off instruction" is inserted on the edge. Note that an "on instruction" needs not be inserted redundantly before the off instruction on the same edge.

Our algorithm allows the granularity of optimisation regions to be adjusted by varying the tunable parameter AFFINITY. If the regions are large enough, the performance and dynamic energy penalties due to switching on/off activities will be insignificant but the opportunities for leakage reduction are also small. In general, the larger a region is, the larger the number of cache lines there will be in the normal mode and the smaller the leakage energy savings will be in the region. Therefore, the regions can be tuned to

```
1   #DEFINE AFFINITY = a value in [0, 1]
2   PROCEDURE CacheOpt()
3   Build the TFG (Definition 2)
4   SetofRegs = FindRegions(TFG, AFFINITY)
5   InsertOnOffInsts

6   PROCEDURE InsertOnOffInsts()
7   Insert one "on inst" at entry to main
8   for every trace entry edge (x, y)
9       Insert one "off inst"
10  for every trace exit edge (x, y)
11      Insert one "on inst"
12  for every trace link edge (x, y)
13      if x.region ≠ y.region
14          Insert one "off inst"
```

Fig. 5. A leakage optimisation for data caches

make tradeoffs between the leakage energy savings and associated overheads (including dynamic energy and execution time penalties).

Example. As in before, we assume that BB_MIN=1000, BB_PROB=50% and AFFINITY = 1/1.2. Consider our running example given in Figure 3(a). In lines 3 – 4, the trace flow graph and the optimisation regions found are given in Figures 3(c) and 3(d), respectively. As a result, the on and off instructions are inserted as shown in Figure 6.

4   Experimental Results

In our experiments, we evaluate the effectiveness of our trace generation algorithm in identifying the hot traces and the effectiveness of our optimisation in reducing the leakage energy of data caches.

We use 15 benchmarks from the Media benchmark suite. All benchmarks are compiled using DEC C 5.6-075 at "O2" on an Alpha 21264-based system. Similar trends in our results are observed at "O3" or under gcc with varying optimisation levels. There are so-called "second data sets" for 12 out of the 15 benchmarks available in the Mediabench web site. The exceptions are pgpencrypt, pgpdecrypt and mesa. For each benchmark, the profiling information is collected using the so-called "second data set" if it exists and the data set that comes with the benchmark otherwise. All benchmarks are simulated using the data sets that come with these benchmarks.

We consider a superscalar out-of-order architecture consisting of two integer multipliers, four integer ALUs for non-multiplication integer operations, one floating point multiplier and four floating point adders. Such an architecture is chosen to match the target architecture of alto, in which our trace-based framework is implemented. We use sim-outorder, an out-of-order cycle-level simulator from SimpleScalar. The simulations for all the benchmarks are run to completion.

In order to make our presentation precise, we use P_{alto} to denote the binary from alto and P_{opt} to denote the binary generated after CacheOpt has been applied.

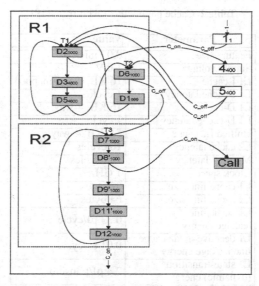

Fig. 6. The result of applying CacheOpt to the running example given in Figure 3. All tunable parameters used are defined in Section 3.3.

4.1 Trace Generation: GenTrace

The three metrics are used: (1) the trace accuracy measured as the cycles spent in the traces, (2) the code size increase due to the duplication of the traces, and (3) the performance degradation due to the introduction of the traces.

Table 1. Five settings for BB_THRESHOLD and BB_PROB

Configuration	BB_THRESHOLD	BB_PROB
CONFIG1	3%	50%
CONFIG2	5%	25%
DEFAULT	5%	50%
CONFIG3	5%	75%
CONFIG4	8%	50%

We evaluate GenTrace below using the five configurations listed in Table 1, where DEFAULT is the default setting. The trace accuracies are over 80% for all benchmarks under all five configurations. The only exception is djpeg for which an accuracy of 49.12% is obtained in CONFIG1. In this special case, a threshold of BB_PROB = 3% results in BB_MIN=703, which is too large to capture all frequently executed paths in the benchmark. The static instruction count increases range from 0.12% in nearly all five configurations for both rawcaudio and rawdaudio to 6.87% in CONFIG4 for cjpeg. The performance changes for all the benchmarks are very encouraging. Out of the 15 benchmarks used, pgpdecrypt and g721encode have small positive or

Table 2. Cache parameters taken from [19]

Parameter	Value
Feature size	0.07 micron
Supply voltage	1.0 V
L1 I-cache	16 KB, direct-mapped
L1 I-cache latency	1 cycle
L1 D-cache	16 KB, 4-way
L1 D-cache latency	1 cycle
Unified L2 cache	512KB, 4-way
L2 cache latency	10 cycles
Memory latency	100 cycles
Clock speed	1 GHz
L1 cache line size	32 bytes
L2 cache line size	64 bytes
L1 cache line leakage energy	0.33 pJ/cycle
L1 deactive mode cache line leakage energy	0.01 pJ/cycle
L1 state-transition (dynamic) energy	2.4 pJ/transition
L1 state-transition latency from deactive mode	1 cycle
L1 dynamic energy per access	0.11 nJ
L2 dynamic energy per access	0.58 nJ

negative speedups configurations under all five configurations, `toast` and `untoast` run between 0.04% to 1.58% slower under all five configurations, and the remaining 11 programs run faster under all five configurations. These performance variations appear to be attributed to the profile-guided code layout pass invoked in the code generation module of `alto` as shown in Figure 1. Our results show that GenTrace is capable of identifying the most frequently executed paths in a program and the associated costs for duplicating these paths as the hot traces in the program are small (relative to the achieved energy savings to be discussed shortly).

4.2   Leakage Optimisation for Data Caches

We will use the DEFAULT configuration to evaluate our data cache leakage optimisation: BB_THRESHOLD = 5%, BB_PROB = 50% and AFFINITY takes four values: 1, 1/1.05, 1/1.5 and 0. We adopt the cache configuration and energy numbers listed in Table 2, which is taken entirely from [19]. The cache state-preserving leakage control mechanism used is from [6]. According to [19], the energy numbers were obtained by circuit simulation for the 0.07 micron process.

Figure 7 depicts the data cache leakage energy savings achieved by CacheOpt. The percentage leakage reduction in a program P_{opt} is given by:

$$\text{cache\_saving} = \frac{O_{\text{static}} - C_{\text{dynamic}} - C_{\text{static}}}{O_{\text{static}}}$$

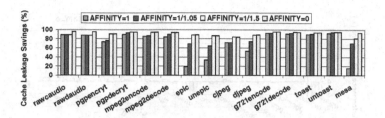

Fig. 7. Percentage cache leakage energy reductions of P_{opt} relative to P_{alto}

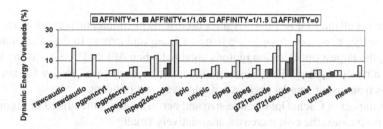

Fig. 8. Dynamic energy overheads measured as $\frac{C_{dynamic}}{C_{static}+C_{dynamic}}$

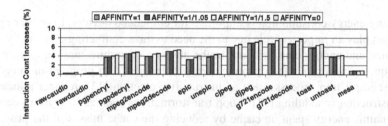

Fig. 9. Code expansion of P_{opt} relative to P_{alto}

where O_{static} denotes the amount of leakage energy consumed in P_{alto} before the optimisation, C_{static} the amount of leakage energy consumed in the optimised P_{opt} and $C_{dynamic}$ the dynamic energy overhead due to the switching on/off activities introduced in P_{opt}. As shown in Figure 7, the leakage energy savings are obtained in all benchmarks at all four AFFINITY values. In addition, they are progressively non-worse as the granularity of optimisation regions (i.e., AFFINITY) decreases. When AFFINITY = 1, the leakage reductions range from 18.59% for `epic` to 92.59% for `g721encode`. In the other extreme when AFFINITY = 0, the leakage reductions are more impressive, ranging from 83.87% for `cjpeg` to 95.74% for `rawcaudio`.

In the Mediabench benchmarks, a small set of data are typically active at a given period of time. As a result, reducing the granularity of optimisation regions tends to increase the total leakage energy saved. While smaller regions lead to higher on/off switching activities, i.e., higher dynamic energy consumption, as illustrated in Figure 8, these overheads are more than or equally outweighed by the leakage energy savings

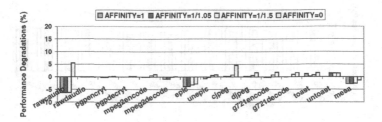

Fig. 10. Performance changes of P_{opt} relative to P_{alto}

achieved at all the four AFFINITY values used. This phenomenon is more pronounced in pgpencrypt, epic, unepic, cjpeg, djpeg and mesa. In the other nine benchmarks, the largest optimisation regions obtained when AFFINITY = 1 are small, resulting in already at least 83.87% leakage reduction in each case. So any further leakage savings from using smaller regions are relatively insignificant.

The impact of CacheOpt on code size and performance is illustrated in Figures 9 and 10. In both cases, the cost increases are relatively small.

5   Related Work

Reducing energy consumption is important for embedded devices. Compiler optimisations can play an important role due to the need to meet conflicting constraints on time, code size and energy consumption. In the absence of architectural support, compiler techniques can improve the dynamic energy behaviour of a program in many phases of the compilation process, such as instruction selection [13], register allocation [7] and instruction scheduling [11]. Loop transformations such as loop tiling can reduce the dynamic energy spent on cache by reducing the cache misses in the program [9]. By exploiting available architectural support in an embedded system, the compiler can generate code to dynamically reconfigure the processor resources to make tradeoffs between performance and energy usage. For example, [16] explore DVS as a means of improving the dynamic energy consumption of a program without increasing its execution time. [18] analyse and evaluate the opportunities and limits of compile-time DVS scheduling.

The on-chip caches are one of the hardware components for leakage reduction since they contain a significant fraction of the transistors in a microprocessor. Flautner *et al* [6] present architectural techniques for reducing the leakage energy of a data cache by periodically putting cache lines into a low-power mode. Motivated by this work, Zhang *et al* [19] describes a loop-based, compiler-directed solution. Essentially, the innermost loops are taken as optimisation regions. Given an innermost loop, all the cache lines are placed in a low-leakage mode at the beginning of the loop and restored to their normal mode at its exits. His experimental results over benchmarks show that this software solution can be competitive with the hardware-based solution [6].

In this work, we present a trace-based approach to reducing data cache leakage energy at link time. Rather than innermost loops, our units of optimisations are the regions constructed from the hot traces. The advantages of using traces are stated earlier. The traces are inherently inter-procedural, spanning both user and library functions (which may contain assembly code). In addition, the frequently executed paths formed by recursive calls are recognisable as traces but not as loops.

There are a number of static or dynamic binary translation systems around [1,3,17]. These systems aim at improving performance or otherwise achieving portability. However, we are the first to investigate the effectiveness of a trace-based, static binary translation framework in supporting energy-oriented optimisations for embedded applications. Working on binaries at link time (i.e., statically) dispenses with an expensive run-time system that would otherwise be required.

Traces are not new. Trace scheduling [5] is a well-known technique for increasing the amount of ILP by scheduling a sequence of basic blocks together, which typically represents a frequently executed path in the program. Traces have a number of extensions such as hyperblocks [14] and regions [8]. In Dynamo [1], the frequently executed paths are identified at run time so as to improve the program performance transparently. These previous works show that a trace-based approach is effective in supporting performance-oriented optimisations. This work demonstrates that the traces also represent a suitable framework to support energy-oriented optimisations.

Our trace generation algorithm identifies the hot traces across procedural boundaries at link time based on an inter-procedural CFG constructed from a binary file. This CFG is imprecise since the targets of some jumps may be unknown or even *illegal* since a branching instruction in one function may jump to the middle of another function. These problems do not exist when the traces are constructed at compile time [5,8,14] or cause less trouble when the traces are constructed at run time [1].

6   Conclusion

This work investigates for the first time the effectiveness of conducting energy-oriented optimisations for data caches in a traced-based compilation framework at link time. We present a simple yet effective algorithm for identifying and constructing the hot traces in a binary program at link time. We also introduce a trace-based optimisation for reducing leakage energy for data caches. The optimisation is simple since traces allow the optimisation regions and on/off insertion points to be identified easily and also effective since significant leakage energy reductions can be obtained for benchmarks at small performance degradations and code size expansions.

Acknowledgements

This work is supported in part by ARC Discovery grants DP0211793 and DP0452623.

References

1. V. Bala, E. Duesterwald, and S. Banerjia. Dynamo: a transparent dynamic optimization system. In *ACM SIGPLAN '00 Conference on Programming Language Design and Implementation*, pages 1 – 12, Vancouver, British Columbia, Canada, 2000. ACM Press.

2. A. Chandrakasan, W. J. Bowhill, and F. Fox. *Design of High-Performance Microprocessor Circuits.* IEEE Press, 2001.
3. J. C. Dehnert, B. K. Grant, J. P. Banning, R. Johnson, T. Kistler, A. Klaiber, and J. Mattson. The transmeta code morphing software: using speculation, recovery, and adaptive retranslation to address real-life challenges. In *1st ACM/IEEE International Symposium on Code Generation and Optimization*, pages 15–24. IEEE Computer Society, 2003.
4. D. Detlefs and O. Agesen. Inlining of virtual methods. In *13th European Conference on Object-Oriented Programming (ECOOP'99)*, pages 258–278, 1999.
5. J. Fisher. Trace scheduling: a technique for global microcode compaction. In *IEEE Transactions on Computers*, pages 478–490, 1981.
6. K. Flautner, N. S. Kim, S. Martin, D. Blaauw, and T. Mudge. Drowsy caches: simple techniques for reducing leakage power. In *29th annual international symposium on Computer architecture*, pages 148–157. IEEE Computer Society, 2002.
7. C. H. Gebotys. Low energy memory and register allocation using network flow. In *34th Annual Conference on Design Automation Conference*, pages 435–440. ACM Press, 1997.
8. R. E. Hank, W.-M. Hwu, and B. R. Rau. Region-based compilation: an introduction and motivation. In *28th ACM/IEEE International Symposium on Microarchitecture*, pages 158–168. IEEE Computer Society Press, 1995.
9. M. T. Kandemir, N. Vijaykrishnan, M. J. Irwin, and W. Ye. Influence of compiler optimizations on system power. In *Design Automation Conference*, pages 304–307, 2000.
10. N. S. Kim, K. Flautner, D. Blaauw, and T. Mudge. Drowsy instruction caches: leakage power reduction using dynamic voltage scaling and cache sub-bank prediction. In *Proceedings of the 35th annual ACM/IEEE international symposium on Microarchitecture*, pages 219–230. IEEE Computer Society Press, 2002.
11. C. Lee, J. K. Lee, T. Hwang, and S.-C. Tsai. Compiler optimization on instruction scheduling for low power. In *13th International Symposium on System Synthesis*, pages 55–60, Madrid, Spain, 2000. ACM Press.
12. L. Li and J. Xue. A trace-based binary compilation framework for energy-aware computing. In *LCTES '04: Proceedings of the 2004 ACM SIGPLAN/SIGBED conference on Languages, compilers, and tools*, pages 95–106. ACM Press, 2004.
13. M. Lorenz, L. Wehmeyer, and T. Dräger. Energy aware compilation for DSPs with SIMD instructions. In *ACM SIGPLAN' 02 Conference on Languages, Compilers, and Tools for Embedded Systems*, pages 94–101. ACM Press, 2002.
14. S. A. Mahlke, D. C. Lin, W. Y. Chen, R. E. Hank, and R. A. Bringmann. Effective compiler support for predicated execution using the hyperblock. In *25th ACM/IEEE International Symposium on Microarchitecture*, pages 45–54. IEEE Computer Society Press, 1992.
15. R. Muth. *ALTO: A Platform for Object Code Modification.* PhD thesis, The University of Arizona, 1999.
16. H. Saputra, M. Kandemir, N. Vijaykrishnan, M. J. Irwin, J. S. Hu, C.-H. Hsu, and U. Kremer. Energy-conscious compilation based on voltage scaling. In *ACM SIGPLAN '02 Conference on Languages, Compilers, and Tools for Embedded Systems*, pages 2 – 11, Berlin, Germany, 2002. ACM Press.
17. D. Ung and C. Cifuentes. Machine-adaptable dynamic binary translation. In *ACM SIGPLAN Workshop on Dynamic and Adaptive Compilation and Optimization*, pages 41–51. ACM Press, 2000.
18. F. Xie, M. Martonosi, and S. Malik. Compile-time dynamic voltage scaling settings: opportunities and limits. In *ACM SIGPLAN' 03 Conference on Programming Language Design and Implementation*, pages 49–62. ACM Press, 2003.
19. W. Zhang. Compiler-directed data cache leakage reduction. In *IEEE Computer Society Annual Symposium on VLSI Emerging Trends in VLSI Systems Design*. IEEE Computer Society, 2004.

Parallelizing User-Defined and Implicit Reductions Globally on Multiprocessors

Shih-wei Liao

Intel Corporation
2200 Mission College Blvd, Santa Clara, CA 95054
shih-wei.liao@intel.com

Abstract. Multiprocessors are becoming prevalent in the PC world. Major CPU vendors such as Intel and Advanced Micro Devices have migrated to multicore processors. However, this also means that computers will run an application at full speed only if that application is parallelized. To take advantage of more than a fraction of compute resource on a die, we develop a compiler to parallelize a common and powerful programming paradigm, namely reduction. Our goal is to exploit the full potential of reductions for efficient execution of applications on multiprocessors, including multicores. Note that reduction operations are common in streaming applications, financial computing and HPC domain. In fact, 9% of all MPI invocations in the NAS Parallel Benchmarks are reduction library calls. Recognizing *implicit* reductions in Fortran and C is important for parallelization on multiprocessors. Recent languages such as Brook Streaming language and Chapel language allow users to specify reduction functions. Our compiler provides a unified framework for processing both implicit and user-defined reductions. Both types of reductions are propagated and analyzed interprocedurally. Our *global* algorithm can enhance the scope of user-defined reductions and parallelize coarser-grained reductions. Thanking to the powerful algorithm and representation, we obtain an average speedup of 3 on 4 processors. The speedup is only 1.7 if only intraprocedural scalar reductions are parallelized.

Keywords: Reduction, multiprocessor, multicore, reduction recognition, interprocedural analysis, data flow analysis, parallelization, implicit reductions, user-defined reductions.

1 Introduction

With the arrival of multicore CPUs in the PC market [7], the general public can readily use multiprocessors for the first time. However, only a parallel application can utilize all the cores on a die. To effectively leverage multicores, we target the parallelization of reduction operations. Reductions and scans are ubiquitous abstractions of compute operations. As a result, Blelloch has advocated them as the principal abstractions for parallel computation [6]. Our parallelization of reduction can enable efficient execution of this powerful paradigm on multicores.

A reduction is the application of an associative operation (for instance, addition, multiplication, and finding minimums and maximums) to combine a data set. Because of the associativity of a reduction operation, the compiler may reorder the computation,

C. Jesshope and C. Egan (Eds.): ACSAC 2006, LNCS 4186, pp. 189–202, 2006.
© Springer-Verlag Berlin Heidelberg 2006

and in particular, may execute portions of the computation in parallel. Reduction operations are prevalent in streaming applications, financial computing and HPC domain [1][2][8][10][11][13]. For instance, MPI provides reduction library routines that account for about 9% of all MPI calls in the NAS Parallel Benchmarks (NPB) version 3.2 [5].

A reduction can be explicit or implicit. The former is specified in the language or in the library API; while the latter requires compiler or runtime analysis for detection. Explicit reduction operators date back to APL in the 60s [8]. Because of the importance of reductions, OpenMP supports reduction clauses, while MPI and HPF provide reduction libraries. Recent languages such as the Brook Streaming language and the Chapel language allow users to specify reduction functions. Identity, accumulating, and combining functions can be specified in Chapel which is part of the DARPA program for High Productivity Computing Systems.

Implicit reductions are prevalent in HPC domain. Recognizing implicit reductions in traditional languages and parallelizing them is essential for achieving high performance on multiprocessors. Our compiler currently handles Brook, C and Fortran languages, which contain both explicit and implicit reductions.

To unify the processing of both kinds of reductions, we build a compiler that detects implicit reductions, checks explicit reductions, and represents both implicit and user-defined reductions uniformly in the intermediate representation (IR). Both implicit and user-defined reductions are propagated and analyzed globally. Specifically, our compiler operates in three steps:

1. Local checking and representation of user-defined reductions in annotations on IR.
2. Local detection and annotation of implicit reductions. Section 3 describes our algorithm to detect reductions.
3. Using the uniform representations in "1" and "2", we perform interprocedural analysis and checking to obtain the best granularity in parallelization. The algorithm has been implemented in our fully functional parallelizers.

This paper makes the following contributions:

- **Unified processing of implicit and user-defined reductions.** We check user-defined reductions and represent them in the same fashion as representing implicit reductions. We present a general algorithm for processing both kinds of reductions.
- **A powerful and interprocedural reduction recognition algorithm.** We present a powerful algorithm for finding reductions on both scalar and array variables. First, the algorithm extends beyond previous approaches in its ability to locate reductions to array regions, even in the presence of arbitrarily complex data dependences. As an important example, the algorithm can locate reductions on indirect array references through index arrays. Second, our algorithm locates interprocedural reductions, reduction operations that span multiple procedures. We show that these global reductions occur in some computationally-intensive loops.

- **Extensive evaluation of importance in benchmarks.** We measure the impact of reduction recognition on parallelization of a collection of programs. These results demonstrate that parallelizing reductions makes a tremendous difference in the amount of the computation that can be parallelized.

The rest of the paper is organized as follows. Section 2 discusses the scope of our reduction analysis. Section 3 describes the interprocedural reduction recognition algorithm. Section 4 provides results indicating the frequency with which reductions occur in the benchmarks and quantifying their impact on the parallelization of these programs. The related work is presented in Section 5. Section 6 summarizes the paper.

2 Scope of Our Reduction Analysis

A reduction is the application of an associative operation to combine a data set. Reduction recognition and checking is an important component of enabling parallelism on multicores.

2.1 User-Defined Reductions

Our compiler first performs local checking on user-defined reductions. Our algorithm can parallelize the associative functions such as addition, multiplication, and finding minimums and maximums. For example, *foo* is a reduction, but compiling *bar* will produce an error message that identifies *bar* as a non-associative function. Note that *reduce* is a keyword in the Brook language.

```
reduce void foo(type(x), reduce int result)
{
      result = result + x;
}

reduce void bar(type(x), reduce int result1)
{
      result1 = result1 / x;
}
```

In our intermediate representation, we represent user-defined reductions in annotations. Reduction operators and variables are captured in the annotation. *foo* is annotated with a reduction annotation. As Section 3 explains, each enclosing program region may have a reduction annotation attached for *result*. Those annotations are propagated and attached as part of our interprocedural reduction recognition algorithm in Section 3.

For instance, in the following code, *result* is a reduction variable at the inner loop level, but not at the outer loop level. The reason is that our compiler recognizes that the read access to *result* in the statement *S2* makes the variable no longer reducible at the outer loop level. Even if the programmer removes the statement *S2*, *result* is still not reducible at the outer level because the statement *S1* is not reducible. Both *S1* and *S2* need to be removed for *result* to become a reduction variable at the outer level.

```
for (I = 0; I < M; I++) {   // no reduction annotation
    // Statement S1: no reduction annotation
    bar(C, result);
    // Statement S2
    d = ... result ...;
    // reduction annotation on the result variable
    for (J = 0; J < N; J++) {
        // reduction annotation on the result variable
        foo(B, result);
        ...
        // reduction annotation on the result variable
        foo(A, result);
    }
}
```

As shown above, reductions may span across multiple loops or functions. By propagating reduction summaries across program region boundaries, we are able to parallelize larger amounts of codes, with much lower parallelism overhead. Note that implicit reductions may also span across multiple program regions. One such example is the reductions on the *FLN* array in the *spec77* program in the Perfect Club benchmark [19]. Parallelizing *multiple* reductions on the same *FLN* array *interprocedurally* in the *spec77* benchmark is important for achieving scalability and speedups on multiprocessors.

2.2 Implicit Reductions

Our algorithm can analyze both scalar reductions and array reductions, as presented below. In addition, we want to recognize reductions which consist of multiple updates to the same variable.

2.2.1 Scalar Reductions
A summation of an array *A[0:N-1]* is typically coded as:

```
for (I =  0; I < N; i++)
    SUM = SUM + A[i];
```

The values of the elements of the array *A* are reduced to the scalar *SUM*. As shown in this example, reductions, when coded in sequential programming languages, are not readily recognizable as commutative operations. However, most parallelizing compilers will recognize scalar reductions such as this accumulation into the variable *SUM*. Such reductions can be transformed to a parallel form by creating a private copy of *SUM* for each processor, initialized to 0. Each processor updates its private copy with the computation for the iterations of the *I* loop assigned to it, and following execution of the parallel loop, atomically adds the value of its private copy to the global *SUM*.

2.2.2 Regular Array Reductions
To discover coarse granularity of parallelism, it is important to recognize reductions that write to not just simple scalar variables but also to array variables. Reductions on

array variables are also common and are a potential source of significant improvements in parallelization results.

There are several variations on how array variables can be used in reductions. For example, we can simply replace the *SUM* variable by an array element:

```
for (I = 0; I < N; I++)
    B[J] = B[J] + A[I];
```

Or, the reduction may write to the entire or a section of an array:

```
for (I = 0; I < N; I++) {
    // ... a lot of computation to calculate A(I,1:3)
    for (J = 1; J <= 3; J++)
        B[J] = B[J] + A[I,J]
}
```

Suppose, in this example, the calculations of *A[I,1:3]* for different values of *I* are independent. Standard data dependence analysis would find the *I* loop (the loop with index *I*) not parallelizable because all the iterations are reading and writing the same locations *B[1:3]*. It is possible to parallelize the outer loop by having each processor accumulate to its local copy of the array *B* and then sum all the local arrays together.

2.2.3 Sparse Array Reductions

Sparse computations pose what is usually considered a difficult construct for parallelizing compilers. When arrays are part of subscript expressions, a compiler cannot determine the location of the array being read or written. In some cases, loops containing sparse computations can still be parallelized if the computation is recognized as a reduction. In the example below, we observe that the only accesses to the sparse vector *HISTOGRAM* are commutative and associative updates to the same location, so it is safe to transform this reduction to a parallelizable form.

```
for (I = 0; I < N; i++)
    HISTOGRAM[A[I]] = HISTOGRAM[A[I]] + 1;
```

It is possible to parallelize the code by having each processor compute a part of the array *HISTOGRAM* and collect the information in a local histogram, and sum the histograms together at the end. Our reduction analysis can parallelize this reduction even when the compiler cannot predict the locations that are written.

3 Reduction Recognition

Section 2.1 describes the checking and representation of user-defined reductions, which is the first phase of our reduction analysis. We present the phase 2 and 3 of the analysis in this section: locating reductions and performing interprocedural analysis as part of our array data-flow analysis. The algorithm has been implemented in our fully functional parallelizer in SUIF.

As defined previously, a reduction occurs when a location is updated on each loop iteration, where a commutative and associative operation is applied to that location's previous contents and some data value. We have implemented a simple, yet powerful approach to recognizing reductions, in response to the common cases we have encountered in experimenting with the compiler. The reduction recognition algorithm for both scalar and array variables is similar, as scalar reductions are just a degenerate version of array reductions. This section focuses on array reduction recognition, which is integrated with the array data-flow analysis in the SUIF Compiler.

3.1 Problem Formulation for Reduction Analysis

The formulation of our reduction recognition algorithm is different from that used in previous compilers, and is powerful enough to allow our compiler to parallelize all the examples in Section 2. We model a reduction operation as consisting of a series of commutative updates. An update operation consists of reading from a location, performing some operation with it, and writing the result back to the same location. We say that a (dynamic) series of instructions contains a reduction operation to a data section r if all the accesses to locations in r are updates that can commute with each other without changing the program's semantics. Under this definition, it is easy to see that the examples above contain a reduction to, respectively, the regions *SUM*, *B[J]*, *B[1:3]* and *HISTOGRAM[1:M]* where M is the size of the array *HISTOGRAM*.

Not only is this model powerful, the analysis technique can be easily integrated with interprocedural array data-flow analysis. We will show how the reduction analysis is a simple extension of array data-flow analysis. The representation of array sections is common to both array data-flow analysis and array reduction analysis. The basic unit of data representation is a system of integer linear inequalities, whose integer solutions determine array indices of accessed elements. As described in our previous work [3], the denoted index tuples can also be viewed as a set of integral points within a polyhedron. The accessed region of an array is represented as a set of such polyhedra.

3.2 Interprocedural Reduction Recognition

The reduction recognizer is integrated with our array data-flow analysis. We will first describe the criteria for reductions and then the integration with the interprocedural dataflow analysis framework. The basic unit of data representation is a system of linear inequalities, whose integer solutions determine array indices of accessed elements. In addition, we add to the array section descriptor all the relationships among scalar variables that involve any of the variables used in the array index calculation.

3.2.1 Locating Reductions

The reduction recognition algorithm searches for computation that meets the following criteria.

1. The computation is a commutative update to a single memory location A of the form, A = A op ..., where op is one of the commutative operations recognized by the compiler. Currently, the set of such operations includes +, *, MIN, and MAX. The MIN (and, similarly, MAX) reductions of the form "if (A[i] < tmin) tmin = A[i]" are also supported.

2. In the loop, the only other reads and writes to the location referenced by A are also commutative updates of the same type described by op.

3. There are no dependences on any operands of the computation that cannot be eliminated either by a privatization or reduction transformation.

This approach allows any commutative update to an array location to be recognized as a reduction, even without precise information about the values of the array indices. This point is illustrated by the sparse reductions in Section 2.2.3. The reduction recognition correctly determines that updates to *HISTOGRAM* are reductions, even though *HISTOGRAM* is indexed by another array *A* and so the array access functions for *HISTOGRAM* are not affine expressions.

In the following, we will first summarize our array data-flow analysis and then present our interprocedural reduction analysis in the data-flow analysis framework.

3.2.2 Array Data-Flow Analysis

As described in our previous work [3], the bottom-up phase of our array data-flow analysis summarizes the data that has been read and data that has been written within each loop and procedure. The bottom-up algorithm analyzes the program starting from the leaf procedures in the call graph and analyzes a region only after analyzing all its subregions. Note that this part of reduction recognition algorithm applies best to Fortran programs. We can only apply this propagation and analysis to a subset of non-Fortran programs where we can disambiguate function pointers and the memory aliases on commutative updates. Simple recursions are handled via fixed point calculations. We do not deal with complicated cases. Fortunately the reductions in our non-Fortran workload typically do not involve complex aliasing and pointers.

We compute the union of the array sections to represent the data accessed in a sequence of statements, with or without conditional flow. At loop boundaries, we derive a loop summary by performing the closure operation, which projects away the loop index variables in the array regions. We summarize the sections of data accessed in a loop to eliminate the need to perform n^2 dependence tests for a loop containing n array accesses. At procedure boundaries, we perform parameter mapping, reshaping the array from formal to actual parameter if necessary. At each loop level, we apply a data dependence test and privatization test to the read and written data summaries [3][4].

3.2.3 Integration into Data-Flow Analysis Framework

In terms of the data-flow analysis framework, reduction recognition requires only a flow insensitive examination of each loop and each procedure body. Array reduction recognition is integrated into the array data-flow analysis from the previous section. Whenever an array element is involved in a commutative update, the array analysis derives the union of the summaries for the read and written sub-arrays and marks the system of inequalities as a reduction of the type described by op, where op is either +, *, MIN, MAX, or user-specified reductions. When meeting two systems of inequalities during the interval analysis, the resulting system of inequalities will only be marked as a reduction if both reduction types are identical.

3.2.4 Interprocedural Algorithm

Working in a bottom-up manner, the interprocedural algorithm starts by detecting statements that update a location via an addition, multiplication, minimum, maximum, or user-specified operator. The algorithm keeps track of the operator and the reduction region, which is calculated in the same manner as above if an array element has been updated. To calculate the reductions carried by a sequence of statements, we find the union of the reduction regions for each array and each reduction operation type. The result of the union represents the reduction region for the sequence of statements if it does not overlap with other data regions accessed via non-commutative operations or other commutative operations. At loop boundaries, we derive a summary of the reduction region by projecting away the loop index variables in the array region. Again, the summary represents the reduction region for the entire loop if it does not overlap with other data regions accessed.

The way we determine if a loop is parallelizable is as follows. We first apply the data dependence test and the privatization test on the read and write summaries and determine whether there is any dependence. If not, the loop is parallelizable and reductions are not necessary. Otherwise, we check if all data dependences on an array result from its reduction regions. If so, we parallelize the loop by generating parallel reduction code for each such array.

4 Experimental Results

Our reduction algorithm automatically parallelizes the reduction operations in sequential applications without relying on user directives. Parallel programs generated by our compiler are executed on cache-coherent shared address-space multi-processors. We will first describe our experimental setup in Section 4.1, evaluate the frequency of reductions and the coverage and the granularity of parallelism in Section 4.2, and present the performance results in Section 4.3.

4.1 Experimental Setup

The reduction recognition algorithm described above is implemented in the SUIF compiler. The following collection of results were obtained with the SUIF compiler, which takes input programs and generates parallel SPMD (Single Program Multiple Data) code with calls to our own runtime thread package.

Our runtime thread package supports parallel execution on a variety of machines, including the bus-based SMP (Symmetric Multi-Processors) such as the Silicon Graphics Challenge series, and the CC-NUMA (Cache-Coherent Non-Uniform Memory Access) architectures such as the Stanford DASH, the Stanford FLASH, and the Silicon Graphics Origin series.

4.2 Role of Reduction in Parallelization

We present measurement on how often the commutative update operations must be converted to parallelized reductions in order to parallelize loops in the benchmark programs. To evaluate our reduction algorithm, we present two sets of results, one without using reduction analysis and the other with reduction analysis. The former is obtained by using the baseline system, which includes interprocedural data dependence analysis, interprocedural scalar analysis, and interprocedural array privatization analysis. The latter uses array reduction analysis, in addition to the analyses in the baseline system.

To evaluate the applicability of our reduction recognition algorithm, we apply our algorithm on the LowPass benchmark [9] in Brook and the NAS parallel benchmark [5]. Table 1 provides the program description and the number of lines of code for each program. LowPass is a Brook program that uses explicit reduction. The NAS Parallel Benchmarks is a suite of eight programs used for benchmarking parallel computers. NASA provides sample sequential programs plus application information, with the intention that they can be rewritten to suit different machines. We use all the NASA sample programs except for *embar*. We substitute for *embar* a version from Applied Parallel Research (APR) that separates the first call to a function, which initializes static data, from the other calls.

Table 1. Benchmarks and their descriptions

Program	No. of lines	Description
LowPass	109	9-tap low pass filter using stencil and convolution
appbt	4457	block tridiagonal partial differential equation solver
applu	3285	parabolic/elliptic partial differential equation solver
appsp	3516	scalar penta-diagonal partial differential equation solver
buk	305	integer bucket sort of a random sequence
cgm	855	unstructured sparse solver using conjugate gradient
embar	135	parallel random number generator
fftpde	773	3-D partial differential equation of fast Fourier transform
mgrid	676	3-D multigrid solver for computing potential field

4.2.1 Static Measurements

Table 2 presents a count of the number of loops containing reductions that must be parallelized in order to parallelize the loop. The interprocedural and intraprocedural categories divide the reductions into those that spam multiple procedures and those that do not. Note that some of the reductions classified as intraprocedural are in loops that contain procedure calls; a reduction is only classified as interprocedural if the commutative update operation and the loop in which it is a reduction are in different procedures. We also divide the loops into those containing only scalar reductions, only array reductions, or both types of reductions. The column labeled "number of parallel loops with reduction" gives the number of loops in all categories that require parallel reductions in order to be parallelized. Note that in Table 2 we only count the outermost parallel loop in a loop nest, even if the inner ones may also be parallel.

The second column from the right end shows the number of loops that are parallelized without parallel reductions. The last column reports the total number of outermost parallel loops. Note that the number of parallel loops without reduction plus the number of loops requiring reduction does not necessary equal the number of parallel loops. This is because when an outer loop in a nest is parallelized, we only count the nest once, even if parallelizing its inner loops is also possible. Thus, sometimes parallelizing a reduction allows us to parallelize an outer loop in a nest; when the reduction is suppressed, parallelizing some inner loops may still be possible.

From this table, we see that parallelizable reductions occur in almost all of the programs. Clearly, parallelized reductions are widely applicable. We note that most of the reductions are intraprocedural reductions on scalar variables. Array and interprocedural reductions occur less often. However, as we will see in subsequent results, the array and interprocedural reductions can have a tremendous impact on performance.

Table 2. Impact of reductions (static measurements)

Program	No. of parallel loops with interprocedural reduction			No. of parallel loops with intraprocedural reduction			No. of parallel loops w/ red.	No. of parallel loops w/o red.	Total no. of parallel loops
	scalar	array	both	scalar	array	both			
Low-Pass	0	1	0	0	1	0	1	4	5
appbt	0	3	0	3	3	0	9	161	169
applu	0	3	0	3	4	0	10	126	136
appsp	0	3	0	3	3	0	9	157	166
buk	0	0	0	1	0	0	1	3	4
cgm	0	0	0	4	2	0	6	13	19
embar	0	0	1	2	1	0	4	2	5
fftpde	0	0	0	4	0	0	4	21	25
mgrid	0	0	0	5	0	0	5	33	38
Total	0	10	1	25	14	0	49	520	567

4.2.2 Coverage and Granularity

The previous section presents static counts of the parallelizable loops found with and without reductions. Static loop counts, though, are not good indicators of whether parallelization is successful. Specifically, parallelizing just one outermost loop can have a profound impact on the performance of a program. Dynamic measurements provide much more insight into whether a program may benefit from parallel reductions. Thus, we present a series of results gathered from executing the program on parallel machines. Table 3 shows whether the reduction loops are ones in which the program spends its time. We use two dynamic measurements which we call *parallelism coverage* and *parallelism granularity*. Parallelism coverage gives the percentage of the sequential execution time spent in parallelized regions of the code. Parallelism coverage gives us a first order approximation of how well the parallel program can be expected to perform; programs with low coverage do not perform well. By Amdahl's law, a program with parallelism coverage of 80% can at most speed up by 2.5 on 4 processors. High coverage is indicative that the parallelizer is locating significant amounts of parallelism in computation.

Parallelism granularity is the average length of computation between synchronizations in the parallel regions. Due to overheads of synchronization and data communication, programs with low granularity do not perform well. Table 3 lists the programs

Table 3. Coverage and granularity information on the programs on which parallel reductions have an impact

Program	Parallelism coverage			Parallelism granularity		
	no reduc-tion (%)	use reduc-tion (%)	ratio of no reduce. vs. use reduc.	no reduc-tion (msec)	use reduc-tion (msec)	ratio of no reduce. vs. use reduc.
LowPass	92	98	94%	0.8	0.9	89%
appbt	97.9	99.4	98%	12.8	13.1	98%
cgm	4.2	96.4	4%	0.86	18.4	5%
embar	0	100.0	0%	0.009	8133.6	0%

for which reduction recognition is important to discover coarser granularity of parallelism.

We obtain our coverage and granularity data on a uniprocessor Challenge. Table 3 reports *only* those programs for which parallel reductions increase more than 2% of the coverage or more than 2% of the granularity. We observe from these results that reductions are critical in extracting parallelism from 4 out of the 9 programs. Coverage is above 80% for all 4 programs. Granularity is above 0.9 millisecond for all 4 programs. In our experience, granularities on the order of 1 millisecond are high enough to yield speedup.

Recall from the previous section that *LowPass, appbt,* and *embar* all contain inter-procedural reductions. These interprocedural loops are the main reasons for the increased coverage and granularity. Despite the fact that interprocedural reductions are not all that common, when they do occur, because interprocedural loops often contain a significant amount of work, they can greatly impact performance. All of the 4 programs in Table 3 contain array reductions.

4.3 Performance Improvement

While parallel speedups measure the overall effectiveness of a parallel system, they can be highly machine dependent. Since parallel reductions incur more overhead than simple parallelization, not only do speedups depend on the number of processors, they are sensitive to many aspects of the architecture, such as the cost of synchronization, the interconnect bandwidth, and the memory subsystem. Thus, we evaluate the effectiveness of our reduction algorithm both the SMP (Challenge) and the CC-NUMA machine (Silicon Graphics Origin).

Table 4 compares the speedups of the 4 programs on a four-way SMP with and without parallelized reductions. We observe that *LowPass, cgm,* and *embar* benefit from parallelized reductions. The speedups for *cgm* and *embar* are quite significant, as compared with speedups of approximately 1 without reduction. Table 4 also explains the reasons for the increased speedups. The sparse reductions and the interprocedural reductions are the key to improving the performance of these programs.

Table 4. Performance improvement due to reduction on a 4-way SMP

Program	Time of sequen-tial version (sec)	Speedups			Reasons for improvement		
		no reduc-tion	use re-duction	relative improve-ment	sparse reduction	inter-proce-dural re-duction	intra-proce-dural re-duction
LowPass (4k elts)	3.7	1.2	1.3	10%		YES	YES
appbt ($12^3 *5^2$ grid)	10.1	2.9	2.9	0%			
cgm (1.4k elements)	5.4	1.0	3.5	250%	YES		YES
embar (256 it-erations)	4.6	1.0	4.0	300%	YES	YES	

The difference in parallel coverage observed earlier for these programs translates into positive effects on parallelization. The coverage of *LowPass* and *appbt* increases only slightly, and hence the performance is almost the same. The parallelization of *appbt* relies on the array privatization technique, not on the array reduction technique.

Table 5. Performance improvement due to reduction on a 4-way CC-NUMA

Program	Time of sequen-tial version (seconds)	Speedups			Reasons for improvement		
		no reduc-tion	use re-duction	relative improve-ment	sparse reduction	inter-proce-dural re-duction	intra-proce-dural re-duction
LowPass (32k elts)	2.4	1.1	1.3	20%		YES	YES
appbt ($34^3 *5^2$ grid)	939.4	3.6	3.7	3%			YES
cgm (14k elts)	87.8	1.0	2.9	190%	YES		YES
embar (64k it-erations)	1009.7	1.0	4.0	300%	YES	YES	

Table 5 presents the performance data on a CC-NUMA machine. The speedups for *cgm* and *embar* are also significant. We are able to use the large data set to obtain good speedups. The running time is too small otherwise. As a result, we do not use the same input data set from Table 4.

5 Related Work

User-defined reductions and scans date back to APL days. The recent languages, Chapel, Fortress and X10 all have reduction operators [2][12][14]. These languages are part of the DARPA program for High Productivity Computing Systems. Chapel allows its users to specify the identification, accumulation, and combining functions for reductions and scans [2]. Our compiler provides a unified framework for processing both implicit and user-defined reductions. Both implicit and user-defined reductions are propagated and analyzed globally. Our global algorithm can enhance the scope of user-defined reduction globally and obtain coarser-grained reductions.

Reduction recognition approaches have been proposed that rely on symbolic analysis or abstract interpretation to locate many kinds of complex reductions [15][16][17]. However, it is unclear whether the significant additional expense of these approaches is justified by the types of reductions that appear in practice.

Most previous array reduction algorithms need to constrain the array index function to be affine. Our algorithm can perform reductions even when the compiler cannot predict the locations that are written. The formulation of our reduction recognition algorithm is different from that used in previous compilers and is powerful enough to allow our compiler to parallelize more cases. For example, although important, sparse array reductions are not being sufficiently exploited as a source of parallelism in today's parallelizing compilers. We also found that coarser grain interprocedural computations are particularly beneficial when parallelizing reductions because the overhead of the reduction can be amortized over a larger parallel computation. In comparison, previous compilers [18] did not parallelize interprocedural sparse reductions with integrated explicit reductions as aggressively.

6 Conclusion

Reductions are powerful programming paradigms. Our region-based interprocedural compiler provides a unified framework for processing both implicit and user-defined reductions. Our work is distinguished by its ability to integrate explicit reductions and to parallelize interprocedural and sparse reductions.

We have shown through extensive measurements that parallelizing reductions is an important component in leveraging multiprocessors. Finally, our experimental results show that many of the parallelizable loops do not require interprocedural reduction analysis. However, the coarse-grained loops parallelized with our reduction analysis often contain a significant portion of the overall computation of the program and, as shown in Section 4, can make a substantial difference in overall performance. Thus, parallelizing reductions is an essential component in obtaining excellent parallel codes for multiprocessors.

References

1. Buck. Brook Language Specification. In *http://merrimac.stanford.edu/brook*, Oct. 2003.
2. S. Deitz, D. Callahan, B. Chamberlain, L. Snyder. Global-View Abstractions for User-Defined Reductions and Scans. In *Proceedings of the ACM SIGPLAN Symposium on Principles and Practices of Parallel Programming*. New York, New York, March 2006.

3. M. Hall, S. Amarasinghe, B. Murphy, S. Liao, M. Lam. Detecting Coarse-Grain Parallelism Using an Interprocedural Parallelizing Compiler. In *Proceedings of Supercomputing,* San Diego, CA, December 1995.

4. M. Hall, J. Anderson, S. Amarasinghe, B. Murphy, S. Liao, E. Bugnion and M. S. Lam. Maximizing Multiprocessor Performance with the SUIF Compiler. In *IEEE Computer, 29(12),* December 1996.

5. D. Bailey, T. Harris, W. Saphir, R. Van der Wijngaart, A. Woo, M. Yarrow. The NAS Parallel Benchmarks 2.0. Technical Report RNR-95-020, NASA Ames Research Center, Moffet Field, CA, December 1995.

6. G. E. Blelloch. Vector Models for Data Parallel Computing. MIIT Press, Cambridge MA. 1990.

7. Intel Multi-Core and AMD Multi-Core Technology. In *http://www.intel.com/multi-core/* and *http://multicore.amd.com/en/,* June 2006.

8. K. Iverson. A Programming Language. John Wiley & Sons. 1962.

9. S. Liao, Z. Du, G. Wu, G. Lueh. Data and Computation Transformations for Brook Streaming Applications on Multiprocessors. In *IEEE/ACM International Symposium on Code Generation and Optimization,* New York, NY, March 2006.

10. High Performance Fortran Forum. High Performance Fortran Specification Version 2.0, January 1997.

11. W. Gropp, E. Lusk, A. Skjellum. Using MPI (2nd edition): Portable Parallel Programming with the Message-Passing Interface. MIT Press, 1999.

12. P. Charles, C. Donawa, K. Ebcioglu, C. Grothoff, A. Kielstra, C. von Praun, V. Saraswat, V. Sarkar. X10: An Object-oriented Approach to Non-uniform Cluster Computing. In *Proceedings Of the Conference on Object-Oriented Programming Systems, Languages, and Applications (OOPSLA) – Onward! Track,* October 2005.

13. Official OpenMP Specifications Version 2.5. In *http://www.openmp.org,* May 2005.

14. Fortress: A New Programming Language for Scientific Computing. In *http:// research. sun.com/ projects/plrg/fortress0618.pdf,* 2005.

15. Z. Ammarguellat and W. Harrison. Automatic Recognition of Induction Variables and Recurrence Relations by Abstract Interpretation. In *Proceedings of the SIGPLAN '90 Conference on Programming Language Design and Implementation.* White Plains, NY, June 1990.

16. M. Haghighat and C. Polychronopoulos. Symbolic Analysis: A Basis for Parallelization, Optimization and Scheduling of Programs" In *Proceedings of the Sixth Workshop on Languages and Compilers for Parallel Computing,* Portland, OR. August 1993. Springer-Verlag Lecture Notes in Computer Science.

17. M. Haghighat and C. Polychronopoulos. Symbolic Analysis for Parallelizing Compilers. In *ACM Transactions on Programming Languages and Systems,* Volume 18, Issue 4, July 1996.

18. B. Pottenger and R. Eigenmann. Parallelization in the Presence of Generalized Induction and Reduction Variables. In *Proceedings of the 1995 ACM International Conference on Supercomputing,* June 1995.

19. L. Pointer. Perfect: Performance Evaluation for Cost Effective Transformations Report 2. In *Technical Report 964, University of Illinois, Urbana-Champaign,* March 1990.

Overload Protection for Commodity Network Appliances

Luke Macpherson

The University of New South Wales and National ICT Australia
Sydney, Australia
lukem@cse.unsw.edu.au

Abstract. Performance degradation under overload is a well known problem in networked systems. While this problem has been explored extensively in the context of TCP-based web servers, other applications have unique requirements which need to be addressed.

In existing admission control systems, the cost of admission control increases with the load to the system. This is acceptable for responsive TCP-based loads, but it is not effective in preventing overload for unresponsive workloads.

We present a solution where admission control cost is a function of the traffic admitted to the system, allowing our approach to maintain peak throughput under overload.

We have implemented our approach in a real system and evaluated its effectiveness in preventing overload for a number of demanding network workloads. We find that our solution is effective in eliminating performance degradation under overload, while having the desirable property of being simple to implement in commodity systems.

1 Introduction

All real systems have finite resources, and all systems are subject to physical constraints such as processor speed, memory capacity, bandwidth, latency, power consumption etc. It will therefore always be possible to demand more of a system than it can physically provide. It is a simple matter of applying enough load to a system that it no longer has enough resources to process all of the applied load. We must, therefore, accept that it is always possible that a system may become overloaded, and consider the behaviour of systems when that situation occurs.

It is desirable that a system maintain maximum throughput under sustained high load, however, performance degradation under overload is a common characteristic of many operating systems. The extreme case of such performance degradation is livelock, where given a suitably high load, the throughput of the system drops to zero.

The problem of overload becomes increasingly evident as the disparity between network speed and other processing resources increases. For this reason, we are particularly interested in solving the problem of overload as experienced

C. Jesshope and C. Egan (Eds.): ACSAC 2006, LNCS 4186, pp. 203–218, 2006.

in commodity network appliances such as routers, firewalls and network attached storage products. Such products typically have limited CPU resources and are commonly available with high-speed network interfaces.

Most current work on overload focusses on admission control for web-servers. These approaches have a number of shortcomings when applied to our target application. Admission control in web-servers is typically performed on a per-TCP-connection basis. Such an approach does not generalise to other network applications well. Current approaches also have an admission control cost which increases with applied load. This leads to degradation under overload and is particularly unacceptable for systems with limited resources.

This paper describes a protocol-independent admission control implementation whose resource consumption is independent of the load applied to the system. Unlike existing approaches, admission control is achieved by careful use of the network interface's DMA interface, allowing a commodity network interface to perform rate-limiting on incoming packets (Section 2.1). We also implement a new approach to determining the maximum throughput of a system, by using network traffic analysis to measure and control the performance of the system at runtime (Section 2.2).

We have implemented our approach in FreeBSD, and evaluated it by comparing the performance of our solution to an unmodified system, and a hypothetical ideal solution (Section 3). We show that our approach solves the problem of performance degradation under overload, without requiring significant modification to the operating system.

2   The Edge Limiting Approach

We will now examine mechanisms for eliminating performance degradation which may be implemented within an operating system using commodity hardware. Our goal is to enable data-paths consisting of both degradable and non-degradable resources to have the overall characteristics of a non-degradable resource. That is to say, regardless of the composition of the data-path, we want to prevent the overall performance of the data-path from degrading under overload.

Our approach to solving this problem is to create a rate-limiting resource by causing a non-degradable logical resource to become saturated early in the data path, at the maximum capacity of the data-path. This prevents all other resources on that data-path from exposure to data rates beyond their maximum capacities, thereby preventing performance degradation under overload from occurring.

This approach has two distinct requirements: a way to control the rate at which data enters the system, and a way to determine the maximum capacity of the system. This section will discuss how these two requirements can be implemented in a real operating system, using a commodity Gigabit Ethernet interface.

2.1   Rate Control Mechanisms

Our approach requires the ability to rate-limit network traffic entering the system. This requirement is orthogonal to the way in which feedback is propagated within the system. We propose the placement of a controllable rate-limiting resource at the edge of the system, to limit the data rate seen by the rest of the system. This rate-limiting resource is responsible for discarding packets when the system's capacity to process them has been exceeded.

It is important that the resource be placed as close to the edge of the system as possible. This requirement precludes the use of software rate-control mechanisms, since packets must be discarded before they consume precious resources, such as peripheral and memory bus bandwidth. Since we require the use of commodity hardware, we will examine rate-limiting mechanisms which can be implemented in the driver, and which cause packets to be dropped by the network interface before they can be copied to main memory using DMA.

The following rate-limiting mechanisms leverage the behaviour of the network interface when all receive buffers in the DMA descriptor ring have been used, which is to drop any subsequent incoming packets. This approach gives the behaviour of a non-degradable resource, because packets which are discarded do not consume any additional system resources. Resource consumption of the discarded packet is limited to processing on the network interface, which is capable of handling the full load of the network link.

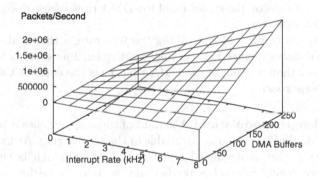

Fig. 1. Model of rate-limiting mechanism

Figure 1 shows the relationship between the achieved packet rate, the number of packets dequeued per interrupt and the interrupt frequency. Given this model, we can choose to control the incoming packet rate by adjusting the number of packets dequeued per interrupt, or by adjusting the interrupt frequency.

Controlled dequeue rate: This rate-limiting mechanism is implemented by controlling the rate at which packets are dequeued from the DMA ring by the driver.

Traditional driver implementations aim to dequeue as many packets from the DMA ring as possible before returning from the interrupt handler. We modify this behaviour by dequeuing only the appropriate number of packets to maintain the desired data rate. Excess packets are left in the DMA ring, while consumed packets are freed in the DMA ring. If the incoming data rate exceeds the packet dequeue rate, the DMA ring becomes full, and the network interface begins dropping packets. If the network supports flow control, the rate-limit will be propagated through the network, causing the sender to be blocked.

The main advantage of this approach is that it is extremely simple to implement, requiring only a few lines of code in the driver's interrupt service routine. The disadvantage of this approach is that it incurs additional per-packet latency, as packets must sit in the DMA ring until the driver is ready to process them. The average incurred latency can be calculated as the size of the DMA ring divided by the data rate.

Controlled free rate: An alternative to the controlled-dequeue-rate approach is to dequeue packets as soon as they are available, but delay notification of packet consumption to the network interface. In this solution we free packets in the DMA ring at the desired packet rate.

Because network interfaces typically consider a slot in the DMA ring to be either full or empty, the driver must introduce a third state to keep track of slots which are no longer in use, but which have not yet been returned to the network interface for reception of additional packets. How cleanly this can be implemented depends on the structure of the DMA ring, whose design is dictated by the network interface.

The primary advantage of controlling the free rate is that it does not incur any additional latency, since packets may be dequeued as soon as the interrupt is raised, rather than waiting in the DMA ring, as is the case for the controlled-dequeue-rate approach.

DMA ring length modulation: A variant of these approaches is to control the number of DMA buffers which are available in the receive ring. At fixed intervals, the entire DMA ring is dequeued and freed. This approach is suitable when the receive-processing interval is predictable, as is the case for many Gigabit Ethernet interfaces which support interrupt moderation.

Like the controlled-free-rate approach, the difficulty of implementing DMA ring length modulation depends on the data structures defined by the network interface.

2.2   Determining Maximum Throughput

There are many ways to determine the maximum throughput of the system. One is to have every resource along the data-path detect when it is overloaded. When a resource becomes overloaded, that information could be propagated to the data source. This is the approach taken by the staged event-driven architecture (SEDA) [14].

Although detection of overload within an individual resource is simpler than detecting overload in the system as a whole, retrofitting such detection to an existing system is a difficult task. Providing explicit flow control requires that overload detection and feedback mechanisms be built into each component. We therefore seek alternative methods of detecting overload which have less impact on the overall system structure.

One method which has been proposed to solve this problem is to use resource monitoring to detect when a system has become overloaded [13,10,11,12]. Unfortunately, resource monitoring is often a poor indicator of overload, since many optimisations take advantage of any spare resources which are available. Additionally, resource consumption may not be a function of network load if the resources are being consumed by some independent process.

An alternative approach is to use traffic monitoring to detect overload. Such a monitor would observe the response of the system to incoming traffic in order to determine that the system is performing sub-optimally. If overload is detected, the monitor should reduce the data rate entering the system by directly controlling data source(s) in the system. The advantage of this approach is that it is relatively simple to retrofit to an existing system, and it is more accurately able detect the occurrence of overload than simple resource monitoring schemes.

Traffic monitoring and rate selection: The goal of the rate selection algorithm is to determine the maximum throughput of the system at runtime. A rate-limiting mechanism may then be used to limit the input rate to the maximum throughput of the system.

There are a number of properties which may be monitored in order to detect overload. Such properties include throughput, latency, request rate vs. response rate, and other properties depending on the nature of the network traffic being monitored. Such traffic analysis may be performed passively, using traffic already entering the system, or actively, by inserting additional probe traffic into the system.

Once a given property can be monitored, the rate selection algorithm needs to know what behaviour is indicative of overload. In the case of throughput, the characteristic behaviour of an overloaded resource is throughput which decreases with increased load. In the case of latency, a significant jump in latency may be observed as the system becomes overloaded. We expect that other properties will provide additional behaviours which can be used to detect overload.

We have implemented throughput monitoring by instrumenting the network interface driver. We use a simple feedback system, which continually performs small changes to the input rate of the system, and observes the output rate. If throughput decreases over the control period, the search direction is reversed. This allows the control algorithm to stay near the system's peak throughput.

2.3   Limitations

We are forced by commodity network hardware to share a single DMA ring between multiple data-paths. This makes it impossible to apply individual rate-limits to each individual data-path, because when one data-path is rate limited, the throughput of other data-paths which are prefixed by the same DMA ring are also necessarily reduced. This situation could be resolved by having hardware that supports packet demultiplexing into multiple queues, or by limiting each network interface to a single data-path.

In practice many applications, such as those typically used in network appliances, put the majority of traffic through a single data-path. Therefore despite this limitation, our approach achieves useful results.

3   Experimental Evaluation

In order to evaluate the ability of our approach to eliminate performance degradation under overload, we have implemented it in the FreeBSD kernel's *em* device-driver for Intel's Gigabit Ethernet chip-set.

For our approach to be deemed successful, it must prevent the system from experiencing degraded throughput under overload. In order to show this, we establish a scenario where livelock is a problem in the FreeBSD implementation, then compare the behaviour of the standard kernel to one with our own modifications.

Instead of making quantitative comparisons with existing work, we compare our approach to the ideal throughput of an unmodified system. If our approach is able to maintain maximum throughput under overload, then we have achieved the ideal result for our system. Anything greater than this would indicate that additional optimisation had occurred, however such optimisation is orthogonal to the problem of eliminating performance degradation. Anything less than ideal indicates that additional overheads have been introduced.

3.1   Kernel Configuration

For the purpose of evaluating our system, we will be comparing two different configurations of the FreeBSD kernel, which we refer to as the *standard* and *dynamic* configurations. No kernel modifications are made between the different benchmarks, and no hand-tuning of the control algorithm has been done for specific applications. This section will summarise the similarities and differences between the two configurations.

The standard configuration has minimal changes when compared to the generic kernel configuration[1]. The primary change is that the timer interrupt rate was increased from 100Hz to 1000Hz[2] The interrupt moderation setting of the Ethernet driver was left at the default 8000 interrupts per second. Reducing this value could be expected to improve peak performance by decreasing interrupt overheads.

---

[1] The generic kernel is the *GENERIC* kernel and corresponding kernel configuration file distributed with *FreeBSD 5.3-RELEASE*.

[2] This change is a typical network optimisation in FreeBSD, and has become the default in recent FreeBSD releases. It was made to allow comparison against the FreeBSD polling implementation, which requires this setting.

The dynamic configuration implements our proposed solution, and consists of the standard configuration, with the addition of a controlled-dequeue-rate based rate-limiting mechanism in the driver, a control thread to determine the appropriate receive rate based on throughput monitoring, and some statistics collection required by the control loop. The interrupt moderation settings remain the same as for the standard configuration.

3.2   Hardware Description

The FreeBSD machine being tested was based on an Intel Xeon 2.66GHz processor with hyper-threading disabled[3], 1GB RAM, and an Intel PRO/1000 Gigabit Ethernet adapter[4] connected via PCI-X. A D-Link DGS-1216T managed Gigabit Ethernet switch was used, and was configured with pause frames disabled on all ports. This was done to prevent flow control information from propagating within the network, which was necessary to ensure that the full range of loads could be applied to the machine being tested.

3.3   Firewall Benchmark

The firewall benchmark is designed to simulate an overloaded network firewall. The benchmark utilises *ipbench* [15] to generate a prescribed load on the firewall, then measures the throughput and CPU utilisation at that load.

Firewall configuration: Figure 2.1 shows how our hardware was configured for benchmarking. The configuration consists of two VLANs, each containing four hosts connected via a Gigabit Ethernet switch. The two VLANs are connected via a single FreeBSD machine acting as router and simple firewall. The hosts on the first VLAN run the ipbench distributed network benchmark's UDP load generator, while the hosts on the second VLAN run UDP echo servers.

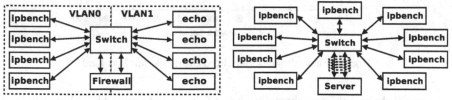

2.1: Firewall configuration.   2.2: NFS configuration

The FreeBSD firewall is configured to use the *pf* packet filter, with a simple rule-set that checks that all packets have reasonable and valid protocol headers, and that the source and destination addresses are valid before forwarding.

---

[3] Hyper-threading was disabled because SMP is not supported by FreeBSD's polling implementation, and because it makes CPU idle time measurement more difficult.

[4] Both ports of a dual-port card were used for the firewall benchmark, two ports of a quad-port card were used for the NFS benchmarks.

The ipbench distributed benchmark was run on the hosts in VLAN0. These hosts generate 512-byte UDP packets at a specified data-rate, which we refer to as the *applied load*. The UDP packets traverse the switch and firewall, to the hosts on VLAN1, which are running UDP echo servers. The UDP echo servers simply send an identical copy of the UDP payload back to the ipbench host, which again must travel via the switch and firewall. The ipbench host then records the rate of echo replies, which we refer to as the *achieved throughput*.

We note that packets must traverse the firewall twice before they are measured as achieved throughput. It is also worth noting that the firewall's input packet rate on VLAN0 will be higher than the firewall's input packet rate on VLAN1 when the firewall is overloaded. This is because some packets from VLAN0 will be dropped before they are seen by VLAN1. Therefore, those packets which are dropped before reaching VLAN1 will never be echoed, and hence cannot generate additional load on the firewall.

Firewall measurements: This section discusses measurements taken to evaluate our implementation. We begin by establishing a performance baseline for the standard configuration, by comparing applied load with achieved throughput. We then compare our dynamic configuration to the standard configuration on the basis of achieved throughput, CPU utilisation and cycles per delivered packet, under a variety of applied loads.

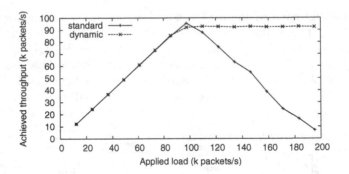

Fig. 2. Firewall: achieved throughput vs. applied load

Figure 2 shows achieved throughput as a function of applied load in the firewall benchmark, for both the standard and dynamic configurations. The standard line establishes the baseline throughput of the firewall benchmark. The results for the standard configuration show that the system does indeed exhibit significant performance degradation under overload.

The dynamic line in Figure 2 shows the effect of introducing our rate-limiting to the system. The dynamic line shows that limiting the receive rate by controlling the number of packets dequeued per interrupt causes the receive DMA ring to behave as a non-degradable resource, preventing performance degradation under overload.

Our approach comes within 5% of the ideal result of matching the peak throughput of the standard configuration, while avoiding the effects of performance degradation under overload. The slight decrease in peak throughput when compared with the standard configuration can be attributed to our rate selection algorithm needing to occasionally select throughputs above and below the maximum rate achieved by the standard configuration in order to detect overload.

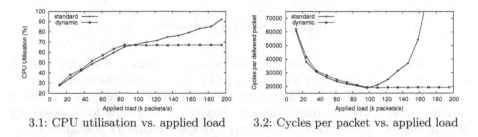

3.1: CPU utilisation vs. applied load   3.2: Cycles per packet vs. applied load

Fig. 3. Firewall CPU usage

We measure CPU utilisation by counting the percentage of cycles spent in a low-priority user process. This lets us accurately determine the number of cycles left for other user processes for a given load. In Figure 3.1, we see that the dynamic configuration incurs slight overheads when compared to the standard configuration, however once overload is reached, the dynamic configuration does not increase its CPU utilisation with applied load, showing that our rate-limiting mechanism is effective in preventing the system from exposure to excessive network loads.

Once the system becomes overloaded, the standard configuration begins wasting cycles on packets which are later discarded. This can be seen in Figure 3.2, where cycles per delivered packet increases considerably with applied load. Meanwhile the dynamic configuration maintains consistent overheads even when overloaded, since it does not waste resources handling packets which are not processed to completion.

3.4   NFS Benchmark

The NFS benchmark is designed to test the behaviour of an NFS server under overload. We utilise ipbench to generate very high NFS request rates, and monitor the corresponding response rate.

NFS configuration: The NFS benchmark configuration consists of nine load generators running ipbench, a Gigabit Ethernet switch, and a FreeBSD NFS server, as shown in Figure 2.2. The load generators are connected to the Gigabit Ethernet switch, which is in turn connected to the NFS server via two Gigabit Ethernet links, which are trunked using FreeBSD's Fast EtherChannel (FEC) netgraph module.

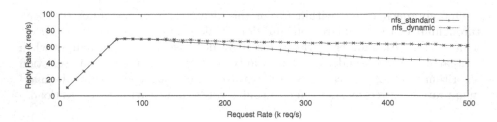

Fig. 4. NFS: replies vs. requests

It is important to note that the rate-limiting is performed in the network driver, which is not aware of the existence of FEC. We could have instead configured the NFS server with multiple independent Internet addresses, however we chose to use port trunking because it allowed us to generate loads exceeding one Gigabit-per-second while maintaining a simple benchmark configuration.

The NFS server is configured to serve data from an RAM-backed filesystem. This configuration was chosen primarily because we did not have access to a high-performance disk array for benchmarking purposes.

Load was generated using ipbench, which was configured to generate read and write requests with equal probability. Individual request sizes were randomly selected between 16 and 1024 bytes. All NFS operations were performed on a single 400 megabyte file.

NFS measurements: The results of the NFS benchmark are shown in Figure 4. We see that the results of the NFS benchmark have similar characteristics to the results of the firewall benchmark. For both the standard and dynamic configurations, response rate matches the request rate for request rates which are less than the maximum capacity of the system (in this case, 70,000 requests per second). Once the system becomes overloaded, the standard configuration experiences gradual and continuous performance degradation as the applied load increases.

The rate of performance degradation of the standard configuration is considerably lower than that seen in the firewall benchmark. This tells us that the kernel is doing less work on incoming requests before discarding them than is the case for the firewall benchmark. While the rate of performance degradation has improved, it is clear that performance degradation under overload is significant. Changing the amount of work done by enabling additional packet processing features (such as a packet filter) would increase the rate of degradation.

We observe that the dynamic configuration still displays a small amount of performance degradation under overload. Because all measurements are performed by ipbench, results indicate the behaviour of the entire benchmark configuration. Therefore the observed decrease may be the result of packet loss which occurs externally to the NFS server.

3.5   Summary of Results

Our results show that the dynamic configuration performs well when subjected
to overload. Unlike the unmodified case, peak throughput is maintained independently of applied load. Cycles expended per delivered packet do not increase,
indicating that the cost of our admission control mechanism does indeed scale
with the number of packets admitted, rather than the packets arriving at the
admission controller.

Our results also show that the dynamic configuration provides identical peak
performance to an unmodified system. This demonstrates that traffic monitoring
has been successful in determining the appropriate admission control rate for the
system.

4   Related Work

This section examines a number of existing systems by comparing their features
for a number of criteria which are relevant to system behaviour under overload.
Specifically, we are interested in the cost of admission control in the system,
whether it is possible to cause performance degradation with that admission
control in place, the granularity at which admission control is performed, and
the feedback mechanism used to decide how much load to admit into the system.
The table in Figure 5 gives a summary of these features for a number of existing
systems.

System	Admission control cost	Performance degrades	Granularity	Feedback mechanism	OS restructure	Ref.
ERL	$O(admitted)$	N	Packet	Full queue	Y	[7]
Hardware LRP	$O(admitted)$	N	Socket	Full queue	Y	[5]
Software LRP	$O(total)$	Y	Socket	Full queue	Y	[5]
SRP	$O(total)$	Y	Socket	Full queue	Y	[4]
SYN Policing	$O(total)$	Y	TCP	Resource monitor	N	[13, 10, 11, 12]
WebQoS	$O(total)$	Y	HTTP Request	Queue length	N	[1]
Yaksha	$O(total)$	Y	HTTP Request	Response time	N	[6]
Quorum	Independent	N	HTTP Request	Response time	N	[3]
SEDA	$O(total)$	Y	Multiple	Multiple	N	[14]
Edge limiting	$O(admitted)$	N	Packet	Throughput	N	

Fig. 5. Existing admission control approaches

4.1   Admission Control

In order for a system to provide acceptable behaviour under overload, it must
implement some form of admission control. This section examines the admission
control mechanisms used in a number of existing systems.

One early instance of kernel-level admission control can be seen in Mogul
and Ramakrishnan's work on eliminating receive livelock (ERL) in an interrupt-
driven kernel [7]. This solution services queues in a round-robin fashion from

within a polling thread, and limits the number of packets which may be handled each time a queue is serviced.

While the main intent of this work was to curtail excessive interrupt rates, the solution provided a simplistic form of admission control by temporarily disabling input from the network interface when queues became full. This method of admission control is too coarse to work well on modern network interfaces, which tend to support very high packet rates, and transfer many packets per interrupt.

Lazy receiver processing (LRP) [5] used early packet demultiplexing to separate individual data-paths within the system. There were two implementations of LRP, a hardware based solution that demultiplexed packets based upon ATM virtual circuit identifiers, and a software implementation that demultiplexed packets based upon IP header fields. Admission control was performed by dropping packets that destined for a socket whose queue was full.

TCP SYN policing [13] is an admission control system which limits the rate of TCP connection establishment by rejecting the connection setup packets of a TCP connection. It has been used particularly in the context of web servers, whose network behaviour is typically characterised by large numbers of short-lived TCP connections. Admission control occurs by only allowing TCP SYN packets to enter the system at a controlled rate. This approach is only effective for loads which are responsive to such feedback, rather than performing load shedding at the overloaded host.

The staged event-driven architecture (SEDA) [14] wraps every stage in a data-path with its own admission controller and feedback loop. This results in load shedding at many points in the system, depending on which stage of the data-path is overloaded. Non-admittance to a stage allows upstream stages to respond by altering their behaviour in order to reduce the load applied to the downstream stage.

4.2   Admission-Control Cost

We are interested in whether the cost of performing admission control scales with the number of admitted requests, $O(admitted)$, or with the total number of requests, $O(total)$. If the admission control mechanism itself scales according to the total number of requests, then the admission control mechanism may itself be subject to overload, for large enough input loads. If an admission control mechanism scales with the number of accepted requests, it will not contribute to performance degradation under overload.

The ERL approach of disabling input from the network interface is inherently $O(admitted)$, since the system only performs processing on data once it has already passed the admission control mechanism. This results in short bursts of traffic being admitted to the system during overload, rather than applying a consistent load to the host.

The hardware-based LRP approach is able to discard traffic at the network interface when a socket's queue is full, and hence achieves $O(admitted)$ performance. The software LRP approach must perform packet processing on every packet entering the system prior to performing admission control. Therefore, the software LRP approach is only able to achieve $O(total)$ performance, and given suitably high loads will exhibit performance degradation.

In a similar manner to software LRP, *signaled receiver processing* (SRP) [4] also performs work on all packets entering the system prior to admission control. SRP is therefore also subject to performance degradation under overload, due to the expenditure of resources on packets which are later discarded.

SYN policing is strongly dependent on the behaviour of the client. Fundamentally, the performance is $O(total)$, since all packets are examined for the SYN flag when admission control is occurring, however the extent to which performance degradation occurs is determined by the ratio of SYN packets to other network traffic.

4.3 Performance Under Overload

Systems whose admission-control cost is $O(total)$ exhibit degraded throughput under overload. The rate at which degradation occurs in such systems is dependent on resource consumption which occurs prior to admission control. The less work which is performed prior to admission control, the slower a system's degradation will be. For this reason, late admission control is still better than no admission control, even though some performance degradation will still be present in the system.

Those systems whose admission control cost is $O(admitted)$ or better will not experience degraded throughput under overload. Of those systems whose performance does not degrade under overload, we recognise two sub-categories; those whose peak performance is comparable with that of a standard system, and those whose peak performance is significantly lower.

4.4 Differentiation

Admission control may be performed at different granularities depending on the requirements of the system. Most systems perform admission control on either a per-packet, per-TCP-connection, or per-user basis.

Performing admission control on a per-packet basis is primarily used because it does not require specific knowledge about the contents of a packet in order for admission control to take place. This approach has the advantage that admission control cost can be made independent of the load applied to the admission controller, allowing the approach to scale to very high applied loads. The disadvantage is that it is not possible to preferentially treat packets based on their contents.

Admission control on a per-TCP-connection basis has been proposed as a solution for protocols such as HTTP. The advantage of this approach is that existing connections can be prioritised over new connections. The disadvantage of this approach is that it requires that the admission controller be able to process the IP and TCP packet protocol fields, in order to differentiate between incoming packets. Such processing consumes resources for each additional packet received, even if that packet is not admitted.

Admission control can also be performed at higher levels, according to information available to the application-level protocol. Such information could be used to perform per-user service differentiation [13].

While the granularity at which admission control is performed is conceptually orthogonal to the cost of admission control, the cost of admission control is closely related to the implementation details of session differentiation.

There are two classes of admission control implementation; those which perform admission control at the network interface, and those which perform admission control during protocol processing on the host CPU. Performing admission control at the network interface is necessary to achieve $O(admitted)$ scalability, however performing session differentiation at greater granularities requires increased processing capacity on the network interface itself.

For commodity IP over Ethernet, performing admission control at the network interface on a per-packet basis is simply a matter of accepting packets at the appropriate rate. Performing admission control at higher levels requires the examination of higher level protocol fields in order to differentiate between packets. Such functionality is typically not available in commodity Ethernet interfaces, however in other research contexts, such as user-level network protocol implementations, programmable Ethernet interfaces have been modified to perform hardware packet filtering into multiple input queues [8].

For TCP/IP over ATM, performing admission control at the network interface on a per-connection basis is feasible, since TCP connections may be mapped to individual ATM virtual circuits [9, 2]. This is the approach taken by the hardware-based implementation or LRP [5].

4.5   Feedback

This section will examine feedback mechanisms that are used to control the acceptance rate of the admission controller. There are three fundamental approaches that are taken in the literature, explicit flow control, resource-based feedback, and performance monitoring.

Explicit flow control is used in systems that are structured with queues between connected components. Such systems allow upstream components to signal downstream components that they are overloaded, by allowing their incoming queues to become full. Upon encountering a full receive queue, the downstream component can presume that the upstream component is unable to process the incoming data-stream at the required rate, and is overloaded.

Resource-based feedback is implemented by monitoring key system resources, such as CPU time and memory consumption, in an attempt to determine when a system has become overloaded. The main problem with resource-based feedback is that resource usage is not always an accurate indicator of overload.

The third feedback mechanism which is commonly used is performance monitoring. Most systems use some variation of response time measurement, where the feedback mechanism uses a control loop to maintain response time guarantees. For example, SEDA, Yaksha and Quorum aim to maintain a well-defined percentage of traffic above a minimum response time.

5   Conclusion

Current admission control schemes are not suitable for use in scenarios where network traffic is not responsive, because the cost of admission control in the system scales with the load applied to the system. Meanwhile, older approaches such as hardware-based LRP and ERL do not work on current commodity hardware.

We have presented an approach to admission control where the cost of admission control is a function of the traffic admitted to the system. This approach allows peak throughput to be maintained under overload, even in the presence of non-responsive, non-TCP workloads.

We have implemented our approach in a real system and evaluated its effectiveness in preventing overload in two common network appliance applications: firewalls and networked attached storage (NFS). We have shown that our solution is effective in eliminating performance degradation under overload for these systems, while maintaining the desirable property of being simple to implement in existing operating systems using commodity hardware.

References

1. Nina Bhatti and Rich Friedrich. Web server support for tiered services. *IEEE Network*, 13(5):64–71, 1999.
2. Richard Black, Paul T. Barham, Austin Donnelly, and Neil Stratford. Protocol implementation in a vertically structured operating system. In *Proceedings of the 22nd Annual IEEE Conference on Local Computer Networks*, pages 179–188. IEEE Computer Society, 1997.
3. Josep M. Blanquer, Antoni Batchelli, Klaus Schauser, and Rich Wolski. Quorum: Flexible quality of service for internet services. In *2nd Symposium on Networked Systems Design and Implementation*, Boston, MA, USA, May 2005.
4. Jose Brustoloni, Eran Gabber, Abraham Silberschatz, and Amit Singh. Signaled receiver processing. In *Proceedings of the 2000 USENIX Annual Technical Conference*, pages 211–223, San Diego, CA, USA, 2000.
5. Peter Druschel and Gaurav Banga. Lazy receiver processing (LRP): A network subsystem architecture for server systems. In *2nd OSDI*, pages 261–275, Seattle, WA, USA, Oct 1996.
6. Abhinav Kamra, Vishal Misra, and Erich M. Nahum. Yaksha: a self-tuning controller for managing the performance of 3-tiered web sites. In *Quality of Service - IWQoS 2004, 12th International Workshop*, pages 47–56, Montreal, Canada, 2004.
7. Jeffrey C. Mogul and K. K. Ramakrishnan. Eliminating receive livelock in an interrupt-driven kernel. In *1996 USENIX Techn. Conf.*, pages 99–111, San Diego, CA, USA, Jan 1996.
8. Ian Pratt and Keir Fraser. Arsenic: A user-accessible Gigabit Ethernet interface. In *20th INFOCOM*, Apr 2001.
9. Dickon Reed and Robin Fairbairns. *Nemesis Kernel Overview*, May 1997.

10. Thiemo Voigt. Overload behaviour and protection of event-driven web servers. In *Proceedings of the International Workshop on Web Engineering*, Pisa, Italy, May 2002.

11. Thiemo Voigt and Per Gunningberg. Adaptive resource-based web server admission control. In *7th IEEE Symposium on Computers and Communication*, Taormina/Giardini Naxos, Italy, 2002.

12. Thiemo Voigt and Per Gunningberg. Handling multiple bottlenecks in web servers using adaptive inbound controls. In *Seventh International Workshop on Protocols for High-Speed Networks*, Berlin, Germany, 2002.

13. Thiemo Voigt, Renu Tewari, Douglas Freimuth, and Ashish Mehra. Kernel mechanisms for service differentiation in overloaded web servers. In *Proceedings of the 2001 USENIX Annual Technical Conference*, pages 189–202, Boston, MA, USA, 2001.

14. Matt Welsh and David Culler. Adaptive overload control for busy internet servers. In *Proceedings of the USENIX Symposium on Internet Technologies and Systems*, Seattle, WA, USA, 2003.

15. Ian Wienand and Luke Macpherson. ipbench: A framework for distributed network benchmarking. In *AUUG Winter Conference*, Melbourne, Australia, Sep 2004.

An Integrated Temporal Partitioning and Mapping Framework for Handling Custom Instructions on a Reconfigurable Functional Unit

Farhad Mehdipour[1], Hamid Noori[2], Morteza Saheb Zamani[1], Kazuaki Murakami[2], Mehdi Sedighi[1], and Koji Inoue[2]

[1] Computer and IT Engineering Department, Amirkabir University of Technology, Tehran, Iran
{mehdipur, szamani, msedighi}@ce.aut.ac.ir
[2] Department of Informatics, Graduate School of Information Science and Electrical Engineering, Kyushu University, Japan
noori@c.csce.kyushu-u.ac.jp,
{murakami, inoue}@i.kyushu-u.ac.jp

Abstract. Extensible processors allow customization for an application by extending the core instruction set architecture. Extracting appropriate custom instructions is an important phase for implementing an application on an extensible processor with a reconfigurable functional unit. Custom instructions (CIs) usually are extracted from critical portions of applications. This paper presents approaches for CI generation with respect to the RFU constraints to improve speedup of the extensible processor. First, our proposed RFU architecture for an adaptive dynamic extensible processor called AMBER is described. Then, an integrated temporal partitioning and mapping framework is presented to partition and map the CIs on the RFU. In this framework, a mapping aware temporal partitioning algorithm is used to generate CIs which are mappable on the RFU. Temporal partitioning iterates and modifies partitions incrementally to generate CIs. In addition, a mapping algorithm is presented which supports CIs with critical path length more than the RFU depth.

1 Introduction

Synthesis of application-specific instruction-set processors (ASIPs) has been an important design methodology for system-on-chip processors in the last decade. ASIPs have more potential to meet the high-performance demands of embedded applications, compared to general purpose processors (GPPs) but the synthesis of ASIPs traditionally involved the generation of a complete instruction set architecture for the targeted application. On the other hand, GPPs are very flexible but may not offer the necessary performance.

Another method for providing enhanced performance is application-specific instruction set extension. An important feature of this design method is extending an existing processor core with units specialized for a given domain, rather than designing a custom processor completely. By creating application-specific extensions to an instruction set, the critical portions of an application's dataflow graph (DFG) can be accelerated by using custom functional units. The nodes of these DFGs are the instructions of critical potion of applications and the edges of DFGs represent the

C. Jesshope and C. Egan (Eds.): ACSAC 2006, LNCS 4186, pp. 219–230, 2006.

dependency between instructions. In our method, custom instruction is a sequence of instructions that are extracted from hot basic blocks (HBBs). HBBs are basic blocks which are executed more than a predefined number of times and a basic block is a sequence of instructions that terminates by a control instruction.

Using an extensible processor with a reconfigurable functional unit proposes favorable tradeoff between efficiency and flexibility, while keeping design turnaround times much shorter. The reconfigurable part of an extensible processor executes critical portions of an application to gain better performance. It can be coarse grain or fine grain. The former, demands for less configuration memory. Also mapping of instructions on it is easier. The latter is more flexible but it is slower comparing with the coarse grain one.

Extracting CIs from applications is an important stage in accelerating application execution. Some generated CIs cannot be mapped to reconfigurable hardware because some RFU constraints, like physical constraints, cannot be considered at this stage. We call this kind of CIs *rejected CIs*. Two different strategies are used for rejected CIs. In the first case, rejected CIs are run on the base line processor, and so, this offers no speedup. As the second strategy, we suggest using approaches to recover and execute rejected CIs on the RFU rather than the base processor. To achieve this goal, two approaches are proposed. In the first approach, a CI generation tool is used to regenerate the CIs from HBBs according to the RFU constraints. As another approach, we propose a novel framework for generating CIs. This framework generates CIs in such a way that they can be executed on the RFU. Besides, it partitions rejected CIs to multiple mappable CIs. We utilize the same well-known *temporal partitioning* concept for this purpose.

In Section 2, we highlight some related work. The RFU architecture is described in Section 3. Section 4 discusses the design flow proposed for generating CIs. In Section 5, experimental results are presented and finally, Section 6 concludes the paper.

2 Related Works

Identifying optimal set of custom instruction to improve the computational efficiency of applications has received a lot of attention recently. PRISC [13] and Chimaera [17] provide compilation tools that attempt to automatically generate mappings for the reconfigurable logic. Custom instructions tend to be relatively small, due in part to the difficulty of the matching problem and the size of the programmable fabric available. DISC [16] is another system that requires CIs to be identified and programmed manually. The main focus of DISC is in the management of the loading of custom instructions.

Research in reconfigurable computing is often more in line with our goal. Researches in reconfigurable computing investigate the identification of application sections that are mapped to a reconfigurable fabric. Most of CI extraction methods attempt to identify patterns within a basic block. In [7] the authors combine template matching and generation based on the occurrence of patterns which usually led to small templates. Template matching is done based on graph isomorphism. Methods presented in [5], [8] impose further constraints by allowing multiple input-single output patterns. Arnold et al. [1] avoids the exponentially increasing of these patterns by using an iterative technique that detects 2-operator patterns, replace their occurrences in DFG and repeats the process. Atasu et al. [2] search a full binary tree and decides at each step whether or not to include a particular instruction in a pattern. The potential exponential search space is pruned based on input/output constraints. They attempt to find maximal subgraphs of application data flow graph, but it does not take into account the underlying structure of the execution hardware. Clark et al. [4] search possibly good patterns by starting with small patterns and expanding them considering the input, output and convexity constraints [18].

The general goal of this work is presenting methods for CI generation, specifically for recovering the rejected CIs. We propose approaches for generating CIs for AMBER, an adaptive dynamic extensible processor presented in [11]. AMBER uses a coarse grain reconfigurable functional unit with fixed resources. Some of the generated CIs might be rejected because of violating RFU constraints. Rejection of CIs decreases the speedup. We do not use any pruning algorithm for making smaller CIs from rejected CIs because obviously by using bigger CIs more speedup can be obtained. Our main contribution is in using an RFU architecture-aware temporal partitioning algorithm, which iteratively attempts to partition and generate appropriate CIs. These CIs are maximal subgraphs extracted from data flow graph of non-mappable CI.

For this purpose, we use an integrated temporal partitioning and mapping framework. The idea behind temporal partitioning is that functions that are too large to fit on a programmable hardware can be partitioned into several modules which are then successively downloaded into the hardware in accordance with a predefined schedule [6]. Different algorithms have been presented for temporal partitioning. Bobda [3] proposed two methods to solve temporal partitioning problem. The first one was an enhancement of the well-known list vector space. The second method uses a spectral placement to position the modules in a three-dimensional vector space. Karthikeya et al. [6] proposed algorithms for temporal partitioning and scheduling of large designs on area constrained reconfigurable hardware. *SPARCS* [12] is an integrated partitioning and synthesis framework, which has a temporal partitioning tool to temporally divide and schedule the DFGs on a reconfigurable system. Tanougust et al. [15] attempted to find the minimum area while meeting timing constraints during temporal partitioning. In [14], Spillane and Owen focused on finding a sequence of conditions for activating an appropriate component at a particular time and optimizing successive configurations to achieve the desired trade-offs among reconfiguration time, operation speed and area.

In [9], a new design flow was proposed for the compilation of data flow graphs for a reconfigurable system. This design flow consists of temporal partitioning and physical design phases with a feedback loop. In this paper, we propose a modified version of this design flow for generating appropriate CIs as a general methodology and use is specifically for AMBER RFU. This framework attempts to take advantages of the basic design flow to generate CIs and improve target extensible processor speedup.

3   RFU Architecture

In [11] an adaptive extensible processor (AMBER) was presented which has the capability of tuning its extended instructions to the running application. For this extensible processor, a coarse grain reconfigurable functional unit (RFU) was designed which is an array of functional units (FUs). FUs support all fixed point instructions of the base line processor except multiplication, division and load. A quantitative approach [4] was used to determine the number of inputs, outputs, nodes, routing resources and other architectural specifications. Twenty-two applications of Mibench [19] were used to provide quantitative analysis. Also, a mapping tool was developed to map CIs on the RFU. The details of RFU design and its integration with the base processor is out of the scope of this paper, therefore, for completeness we only describe the specification of the final architecture.

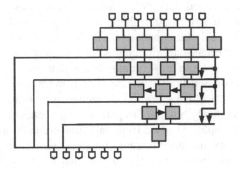

Fig. 1. Block diagram of RFU designed for AMBER.

According to the obtained results, eight inputs, six outputs and 16 FUs brought about a reasonable CI rejection rate (about 10%). Rejection rate represents the percentage of CIs that can not be mapped on the RFU according to its defined constraints. In addition, a proper topology for RFU connections was achieved based on the quantitative analysis (Fig. 1). In the proposed architecture, there are left to right connections in the 4th row and right to left connections in the 3rd row. Outputs of FUs in each row are fully connected to inputs of FUs in subsequent row. In addition, there are extra vertical connections, as in Fig. 1, between non-subsequent rows to keep the CI rejection rate low.

4   Integrated Temporal Partitioning and Mapping

Initial CIs for AMBER can be extracted from hot basic blocks of applications according to the algorithm presented in [12]. Two different approaches for generating appropriate CIs are used. Appropriate CI set means the set of CIs which satisfy the RFU primary constraints and may have the capability of being mapped successfully on the RFU. RFU *primary constraints* are the architectural constraints including the number of inputs, outputs and nodes. We used two different approaches for generating CIs. The first CI generation approach (*CIGen*) considers RFU *primary constraints* for mapping but it cannot consider all of the constraints such as routing resources constraints. For considering the physical constraints during CI generation physical design process need to be done. Therefore, for rejected CIs, *CIGen* follows a conservative method to generate appropriate CIs.

4.1 The *Integrated Framework*

Integrated Framework is the second CI generation approach that performs an integrated temporal partitioning and mapping process to generate mappable CIs. The proposed design flow is shown in Fig. 2. This design flow takes rejected CIs and attempts to partition them to appropriate CIs those have the capability of mapping on the RFU. Each CI is partitioned into two or more CIs.

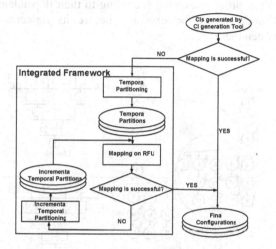

Fig. 2. Integrated temporal partitioning and mapping for supporting large CIs.

Initial temporal partitioning algorithm is done according to [9]. In this stage, RFU *primary constraints* are considered. The generated CIs are accepted and finalized if they can be mapped on the RFU. For each partition generated in the previous step, the mapping process is done and the generated CI is considered as appropriate if it can be mapped on the RFU successfully. Otherwise, an incremental temporal partitioning algorithm modifies the partition by moving some of nodes to the subsequent partition. In the next step, the mapping process is repeated. This process is done iteratively while all partitions are mapped successfully on the RFU. Fig. 3 shows an example of a rejected CI which is finally partitioned into two partitions and mapped on the RFU successfully. This framework has the following advantages:

- Reducing the number of rejected CIs: This can affect the overall performance by partitioning the rejected CIs to CIs which can be mapped on the RFU.
- Using a mapping-aware temporal partitioning process: This process attempts to prevent the rejection of CIs by modifying CIs according to the feedbacks obtained from the mapping process. In fact, only *primary constraints* of the RFU can be considered in the *CIGen* but it is unaware of such mapping information as routing resource constraints. In *Integrated Framework*, CIs are partitioned in such a way that they can be mapped on the RFU.

4.2 Incremental Temporal Partitioning Algorithm

In *Integrated Framework*, an incremental temporal partitioning process is performed iteratively until all partitions are mapped on the RFU successfully. Each partition which does not satisfy RFU constraints is modified by selecting and moving proper nodes to the subsequent partition and then a new iteration starts. An incremental temporal partitioning algorithm tries to modify partitions during the iteration process. This algorithm chooses the nodes with highest *ASAP* level first. The *ASAP* level of nodes represents their order to execute according to their dependencies [10]. In other words, a parent node should be executed before its descents because of data dependencies between them.

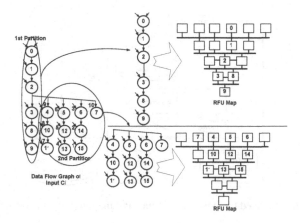

Fig. 3. An example of CI generation using the *Integrated Framework*.

All nodes in a partition are sorted according to their *ASAP* level and the node with the highest *ASAP* level is selected and moved to the subsequent partition. In Fig. 3, the order in which are selected and moved to the next partition is 15, 13, 11, 9, 14, 12, 10, 8, 3 and 7. The nodes are moved until all the generated partitions satisfy the RFU architectural constraints.

4.3 Mapping Procedure

Mapping process in the *Integrated Framework* is the same as the well-known placement problem. Mapping process can be defined as the placement of the DFG nodes on a fixed architecture RFU, to determine the appropriate positions for DFG nodes on the RFU. Assigning CI instructions or DFG nodes to FUs is done based on the priority of the nodes.

We calculated *slack* of nodes [10] to determine their priority for partitioning. Slack of each node represents its criticality. For example, slack equal to *0* means that it is on the critical path of DFG and should be scheduled with the highest priority. On the other hand, for the nodes with the same criticality, *ASAP* level of them determines their mapping order. Therefore, in the first step, *ASAP, ALAP*[1] and *slack* values of

---

[1] As Late As Possible.

each node in DFG are determined [9, 10]. Assigning a position for each selected node starts by determining an appropriate row for that node. Row number is set to the last row if the selected node is on a critical path with the length more than or equal to RFU depth. Otherwise, row number is selected according to *slack* and *ALAP* of the selected node and the number of un-occupied cells available in the RFU rows.

For the nodes which do not belong to any critical path with length more than the RFU depth, their starting row is set to *ALAP- slack -1*. This means that we reserve FUs of lower rows for the nodes belong to critical path. For this purpose, we prevent the occupation of FUs in the lower RFU rows by the nodes which do not belong to critical paths. Therefore, spiral shaped mapping of nodes is being possible for long length critical paths. After determining the row number, an appropriate column is determined for the selected node. Column number is determined according to the minimum connection length criterion. All non-occupied cells of the RFU in the determined row are checked to find an FU which gives the minimum connection length between the selected node and its dependent nodes positioned on the RFU.

For each row, a maximum capacity is considered to prohibit gathering many nodes in a row. Capacity of rows is determined with respect to longest critical path and the number of critical paths in the DFG. Row number is decreased and a new attempt starts if there is not any cell to assign the selected node. The pseudo code of the mapping algorithm is as follows:

Mapping Algorithm:

- Determine *ASAP* level of each node in the input DFG,

- Determine *ALAP* level of each node in the DFG,

- Calculate *slack* for each node in the DFG.

for *s= 0* to *Maximum slack* value

  - Create List of Nodes with *slack* equal to *s*

    for all nodes in the list

  - Determine appropriate position for the selected node from the list

  - if the number of nodes mapped on the *RFU* is equal to the DFG node number then mapping process is terminated successfully

Determine appropriate position for a selected node:

if *ALAP- slack >= RFUDepth*

  StartRow= RFUDepth;

else

   StartRow= ALAP- slack - 1;

for *Row= StartRow* to *0*

  -if there is un-occupied column in the selected row and the selected row has sufficient capacity, select a column with minimum connection length.

Referring to the RFU architecture in Fig. 1 and its routing resources, though the RFU depth is equal to 5, our mapping algorithm can map CIs whose critical path length are at most equal to 8. In Fig. 3, corresponding DFG of the first partition has a critical path longer than the RFU depth, and so it takes advantage of a spiral shaped mapping. This kind of mapping results in effective usage of routing resources (horizontal connections of the third and forth rows) and FUs.

5   Experimental Results

SimpleScalar tool set (PISA configuration)[20] and 22 applications of Mibench [19] were used for doing experiments. The base line processor of AMBER was MIPS324K with five stage pipeline, 32KB L1 data cache (1 clock cycle latency); 32KB L1 instruction cache (1 clock cycle latency) and 1MB unified L2 cache (6 clock cycle latency). RFU was implemented using Synopsys tools with Hitachi $0.18\mu m$ library. The RFU area size is $1.15mm^2$. It was assumed that the RFU has a variable latency based on the length of the longest critical path. Regarding base processor frequency (166MHz) and RFU delay, CIs with critical path length less than or equal to 5 take 1 clock cycle and CIs including critical path length more than 5 take 2 clock cycles for execution on the RFU.

Initial CIs were generated according to the method proposed in [11]. Experiments showed that the CI rejection rate with respect to RFU architectural constraints was about 10%. In 9 of the 22 applications, there was not any rejected CI, which means that

Table 1. Mibench Applications, their CI rejection rates and maximum and minimum length of Cis

App. No.	Application Name	CI Rejection % (Considering Execution Freq)	Min. CI length	Max. CI length	Min. length of Rejected CIs
1	adpcm(enc)	0	5	7	-
2	adpcm(dec)	0	5	7	-
3	bitcounts	2.3	4	20	20
4	blowfish	43.2	5	16	15
5	blowfish (dec)	43.2	5	16	15
6	basicmath	0	3	11	-
7	cjpeg	11.7	5	59	11
8	crc	0	5	5	-
9	dijkstra	0	4	9	-
10	djpeg	28.8	4	48	8
11	fft	3.4	3	16	16
12	fft (inv)	3.4	3	16	16
13	gsm (dec)	2.8	5	14	14
14	gsm (enc)	6.5	4	26	13
15	lame	11.9	3	13	7
16	patricia	0	3	6	-
17	qsort	0	5	7	-
18	rijndael (enc)	40.6	5	16	10
19	rijndael (dec)	35.4	5	18	10
20	sha	1.9	5	18	7
21	stringsearch	0	5	9	-
22	susan	0	6	10	-

all CIs in these applications were mapped on the RFU successfully. Rejected CIs of remaining 13 applications are as input of our Integrated Framework. Table 1 shows the applications, the percentage of rejected CIs considering the RFU constraints and execution frequency of CIs, minimum and maximum length of initial CIs and minimum length of rejected CIs. Application names with rejected CIs are shown in bold face.

As mentioned in Section 3, for generating appropriate CIs two approaches including *CIGen* and *Integrated Framework* were used. For CIs generated by *CIGen*, the mapping process was done and some of them were rejected again at the mapping stage because of the RFU violation of routing resource constraints. In this method, CIs were generated using a more conservative approach. Some of the CIs can not be supported and are rejected. Fig. 4 shows that 10 applications already have CIs which are non-mappable on RFU. These rejected CIs have to execute on the base line processor and offer no speedup.

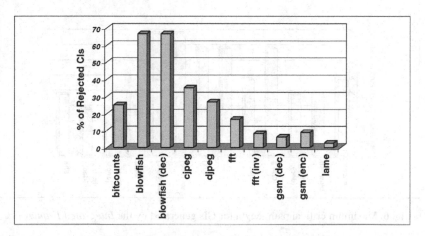

Fig. 4. Percentage of rejected CIs generated by *CIGen*

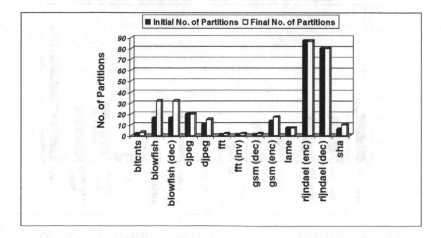

Fig. 5. Initial and final number of partitions generated by the *Integrated Framework*

In the second approach, we used the *Integrated Framework* to generate appropriate CIs. Using this approach, which iteratively generates CIs, all CIs were successfully mapped on the RFU during partitioning process. This is one of the most important advantages of the proposed design flow. Fig. 5 shows the initial and final number of partitions (CIs) generated for each application using the *Integrated Framework*. Initial number of CIs is the number of partitions generated by the temporal partitioning algorithm. In addition, the final number of partitions means the number of CIs that are generated after performing the iterative process to modify and generate appropriate CIs.

Fig. 6 shows the maximum length of the critical path for the generated CIs. According to the results obtained, for *cjpeg, fft, fft(inv), gsm(end)* and *gsm(dec)*, the mapping algorithm took advantage of spiral shape mapping to handle critical paths with length more than 5.

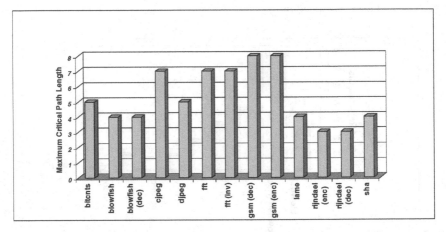

Fig. 6. Maximum critical path length for CIs generated by the *Integrated Framework*

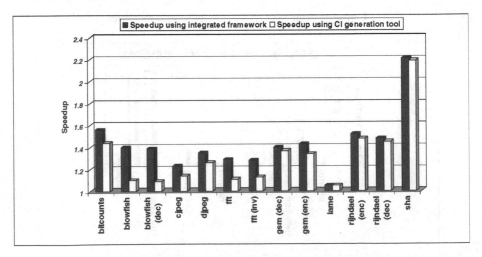

Fig. 7. Speedup comparison between *CIGen* and the *Integrated Framework*

Finally, Fig. 7 shows the speedup comparison for *CIGen* and the *Integrated Framework*. The *Integrated Framework* generated CIs all of which can be mapped on the RFU, because, temporal partitioning stage is properly aware of the mapping process result and is iteratively done according to the feedbacks obtained from the mapping phase. According to Fig. 7, speedup increases using the *Integrated Framework*. For *lame, CIGen* and the *Integrated Framework* generated similar CIs, therefore, the *Integrated Framework* does not offer more improvement for *lame* in compared to *CIGen*.

6 Conclusion

In this paper, an integrated framework was presented to address generating appropriate custom instructions and mapping them on RFU of an adaptive extensible processor. First, an RFU was presented for AMBER, a dynamic adaptive extensible processor. Some CIs of the attempted applications were rejected because of RFU primary constraints. One method for generating appropriate CIs is applying the RFU constraints to the CI generation tool and extracting the CIs which meet these constraints (*CIGen*). Using *CIGen* may still cause some generated CIs to be rejected. This approach does not have the capability of considering constraints such as routing resource constraints before mapping since it is unaware of the mapping process result. The *Integrated Framework* is the second approach which uses a mapping-aware temporal partitioning algorithm for generating appropriate CIs. In this framework, each rejected CI is partitioned to smaller partitions and iteratively modified to meet the RFU constraints. The experimental results showed that for the attempted benchmarks, the algorithm successfully mapped all CIs on the RFU. Our proposed mapping algorithm uses spiral shaped paths to cover CIs with critical paths longer than the RFU depth. Also, the *Integrated Framework* brought about more speedup enhancement comparing with *CIGen* by generating CIs which have less running time on the RFU.

Acknowledgement

The authors would like to thank *System LSI* Laboratory of Kyushu University for providing the necessary facilities and equipments. This work has been supported by Iran Telecommunication Research Center *(ITRC)*.

References

[1] Arnold, M., Corporaal, H., Designing domain-specific processors. In Proceedings of the Design, Automation and Test in Europe Conf, 2001, pp. 61-66.
[2] Atasu, K., Pozzi, L., Lenne, P., Automatic application-specific instruction-set extensions under microarchitectural constraints, 40th Design Automation Conference, 2003.
[3] Bobda, C., Synthesis of dataflow graphs for reconfigurable systems using temporal partitioning and temporal placement, Ph.D thesis, Faculty of Computer Science, Electrical Engineering and Mathematics, University of Paderborn, 2003.

[4] Clark, N., Kudlur, M., Park, H., Mahlke, S., Flautner, K., Application-specific processing on a general-purpose core via transparent instruction set customization, In Proceedings of the 37th annual IEEE/ACM International Symposium on Microarchitecture, 2004.

[5] Halfhill, T.R., MIPS embraces configurable technology, Microprocessor Report, 3 March 2003.

[6] Karthikeya, M., Gajjala, P., Dinesh, B., Temporal partitioning and scheduling data flow graphs for reconfigurable computer, IEEE Transactions on Computers, vol. 48, no. 6, 1999, pp.579–590.

[7] Kastner, R. Kaplan, A., Ogrenci Memik, S., Bozorgzadeh, E., Instruction generation for hybrid reconfigurable systems, ACM TODAES, vol. 7, no. 4, 2002, pp. 605-627.

[8] Lee, C., Potkonjak, M., Mangione-Smith, W.H., MediaBench: A tool for evaluating and synthesizing multimedia and communications systems, In Proceedings of the 30-th Annual Intl. Symp. On Microarchitecture, 1997, pp 330-335.

[9] Mehdipour, F., Saheb Zamani, M., Sedighi, M., An integrated temporal partitioning and physical design framework for static compilation of reconfigurable computing system, International Journal of Microprocessors and Microsystems, Elsevier, vol. 30, no. 1, Feb 2006, pp. 52-62.

[10] Micheli, G.D., Synthesis and optimization of digital circuits, McGraw-Hill, 1994.

[11] Noori, H., Murakami, K., Inoue, K., General overview of an adaptive dynamic extensible processor architecture, Workshop on Introspective Architecture (WISA'2006) , 2006.

[12] Ouaiss, I., Govindarajan, S., Srinivasan, V., Kaul M., Vemuri R., An integrated partitioning and synthesis system for dynamically reconfigurable multi-FPGA architectures, In Proceedings of the Reconfigurable Architecture Workshop, 1998, pp. 31-36.

[13] Razdan, R., Smith, M.D., A high-performance microarchitecture with hardware-programmable functional units, In Proceedings of the 27th Annual International Symposium on Microarchitecture, 1994, pp. 172-180.

[14] Spillane, J., Owen, H., Temporal partitioning for partially reconfigurable field programmable gate arrays, IPPS/SPDP Workshops, 1998, pp. 37-42.

[15] Tanougast, C., Berviller, Y., Brunet, P., Weber, S., Rabah, H., Temporal partitioning methodology optimizing FPGA resources for dynamically reconfigurable embedded real-time system, International Journal of Microprocessors and Microsystems, vol. 27, 2003, pp. 115-130.

[16] Writhlin, M., Hutchings, B., A dynamic instruction set computer, In Proceeding IEEE Symposium on Field Programmable Custom Computing Machines, IEEE Computer Society Press, 1995, pp. 99-107.

[17] Ye, Z.A., et al., Chimaera: A high-performance architecture with tightly-coupled reconfigurable functional unit, In Proceeding of 27th ISCA, 2000, pp. 225-235.

[18] Yu, P., Mitra, T., Characterizing embedded applications for instruction-set extensible processors, In Proceedings of Design and Automation Conference, 2004, pp. 723- 728.

[19] http://www.eecs.umich.edu/mibench.

[20] http://www.simplescalar.com.

A High Performance Simulator System for a Multiprocessor System Based on a Multi-way Cluster

Arata Shinozaki[1], Masatoshi Shima[1], Minyi Guo[2], and Mitsunori Kubo[1]

[1] Future Creation Lab., Olympus Corp., Shinjuku-ku, Tokyo 163-0914, Japan
{arata_shinozaki, masatoshi_shima, mi_kubo}@ot.olympus.co.jp
[2] School of Computer Science and Eng., University of Aizu, Aizu-Wakamatsu,
Fukushima 965-8580, Japan
minyi@u-aizu.ac.jp

Abstract. In the ubiquitous era, it is necessary to research on the architectures of multiprocessor system with high performance and low power consumption. A processor simulator developed in high level language is useful because of its easily changeable system architecture which includes application specific instruction sets and functions. However, there is a problem in processing speed that both PCs and workstations provide insufficient performance for the simulation of a multiprocessor system. In this research, a simulator for a multiprocessor system based on the multi-way cluster was developed. In the developed simulator system, one processor model consists of an instruction set simulator (ISS) process and several inter-processor communication processes. In order to get the maximization of the simulation performance, each processor model is assigned to the specific CPU on the multi-way cluster. Also, each inter-processor communication process is implemented using MPI library, which can minimize the CPU resource usage in a communication waiting state. The evaluation results of the processing and communication performance using a distributed application program such as JPEG encoding show that each ISS process in the developed simulator system consumes approximately 100% CPU resources for keeping enough inter-processor communication performance. This result means that the performance increases in proportion to the number of integrated CPUs on the cluster.

1 Introduction

In the ubiquitous era, micro processors are widely used in many applications including not only PCs and PDAs but also home appliances and cars. For these applications, high performance parallel computing is required for multimedia codec processing, digital signal processing, and secure communication processing. Performance improvement by increasing the operating frequency of a processor is reaching the upper-bound because of leakage current and power consumption [1]. Both multi-core processor systems and multiprocessor systems [2, 3] are effective solution to improve performance without increasing operating frequency. However, they still consume a lot of power. To solve these problems, it becomes necessary to research on the architecture of heterogeneous multiprocessor system with application-specific instruction sets and functions, so that it optimizes the balance between high performance and low power consumption, and lowers the redundancy of processing.

C. Jesshope and C. Egan (Eds.): ACSAC 2006, LNCS 4186, pp. 231–243, 2006.
© Springer-Verlag Berlin Heidelberg 2006

In general, a simulator developed in a high level language is useful for the research on the architecture of a processor system, because the system architecture can be easily changeable [4-8] with additional application specific instruction sets and functions. However, there is a problem that both PCs and workstations provide insufficient performance for the simulation of a multiprocessor system.

In this research, a simulator system for a multiprocessor system was developed based on a multi-way cluster. It is expected to provide high parallelism and high performance with multiple CPUs on each node. This paper shows the usefulness of the developed simulator system according to the evaluation results on the processing capability and communication performance using a distributed processing application.

2   PE and PE Network

Fig. 2.1 shows a schematic diagram of a multiprocessor system. In the part (a), each CPU is a Processing Element (PE). The system bus connecting the CPUs is called a PE Network. From this point of view, a part of multiprocessor system can be simplified as PEs connected by a PE Network.

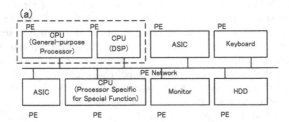

Fig. 2.1. Schematic Diagram of a Multiprocessor System

A PE can be also viewed as a processor, which contains a general purpose processor, a DSP, and a processor specific for special function, with application specific instruction sets and functions. Furthermore, a PE contains peripherals including a monitor, a keyboard, or a HDD. Similarly, PE Network can be viewed as a peripheral bus, a system bus, the Internet, or other networks. The following sections show that the simulator system can connect various PEs with common network interface and protocol. Then, they show the simulator system is useful for the simulation of a heterogeneous multiprocessor system.

3   Simulator System

3.1   Simulator System

Fig. 3.1 shows the simulator system architecture. The simulator system consists of a simulation engine, a control center (CC), and a GUI.

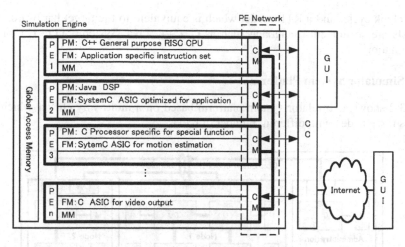

Fig. 3.1. Simulator System Architecture

The simulation engine consisted of (1) PEs, (2) PE Network, and (3) Global Access Memory. Every PE is constructed from (a) Processing Module (PM), (b) application-specific Function Module (FM), (c) Memory Module (MM), and (d) Communication Module (CM). A PM is a core information processing engine. An FM provides application specific instruction sets and functions.

For example, PE1 integrates a general purpose CPU as a PM extended its function with an application specific instruction set as an FM. PE2 accelerates a DSP with an ASIC optimized for an application as an FM. In PE3, a processor specific for special function cooperates with an ASIC for motion estimation, which requires high accuracy and massive data processing in video processing.

An MM is the registers and local memory of a PM and an FM. An MM also serves as a memory for inter-PE communication. MM stores information sent and received over the PE network, because the MM is accessible from CMs. A CM is the protocol-independent general model of PE Network. There is no special module which connects CMs. The connection information provided in each CM decides the structure of PE Network. Also, system information is sent and received through CMs. The Global Access Memory stores information shared between PEs such as large amount of video data.

The CC analyzes information of user's operations, sends control information to the simulation engine, receives simulation results from it, and controls the whole system. The CC also works as the gateway of the simulation engine, and operates the simulation engine as if it were a part of a large information processing system.

As the GUI is independent from a platform it runs, it can operate the simulation engine through the CC over various networks.

PMs and FMs can be implemented with the following various models focusing on different functions and abstraction levels: an untimed function model which simulates only function without time concept, an instruction set model which simulates only the behavior of instructions, a cycle-accurate model [9, 10] which defines the behavior in each clock cycle, and a RTL model which is equivalent to the target hardware. These models are written in a language such as C, C++, Java, SystemC [11, 12], or their combination.

3.2 Simulator System Platform

Fig. 3.2 shows a simulator system platform based on a multi-way cluster which integrates three nodes with different number of CPUs.

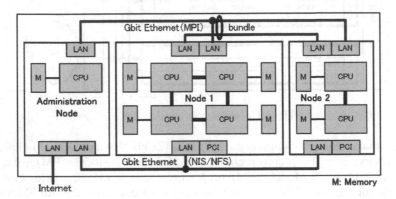

Fig. 3.2. Simulator System Platform

A one-way administration node executes the GUI and the CC, and controls the whole simulator system. Each of 6PEs is assigned to the specific CPU in a four-way node 1 and a two-way node 2 for high-speed simulation. Mainly, the node 1 processes main program and the node 2 executes pre-processing, post-processing, and external I/O processing.

The intra-node communication is implemented with high-speed system bus and memory bus exclusively used for the specific CPU. The simulator system platform implemented Opteron CPU [13] operated in 2.4GHz. One CPU can directly connect up to three adjacent CPUs through HyperTransport [14], which is bidirectional multi-channel system bus possible to transfer data at 6.4GBytes/sec. Each CPU has 4GB memory directly-accessible at 3.2GBytes/sec.

The inter-node communication is implemented with a Gigabit-Ethernet. The Ethernet cables can be logically bundled to avoid performance degradation caused by the limit of bandwidth. Inter-PE communication model is implemented using MPI [15] library which can program the timing of a request for communication and the sequence of communication handshake.

MMs and the Global Access Memory are implemented as shared memory on the OS. If the shared memory is created on other CPUs, a PM, an FM and a CM can access them in high speed through HyperTransport.

SuSE Linux 9.1 Professional (kernel 2.6) [16] facilitates process assignment to each CPU, process control, MPI programming, and the creation of shared memory under 64-bit environment.

3.3   Implementation of Simulator System

Each PM of 6 PEs is implemented with a proprietary MIPS R2000/3000 instruction set [17] simulator (ISS) in C++. An ISS can simulate each step of instruction behavior, and it is suitable for the high-speed verification of algorithm of applications. For the inter-PE communication, system call 1 instruction (syscall1) and system call 2 instruction (syscall2) were expanded from the system call instruction in the MIPS instruction set. Syscall1 requests to send data for the data receiving PE, and syscall2 notifies that the data receiving PE finished using data for the data sending PE.

MMs are implemented with 256KB local memory and registers. The registers consist of general-purpose registers, exception registers, and extended system control registers. The Global Access Memory is composed of 4MB internal bulk memory on the node 1, 4MB external memory, and also 4MB media memory on the node 2.

3.4   Details of Simulator System

3.4.1   Process Organization and CPU Assignment
Fig.3.3 shows process organization and CPU assignment for the communication between PE1 and PE2 / PE3. The PE is implemented with one PM process, i.e., MIPS ISS, and CM processes consisted of pairs of sending process and receiving process. These pairs are used for (1) inter-PE communication and (2) communication with the CC. All processes of a specific PE is assigned to a corresponding CPU. Therefore, all the processes in the PE are possible to use almost 100% of the specific CPU resources. All the processes are accessible to the registers and the local memory in the MM. Fig. 3.4 shows the local memory map.

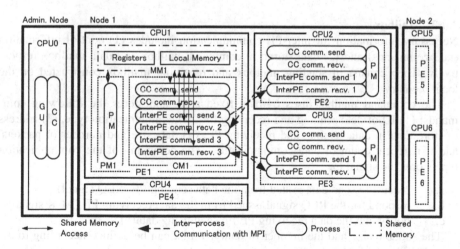

Fig. 3.3. Process Organization and CPU Assignment

3.4.2   Communication Module (CM)
A CM is implemented using MPI library as native code on the multi-way cluster, and works with a pair of a sending process and a receiving one. MPI enables to write the detailed sequence of the communication handshake as intended.

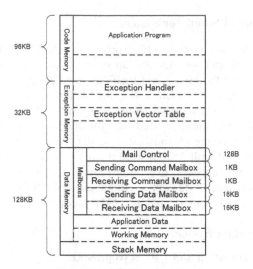

Fig. 3.4. Local Memory Map

When the simulator extends the network structure by increasing or decreasing the pair of the CM processes, these CM processes are required to minimize the influence on the PM process. Then, every sending process or receiving process minimizes its CPU resource usage, organized with a loop starting from MPI_Recv() function to block its execution and sleep in a waiting state. This enabled the PM process to use almost 100% of the specific CPU resources.

3.4.3 Mailbox

Necessary information for inter-PE communication includes (1) control information (i.e., commands) and (2) data stored in command mailbox and data mailbox respectively. They consist of sending mailbox and receiving mailbox constructed on the local memory.

The command mailbox uses 64-byte fixed area, and stores the following commands: (1) ID of data sending and receiving PE, (2) communication type, (3) address to store data in data sending and receiving PE, (4) data size and number of packets, and (5) repeat count of data communication. The command of the communication type stores the signal to:

a.   request to send data issued from the data sending PE (REQ signal)
b.   respond for the REQ signal issued from the data receiving PE (ACK signal)
c.   notify that the data receiving PE finished using data(FIN signal)

The suitable size and the number of data mailbox can be defined according to the characteristics of the application.

The Mail Control was constructed at the top of mailbox area. It manages communication status using the following register and flags:

A.   Sending Session Counter (SSC) to count the number of communication session

B.   Sending Mailbox Full (SMF) to notify whether the sending mailbox is empty to the PM process

C.   Receiving Mailbox Full (RMF) to notify whether the receiving data mailbox receives data to the PM process

3.4.4 Sequence of Communication

Fig. 3.5 shows the sequence of the inter-PE communication to send data from PE1 to PE2 with a single communication buffer. PM1 app. and PM2 app. express the description of application program running on PM1 and PM2 respectively. PM1 and PM2 express the behavior of PMs which application programs cannot detect, for example the control of a flags and mailboxes etc.

(flow)

(1) [PM1 app.] stores sending commands including the REQ signal and the address to indicate the top of sending data to the sending command mailbox.

(2) [PM1 app.] stores sending data to the sending data mailbox.

(3) [PM1 app.] executes syscall1.

(4) [PM1] sets SCC and SMF.

(5) [PM1] extracts the ID of PE2 from the sending command mailbox, then, sends the sending commands including the REQ signal to CM2

(6) [CM2] receives the commands including the REQ signal, and returns from a waiting state.

(7) [CM2] stores the sending commands including the ACK signal and the address to indicate the top of the receiving data to the sending command mailbox.

(8) [CM2] sends the sending commands including the ACK signal to CM1

(9) [CM1] receives the commands including the ACK signal, and returns from a waiting state.

(10) [CM1] sends the sending data in the sending data mailbox to CM2

(11) [CM1] clears SMF, and waits the next commands by MPI_Recv(). PM1 app. becomes able to store the sending commands and data for the next session to the sending mailboxes.

(12) [CM2] receives the data in the receiving data mailbox.

(13) [CM2] sets RMF, and enters a waiting state by MPI_Recv().

(14) [PM2 app.] detects RMF, and stores the received data to the working memory

(15) [PM2 app.] sets the sending commands including the FIN signal to the sending command mailbox.

(16) [PM2 app.] executes syscall2.

(17) [PM2] clears RMF.

(18) [PM2] extracts the ID of PE1 from the sending command mailbox, then, send the sending commands including the FIN signal to CM1

(19) [CM1] receives the commands including the FIN signal, and returns from a waiting state.

(20) [CM1] clears SSC, and enters a waiting state by MPI_Recv(). After that, PM1 app. can execute syscall1.

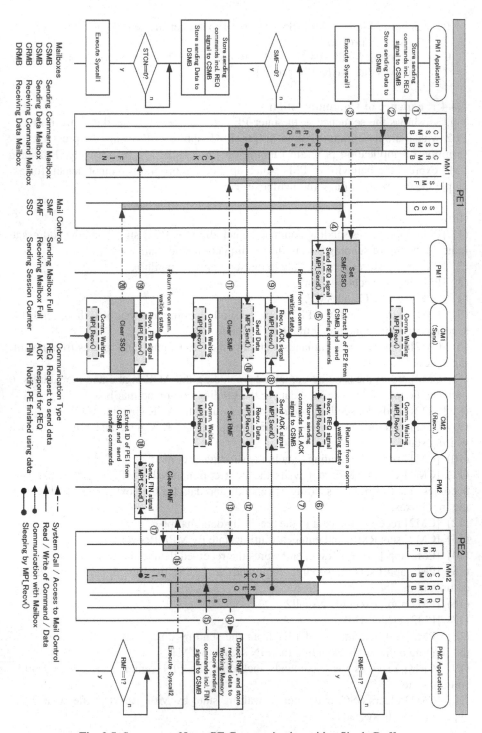

Fig. 3.5. Sequence of Inter-PE Communication with a Single Buffer

4   Performance Evaluation

This section shows the basic processing performance of PE without CM processing and the basic communication performance of CM without PM processing. After that, we will evaluate the processing and communication performance of this simulator system and its usefulness, using an application -- JPEG encoding program.

4.1   Performance Evaluation of PM Processing

The following five application programs were selected for performance evaluation of PM processing: (1) transposition of 32x32-bit matrix, (2) two-dimensional DCT for 8x8-element matrix, (3) a test program for arithmetical and logical instructions (4) a test program for branch and jump instructions, and (5) a test program for memory access instructions. Each application program executed 1G instructions on each of 1 PE, 2 PEs, 4 PEs, or 6 PEs without inter-PE communication, measuring the processing time to evaluate the processing performance of ISSs as PM. Fig. 4.1 shows the average processing performance and CPU resource usage of PM.

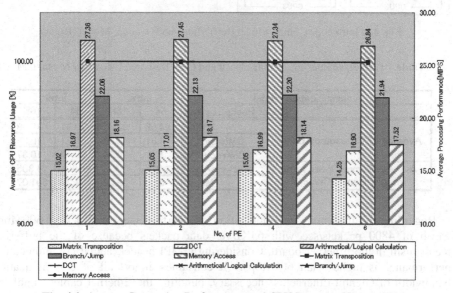

Fig. 4.1. Average Processing Performance and CPU Resource Usage of PM

This instruction simulator caches decoded instructions. Therefore, the processing performance of PM depends on the cache hit rate. In terms of matrix transposition, which shows the lowest performance, the average processing performance of PM was over 14MIPS in 6PE case. The performance is only 5% lower than that in 1 PE case. Other application programs show almost the same results. For each PE was assigned to the specific CPU, the CPU resource usage in all of application programs shows almost 100% as expected.

4.2 Performance Evaluation of CM Processing

On the intra-node and inter-node communication models shown in Fig. 4.2, (1) 64-byte packets same as a command mailbox and (2) 16K-byte packets same as a data mailbox were sent and received sequentially in 60 seconds. Each communication channel has no dependency. The average of inter-PE communication speed of all channels and the CPU resource usage were calculated. To measure the communication performance while all PMs consume almost 100% of CPU resources, the execution priority of each CM process was set to be low. Table 4.1 shows the results of the measurement.

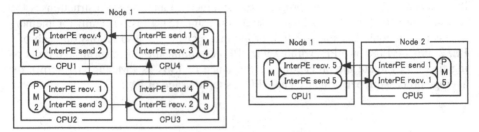

Fig. 4.2. Intra-node Comm. Model (left) / Inter-node Comm. Model (Right)

Table 4.1. Average Inter-PE Comm. Speed and CPU Resource Usage of PM and CM

Communication Model		Intra.		Inter.	
Size of Packet[Bytes]		64	16K	64	16K
	PM[%]	94.58	98.87	73.31	79.58
Average CPU Resource Usage	CM(send)[%]	4.31	0.38	6.21	10.05
	CM(recv.)[%]	1.11	0.74	20.49	10.37
Average Comm. Speed in All	[Packets/sec]	1,222	476	63,991	4,805
InterPE Comm. Channel	[Mbps]	0.60	59.52	31.26	601.07

Regarding the inter-node communication, the performance of CM kept 600Mbps worth of 4800 packets/sec with 64KByte data packets because of the buffering mechanism in the Ethernet board. Considering a MPI header, actual communication performance is higher than 600Mbps. It consumes almost all of communication bandwidth of Gigabit-Ethernet. If necessary, bundling the Ethernet cables is able to expand the bandwidth. For an application in which communication plays an important role, it is possible to increase communication speed by lowering the CPU resource usage of PM. The same can be said for the intra-node communication.

On the other hand, regarding the intra-node communication, communication speed is 1200 packets/sec with 16KB packets and 500 packets/sec with 64B packets using 4 channels, while PM consumes about 95% CPU resources. If much higher communication speed is required, it is possible to share the information without communication by constructing mailboxes on the Global Access Memory based on the characteristics of the multi-way cluster.

4.3 Performance Evaluation of Simulator System Using JPEG Encoding Application Program

The JPEG encoding application is divided into six sub-programs and executed on each PE as shown in Table 4.2. An input image is specified with the format of 24-bit-depth bitmap file, the size of VGA (640x480), the sampling factor of 4:2:2, and the quality of 75. Table 4.2 shows the processing performance of PM, the CPU resource usage of PM, the times and the processing rate defined below, the data size in inter-PE communication, and the performance of CM processing.

- PE operating time   = the elapsed time from the beginning of processing to the end of it on each PE
- PM operating time   = the time consumed as a user process out of PE operating time
- PM waiting time   = PM operating time * (No. of instructions executed in a communication waiting state / No. of all instructions)
- PM processing time   = PM operating time – PM waiting time
- CM communicating time = PE operating time – PM operating time
- PE processing rate   = (PM processing time + CM communicating time) / PE operating time

Table. 4.2. Simulator System Performance Using JPEG Encoding Application Program

Assigned Node	Node 2	Node 1				Node 2	
Assigned PE	PE5	PE1	PE2	PE3	PE4	PE6	Average
Function	Bitmap File Reading	RGB to YCrCb	Down Sampling	DCT/ Quantizati on	Huffman/R un-length	JPEG File Writing	
PM Processing Performance[MIPS]	15.29	14.03	14.58	14.08	14.06	15.68	14.62
PM CPU Resource Usage	99.32%	99.52%	99.95%	99.97%	99.90%	99.95%	99.77%
PE Operating Time[sec]	21.41	21.40	21.40	21.40	21.40	21.41	
PM Operating Time[sec]	21.24	21.20	21.31	21.31	21.28	21.32	
PM Processing Time[sec]	0.36	3.07	1.55	8.16	2.19	0.02	
PM Waiting Time[sec]	20.88	18.13	19.76	13.15	19.08	21.30	
CM Commnicating Time[sec]	0.17	0.20	0.09	0.09	0.13	0.09	
PE Processing Rate	2.50%	15.28%	7.65%	38.55%	10.84%	0.50%	12.55%
Size of Receiving Data[KBytes]	0	900	900	600	1200	~600	
Size of Sending Data[KBytes]	900	900	600	1200	~600	0	
CM Processing Performance [MBytes/sec]	5.05	8.75	16.10	19.75	~14.06	~6.73	

Each PM could achieve over 14MIPS performance with CM processing. CM could achieve over 5MBytes/sec communication performance using less than 1 % CPU resources. The performance of PM itself is equivalent to the performance in the case of single PM processing without CM processing shown in Fig. 4.1. The performance of CM is higher than that of CM processing without PM processing, which is shown in Table 4.1. However, this JPEG encoding application used only single communication buffer and could send the next data only after detecting the execution of data processing. As a result, 90% of PE operating time was consumed for a waiting state, and the simulation time exceeded 20 seconds for the encoding of one JPEG picture. In the next step, the communication waiting time will be reduced using multiple communication buffer and overlapping PM processing and CM processing to improve the performance.

One of the performance improvement methods is averaging the processing times in all of PMs and optimizing the partitioning of functions assigned to each PE by detecting performance bottlenecks. This simulator system enables researchers to profile and detect the bottlenecks of the processing time and waiting time of each PE. For example, the result in Table 4.2 implies that PE3 is one of bottlenecks consuming the longest processing time, and partitioning them into DCT and quantization will be effective. Also, it implies PE6 consumes less than 1% PE processing rate, and combining it with PE4 will be effective. Thus, the simulator system is useful to optimize the partitioning of functions, and research new additional instruction sets and application specific functions. As a result, the simulator system is suitable to research the architecture of a heterogeneous multiprocessor system.

5 Conclusion

This research focused on a simulator system for a multiprocessor system based on the high performance multi-way cluster integrated multiple CPUs on each processing node. The implemented simulator system maximized its performance, assigning each PE to the specific CPU on the multi-way cluster and implementing CM with MPI which can minimize the CPU resource usage in a communication waiting state. The simulator system executed application at over 14MIPS on each PM, achieving communication performance at over 5MBytes/sec with the distributed processing of JPEG encoding using single communication buffer. Thus, this showed that the implemented simulator system is useful for the simulation of distributed application on a multiprocessor system.

This paper showed that the implemented simulator system enables to profile application processing time and waiting time of each PE, detect bottlenecks, optimize the partitioning of functions in available PE resources, and research additional new instruction sets and application specific functions for the architecture of a heterogeneous multiprocessor system suitable for the ubiquitous era.

In the future, extending the current simulator system, we will research and develop a full-scale simulator system suitable for a multi-stream application with new sets of PE including ISSs and cycle-accurate models with additional instruction sets, application specific untimed function models, and RTL models in a system description language such as SystemC. The simulator system will promote the research on the target multiprocessor system.

References

1. Matsuzawa, A., Issues of Current LSI Technology and the Future Technology Direction. IEICE Transactions vol. J87-C No.11, pages 802-809, 2004.
2. Pham, D., et al., The Design and Implementation of a First-Generation CELL Processor – A Multi-Core SoC. ICICDT 2005 pages 49 – 52, 2005

3. Intel PentiumD Processor, http://www.intel.com/products/processor/index.htm (March, 2006)
4. Imafuku, S., Ohno, K., and Nakashima, H. Reference filtering for distributed simulation of shared memory multi-processor. In Proc. 34th Annual Simulation Symposium, pages 219—226, May 2001.
5. Mukherjee, S., Reinhardt, S., Falsafi, B., Litzkow, M., Huss-Lederman, S., Hill, M., Larus, J., and Wood, D. Wisconsin Wind Tunnel II: A fast and portable parallel architecture simulator. In Proc. Workshop on Performance Analysis and Its Impact on Design, June 1997.
6. Rosenblum, M., Herrod, S., Witchel, E., and Gupta, A. Complete computer system simulation: The SimOS approach. IEEE Parallel & Distributed Technology, 3(4): 34—43, 1995.
7. Veenstra, J., and Fowler, R. Mint: A front end for efficient simulation of shared-memory multi-processor. In Proc. MASCOTS'94, pp. 201—207, 1994.
8. Cmelik, R., and Keppel, D. Shade: A fast instruction set simulator for execution profiling. In Proc. of 1994 ACM SIGMETTRICS Conference on Measurement and Modeling of computer systems, Philadelphia, 1996.
9. Shima, M., Shinozaki, A., Sato, T. Cycle-Accurate Processor Modeling Written in Java Lan-guage. IEICE CPSY2002-53, pages 13-18, 2002.
10. Shima, M., Shinozaki, A., Ohta, S., Ito, K. Cycle-Accurate System Modeling in Java. IEICE VLD2002-146, pages 1-6, 2003.
11. Grotker, T., Liao, S., Martin, G., Swan, S. System Design with SystemC, Kluwer Academic Publishers, 2003.
12. SystemC Community. http://www.systemc.org/ (March, 2004).
13. AMD Opteron Processor, http://www.amd.com/us-en/Processors/ProductInformation/0,,30_118_8825,00.html (Current March, 2006).
14. HyperTransport Consortium, http://www.hypertransport.org/ (Current March, 2006).
15. Pacheco, P., Parallel Programming with MPI. Morgan Kaufmann Publishers, CA, USA, 1997.
16. SUSE Linux, http://www.novell.com/linux/ (Current March, 2006)
17. Kane, G., Heinrich, J. MIPS RISC ARCHITECTURE. Prentice Hall PTR, New Jersey, USA, 1992.

Hardware Budget and Runtime System for Data-Driven Multithreaded Chip Multiprocessor

Kyriakos Stavrou, Pedro Trancoso, and Paraskevas Evripidou

Department of Computer Science, University of Cyprus
75 Kallipoleos Ave., P.O. Box 20537, 1678 Nicosia, Cyprus
{tsik, pedro, skevos}@cs.ucy.ac.cy

Abstract. The Data-Driven Multithreading Chip Multiprocessor (DDM-CMP) architecture has been shown to overcome the power and memory wall limitations by combining two key technologies: the use of the Data-Driven Multithreading (DDM) model of execution, and the Chip-Multiprocessor architecture. DDM is able to hide memory and synchronization latencies providing significant performance gains whereas the use of of the CMP architecture offers high-degree of parallelism at low complexity design and is therefore power efficient.

This paper presents the hardware budget analysis and the runtime support system for the DDM-CMP architecture. The hardware analysis shows that the DDM benefits may be achieved with only a 17% hardware cost increase compared to a traditional chip-multiprocessor implementation. The support for the runtime system was designed in such a way that allows the DDM applications to execute on the DDM-CMP chip using a regular, non-modified, Operating System and CPU cores.

1 Introduction

To deliver performance as predicted by Moore's Law, computer architects have relied on extracting higher degrees of Instruction Level Parallelism (ILP) using more complex structures and larger cache hierarchies. While this approach has worked well in the past, it is currently only resulting in diminishing returns [1]. This is due to the inability of current architectures in surpassing two major obstacles: the *memory* and *power walls*. Both walls can be traced back to the von Neumann model of execution that has dominated the computer architecture field since the advent of digital computers. The memory wall problem is due to the imbalance between the speed of microprocessors and that of main memory, while the power wall is due to the high frequencies and complexity in modern microprocessors.

Data-Driven Multithreading (DDM) [2,3] is an alternative model of execution that does *not* suffer from the previously mentioned limitations. DDM has been shown, in our previous work [2,3], to be able to tolerate the memory and synchronization latencies by allowing the computation processor to produce useful work while a long latency event is in progress. In this model, the synchronization part of the program is separated from the communication part allowing it

C. Jesshope and C. Egan (Eds.): ACSAC 2006, LNCS 4186, pp. 244–259, 2006.
© Springer-Verlag Berlin Heidelberg 2006

to hide the synchronization and communication delays [2]. While such computation models usually require the design of dedicated microprocessors, Kyriacou *et al.* [2] showed that the DDM benefits may be achieved using commodity microprocessors. The only additional requirement is a small hardware structure, the *Thread Synchronization Unit* (TSU).

State-of-the-art microprocessors have a high transistor density, execute at very high frequencies, include large cache memories and rely heavily on out-of-order and speculative execution. For the implementation of these techniques, multiported and even replicated devices are required. This, however, leads to an exponential increase at the gate level whereas getting the power consumption out of hand [4]. As such, major microprocessor manufacturers have shifted their strategy to multicore chips in order to avoid the memory and power walls. CMPs utilize the increasing number of on-chip transistors not through more complex designs but by replicating simpler cores. Although this is a working solution today, CMPs' scalability potential is likely to be limited by the memory wall.

DDM-CMP is a single-ISA homogeneous chip multiprocessor that supports the Data-Driven Multithreading model of execution [5]. As such, it is able to combine the advantages of the DDM model with those of the CMP architecture offering the potential for better scalability. DDM-CMP has been shown able to deliver very high performance speedup combined with significant power reduction [5,6].

While our previous work focused on the DDM model [2,3,12] and more recently on high-level issues of DDM-CMP [5,6], such as estimations of the performance and power benefits, in this paper we go a step further and present an analysis of the hardware budget for the DDM-CMP. As a result we can now accurately determine the number of cores that may be included in a chip with the same hardware budget as other traditional CPUs. In this paper we show that, in the same hardware budget of a modern high-end single-chip microprocessor, it is possible to build a DDM-CMP chip with 16 cores. The extra hardware cost for supporting execution under the DDM model are shown to be less than 17% of the total area. Moreover, we present and validate the Runtime Support System of DDM-CMP. A careful design of this system allows the execution of both regular and DDM applications without any modification to the CPU or the OS. This system was validated using a functional Simics-based [7] full system simulator.

The rest of this paper is organized as follows. Section 2 presents the DDM-CMP architecture, Section 3 describes the DDM-CMP chip whereas Section 4 the DDM-CMP runtime support system. The validation is presented in Section 5, and Section 6 discusses the conclusions and future work.

2   The DDM-CMP Architecture

2.1   The Data-Driven Multithreading Model of Execution

Data-Driven Multithreading (DDM) provides effective latency tolerance by allowing the computation processor produce useful work, while a long latency event is in progress. This is achieved by scheduling a thread for execution only when its input data have been produced and prefetched. Efficient prefetching of the input data may be achieved through the *CacheFlow* policies [8].

The DDM model of execution has been evolved from the dataflow model of computation [9,10,11]. In particular, it originates from the dynamic dataflow Decoupled Data-Driven (D^3) graphs [12,13], where the synchronization part of a program is separated from the computation part. The computation part represents the actual instructions of the program executed by the computation processor, while the synchronization part contains information about data dependencies among threads and is used for thread scheduling.

A program in DDM is a collection of re-entrant code blocks. A code block is equivalent to a function or a loop body in the high-level program text. Each code block comprises of several threads. A thread is a sequence of instructions equivalent to a basic block. A producer/consumer relationship exists among threads. In a typical program, a set of threads, called the *producers*, create data used by other threads, called the *consumers*. Scheduling of code blocks, as well as scheduling of threads within a code block is done dynamically at run time according to data availability. The instructions within a thread are fetched by the CPU sequentially in control-flow order. Nevertheless, the CPU can reorder the sequence of instructions internally to exploit the advantages of out-of-order execution.

At compile time a program is partitioned into a *data-driven synchronization graph* and *code threads*. Each node of the graph represents one thread associated with its *Synchronization Template*. Each thread is identified by the thread number (*Thread#*) consisting of the triplet (*Context, Block, ThreadID*). The *Context* field is set at run time to distinguish between multiple invocations of the same code block or thread. This is useful for the implementation of multiple invocations of functions and loop bodies. The *Block* field identifies the code block, while the *ThreadID* identifies the thread within the code block. The synchronization template of each thread contains the following information: *Ready Count, Instruction Frame Pointer (IFP), Data Frame Pointer (DFP)* and *Consumer threads* (*Consumer1* and *Consumer2*). The *Ready Count* is set by the compiler and corresponds to the number of input values , i.e. producers to the thread. This value is decremented at runtime and a thread is enabled, *i.e.* it is ready for execution when its Ready Count reaches zero. Whenever the thread completes its execution, it uses the *Consumer thread pointers* to decrement their ready count. When a thread is to be executed, its code and data blocks must be specified. This information is provided by *IFP* and *DFP*. *IFP* is a pointer to the address of the first instruction of the thread, whereas *DFP* is a pointer to the data frame assigned for the thread/code block.

TSU: Hardware Support for DDM. The purpose of the *Thread Synchronization Unit* (TSU) is to provide hardware support for data-driven thread synchronization on conventional microprocessors. The TSU is made out of three units: the *Thread Issue Unit* (TIU), the *Post Processing Unit* (PPU) and the *Network Interface Unit* (NIU). When a thread completes its execution, the PPU updates the *Ready Count* of its consumer threads, determines whether any of those threads became ready for execution and if so, it forwards them to the TIU. The function of the TIU is to schedule and prefetch threads deemed executable by the PPU. The NIU is responsible for the communication between the TSU and the interconnection network. The internal structure of the TSU is shown in Figure 1. A more detailed presentation of the DDM model and its components can be found in [3].

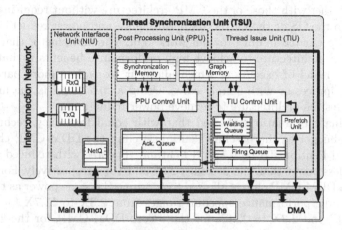

Fig. 1. Thread Synchronization Unit (TSU) and its relationship with the execution processor

CacheFlow. Although DDM can tolerate communication and synchronization latency, scheduling based on data availability may have a negative effect on locality. To overcome this problem, the scheduling information together with software-triggered data prefetching, are used to implement efficient cache management policies. These policies are named CacheFlow. A presentation and evaluation of the CacheFlow policies can be found in [8]. The most effective CacheFlow policy contains two optimizations, *False Conflict Avoidance* and *Thread Reordering*. False Conflict Avoidance prevents the prefetcher from replacing cache blocks required by the threads deemed executable and so reduces cache misses. Thread Reordering attempts to exploit both temporal and spatial locality by reordering the threads still waiting for their input data.

The DDM model used on a Data-Driven Network-Of-Workstations [14] architecture tolerates well both the communication and synchronization latency. Although Dataflow is known to reduce memory access locality, DDM together with CacheFlow was shown to reduce the local memory latency resulting in very high speedup values [2]. In particular, for a set of SPLASH-2 benchmarks [15], the use of DDM without CacheFlow, increases the cache miss rate from 7.1% to 9.8%. Adding CacheFlow reduces it to only 1.4% [8]. Overall, for 16- and 32-node machines, the authors observed performance speedup, compared to the sequential single node execution, of 14.4× and 26.0×, respectively.

More details about the DDM model of execution as well as the analysis of its performance potential can be found in [2,3].

2.2 The Data-Driven Multithreading Chip Multiprocessor

DDM-CMP is a chip multiprocessor able to support the Data-Driven Multi-threading model of execution. DDM-CMP combines the benefits of the DDM model together with those of the CMP architecture without requiring any modification to the OS or the CPUs. Its performance and power reduction potential have been presented in our previous work [5,6]. The main factor that allows the DDM-CMP architecture to achieve high performance benefits is that it utilizes the DDM model of execution, which allows it to explore more parallelism on Chip Multiprocessor with simple cores. Using *simple* cores is the main reason that enables the architecture to achieve power reductions.

Preliminary evaluations showed that with equal frequency, technology and hardware budget as the baseline Pentium 4 chip, the DDM-CMP chips with 4 unmodified Pentium III core and 8 Pentium III cores with reduced cache sizes consume less power than the baseline, 22% and 19%, respectively. For a scenario where the DDM-CMP chip is allowed to consume the same power as the baseline processor, the performance speedup ranges from 2.3X to 11.7X for the 4 core DDM-CMP and 2.3X to 22.6X for the 8 core DDM-CMP, for the 4 SPLASH-2 [15] benchmarks studied.

3   DDM-CMP Chip

3.1   Chip Layout

The DDM-CMP chip includes the execution cores along with all other units that are required in order to operate as a shared-memory chip multiprocessor and support the DDM model of execution. The extra hardware required to enable the on-chip CPUs to operate as a shared-memory chip multiprocessor is an on-chip interconnection network along with the necessary logic to guarantee data consistency. These extra units are referred as the *"CMP Hardware Support"*. To support the DDM model, the chip also includes one TSU per execution core and a communication media between the TSUs. These extra units are referred as the *"DDM Hardware Support"*. Without loss of generality, Figure 2 depicts the layout of a DDM-CMP chip with only 4 cores.

Instead of requiring ISA extensions to support the CPU-TSU communication we use simple memory read and write operations. This is achieved by having the TSU as a memory-mapped device. Therefore, the execution core (CPU), of the DDM-CMP chip can be *any* commodity microprocessor that supports memory-mapped devices. As the vast majority of today's microprocessors meet the requirement, this is not a limitation. In the current implementation, the basic core chosen for the DDM-CMP chip is the PowerPC405 [16]. The use of simple, embedded processors is justified by Olukotun *et al.* [4] who showed that

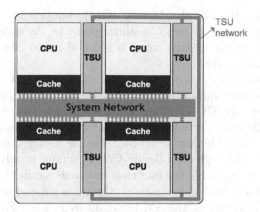

Fig. 2. The layout of DDM-CMP chip with 4 cores

the simpler the cores of the multiprocessor, the higher their frequency can be. In addition, embedded processors are smaller and therefore we are able to include more cores in the same chip. The reason we have selected this specific embedded processor, is that it is the processor used in the hardware prototype platform currently under development.

The *System Interconnection Network* enables the communication between the CPUs and the rest of the memory hierarchy. Additionally, it serves as the necessary media for the enforcement of memory consistency between the on-chip caches. CPU-TSU communication also uses this network as the TSUs are memory mapped devices. Nevertheless, to avoid congestion on the primary data path, a dedicated network, the *TSU Network*, serves the communication between the TSUs.

3.2 Hardware Budget Analysis

To estimate the hardware budget of the DDM-CMP chip we performed a detailed analysis for each of its units. Specifically, we analyzed the total hardware requirements of the TSUs, the two interconnection networks and the CPUs. The number of entries for the different TSU structures, is borrowed from the D^2NOW configuration [14], the predecessor of DDM-CMP. That TSU configuration proved to be efficient for the execution of the SPLASH-2 [15] benchmarks.

As depicted in Figure 1, the TSU consists mainly of memory units and a small number of logic units. The largest units of the TSU are the Graph and Synchronization Memory, which keep the Synchronization Graph of the program (see Section 2.1). Both these structures are indexed with the Thread#. As a thread can be stored in any available entry, both structures are implemented as Content Addressable Memories (CAM) [1].

---

[1] As these units have only 64 entries, implementing them as content addressable memories, will not result in a performance penalty.

For each thread, the Graph Memory (GM) contains its Thread#, its two Data-Frame-Pointers and its two Consumer-pointers. As each of these fields is 32-bits long the total size of each entry in the GM is 160 bits. The current GM is configured with 64 entries.

To allow threads with more than two Data Frame or Consumer pointers, two additional memory units exist on the TSU, the Data Frame Pointer (DFP) and the Consumer lists (CON). These units are simple Direct-Mapped memory structures with 128 entries, each of which 32 bits long.

The Synchronization Memory (SM) contains the Ready-Count counters of the execution threads. Although each Ready-Count counter is only 4 bits long, what increases the size of the SM is the fact that one such counter exists for each parallel invocation of a thread. As such, each thread is allowed to have 64 dynamic instances, with each entry of the SM being 32 bytes long. For consistency, SM must have the same number of entries as the GM, i.e. 64.

The Waiting Queue (WQ) is a Direct Mapped structure that keeps the Thread# and the Index of the threads deemed executable. The WQ has 16 entries of 64 bits (both Thread# and Index are 32 bits long). According to the CacheFlow policies (see Section 2.1), when a prefetch request is issued for a thread of the WQ, this thread is moved in the Firing Queue (FQ). This FIFO structure has 16 entries and holds for each thread its Thread#, its Index, its Instruction Frame Pointer and finally its Data Frame Pointer. As such, the total size of an FQ entry is 128 bits.

The threads that have completed their execution are held in the Acknowledgment Queue (AQ). This simple FIFO structure has 64 entries, each of which is 80 bits long. The Thread# and the Index require 64 bits, whereas the other 16 bits concern information that is necessary for the post-processing phase.

Finally, two more FIFO structures exist in the Network Interface Unit (NIU) of the TSU, the Transmit and the Receive Queue. Each queue has 64 32-bit long entries.

To estimate the hardware budget for the memory units of the TSU we used CACTI [17], a well known tool for on-chip cache area estimation. Table 1 summarizes the way TSU memory units were modeled as a caches. For the FIFO and Direct Mapped units we used the area results concerning the data array of the modeled cache whereas for the CAM units the total cache area. As CACTI's results are in terms of area and not transistor count, we determined the #transistor/area ratio using a known cache example. We modeled in CACTI, the Data-Cache of a 180nm Pentium III processor and compared its area with the processor's floorplan and total number of transistors. For the 180nm technology, this ratio was found to be 185K transistors per mm^2. Based on this analysis, the memory units of the TSU require a total number of 584K transistors.

For the logic units of the TSU, we used a different approach. Specifically, we used hardware synthesis estimations and concluded that they require approximately 35K transistors. Therefore, the total transistor count for the TSU was found to be 620K.

The transistor count for the System Interconnection Network was estimated based on the results reported in [18]. Specifically, the authors report the System

Table 1. The configuration of each memory unit of the TSU

Real Configuration	GM	SM	WQ	FQ	AQ	DFP	CON	NIU
- Memory Type	CAM	CAM	DM	FIFO	FIFO	DM	DM	FIFO
- Number of entries	64	64	16	16	64	128	128	64
- Size per entry (bits)	160	256	64	128	80	32	32	32
Configuration in CACTI	**GM**	**SM**	**WQ**	**FQ**	**AQ**	**DFP**	**CON**	**NIU**
- Associativity	FA	FA	DM	DM	DM	DM	DM	DM
- Cache Size	1280	2048	128	256	640	512	512	256
- Block Size	10	32	8	16	10	8	8	16
- Associativity	FA	1	1	1	1	1	1	1
- Read/Write Ports	0	0	0	0	0	0	0	0
- Exclusive Read Ports	1	1	1	1	1	1	1	1
- Exclusive Write Ports	1	1	1	1	1	1	1	1
- Number of sub-banks	1	1	1	1	1	1	1	1
Transistor Count($\times$1000)	**179**	**179**	**21**	**30**	**51**	**32**	**32**	**60**

Interconnection Network together with the necessary Cache Coherency logic to be approximately 3.125mm^2 *per core* for the 180nm technology. According to the previously determined #transistor/area ratio, this is approximately equal to 580K transistors. Although, the TSU network is simpler and thus most likely smaller than the System Interconnection Network, we will consider both to have the same requirements, which is an overestimation. Finally, the execution core of the DDM-CMP chip, the PowerPC405, accounts for approximately 5.2 million transistors [19].

Overall, the hardware budget for each DDM-node, including all necessary hardware support units, is about 7 million transistors. Table 2 summarizes the transistor budget decomposition for a DDM-CMP node. All values reported are *per-node* and represent thousands of transistors.

Table 2. DDM-CMP node transistor-budget decomposition. The values reported concern the portion for each DDM-CMP node. Numbers represent thousands of transistors.

DDM Hardware Support			CMP Hardware Support	CPU
TSU memory	TSU Logic	TSU Network overhead	CMP Overhead	CPU
584	35	580	580	5200

Figure 3 presents a relative analysis of the real estate of a DDM-CMP node. The CPU accounts for 74.5% of the area budget, while the CMP and DDM hardware support account for 8.3% and 17.2% respectively. This is a good indication that the performance benefits of DDM can be achieved at a minimal hardware cost of 17.2%.

From the information reported in [20], the number of transistors used in implementing Intel Pentium 4 3.2GHz 1MB L2 cache 90nm technology is approximately 125 million, while the number of transistor used in a DDM-CMP node is

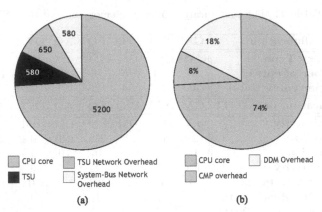

Fig. 3. (a) Transistor count ×1000 for each unit of a DDM-CMP node. (b) Percentage of the area budget for the CPU core, the DDM overhead and the CMP overhead

7 million. Therefore, given the same hardware budget we can build a DDM-CMP chip with 16 cores.

4 DDM-CMP Runtime System and Support

A primary target of the DDM-CMP architecture is to be able to execute not only DDM applications, but also conventional, non-DDM binaries. To meet this goal, a runtime support system that does not require modifications of the Operating System or the CPU cores has been designed. As such, the runtime system has to satisfy two important requirements. First, when an application is executed in parallel in a shared-memory multiprocessor, the execution CPUs need to have access to the same virtual address space. This is also true in the DDM model of execution. Secondly, as the TSU space is limited, a mechanism that dynamically loads and unloads its internal structures with the proper data is required.

To meet these requirements, we designed a simple, lightweight user level process, the *DDM-Kernel*, which is presented in the next section.

4.1 The DDM-Kernel

A DDM-application starts its execution by launching n DDM-Kernels. Each Kernel is run by a different process on a different CPU. The application completes its execution when all its kernels have done so. This approach guarantees a common virtual address for all CPUs, the first requirement the runtime support system must meet.

Figure 4 depicts the pseudocode of the DDM-Kernel. Its first operation is to transfer the execution to the address of the first instruction of the Inlet Thread (the first thread of each Code-Block is called the *"Inlet Thread"*) of the first Code-Block it will execute. The rest of its code is a simple loop, which purpose is explained later on.

The primary responsibility of *Inlet Threads* is to load the TSU with all threads of their Code-Block (Figure 5-(a)). The information regarding these threads is inserted in the application's code during compilation. At this point, the operation of the DDM-Kernel guarantees that the TSU will contain the necessary information to execute all threads of that Code-Block.

On the other hand, the last thread of a Code-Block is the block's *Outlet Thread* (Figure 5-(b)). Its primary operation is to clear the resources allocated on the TSU for that block. When such a command is sent to the TSU, all its internal state is flushed. The inlet and outlet threads enable the DDM-Kernel to meet its second goal, the dynamic loading/unloading of the TSU.

```
                goto (first_instruction_of_INLET_THREAD)

THREAD_SELECT:     address = readReadyThreadFromTSU();
                   goto address;
```

Fig. 4. The pseudocode of the DDM-Kernel

The *THREAD_SELECT* loop, combined with the TSU's post-processing phase, guarantee that execution will be transfered to subsequent threads. Specifically, the last operation of all threads is to inform their TSU that they have completed their execution and jump to a special loop in the DDM-Kernel named the *THREAD_SELECT* loop (Figure 5-(a)-(b)-(d)). Acknowledging the thread completion is achieved by sending a special flag to the corresponding TSU which triggers the post-processing phase. As a result, the next thread deemed for execution is found.

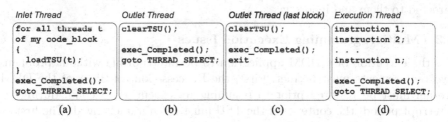

| Inlet Thread | Outlet Thread | Outlet Thread (last block) | Execution Thread |

```
for all threads t    clearTSU();          clearTSU();          instruction 1;
of my code_block                                               instruction 2;
{                    exec_Completed();    exec_Completed();    . . .
   loadTSU(t);       goto THREAD_SELECT;  exit                 instruction n;
}
exec_Completed();                                              exec_Completed();
goto THREAD_SELECT;                                            goto THREAD_SELECT;
```

| (a) | (b) | (c) | (d) |

Fig. 5. The pseudocode of DDM threads. The first thread of a block is named *Inlet Thread* and the last *Outlet Thread*

The *THREAD_SELECT* loop performs two simple operations: reads from the TSU the address of the next available thread and branches to that address. When the CPU requests this address, the TSU first tests whether a ready thread exists, *i.e.* checks if a thread has Ready Count equal to 0. If this is the case, it returns the address of its first instruction. In case no ready thread exists, it returns the address of the *THREAD_SELECT* loop (Figure 5-(d)).

As it was mentioned earlier, upon their completion, all threads jump to the address of the *THREAD_SELECT* loop. However, the outlet thread of the *last* block, is set by the compiler to force the DDM-Kernel to exit (Figure 5-(c)).

4.2   On-Chip Communication

The DDM-Kernel operation reveals the need for three different communication paths: between TSUs, between a CPU and its TSU and between CPUs and the System Network.

Communication between the TSUs is necessary for the correct operation of the DDM-model. For this communication path, a dedicated network named *TSU-Network* (Figure 2) exists. In the current design, this network is implemented using a simple broadcast bus.

As explained in the previous section, a two-way communication path between the CPU and the TSU is also necessary. To read data from the TSU, the CPU places the address of the corresponding memory mapped device on the system-network. Snooping the network, the TSU mapped to that specific address identifies that the request is directed to itself. Subsequently, the TSU places on the network the requested data. This request is *not* sent to the main memory as the network's logic, through the address decoding, determines that it is targeted for a memory mapped device. In order to send data to the TSU, a similar process is followed. Specifically, the CPU places the address of the target device on the system-network followed by the data. The TSU that corresponds to that address reads and manipulates these data.

The communication between the CPU and the memory hierarchy is the same as in any CMP. Specifically, the CPU's memory controller places the address of the requested data on the network. The network's logic identifies that this address is for the main memory and forwards the request. At the same time, the TSUs, by snooping the network, will identify that the specific request is not directed to them and ignore it.

4.3   Multiprogramming Execution Issues

For the execution of a DDM application to be interruptible without problems, two requirements must be met. First, the Process-Control-Block of the DDM-Kernel must be restored prior to resuming its execution. Second, during the interrupt period, the contents of the TSU must remain unchanged. The first requirement is guaranteed by the operating system context switch procedure. The second requirement is enforced by the TSU, by saving the Process ID (PID) of its corresponding DDM-Kernel (Kernel-ID). For a process to update the state of the TSU, its PID must match with the TSU's Kernel-ID. By satisfying these requirements, the DDM-Kernel implementation allows the simultaneous execution DDM and non-DDM applications.

4.4   DDM-CMP Compiler Support

For a thorough evaluation of the architecture it is necessary to have an appropriate compiler. A compiler for the DDM model of execution needs to identify independent parallelizable loop iterations and function calls. These are the portions of code that will be converted into DDM-threads. Additionally, the DDM-compiler must provide some guarantees specifically regarding the DDM model. For example, it must assure that the Code-Blocks are small enough to fit in the internal queues of the TSU.

However, at the early stages of the development of a novel architecture such as the DDM-CMP, hand-coded application results [2,3,12] and pragma-based directives for code generation are an acceptable way to do initial testing. Currently we support a semi-automatic code generation through the *DDM Preprocessor*. This process resembles the one followed for OpenMP programs where special pragma directives are inserted in the source code. The *DDM directives* allow the user to specify the thread's code and Code-Blocks' boundaries. The *DDM Preprocessor* then adds in the native code instructions for the creation of the DDM threads and the DDM-Kernels.

Figure 6 depicts an example of a program that uses such pragma directives. Specifically, in line 01 the *BLOCK_START* pragma is used to inform the complier that a new DDM Code-Block starts. This Code-Block ends at line 16 with the *BLOCK_END* pragma instruction. Lines 03-07 and 09-13 define threads 1 and 2, respectively. The code of a thread is enclosed within the *THREAD_START* and *THREAD_END* pragma directives. With the *THREAD_START* pragma the user defines the Thread# of the thread, the Thread# of its consumers and the DDM-Kernel/CPU that will run it.

The *BLOCK_START* pragma has the effect of adding to the native code a proper *Inlet Thread* for the specific block. Similarly, the *BLOCK_END* pragma, leads to adding an *Outlet Thread* to the code. The necessary information for these threads is taken from the included *THREAD_START* pragma directives. Additionally, the *THREAD_START* pragma, defines the first instruction of the thread. Finally, the *THREAD_END* pragma directive, defines the last instruction of the thread and makes the compiler insert in its place a branch to the *THREAD_SELECT* loop. An example of the generated code is shown in Figure 8.

```
00  ...
01  #PRAGMA DDM BLOCK_START BLOCK 1
02
03    #PRAGMA DDM THREAD_START THREAD 1 CONSUMERS 2,4 KERNEL 1
04      for(i=0;i<effort;i++)
05        for(j=0;j<effort;j++)
06          Out1+=(i*j+j)/(j+1);
07    #PRAGMA DDM  THREAD_END
08
09    #PRAGMA DDM THREAD_START THREAD 2 CONSUMERS 5,6,8 KERNEL 1
10      for(i=0;i<effort;i++)
11        for(j=0;j<effort;j++)
12          Out2+=(i*j+j)/(j+Out1);
13    #PRAGMA DDM THREAD_END
14
15  ...
16  #PRAGMA DDM BLOCK_END
17  ...
```

Fig. 6. An example program that uses the DDM pragmas

5   Runtime Support System Validation

We validate the proposed DDM-Kernel using a functional, Simics-based [7] full system simulator using a variety of different applications. Due to space limitations, we only present one example. This synthetic application was designed to have a relatively complex thread dependency graph in order to test the correct execution of the TSU and DDM-Kernel. Also, the core code of each thread may be artificially increased by performing more iteration of the same operation. We call this number of iterations the *loop effort*. As the iterations result from the use of two nested loops we represent this effort in terms of $n \times n$. Figure 7 depicts the threads and the corresponding synchronization graph for the program used.

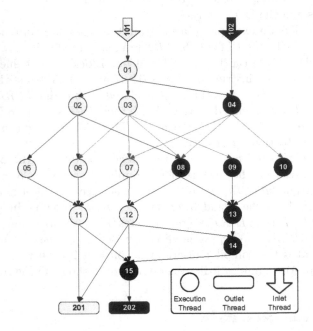

Fig. 7. The Synchronization Graph of the program used for the experiments

The different tones of the threads represented in Figure 7 represents the static assignment of each thread to a particular processor. Therefore, all light threads will execute on processor A while all dark threads will execute on processor B.

This program is written using the *pragma* directives as presented in Section 4.4. An excerpt of this program is shown in Figure 6. After this program is passed through the DDM-CMP preprocessor, it outputs the code including the corresponding DDM-Kernel and Threads. An excerpt of the the *main*, together with the DDM-Kernel code, is shown in Figure 8-(a). An excerpt of the thread code is presented in Figure 8-(b).

```
int main(int argc,char *argv[]){
  ...
  //CREATE THE DDM KERNELS
  for(i=0;i<NO_OF_DDM_KERNELS;i++) {
    pid=fork();
    if(pid==0) { //CHILD CODE
      ownTSU=&(tsuArray->tsu[i]);
      //Bind the DDM Kernel to a processor
      bindprocessor( getpid(), (i+1)) );
      //Move execution to DDM kernel
      kernelNumber=i+1;
      goto DDM_KERNEL;
      return 0;
    }
  }
  ...

  //The DDM KERNEL
  DDM_KERNEL:
    switch(kernelNumber) {
      case 1: loadTSU(
                ownTSU,   //Execution TSU
                101,101,0,//ThrID,IFP,RC
                1,0,0,0); //Cons 1,2,3,4
              goto THREAD_SELECT;
              break;
      ...
    }

  //The THREAD SELECT LOOP
  THREAD_SELECT:
    threadUnderExecution=
      currentlyExecutedThread(ownTSU);

    switch(threadUnderExecution) {
      case 101: goto INLET_BLOCK01_KERNEL01;
                break;
      ...
      case 2:   goto THREAD02;
                break;
      ...
    }
  ...
```

(a)

```
// B L O C K   0 1
//Inlet thread Block 01-Kernel 01
INLET_BLOCK01_KERNEL01:
    //LOAD THREAD01
    loadTSU(
      ownTSU,     //Execution TSU
      1,1,1,    //ThrID, IFP, RC
      2,3,4,0);//Cons 1,2,3,4
    ...

    threadCompletedExecution(ownTSU);
    goto THREAD_SELECT;
...

THREAD02:
    tmp_Out=0;
    tmp_In01=threadResults->result[1];

    for(i=0;i<effort;i++)
      for(j=0;j<effort;j++)
        tmp_Out+=(i*j+j)/(j+tmp_In01);

    threadResults->result[2]=tmp_Out+1;
    threadCompletedExecution(ownTSU);

    goto THREAD_SELECT;

    ...

OUTLET_BLOCK01_KERNEL01:
    (*numberOfLiveKernels)--;
    exit(0);
```

(b)

Fig. 8. (a) Main and DDM-Kernel and (b) Thread code

The program was implemented using the available tools and executed on the functional DDM-CMP Simics-based simulator. The correct execution of the Runtime System was validated by comparing the results of this, and other similar programs, against the execution of their corresponding serial code.

6 Conclusions and Future Work

DDM-CMP is a single-ISA homogeneous chip multiprocessor that overcomes memory and power limitations. This is achieved by combining two key technologies. First, the use of the Data-Driven Multithreading model of execution, which is an efficient dataflow-oriented implementation that has minimal hardware requirements and tolerates long latencies by allowing the processor to produce useful work while a long latency event is in progress. Second, chip-multiprocessor architectures offer high-degree of parallelism at low complexity design and therefore are power efficient.

This paper presented the design and implementation details of the DDM-CMP chip. The main contributions include the detailed hardware budget analysis and the runtime support system description and validation. The analysis showed that the DDM benefits may be achieved with only a 17% hardware cost increase compared to a simple chip-multiprocessor implementation. The analysis also showed that in the hardware budget as a state-of-the-art single-chip uniprocessor it is possible to build a 16-core DDM-CMP chip. Finally, DDM applications are shown to execute on the DDM-CMP chip using a regular, non-modified, Operating System. To achieve this, a simple user-level process used to coordinate the DDM application execution, the DDM-Kernel, was presented and validated.

Based on the design presented in this paper we are currently pursuing the implementation of a Xilinx-based hardware prototype to validate the concepts here presented. In addition, we are developing a fully automated compiler for DDM.

References

1. Arvind, Asanovic, K., Chiou, D., Hoe, J.C., Kozyrakis, C., Lu, S.L., Oskin, M., Patterson, D., Rabaey, J., Wawrzynek, J.: Ramp: Ramp: Research accelerator for multiple processors - a community vision for a shared experimental parallel hw/sw platform. Technical Report UCB//CSD-05-1412 (2005)
2. Kyriacou, C., Evripidou, P., Trancoso, P.: Data-Driven Multithreading Using Conventional Microprocessors. IEEE Transactions on Parallel and Distributed Systems (2005)
3. Kyriacou, C.: Data Driven Multithreading using Conventional Control Flow Microprocessors. PhD dissertation, University of Cyprus (2005)
4. Olukotun, K., et al.: The Case for a Single Chip Multiprocessor. In: Proc. of the 7th ASPLOS. (1996) 2–11
5. Stavrou, K., Evripidou, P., Trancoso, P.: DDM-CMP: Data-Driven Multithreading on a Chip Multiprocessor. In: Proc. of the 5th SAMOS. (2005)
6. Trancoso, P., Evripidou, P., Stavrou, K., Kyriacou, C.: A Case for Chip Multiprocessors based on the Data-Drive Multihreading Model. International Journal on Parallel Processing (2005)
7. Magnusson, P.S., Christensson, M., Eskilson, J., Forsgren, D., Hallberg, G., Hogberg, J., Larsson, F., Moestedt, A., Werner, B.: Simics: A Full System Simulation Platform. IEEE Computer 35(2) (2002) 50–58
8. Kyriacou, C., Evripidou, P., Trancoso, P.: Cacheflow: A short-term optimal cache management policy for data driven multithreading. In: EuroPar-04. (2004) 561–570
9. Dennis, J.B., Misunas, D.P.: A preliminary architecture for a basic data-flow processor. In: Proceedings of the 2nd annual symposium on Computer architecture. (1975) 126–132
10. Dennis, J.B.: First version of a data flow procedure language. In: Programming Symposium, Proceedings Colloque sur la Programmation. (1974) 362–376
11. Arvind, R., Kathail, V.: A multiple processor data flow machine that supports generalized procedures. In: Proceedings of the 8th annual symposium on Computer Architecture. (1981) 219–302

12. Evripidou, P.: D3-machine: A Decoupled Data-Driven Multithreaded Architecture with Variable Resolution Support. Parallel Computing **27**(9) (2001) 1197–1225
13. Evripidou, P., Gaudiot, J.: A decoupled graph/computation data-driven architecture with variable resolution actors. In: Proc. of ICPP 1990. (1990) 405–414
14. Evripidou, P., Kyriacou, C.: Data driven network of workstations (D2NOW). J. UCS **6**(10) (2000) 1015–1033
15. Woo, S., Ohara, M., Torrie, E., Singh, J., Gupta, A.: The SPLASH-2 Programs: Characterization and Methodological Considerations. In: Proc. of 22nd ISCA. (1995) 24–36
16. IBM Microelectronics Division: The PowerPC 405(tm) Core (1998)
17. Shivakumar, P., Jouppi, N.P.: Cacti 3.0: An integrated cache timing, power and area model. Technical report, Compaq Computer Corporation Western Research Laboratory (2001)
18. Burns, J., Gaudiot, J.L.: Area and System Clock Effects on SMT/CMP Processors. In: Proceedings of the 2001 International Conference on Parallel Architectures and Compilation Techniques (PACT 2001). (2001) 211–218
19. Topelt, B., Schuhmann, D., Volkel, F.: Embedded Forum, Day Two: Information Appliances Not Dead Yet. www.findarticles.com/p/articles/mi_zdext/is_200106/ai_ziff3378/pg_2 (2001)
20. Intel: Intel microprocessor quick reference guide. (www.intel.com/pressroom/kits/quickreffam.htm)

Combining Wireless Sensor Network with Grid for Intelligent City Traffic

Feilong Tang, Minglu Li, Chuliang Weng, Chongqing Zhang,
Wenzhe Zhang, Hongyu Huang, and Yi Wang

Department of Computer Science and Engineering,
Shanghai Jiao Tong University, Shanghai 200030, China
tang-fl@cs.sjtu.edu.cn

Abstract. Intelligent city traffic for travelling navigation, traffic prediction and decision support needs to collect large-scale real-time data from numerous vehicles. As a small, economical yet reasonably efficient device, wireless sensors can conveniently serve for this purpose. In this paper[1], we investigate how to deploy wireless sensor networks in buses to gather traffic data for intelligent city traffic. The paper presents a self-organization mechanism and a routing protocol for the proposed sensor networks. Our work has three advantages: (1)adaptive network topology, which satisfies highly mobile city traffic environment, (2)directed data transmission, saving energy consumption of sensor nodes with limited power resource, and (3)longer lifetime because of fewer redundant network communication and balanced power usage of sensor nodes in a network.

1 Introduction

Wireless sensor networks will play a key role in sensing, collecting, and disseminating information about environmental phenomena. With the advances in computation, communication, and sensing capabilities, large scale sensor-based distributed environments are becoming a reality. There are a wide range of applications for sensor networks with differing requirements. Such distributed sensor networks allow us to continuously monitor and record the state of the physical world which can be used for a variety of purposes such as transportation, medicine, surveillance, environment monitoring and protection, security, defense, science and engineering[1,2,3,4,5,6,7].

Intelligent traffic management is a very important issue. For this purpose, Shanghai municipality launched a project ShanghaiGrid in 2003. The main issues in this project are to collect real-time traffic data from buses and taxis, handle these data with Grid technologies, and finally provide citizens with intelligent services. For solving the first issue, some GPS terminals have been deployed in a

---

[1] This paper is supported by 973 Program of China (2002CB312002), National Natural Science Foundation of China(60473092, 90612018, 60503043), Natural Science Foundation of Shanghai Municipality of China (05ZR14081), and ShanghaiGrid from Science and Technology Commission of Shanghai Municipality (05DZ15005).

C. Jesshope and C. Egan (Eds.): ACSAC 2006, LNCS 4186, pp. 260–269, 2006.

part of vehicles. However, many drivers especially taxi drivers dislike using GPS devices because they are expensive and inconvenient. Sensors are an appropriate substitute for sensing traffic data from various vehicles to analyze traffic status, plan travelling routes and so on.

A sensor network is composed of a large number of sensor nodes that are densely deployed either inside the phenomenon or very close to it. Each of these scattered sensor nodes has capabilities to collect data and route data back to the sink. After deployment, topology changes are due to change in sensor nodes' position, reachability (due to jamming, noise, moving obstacles, etc.), available energy, malfunctioning, and task details. In our target environment, the topology of a sensor network for sensing traffic data changes very frequently because sensors keep continuously mobile. Protocols and algorithms for these sensor networks must possess self-organizing capabilities [8,9,10,11,12,13].

Sensor nodes mainly use a broadcast communication paradigm. They are inherently resource constrained in power, computation and storage capacities. Power consumption of a sensor node can be divided into three domains: sensing, communication, and data processing. Energy expenditure in data communication is much more compared to others[14]. Therefore, energy consumption of a sensor node significantly increases with transmission distance. In order to maximize lifetime of a network, nodes in our sensor network communicate in the following way.

- In a sensor network, only one node closest to the *sink* can directly transmit data to it in a hop. We call such a sensor node as a *super node*.
- Other sensor nodes can directly communicate only with neighbor nodes. They send data back to the *sink* in a multihop fashion, through the *super node*.
- Each sensor node only relays data from nodes farther from the *super node* in distance.
- All nodes work as the *super node* in turn by elections. After an election, the sensor network keep a stable topology for a period of time. During this period, the *super node* keeps the closest to the *sink*.

The goal of this paper is to investigate feasibility to deploy wireless sensor networks for intelligent traffic. We proposes a model for self-organization of sensor networks that are used to collect traffic information for decision support and intelligent prediction such as road status (free or jammed), the best path to an expected destination, estimated time that the next bus is going to arrive at a stop. And then we design a protocol for routing traffic data to the Grid system.

2   Related Work

Routing for wireless sensor networks has recently received a lot of attention. Many algorithms have been proposed in research literatures.

Flooding is a classical mechanism to relay data in sensor networks without the need for topology maintenance. In flooding, each node receiving a data or management packet broadcasts it to all of its neighbors, unless a maximum number of hops for the packet is reached or the destination of the packet is the node itself. Flooding is a simplest routing protocol, but with several serious deficiencies such as implosion, overlap and resource blindness[11,15].

Gossiping, a derivation of flooding, sends data to one randomly selected neighbor, which picks another random neighbor to forward the packet and so on. Gossiping avoids implosion problem by just selecting a random node to send the packet rather than broadcasting, however, message propagation takes longer time[11,16].

SPIN is a family of adaptive protocols and addresses the deficiencies of classic flooding by considering resource adaptation and data negotiation between nodes in order to eliminate redundant data and save energy. In SPIN, whenever a node has available data, it broadcasts a description of the data instead of all the data and sends it only to the sensor nodes that express interest to save energy[15,17].

Directed Diffusion has become a breakthrough in data-centric routing, where the sink sends out interest, which is a task description, to all sensors. The task descriptors are named by assigning attribute-value pairs. Each sensor node then stores the interest entry in its cache. The interest entry contains a timestamp field and several gradient fields. As the interest is propagated throughout the sensor network, the gradients from the source back to the sink are set up. When the source has data for the interest, the source sends the data along the interest's gradient path[13,18].

LEACH is a 2-level hierarchical routing protocol which attempts to minimize global energy dissipation and distribute energy consumption evenly across all nodes. The nodes self-organize into local clusters with one node in each cluster acting as a cluster head, based on the received signal strength. The head works as a routers to the sink. Cluster members send data to the cluster head(low energy transmission) which in turn sends it to the base station(high energy transmission). Energy dissipation is evenly spread by dissolving clusters at regular intervals and randomly choosing the cluster heads. However, LEACH uses single-hop routing where each node can transmit directly to the cluster-head. Therefore, it is not applicable to networks deployed in large regions [19].

The above protocols need to be improved to address higher topology changes and higher scalability for highly mobile traffic system.

3   Background

Our research focuses on how to collect real-time traffic data from buses for ShanghaiGrid, which is a long term research plan sponsored by Science and Technology Commission of Shanghai Municipality (STCSM) to provide intelligent traffic services for citizens and Shanghai government. As the most important part of digital city and city Grid plan, ShanghaiGrid concentrates on constructing metropolis-area information Grid infrastructure, establishing an open standard, and developing a set of system softwares for the information Grid for widespread upper-layer applications from both research communities and official departments. By means

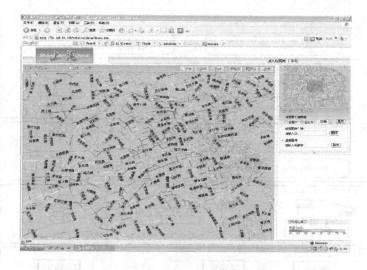

Fig. 1. Prediction of road traffic status

of flexible, secure and open standards, data information and dedicated services among virtual organisations, this project will build an information Grid testbed for Shanghai and support typical applications of Grid based traffic-jam control and guidance.

The ShanghaiGrid project is built on four major computational aggregations and networks in Shanghai, i.e. the CHINANET (public internet backbone built by China Telecom), the SHERNET (Shanghai Education and Research Network), Shanghai Supercomputing Center, and campus networks in Shanghai Jiao Tong University, Tongji University and Shanghai University, and is planned to enable the heterogeneous and distributed resources to collaborate into an information fountain and computation environment for research, education and metropolis management applications, seamlessly and transparently. To achieve the goal, the project consists of four interdependent sub-projects: the research and investigation on requirements, protocols and standards of information Grid infrastructure, the development of system software and establishment of major Grid nodes, the development of decentralized virtual research platform, and research on metropolis Grid applications.

Relying on the growing network infrastructure and abundant scientific research resources, the ShanghaiGrid project will construct the first metropolis-area information Grid to provide tremendous data manipulations and ubiquitous information services for variety of organizations. Especially, the traffic-congestion control and guidance application are planned to take advantage of Grid computing to integrate traffic data collection, traffic monitoring and supervising, traffic information supply and traveller guidance, in order to make the traffic system run more efficient and people easier to travel within the city [20,21,22,23]. Fig.1 is an example for prediction of the road traffic status, where traffic flow is depicted by different colours.

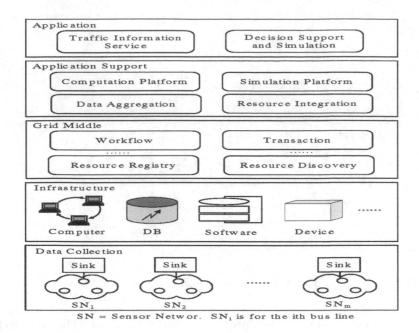

Fig. 2. The architecture of city Grid with sensor networks

As mentioned above, current data collection in this project mainly relies on GPS systems. We argue that the wireless sensor network is a better substitute because: (1) GPS data is often lost owing to high building, bad weather and other disadvantageous factors, and (2) a sensor is more economical than a GPS terminal. We propose an architecture where real-time traffic data is collected by sensor networks for ShanghiGrid, as shown in Fig.2, which consists of five layers. The application layer means actual intelligent traffic services, mainly including estimation of road status for traffic-congestion control, prediction of arrival time of the next bus, the best travelling path to a specified destination, decision support and simulation. The next application support layer provides application-specific environment and tools. The Grid middle layer is the core of ShanghaiGrid, which is responsible for task management, data service, scheduling, workflow, transaction etc., based on Grid technologies. Grid resources form the infrastructure layer. This paper concentrates on the data collection layer, which collects real-time traffic data based on sensor networks.

4   Sensor Network Design

As a part of intelligent traffic service, our sensor networks take charge of collection of real-time traffic data such as passenger number, speed and direction of vehicles, the number of bus line. In this paper, we present how to design sensor networks to gather data from buses. Sensing taxi data will be reported in near future.

There are hundreds of bus lines and thousands of taxies in Shanghai. Based on practical situation, public traffic generally complies with the following model.

- Each bus line that consists of hundreds of buses often covers 10 to 20 kilometers.
- Each bus line associates with a scheduling office, located at an end of the traffic line to schedule these buses.
- Buses move back and forth on the line one by one.
- Each bus stays at the scheduling office for a few minutes before the next round, during which it is the bus closest to the scheduling office.

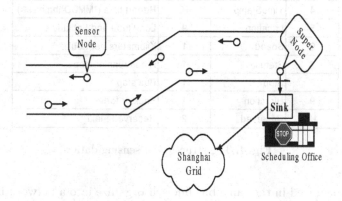

Fig. 3. A sensor network for collection of bus information

4.1   Topology of a Sensor Network

Design of a scalable sensor network and efficient routing protocol to collect traffic information for intelligent traffic poses many significant challenges because of

- continuous movement of sensors. The super node that directly communicates with the stable *sink* has to change continuously.
- limited computation, communication, and storage resources at sensor nodes. Data has to be routed back to the *sink* in an energy-efficient way.

We deploy sensors in each bus. A bus line forms a sensor network with a number of ordinary sensor nodes, a super sensor node and a sink, as shown in Fig. 3. All sensor nodes have the capabilities to observe, temporarily store and route data back to the *sink* by a multihop routing mechanism at any given time/period of the measurement. Moreover, a super node acts as a gateway of a sensor network. The sink may communicate with the Shanghai Grid via Internet or satellite. Sensor nodes do not transmit data from different sensor networks through checking their bus line numbers. In the same network, sensor nodes only route data from nodes further from the super node.

4.2   Sensor Network Model

We model a bus line in L={O,B,BS}, where O is a scheduling office for a bus line, one scheduling office for each bus line; B={B_1,B_2,...,B_n} is a set of of buses that move on the same bus line and BS is a set of bus stops. Each bus is equipped with a sensor node.

No	Name	Length (Byte)	Description
1	LineID	1	ID of the bus line
2	BusID	1	ID of the bus
3	Passenger	1	Number of passengers
4	TimeStamp	10	Report time ("MMDDhhmmss")
5	Location	9	Longitude and Latitude
6	Speed	1	Kilometers per hour
7	Status	1	A bus runs or stops
8	Stop	1	Bus stop
9	Direction	1	Back or forth
10	Reserved	2	Reserved Field

Fig. 4. The structure of sensing data

Sensors deployed in the same bus line self-organize into a network by an election. A sensor network in a bus line L can be modelled as SN(L)={Sink, Super, S, D}, where the Sink is a communication node deployed in the scheduling office, and interconnects with Shanghai Grid, Super is the super node, S={S_1,S_2,...,S_n} is a sensor set and D={D_1,D_2,...,D_n} is a sensing data set. Sensor S_i (i=1,2,...n) is deployed on the bus B_i. It collects data D_i all the time and transmits D_i to the sink node every 18 seconds. D_i and D_j (i,j=1,2,...,n, i$\neq$j) have the same data structure but different values. Note that the value(s) of D_i change(s) continuously. The data structure of D_i is illustrated in Fig. 4.

4.3   Election of a Super Node

Energy consumption of a sensor node contains data processing and data transmission. The longer transmission distance, the more energy consumption for data transmission. We assume a node can directly communicate with only its neighbors to reduce its energy consumption by adjusting transmission power of the node.

Election of a super node occurs periodically. Whenever a sensor node detects that a signal from the sink exceeds a threshold, it initiates an election to run for a super node. We call such a sensor node as a candidate super node. In fact, the super node from a successful election is that the closest to the sink. Election algorithm includes the following two phase.

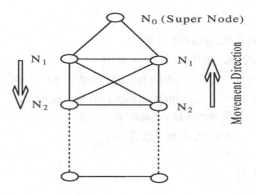

Fig. 5. A topology after an election

Initiation of an election. A candidate super node sends an ELECTION message to its two neighbors. The message contains a node name N_0, a bus line number and an election time.

Promulgation of the ELECTION message. After a sensor node receives an ELECTION message from the node N_i with the same direction, it changes the node name into N_{i+1}, then relays the message to further nodes. This process continues until the end of this bus line.

An election forms a hierarchical graph with two nodes in every level except the super node N_0, as shown in Fig. 5, where a solid line between two sensor nodes denotes a hop transmission. The two nodes with the same name N_i move towards reverse directions. Note that a node with the name N_i only routes an ELECTION message from nodes with the name N_{i-1}.

4.4   Routing Traffic Data

In our sensor networks, sensor nodes collect traffic data from buses and then send them back to the sink by a multihop fashion. A node works as both a data source and a router, however, any node only routes sensing data from the same network. The super node is a sole sensor that can communicate with the sink in a hop. Routing traffic data is based on the topology generated from an election, where each sensor node associates with a logical name N_i. Between two elections, data transmission can happen many times.

Sensor nodes route traffic data using the directed routing algorithm (see Fig.6), where S is a set of nodes in a sensor network, N_i represents a sensor node with a logical name N_i generated from the last election.

In our routing algorithm, a sensor node only relays traffic data from its own sensor network. It can be realized by checking the LineID in the data D_j because data sensed from different bus lines carries different LineIDs. As a result, each sensor network only reports the traffic data from its own bus line. In addition, a sensor only routes the data from the node that moves to the same direction and is farther from the super node than itself, which reduces redundant communication.

> *Imput*: traffic data D_j
> *Output*: transmission of the D_j
> N_i receives traffic data D_j from N_j
> If N_j in S   //transmit data from its own network
>   If $j > i$ //transmit data for farther nodes
>   If N_j moves to the same direction
>   broadcast the data D_j
>   EndIf
>   EndIf
> EndIf

Fig. 6. Routing algorithm for the node N_i

In our sensor network, the farther from the super node a sensor with the name N_i is, the more i becomes.

5   Conclusions and Future Work

We have investigated a deployment of wireless sensor networks in buses to gather traffic data for intelligent city traffic. The paper presented a self-organization mechanism and a routing protocol for the proposed networks. Our method has adaptive network topology, directed data transmission and longer lifetime.

We are going to study how to deploy and design sensor networks in more than eight thousand of taxis to provide more precise traffic services.

References

1. S. Tilak, N.B. Abu-Ghazaleh and W. Heinzelman. A Taxonomy of Wireless Micro-Sensor Network Models. ACM SIGMOBILE Mobile Computing and Communications Review, 2002,1(2):1-8.
2. Q. Han, S. Mehrotra and N. Venkatasubramanian. Energy Efficient Data Collection in Distributed Sensor Environments.
3. J. Agre and L. Clare. An integrated architecture for cooperative sensing networks, IEEE Computer Magazine (May 2000) 106-108.
4. N. Bulusu, D. Estrin, L. Girod, J. Heidemann. Scalable coordination for wireless sensor networks: self-con.guring localization systems, International Symposium on Communication Theory and Applications (ISCTA 2001), Ambleside, UK, July 2001.
5. A. Cerpa, J. Elson, M. Hamilton and J. Zhao. Habitat monitoring: application driver for wireless communications technology, ACM SIGCOMM2000, Costa Rica, April 2001.
6. C. Jaikaeo, C. Srisathapornphat and C. Shen. Diagnosis of sensor networks, IEEE International Conference on Communications ICC'01, Helsinki, Finland, June 2001.

7. M. Srivastava, R. Muntz and M. Potkonjak. Smart Kindergarten: Sensor-based Wireless Networks for Smart Developmental Problem-solving Environments (Challenge Paper). In Proc. 7th Ann. Intl. Conf. on Mobile Computing and Networking, pages 132-138, Rome, Italy, July 2001. ACM.

8. S. Cho and A. Chandrakasan. Energy-efficient protocols for low duty cycle wireless microsensor, Proceedings of the 33rd Annual Hawaii International Conference on System Sciences, Maui, HI Vol. 2 (2000).

9. W.R. Heinzelman, J. Kulik and H. Balakrishnan. Adaptive protocols for information dissemination in wireless sensor networks, Proceedings of the ACM MobiCom99, Seattle, Washington, 1999, pp. 174-185.

10. C. Intanagonwiwat, R. Govindan and D. Estrin. Directed diffusion: a scalable and robust communication paradigm for sensor networks, Proceedings of the ACM MobiCom'00, Boston, MA, 2000, pp. 56-67.

11. I.F. Akyildiz, W.L. Su, Y.Sankarasubramaniam, E. Cayirci. A survey on sensor networks, IEEE Communications Magazine, 2002, 40(8):102-114.

12. A. Cerpa and D. Estrin. ASCENT: adaptive self-configuring sensor networks topologies, UCLA Computer Science Department Technical Report UCLA/CSDTR-01-0009, May 2001.

13. C. Intanagonwiwat, R. Govindan and D. Estrin, Directed Diffusion: A Scalable and Robust Communication Paradigm for Sensor Networks, Proc. of ACM MobiCom 00, Boston, MA, 2000, pp. 56-67.

14. I.F. Akyildiz, W. Su, Y. Sankarasubramaniam, E. Cayirci. Wireless sensor networks: a survey. Computer Networks 38 (2002) 393-422.

15. W. R. Heinzelman, J. Kulik, and H. Balakrishnan, Adaptive Protocols for Information Dissemination in Wireless Sensor Networks, Proc. of ACM MobiCom 99, Seattle, WA, 1999, pp. 174-185.

16. S. Hedetniemi, S. Hedetniemi and A. Liestman. A Survey of Gossiping and Broadcasting in Communication Networks, Networks, vol. 18, 1988.

17. W. Heinzelman, J. Kulik and H. Balakrishnan. Adaptive protocols for information dissemination in wireless sensor networks, in the Proceedings of the 5th Annual ACM/IEEE International Conference on Mobile Computing and Networking (MobiCom99), Seattle, WA, August 1999.

18. D. Estrin, et al. Next century challenges: Scalable Coordination in Sensor Networks, in the Proceedings of the 5th annual ACM/IEEE international conference on Mobile Computing and Networking (MobiCom99), Seattle, WA, August 1999.

19. W.R. Heinzelman, A. Chandrakasan and H. Balakrishnan. Energy-efficient communication protocol for wireless microsensor networks. IEEE Hawaii International Conference on System Sciences, 2000.

20. G.W.Yang, H.Jin, M.L.Li et al. Grid Computing in China. Journal of Grid Computing, June 2004, 2(2): 193-206.

21. F. L. Tang, M. L. Li and J. Z. X. Huang. Real-time transaction processing for autonomic Grid applications. Engineering Applications of Artificial Intelligence, 17(7), 2004, pp 799-807.

22. F. L. Tang, M. L. Li and J. Z. X. Huang. Automatic Transaction Compensation for Reliable Grid Applications. To apper in Journal of Computer Science & Technology.

23. M.L. Li, H. Liu, F. L. Tang et al.. ShanghaiGrid in Action: the First Stage Projects Towards Digital City and City Grid. International Journal of Grid and Utility Computing, Vol. 1, No. 1, 2005, pp. 22-31.

A Novel Processor Architecture for Real-Time Control

Xiaofeng Wu[1], Vassilios Chouliaras[2], Jose Nunez-Yanez[3],
Roger Goodall[2], and Tanya Vladimirova[1]

[1] Surrey Space Center, Department of Electronic Engineering, University of Surrey,
Guildford, UK GU2 7XH
{X.Wu, T.Vladimirova}@surrey.ac.uk

[2] Department of Electronic and Electrical Engineering, Loughborough University,
Leicestershire, UK LE11 1SN
{V.A.Chouliaras, R.M.Goodall}@lboro.ac.uk

[3] Department of Electronic Engineering, University of Bristol,
Bristol, UK BS8 1UB
J.L.Nunez-Yanez@bristol.ac.uk

Abstract. This paper describes a control system processor architecture based on $\Delta\Sigma$ modulation ($\Delta\Sigma$-CSP). The $\Delta\Sigma$-CSP uses 1-bit processing which is a new concept in digital control to remove multi-bit multiplications. A simple conditional-negate-and-add (CNA) unit is proposed for most operations of control laws. For this reason, the targeted processor is small and very fast, making it ideal for embedded real-time control applications. The $\Delta\Sigma$-CSP has been implemented as a VLSI hard macro in a high-performance $0.13\mu m$ silicon process. Results show that it compares very favorably to other digital processors in terms of area and clock frequency.

1 Introduction

Many analogue-to-digital (A/D) and digital-to-analogue (D/A) converters employ an intermediate $\Delta\Sigma$ modulating stage for high quality data conversion [1]. The $\Delta\Sigma$ modulator converts signals into a simple bit-stream, i.e. 1-bit signals that can be stored in 1-bit registers. This bit-stream contains all the useful information of the input, thus making it possible to perform signal processing directly on those 1-bit signals. $\Delta\Sigma$-based signal processing has been widely investigated in the context of finite-impulse-response (FIR) filters [2], infinite-impulse-response (IIR) filters [3] and audio processing [4]. Moreover these systems are able to interface to analogue signals directly as the decimating filter for A/D converters and interpolating filter for D/A converters are removed. For this reason, integration of $\Delta\Sigma$ modulators in control system processing has been studied [5].

The actual implementation of control laws is part of the design process which most control engineers strive to achieve in as straightforward and transparent way as possible. $\Delta\Sigma$-based control systems can be implemented as software running in existing digital processors, but this doesn't result in a cost effective

C. Jesshope and C. Egan (Eds.): ACSAC 2006, LNCS 4186, pp. 270–280, 2006.
© Springer-Verlag Berlin Heidelberg 2006

solution, particularly taking the 1-bit feature into consideration. We therefore propose a novel $\Delta\Sigma$-based control system processor for demanding control applications and evaluate its hardware performance compared with other digital processors running a control example.

2 1-bit Processing

1-bit processing is a new concept in digital control. Fig. 1 shows the diagram of such a system. Here PDM means pulse density modulation. In 1-bit processing, however, the continuous signal is shaped into a single bit-stream via $\Delta\Sigma$ modulation. A digital $\Delta\Sigma$ modulator is placed after the controller in the main loop, resulting in a 1-bit signal after control processing. As a result, the processed 1-bit signal is used to control physical systems directly through PDM which works similarly to pulse-width-modulation (PWM).

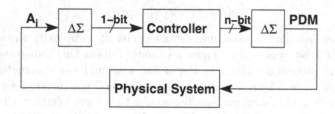

Fig. 1. 1-bit control system

2.1 $\Delta\Sigma$ Modulation

Fig. 2 shows a $\Delta\Sigma$ modulator, in which several integrators are cascaded in the forward loop to create a higher order filter, with each integrator receiving an additional input from the quantiser. The output of the quantiser is a binary value ($\pm\Delta$).

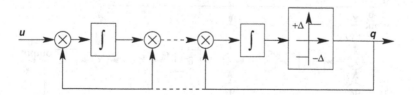

Fig. 2. $\Delta\Sigma$ modulation

Each sample q has its corresponding part on the original input u but with quantisation noise [6]. When the sampling frequency is sufficiently high, this quantization noise can be ignored as the noise spectrum within the signal bandwidth is much smaller than the input signal spectrum.

2.2   Controller Structure

1-bit processing requires a very fast sampling frequency which may result in long word-lengths for both coefficients and variables within the controller, primarily because the differences between successive values of the input and output become increasingly small. This is related to the known problems of coefficient sensitivity with conventional forms of control system processing using the shift operator z [7]. This feature becomes particularly critical with the much higher sample rates required for 1-bit signal processing. It has been recognized that alternative forms, using the δ-operator, overcome a number of these problems [8].

The δ-operator is defined as

$$\delta = q - 1. \tag{1}$$

in which q is the shift operator. Hence, the equation $y = \delta^{-1}x$ is implemented as

$$y(n + 1) = x(n) + y(n). \tag{2}$$

This paper concentrates on minimising the circuit complexity through taking advantage of 1-bit processing. Thus, a canonic δ-form that integrates the $\Delta\Sigma$ modulator is proposed, shown in Fig. 3 for a second order structure. Notice that the input u is a 1-bit signal from the 1-bit A/D converter. As a result, all multiplications in this structure are between a 1-bit signal (either +1 or -1) and a multi-bit coefficient, which just changes the sign of the multi-bit coefficient. Multiplication therefore becomes a simple 'conditional-negate', removing the need for multi-bit multipliers in the calculations. Variable x_1 and x_2 are multi-bit and the gain k is a power of 2 scaling factor which requires only a simple shift operation and avoids the need for a multiplication which otherwise would increase the circuitry complexity. For VLSI implementation, this structure shows great advantages over traditional designs as both the circuit complexity and computation latency are greatly reduced.

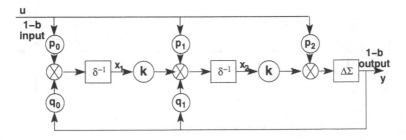

Fig. 3. The canonic δ-form for 1-bit processing

The transfer function (not including the $\Delta\Sigma$ modulator) of the controller in Fig. 3 therefore can be written as:

$$\frac{Y}{U} = \frac{p_0 k^2 \delta^{-2} + p_1 k \delta^{-1} + p_2}{q_0 k^2 \delta^{-2} + q_1 k \delta^{-1} + 1}. \tag{3}$$

Consider for example a generalised single-input single-output controller of second order. Its transfer function can be represented by

$$H(s) = \frac{a_1 s^2 + a_2 s + a_3}{s^2 + b_1 s + b_2}. \tag{4}$$

From Eq. 1, the δ operator approximates to sT when the sampling time T is very small. Here s is the Laplace operator. Hence, from Eq. 3 and Eq. 4, the coefficients are obtained:

$$\begin{aligned} p_0 &= a_3 T^2 k^{-2}, \\ p_1 &= a_2 T k^{-1}, \\ p_2 &= a_1, \\ q_0 &= b_2 T^2 k^{-2}, \\ q_1 &= b_1 T k^{-1}. \end{aligned} \tag{5}$$

Here k is used to scale up the coefficients which are very small due to the high sampling frequency.

3   Processor Architecture

The $\Delta\Sigma$-CSP is reasonably simple by considering all the necessary elements needed to perform a control law.

3.1   Word Length

The $\Delta\Sigma$-CSP adopts a fixed-point arithmetic format because the floating-point arithmetic is expensive in terms of speed, power and complexity. However the word length needs to be carefully chosen to ensure that the full value and dynamic range of the variables can be accommodated.

A simple criterion used to determine the number of fractional bits is described in [9], and a reasonable number of fractional bits would be in the range of 8-16 bits, which will support a wide range of controllers. A 24-bit fixed-point format is chosen for one-bit processing, which contains 16 fractional bits, 7 integer bits and 1 sign bit. This format accommodates a signal with an amplitude between -128 to 128, which is sufficient for most control applications as the input/output is only -1 or 1 and no multipliers are needed in one-bit processing. Because there are no multiplications, no overflow or underflow bits are specified.

3.2   Instruction Set Architecture (ISA)

The ISA of the proposed programmable solution is given in Table 1. The instruction set is fairly small and specialised to control law implementation.

Each instruction contains three elements: an opcode, an I/O address and a data RAM address. These elements decide the word length to represent an

Table 1. $\Delta\Sigma$-CSP opcodes

Binary code	Opcode	Function description
000	HLT	No operation
001	RDW	Read data from the program RAM
010	WRB	Output the result to the digital output ports
011	WRW	Write the intermediate states to the data RAM
100	SRS	Right shift
101	CNA	Conditional negate and accumulate
110	SET	Set the sampling frequency for the timer
111	WPC	Set the start value for the program counter

instruction. In this processor design, we use 16-bit word format, which includes 3 bits for opcode, 4 bits for digital I/O and 9 bits for data RAM. The processor has only 8 opcodes (see Table 1) to accomplish all the necessary operations for a control system. 8 digital inputs and 8 digital outputs are provided in the I/O block which allows a maximum of 8 inputs and 8 outputs for an MIMO (multi-input and multi-output) control system. As there are 9 bits to represent an address of the data RAM, it allows access to a RAM with a maximum size of $512 * 24b$. This is enough to perform a complex control system as only the states, which are used in the next sample calculations, will be written to the data RAM.

3.3   Microarchitecture

Fig. 4 depicts the block diagram of the $\Delta\Sigma$-CSP. All calculations take place in the arithmetic and logic unit (ALU). Memories are used to store coefficients and instructions. The following major microarchitecture blocks are identified:

Program Counter. The program counter maintains the memory of the currently executing instructions of the control law in the program RAM. It starts at an initial location and is incremented by 1 on every clock cycle. The program counter contains an initial address, from which the control loop begins. When the control law has executed, the program counter stops counting via a 'HLT' instruction and awaits the next sample trigger event. The initial address is reloaded in the program counter and execution begins once again.

Decoder. In the decoder, the instructions are extracted into three parts: opcode, I/O address and memory address. The decoder also generates control logic signals which control memory and digital I/O accesses by enabling read and write signals to the memories and the digital I/O block.

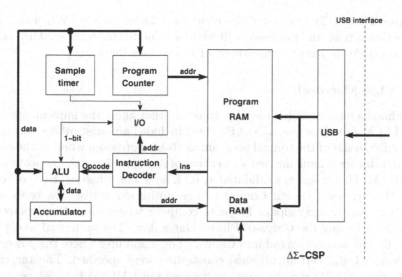

Fig. 4. $\Delta\Sigma$-CSP diagram

Arithmetic and Logic Unit. The ALU takes the opcode and three inputs from I/O, accumulator and data RAM respectively for each calculation.

For a controller structure of the type as shown in Fig. 3, the conditional-negate-and-add (CNA) unit, is utilized to perform most operations of control laws. The CNA unit performs the operation

$$D = \ominus B|A + C, \tag{6}$$

where B is either a coefficient or a state variable, A is a 1-bit signal, and C is a state variable. $\ominus$ is a symbol which means conditional-negate. Hence $\ominus B|A$ conditional-negates B given a condition of A. A is from either input u or output y. If A is 1, $\ominus B|A$ gives B. Otherwise, $\ominus B|A$ gives $-B$. Finally, to complete the CNA operation, the result of the conditional-negation is added to the state variable C and is stored in the accumulator, ready for the next arithmetic operation.

The other arithmetic unit is the shift operation. The scaling factor k in the main loop is a very small power of 2 value in order to enlarge the coefficients. Hence when realised in hardware, it corresponds to a signed shift right operation. Other arithmetic operations such as add, subtract, multiply or divide are not necessary. In addition, very few logic operations are necessary for control system processing [10], and as a result, no Boolean unit is included in this design.

Accumulator. After processing in the ALU, each result is stored in the accumulator for the following instruction at the next clock cycle. Note that the data in this accumulator will be cleared as soon as a 'HLT' instruction is read. This operation is necessary because the final result of each control loop cannot be brought in the calculations at the next sample time.

Sample Timer. The sample timer contains a 24-bit register. When the 'SET' instruction is read, the processor will write a value to this register. This value is used to decide the sample time along with the clock frequency.

3.4   VLSI Macrocell

We defined a number of high-level parameters that affect the implementation of the VLSI Macrocell of the $\Delta\Sigma$-CSP. These included amongst others parameters to specify the size of the control program in 16-bit words and whether the control program storage is implemented as an array of flops or using a single-port embedded SRAM. The design was validated at RTL level and subsequently synthesized using the Synopsys Design Compiler. The optimized netlist was re-validated and then read into Synopsys Physical compiler where an optimal placement was achieved using the Gates-to-Placed-Gates flow. The optimized and placed netlist was subsequently read into Cadence SoC encounter where the power plan was designed and certain physical constraints were specified. The target frequency was 400 MHz and the target technology was UMC $0.13\mu m$, 8-layer copper process.

Fig. 5 depicts the Floorplan (placed database) and final layout (routed) database. The major identifiable blocks are:

- USB Core: This is to the left of the Floorplan and occupies approximately 50% of the total silicon area. We used the USB 1.0 interface core and synthesized it for a clock frequency of 48 MHz.
- $\Delta\Sigma$-CSP Program RAM: An array of flops for storing the control program and associated multiplexing logic.
- Data RAM: Coefficient/Data RAM. Implemented as an embedded memory of 512 words by 24 bits.
- BCSP Core: The processing logic of the $\Delta\Sigma$-CSP.

The design was routed in Cadence SoC encounter and the following results were obtained and shown in Table 2:

Table 2. Results of the design

Frequency (MHz)	355 (DC target 400 MHz)
Std cells (RAMs)	10505(3)
area	$1194\mu m \times 594\mu m = 709438\mu m^2$
Core Utilization	64.5%

3.5   System Performance

The $\Delta\Sigma$-CSP performance is compared to the direct implementation by implementing a 4th order controller. The results are further compared to a conventional

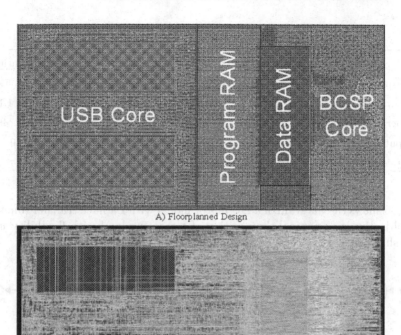

A) Floorplanned Design

B) Routed Design

Fig. 5. Flop-based $\Delta\Sigma$-CSP

control system processor (CSP) [11] and also many other processors. The transfer function of the example controller is

$$H(s) = \frac{1}{(1 + 1.4\frac{s}{w} + \frac{s^2}{w^2})^2}, \tag{7}$$

where $w = 2\pi$.

Table 3 shows the comparison results. From the table, the direct implementation is more than 9 times faster than the $\Delta\Sigma$-CSP to process control laws. But the $\Delta\Sigma$-CSP is still the fastest programmable solution compared to other processor implementations. The power consumption suggests that the $\Delta\Sigma$-CSP is most power efficient as well.

4 Motor Control Application

To thoroughly evaluate the performance of 1-bit processing and $\Delta\Sigma$-CSP in real-life control applications, we demonstrate a practical DC motor controller in this section.

Table 3. Comparison results

	direct impl.	$\Delta\Sigma$-CSP	CSP	TMS320C31	Strong-ARM	PentiumIII
Frequency(MHz)	139	355	50	60	233	500
Clock cycles/instruction	N/A	1	1	2	1.79	1.15
Number of instructions	N/A	24	23	48	43	49
Computation time(μs)	0.0072	0.0676	0.46	1.603	0.331	0.113
Power consumption(w)	0.004	0.28	0.82	2.6	1	> 20

Fig. 6 shows the diagram of a DC motor model with Laplace transfer functions. The objective is to control the position of a rotating load with flexibility in the drive shaft.

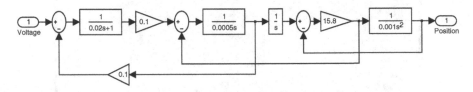

Fig. 6. DC motor diagram

A 4th order position controller was designed including a PI filter, a phase advance filter and a notch filter to minimise the effect of the resonance caused by the flexibility. The Laplace transfer function for the control system is

$$H(s) = \frac{0.0001s^4 + 0.001s^3 + 0.25s^2 + 0.2501s + 0.001}{0.0001s^4 + 0.011s^3 + 0.11s^2 + s}. \tag{8}$$

A hardware-in-loop methodology is adopted to verify the feasibility of the $\Delta\Sigma$-CSP. The DC motor and the $\Delta\Sigma$ modulator are both modelled in the computer with C++. The $\Delta\Sigma$-CSP architecture is realised with the FPGA technology.

The coefficients are represented in a 24-bit fixed-point word format, which results in a maximum error of 0.524% when the sampling frequency is selected at $1kHz$. Because the accuracy of the coefficients should be the same as that of overall control system (typically within 5%) [12], the coefficients can be safely engaged in calculations to perform the control law in the $\Delta\Sigma$-CSP.

The step response of the hardware-in-loop simulation is compared with that of the digital simulation which was carried out in Matlab. The digital simulation takes Eq. 8 as a continuous control system in Simulink. The results are shown in Fig. 7(a). A small area of the simulation results is enlarged as shown in graph (b) because this area is where the peak response of the control system happens. The only difference is that the motor oscillates a bit more heavily with the hardware-

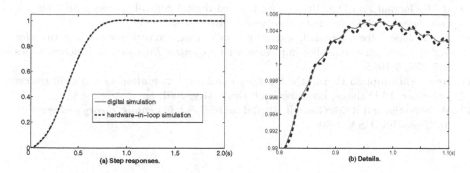

(a) Step responses.   (b) Details.

Fig. 7. Comparisons between the hardware-in-loop simulation and the digital simulation

in-loop simulation. This is due to the effect of pulse density modulation, and will not affect the whole system performance.

5   Conclusion

The $\Delta\Sigma$-CSP is an extremely small and fast application-specific processor. Despite its simplicity, the $\Delta\Sigma$-CSP outperforms even the fastest of the other processors by a significant margin.

At the moment, we are investigating the possibility of very high parallel VLSI architectures consisting of tens to hundreds of $\Delta\Sigma$-CSP cores in an ASIC format.

References

1. James C. Candy. *Oversampling delta-sigma data converters: theory, design, and simulation.* Institute of Electrical and Electronics Engineers, New York, 1992.
2. S. Kershaw, S. Summerfield, M. Sandler, and M. Anderson. Realisation and implementation of a Sigma-Delta bitstream FIR filter. In *IEE Proc.-Circuits Devices Syst.*, volume 143, pages 267–273, October 1996.
3. Simon Kershaw. *Sigma-Delta Bitstream Processors Analysis and Design.* PhD thesis, Kings College, July 1996.
4. J.A.S. Angus and S. Draper. An improved method for directly filtering $\sigma - \delta$ audio signals. In *Proc. AES 104th convention*, Amsterdam, The Netherlands, 1998.
5. Xiaofeng Wu and Roger Goodall. One-bit processing for digital control. *IEE proceedings on Control Theory Applications*, August 2005.
6. Sasan H. Ardalan and John J. Paulos. An analysis of nonlinear behavior in delta-sigma modulators. In *IEEE Transactions on Circuits and Systems*, volume 34, pages 593–604, 1987.
7. B. Liu. Effect of finite wordlength on the accuracy of digital filters — a review. In *IEEE Transactions. Circuit Theory*, volume CT-18, pages 670–677, 1971.
8. R.C. Agarwal and C.S. Burrus. New recursive digital filter structures having very low sensitivity and roundoff noise. *IEEE Trans. Circuits Syst.*, CAS-22(12), 1975.

9. R.M. Goodall and D.S. Brown. High speed digital controllers using an 8-bit microprocessor. *Software and Microsystems*, 4:109–116, 1985.

10. Simon Jones, Roger Goodall, and Mark Gooch. Targeted processor architectures for high-performance controller implementation. *Control Engineering Practice*, pages 867–878, 6 1998.

11. Rene A. Cumplido Parra. *On the design and implementation of a control system processor*. PhD thesis, Loughborough University, 2001.

12. W. Forsythe and R. M. Goodall. *Digital control: Fundamentals, theory and practice*. McGraw-Hill, USA, 1991.

A 0-1 Integer Linear Programming Based Approach for Global Locality Optimizations

Jun Xia, Li Luo, and Xuejun Yang

School of Computer Science, National University of Defense Technology,
Changsha 410073, Hunan, China
ddk@nudt.edu.cn

Abstract. Compiler optimizations aimed at improving cache locality are critical in realizing the performance potential of memory subsystem. For scientific programs, loop and data transformations are two important compiler optimization methods to improve cache locality. In this paper, we combine loop and data transformations and present a 0-1 integer linear programming (0-1 ILP) based approach that attempts to solve global locality optimization problems. We use the treelike memory layout graph (TMLG) to describe a program's locality characteristics, formulate the locality optimization problems as the problems of finding the optimal path sets in TMLGs, and then use 0-1 ILP to find the optimal path sets. Our approach is applicable not only to perfectly nested loops but also to non-perfectly nested loops. Moreover, the approach is suitable for handling the circumstances that arrays are accessed not only along dimensions but also along diagonal-like directions. The experimental results show the effectiveness of our approach.

Keywords: Cache locality, compiler optimizations, memory layouts, loop transformations, data transformations, integer linear programming.

1 Introduction

As the memory speed can not keep up with the speed of microprocessors, memory subsystem has become one of the main performance bottlenecks of the whole computer system. To minimize the impact of this speed gap, memory hierarchies have been used extensively in current computer systems. The performance of programs is determined to a great extent by the use of memory hierarchies and the effective use of caches in memory hierarchies can be made by exploiting programs' cache locality. Loop transformations and data transformations are two important compiler optimization methods to improve programs' cache locality. Loop transformations improve cache locality by iteration space transformations and scheduling techniques, while data transformations improve cache locality by data space transformations.

Loop transformations can improve both temporal and spatial locality, and the effect of loop transformations is local. As loop transformations have the above advantages, many researchers [1-3] have used loop transformations to optimize cache locality over the last decade. Wolf and Lam [1] show how to use unimodular loop transformations followed by tiling loops that carry some form of reuse to improve locality. Li [2] optimizes cache temporal and spatial locality by using loop transformations to reduce

C. Jesshope and C. Egan (Eds.): ACSAC 2006, LNCS 4186, pp. 281–294, 2006.
© Springer-Verlag Berlin Heidelberg 2006

the column heights of the *global data reuse matrix* of a set of array references. McKinley et al. [3] present a method that considers loop fusion, distribution, permutation, and reversal for improving locality.

Loop transformations must be legal and therefore are constrained by data dependences. In addition, imperfectly nested loops and explicitly parallelized programs are in general difficult to be optimized by loop transformations. The above disadvantages of loop transformations have led a great number of researchers [4-7] to consider improving cache locality by data transformations. Data transformations aren't constrained by data dependences and in many cases they can successfully optimize the cache locality of the arrays referenced in imperfectly nested loops and explicitly parallelized programs. Clauss et al. [4] use the parameterized polyhedra theory and Ehrhart polynomials to assure that the data layout corresponds exactly to the utilization order of these data. Kandemir et al. [5] present a hyperplane based approach for optimizing spatial locality in loop nests. Leung [6] optimizes spatial locality by using data transformations to reduce the column heights of *access matrices*. Xia et al. [7] present a projection-delamination technique for optimizing spatial locality and a data transformation framework based on it.

Data transformations have no effect on temporal locality and the effect of data transformations is global. As loop and data transformations have advantages and disadvantages on optimizing cache locality respectively, there have some researchers [8-10] who unify loop and data transformations to optimize cache locality. Cierniak and Li [8] use loop permutations and array dimension permutations in an exhaustive search to determine the appropriate loop and data transformations for a single nest. Kandemir et al. [9] present a matrix-based approach for optimizing the global locality using loop and data transformations. Kandemir et al. [10] use *integer linear programming* (ILP) and the *memory layout graph* (MLG) to find the best combination of loop and data layout transformations for optimizing the global locality.

In this paper, we combine loop and data transformations and present a *0-1 integer linear programming* (0-1 ILP) based approach that attempts to solve the global locality optimization problems. We use the *treelike memory layout graph* (TMLG) to describe a program's locality characteristics, formulate the locality optimization problems as the problems of finding the optimal path sets in TMLGs, and then use 0-1 ILP to find the optimal path sets. The 0-1 ILP formulation obviates the need for any heuristic and can allow us to solve locality optimization problems optimally within our loop transformation space, data transformation space and cost model. Our approach is inspired by the approach used by Kandemir et al. [10] to solve the locality optimization problems. Kandemir et al. [10] use the MLG to describe a program's locality characteristics. An MLG is built from several *nest graphs* (NGs), and an NG is built from several *loop graphs* (LGs). Their approach can only be applicable to perfectly nested loops and can be only suitable for handling the circumstances that arrays are accessed along dimensions. To make our approach applicable not only to perfectly nested loops but also to non-perfectly nested loops, we improve on the NG and the LG and redefine them. We call the redefined NG and LG as the *redefined nest graph* (RNG) and *redefined loop graph* (RLG) respectively. To make our approach suitable for handling the circumstances that arrays are accessed not only along dimensions but also along diagonal-like directions, we find all possible optimal memory layouts for each array and use them to compose its data transformation space. At last, we determine an optimal memory layout for each array and find its corresponding data transformation matrix to optimize cache locality. From the above we can see that the application scope of our approach is more extensive than the approach in [10]. The experimental results show that our approach is very effective in improving the performance of the test programs and the use of 0-1 ILP formulation doesn't increase the compilation time significantly.

The rest of this paper is organized as follows: Section 2 outlines the basic notation and assumptions. Section 3 presents the method for finding the optimal memory layouts of arrays. Section 4 introduces the TMLG and gives the method of constructing it. Based on the TMLG, Section 5 presents our approach in detail. Section 6 gives and discusses the experimental results. Section 7 concludes the paper.

2 Technical Preliminaries

We view the iteration space of a loop nest of depth n as an n-dimensional polyhedron where each point is denoted by an $n \times 1$ column vector $\overline{I} = (i_1, i_2, \cdots, i_n)^T$. We call $\overline{I}$ as the *iteration vector* and show the lower and upper limits for a loop i as li and ui respectively. Similarly, every m-dimensional array X declared in the program defines an m-dimensional polyhedron (namely data space), each point of which represents an array element and can be denoted by an $m \times 1$ column vector. We assume that all loop bounds and subscript expressions are affine functions of enclosing loop indices and symbolic constants. Under the above assumptions, the reference can be represented as $A\overline{I} + \overline{o}$, where $m \times n$ matrix A is called as the *access matrix* and $m \times 1$ column vector $\overline{o}$ is called as the *offset vector* [1]. Without loss of generality, we assume the default memory layout is column-major for all arrays.

3 Optimal Memory Layouts

As the innermost loop is the most frequently accessed loop in all the loops of a given loop nest, we always hope the innermost loop can get the best locality. Given an m-dimensional array B's certain reference $A\overline{I} + \overline{o}$, where $\overline{I} = (i_1, i_2, \cdots, i_n)^T$ and $A = (\overline{\alpha}_1, \cdots, \overline{\alpha}_n)$, according to $\overline{\alpha}_n$, we discuss the locality exhibited by this reference in the following three circumstances:

1. If $\overline{\alpha}_n = \overline{0}$, the reference will exhibit temporal locality in the innermost loop.

2. If $\overline{\alpha}_n$ is a column vector with the first element non-zero and all the other elements zeros, the reference will exhibit spatial locality in the innermost loop with strong possibility.

3. If $\overline{\alpha}_n$ belongs to all the other circumstances, the reference will exhibit bad locality in the innermost loop with strong possibility.

From the above, we can see $\overline{\alpha}_n$ contains locality information the reference $A\overline{I} + \overline{o}$ exhibits. If $\overline{\alpha}_n$ belongs to the third circumstance, we can do data transformations on array B such that it can be accessed along columns. If a non-singular matrix M can make $M\ \overline{\alpha}_n$ become a column vector with the first element non-zero and all the other elements zeros, array B will be accessed along columns after it is transformed by M. We can use the following method to find M.

First we find a basis of $\overline{\alpha}_n$'s orthogonal space. Suppose this basis is $\overline{\beta}_1, \cdots, \overline{\beta}_{m-1}$. Then we find a column vector $\overline{\beta}_m$ that can make $\overline{\beta}_1, \cdots, \overline{\beta}_m$ linearly independent, and use them to construct a non-singular matrix M, where $(\overline{\beta}_m)^T$ is the first row of M and $(\overline{\beta}_1)^T, \cdots, (\overline{\beta}_{m-1})^T$ are all the other rows. Therefore according to $\overline{\alpha}_n$, we can find a data transformation matrix M that can optimize the spatial locality of array B's reference $A\overline{I} + \overline{o}$. We call $\overline{\alpha}_n$ as an *optimal memory layout* of array B.

Assume array B is referenced s times and let $\overline{\gamma}_1, \cdots, \overline{\gamma}_s$ be the last columns of these s references' access matrices respectively. Assume $\overline{\gamma}_1, \cdots, \overline{\gamma}_s$ are non-zero column vectors and therefore all of them are the optimal memory layouts of array B. If we can find a non-singular matrix M that can make each of $M\overline{\gamma}_1, \cdots, M\overline{\gamma}_s$ become a column vector with the first element non-zero and all the other elements zeros, then we call the optimal memory layouts $\overline{\gamma}_1, \cdots, \overline{\gamma}_s$ are *consistent*, which means we can use the same data transformation matrix to optimize the spatial locality of all these s references simultaneously; otherwise we call they are *not consistent*. We can prove that if any two of the optimal memory layouts $\overline{\gamma}_1, \cdots, \overline{\gamma}_s$ are linearly dependent, then they are consistent; otherwise they are not consistent. According to the linear relationship among $\overline{\gamma}_1, \cdots, \overline{\gamma}_s$, we can divide them into several groups such that any two vectors from the same group are linearly dependent while any vector from one group is linearly independent with any vector from the other groups. Then we can select any vector from each group to denote the optimal memory layout the group is representative of and use them to compose array B's data transformation space. Any vector from this data transformation space is a candidate of array B's final optimal memory layout.

4   Constructing TMLG

Given a loop nest, we use a TMLG to describe this loop nest's locality characteristics. A TMLG is constructed from RNGs and each RNG corresponds to a sub-nested loop of a given loop nest. Moreover, a RNG is constructed from RLGs and each RLG corresponds to a loop of a given sub-nested loop.

Input: Loop nest L_1;

Output: All the sub-nested loops of L_1 with their corresponding attributes;

$L = L_1$; $attribute$=NULL; $\Phi = \varnothing$;

FindSN (L , $attribute$)

{ Starting from the outermost loop of L , find all the perfectly close loops $i_1, \cdots, i_s$ (where loop i_1 is the outermost loop) and use them with all the non-loop structure statements enclosed by them to compose sub-nested loop SN;

Set SN's attribute to $attribute$; $\Phi = \Phi \cup \{ SN \}$;

IF loops $i_1, \cdots, i_s$ do not enclose any loop nest THEN Return;

ELSE

FOR each loop nest L' enclosed by loops $i_1, \cdots, i_s$

{ FindSN (L', SN) }}

Fig. 1. The recursive algorithm of finding all the sub-nested loops of L_1

```
DO i₀=li₀,ui₀    SN₁
 DO i₁=li₁,ui₁
  DO i₂=li₂,ui₂
   DO i₃=li₃,ui₃
    {X(i₁,i₂+i₃),Y(i₁+i₃,i₂+i₃,2i₁+i₂),
     Z(i₃+i₃,i₁+i₃),W(i₂+2i₃,i₁+3i₃)}  SN₂
   ENDDO
  ENDDO
 ENDDO
 DO i₁=li₁,ui₁
  DO i₂=li₂,ui₂    SN₃
   {X(i₂,i₁)}
   DO i₃=li₃,ui₃
    DO i₄=li₄,ui₄
     {Y(i₁+2i₃+i₄,i₁+i₂+i₄,i₂+4i₃+i₄),
      Z(i₁+i₄,i₂+i₃),W(2i₄,i₂+2i₄)}  SN₄
    ENDDO
   ENDDO
   DO i₅=li₅,ui₅
    DO i₆=li₆,ui₆
     {Y(i₁+i₁+3i₅,i₁+i₆,i₁+2i₂+6i₅+i₆),  SN₅
      V(i₁+3i₅+2i₆,i₁+2i₅+3i₆)}
    ENDDO
   ENDDO
  ENDDO    SN₃
 ENDDO
ENDDO    SN₁
```

```
DO i₀=li₀,ui₀
 DO i₁=li₁,ui₁
  DO i₂=li₂,ui₂
   DO i₃=li₃,ui₃
    {X(i₁,i₂+i₃),Y(i₁+i₃,i₂+i₃,-i₂+2i₃),
     Z(i₃+i₃,i₂+i₃),W(i₃,i₂)}
   ENDDO
  ENDDO
 ENDDO
 DO i₁=li₁,ui₁
  DO i₂=li₂,ui₂
   {X(i₂,i₁)}
   DO i₃=li₄,ui₄
    DO i₄=li₃,ui₃
     {Y(i₁+2i₃+i₄,i₁+i₂+i₄,2i₃-i₂+i₄),
      Z(i₂+i₃,i₁+i₄),W(i₂,-2i₂+2i₄)}
    ENDDO
   ENDDO
   DO i₆=li₆,ui₆
    DO i₅=li₅,ui₅
     {Y(i₁+i₁+3i₅,i₁+i₆,i₁-i₆),
      V(i₅-i₆,i₁+5i₆)}
    ENDDO
   ENDDO
  ENDDO
 ENDDO
ENDDO
```

(a)   (b)

Fig. 2. (a)The loop nest and its sub-nested loops. (b) The optimized code of the loop nest.

4.1 Sub-nested Loop

A *sub-nested loop* of a loop nest is composed of all the perfectly close loops ('perfectly close' means there are not any statement among the loops) of this loop nest and all the non-loop structure statements enclosed by these loops. We attach an attribute to each sub-nested loop and use this attribute to record the sub-nested loop's parent sub-nested loop. The recursive algorithm of finding all the sub-nested loops of a given loop nest is presented in Fig. 1.

From this algorithm we can see if the loop nest is a perfectly nested loop, it has only one sub-nested loop, namely the loop nest itself; if the loop nest is a non-perfectly nested loop, it has more than one sub-nested loop, and if we think of each sub-nested loop as a node and connect it with its parent sub-nested loop according to its attribute, then we will get a tree. Consider the loop nest in Fig. 2(a). It is a non-perfectly nested loop and the array references used by this loop nest is enclosed by '{' and '}'. The actual computations performed inside the nest are irrelevant for our purposes. Following the algorithm in Fig. 1, we can find out the loop nest's five sub-nested loops SN_1, SN_2, SN_3, SN_4 and SN_5 (which are enclosed by dashed lines respectively). SN_1 contains no statement and its attribute is NULL. Both the attributes of SN_2 and SN_3 are SN_1 and both the attributes of SN_4 and SN_5 are SN_3. The tree composed of these five sub-nested loops is shown in Fig. 3(c).

4.2 Constructing RNG and RLG

Given a sub-nested loop, we construct a RLG for each loop of this sub-nested loop that can be placed in the innermost position. A RLG is constructed using *node-rows* which correspond to arrays accessed in the sub-nested loop. For each array, we insert a node-row into RLG. The nodes in a node-row denote the optimal memory layouts in the data transformation space of the array that the node-row corresponds to. In a given RLG, the node-rows are placed one after another from the top down. Between the two consecutive node-rows X and Y (that correspond to arrays X and Y respectively), there are Layout(X) × Layout(Y) edges where Layout(.) returns the number of the optimal memory layouts in a given array's data transformation space. In addition to the node-rows, the RLG has a start node and a terminal node. Each node in the first node-row is connected to the start node and each node in the last node-row is connected to the terminal node.

Under the condition that the innermost loops enclosing all references of an array are unchanged, we have presented the method of determining this array's data transformation space in Section 3. However, we consider not only data transformations but also simple loop permutation transformations inside sub-nested loops to improve cache locality in this paper, and hence according to loop permutation transformations, it is possible that the innermost loops enclosing these references are changed. Based on the method presented in Section 3, we determine an array's data transformation space as follows:

Assume array B is referenced s times in a loop nest and these s references are $A_1 \overline{I}_1 + \overline{o}_1, \cdots, A_s \overline{I}_s + \overline{o}_s$ respectively, where $A_k = (\overline{\gamma}_{k1}, \cdots, \overline{\gamma}_{kn_k})$. Without loss of generality, we assume $\forall 1 \leq k \leq s$, reference $A_k \overline{I}_k + \overline{o}_k$ occurs in sub-nested loop SN_k, the loops $i_{k1}, \cdots, i_{kp_k}$ in SN_k can be placed in the innermost position of SN_k and $i_{k1}, \cdots, i_{kp_k}$ are the q_{k1} th, $\cdots$, the q_{kp_k} th element of $\overline{I}_k$ respectively. Therefore, $\forall 1 \leq k \leq s$, all the non-zero column vectors among $\overline{\gamma}_{kq_{k1}}, \cdots, \overline{\gamma}_{kq_{kp_k}}$ are array B's optimal memory layouts. Then using the method presented in Section 3, we can divide these optimal memory layouts into several groups and select any vector from each group to compose array B's data transformation space.

Continue the example in Fig. 2(a). Assume in SN_2, loops i_1, i_2 and i_3 can be placed in the innermost position of SN_2; in SN_3, loops i_1 and i_2 can be placed in the innermost position of SN_3; in SN_4, loops i_3 and i_4 can be placed in the innermost position of SN_4; in SN_5, loops i_5 and i_6 can be placed in the innermost position of SN_5. Following the above method, we can find array X's data transformation space is $\left\{(1 \quad 0)^T, (0 \quad 1)^T\right\}$, array Y's data transformation space is $\left\{(1 \quad 0 \quad 2)^T, (0 \quad 1 \quad 1)^T, (1 \quad 1 \quad 0)^T\right.$ $\left., (1 \quad 1 \quad 1)^T\right\}$, array Z's data transformation space is $\left\{(1 \quad 0)^T, (0 \quad 1)^T, (1 \quad 1)^T\right\}$, array W's data transformation space is $\left\{(2 \quad 3)^T, (1 \quad 1)^T\right\}$ and array V's data transformation space is $\left\{(3 \quad 2)^T, (2 \quad 3)^T\right\}$. The RLG corresponding to loop i_1 in SN_2 is shown in Fig. 3(a).

Given a sub-nested loop, we construct its corresponding RNG as follows: A RNG has a start node (marked with St) and a terminal node (marked with Tr). After we have constructed a RLG for each loop of the sub-nested loop that can be placed in the innermost position, we connect all RLGs' start nodes to the RNG's start node and all RLG's terminal nodes to the RNG's terminal node, and hence get the RNG corresponding to the sub-nested loop. If the sub-nested loop contains no array, we use a single node to denote its RNG. The RNG corresponding to SN_2 in Fig. 2(a) is shown in Fig. 3(b).

4.3 Treelike Memory Layout Graph

Given a loop nest, we construct a tree T by thinking each sub-nested loop of the loop nest as a node and connect it with its parent sub-nested loop according to its attribute. Then we replace each node in T with the RNG corresponding to the sub-nested loop that is denoted by the node, and hence get the loop nest's corresponding TMLG. The TMLG corresponding to the loop nest in Fig. 2(a) is shown in Fig. 4.

From the above we can see that a TMLG corresponding to a loop nest is a tree-like structure formed by the connections among RNGs. If we think of each RNG in the TMLG as a node, then the TMLG is a tree. We call the start node of the RNG denoted by this tree's root node as the *root node* of the TMLG (if the RNG denoted by this tree's root node is a single node, this single node is the root node of the TMLG). Moreover, we call the terminal nodes of the RNGs denoted by this tree's leaf nodes as the *leaf nodes* of the TMLG. For each RNG which is not a single node, we define a path from the RNG's start node St to its terminal node Tr is a *path* of this RNG. In addition, we define the *path set* of a TMLG is the path set that is composed of the paths from the TMLG's root node to its all leaf nodes and that satisfies the condition that for all paths passing the same RNG, their partial paths in this RNG are all identical. From this definition, we can see the path set of a TMLG visits all the RNGs and as long as the paths of all the RNGs are determined, the path set of the TMLG is determined too. A path set of the TMLG corresponding to the loop nest in Fig. 2(a) is shown in Fig. 4 (the path set is denoted by the bold lines). If a RLG corresponding to

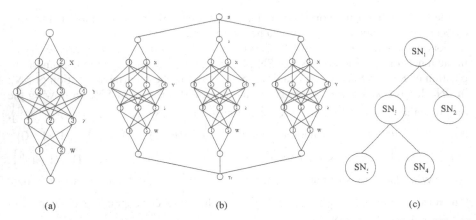

Fig. 3. (a) The RLG corresponding to loop i_1 in SN_2. (b) The RNG corresponding to SN_2. (c) The tree composed of the sub-nested loops in Fig. 2(a).

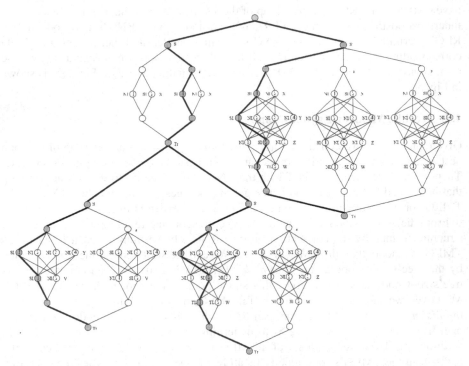

Fig. 4. The TMLG, node costs and a (an optimal) path set corresponding to the loop nest in Fig. 2(a)

a loop in a sub-nested loop is visited by the path set of the TMLG, it means this loop should be placed in the innermost position of this sub-nested loop for best locality. In addition, if a node in a node-row is touched by the path set, it means the optimal memory layout denoted by this node should be selected as the final optimal memory layout of the array that this node-row corresponds to.

4.4 Node Costs

A *node cost* is the estimation of the cache misses and only nodes in node-rows have costs associated with them. We use notation $V_Q^{xl}[j]$ to denote j th node of a node-row for array Q in the RLG l of the RNG x. Then, we define $Cost(V_Q^{xl}[j])$ as the number of cache misses incurred due to array Q in the sub-nested loop x when the optimal memory layout denoted by node $V_Q^{xl}[j]$ is selected as the final optimal memory layout of array Q and the loop l is placed in the innermost position of the sub-nested loop x. The *cost* of a TMLG's path set is the sum of the costs of all the nodes that are in node-rows and that are contained by the path set. We use the following simple method to estimate node costs.

Assume $A\overline{I} + \overline{o}$ is a reference of array Q in the sub-nested loop x and the loop index of the loop l is the q th element of iteration vector $\overline{I}$. Let $\overline{\alpha}_1$ be the q th column of A and $\overline{\alpha}_2$ be the optimal memory layout denoted by node $V_Q^{xl}[j]$. Suppose the loop l is placed in the innermost position and $\overline{\alpha}_2$ is selected as the final optimal memory layout of array Q. Therefore, from Section 3 we can know if $\overline{\alpha}_1$ is a zero column vector, $A\overline{I} + \overline{o}$ will exhibit temporal locality and we let the number of cache misses incurred due to $A\overline{I} + \overline{o}$ be TL; if $\overline{\alpha}_1$ is a non-zero column vector and dependent with $\overline{\alpha}_2$, $A\overline{I} + \overline{o}$ will exhibit spatial locality with respect to $\overline{\alpha}_2$ and we let the number of cache misses incurred due to $A\overline{I} + \overline{o}$ be SL; if $\overline{\alpha}_1$ is a non-zero column vector and independent with $\overline{\alpha}_2$, $A\overline{I} + \overline{o}$ will exhibit no locality with respect to $\overline{\alpha}_2$ and we let the number of cache misses incurred due to $A\overline{I} + \overline{o}$ be NL. We let TL<SL<NL. The node costs of the TMLG corresponding to the loop nest in Fig. 2(a) are shown in Fig. 4.

5 Our Approach

5.1 Problem Statement

Our goal in this paper is to minimize the number of cache misses thereby reducing the time spent due to memory stalls. We achieve this goal by selecting an innermost loop for each sub-nested loop, which encloses array references in question, in a given loop nest and selecting an optimal memory layout for each considered array referenced in this loop nest. The above operations to achieve this goal correspond to finding a path set of the TMLG with minimized cost. We call a TMLG's path set with minimized cost as this TMLG's *optimal path set* and use 0-1 ILP to find the optimal path set.

5.2 Integer Variables and Objective Function

We use notation $H_{PQ}{}^{xl}$ to denote all the Layout(P)×Layout(Q) edges between two consecutive node-rows P and Q for a RLG l of a RNG x. Notation $H_{PQ}{}^{xl}[j,k]$, on the other hand, denotes the edge between the jth node of node-row P and the kth node of node-row Q for a RLG l of a RNG x. We also use $H_{PQ}{}^{xl}[j,k]$ to denote the 0-1 *integer variable* associated with the edge denoted by $H_{PQ}{}^{xl}[j,k]$. Given a path set of a TMLG, $H_{PQ}{}^{xl}[j,k]$ has a value of 1 if the edge denoted by it belongs to the path set; otherwise its value is 0.

Given a path set of a TMLG, if the kth node of a node-row Q in a RLG l of a RNG x is touched by this path set, there must have $\sum_{j=1}^{Layout(P)} H_{PQ}{}^{xl}[j,k]=1$, where P is the node-row connected to Q directly; otherwise there must have $\sum_{j=1}^{Layout(P)} H_{PQ}{}^{xl}[j,k]=0$. Therefore, the cost of this path set can be denoted as

$$\sum_x \sum_l \sum_Q \sum_{k=1}^{Layout(Q)} ((\sum_{j=1}^{Layout(P)} H_{PQ}{}^{xl}[j,k])Cost(V_Q{}^{xl}[k])) \tag{1}$$

The *objective* of the global locality optimization problem is then to select a path set in a given TMLG such that the value denoted by Formula (1) is minimized.

5.3 Constraints

After the objective function is determined, the constraints for 0-1 integer variables should be determined to ensure that the selected edges and nodes can form a path set of a given TMLG. There are three conditions that need to be satisfied:

1. The RNG path condition
The selected edges and nodes in each RNG that is not a single node can form a path of the RNG. We can express this condition in terms our integer variables as

$$\forall k \in [1...Layout(Q)] \sum_{j=1}^{Layout(P)} H_{PQ}{}^{xl}[j,k] = \sum_{s=1}^{Layout(R)} H_{QR}{}^{xl}[k,s].$$

Here, P, Q and R are three arrays corresponding to three consecutive node-rows in the RLGs.

2. The single RNG path condition
The selected edges and nodes in each RNG that is not a single node can only form a single path of the RNG. We can formalize this condition as

$$\sum_{j=1}^{Layout(P)} \sum_{k=1}^{Layout(Q)} H_{PQ}{}^{xl_1}[j,k] + \cdots + \sum_{j=1}^{Layout(P)} \sum_{k=1}^{Layout(Q)} H_{PQ}{}^{xl_n}[j,k] = 1.$$

Here, $l_1, \cdots, l_n$ are all the RLGs of the RNG x and P and Q are any two consecutive node-rows in x.

3. The static memory layout condition

As we only consider static data transformations, each array should only have a unique memory layout. It indicates that if a node of array Q is selected in sub-nested loop x, the same node should also be selected in any sub-nested loop x' that accesses array Q. We can formalize this condition as

$$\forall k \in [1 \ldots Layout(Q)]:$$

$$\sum_{j=1}^{Layout(P_1)} H_{P_1Q}{}^{x_1 l_1{}^1}[j,k] + \sum_{j=1}^{Layout(P_1)} H_{P_1Q}{}^{x_1 l_2{}^1}[j,k] + \cdots$$

$$= \sum_{j=1}^{Layout(P_2)} H_{P_2Q}{}^{x_2 l_1{}^2}[j,k] + \sum_{j=1}^{Layout(P_2)} H_{P_2Q}{}^{x_2 l_2{}^2}[j,k] + \cdots = \cdots$$

$$= \sum_{j=1}^{Layout(P_v)} H_{P_vQ}{}^{x_v l_1{}^v}[j,k] + \sum_{j=1}^{Layout(P_v)} H_{P_vQ}{}^{x_v l_2{}^v}[j,k] + \cdots.$$

Here, array Q only occurs in the sub-nested loops $x_1, \cdots, x_v$, $P_1, \cdots, P_v$ are the arrays whose node-rows are directly connected to that of array Q in $x_1, \cdots, x_v$ respectively, and $l_1{}^s, l_2{}^s, \cdots$ are all the RLGs of the RNG x_s.

5.4 Example

Using the Cplex integer programming tool, we find an optimal path set of the TMLG in Fig. 4 (the optimal path set is denoted by the bold lines in Fig. 4). The optimal path set gives a static optimal solution of the locality optimization problem of the loop nest in Fig. 2(a). According to it, we determine : Loop i_1, i_2, i_3 and i_5 are the innermost loops for SN_2, SN_3, SN_4 and SN_5 respectively; the final optimal memory layouts for arrays X, Y, Z, W and V are $(1 \quad 0)^T$, $(1 \quad 0 \quad 2)^T$, $(0 \quad 1)^T$, $(2 \quad 3)^T$ and $(3 \quad 2)^T$ respectively. According to these optimal memory layouts, we can find the data transformation matrices for optimizing spatial locality of X, Y, Z, W and V. After we do the determined loop and data transformations on the loop nest in Fig. 2(a), the optimized code is shown in Fig. 2(b).

6 Experimental Results

In this section, we report our experimental results obtained on a PC with a single 2GHz Intel Pentium 4 processor. This processor has an 8KB, four-way set associative L1 data cache and a 512KB, eight-way set associative L2 cache. Both the line sizes of the L1 data cache and the L2 cache are 64Bytes. The memory size is 512MB.

For this study, we select 14 programs whose characteristics are shown in Table 1. All of the programs manipulate double-precision arrays, are written in FORTRAN, and compiled using the native g77 compiler. *matmult* is a routine that multiplies two matrices; *syr2k* is a banded matrix update routine from BLAS; *stencil* is a five-point stencil computing code; *htribk* is a test program from Eispack; *mxm, cholsky, vpenta*

Table 1. Test programs in our experiment set

Program	Problem size	Var	Constr	Time 1	Time 2
matmult	1024×1024 matrices	60	38	0.06	0.13
syr2k	1024×1024 matrices	108	58	0.06	0.16
stencil	1024×1024 matrices	24	16	0.09	0.13
htribk	1024×1024 matrices	108	83	0.08	0.25
mxm	1024×1024 matrices	60	40	0.06	0.19
cholsky	The size parameters are set to 2500	212	150	0.1	0.34
vpenta	920×920 arrays 920×920×3 arrays	298	237	0.11	0.36
cfft2d1	1024×1024 matrices	16	15	0.06	0.23
adi	1024×1024×3 arrays	126	65	0.08	0.16
amhmtm	1024×1024 matrices	128	86	0.07	0.19
bmcm	1024×1024 matrices	36	31	0.06	0.2
mxmxm	1024×1024 matrices	104	66	0.09	0.16
transpose	4096×4096 matrices	32	23	0.09	0.13
test	1024×1280 array 1280×1280 array	112	58	0.06	0.14

```
DO i1=1,N
  DO i2=1,N
    X(i1+i2,i1+2*i2)
      =Y(2*i1+i2,3*i1+i2)
  ENDDO
ENDDO
DO i1=1,N
  DO i2=1,N
    Y(3*i1+2*i2,2*i1+3*i2)
      =X(2*i1+2*i2,3*i1+2*i2)
  ENDDO
ENDDO
```

Fig. 5. Program *test*

and *cfft2d1* are four test programs from Spec92/NASA benchmark suite; *adi* is one of Livermore kernels; *amhmtm* and *bmcm* are two subroutines from program WSSI in Perfect Club benchmarks; *mxmxm* is a routine from [8] that multiplies three matrices; *transpose* is a routine from a large computational chemistry application [11]; *test* is a program shown in Fig. 5 and we use it to compare our approach with the approach in [10]. The fourth and the fifth columns give the number of 0-1 integer variables (*Var*) and the number of constraints (*Constr*). The *Time 1* column gives the times (in *seconds*) required to find optimal solutions using Cplex and the *Time 2* column gives the times (in *seconds*) required to compile the optimized programs. From Table 1 we can see the times taken to find optimal solutions are not very high and the time taken to find a solution constituted at most 36 percent of the total compilation time.

We use the following method to test each program: First, we take the original unoptimized code as input and test it with g77 compiler option -O0, option -O3 and options -O3 -funroll-loops respectively. Then, we take the code optimized by the approach proposed in this paper as input and test it with g77 compiler option -O0, option -O3 and options -O3 -funroll-loops respectively. Compiler option -O0 denotes no optimization and option -funroll-loops denotes loop unrolling optimization. The performance results are presented in Table 2.

From Table 2 we can see that except for *mxm* our approach can improve the performance of the rest of 13 programs significantly. With no optimization turned on (-O0), our approach improves the performance of the original codes on average by a factor of 5. In all codes excluding *mxm*, the code generated with our approach without any additional optimizations (-O0) outperforms the best compiler-optimized version (-O3 -funroll-loops) of the original code. The main reason for this result is that the native compiler couldn't use necessary data transformations to improve the locality of arrays and the imperfect nest structure prevented the loop transformations in some codes. With the best compiler optimizations turned on, our approach improves the performance of the original codes on average by a factor of 15 excluding *mxm*. This

Table 2. Performance results

Ver	Time		Speedup
-O0	118.03	13.67	8.63
-O3	114.19	3.62	31.5
-O3+	114.93	3.4	33.8

(a) matmult

Ver	Time		Speedup
-O0	35.18	6.05	5.81
-O3	25.41	2.37	10.7
-O3+	25.92	2.14	12.1

(b) syr2k

Ver	Time		Speedup
-O0	2.734	0.3125	8.75
-O3	2.719	0.1719	15.8
-O3+	2.734	0.1563	17.5

(c) stencil

Ver	Time		Speedup
-O0	303.77	63.24	4.80
-O3	225.97	36.96	6.11
-O3+	215.078	37.26	5.77

(d) htribk

Ver	Time		Speedup
-O0	11.36	11.29	1.01
-O3	4.83	5.07	0.95
-O3+	4.3	4.49	0.96

(e) mxm

Ver	Time		Speedup
-O0	86.55	14.22	6.09
-O3	81.02	7.33	11.1
-O3+	80.66	7.14	11.3

(f) cholsky

Ver	Time		Speedup
-O0	3.34	0.58	5.76
-O3	3.29	0.34	9.68
-O3+	3.29	0.34	9.68

(g) vpenta

Ver	Time		Speedup
-O0	2.07	0.42	4.93
-O3	1.79	0.34	5.26
-O3+	1.76	0.34	5.18

(h) cfft2d1

Ver	Time		Speedup
-O0	3.1094	0.5625	5.53
-O3	2.9688	0.5313	5.59
-O3+	2.9688	0.5313	5.59

(i) adi

Ver	Time		Speedup
-O0	123.95	13.953	8.88
-O3	118.625	3.922	30.2
-O3+	118.953	3.703	32.1

(j) amhmtm

Ver	Time		Speedup
-O0	125	14.766	8.47
-O3	119.25	3.875	30.8
-O3+	119.344	3.6563	32.6

(k) bmcm

Ver	Time		Speedup
-O0	218.77	27.48	7.96
-O3	205.04	7.38	27.8
-O3+	213.68	6.93	30.8

(l) mxmxm

Ver	Time		Speedup
-O0	7.1875	1.2188	5.90
-O3	7.2813	1.0156	7.17
-O3+	7.2969	0.7188	10.2

(m) transpose

Ver	Time			Speedup1	Speedup2
-O0	2.73	2.3	1.07	2.55	2.15
-O3	2.74	1.97	0.87	3.15	2.26
-O3+	2.44	1.99	0.87	2.80	2.29

(n) test

In (a) to (m), the second column gives the times (in *seconds*) spent running the versions taking the original (unoptimized) code as input and taking the code optimized by our approach as input in its first subcolumn and the second subcolumn respectively; the third column gives the speedups of the code generated with our approach relative to the original code with the same compiler optimization options. In (n), the second column gives the times (in *seconds*) spent running the versions taking the original (unoptimized) code as input, taking the code optimized by the approach in [12] as input and taking the code optimized by our approach as input in its first subcolumn, the second subcolumn and the third subcolumn respectively; the third and the fourth columns give the speedups of the code generated with our approach relative to the original code and the code generated with the approach in [12] with the same compiler optimization options. Symbol –O3+ denotes -O3 -funroll-loops options.

shows optimizing locality with data transformations is very important even in the cases where loop unrolling and O3-level optimizations are applicable. From Table 2 we also can see that loop unrolling does not always improve the performance. In addition, from the performance results of program *test* we can see the approach in [10] is not suitable for handling the circumstances that arrays are accessed along diagonal-like directions whereas our approach is suitable, and therefore the versions generated with our approach outperform the versions generated with the approach in [10].

7 Conclusions

The performance of programs is determined to a great extent by the locality exhibited by memory accesses. In this paper, we combine loop and data transformations and present a 0-1 ILP based approach to solve the global locality optimization problems based on the TMLG. As our approach combines loop and data transformations, it can optimize both temporal locality and spatial locality. The experimental results show our approach can improve the performance of the test programs significantly.

References

1. M.Wolf and M.Lam. A data locality optimizing algorithm. In *Proc. SIGPLAN Conf. Prog. Lang. Des. & Impl.*, Toronto, Canada, pp. 30-44, 1991.
2. W.Li. Compiling for NUMA parallel machines. PhD dissertation, Cornell University, Ithaca, NY, 1993.
3. K.McKinley, S.Carr and C.W.Tseng. Improving data locality with loop transformation. ACM Transactions on Programming Languages and Systems, 18(4): 424-453, 1996.
4. P.Clauss and B.Meister. Automatic memory layout transformations to optimize spatial locality in parameterized loop nests. ACM SIGARCH Computer Architecture News, 28(1): 11-19, 2000.
5. M.Kandemir, A.Choudhary, N.Shenoy, P.Banerjee and J.Ramanujam. A hyperplane based approach for optimizing spatial locality in loop nests. In the Proceeding of 1998 ACM International Conference on Supercomputing, Melbourne, Australia pp. 69-76, 1998. .
6. S.Leung. Array restructuring for cache locality. Dept. Computer Science and Engineering, University of Washington, Technical Report UW-CSE-96-08-01, 1996.
7. Jun Xia, Xuejun Yang, Lifang Zeng and Haifang Zhou. A projection-delamination based approach for optimizing spatial locality in loop nests. Chinese Journal of Computers, 26(5): 539-551, 2003.
8. M.Cierniak and W.Li. Unifying data and control transformations for distributed shared memory machines. In *Proc. SIGPLAN Conf. Prog. Lang. Des. & Impl.*, La Jolla, CA, pp.205-217, 1995.
9. M.Kandemir, A.Choudhary, J.Ramanujam and P.Banerjee. A matrix-based approach to global locality optimization. Journal of Parallel and Distributed Computing, 58:190-235, 1999.
10. M.Kandemir, P.Banerjee, A.Choudhary, J.Ramanujam, and E.Ayguade. Static and dynamic locality optimizations using integer linear programming. IEEE Transactions on Parallel and Distributed Systems, 12(9): 922-940, 2001.
11. High Performance Computational Chemistry Group. NWChem: A computational chemistry package for parallel computers, version 1.1. Richland,Wash: Pacific Northwest Laboratory, 1995.

Design and Analysis of Low Power Image Filters Toward Defect-Resilient Embedded Memories for Multimedia SoCs

Kang Yi[1], Kyeong Hoon Jung[2], Shih-Yang Cheng[3],
Young-Hwan Park[3], Fadi Kurdahi[3], and Ahmed Eltawil[3]

[1] School of Computer Sceince and Electronic Engineering,
Handong Global University, Pohang, Korea
yk@handong.edu
[2] Department of Electrical Engineering, Kookmin University, Seoul, Korea
khjung@kookmin.ac.kr
[3] Department of EECS, University of California, Irvine, CA 92697-265
{shihyanc, younghwp, kurdahi, aeltawil}@uci.edu

Abstract. In the foreseeable future, System-on-Chip design will suffer from the problem of low yield especially in embedded memories. This can be a critical problem in a multimedia application like H.264 since it needs a huge amount of embedded memory. Existing approaches to solve this problem are not feasible given the higher memory defect density rates in technologies below 90 nm. In this paper, we present a new defect-resilience technique which employs the directional image filter in order to recover data from corrupted embedded memory. According to the analysis based on simulation the proposed filter can greatly improve the visual quality of the defected H.264 video streams with errors in data memory reaching up to 1.0% memory BER (Bit Error Rate) with lower power consumption relative to conventional median filter. Therefore, the proposed method can be a good solution to overcome the problem of low yield in multimedia SoC memory without suffering from additional redundant memory overhead.

Keywords: Low power image filter design, Embedded memory, Memory yield enhancement, Memory-error resilient design, BIST, BISR, H.264 codec.

1 Introduction

The ever-shrinking design geometries are allowing system designers to integrate larger memories on-chip. Integrating memories and processing core (random logic) into a single chip has the following benefits: (1) higher performance, (2) reduced power consumption, (3) lower parts cost, (4) less inter-chip communication complexity, and (5) smaller number of packages on a system board. Embedded memories are expected to account for most of the silicon die area in the near future SoC (System-on-a-Chip) design as the system-on-chips are moving from logic dominant to memory dominant to meet the application requirements [9]. According to the 2001 International Technology Roadmap for Semiconductor the embedded

C. Jesshope and C. Egan (Eds.): ACSAC 2006, LNCS 4186, pp. 295–308, 2006.
© Springer-Verlag Berlin Heidelberg 2006

memories are going to occupy from 54% to 94% of silicon real estate by year 2014 [1,2]. In particular, multimedia application such as H.264 video decoders require significant amount of memory to store intermediate frame data. Thus, the rapid growth in multimedia content and the corresponding increase in demand for high performance and low-power terminals has exerted increased pressure to integrate these large memories into a System-on-Chip.

However, the lower yield of embedded memory is becoming a barrier to the widespread of very deep submicron technology adoption in SoC. Because memory design uses the most aggressive design rules, memory circuits are more susceptible to the manufacturing errors than random logic circuits. The situation is likely to get worse with the random dopant fluctuation (RDF) problem under 100 nm technology [7]. Therefore, the increasing embedded memory size on a chip may result in the lower SoC yield and higher manufacturing chip cost. Thus, the embedded memory yield is becoming a key issue for the overall SoC yield improvement.

In order to combat this memory yield problem memory repair is typically performed after manufacturing using redundancy. Spare columns and rows are used to replace the defective parts of the memory [3, 4]. These methods show a reasonable yield improvement for the current technology by repairing defective memories with up to 0.003% error rate. But, these existing techniques do not work properly with the very deep-submicron technologies because these methods require too much overheads in terms of the area for the higher defect density of future nano device technology. According to [4] the redundancies to repair memory with even 0.1% BER (Bit Error Rate) require at least 67% of area overhead.

In this paper, we present a new approach that handles embedded memories with higher defect densities than current technologies. Our approach essentially pushes the task of repair from the circuit level up to the application level. To illustrate this approach we focus in this paper on one representative application which is the H.264 video decoder. H.264 is a promising multimedia application which is also memory-hungry. To achieve 100% error free huge embedded memory is an almost impractical assumption especially for advanced processes. Instead of fixing the errors at the circuit (or bit-exact) level, we compensate for them at the application level. There exist a multitude of techniques to do so. One of these techniques is to perform simple spatial filtering on the individual video frames. In this paper, we focus on this approach and present a family of spatial filters that can recover the defect pixel values with simple and yet effective image processing algorithms as depicted in Fig 1. We also analyze the performance and power consumption of these filters in software implementation. With these filters, we can guarantee 100% application-level recovery from errors in embedded memories with up to 0.1% BER as well as current technology memory with BER of 0.001%.

The next chapter explains the background knowledge about defect memory problems in H.264 application and summarizes the related previous works. In Chapter 3, we define the problem for filter design and in Chapter 4 we design new filters for simple and enhanced image processing to recover defective pixel values. In Chapter 5, we show the experimental results and discuss the implication. Finally, in Chapter 6, we conclude our work with future research directions.

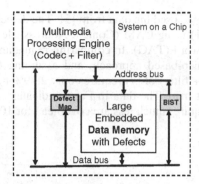

Fig. 1. Our System Architecture with Memory Error-Resilient H.264 decoder : our system has large memory which is defect location. The Defect map and BIST will be used for the problem.

2 Background

In [7], it was shown that one does not need to discard the manufactured chips with memory defects only if we implement the error resilience features at the design time with application specific data redundancies. In [7], we found that it is possible to compensate for the loss due to imperfect data memories using application-level error concealment techniques. By nature, multimedia data has redundancies and such a redundancy may be used to recover data properly. Therefore, H.264 is an ideal example to demonstrate the embedded memory yield enhancement by our approach. Assume an HDTV decoder with 1920 x 1080 pixels image size per frame and the decoded frame image is stored in a memory called Decoded Picture Buffer (DPB) which can be used later for inter-prediction task. Since 4:2:0 sampling mode is assumed and each components has 8 bits per pixel the DPB size is 24Mbits per frame. Since 2 – 5 frames are usually required as a reference frame, at least 48 Mbits of data memory is required. Currently, this DPB memory exists as an external memory chip connected to the main processor chip. As device geometries continue to shrink, the forthcoming SoC design is going to integrate this external memory into a chip. As mentioned before, such huge memories with future VDSM technology will suffer from higher defect rate resulting in lower SoC yield problem.

Fig 2 shows overall structure of our H.264 decoder with memory defect resilient feature. A defect map memory stores the defect pixel location and is used for error concealment schemes with image filter. The image filter is applied only to the defect pixels to get the correct pixel value for each defect pixel reading operation. We may assume that the defect map is constructed at the manufacturing test time. Alternatively, we may assume that it is reconstructed at each power up time by scanning memory reflecting the changing memory status.

Fig 3 shows the overhead of using defect map compared with the existing redundancy approach in [4] and [5] for 100% embedded SRAM yield. Note that the Y-axis in Fig 2 is a log scale. The redundancy scheme in [4] can at most repair only 0.003% defects thus the data used for that level of defects is based on approach in [4].

For higher defect rates we used the data from [5]. The defect map can be implemented in one of two ways: (1) using CAM (Content-Addressable Memory) and (2) using a tag bit for every data word (TAG). In comparing redundancy-based approaches with the proposed defect map-based approach, and assuming 0.1 % memory BER, our approach (defect map + filter) of [7] requires only 2.29% memory area overhead with the CAM-based defect map. The data in Fig 3 indicates clearly that the defect map with filter approach requires much less area overhead for 100% memory yield.

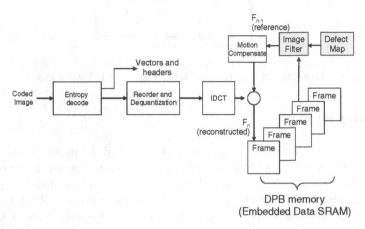

Fig. 2. H.264 decoder with error resilience feature by defect map and filtering

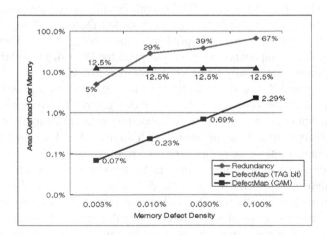

Fig. 3. Overhead Comparison between defect resilience schemes

3   Problem Definition (Filter Design Constraints)

We are going to design filters under the following assumptions and design requirements.

(1) The filters are for the H.264 decoder side.
(2) The errors come not from transmission but from the *storage defect* for the image reference frame data.
(3) The filters work on the Y,U and V domain only.
(4) The defects are distributed in a *randomly uniform fashion*.
(5) The defect rates to cover are in the range *from 0.001% to 1.0%*.
(6) Every defect location is known by defect map.
(7) The filter will only target the defect pixels whose locations are in the defect map.
(8) Our memory defect model is based on the stuck-at fault model in bit level.
(9) The defective pixel map is provided for each Y, U, and V component as separate and independent memories and the defect map memory is assumed to be error free, which is reasonable assumption for the defect map is quite small.
(10) The filter should not be too complicated. The filter overhead to overall system should be minimized.

4 Our Filter Design

The best image filter for error concealment shown in [7] is the median filter which sorts the neighboring eight pixels and finds the median value [10]. This filter shows relatively high PSNRs and good visual quality. However, the problem with the median filter is that it blurs the image when used repeatedly, which makes it inappropriate to use for the higher error rate cases. The other problem is that the median filter requires complex processing as pixel values have to be sorted and therefore consumes a lot of power. One difference between our problem and the traditional image error concealment problem is that the error rates of memory for our problem domain are typically smaller than those assumed in the traditional image processing area. Thus, we don't need to use the existing complex image processing filters to recover the image. In this section, we develop several special image filters which are adjusted for our unique situation.

4.1 Basic Filter Designs

We devised a set of basic simple filters based on the idea that image pixel value can be recovered by finding image direction [11]. Basically, our filters consider only the 3 x 3 pixels around each of the defective pixel to find the image direction as shown in Fig 4 in order to minimize the filter complexity.

(1) **Two pixel mean value filter (MEAN2 filter):** This filter finds the defect pixel value as the mean value of two pixels horizontally neighboring the defective pixel. This filter is the lowest cost filter but works well at very low error rates. For example, The MEAN2 filter for P8 is computed as follows :

$$\text{Pixel\_value (P8)} \leftarrow (\text{pixel\_value(P0)} + \text{pixel\_value (P4))}/2$$

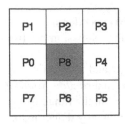

Fig. 4. A 3 x 3 array of pixels round defect pixel P8 : Every filter of our paper assumes this basic 3x3 pixel array to find the correct value of the defect pixel P8

- **Directional filter (DIR filter):** This is an advanced version of blind mean of two pixel filter (MEAN2). Instead of taking the mean of horizontally adjacent two pixels, this filter tries to find the better direction among four possible directions (horizontal, vertical, and two diagonals) of image. Basically, our new filter consists of two phases: the image direction identification phase and the computing the pixel value phase. In the phase 1 the image direction is detected by the absolute differences of two pixel pair for each direction. The direction related to the pixel pair with the least difference is considered the image direction. Fig 5 explains the four candidate directions. DIR filter shows very good performance (PSNR and visual) only if the surrounding pixels are all sound (non-defect pixel or non-boundary cases). According to our analysis of defect images with 1.0% memory BER, DIR filter can compare four all directions properly only for about 53% cases and it fails to decide the direction at all for about 0.02%.

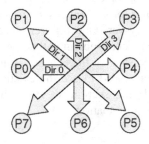

Fig. 5. Directional filter with four candidate directions : DIR filter decide the image direction among the four candidate directions by the pixel value difference computation of the pairs

- **Extended Directional Filter (EXT filter):** In some cases DIR filter fails finding image direction because there are too many corrupted pixels around the defect pixel. In this case, Extended Directional (EXT) filter may be an alternative method. The EXT filter uses more pixels to detect image direction in phase 2 of DIR filter by searching the 5x5 surrounding pixels as shown in Fig 6. According to our observation, EXT filter evaluates all four directions at about 75% cases. It shows relatively higher performance but is more complicated than DIR filter.

Table 1 summarizes the filter performance results with "foreman" video image (encoded with QP=28) with 1.0% BER in memory. In the table 1, "Median_filter1" column shows the median pixel value excluding the neighboring defect pixels while "Median_filter2" column shows median filter including every eight neighboring pixels. The results in Table 2 show that DIR filter and EXT filter outperform the median filters for luma but are not as good as median filters for chroma.

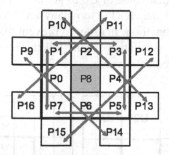

Fig. 6. Pixels used for EXT filter : 5x5 pixels are used for more reliable image direction detection for Y component in phase 2 of EXT filter

Table 1. PSNR of filters for foreman video image with 1.0% error

Components	Median filter1	Median filter2	DIR filter	EXT filter
Y	28.73	28.54	29.95	32.06
U	38.55	38.37	33.53	34.81
V	39.63	39.85	36.16	36.56

4.2 Enhanced Chroma Filter Designs

In Table 1, it is clear that we need to develop better filters for the chroma image components (U and V). The required filters must match the quality but achieve lower cost (power) than median filter. We designed two alternative chroma filters. For these new filters we have an assumption that every luma values are available because these filters use luma component to evaluate image direction. To support this assumption we should use the luma filters twice per pixel to get the correct luma pixel values.

- **Four Directional UV filter (UV4 filter):** The UV4 filter is designed for U and V components only. When we have many consecutive defect pixels there are higher probabilities that every four directions are discarded from the candidates resulting in unfiltered pixels. As a result, with an increasing defect density, we may have more unfiltered condition with DIR filter. Because the distortion of chroma is known to be less sensitive to human eyes, the sampling rate of luma to chroma is already assumes 4:1. Because of this sampling rate if we have peculiar value for a chroma of a pixel, the image may be degraded with big ugly spot. Thus, we need a new filter that does not miss any pixel even under the higher defect density. Our idea is to use luma information in the corresponding positions with the chroma component that we want to filter without failure. Fig 7 shows the required luma pixels for defective chroma value U8. The image direction detection idea is similar to that of the DIR filter.

If the estimated direction is horizontal in Y component, we take the mean value of U4 and U0 to find the filtered U8 value in U component. Assume that the estimated direction from UV4 filter is U0 and U4. But, if U0 is also a defective pixel our strategy is to apply the same filter for U0 to get the estimate of its correct value and use that value of U0 to get an estimate of the U8 value. Under extreme conditions this may lead to too many levels of recursion which results in additional power consumption. In order to prevent that, we restrict the number of recurrence depth. Our simulation results tell the recursion depth one is enough for the quality of filtered color value.

U1	U2	U3
U0	U8	U4
U7	U6	U5

Y6	Y7	Y8	Y9	
Y5	Y0	Y1	Y10	
Y4	Y2	Y3	Y11	
Y15	Y14	Y13	Y12	

Fig. 7. Directional UV filter concept with lumma : one pixel in Chroma (U8) corresponds four pixels in Lumma (Y0~Y3). We use Y0 ~ Y15 to find the image direction of U8.

- **Eight Directional UV filter (UV8 filter):** The Eight Directional UV filter (UV8) is a modified version of UV4 filter. Instead of taking the mean value of two pixels, it just copies the neighboring pixel value. The UV8 filter is based on the idea that the neighboring pixel values in chroma are not so different and the color difference is less sensitive to the human eyes. The computation complexity of UV8 and quality is usually comparable to UV4.

5 Experimental Results and Filter Analysis

We estimate the performance and power consumption of filters to decide which filter combination is the best for our problem. We assume that our target H.264 system-on-a-chip consists of DSP core plus embedded memories as shown in Fig 8. Therefore, our filter will be implemented in forms of a program code added to the H.264 decoder

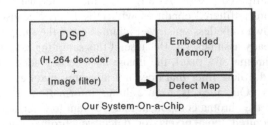

Fig. 8. Our System Configuration with DSP and embedded memory

program code launched on a DSP processor. The DSP processor used in our experiment is TMS320C5510 with 1.6 V supply voltage.

We used Code Composer Studio from TI [12] to compute the clock cycles and utilization of each filter. We used the power computing provided by TI web site [13] to get the estimated DSP power by entering frequency and utilization. Our final power consumption data includes memory power of defect map (CAM) and DPB (SRAM) as well as the core power consumption as shown in the following equation.

$Total\_ Power = Core\ Power + Defect\ Map\ Power + DPB\ Power$
$Total\_Cycles = Cycles/Pixel \times P_{pixel} \times Image\_Size/Frame \times Frame\_Num/Sec$
$P_{pixel} = 1-(1- P_{bit})^{Pixel\_Depth}$

In the above equations, P_{pixel} is a pixel error rate, P_{bit} is a bit error rate, Pixel_Depth is the number of bits for each pixel component (8 for our case), and Cycles/Pixel means the number of instruction cycles for each filter execution on a DSP.

We applied all of our filter combination in one of two manners : *priority and weighted selection*. The priority selection with notation *filterA>filterB* means that primary we use the filterA and then we use the filterB only if filterA fails finding the proper value (because of too much defect pixels or boundary pixel case). And, the notation *filterA+filterB* means applying two filter at the same time equally and selecting one of the results according to some criteria. In the following pseudo code, we summarize the priority and weighted combination. A priority combination approach consumes less power compared with weighted combination.

```
Function FilterA>FilterB (pic : pixel_position ) {
    New_value ← Compute Filter A (pic)
    IF (Filter A fails to find the filtered value)
        New_value ← Compute Filter B(pic)
    Pixel_value(pic) ← New_value
}

Function FilterA+FilterB (pic : pixel_position ) {
    (New_value1, quality_metric1) ← Compute Filter A (pic)
    (New_value2, quality_metric2) ← Compute Filter B(pic)
    IF (quality_metric1 is better than quality_metric2)
        Pixel_value(pic) ← New_value1;
    ELSE
        Pixel_value(pic) ← New_value2
}
```

Our assumptions on the input streams are that: (1) videos are encoded with quantization parameter QP= 28 for all the I, B, and P frames and (2) the frames are transferred in a IPBPBPBP... sequences, and (3) one I frame comes every 60 frames. We use a sample H.264 video sequence named "foreman", at 30fps and 144 x 176 (QCIF) frame image size with 4:2:0 sampling rate. We assume our target system has five reference frames in all cases. Every PSNR value is computed relative to the original sample YUV format video image before encoded in H.264. The PSNR value is computed by the following equation.

$$MSE = \frac{\sum \left[f(i, j) - F(i, j) \right]^2}{N^2}$$

$$PSNR = 20 \log_{10} \left(\frac{255}{\sqrt{MSE}} \right)$$

Where $f(i,j)$ and $F(i,j)$ are the pixels at location (i,j) of the output and reference images, respectively.

First, we evaluate the chroma filters. We apply different filter combinations to our 1.0% error image and we measure the performance (the quality of image measured by PSNRs) and the cost (consumed power). The candidate filters for chroma are DIR, EXT, UV4, UV8, and their combinations. We also compare our filter results with those of the median filter used in [7]. Because the luma filter quality influences the result of UV4 and UV8 filter, we set luma component to be error-free for UV filter performance experiments. Considering both the power consumption and quality, best choice seems to be (DIR>UV8) and (DIR>Median) from experiments.

Secondly, The chroma (Y) filter candidates are tested. The candidate filters for luma are DIR, EXT, MED (MEDIAN filters), and their combinations. In order to decide the visual quality of only luma, we set chroma component error free. From the experiments we find that DIR, DIR>EXT and DIR>MED are good choices in terms of power and quality.

Finally, we put together the best filter choices for luma and chroma and try to find the best filter combinations. From the experiments, we find DIR>EXT for luma and DIR>MED for chroma is the best choice in terms of both power and quality of image. Table 2 shows the experimental result of filters with PSNR values and power consumption data including defect map and DPB power as well as core power consumption at BER 1.0%. This filter combination saves about 64% of filter power compared with the median filter as shown in Table 2.

Fig 9 shows the video image of 29th frame of foreman with 1.0% memory BER and filtered image with median and our best. Note that median filter (c) and our filter (d) show no significant difference from the originally encoded image (a) without error.

Table 2 and Fig 9 show that our best filter combination achieves compatible visual quality with MED filter application while consuming less power.

Fig 10 and Fig 11 show the PSNR values of Y, U component respectively for each different filter at different defect densities. The result of V component is very similar to that of U component. We can have a range of filter choice according to defect density. Some filters show same result with less complexity and less overhead at different defect density. With mean2 filter we can achieve the same quality as median or DIR filters as shown Fig 10 and Fig 11 to save power consumption. If our goal is to select the highest quality filter with lower power consumption, at the BER range below 0.1% then we will choose mean2 filter. At the BER below 0.001% we do not need to apply any filtering. Note that 1.0% BER is at least 1000 times larger error rate

Table 2. Filter Test Result (Luma Error=1.0%, Chroma Error=1.0%)

Y filter	UV filter	Y	U	V	Visual Qulaity	Power Consumption (mW)
DIR	DIR>UV8	29.95	38.72	39.86	Poor	18.50
DIR>EXT	DIR>UV8	31.72	38.62	39.85	Poor	18.61
DIR>MED	DR>UV8	29.86	38.72	39.86	Poor	18.55
DIR	DIR>MED	29.95	38.68	39.95	Acceptable	9.80
DIR>EXT	DIR>MED	31.72	38.68	39.95	Acceptable	**9.91**
DIR>MED	DIR>MED	29.86	38.67	39.93	Acceptable	9.80
MED	MED	28.54	38.37	39.85	Acceptable	27.53

(a) encoded original image (QP=28,I=30)

(b) corrupted image Bit Error Rate=1.0%

(c) median filter result from the corrupted

(d) our low power filter result from corrupted

Fig. 9. Comparison with Corrupted and Recovered Foreman Video Capture : encoded image without error (a) and filtered image (c) and (d) from corrupted image show almost same visual quality. Our best filter result and median filter results shows almost as visual quality.

than the current technologies. So, currently most cases will choose mean2 filter or just leave the defect pixel as it is. But, as the technology advances the DIR>EXT filter is more likely to be chosen.

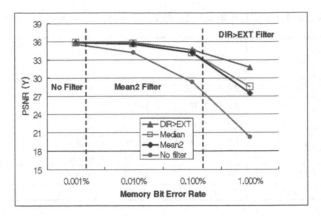

Fig. 10. Luma (Y) Filter Choice at Various Defect Densities : DIR>EXT filter is adequate for high BER and mean2 filter for low error rate. For BER< 0.001% we don't need any filter.

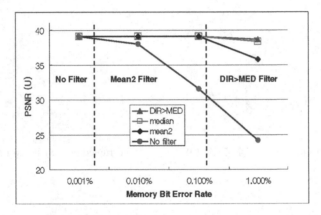

Fig. 11. Chroma (U) Filter Choice at Various Defect Densities : DIR>MED filter is adequate for high BER and mean2 filter for low error rate. For BER< 0.001% we don't need any filter.

Summarizing from the above observation, we can conclude the filter choice as follows:

(1) At BER $\leq$ 0.001%, any filter is not required for all cases.
(2) At BER in the range of 0.001% through 0.1%, mean2 filter is the best choice for all cases.
(3) At BER $\geq$ 0.1%, DIR>EXT is the best filter for luma and DIR>MED is the best filter for chroma.

Fig 12 shows the core power + DPB memory power consumption from our filter selection and median filter for a range of defect memory density. We excluded the defect map power from Fig 12 to highlight the power saving effect by the proper filter selection. In Fig 12, "Median" means power consumption by median filter and "Our Best" means the power consumed by our filters choice above. At higher defect densities, savings of 3.2 x to 12 x in power are observed.

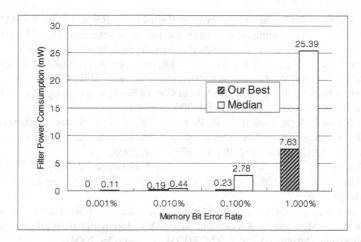

Fig. 12. Power Consumption Data by our Best Filters and Median Filter : Our filter shows about 12 times energy saving compared with median filter at 1.0% BER.

6 Conclusion

In this paper, we addressed the problem of high memory defect density in the near future nano technology era. It is a well known problem that the increasing embedded memory defect density is one of the hardest problems in memory-hungry SoC design. Our approach is based on the idea that we can recover data errors from defective memories at the application level. This is done by making use of the characteristics in the multimedia application itself. For multimedia filtering can be employed to perform such application-specific error recovery. Our newly designed directional filters coupled with defect map hardware recover the image in defective memory while consuming less power and area than conventional approaches. Our new filters show about 64 % power saving relative to conventional median filters. Our simulation results show that the new scheme achieves 3.3 to 12 times power reduction at higher defect density in memory. For the future, we are working to find more efficient filters exploiting the temporal features of H.264 as well as spatial features.

References

1. Shoukourian, S., Vardanian, V., Zorian, Y., "SoC yield optimization via an embedded-memory test and repair infrastructure", Design & Test of Computers, IEEE Volume 21, Issue 3, May-June, Page(s):200 – 207, 2004.
2. Y. Zorian, S. Shoukourian. "Embedded-Memory Test and Repair: Infrastructure IP for SoC Yield," IEEE Design and Test of Computers, vol. 20, no. 3, pp. 58-66, May/June, 2003.
3. T. Gupta, A.H. Jayatissa, "Recent advances in nanotechnology: key issues & potential problem areas," in Proceedings of IEEE Conference on Nanotechnology, Vol. 2, pp. :469 - 472, 2003.

4. J. F. Li , R.-F. Huang, and C.-W. Wu, "A Built-In Self-Repair Design for RAMs with 2-D Redundancy", Proceedings of ITC International Test Conference, pp. 393 – 402, 2003.
5. L. Anghel, N. Achouri, M. Nicolaidis. "Evaluation of Memory Built-in Self Repair Techniques for High Defect Density Technologies," Proc., pp. 315-320, 10th IEEE Pacific Rim International Symposium on Dependable Computing (PRDC'04), 2004.
6. S. Prihar et. Al. " A High Density 0.10um CMOS Technology Using Low-L Dielectric and Copper Interconnect." Proc. of IEDM, 2002.
7. F. J. Kurdahi, A. M. Eltawil, Y.-H. Park, R. N. Kanj, S. R. Nassif, "System-Level SRAM Yield Enhancement", Proceedings of the 7th International Symposium on Quality Electronic Design, (ISQED 2006), pp. 179 – 184, 2006.
8. K. Pagiamtzis, A. Sheikholeslami, "Contents-Addressable Memory (CAM) Circuits and Architectures : A Tutorial and Survey", IEEE journal of Solid-State Circuits, vol 41, No. 3, March 2006.
9. S. Hamdioui, G. Gaydadjiev, A. J. Goor, "The State-of-art and Future Trends in Testing Embedded Memories", Records of the 2004 International Workshop on Memory Technology, Design and Testing (MTDT'04), pp. 54 – 59, 2004.
10. Digital Image Processing, Gonzalez & Woods, Prentice Hall, 2002
11. Kyeong-Hoon Jung, Choong Woong Lee, "Projection-based error resilience technique for digital HDTV," Proc. HDTV Workshop, pp.8.A.2.1-8.A.2.9, Torino, Italy, Oct. 1994.
12. http://focus.ti.com/dsp/docs/dspsupport.tsp?sectionId=3
13. http://www-s.ti.com/sc/psheets/spra972/spra972.zip

Entropy Throttling:
A Physical Approach for Maximizing Packet Mobility in Interconnection Networks

Takashi Yokota[1], Kanemitsu Ootsu[1],
Fumihito Furukawa[2], and Takanobu Baba[1]

[1] Department of Information Science, Utsunomiya University,
7-1-2 Yoto, Utsunomiya-shi, Tochigi, 321-8585 Japan
yokota@is.utsunomiya-u.ac.jp
[2] Learning Technology Laboratory, Teikyo University,
1-1 Toyosato-dai, Utsunomiya-shi, Tochigi, 320-8551 Japan

Abstract. A large-scale direct interconnection network usually consists of enormous number of simple routers. However, its behavior is sometimes very complicated. Such a complicated behavior prevents us from accurate understanding and efficient control of the network. Among serious problems in interconnection networks, congestion control is of extreme importance since network performance is drastically degraded by a congested situation. We focus our discussion on throttling, injection limitation in other words, as one of the most hopeful solutions to the congestion problem. Our approach is inspired from physics. We define entropy as a desirable metric for representing the network's congestion level. We also define packet mobility ratio as a proper approximation of entropy. Thus we reach a new throttling method called 'Entropy Throttling' that is based on theoretical discussion on congestion. Evaluation results by our simulator reveal effectiveness of the proposed method.

1 Introduction

Interconnection network is a vital component in today's state-of-the-art massively parallel systems[1,2]. Most of large-scale direct interconnection networks are composed of many routers. Routers are connected to each other and they relay packets until reaching their destinations. Large-scale networks do not employ centralized control mechanisms to answer the scalability requirement. Thus, routers operate independently.

This principle causes serious performance problem in some congested situations. Each router operates by itself, i.e., it can use only localized information. Thus, globally optimal control is difficult (or very costly). This results in serious congestion under a heavy traffic load. In general, network throughput is proportional to traffic load when the network is not congested. However, once the network is congested, throughput is drastically degraded to very poor performance level.

C. Jesshope and C. Egan (Eds.): ACSAC 2006, LNCS 4186, pp. 309–322, 2006.
© Springer-Verlag Berlin Heidelberg 2006

To answer this congestion problem, *throttling* (in other words, *injection limitation*) is a hopeful solution. That is, we measure the network's congestion level properly by using some metric. When the metric exceeds a given threshold, we limit packet injection into the network until the metric indicates uncongested.

Major issues for implementing throttling method are (1) selecting proper metric(s) and (2) obtaining proper threshold. Many researches have proposed their throttling methods. However, some of them lack theoretical background and some others require long time to reach optimal situation.

This paper discusses congestion mechanisms and their relation to network metrics. We propose an appropriate metric for efficient throttling. The rest of this paper is organized as follows. In Section 2, we first show generation, formulation and vanishment of congestion, and at the same time, some major network metrics are shown. We show that *entropy* metric illustrates congestion level appropriately. Based on the discussion results, Section 3 shows a practical metric derived from entropy, *packet mobility*, and proposes a novel throttling method called *Entropy Throttling*. Section 4 shows our evaluation results. We show some important related work in Section 5. Finally, Section 6 concludes this paper.

2   Network Congestion Metrics

2.1   Transient Congestion Behaviors

An interconnection network offers proportional throughput to its input traffic load, when the network is not congested. Once the traffic load exceeds a certain threshold, the network performs poorly. Basically, throttling methods aim at controlling traffic load not to exceed the threshold. Thereby the network can offer its maximum performance.

We can consider fully controlled situations by an ideal throttling method. The ideal method should detect an early sign of the onset of congestion, so that it can throttle packet injection. At the first step of this study, we have deeply investigated the network behavior to capture the early sign properly.

We have shown some typical behaviors of congestion by using cellular automata (CA) models[3,4,5]. Under critical traffic load conditions, a probabilistic fluctuation causes a small-scale congestion. The small congestion absorbs its surrounding packets and then it grows to a large congestion cluster. In this situation, most packets are absorbed and the system becomes heavily congested. The congestion cluster shows an equilibrium state where incoming and outgoing packets are balanced. When the traffic load is closed to the threshold, the congestion cluster moves according to the network's routing algorithm and vanishes.

We have shown the congestion mechanisms by using CA model[3,4,5]. **Figure 1** shows formulation, movement and vanishment of a congestion cluster in two-dimensional torus topology. The CA model is composed of paths and nodes, which form lattice-shaped texture. A dot represents a packet. Packets move unidirectionally in x- and y-axis, i.e., rightward and downward, respectively. This simplified model illustrates congestion process clearly.

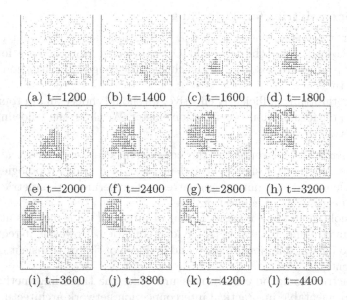

Fig. 1. Congestion cluster in cellular automata model

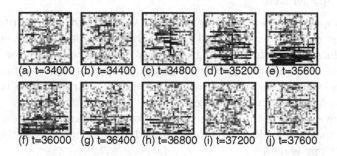

Fig. 2. Congestion cluster in interconnection network simulator

We have also found similar congestion cluster in our interconnection network simulator. **Figure 2** shows congestion behaviors in 32×32 two-dimensional torus network. A simple dimension-order routing algorithm is applied. Each dot represents occupation level of packet buffers in each router. A dark dot shows that the packet buffer is full and a white dot means empty buffer. Traffic load is carefully selected around a critical load condition.

In critical load conditions, congestion clusters occur intermittently. In more heavier load conditions, such congestion clusters continuously emerge. Thus, the ideal throttling method should capture an early stage of congestion emergence. Thereby the early congestion should disappear and the system should be an uncongested situation.

2.2   Proper Metrics for Throttling

Even when the traffic load is stable, a fluctuation causes transient congestion cluster if the load is near the threshold. Once the congestion cluster is formulated, since most packets are absorbed in the cluster, the congestion situation continues for a long time.

To make throttling sufficiently effective, we should choose an appropriate metric to avoid the formulation of congestion cluster. We claim the following features for the metric.

(1) The metric should represent the congestion level properly at all instants of time. The metric should be independent of network topologies, routing algorithms, and communication patterns. Furthermore, the metric shows instantaneous value of congestion level.
(2) Threshold should be constant. Tuning of threshold value may result in a good performance under a stable traffic load condition. However, it requires long time to offer stable performance and it does not follow transient congestion sufficiently.
(3) The metric should be easy to measure, since the throttling method should be implementable in practical interconnection network architecture.

2.3   Entropy Metric

We have proposed an *entropy* metric to represent congestion level properly[3,4]. The entropy measure was inspired from thermodynamics, i.e., by substituting molecules for packets, free moving situation is explained as vapor phase and congested situation as solid (or liquid) phase. Entropy is capable of representing such phases; when the system is in a *vapor* phase, entropy value is high, and when in a *solid* phase, entropy becomes low.

We define *entropy* in interconnection networks as follows.

Assume that a traveling packet (identified with i) has a velocity v_i at any instant. Entropy is defined

$$H = \frac{1}{N_{tp}} \sum_i v_i^{-1} \log_2 v_i \tag{1}$$

where N_{tp} is the number of traveling packets in the network.

Generally, velocity is defined as differentiation of position with respect to time. We define the velocity v_i as follows. We use an approximate value as the velocity, that is, $v_i \approx h_i/\Delta t$ where h_i is number of hops of the traveling packet in a Δt time. h_i represents the packet's traveling distance. We do not discuss traveling directions for simplification; only the number of hops is used.

We measure traveling distance for all the packets in the whole network and determine statistical distribution for each of possible traveling distance dh value. Let n_h be the number of packets whose traveling distance is h, where $0 \leq h \leq \Delta t$. Thus our first approximation of the original entropy H is represented as follows.

$$H_{\Delta t} = \sum_{h=1}^{\Delta t} \frac{n_h}{N_{tp}} \log_2 h. \tag{2}$$

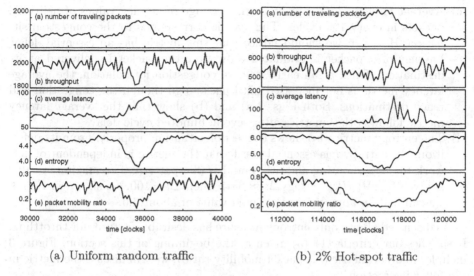

(a) Uniform random traffic   (b) 2% Hot-spot traffic

Fig. 3. Some network metrics at an intermittent congestion

When the system is in a non-congested situation, packets travel long distance in Δt time. Thus, it results in a large entropy value. In a congested situation, since not a few packets are captured in a congested area, their short traveling distances decrease the entropy value. Thus, the entropy value properly represents the system's congestion level.

Now, we show that the entropy satisfies the criteria listed above and other metrics are inadequate for throttling control. We discuss (a) number of traveling packets in the network (N_{tp}), (b) throughput (th)[1], (c) average latency (lat), and (d) entropy ($H_{\Delta t}$) as candidates of throttling metrics.

Figure 3 shows time sequences of some network metrics in uniform random traffic pattern (Fig. 3(a)) and 2% hot-spot traffic (Fig. 3(b)). The network is 32×32 two-dimensional torus and simple dimension-order routing is used. Figure 2 shows snapshot views of Fig. 3(a). In Fig. 3(b), 2% of packets are destined to the center node $(16, 16)$ and other remaining packets are randomly destined.

We can find that all the metrics (a) to (d) can represent congestion situation at some degree. At the same time, we can find some differences.

(a) Number of traveling packets (N_{tp}) properly represents congestion level. Although, absolute N_{tp} values shown in Figs. 3 (a) and (b) are different. For example, there are over 1000 packets traveling in uniform random traffic, however, only about 100 packets in hot-spot traffic.

(b) Throughput (th) is given as the number of delivered packets in every 100 cycles. In uniform random traffic, this metric represents congestion level at some degree, although, noisy fluctuations are also found. However, this metric is not useful in hot-spot traffic as shown in Fig. 3(b).

---

[1] i.e., number of delivered packets.

(c) Average latency (lat) is given as the average of latency values of delivered packets in every 100 cycles. This metric corresponds to the congestion situation. However, we should notice that this metric has an essential delay. Latency of a packet is evaluated only after the packet is delivered at its destination. Thus, at an early stage of congestion formulation, the average latency metric is not increased until packets go though the congestion and reach destinations. Both Figs. 3(a) and (b) show that the average latency metric follows other metrics after several hundred cycle delay.

(d) The entropy metric also shows congestion situation properly. From its definition, the entropy has essential merit that the metric is independent of network topology, routing algorithm, and traffic pattern. The maximum value is given by Δt; $H_{\Delta t}^{max} = \log_2 \Delta t \approx 6.64$ when $\Delta t = 100$. As shown in Fig. 3, we can find an appropriate threshold value of about 4.0.

As discussed above, only entropy measure has desirable features for throttling. It satisfies our criteria (1)–(3) given at the beginning of this section. Figure 3 includes another metric ((e) packet mobility ratio), we will discuss the metric in the following section.

3 Entropy Throttling

3.1 Approximation of Entropy

Despite its preferable features, the entropy measure is impractical to implement in actual routers. Equation (2) requires to measure packets' moving distances in each Δt period. To measure the entropy with proper accuracy, Δt should not be so small, for a typical example, $\Delta t = 100$ [cycles].

One possible solution is adding some information into packets. As the additional information squeezes communication bandwidth, we cannot employ this scheme.

Another solution is proper approximation of the entropy. We further approximate (2) to match the practical router and interconnection network organization. The impracticability comes from the long measuring period, i.e., $\Delta t \gg 0$. We discuss the limit where $\Delta t \to 0$. That is,

$$\lim_{\Delta t \to 0} H_{\Delta t} = \lim_{\Delta t \to 0} \left(\sum_{h=1}^{\Delta t} \frac{n_h}{N_{tp}} \log_2 h \right). \tag{3}$$

Actually, at the $\Delta t \to 0$ limit, each packet moves at most one hop. That is,

$$h_0 = \begin{cases} 1, & \text{if the packet moves} \\ 0, & \text{otherwise.} \end{cases} \tag{4}$$

Note that $\lim_{\Delta t \to 0} \frac{n_h}{N_{tp}}$ shows the ratio of moved packets at any instants of time. We introduce a new metric, packet mobility ratio, as follows.

$$p_m = \lim_{\Delta t \to 0} \frac{n_h}{N_{tp}} \tag{5}$$

Here, we introduce rough approximation of entropy by using the p_m metric.

$$H_{(0)} = \kappa p_m. \tag{6}$$

Equation (6) leads us to a practical and efficient entropy measure. All we need to measure the entropy is counting the numbers of moved and unmoved packets. Figures 3 (a) and (b) show the packet mobility ratio in uniform random pattern and 2% hot-spot traffic one, respectively. We can find that the metric properly represents congestion level.

3.2   Measurement Circuit

Here, we discuss how we can practically measure the packet mobility ratio. We assume some dedicated registers for measuring the metric and we propose a measurement circuit which can be embedded in two-dimensional mesh/torus networks. **Figure 4** shows the circuit. Each router has a register named 'MCR' (mobility counter register). MCR has two values, n_{ab} and n_{ob}. n_{ob} stands for the number of occupied buffers which contain at least one flit of packet. n_{ab} is the number of active buffers whose packets are not blocked.

Each router sends its MCR to the center direction in its row, and at the same time, each router adds the incoming MCR values with its own MCR. Thus each center node has a partial sum $\sum_i MCR_{i,j}$, and the partial sum is broadcasted by using outbound links. By applying the similar operation in vertical direction, we can calculate $\sum_{i,j} MCR_{i,j}$ effectively. The resulting value is composed of (N_{ob}, N_{ab}) where $N_{ob} = \sum n_{ob}$ and $N_{ab} = \sum n_{ab}$. The entropy value can easily be calculated by $p_m = N_{ab}/N_{ob}$.

The measurement circuit, given in Fig. 4, can be easily embedded in two-dimensional mesh/torus networks. The circuit can share physical links with packet communication. Each router sends a necessary register to its adjacent router only when its MCR and partial sum values change. But it should wait sending if the physical link is occupied by packet communication. This cycle-stealing method does not affect packet communication performance but delays the entropy calculation. The latency is not fatal to our purpose since physical links are not always occupied by packet communication. A textbook says that more than 50% of time is open [2]. We will evaluate the essential delay in Section 4.4. Actually, the virtual control channel (VCC, [6]) and Cross-Line[7,8,9] methods make efficient use of this fact. Thus, the measurement circuit can update the entropy measure in $O(N)$ time for $N \times N$ networks.

3.3   Entropy Throttling

After the approximated entropy value is measured, throttling method is quite simple. The entropy measurement circuit delivers the resulting entropy value to each router. Each router checks the entropy value for sinking below a certain threshold. If the entropy becomes lower than the threshold, router should prohibit new packet injection. We call the novel throttling method *Entropy Throttling*. We assume the threshold R_{th} and we will discuss its actual value in the next section.

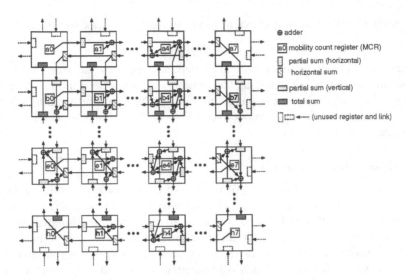

Fig. 4. Entropy measurement circuit

4   Evaluation

We have implemented the Entropy Throttling method in our interconnection network simulator to evaluate the effectiveness. Since the Entropy Throttling is independent of routing algorithms, we use simple dimension-order routing and minimum adaptive routing algorithms for evaluation. Network topology is two-dimensional torus of 32×32 size. It is a conscious choice to use 32×32 torus, since larger-scale networks are critical to congestion. We use eight-flit packets and virtual cut-through flow control. Each virtual channel has its own packet buffer at each input port of the router. The capacity of packet buffer is 16 flits. A Packet can be forwarded one hop at each clock cycle, if the packet is not blocked.

4.1   Random Traffic Performance

Figure 5 illustrates the network performance of dimension-order routing under the uniform random traffic pattern. Figure 5(a) shows the normalized throughput and Fig. 5(b) shows average latency curves. In these graphs, "no TC" means "no throttling control." Other curves labeled "$R_{th} = w$" show particular performance curves of Entropy Throttling with the threshold $R_{th} = w$.

In our evaluations, each node generates a packet in a given interval. Normalized offered traffic value is the inverse of the packet generation interval. Note that packet injection into the network is actually postponed while the corresponding router is not ready to receive the packet.

Each simulation runs 200,000 cycles, and network metrics are measured in the latter 100,000 cycles in order to omit initial conditions. Normalized throughput is

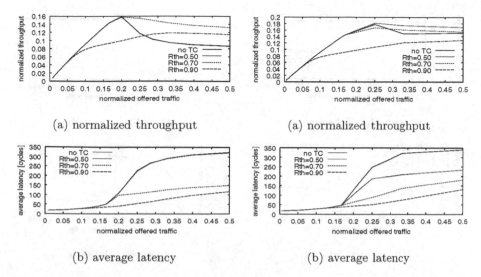

(a) normalized throughput

(a) normalized throughput

(b) average latency

(b) average latency

Fig. 5. Dimension-order routing, uniform random traffic

Fig. 6. Adaptive routing, uniform random traffic

a ratio of the number of delivered packets to a theoretical maximum throughput. Similarly, 'average latency' shows the average of latency of delivered packets. These metrics are measured in every 100 cycles.

Figure 5(a) shows that Entropy Throttling properly controls network throughput even under heavy traffic load, if a proper threshold (i.e., $R_{th} = 0.7$ in this graph) is given. Furthermore, Fig. 5(b) reveals considerable reduction in average latency to about 50 percents. Note that the $R_{th} = 0.5$ curve is mostly overlapped and we cannot discriminate from 'no TC'.

Figure 6 shows adaptive routing performance under uniform random traffic pattern. This figure also shows the effectiveness of Entropy Throttling.

4.2 Hot-Spot Traffic Performance

Figures 7 and 8 show 2% hot-spot performance of dimension-order and minimum adaptive routing, respectively. Simulation conditions are similar to those of Figs. 5 and 6, except that 2% of packets are destined to a center node, $(16, 16)$ in the 32×32 two-dimensional torus network.

Figures 7(a) and 8(a) show that no significant differences are observed regardless of the throttling method. In this traffic pattern, a particular bottleneck, i.e., the hot-spot, limits the whole network's performance. That is why the throttling method offers little improvement in threshold under the hot-spot traffic pattern.

However, average latency is significantly improved in both deterministic and adaptive routing. Figures 7(b) and 8(b) illustrate the fact and we can find more than 50% reduction in average latency.

Furthermore, we can find that the appropriate threshold value is $R_{th} = 0.7$ also in this traffic pattern. This fact shows that the proposed Entropy Throttling

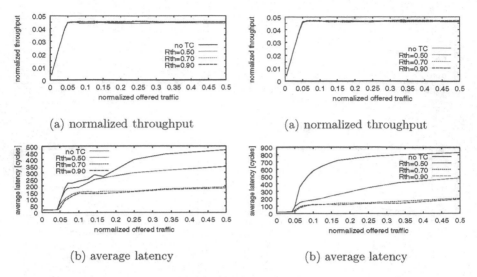

(a) normalized throughput   (a) normalized throughput

(b) average latency   (b) average latency

Fig. 7. Dimension-order routing, 2% hot-spot traffic

Fig. 8. Adaptive routing, 2% hot-spot traffic

does not need dynamic tuning of threshold value. We find that $R_{th} = 0.7$ is the proper threshold value for uniform random and hot-spot traffic and also deterministic and adaptive routing algorithms.

4.3   Observation of the Throttling Effects

Figures 5, 6, 7 and 8 show statistical results. We show dynamical feature of the proposed throttling method in **Figures 9 and 10**. They show time sequence of average latency, entropy and packet mobility ratio values at starting 5,000 cycles in simulation. The network is 32×32 two-dimensional torus and simple dimension-order routing algorithm is used. Simulation conditions are the same as other evaluations and performance curves are shown in Fig. 5.

Figure 9 shows the network behavior without throttling control, and Fig. 10 shows the proposed Entropy Throttling with $R_{th} = 0.7$ threshold value.

Figures 9(a) and 10(a) show network metrics when average packet generation interval is 32 cycles (normalized offered traffic is (packet length)/(interval) = $8/32 = 0.25$. At this traffic load, the network becomes heavily congested. The packet generation interval is 44 cycles in Figs. 9(b) and 10(b). This represents normalized offered traffic as $8/44 \approx 0.18$.

Figure 10(a) shows that Entropy Throttling acts a considerably different behavior from that of un-throttled case shown in Fig. 9(a). The Entropy Throttling properly controls the congestion situation. Oscillation phenomena, whose duration is several hundred cycles, are observed in Fig. 10(a). This shows that the throttling method controls congestion formulation.

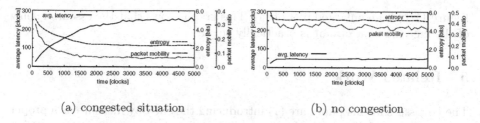

(a) congested situation   (b) no congestion

Fig. 9. Time sequence of average latency, entropy and average packet mobility

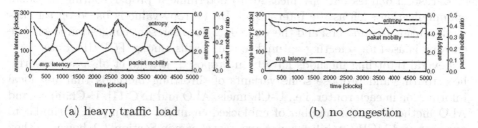

(a) heavy traffic load   (b) no congestion

Fig. 10. Time sequence of average latency, entropy and average packet mobility (under Entropy Throttling with $R_{th} = 0.7$)

In non-congested situations (as shown in Figs. 9(b) and 10(b)), no significant difference is observed. This shows that the throttling method is harmless when the traffic is smooth.

4.4   Response of the Entropy Circuit

As described in Section 3.2, our proposed entropy circuit has an essential delay caused by cycle-steal use of physical links. We measured transient behavior of the entropy circuit. In a particular simulation at the normalized offered traffic load of 0.1, we changed the traffic pattern from uniformly random to 2% hot-spot. Figure 11 shows the time sequence plot of the approximated entropy (R_m) that is measured by the entropy circuit, accompanied by the average packet mobility.

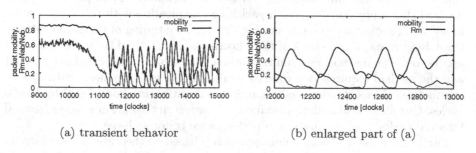

(a) transient behavior   (b) enlarged part of (a)

Fig. 11. Response of the entropy circuit

Figure 11(b) is an enlarged plot of (a). This graph shows that the essential delay of the measurement circuit is practically small.

5 Related Work

The key issues in this paper are (1) introducing the entropy measure as a proper representation of congestion level, and (2) applying the entropy to throttling control.

Bernstein defines entropy measure to determine a proper routing in global communication such as the Internet[10]. His entropy value is based on the network routing parameters, and the value does not represent congestion level. The entropy is used for selecting optimal routing paths among TCP/IP routers.

Several throttling methods have been proposed. Baydal et al. assume wormhole routing and propose some variants of throttling methods that use local information in each router, i.e., U-Channels, ALO and INC[11]. U-Channels and ALO methods use the number of unblocked channels. This metric is similar to our proposed MCR (mobility count register) shown in Section 3.2, however, they use the information only locally while our method calculates the whole value. INC method measures the amount of packet flow in a certain interval of time. Their methods only use localized information and do not reflect global congestion situation.

DRIL, proposed by Lṕes et al.[12], and CLIC, proposed by Obaidat et al.[13], also use localized information and do not use the whole congestion situation. Although localized information is somewhat practical in highly parallel networks, localized methods cannot sufficiently control congestion formulation because the congestion is a result of global behavior of routers.

Thottethodi et al. have proposed an adaptive throttling method [14,15]. Their method throttles packet injection by means of the number of traveling packets in packet buffers. They use an independent communication mechanism from packet communication and and use meta-packets to gather congestion information in the whole network. Throttling is determined by the resulting (gathered) information. This method is similar to our proposed method in the sense that both methods collect local information and forms a global measure to determine throttling. However, our method is different in the following two points. (1) Our method shares physical links with packet communication with relatively low latency, and (2) our method does not require dynamic tuning of threshold value of throttling. A major drawback of the Thotthethodi's method is long latency and oscillation. The method determines optimal threshold by hill-climbing method and the method requires long time to attain a stable performance. Furthermore, the method shows drastic oscillation whose duration is about 5,000 to 10,000 cycles. Our method also shows oscillation, however, its duration is short (several hundred cycles) and fluctuation in performance is not so large.

Furthermore, we claim that our approach is based on theoretical discussion on congestion metric. Many of the existing methods use simple metrics. For example, Baydal et al. shows an empirical rule that the network saturates when the number of free channel is decreased under 30% of useful channels[16]. Another example, Thotthethodi's method given in [14], uses the number of traveling packets in packet buffers. This metric is similar to the number of traveling packets, but the metric is not appropriate as we discussed in Section 2.2.

6   Conclusions

Most large-scale interconnection networks are composed of a lot of independent routers. Routers work autonomously under certain distributed control mechanisms. Difficulties in proper control of routers are brought from the fact. A large-scale interconnection network is a complex system, where we do not have sufficient knowledge on its behavior.

Network congestion is one of serious problems. Especially in large-scale interconnection networks, since no effective centralized control is given, congestion degrades the network performance drastically. Such situation is very similar to heavy traffic jams which we sometimes experience in usual life.

We focus our discussion on congestion control, especially on injection limitation (throttling). Since congestion is caused as a result of network's dynamic behavior, we first show transient congestion phenomena. Then we discuss possible metrics for representing congestion level properly, and we show the entropy measure has desirable features. The entropy is a simple derivation of thermodynamics entropy.

Furthermore, we introduce packet mobility ratio as an appropriate approximation of the entropy. The approximated entropy can be measured by a simple circuit which can be embedded in two-dimensional mesh/torus networks. We propose *Entropy Throttling* by using the entropy metric. The proposed method is based on our theoretical discussion and the method does not need dynamic tuning.

Evaluation results reveal that the proposed method is effective in controlling congestion. The results present a proper threshold $R_{th} = 0.7$, which is applicable to uniform random and 2% hot-spot traffic patterns under deterministic and adaptive routing algorithms. Since the threshold value is theoretically independent of actual interconnection network methods and no dynamic tuning is required, the proposed method is expected to be applicable to a wide range of applications.

Acknowledgements. This research was supported in part by Grant-in-Aid for Scientific Research ((B)18300014 and (C)16500023) and Young Scholarship (14780186) of Japan Society for the Promotion of Science (JSPS).

References

1. Duato, J., Yalamanchili, S. and Ni, L.: Interconnection Networks: An Engineering Approach. Morgan Kaufmann Pub., 2003.
2. Dally, W. J. and Towles, B.: Principles and Practices of Interconnection Networks. Morgan Kaufmann Pub., 2004.

3. Yokota, T., Ootsu, K., Furukawa, F. and Baba, T.: A Cellular Automata Approach for Large-Scale Interconnection Network Simulation. IEICE Technical Report, CPSY2005–32, Dec. 2005.
4. Yokota, T., Ootsu, K., Furukawa, F. and Baba, T.: A Cellular Automata Approach for Understanding Congestion in Interconnection Networks. IPSJ Trans. Advanced Computing Systems, 2006. (to appear).
5. Yokota, T., Ootsu, K., Furukawa, F. and Baba, T.: Phase Transition Phenomena in Interconnection Networks of Massively Parallel Computers. Journal of Physical Society of Japan, Vol.75, No.7, 2006. (to appear)
6. Yokota, T., Matsuoka, H., Okamoto, K., Hirono, H. and Sakai, S.: Virtual Control Channel and its Application to the Massively Parallel Computer RWC-1. Proc. Int. Conf. on High Performance Computing (HiPC97) pp.443–448, Dec. 1997.
7. Nishitani, M., Ezura, S., Yokota, T., Ootsu, K. and Baba, T.: Preliminary Research of a Novel Routing Algorithm Cross-Line Using Dynaic Information. Proc. IASTED PDCS 2004, pp.107–112, Nov. 2004.
8. Yokota, T., Nishitani, M., Ootsu, K., Furukawa, F. and Baba, T.: Cross-Line — A Globally Adaptive Control Method of Interconnection Network. Proc. ISHPC–VI, Sep. 2005.
9. Yokota, T., Ootsu, K., Furukawa, F. and Baba, T.: Cross-Line: A Novel Routing Algorithm that Uses Global Information. IPSJ Trans. Advanced Computing Systems, Vol.46, No.SIG 16 (ACS 12), pp.28–42, Dec. 2005.
10. Bernstein, H. J.: Some Comments on Highly Dynamic Network Routing. Tech. Rep. 371, Computer Science Dept., New York Univ., May 1988.
11. Baydal, E., López, P. and Duato, J.: A Family of Mechanisms for Congestion Control in Wormhole Networks. IEEE Trans. Parallel and Distributed Systems, Vol.16, No.9, pp.772–784, Sep. 2005.
12. López, P., Martínez, J. M. and Duato, J.: DRIL: Dynamically Reduced Message Injection Limitation Mechanism for Wormhole Networks. Proc. 1998 ICPP, pp.535–562, 1998.
13. Obaidat, M. S., Al-Awwami, Z. H. and Al-Mulhem, M.: A new injection limitation mechanism for wormhole networks. Computer Communications, Vol.25, pp.997–1008, 2002.
14. Thottethodi, M., Lebeck, A. R. and Mukherjee, S. S.: Self-Tuned Congestion Control for Multiprocessor Networks. Proc. HPCA–7, pp.107–118, 2001.
15. Thottethodi, M., Lebeck, A. R. and Mukherjee, S. S.: Exploiting Global Knowledge to Achieve Self-Tuned Congestion Sontrol for k-Ary n-Cube Networks. IEEE Trans. Parallel and Distributed Systems, Vol.15, No.3, pp.257–272, Mar. 2004.
16. Baydal, E., López, P. and Duato, J.: A Congestion Control Mechanism for Wormhole Networks. Proc. 9th Euromicro Workshop on Parallel and Distributed Processing (EUROPDP'01), pp.19–26, Feb. 2001.

Design of an Efficient Flexible Architecture for Color Image Enhancement

Ming Z. Zhang, Li Tao, Ming-Jung Seow, and Vijayan K. Asari

Computational Intelligence and Machine Vision Laboratory
Department of Electrical and Computer Engineering
Old Dominion University, Norfolk, VA 23529, USA
{mzhan002, ltaox001, mseow, vasari}@odu.edu

Abstract. A novel architecture for performing digital color image enhancement based on reflectance/illumination model is proposed in this paper. The approach promotes the log-domain computation to eliminate all multiplications, divisions and exponentiations utilizing the approximation techniques for efficient estimation of $\log_2$ and inverse-$\log_2$. A new quadrant symmetric architecture is also incorporated into the design of homomorphic filter to achieve very high throughput rate which is part of V component enhancement in Hue-Saturation-Value (HSV) color space. The pipelined design of the filter features the flexibility in reloading a wide range of kernels for different frequency responses. A generalized architecture of max/min filter is also presented for efficient extraction of V component. With effective color space conversion, the HSV-domain image enhancement architecture is able to achieve a throughput rate of 182.65 million outputs per second (MOPS) or equivalently 52.8 billion operations per second on Xilinx's Virtex II XC2V2000-4ff896 field programmable gate array (FPGA) at a clock frequency of 182.65 MHz. It can process over 174.2 mega-pixel (1024×1024) frames per second and consumes approximately 70.7% less hardware resource when compared to the design presented in [10].

Keywords: color image enhancement, reflectance/illumination model, HSV-domain image processing, log-domain computation, 2D convolution, multiplier-less architecture, homomorphic filter, quadrant symmetric architecture, parallel-pipelined architecture.

1 Introduction

Physical limitations exist in the sensor arrays of imaging devices, such as CCD and CMOS cameras. Often, the devices cannot represent scenes well that have both very bright and dark regions. The sensor cells are commonly compensated with the amount of saturation from bright regions, fading out the details in the darker regions. Image enhancement algorithms [1], [2] provide good rendering to bring out the details hidden due to dynamic range compression of the physical sensing devices. However, these algorithms fail to preserve the color relationship among RGB channels which result in distortion of color information after

C. Jesshope and C. Egan (Eds.): ACSAC 2006, LNCS 4186, pp. 323–336, 2006.
© Springer-Verlag Berlin Heidelberg 2006

enhancement. The recent development of fast converging neural network based learning algorithm called Ratio Rule [3], [4] provides excellent solution for natural color restoration of the image after gray-level image enhancement. Hardware implementation of such algorithms is absolutely essential to parallelize the computation and deliver real time throughputs for color images or videos containing extensive transformations and large volumes of pixels. Implementation of window related operations such as convolution, summation, and matrix dot products which are common in enhancement architectures demands enormous amount of hardware resources [5], [6]. Often, large number of multiplications/divisions is needed [7]. Some designs compromise this issue by effectively adapting the architectures to very specific forms [5], [6], [8] and cannot operate on different sets of properties related to the operation without the aid of reconfiguration in FPGA based environment. We propose the concept of log-domain computation [9] to solve the problem of multiplication and division in the enhancement system and significantly reduce the hardware requirement while providing high throughput rate.

We proposed a hardware-efficient architecture in [10] for enhancement of the digital color images using a Ratio learning algorithm [3], [4]. The enhancement scheme works very well in general for color images with uniformed or non-uniformed darkness. In this paper, we propose an alternative design of the system to significantly reduce hardware requirement while achieve similar fidelity in the enhanced images. The new architecture processes the images in HSV-domain with the homomorphic filter and converts the enhanced images back to RGB representation with highly effective conversion factor [11], [12].

2   Concept of the Design

In section 2.1, we describe the concept of the design proposed in the machine learning based image enhancement system. We then carry this concept and apply it to HSV-domain image enhancement with the discussion in section 2.2. This leads to the theory for optimal design in which we extended the idea from section 2.2 to section 2.3.

2.1   Enhancement Based on Framework of Ratio Learning Algorithm

The color image enhancement with Ratio Rule comprises three steps [10]. The first step is to boost separate RGB components to bring out the details hidden in dark regions of the image. This technique introduces color distortion in the enhanced image. The second step is to characterize the relationship between the components and train the synaptic weights of the fully connected neural network. In final step, the boosted RGB components are fed into the neural network for color balancing to restore the natural color which exists in the original image back to the enhanced image. The final step affectively corrects the distorted relationship of RGB channels for natural color rendition. This enhancement concept can be applied to HSV-domain as an alternative mechanism to avoid color distortion.

2.2 HSV-Domain Enhancement

Color distortion correction can be avoided for color image enhancement in HSV-domain. Only the V component in HSV needs to be enhanced instead of boosting separate RGB channels in RGB color space. Extraction of the V component is defined as

$$V(x, y) = \max(RI(x, y), GI(x, y), BI(x, y)), \tag{1}$$

where the $I(x, y)$ is the input image. The V component is enhanced by a homomorphic filter defined as

$$Venh(x, y) = e^{\left(\ln\left(\frac{V(x,y)}{2^P}\right)*h(x,y)\right)} \times D, \text{ or}$$

$$Venh(x, y) = 2^{\left(\log_2\left(\frac{V(x,y)}{2^P}\right)*h(x,y)\right)} \times D \tag{2}$$

for logarithmic based two expression where the * denotes convolution operation, $h(x, y)$ is the spatial-domain filter coefficients from its corresponding high-boosting homomorphic transfer function in frequency domain, P is the resolution of the pixel, D is the de-normalizing factor, and $V_{enh}(x, y)$ is enhanced intensity value of the image. This enhancement model assumes that the detail (reflectance components) in the image is logarithmically separable [12], [13]. The convolution or digital filter operation can be defined as

$$Venhl(x, y) = \sum_{m=-a}^{a} \sum_{n=-a}^{a} Vnl(x - m, y - n) \times h(m, n), \tag{3}$$

where $a = (K - 1)/2$ for $K \times K$ filter kernel, V_{nl} is the normalized logarithmic scaled version of $V(x, y)$ and V_{enhl} is the result from performing 2D convolution. The quadrant symmetry property of the homomorphic filter operation defined in (2) allows us to optimized (3) to reduce the number of multiplications by $3/4$, which we proposed in [14]. The folded version of (3) can be expressed as

$$Venhl(x, y) = \sum_{m=0}^{\frac{K}{2}-1} \sum_{n=0}^{\frac{K}{2}-1} Vnl\left(x \pm m + \tfrac{K}{2}, y \pm n + \tfrac{K}{2}\right) \times h(m, n)$$
$$+ Vnl(x, y) \times h\left(\tfrac{K}{2}, \tfrac{K}{2}\right)$$

$$Venhl(x, y) = \sum_{m=0}^{\frac{K-1}{2}} \sum_{n=0}^{\frac{K-1}{2}} h(m, n) \tag{4}$$
$$\times \begin{bmatrix} Vnl\left(x + m - \tfrac{K}{2} + 1, y + n - \tfrac{K}{2} + 1\right) \\ + Vnl\left(x - m + \tfrac{K}{2}, y + n - \tfrac{K}{2} + 1\right) \\ + Vnl\left(x + m - \tfrac{K}{2} + 1, y - n + \tfrac{K}{2}\right) \\ + Vnl\left(x - m + \tfrac{K}{2}, y - n + \tfrac{K}{2}\right) \end{bmatrix}$$

for odd and even dimension kernels respectively. The enhanced image can now be transformed back to RGB representation by

$$\{R'G'B'\}_n = \{\{e,p,t\},\{n,e,t\},\{t,e,p\},\{t,n,e\},\{p,t,e\},\{e,t,n\}\} \atop \text{for } i \text{ in } \{\{0\},...\{5\}\}, \tag{5}$$

where $t=1-S$, $n=1-S\times f$, $p=1-S\times(1-f)$, $e=1$, and $\{R'G'B'\}_n$ is the normalized enhanced RGB components. The i and f are the integer and fraction portions of H component in HSV-domain and is defined as

$$H = \begin{cases} 0 + (G-B)/(V - \min(RGB)), & \text{if } V = R \\ 2 + (B-R)/(V - \min(RGB)), & \text{if } V = G \\ 4 + (R-G)/(V - \min(RGB)), & \text{if } V = B. \end{cases} \tag{6}$$

The S component in HSV domain is defined to be

$$S = \frac{V - \min(RGB)}{V}. \tag{7}$$

The final output, $\{R'G'B'\}$, can be calculated as

$$\{R'G'B'\} = \frac{\{R'G'B'\}_n \times Venh}{\max(\{R'G'B'\}_n)}, \tag{8}$$

where $V_{enh} = 2^{Venhl} \times D$. Equations (1)-(8) provide basic framework for the algorithm we propose for hardware design of HSV-domain color image enhancement system.

2.3 HSV-Domain Enhancement with Optimal Color Space Conversion

We have shown the concept of enhancing color images in HSV-domain in section 2.2. It reduces the processing bandwidth needed in hardware design to focus on one channel (V component) rather than concurrently processing on all RGB channels. This approximately cuts the hardware resource by $2/3$ compared to the design discussed in section 2.1. As Li Tao et al demonstrated in the color image enhancement algorithms [11], [12], the color restoration process can be further simplified. She had shown that since H and S components in HSV color space remain constant, the equations (5)-(8) needed for inverse transformation can be replaced by

$$\{R'G'B'\} = \frac{\{RGB\}}{V} \times Venh. \tag{9}$$

This approach should moreover reduce the hardware requirement to more than $2/3$ compared to [10]. In the next section, we show the optimal architectural realization of the equations (1), (2), and (9) in the color image enhancement system.

3   Architecture for Color Image Enhancement

A overview of the block diagram of the system is described in section 3.1. A very tightly coupled system architecture which decomposes the block diagram presented in section 3.1 in to components is discussed in section 3.2. Discussion on the design of data buffer, V component extraction, homomorphic filtering and color space conversion components are explained in sub-sequential sub-sections.

3.1   Overview of the Computational Sequence

A brief overview of the image enhancement system with color restoration is shown in Fig. 1 along with its interface signals. The architecture features RGB streaming input with the options of specifying the image width on 'Imsize' bus, and reloading of kernel coefficients through 'KernBus' for the convolution operation. The output buses include the enhanced RGB components. The computational sequence takes place as follows. The input pixels are buffered just enough to create internal parallel data bus (PDB) to maximize the fine grained parallelism for massive parallel processing. The V component is extracted from PDB. This component is converted to $\log_2$ scale and filtered through a flexible 2D convolution architecture optimized for quadrant symmetric kernels. Lastly, the output from the homomorphic filtering process is combined with the original RGB components to restore color back from HSV-domain.

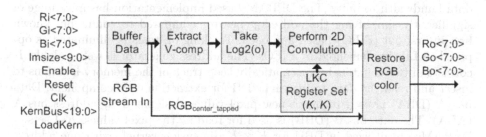

Fig. 1. Block diagram illustrates the overall sequence of computation which takes place within the system along with its interface signals

3.2   The Tightly Coupled System Architecture

The tightly coupled system architecture is illustrated in Fig. 2. It mainly consists of three units, the data buffer unit (DBU), the homomorphic filter unit (HFU), and the HSV to RGB conversion (HRC) arithmetic. The integration of these units contributes to consistent and highly parallel-pipelined design to maximize hardware utilization and delivery optimal peak performance which might be degraded in a loosely coupled or unevenly pipelined system. The design of these units is discussed in greater detail in the following sub-sections.

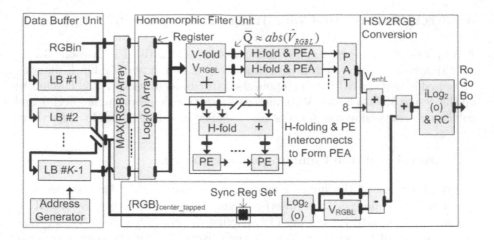

Fig. 2. System Architecture illustrates the coupling of three main units to achieve optimal peak performance

3.3 Data Buffer Unit

The DBU is implemented with dual port RAMs (DPRAMs) as shown in Fig. 3. One set of DPRAMs is utilized to form line buffer (LB) to create massive internal parallelism for concurrent processing. Each line of the image is store in one LB with the pixels fetched in raster-scan fashion. This reduces the input data bandwidth to unity. The DPRAM based implementation has advantage of significantly simplifying the address generator compared to commonly known first-in-first-out (FIFO) based approach. Tracking of items is eliminated as opposed to LBs implemented by FIFOs. The address generator is well scalable. It consists of two counters to automatically keep track of the memory locations to insert and read the data to internal PDB for extraction of V component. Data bus A (DBA) is used to insert new pixel values designated by address bus A (ABA). The data bus B (DBB) is used for reading the pixel values. K-1 sets of DPRAMs are utilized in DBU for $K \times K$ dimension kernels with one address generator.

3.4 Extraction of V Component

The V component is extracted by a max filter presented in [15]. The concept was extended from the architecture for 2D uniform filter. For 1D max filter, which is what we need in this design, a pipelined adder tree (PAT) style can be utilized. A generalized 1D max filter architecture for N nodes is shown in Fig. 4. The design utilizes the signs from subtractions in the PAT structure to successively filter and merge until a maximum value is found at the end of last pipeline stage. An array of K 3-to-1 max filters is necessary as illustrated in MAX(RGB) Array block of Fig. 2. This architecture works for min finder as well by swapping the inputs fed to 2-to-1 multiplexer (mux).

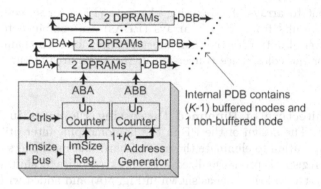

Fig. 3. Detail architecture of the DBU shown in Fig. 2. Each LB is constructed with 2 BRAMs to store RGB components. (K-1) sets of BRAMs are needed for $K \times K$ dimension kernels.

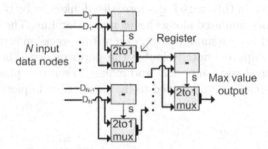

Fig. 4. Elementary architecture of the max filter is used to extract the V component. K elements of 3-to-1 max filters are needed in the MAX(RGB) Array shown in Fig. 2.

3.5 Architecture of the Homomorphic Filter

The HFU coupled with an array of the log_2 scaled version of V component is illustrated in Fig. 2. The quadrant symmetry property of the 2D convolution operation indicated by (4) allows the computation to concentrate on one quarter of the kernel through folding. The vertical folding of data is accomplished by linearly fold the data from the last stage of internal PDB with adders. This halves the processing bandwidth. To normalize a value v ($log_2(v/2^N) = log_2(v) - N$), which is negative, given the fact that image pixels are positive and log_2 of negative number is undefined, the absolute value can be logically approximated by taking the inverted output ($\overline{Q} \approx N - log_2(v) = \overline{log_2(v)}$) of the registered result from vertical folding. This procedure inherently utilizes the V-fold pipeline stage rather than introducing additional stage and resource to compute the absolute value of the normalized v. To reduce the processing bandwidth by another half, the horizontal folding is performed, taking account of the delay in systolic architecture [14]. The registered results of the H-fold stage are sent to arrays of processing elements (PEs) for successive filtering. The partial results from the PE arrays (PEAs) are combined together by a PAT. The overall output of the homomorphic filter for each channel is kept in $\log_2$ scale for the color space conversion in the HRC architecture as shown in Fig. 2.

3.5.1 Architecture of Pipelined Processing Elements in Homomorphic Filter.

The design of the PE in the homomorphic filter utilizes the log-domain computation to eliminate the need of hardware multipliers [9]. The data from H-fold register is pre-normalized without extra logics by shifting the bus. It is then converted to $\log_2$ scale as shown in Fig. 5(a) and added with $\log_2$ scaled kernel coefficients (LKC) in LKC register set. The result from last stage is converted back to linear scale with range check (RC). If the overflow or underflow occurs, the holding register of this pipeline stage is set or clear, respectively. Setting and clearing contribute the max and min values representable to N-bit register. The output of this stage is de-normalized, likewise by bus shifting, before it is successively accumulated along the accumulation line. The $\log_2$ architecture shown in Fig. 5(b) is very similar to [9], except full precision is used and registers are introduced to approximately double the performance. The maximum logic delay is reduced to single component and makes no sense to pipeline beyond this point. Interested readers are referred to [9] for detailed implementation.

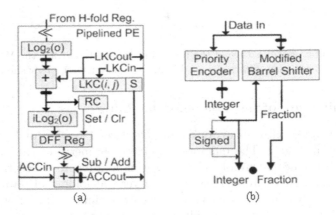

Fig. 5. Architecture of the PE in the homomorphic filter (a), and the pipelined $\log_2$ module (b)

3.6   HSV to RGB Color Space Conversion

The HRC unit inverse transforms the enhanced image in HSV color space back to RGB representation. As illustrated in Fig. 2, the center-tapped RGB components from DBU pass through synchronization register set to compensate the latencies associated with HFU. The synchronized RGB components are converted to $\log_2$ scale. Furthermore, the V component at this node is also determined with the architecture shown in Fig. 4. The V_{enhl} output is first de-normalized by adding constant 8 in log-domain which is equivalent to multiplication of de-normalizing factor $D = 2^8$. The division in (9) is calculated by subtraction in log-domain as illustrated in Fig. 2. The final output of the enhanced RGB components is computed by taking the inverse-$\log_2$ of the sum of the resultant subtraction and V_{enhl}. This completes the discussion on the design of image enhancement system. The simulation and error analysis of the architecture is discussed next.

4   Simulation and Error Analysis

Images with non-uniform darkness are used in the simulation of the hardware algorithm. The parameter set for the test is as follows:

- 8-bit unsigned pixel resolution
- Transfer function of the homomorphic filter [16]:
- Boost ratio: 2
- Cutoff frequency: 0.1
- Filter order: 2
- 1/4/15-bit coefficient sign, integer, and fraction for $\log_2$ scaled homomorphic filter coefficients (transfer function quantitized accordingly), respectively
- 9/4-bit integer/fraction in accumulation line of PEs in homomorphic filter
- Full precision $\log_2$/inverse-$\log_2$ fractions
- 7×7 window for homomorphic filter.

4.1   Simulation

The image is sent to the architecture pixel by pixel in raster scan fashion. After the initial latency of the system (i.e. Imsize×$(K$-$1)/2+(K$+$1)/2+15+D_{PAT}$ cycles, where D_{PAT} is the latency of PAT), the output becomes available and is collected for error analysis. The overall output of the enhancement architecture is recorded to give pictorial view of the enhanced image for quick evaluation of the visual quality. Typical test image is shown in Fig. 6(a) where the shadow regions exist as the consequence of the saturation in bright region. The outputs of the system produced by Matlab software and hardware simulation are illustrated in Fig. 6(b) and 6(c) respectively. As one can see that majority of the detail hidden in the dark regions of the original image are brought out while the natural color is preserved. The enhanced image produced in hardware simulation is slightly brighter than the one computed by Matlab software. Overall, the visual quality is very satisfied with least areas of shadow regions. The error introduced from replacing equations (5)-(8) by (9) is shown in Fig. 6(d) with 50

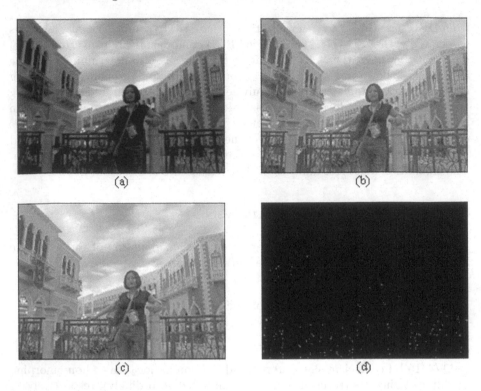

Fig. 6. Images shown from (a) to (d) are the test color image with non-uniformed darkness, the Matlab software output image, the result from hardware simulation, and the error introduced with 50 times magnification for replacing equations (5)-(8) by (9)

times magnification. The simplification induces negligible magnitude of error at extremely dark regions of the image.

4.2   Error Analysis

Typical histograms of the error between software algorithm and hardware simulation are shown in Fig. 7 for the test image. The error produced in homomorphic filter illustrated in Fig. 7(a) has average error of 2.91 pixel intensity. The average error of overall system in Fig. 7(b) is slight larger than 2.91. Simulation with large set of images shows majority of the errors in this system is less than 5 to 10 pixel intensities with the average errors around 4. This error measure includes the fact that the hardware simulation is bounded to approximation error and specific number of bits representable in the architecture where the software algorithm is free from these constraints. While the hardware simulation shows very attractive results, the efficiency of hardware utilization and its performance, which is discussed in the follow up section, is even more impressive.

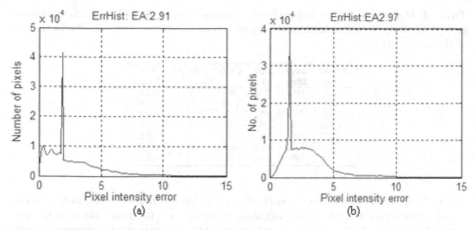

Fig. 7. Error histograms of the homomorphic filter and the system are shown in (a) and (b) from enhancement of the test image with average errors of 2.91, and 2.97 pixel intensities respectively. Typically, the error is less than 5 to 10 with the average error around 4.

5   Hardware Utilization and Performance Evaluation

5.1   Hardware Utilization

The hardware resource utilization is characterized based on the Xilinx's Virtex II XC2V2000-4ff896 FPGA and the Integrated Software Environment (ISE). The particular FPGA chip we target has 10,752 logic slices, 21,504 flip-flops (FFs), 21,504 lookup tables (4-input LUTs), 56 block RAMs (BRAMs), and 56 embedded 18-bit signed multipliers in hardware; however, we do not utilize the built-in multipliers. The resource allocation for various sizes of the kernels in homomorphic filter is shown in Table 1 with the resolution parameters listed in section 4. For 9×9 kernels in homomorphic filter, the computational power is approximately 81 multipliers which is significantly less compare to [10] with similar setting where 243 multipliers and 150 dividers are needed if conventional approach is taken. With the concept of log-domain computation the amount of hardware resource available become feasible in this implementation. The maximum windows can be utilized on target FPGA consumes 85% of the logic slices (4 slices is equivalent to 1 configurable logic block), 51% of the FFs, 49% of LUTs and 32 BRAMs (2 BRAMs for each line of RGB components). Table 2 shows the proposed design uses approximately 70.7% less logic slices on average compared to the architecture presented in [10].

5.2   Performance Evaluation

The critical timing analysis of Xilinx's ISE shows that the 182.65 MOPS, or equivalently 52.8 ((17×17) ×182.65e6) billion operations per second, is the most optimal throughput achievable with the maximum clock frequency of 182.65

Table 1. Hardware resource utilization for various sizes of the kernels in the homomorphic filter along with its corresponding performance indicates the overall effectiveness of the architecture

Kernel Size	Logic Slices	Slice FFs	LUTs	BRAMs	Perf (MOPS)
5×5	14%	8%	7%	8	182.65
7×7	21%	12%	11%	12	182.65
9×9	30%	18%	17%	16	182.65
11×11	41%	25%	23%	20	182.65
13×13	54%	32%	31%	24	182.65
15×15	68%	41%	39%	28	182.65
17×17	85%	51%	49%	32	182.65

Table 2. Comparison on the resource allocations and performance between the proposed architecture and the implementation presented in [10] illustrates that the proposed design uses significantly less hardware resource and gains higher system throughput while it achieves very similar quality in the enhanced images. It reduced 70.7% logic slices on average.

Kernel Size	Logic Slices Reduction	Performance Improvement
5×5	74.1%	124%
7×7	70.4%	124%
9×9	67.7%	124%

MHz. Further evaluation of pipelining the critical path suggests that increasing the level of pipelining does not gain significant throughput rate. This directly indicates the impact of the design with tightly coupled interfaces and well pipelined system. Given 1024×1024 image frame, it can process over 174.2 frames per second without frame buffering at its peak performance. This tremendous gain in the performance while consuming significantly less hardware resources would have been extremely difficult to achieve without the log-domain computation. The additional benefit is that the filter coefficients are not hardwired, which gives the highest flexibility in reloading the coefficients without the need of dynamic reconfiguration for different characteristics of the transfer functions. While Table 2 shows significant percentage of the hardware resource reduction, it also indicates that the performance of the proposed approach increases to 124% when compared to the design we presented in [10].

6   Conclusion

A novel architecture for performing color image enhancement has been presented. The approach utilized log-domain computation to eliminate all multiplications, divisions and exponentiations. Log_2 and inverse-log_2 computations were performed based on the approximation techniques with improved performance. A new high performance quadrant symmetric architecture was also presented to provide very high throughput rate for the homomorphic filter in the image enhancement where the V component of the image in HSV-domain was boosted. A generalized architecture for max/min filter was also presented as part of the extraction of V component. Tight system integration was also achieved along with very effective color space conversion mechanism to minimize degradation of system's performance. It has been observed that the system is able to sustain a throughput rate of 182.65 million outputs per second (MOPS) or equivalently 52.8 billion operations per second with 17×17 homomorphic filter on Xilinx's Virtex II XC2V2000-4ff896 FPGA at a clock frequency of 182.65 MHz. Given 1024×1024 image frame, it can process over 174.2 frames per second without frame buffering at its peak performance. It was further observed that the proposed architecture requires approximately 70.7% less logic slices on average when compared to the architecture for gray-level image enhancement [10].

References

1. Caselles, V., Lisani, J.L., Morel, J.M., Sapiro, G.: Shape Preserving Local Histogram Modification. IEEE Trans. Image Process. 8 (2) (1999) 220–230
2. Jobson, D.J., Rahman, Z., Woodell, G.A.: A Multi-scale Retinex for Bridging the Gap between Color Images and the Human Observation of Scenes. IEEE Trans. Image Process. 6 (7) (1997) 965–976
3. Seow, M.J., Asari, V.K.: Ratio Rule and Homomorphic Filter for Enhancement of Digital Color Image. Journal of Neurocomputing (2006) (in print).
4. Seow, M.J., Asari, V.K.: Associative Memory using Ratio Rule for Multi-valued Pattern Association. Proceedings of the IEEE International Joint Conference on Neural Networks, Portland, Oregon (2003) 2518–2522
5. Breitzman, A.F.: Automatic Derivation and Implementation of Fast Convolution Algorithms. PhD Dissertation, Drexel University (2003)
6. Jamro, E.: Parameterised Automated Generation of Convolvers Implemented in FPGAs. PhD Dissertation, University of Mining and Mentallurgy (2001)
7. Wong, A.: A New Scalable Systolic Array Processor Architecture for Discrete Convolution. MS Thesis, University of Kentucky (2003)
8. Yli-kaakinen, J., Saramaki, T.: A Systematic Algorithm for the Design of Multiplierless FIR Filters. Proceedings of the IEEE International Symposium Circuits and Systems, Vol. 2. Sydney, Australia (2001) 185–188
9. Zhang, M.Z., Ngo, H.T., Asari, V.K.: Design of an Efficient Multiplier-Less Architecture for Multi-dimensional Convolution. Lecture Notes in Computer Science, Vol. 3740. Springer-Verlag, Berlin Heidelberg (2005) 65–78
10. Zhang, M.Z., Seow, M.J., and Asari, V.K.: A High Performance Architecture for Color Image Enhancement Using a Machine Learning Approach. International Journal of Computational Intelligence Research – Special Issue on Advances in Neural Networks, Vol. 2. No. 1. (2006) 40–47
11. Tao, L. and Asari, V.K.: An Adaptive and Integrated Neighborhood Dependent Approach for Nonlinear Enhancement of Color Images. SPIE Journal of Electronic Imaging, Vol. 14. No. 4. (2005) 1.1-1.14
12. Tao, L. and Asari, V.K.: An Efficient Illuminance-Reflectance Nonlinear Video Stream Enhancement Model. IS&T/SPIE Symposium on Electronic Imaging: Real-Time Image Processing III, San Jose, CA, (2006)
13. Stockham Jr., T.G.: Image Processing in the Context of a Visual Model. Proceedings IEEE Vol. 60. (1972) 828–842

14. Zhang, M.Z., Ngo, H.T., Livingston, A.R. and Asari, V.K.: An Efficient VLSI Architecture for 2-D Convolution with Quadrant Symmetric Kernels. IEEE Computer Society Proceedings of the International Symposium on VLSI – ISVLSI 2005, Tampa, Florida, (2005) 303-304

15. Zhang, M.Z., Seow, M.J. and Asari, V.K: A Hardware Architecture for Color Image Enhancement Using a Machine Learning Approach with Adaptive Parameterization. International Joint Conference on Neural Networks – IJCNN 2006, Vancouver, BC, Canada, (2006) (accepted).

16. Kovesi, P.D.: Homomorphic filter: http://www.csse.uwa.edu.au/~pk/Research/ MatlabFns/FrequencyFilt/homomorphic.m (accessed on March 2006).

Hypercube Communications on Optical Chordal Ring Networks with Chord Length of Three

Yawen Chen[1,2], Hong Shen[2], and Haibo Zhang[1,2]

[1] Graduate School of Information Science
Japan Advanced Institute of Science and Technology
1-1, Asahidai, Nomi, Ishikawa 923-1211, Japan
{yawen, haibo}@jaist.ac.jp
[2] Department of Computing and Mathematics
Manchester Metropolitan University
Oxford Road, Manchester, M1 5GD, UK
H.Shen@mmu.ac.uk

Abstract. In this paper, we study routing and wavelength assignment for realizing hypercube communications on optical WDM chordal ring networks with chord length of 3. Specifically, we design an embedding scheme and identify a lower bound on the number of wavelengths required, and provide a wavelength assignment algorithm which achieves the lower bound. Our result for this type of chordal ring is about half of that on WDM ring with the same number of nodes.

Keywords: Wavelength Division Multiplexing (WDM), routing and wavelength assignment(RWA), hypercube communication, chordal ring.

1 Introduction

Wavelength Division Multiplexing (WDM) optical networks provide huge bandwidth, and has become a promising technology for parallel/distributed computing applications [11]. In WDM networks, the fiber bandwidth is partitioned into multiple data channels, in which different messages can be transmitted simultaneously using different wavelengths. To efficiently utilize the bandwidth resources and to eliminate the high cost and bottleneck caused by optoelectrical conversion and processing at intermediate nodes, end-to-end lightpaths are usually set up between each pair of source-destination nodes. The lightpath must satisfy the *wavelength-continuity constraint* [13], if there is no wavelength converter facility available in the network. In this case, a connection must use the same wavelength throughout its path. That is to say, the connections in WDM optical networks without wavelength conversion are subject to the following two constraints [13]: 1. *Wavelength continuity constraint*: a lightpath must use the same wavelength on all the links along its path from source to destination node. 2. *Distinct wavelength constraint*: all lightpaths using the same link (fiber) must be assigned distinct wavelengths. Such is referred to as *Routing and Wavelength Assignment* (RWA) problem [13], which is a key problem for

C. Jesshope and C. Egan (Eds.): ACSAC 2006, LNCS 4186, pp. 337–343, 2006.
© Springer-Verlag Berlin Heidelberg 2006

increasing the efficiency of wavelength-routed all-optical networks. RWA tries to minimize the number of wavelengths to realize a communication requirement by taking into consideration both routing options and wavelength assignment options. A number of communication patterns, such as multicast communication, all-to-all communication, broadcasting etc. realized on different type of optical WDM networks have been discussed[7][9][14] .

Hypercube communication is one of the most versatile and efficient communication patterns for parallel computation. One drawback to the hypercube is that the number of connections grows logarithmically with the size of the network. In [12], wavelength assignments for hypercube communications on WDM linear arrays, rings, meshes, and tori were studied. We improved the results in [12] and extended the results to the unidirectional hypercube in [4]. However, the numbers of wavelengths required to realize hypercube communications on the topologies discussed in [4][12] are large if the number of communication nodes is large. In order to reduce the number of required wavelengths, we design the embedding of hypercube communications realized on a special chordal ring networks. The results show that the number of wavelengths can be reduced by adding some chords on the simple regular networks.

The rest of this paper is organized as follows. In Section 2, the lower bound for the number of wavelengths required to realize hypercube communications on chordal ring networks with chord length of 3 is identified and the number of wavelengths is derived. The embedding scheme and the routing scheme are also designed. Comparisons for the numbers of wavelengths between WDM ring and WDM chordal ring with chord length of 3 are given in Section 3. Finally, we conclude the paper in Section 4.

2   RWA of Hypercube Communications on Chordal Ring Networks with Chord Length of 3

2.1   Chordal Ring Networks with Chord Length of 3

As described in [1], a chordal ring is basically a ring network, in which each node has an additional link, called a chord. The number of nodes in a chordal ring is assumed to be even, and nodes are indexed as $0, 1, 2, \ldots, N - 1$ around the N-node ring. We assume that each even numbered node $i(i = 0, 2, \ldots, N - 2)$ is connected to a node $(i + w) \bmod N$, where w is the chord length, which is assumed to be positive odd.

In this paper, we assume the chord length of the chordal ring is 3, which we denote by $CR(n, 3)$ with $N = 2^n$ nodes numbered from 0 to $N - 1$. We assume each link in the network is bidirectional and composed of a pair of unidirectional links with one link in each direction. For H_n, if $(x, y) \in H_n$, then $(y, x) \in H_n$. Assuming that these two communications can be realized by two lightpaths in the same path of opposite directions passing through different fiber links, the same wavelength can be assigned to these two lightpaths. In this case, we can ignore the problem of communication directions in H_n.

2.2 Hypercube Communication Pattern

Two nodes are connected in the hypercube if and only if the binary representations differ by exactly 1 bit. A connection in the hypercube is called a *dimensional i connection* [8] if it connects two nodes that differ in the ith bit position.

For hypercube communication pattern, two nodes of x and y, whose binary representations differ by the ith bit position, are connected by two dimensional i connections of (x, y) and (y, x). We define H_n as the set of hypercube communications with $N = 2^n$ nodes, and DIM_n^i, where $0 \leq i \leq n - 1$, as the set of all the corresponding dimensional i connections. That is,

$$H_n = \bigcup_{i=0}^{n-1} DIM_n^i,$$

$$DIM_n^i = \{(j, j + 2^i), (j + 2^i, j) | j \bmod 2^{i+1} < 2^i\}.$$

For H_n, there are $n \times 2^n = N \log N$ connections and 2^n connections in DIM_n^i for each $0 \leq i \leq n - 1$.

2.3 Wavelength Requirement Analysis

Given a network G and communication pattern H, the congestion for embedding H in G is the minimum among all the embedding schemes for maximum number of paths in H that use the links in G. Let $Cong(H, G)$ denote the congestion of graph H embedded in graph G, and $\lambda_e(H, G)$ denote the number of wavelengths required for realizing communication pattern of H in optical network G by embedding scheme e. Although the objective and techniques of RWA are different from those of embedding, the relevance between congestion and the number of wavelengths is shown by the following lemma [2]:

Lemma 1. $\lambda_e(H, G) \geq Cong(H, G)$.

The congestion of embedding hypercube on linear array [3], denoted by $Cong(H_n, L_n)$, is the minimum over all embedding schemes of the maximum number of hypercube edges that pass any edge of the linear array, which can be obtained by the following lemma.

Lemma 2. $Cong(H_n, L_n) = \begin{cases} (2N - 2)/3, & \text{if n is even;} \\ (2N - 1)/3, & \text{if n is odd.} \end{cases}$

We design the embedding scheme of the nodes in H_n onto $CR(n, 3)$ as follows.

Assume that X is an order of binary representations, and X^{-1} is the reversal order of these binary representations. For example, if $X = a, b, c, d$, then $X^{-1} = d, c, b, a$, and $(X_1 X_2)^{-1} = X_2^{-1} X_1^{-1}$. The node order of X_n is defined recursively as follows:

$X_1 = 0, 1,$
$X_2 = 0X_1, 1X_1^{-1},$
$\vdots$
$X_n = 0X_{n-1}, 1X_{n-1}^{-1}.$

This is also called a binary-reflected Gray code[6].

Embed the ith node of X_n in H_n onto the ith node of $CR(n,3)$. Thus, we establish the 1-1 mapping from the nodes of H_n to the nodes of $CR(n,3)$. We define such an embedding scheme as *reflected embedding* and the corresponding number of wavelengths as λ_r. For the routing scheme of the connections, we design a routing scheme with the assumption of all the communications routed by the shortest path. For the connection of (u,v), if u is even, route the connection along the links $(u, u+3), (u+3, u+4), (u+4, u+7), ..., (v-3, v)$ through the chordal links and the ring links alternatively until it reaches v. If u is odd, route the connection along the links $(u, u+1), (u+1, u+4), (u+4, u+5), ..., (v-1, v)$ through the ring links and the chordal links alternatively until it reaches v. We call such a routing scheme *Shortest Path Alternate Routing*(SPAR). For example, if the source node is 0 and the destination node is 15 for the connection of $(0, 15)$ in H_5, the routing path is $0 \to 3 \to 4 \to 7 \to 8 \to 11 \to 12 \to 15$ by SPAR scheme, as the dashed line is shown in Figure 1. As to the connection of $(1, 14)$, the routing path is $1 \to 2 \to 5 \to 6 \to 9 \to 10 \to 13 \to 14$.

In order to obtain the number of wavelengths required to realize H_n on $CR(n,3)$, we first derive the results on a type of chordal linear array with $N = 2^n$ nodes numbered from 0 to $N-1$, which we denote by $CLA(n,3)$. For $CLA(n,3)$, node $i(i = 0, 2, ..., N-3)$ is connected to a node $i+3$. We divide the set of the links of $CLA(n,3)$ into three sets as follows.

Chordal link set: $E_1 = \{(i, i+3) \mid i = 0, 2, ..., N-3\}$.
Even link set: $E_2 = \{(i, i+1) \mid i = 0, 2, ..., N-3\}$.
Odd link set: $E_3 = \{(i, i+1) \mid i = 1, 3, ..., N-2\}$.

The number of wavelengths required to realize hypercube communications on $CLA(n,3)$ can be obtained in the following lemma.

Lemma 3. *By the reflected embedding scheme and routing scheme of* SPAR, *the number of wavelengths required to realize hypercube communications on* $CLA(n,3)$ *is* $\lfloor N/3 \rfloor$.

Proof. By the reflected embedding scheme and routing scheme of *SPAR*, for each i, $DIM_n^i \cup DIM_n^{i+1}$ are routed on 2^{n-i-2} disjoint $CLA(i+2, 3)$ subarrays and the connections on each subarray with 2^{i+2} nodes do not share any links with the connections on the other subarray. Therefore, the maximum number of wavelengths required to realize $DIM_n^i \cup DIM_n^{i+1}$ is 2^i on the links which are in E_1 and E_3. For n is even, $\lambda_r(H_n, CLA(n,3)) = \lambda_r(\bigcup_{i=0}^{n-1} DIM_n^i, CLA(n,3)) = \lambda_r(\bigcup_{i=0,2,4,...,n-2}(DIM_n^i \cup DIM_n^{i+1}), CLA(n,3)) = 2^0 + 2^2 + 2^4 + ... + 2^{n-2} = N/3 - 1/3$. For n is odd, $\lambda_r(H_n, CLA(n,3)) = \lambda_r(\bigcup_{i=0}^{n-1} DIM_n^i, CLA(n,3)) = \lambda_r(\bigcup_{i=1,3,5,...,n-2}(DIM_n^i \cup DIM_n^{i-1}), CLA(n,3)) + \lambda_r(DIM_n^0, CLA(n,3)) = 2^1 + 2^3 + 2^5 + ... + 2^{n-2} = N/3 - 2/3$, since one wavelength is sufficient to realize DIM_n^0 on the links of E_2.

We first provide the lower bound on the number of wavelengths required to realize H_n on $CR(n,3)$, and then derive the number of wavelengths.

The congestion of embedding hypercube on cycle has been studied as the problem of cyclic cutwidth for hypercube [5]. As far as we know, the problem

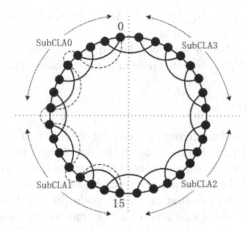

Fig. 1. $CR(5,3)$

of cyclic cutwidth for hypercube is still an open problem [5][10]. The best lower bound known for the cyclic cutwidth for hypercube, denoted by $ccw(H_n)$ in [5], is $ccw \geq \frac{1}{2}lcw(H_n)$. $lcw(H_n)$ is referred to cutwith of hypercube which is equal to congestion of hypercube on linear array. Although the cyclic cutwidth hypercube has not been discovered, a conjecture, $ccw(H_n) = \lfloor 5N/12 \rfloor$, has been made in [5]. So far as has been tested, this conjecture has been held. Based on this conjecture, we obtain the following lemma.

Lemma 4. *If $ccw(H_n) = \lfloor 5N/12 \rfloor$, the number of wavelengths required to realize hypercube communications on $CR(n,3)$ is not less than $\lfloor 5N/24 \rfloor$.*

Proof. Assume that the conjecture of $ccw(H_n) = \lfloor 5N/12 \rfloor$ is held. No matter what the embedding scheme is used, there exists a cut on $CR(n,3)$ that separate two neighborhood nodes x and y, with at lease 2 links connecting x and y, such that at least $\lfloor 5N/12 \rfloor$ or $\lfloor 5N/12 \rfloor - 1$ connections passing through this cut. Since there are at lease 2 links connecting this cut, it can be easily calculated that each of these 2 links must be used at least $\lfloor 5N/24 \rfloor$ times, regardless of the embedding and routing schemes used.

Theorem 1. *The number of wavelengths required to realize hypercube communications on $CR(n,3)$ is $\lfloor 5N/24 \rfloor$.*

Proof. By reflected embedding, connections in $H_n - DIM_n^{n-1} - DIM_n^{n-2}$ embedded on $CR(n,3)$ can be regarded as four H_{n-2} embedded on four $CLA(n-2,3)$, denoted by $SubCLA_i (i = 0,1,2,3)$, as illustrated in Figure 1. Since $SubCLA_0$, $SubCLA_1$, $SubCLA_2$ and $SubCLA_3$ are disjoint and the connections in each $CLA(n-2,3)$ do not share links with the connections in other $CLA(n-2,3)$ by the shortest path, wavelengths can be reused and the same set of wavelengths can be assigned to each $CLA(n-2,3)$. By Lemma 3, the number of wavelengths required for each $CLA(n-2,3)$ is $\lfloor N/12 \rfloor$.

For the connections in $DIM_n^{n-1} \cup DIM_n^{n-2}$, it can be easily proven that the number of wavelengths required is $N/8$.

Therefore, the number of wavelengths required to realize H_n on $CR(n,3)$ is $\lfloor N/12 \rfloor + N/8 = \lfloor 5N/24 \rfloor$ by reflected embedding and routing scheme of $SPRA$.

3   Comparisons

We compare the wavelength requirement for realizing H_n on chordal ring of $CR(n,3)$ and WDM ring. Figure 2 shows the wavelength requirement for WDM ring and $CR(n,3)$ with the same number of process nodes when $3 \le n \le 8$. It can be seen that the wavelength requirement for realizing hypercube communication on $CR(n,3)$ is about half of that on the 2^n-node ring. Although the number of links for $CR(n,3)$ is about one and a half of that for the ring networks, it can be observed that single wavelength fiber can be used for the links in Even link set(E_2) of $CR(n,3)$.

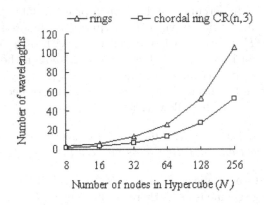

Fig. 2. Wavelength requirement for H_n on ring and $CR(n,3)$

4   Concluding Remarks

In this paper, we discussed routing and wavelength assignment of hypercube communications on optical chordal ring networks of $CR(n,3)$. Specifically, we identified the lower bound on the number of wavelengths required, and designed an embedding scheme and wavelength assignment algorithm which uses a near-optimal number of wavelengths. The results show that the wavelengths requirement to realize the hypercube communication on the chordal ring of $CR(n,3)$ is about half of that on WDM ring networks with the same number of nodes. Since hypercube communication represents a common communication pattern shared by a large number of computational problems, our results have both theoretical and practical significance which increases with the growth of the popularity of WDM optical networks. In our future research, we will continue to study the problem of realizing hypercube communication patterns on general chordal ring networks without the limitation of the chord length.

References

1. B. Arden and H. Lee, "Analysis of chordal ring networks," *IEEE Transactions on Computers*, vol. 30, no. 4, pp. 291–295, 1981.
2. B. Beauquier, J.-C. Bermond, L. Gargano, P. Hell, S. Pérennes, and U. Vaccaro, "Graph problems arising from wavelength routing in all optical networks," in *Proceedings of* WOCS'97, 1997, pp. 366–370.
3. S. Bezrukov, J. Chavez, L. Harper, M. Rottger, and U.-P. Schroeder, "The congestion of n-cube layout on a rectangular grid," *Discrete Mathematics*, pp. 13–19, 2000.
4. Y. Chen and H. Shen, "Wavelength assignment for directional hypercube communications on a class of WDM optical networks," Tech. Rep., 2005.
5. J. Erbele, "The cyclic cutwidth of Q_n," California State University San Bernardino (CSUSB), Tech. Rep., 2003.
6. M. Gardner, *Knotted Doughnuts And other Mathematical Entertainments.* New York: W.H. Freeman and Company, 1986.
7. Q.-P. Gu and S. Peng, "Multihop all-to-all broadcast on WDM optical networks." *IEEE Trans. Parallel Distrib. Syst.*, vol. 14, no. 5, pp. 477–486, 2003.
8. F. T. Leighton, *Introduction to Parallel Algorithms and Architectures: Arrays, Trees, Hypercubes.* Morgan Kaufmann, 1992.
9. L. Ruan, D.-Z. Du, X.-D. Hu, X. Jia, D. Li, and Z. Sun, "Converter placement supporting broadcast in WDM optical networks," *IEEE Transactions on Computers*, vol. 50, no. 7, pp. 750 – 758, July 2001.
10. H. Schroder, H. Schroder, O. Sykora, and I. Vrto, "Cyclic cutwidths of the mesh," in *SOFSEM '99*, 1999, pp. 443–452.
11. Y. Yang and J. Wang, "Cost-effective designs of WDM optical interconnects," *IEEE Transactions on Parallel and Distributed Systems*, vol. 16, no. 1, pp. 51–66, 2005.
12. X. Yuan and R. Melhem, "Optimal routing and channel assignments for hypercube communication on optical mesh-like processor arrays," in *Proceedings of the 5th International Conference on Massively Parallel Processing Using Optical Interconnection IFIP International Conference on Network and Parallel Computing*, 1998, pp. 110–118.
13. H. Zang, J. P. Jue, and B. Mukherjee, "A review of routing and wavelength assignment approaches for wavelength-routed optical networks," *Optical Network Magazine*, vol. 1, no. 1, pp. 47–60, 2000.
14. C. Zhou and Y. Yang, "Wide-sense nonblocking multicast in a class of regular optical WDM networks," *IEEE Transactions on Communications*, vol. 50, no. 1, pp. 126–134, 2002.

PMPS(3): A Performance Model of Parallel Systems

Chen Yong-ran, QI Xing-yun, Qian Yue, and Dou Wen-hua

Computer College, National University of Defense Technology, Hunan, 410073,
PR China
chenyr@nudt.edu.cn

Abstract. In this paper, an open performance model framework
PMPS(n) and a realization of this framework PMPS(3), including memory, I/O and network, are presented and used to predict runtime of NPB
benchmarks on P4 cluster. The experimental results demonstrates that
PMPS(3) can work much better than PERC for I/O intensive applications, and can do as well as PERC for memory-intensive applications.
Through further analysis, it is indicated that the results of the performance model can be influenced by the data correlations, control correlations and operation overlaps and which must be considered in the models
to improve the prediction precision. The experimental results also showed
that PMPS(n) be of great scalability.

Keywords: Performance Model, Parallel, I/O, Convolution Methods.

1 Introduction

Methods of performance evaluations can be broken down into two areas [1]:
structural models and functional/analytical models. Simulators have the advantage of automating performance prediction from the user's standpoint. The
disadvantage is that these simulators capture all the behavior of the processors, simulations can take on an upwards of 1,000,000 times longer than the real
runtime of the application [2].

In the second area of performance evaluation, functional and analytical models, the performance of an application on the target machine can be described
by a complex mathematical equation. When the equation is fed with the proper
input values to describe the target machine, the calculation yields a wall clock
time for that application on the target machine. Various flavors of theses methods have been researched.

The goal of our work is to create a more accurate functional and analytical
models of scientific applications in parallel systems.

2 PMPS(3)

An open performance prediction model of parallel systems based on convolution
methods [3,4,5,6] PMPS(n) is showed in this paper.

C. Jesshope and C. Egan (Eds.): ACSAC 2006, LNCS 4186, pp. 344–350, 2006.

The framework of PMPS(n) is illustrated in Fig. 1. In the framework, we capture n kinds of machine profiles and gather n kinds of application signatures. Generally, the more information is captured (n is larger), the more the result of framework will be precise, and the longer time the predicting will last. The modules in this framework are classified into two parts: n_1 modules are used to analyze the performance of single-processor nodes; n_2 modules are used to analyze the performance of network. In this case, $n = n_1 + n_2$.

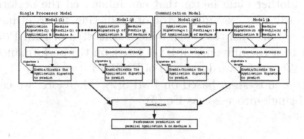

Fig. 1. Performance model of parallel systems

In the PMPS(n), we have considered not only the influence of n kinds of operations of the applications on the prediction, but also the influence of overlaps of operations. We can denote the performance of the single processor as Eq.(1).

$$P_{cpu} = \sum_{i=1}^{m} \left(\sum_{j=1}^{n_1} (W_j BB_i)(Ops_j BB_i / Rate_j BB_i - \sum_{k \ j=1}^{n_1} OverlapT BB_i(Ops_j, Ops_k)) \right). \tag{1}$$

in which:

- m: Total number of base blocks completed by that parallel application;
- n_1: Total number of operation types analyzed in the model;
- $W_j BB_i$: The contribution of the jth operation to the prediction in the BB_i. If the operation takes part in the prediction, it is 1, or it is 0.
- $Ops_j BB_i$: The number of the jth operation in the BB_i, denotes the application signature;
- $Rate_j BB_i$: Ratio of the jth operation in the BB_i, denotes the machine profile;
- $OverlapT BB_i(Ops_j, Ops_k)$: The overlap time of the jth operation and the kth operation in the BB_i.

We can obtain the performance of network by using the same method. Using the performance of single-processor and network as input parameters, the convolution module can predict the runtime T' of application.

Furthermore, we define the accuracy of the prediction of the model in Eq.(2). In which T is wall clock time of the application.

$$Error = \frac{T - T'}{T} 100\% \tag{2}$$

PMPS(n) is an open performance model of the parallel systems based on convolution methods. Generally, when using this model to predict the performance of a system, we only consider the key factors that can influence the performance. For example, the PERC model carried out by San Diego Supercomputer Center is a typical model of PMPS(2). The PERC considered that the single-processor performance is mainly decided by the memory operation, and the scalability is mainly decided by the character of network[3,5]. Using the model to predict the runtime of storage-intensive applications, the error will be less than 20%.

The I/O is another main factor that can influenced the performance of the system enormously. For example, error of predicting the runtime of HYCOM on a 234-node system with that each node is consisted of IBM Power4 is about 30.6%. It is for that the influence of I/O system on the performance hasn't been considered [4]. We put forward a model of PMPS(3) (n_1=2, n_2=1) that includes the factor of I/O subsystem based on PMPS(2). Therefore, we can denote the performance of single-processor as Eq.(3).

$$p_{cpu} = \sum_{i=1}^{m} \left(Ops_m BB_i / Rate_m BB_i + Ops_{IO} BB_i / Rate_{IO} BB_i - OverlapT BB_i(Ops_m, Ops_{IO}) \right). \tag{3}$$

Moreover, if we don't consider the factor of operation overlaps, that is $OverlapT BB_i(Ops_m, Ops_{IO}) = 0$, then we have Eq.(4).

$$p_{cpu} = \sum_{i=1}^{m} \left(Ops_m BB_i / Rate_m BB_i + Ops_{IO} BB_i / Rate_{IO} BB_i \right). \tag{4}$$

3   Experimental Details

In the next section, we will provide detailed results for the P4 Linux cluster. The P4 Linux cluster has 8 processing nodes. Each node has a 2.4GHz Intel Pentium IV processor running Red Hat Linux 7.2 with kernel version 2.4.17. Each processor is equipped with L1 and L2 caches of 8KB and 512KB. Each node has 512M DDR SDRAM memory and a 7200 RPM Ultra-ATA/133 60GB hard disk. All nodes are connected using 100Mb/s Ethernet.

For parallel I/O performance testing, this work centers on the combined use of three I/O system software package to provide both a convenient API and high performance I/O access [9]. The Parallel Virtual File System PVFS [8], the ROMIO MPI-IO implementation ROMIO MPI-IO [10], and the Hierarchical Data Format HDF5 [11] application interface together provide the I/O functionality.

We use NPB [7] as the testing program.In the experiments, part of the NPB benchmarks is used and the size of problems is listed in Table [1]. In order to test I/O operation influence on the prediction result of the PMPS(3) and PERC, we use BTIO [12] in NPBs to test the parallel I/O performance.

Table 1. NPB benchmarks used in this work

Name	Input	Description
CG	Class S/W/A	Conjugate Gradient
FT	Class S/W	Fast Fourier Transform
MG	Class S/W/B	3-D Multi-grid
BT	Class S/W/B	Block Tri-diagonal
SP	Class S/W	Scalar Penta-diagonal
BTIO	Class S/W/B	Test the speed of parallel I/O was provided by the BT

4 Results

4.1 Single-Processor Experimental Results

In Fig. 2, we present the wall clock time, PERC prediction time and PMPS(3) prediction time of NPB kernel benchmarks running in single Intel P4 processor.

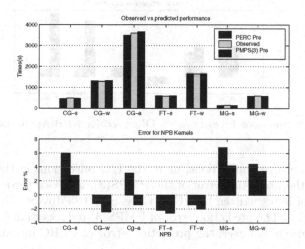

Fig. 2. Single Processor Predictions vs. Observed for NPB Kernels

From the experimental result, we can find that the prediction precision of PMPS(3) don't increase compared with PERC model. The error range of PERC is (-2.2%–6.8%) and that of PMPS(3) is (-2.4%–4.2%). This is for that the kernel programs of NPB are memory-intensive applications. They are mainly used in testing the floating point computing performance, seldom in testing the I/O operations.

For any application workload, the prediction time of PMPS(3) model will be longer than that of PERC. This is mainly because of the difference between the performance prediction formulas of the two models on single processor. As compared to PMPS(3), it has no I/O operation time.

The prediction precision of the PMPS(3) is better than that of PERC when more I/O operations are included in the applications. Fig. 3 shows the experimental result of NPB applications and BTIO. From the results, we can obtain that for BT and SP, the prediction results of PMPS(3) are equivalent to that of PERC, but for BTIO, the prediction results of PMPS(3) are better than that of PERC. The errors of former are 6.9% and 4.6%, while the errors of the latter are 33.5% and 37.9%. The prediction error of PERC in I/O intensive applications is 7 times of that of PMPS(3), which is far beyond the bound we can accept.

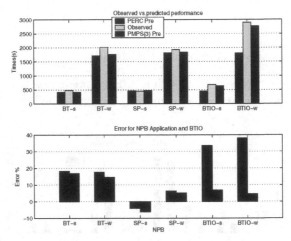

Fig. 3. Single Processor Predictions vs. Observed for NPB Application and BTIO

For I/O intensive applications, more the I/O operations in the whole applications, less the prediction error of the PMPS(3), and vice versa. For example, the number of bytes written by I/O in Class S is 0.83Mbytes and in Class W is 22.12Mbyes [12]. The prediction error of PMPS(3) reduces from 6.9% to 4.6% in the two instances, however, the prediction error of PERC increass from 33.5% to 37.9%.

The prediction error of PMPS(3) and PERC for applications of BT and SP in NPB is greater than that for kernels such as CG, FT and MG. The control flow and data flow in NPB kernel benchmarks is very simple, and the programs have little dependency. So they have little influence on the performance. However, if the signatures of benchmark are closer to the applications, the control flow and data flow in programs will be more complex, and the performance will be more easily influenced by the dependency operations. Moreover, because of the dependency of the programs, the time of the applications predicted by model is much less than that of practice in most instances, and the error is positive. It should be explored further that how the dependency can influences the prediction results in PMPS(n) model [6,13].

4.2   Multi-processor Experimental Results

We analyzed the running time of MG Class B, BT Class B and BTIO Class B in the 8-node P4 cluster separately. For each application, we use 3 parameters of single-processor nodes as the input of Dimemas. They are peak performance of CPU: MaxFlops; testing result of PERC model: PERCFlops and testing result of PMPS(3): PMPSFlops. The wall clock time and the prediction time of the three applications are illustrated in Fig. 4.

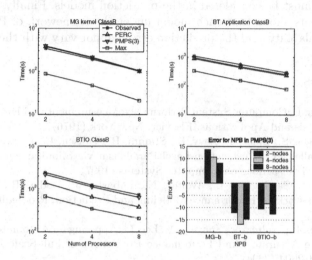

Fig. 4. Observed vs. Predicted times for MG kernel Class B on P4 Clusters

Similarly to the prediction result of the single processor, PMPS(3) can do as well as PERC for memory-intensive applications. For I/O intensive applications, the prediction results of PMPS(3) are much better than that of PERC. This is because of the different input parameters of Dimemas simulator. If the performance parameters entered into the single-processor nodes are more precise, the performance prediction error of the cluster system will be much less. The performance parameters of the single-processor nodes can influence the prediction results of the models greatly.

For any applications, the prediction precision of a model doesn't vary with the number of processor, so the model has good scalability. We can see from Fig. 4 that the change of the number of processor nodes has little influence on the prediction error. Because the scalability depends on the performance parameters of the network.

5   Conclusion

In this paper, we bring forward PMPS(n), a general framework of the performance prediction model of parallel computing system based on convolution methods, and present an implement of PMPS(3) that can cover the prediction of the single-processor nodes performance, I/O performance and network performance. Using the model to predict the performance of NPB benchmarks running in P4 cluster, we can find that PMPS(3) can work much better than PERC for I/O intensive applications, and can do as well as PERC for memory-intensive applications. This shows that PMPS(3) is more generalized. We also find that data dependency, control dependency and operation overlap influenced the running time and the prediction results of the applications through experiments. Such factors must be considered in the prediction models. Finally, the result of the experiments shows that each model under the framework of PMPS(n) has very good scalability, and the prediction error cannot vary with the system size.

References

1. Svobodova, L.:Computer System Performance Measurement and Evaluation Methods: Analysis and Applications. Elsevier, New York (1976)
2. Lo, J., Egger, S., Emer, J., Levy, H., Stamm, R., Tullsen, D.: Converting Thread-Level Parallelism to Instruction-Level Parallelism via Simultaneous Multithreading. ACM Transactions on Computer Systems (1997)
3. Snavely, A., Carrington, L., Wolter, N., Labarta, J., Badia, R., Purkayastha, A.:A Framework for Performance Modeling and Prediction. Proceedings of SC2002 (2002)
4. Carrington, L., Wolter, N., Snavely, A., Lee, C.:Applying an Automated Framework to Produce Accurate Blind Performance Predictions of Full-Scale HPC Applications. UGC2004 (2004)
5. A. Snavely, A., Wolter, N., Carrington, L.:Modeling Application Performance by Convolving Machine Signatures with Application Profiles. IEEE 4th Annual Workshop on Workload Characterization, Austin (2001)
6. Carrington, L., Gao, X.F., Wolter, N., Snavely, A., Lee, C.: Performance Sensitivity Studies for Strategic Applications. UGC2005 (2005)
7. NAS Parallel Benchmarks. http://www.nas.nasa.gov/software/npb (2005)
8. Carns, P.H., Ligon III, W.B., Ross R.B., Thakur, R.: PVFS: A Parallel File System For Linux Clusters. Proceedings of the 4th Annual Linux Showcase and Conference, Atlanta, GA, (2000) 317–327
9. Ross, R., Nurmi, D., Cheng, A., Zingale, M.: A Case Study in Application I/O on Linux Clusters. Proceedings of Supercomputing 2001 (2001)
10. Rajeev Thakur, William Gropp, Ewing Lusk.: On implementing MPI-IO portably and with high performance. In Proceedings of the Sixth Workshop on Input/Output in Parallel and Distributed Systems (1999) 23–32
11. Hierarchical Data Format 5. http://hdf.ncsa.uiuc.edu/
12. Rob,F., Van,W.D.,:NAS Parallel Benchmark I/O Version 2.4. NAS Technical Report NAS-03-002 (2003)
13. David, H., Bronis, S.:Performance Research: Current Status and Future Directions.http://perc.nersc.gov/main.htm (2005)

Issues and Support for Dynamic Register Allocation*

Abhinav Das, Rao Fu, Antonia Zhai, and Wei-Chung Hsu

Department of Computer Science,
University of Minnesota
{adas, rfu, zhai, hsu}@cs.umn.edu

Abstract. Post-link and dynamic optimizations have become important to achieve program performance. A major challenge in post-link and dynamic optimizations is the acquisition of registers for inserting optimization code in the main program. It is difficult to achieve both correctness and transparency when software-only schemes for acquiring registers are used, as described in [1]. We propose an architecture feature that builds upon existing hardware for stacked register allocation on the Itanium processor. The hardware impact of this feature is minimal, while simultaneously allowing post-link and dynamic optimization systems to obtain registers for optimization in a "safe" manner, thus preserving the transparency and improving the performance of these systems.

1 Introduction

The dynamic nature of languages and dynamic program behavior has increased the importance of post-link and dynamic optimization systems. Many such systems have been proposed in the past[4][5][6][11][12]. To deploy optimizations at post-link or run time, these systems need registers. Register acquisition, which, in the context of post-link and dynamic optimization broadly includes obtaining extra registers for optimization, is challenging due to several reasons: (i) compiled binaries have already performed traditional register allocation that tried to maximize register usage; (ii) control and data flow information, which is necessary for performing register allocation, may not be accurately known from analysis of binary. At runtime when code is seen incrementally, flow analysis is more restricted. Thus, there is no efficient software solution for acquiring registers for post-link time optimization, and even more so for dynamic optimization. Software support, such as compiler annotations, and architecture/hardware support, such as dynamic stack register allocation, can potentially ease post-link and runtime register acquisition.

The requirements of register acquisition for post-link and dynamic binary optimization systems are different from traditional and dynamic compilation models. Since register allocation has already been performed, such systems have

---

* This work is supported by a grant from NSF EIA-0220021.

C. Jesshope and C. Egan (Eds.): ACSAC 2006, LNCS 4186, pp. 351–358, 2006.
© Springer-Verlag Berlin Heidelberg 2006

to make very conservative assumptions about register usage. Dynamic binary optimization systems face the additional burden of finding registers with minimal runtime overhead. Post-link time optimization systems do not have a time constraint, since analysis is done off line. Traditionally, these systems rely on binary analysis to find registers that are infrequently used. These registers are freed for optimization by spilling them. For architectures that support variable-size register windows, these optimization systems increase the size of register window to obtain registers. Unfortunately, these software-based schemes make assumptions about code structure that can be easily broken. In this paper, we make the following contributions: (i) Briefly describe existing register acquisition schemes in post-link time and dynamic optimizers, such as Ispike[5] and ADORE[2][4] (ii) Present an architecture feature that enables the use of variable-size register windows to dynamically obtain required registers. In the context of this paper, register allocation means register acquisition as described above.

2 Software-Based Register Allocation

2.1 Fixed-Number Register Allocation

Registers can be allocated statically with help from the compiler or from hardware. The compiler can be instructed to not use certain general purpose registers, which can be later used by dynamic optimization systems. Similarly, hardware can be implemented to allow the use of certain registers only for specific purposes. If the compiler is used for static register allocation, compiler support must be available from compilers and some form of annotation must be provided for the dynamic optimizer to differentiate between supported and unsupported binaries. Hardware can support a fixed number of registers (shadow registers) for optimization. [1] presents a detailed explanation of the limitations involved in using a fixed number of registers. Lu et al. in [4] showed that allocating registers dynamically can significantly improve the performance of runtime optimization systems.

2.2 Dynamic Register Allocation

Register Spilling: Registers used for dynamic optimizations can be obtained by first scanning the optimized trace (a single-entry multiple-exit region of code) to find unused registers, then spilling and restoring these registers at trace entry and exit, respectively. The main challenge in register spilling is where to spill registers. Possible choices are (i) on stack top (ii) on the heap (thread shared or thread private). Each of these has limitations detailed in [1].

Dynamically Increase Variable Register Window Size: The size of frame (of the function to be optimized) is incremented by executing a copy of the *alloc[15]* instruction for the current frame with an increased frame size. Figure 1, shows how extra output registers are dynamically allocated for optimization.

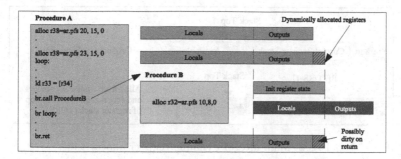

Fig. 1. Mechanism of dynamic register allocation using *alloc* instruction on the IA64 architecture[15]

However, there are some limitations to this approach. It is difficult to find the *alloc* instruction for the register frame of code to be optimized. Scanning the binary may lead to detection of an incorrect *alloc* instruction due to compiler optimizations, such as function splitting. Aggressive compilers use multiple *allocs* to allocate different number of registers down different paths. The presence of multiple *allocs* may lead code scanning in finding the wrong *alloc*. Leaf routines may not have an *alloc* instruction at all, and they use registers from the caller's output frame and global registers. These are described in detail in [1].

Since static scanning has limitations, a dynamic mechanism is needed to find the state of the current register stack. This state information is encoded in an architecturally invisible register called *current frame marker* (CFM). On a function call contents of this register are copied to an architecturally visible application register called *previous function state* (ar.pfs). To determine the register stack state dynamically, we can inject a function call just before trace entry. The injected function call then reads the *ar.pfm* register and passes this value to the dynamic optimizer. Possible methods of injecting a function call are (i) inserting a call instruction before trace entry and (ii) generating a trap by inserting an illegal instruction, for example. For reasons discussed in [1] we need to generate a trap, which has a high overhead (as much as 1789%).

3   Architecture Support

Since the main limitation of existing support is the absence of fast access to current register state information, an easy architecture extension is to expose the CFM register and thus providing the current state information. Doing so, reduces the overhead of finding current state, but does not reduce the overhead of determining if the state is the same as when the trace is generated. If the state has changed, traces need to be regenerated that can result in substantial overhead. With this limitation in mind, we sought features that were free from the above limitations and provided a fast and easy way to obtain additional registers.

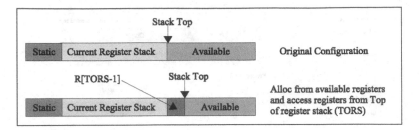

Fig. 2. Main idea of dynamic register allocation

3.1   Main Idea

The main requirements of allocating registers dynamically is a scheme that uses relative addressing to access registers. If we use a fixed method to access registers, compilers can use those registers, and we will have no guarantee of using those registers post-compilation. A disadvantage of fixed register schemes is that optimizations cannot be stacked onto one another. A scheme that can allocate registers on top of existing allocation is better suited to runtime optimization, or in general, incremental post-link optimization. Figure 2, shows the main idea of this approach. In this figure, a new instruction can allocate some number of registers from available architectural registers by only specifying the number of registers needed rather than specifying complete frame information (as is needed in the current implementation of *alloc* instruction). The other aspect shown in the figure is the access mechanism for these registers. Registers are accessed relative to the Top of Register Stack (ToRS). Let us consider some cases and explain how dynamic register allocation will work with such a mechanism, even if the compiler uses this scheme for allocating registers. Suppose that post-link, we want to optimize a loop that already addresses some registers using the top of register stack. Let us assume that optimization requires 2 dynamic registers. We can use a new instruction to increment the size of frame by 2 and adjust the relative offset of instructions already using relative addressing by 2. Note that only those instructions that are in the trace need to be modified, as the state of register frame would be restored upon trace exit. We need another instruction to restore the register frame. Thus, a stack-based approach coupled with relative addressing from top of stack can be effectively used for dynamic register allocation.

3.2   Relative Addressing

In this section, we will discuss implementation details of the relative addressing scheme proposed. There are 128 registers in the IA64 ISA and a 7-bit field is used to address these registers. In the simplest form, a bit can be added to each 7-bit register entry that distinguishes regular access from relative access. We would add an extra bit for each register field thereby increasing the instruction width from 41 bits to 44 bits (maximum of 3 register fields in an instruction).

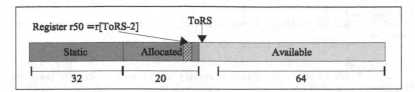

Fig. 3. Case example showing stack allocation of 20 registers highlighting the case where total number of registers accessed is less than 64

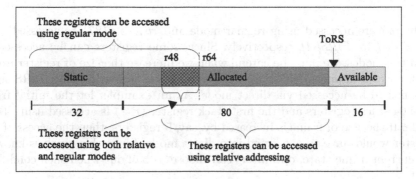

Fig. 4. Example with 80 registers are allocated on the stack highlighting the case where total number of registers accessed is greater than 64

However, we can use a clever trick to ensure that the register address field width is not increased. In this scheme, the 7th bit is used to distinguish between regular access and relative access. Since we are left with only 6 bits for indexing into registers, let us discuss how 128 registers can be accessed using this addressing scheme.

Case 1: Number of Registers allocated by compiler ≤ 64: In this case (Figure 3) all registers can be accessed by both relative and regular access. The number of registers (static and stack) total to less than 64. Thus, they can be accessed by both modes. For regular access the 7th bit is set to zero. If the compiler wants to use relative accessing it is free to do so. In the example shown, 20 stack registers are allocated along with 32 static registers. Register $r51$ is the last allocated register which can be accessed as $r51$ or as $ToRS[-1]$ as the ToRS points to $r52$. The compiler should encode this field as 1000000_2.

Case 2: Number of Registers allocated by compiler > 64: In the example shown in figure 4, the compiler has to use regular mode for registers $r0$ to $r47$. Registers $r48$ to $r63$ can be accessed using regular mode and ToRS mode ($ToRS[-64]$ to $ToRS[-49]$ respectively) and registers $r64$ onwards have to be accessed using relative addressing ($ToRS[-48]$ onwards).

Thus, the addressing mode is implemented such that the width of register field remains the same. In the extreme case, when all 128 registers are allocated,

```
inc_alloc imm7
   imm7 - a 7-bit immediate field used to specify the amount to increment the frame by
Operation:
   if(cfm.sof+imm7) > 96 then Illegal_operation_fault() else cfm.sof += imm7

dec_alloc imm7
   imm7 - a 7-bit immediate field used to specify the amount to decrement the frame by
Operation:
   if(cfm.sof-imm7) < 0 then Illegal_operation_fault() else cfm.sof -= imm7
```

Fig. 5. Instruction format for inc_alloc and dec_alloc instructions

$r0$ to $r63$ are accessed using regular mode and $r64$ to $r127$ are accessed using ToRS[-64] to ToRS[-1], respectively. Since, some registers can be accessed by both the modes, we must be careful when we increase the size of register frame, as it may so happen that some register that was accessed using ToRS mode now has to be accessed via direct mode. As an example, let the initial frame have 64 stack registers and the first stack register ($r32$) is accessed using ToRS mode. If the size of frame is increased by, say, 5 registers, then the access of this register would have to converted into direct mode. Since this involves knowing the current frame state, optimizers can choose to bail out when such conditions exist.

Since a register access on Itanium already performs an indexing operation to access the correct physical register, we believe our implementation does not add to the hardware cost. To reduce the cost of subtracting the offset, the top of register stack can be maintained as part of the current frame in the CFM register.

3.3   New Instructions

Some new instructions must be added to manage dynamic register stack in a way which is slightly different from the *alloc* instruction. The aim is to leverage existing hardware. We add two new instructions for increasing and decreasing the register stack. The first instruction is *inc_alloc* that increments the current register frame size (cfm.sof) by a number specified in the instruction. The second instruction is *dec_alloc* that decrements the sof value in cfm. The format and operation of these instructions are shown in Figure 5.

4   Related Work

Dynamic binary translation poses similar challenges to register acquisition. Register allocation in translation involves mapping source (i.e. the binary to be translated) registers to the target (i.e. the host) machine's registers. Shade[9][10] is a dynamic translation and tracing tool for the SPARC platform. It translates SPARC (v8 and v9) and MIPS 1 instructions for SPARC v8 systems. For native translation, the virtual and the actual number of registers are the same. Since some registers are needed by SHADE, registers in the translated program are remapped to different physical registers and registers are spilled lazily. PIN [13] is a instrumentation tool for 4 architectures IA32, EM64T, IA64 and ARM. It performs native translation for each of these architectures and does register reallocation and liveness analysis. PIN builds register liveness incrementally as it sees more code. When traces are linked, PIN tries to keep a virtual register in the same physical register whenever possible. If this is not possible, it reconciles differences in mapping by copying registers through memory before jumping to another trace. Probst et al. [8] discuss a technique for building register liveness information incrementally for dynamic translation systems.

Post-link optimizers such as SPIKE[6] and Ispike[5] optimize binaries by analyzing profile information. SPIKE needs registers for inserting instrumentation code. It uses register usage information collected by scanning the binary to find free registers, so that register spills can be minimized. Ispike collects profile from hardware counters on the Itanium platform and thus it does not require registers for collecting profile. However, data prefetching optimization requires registers. Ispike uses either free registers by liveness analysis, increments register stack (by looking for *alloc* instruction) or uses post-increment/decrement in prefetch and load operations.

Dynamic optimizers can be similar to dynamic translators if they use translation to build traces. Dynamo [11] is a dynamic optimizer for PA-RISC binaries. When emitting traces to be optimized, Dynamo tries to create a 1-1 mapping between virtual and physical registers. For registers that cannot be mapped, it uses the application context stored in the translator to store the physical registers. DynamoRIO [12] is a system based on Dynamo for x86 systems. ADORE [2][3][4] as described earlier uses *alloc* instruction or spills registers to obtain registers for optimization. Saxena in [14] describes various issues of register allocation for the ADORE system and presents data for finding dead registers in a trace. Jesshope in [17] uses register access by relative addressing to communicate dependencies between variables in dynamically parallelized code. Relative access to registers is not a new idea, but one that is already implemented in Itanium. Our contribution is to provide another base for accessing registers, to tackle the specific problem of register acquisition for post-link and dynamic optimization.

5   Conclusion

Register allocation for post-link and dynamic optimization systems poses interesting challenges as correctness, overhead and transparency are important concerns. In this paper, we have presented a modest hardware addition to the IA64 architecture, as an example, to illustrate how such a feature would simplify dynamic register acquisition. The proposed hardware support ensures correct execution while imposing no performance overheard and transparency limitations. When multiple post-link and dynamic optimizations are present, the proposed hardware allows optimization systems to stack their optimizations on top of each other. The architecture feature described, leverages existing hardware on the Itanium processor, thus will likely be feasible. We believe that given the performance delivered by post-link and dynamic optimization, it will be cost-effective to devote more hardware resources for this purpose.

References

1. Das, A., Fu, R., Zhai, A., Hsu, W.-C.: Issues and Support for Dynamic Register Allocation. Technical Report 06-020, Computer Science, U. of Minnesota, 2006
2. Lu, J., Das, A., Hsu, W-C., Nguyen, K., Abraham, S.: Dynamic Helper-threaded Prefetching for Sun UltraSPARC Processors. MICRO 2005.
3. Jiwei Lu, Howard Chen, Rao Fu, Wei-Chung Hsu, Bobbie Othmer, Pen-Chung Yew: The Performance of Runtime Data Cache Prefetching in a Dynamic Optimization System. MICRO 2003.
4. Jiwei Lu, Howard Chen, Pen-Chung Yew, Wei Chung Hsu: Design and Implementation of a Lightweight Dynamic Optimization System. Journal of Instruction-Level Parallelism, Volume 6, 2004
5. Chi-Keung Luk, Robert Muth, Harish Patil, Robert Cohn, Geoff Lowney: Ispike: A Post-link Optimizer for the IntelItaniumArchitecture. CGO, 2004.
6. R. Cohn, D. Goodwin, P. G. Lowney and N. Rubin: Spike: An Optimizer for Alpha/NT Executables. Proc. USENIX Windows NT Workshop, Aug. 1997.
7. David W. Goodwin: Interprocedural dataflow analysis in an executable optimizer. PLDI, 1997
8. M. Probst, A. Krall, B. Scholz: Register Liveness Analysis for Optimizing Dynamic Binary Translation. Ninth Working Conference on Reverse Engineering(WCRE'02).
9. Cmelik, B. and Keppel, D. 1994: Shade: a fast instruction-set simulator for execution profiling. SIGMETRICS Perform. Eval. Rev. 22, 1 (May. 1994), 128-137.
10. Robert F. Cmelik and David Keppel: Shade: A fast instruction-set simulator for execution profiling. Technical Report 93-06-06, CS&E, U. of Washington, June 1993
11. Bala, V., Duesterwald, E., and Banerjia, S: Dynamo: a transparent dynamic optimization system. PLDI, 2000.
12. Bruening, D., Garnett, T., and Amarasinghe, S: An infrastructure for adaptive dynamic optimization. CGO, 2003.
13. Luk, C.-K., Cohn, R., Muth, R., Patil, H., Klauser, A., Lowney, G., Wallace, S., Reddi, V. J., Hazelwood, K.: Pin: Building Customized Program Analysis Tools with Dynamic Instrumentation. PLDI, June 2005.
14. Saxena, A., Hsu, W.-C.,: Dynamic Register Allocation for ADORE Runtime Optimization System. Technical Report 04-044, Computer Science, U. of Minnesota, 2004
15. Intel®Itanium®Architecture, Software Developer's Manual, Volume 1, 2 and 3: http://www.intel.com/design/itanium/manuals/iiasdmanual.htm.
16. UltraSPARC™III Processor User's Manual: http://www.sun.com/processors/-manuals/USIIIv2.pdf
17. Jesshope, C. R.: Implementing an efficient vector instruction set in a chip multiprocessor using micro-threaded pipelines. Proc. ACSAC 2001, Australia Computer Science Communications, Vol 23, No 4., pp80-88

A Heterogeneous Multi-core Processor Architecture for High Performance Computing

Jianjun Guo, Kui Dai, and Zhiying Wang

School of Computer, National University of Defense Technology,
410073 Changsha, Hunan, China
jjguo@tom.com

Abstract. The increasing application demands put great pressure on high performance processor design. This paper presents a multi-core System-on-Chip architecture for high performance computing. It is composed of a sparcv8-compliant LEON3 host processor and a data parallel coprocessor based on transport triggered architecture, all of which are tied with a 32-bit AMBA AHB bus. The LEON3 processor performs control tasks and the data parallel coprocessor performs computing intensive tasks. The chip is fabricated in 0.18um standard-cell technology, occupies about 5.3mm^2 and runs at 266MHz.

Keywords: SoC, heterogeneous, multi-core, TTA.

1 Introduction

Nowadays, the application domain is shifting from desktop computers and multi-processors to general-purpose computers and embedded systems, especially with the new applications manipulating all kinds of media signals. These developing applications such as graphics, image and audio/video processing put great pressure on high performance processor design. The increasing application demands make the traditional processors inadequate to meet the application requirements, thus high performance processors are in demand. Chip multiprocessors are a natural trend for a workload which has independent threads, which we need to take advantage of the architecture, and we also need to fit a lot of computation into a small area.

As VLSI technology improves to allow us to fabricate hundreds of millions of transistors on a single chip, it is possible to put a complete multiprocessor, including both CPUs and memory, on a single chip. System-on-Chip (SoC) technology is mature now. One of the advances that will be enabled by SoC technology is the single-chip multiprocessor. Single-chip multiprocessors will be useful not just in low cost servers but also to perform video and a wide variety of consumer applications. The advent of single-chip multiprocessors will require us to rethink multiprocessor architectures to fit the advantages and constraints of VLSI implementation.

This paper studies a heterogeneous multi-core SoC architecture which is composed of a LEON3 processor and a data parallel coprocessor (DPC) based on transport triggered architecture (TTA). It can exploit instruction level parallelism (ILP) as much as possible with support of custom function units for special operations. The rest of this paper is organized as follows. Section 2 briefly describes the LEON3

C. Jesshope and C. Egan (Eds.): ACSAC 2006, LNCS 4186, pp. 359–365, 2006.

processor and the transport triggered architecture. Section 3 describes the proposed multi-core SoC architecture and several architecture decisions. In section 4 performance tests and results are given while the last section concludes and discusses the future work.

2   Overview of LEON3 and TTA

In this section, the sparcv8-complicant LEON3 host processor is introduced first, and then the transport triggered architecture follows.

2.1   The LEON3 Processor

LEON3 is a sparcv8-compliant processor developed by Gaisler Research [1]. It provides sufficient research resources which are centered around the LEON3 processor core and includes a large IP library, behavioral simulators, and related software development tools - all the necessary components to create high quality and high performance products allowing us to shorten the development cycle of new cores and tools. So LEON3 was chosen as our host processor. It is designed with the following main features: advanced 7-stage pipelines, separate instruction and data caches, local instruction and data scratchpad rams, hardware multiply, divide and MAC units. It uses AMBA-2.0 AHB bus interface. Additional modules can easily be added using the on-chip AMBA AHB/APB buses. The model is highly configurable, and particularly suitable for SoC designs.

2.2   Transport Triggered Architecture

Transport triggered architecture (TTA) [2] can provide both flexibility and configurability during the design process. It provides support for instruction level parallelism. Based on the flexibility and configurability of TTA, the high performance processor architecture can be specially designed according to the characteristics of specific applications.

In traditional architectures, one instruction execution is operation triggered. In contrast, transport triggered architectures use data transport to trigger execution. In TTA, the instruction set is composed of only one MOVE instruction implementing assignment among registers. Different register classes are provided: operator registers are used to hold operands and result registers are used to hold the computing results while trigger register triggers an operation whenever updated. Here, a standard RISC instruction can be decomposed into a series of MOVE operations. For example, a usual add operation can be presented as follows:

$$add\ r_3, r_2, r_1 \quad => \quad r_1 \text{->} O_{add}; \quad r_2 \text{->} T_{add}; \quad R_{add} \text{->} r_3$$

Transport triggered processors have very small cycle times for instruction execution, because they reduce every operation to a MOVE instruction. Moreover, fine-grained parallelism can be exploited: each basic step previously handled by the pipeline organization is now available to the compiler for parallelism extraction. On the other hand, TTA completely relies on compiler heuristics to achieve higher performance. The transport network required to allow data movement among different registers presents the same challenges as any computer networks including the need to avoid performance bottlenecks. As shown in Fig. 1, the structure of TTA is very simple. Function units (FU) and register files (RF) are connected to buses by sockets.

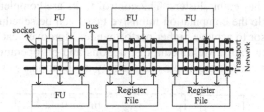

Fig. 1. General Structure of TTA. It is composed of function units and register files, all of which are connected by the transport network.

In TTA, the number of the function units, register files and their ports, buses and bus connections can be configured according to the analyses of application characteristics. This brings the flexibility for the architecture design. In addition, one TTA instruction always contains several parallel data move operations after software optimization. For example, a TTA instruction under 6 buses is shown as follows:

$$r_5 \rightarrow O_{add}; \quad r_2 \rightarrow T_{add}; \quad R_{mac} \rightarrow r_0; \quad r_1 \rightarrow O_{sub}; \quad r_7 \rightarrow T_{sub}; \quad R_{mul} \rightarrow r_3;$$

The maximum number of parallel operations is the same as the number of the buses. Therefore, the increase of the bus number brings increase of performance. In addition, the architecture designer can customize special operations into the instruction set by designing special function units for some special operations [3]. Thus, some critical bottleneck operations in a specific application can be accomplished by special function units to meet performance requirements of the application.

3 Implementation

In this section, the typical benchmark applications used in the experiments will be given first. Then the proposed multi-core SoC architecture will be described and several architecture decisions will be made.

3.1 Typical Benchmark Applications

Several benchmark applications from TI DSP library [7] are selected to do the experiments. FFT is the fast fourier transform as a fast implementation of discrete fourier transform. IIR is the infinite impulse response filter while FIR is the finite impulse response filter. IDCT is the inverse discrete cosine transform frequently used in video processing applications to decode the compressed image. MATRIX is the multiplication of two matrixes. MAX is to find a maximum number from an array. These kernel applications are frequently used in many embedded DSP applications so accelerating these applications is a matter of great significance.

3.2   The Whole Architecture and Function Units Design

The whole SoC architecture is depicted in Fig. 2. It is composed of a LEON3 host processor and TTA-based DPC along with sufficient external interfaces. The TTA-based coprocessor has eight clusters. The control tasks are completed by the LEON3 host processor while the computation intensive tasks can be scheduled to the clusters by the host processor to achieve higher performance. Moreover, each cluster has eight parallel SIMD Data Paths. Multimedia instructions and bit operations are added into the instruction set to accelerate media and security applications.

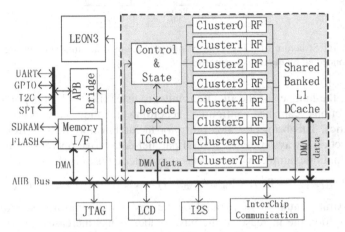

Fig. 2. Overview of the Whole Architecture

The type and number of major operations which is derived from the analysis of simulation results determines the type and number of the function units in TTA to meet the application requirements. According to the type of the operation, designer can quickly decide what function unit to implement; similarly, the number of function units is decided according to the proportion of the equivalent operations. In the simulation independent of architecture, the parallelism upper bound is determined through trace analysis. The number of the buses determines how many operations can be executed at the same time, and so the parallelism upper bound means how many buses should be used. The number of the average active registers shows that how many registers should exist at the same time both to save the hardware cost and to keep the performance.

Specific configuration of function units in each cluster is given as follows. Four integer ALUs perform the common operations including the arithmetical and logical ones. To support many embedded applications better, sub-word parallelism on half-word or byte is added. Two floating-point units perform operations on single and double precision floating-point operands. The floating-point unit is fully pipelined and a new operation can be started every clock cycle except that floating-point divide operation which requires 20 clock cycles and is not pipelined. Three compare units do the compare operation and return a result, which can be used to predicate the conditional transfers by the conditional codes. One CORDIC unit is designed based on the parallelization of the original CORDIC algorithm [4] and to compute many complex functions with a delay of 33 clock cycles.

3.3 Memory System

Research in [5] shows that SRAM is complex and not friendly to compiler and its performance is not necessarily better than traditional cache-based architecture. So we still choose the cache-based architecture. While as illustrated in [6], sharing L2 cache among multiple cores is significantly less attractive when interconnect overheads are taken into account than when the factors of delay and area are ignored. So only L1 cache and large register file system is chosen in our design. The L1 cache is multi-banked and high-bit address interleaved.

256-bit long cache-line is selected to achieve higher performance. Longer cache-line can exploit better data spatial locality and can support vector operations too. The performance of DPC under write-through and write-back policy is compared. The read and write miss ratio for several benchmark applications under write-back policy are shown in Table 1. Performance gains compared with write-through policy is also given in Table 1. From Table 1, it can be seen that write-back policy achieves a better performance and becomes our final choice. It is due to that the write-back policy can work better with the longer cache-line and can save memory bandwidth while the write-through policy will waste more memory bandwidth.

DMA channels are used to allow the host processor or other peripherals to access the processed data quickly. TTA structure depends on scheduling algorithms heavily, so the number of registers for compiler use is performance sensitive. For register file, 8 banked and total 128 registers with 1R/1W port are used in our design as a tradeoff of performance and cost.

Table 1. The Read/Write miss ratio under write-back policy and its performance gains

Application	Read miss ratio	Write miss ratio	Performance gains
FFT	6.10%	2.53%	4.35%
IIR	0.05%	2.09%	7.43%
FIR	0.05%	0.78%	13.27%
IDCT	7.50%	0.00%	2.23%
MATRIX	10.42%	4.17%	0.27%

4 Experimental Results

A prototype chip with the host processor and one cluster is first implemented and tested with different technology to verify our design. The performance comparison is given too.

4.1 Implementation with Different Technologies

The prototype design is first implemented on a FPGA board. The Gidel's PROCStar board is utilized, which comprises three large ALTERA EP1S80F780 devices. The prototype runs at 20MHz and the application tests are all done and passed under this platform. Then under the clock frequency of 266 MHz, the implementation of the prototype design utilizing a 0.18um CMOS standard cell technology resulted in an area of approximate 5.3mm^2 including expected layout overhead with regard to the synthesis results with the Synopsys® Design Compiler®.

4.2 Performance Comparison of the Whole Chip

The performance speedup of several typical applications from TI DSP library [7] on DPC compared with LEON3 is given in Table 2. It can be seen from Table 2 that DPC achieves a considerable speedup compared with LEON3 processor. The extraordinary speedup of IIR and FIR is due to that they use sine operation frequently which can be accelerated by the CORDIC function unit in DPC.

Table 2. The typical applications performance comparison between LEON3 and DPC. The speedup is given here.

Application	Speedup
radix-4 complex 128-dot FFT	3.84
500-dot IIR	348.89
128-dot FIR	3797.11
8x8 IDCT	2.86
64-dot MAX	5.20

5   Conclusions and Future Work

From above, it can be seen that the heterogeneous multi-core architecture composed of LEON3 and DPC achieves higher performance. Moreover, clock gating technology can be easily used to lower power dissipation due to its clear architecture. Given a fixed circuit area, using heterogeneous multi-core architectures instead of homo-geneous chip multi-processors can provide significant performance advantages for a multi-programmed workload. First of all, a heterogeneous multi-core architecture can match each application to the core best suited to meet its performance demands. Second, it can provide improved area-efficient coverage of the entire spectrum of different workload demands, from low thread-level parallelism that provides low latency for few applications on powerful cores to high thread-level parallelism in which simple cores can host a large number of applications simultaneously.

Multiprocessors will be important for media processing because this area is characterized by enormous computing power and by a massive amount of data communication and data storage. In the future we won't be able to solve that with a monolithic processor and memory architecture. We'll need distributed architectures to deal with the performance requirements these systems have. Heterogeneous multi-core technology is a better option.

In this paper we studied a heterogeneous multi-core processor that is very suitable for different applications for its flexibility and configurability. Through the application characteristics analysis and special function unit support, it is easy to modify the architecture to adapt to different applications. Traditional processor architecture is fixed, so the software must be adjusted to map to the hardware structure to gain best performance, whereas the DPC is configurable, so the hardware/software co-design method can be used to achieve a higher performance.

In the future work, the application partition techniques and workload scheduling algorithm between both sides will be our main work. An integrated simulator and development environment for both sides will be developed too.

Acknowledgments. The authors would like to thank Andrea Cilio and his colleagues in Delft technology university of Netherlands for their great help and support to our research work.

References

1. http://www.gaisler.com/cms4_5_3/
2. Henk Corporaal and Hans Mulder. MOVE: A framework for high-performance processor design. In Supercomputing91, Albuquerque, November 1991, p692-701
3. Jan Hoogerbrugge. "Code generation for Transport Triggered Architectures." PhD thesis, Delft Univ.of Technology, February 1996. ISBN 90-9009002-9
4. Jack E. Volder. The CORDIC trigonometric computing technique. IRE Transactions on Electronic Computers, vol. 8, 1959, pp. 330–334.
5. Sadagopan Srinivasan, Vinodh Cuppu, and Bruce Jacob. Transparent Data-Memory Organizations for Digital Signal Processors. In Proc. Int'l Conf. on Compilers, Architecture, and Synthesis for Embedded Systems (CASES'01), November 16-17, 2001, Atlanta, Georgia, USA
6. Terry Tao Ye. On-chip multiprocessor communication network design and analysis. PhD thesis, Stanford University, December 2003
7. http://focus.ti.com/docs/toolsw/folders/print/sprc092.html.

Reducing the Branch Power Cost in Embedded Processors Through Static Scheduling, Profiling and SuperBlock Formation

Michael Hicks, Colin Egan, Bruce Christianson, and Patrick Quick

Compiler Technology and Computer Architecture Group (CTCA)
University of Hertfordshire, College Lane, Hatfield, AL10 9AB, UK
m.hicks@herts.ac.uk

Abstract. Dynamic branch predictor logic alone accounts for approximately 10% of total processor power dissipation. Recent research indicates that the power cost of a large dynamic branch predictor is offset by the power savings created by its increased accuracy. We describe a method of reducing dynamic predictor power dissipation without degrading prediction accuracy by using a combination of local delay region scheduling and run time profiling of branches. Feedback into the static code is achieved with hint bits and avoids the need for dynamic prediction for some individual branches. This method requires only minimal hardware modifications and coexists with a dynamic predictor.

1 Introduction

Accurate branch prediction is extremely important in modern pipelined and MII microprocessors [10] [2]. Branch prediction reduces the amount of time spent executing a program by forecasting the likely direction of branch assembly instructions. Mispredicting a branch direction wastes both time and power, by executing instructions in the pipeline which will not be committed. Research [8] [3] has shown that, even with their increased power cost, modern larger predictors actually save global power by the effects of their increased accuracy. This means that any attempt to reduce the power consumption of a dynamic predictor must not come at the cost of decreased accuracy; a holistic attitude to processor power consumption must be employed [7][9].

In this paper we explore the use of delay region scheduling, branch profiling and hint bits (in conjunction with a dynamic predictor) in order to reduce the branch power cost for mobile devices, without reducing accuracy.

2 Branch Delay Region Scheduling

The branch delay region is the period of processor cycles proceeding a branch instruction in the processor pipeline before branch resolution occurs. Instructions can fill this gap either speculatively, using branch prediction, or by the use of scheduling. The examples in this section use a 5 stage MIPS pipeline with 2 delay slots.

C. Jesshope and C. Egan (Eds.): ACSAC 2006, LNCS 4186, pp. 366–372, 2006.
© Springer-Verlag Berlin Heidelberg 2006

2.1 Local Delayed Branch

In contrast to scheduling into the delay region from a target/fallthrough path of
a branch, a locally scheduled delay region consists of branch independent instructions that precede the branch (see Figure 1). A branch independent instruction
is any instruction whose result is not directly or indirectly depended upon by
the branch to calculate its own behaviour.

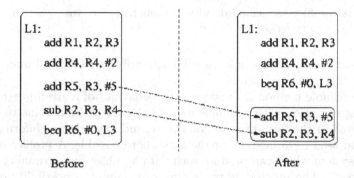

Before   After

Fig. 1. An example of local delayed branch scheduling

Deciding which instructions can be moved into the delay region locally is
straightforward. Starting with the instruction from the bottom of the given basic
block in the static stream, above the branch, examine the target register operand.
If this target register is NOT used as an operand in the computation of the
branch instruction then it can be safely moved into the delay region. This process
continues with the next instruction up from the branch in the static stream, with
the difference that this time the scheduler must decide whether the target of the
instruction is used by any of the other instructions below it (which are in turn
used to compute the branch).

Local Delay Region Scheduling is an excellent method for utilising the delay
region where possible; it is always a win and completely avoids the use of a
branch predictor for the given branch. The clear disadvantage with local delay
region scheduling is that it cannot always be used. There are two situations
that result in this: well optimised code and deeply pipelined processors (where
the delay region is very large). It is our position that, as part of the combined
approach described in this paper, the local delay region is profitable.

3 Profiling

Suppose that we wish to associate a reliable static prediction with as many
branches as possible, so as to reduce accesses to the dynamic branch predictor
of a processor at runtime (in order to save power). This can be achieved to a
reasonable degree through static analysis of the assembly code of a program; it

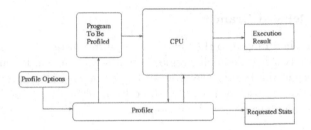

Fig. 2. The profiler is supplied with parameters for the program and the traces/statistics to be logged

is often clear that branches in loops will commonly be taken and internal break points not-taken.

A more reliable method is to observe the behaviour of a given program while undergoing execution with a sample dataset [4]. Each branch instruction can be monitored in the form of a program trace and any relevant information extracted and used to form static predictions where possible. A profiler is any application/system which can produce such data by observing a running program (see Figure 2). The proceeding two sections examine the possibility of removing certain classes of branch from dynamic prediction by the use of run-time profiling.

3.1   Biased Branches

One class of branches that can be removed from dynamic prediction, without impacting on accuracy, are highly biased branches. A biased branch is a branch which is commonly taken or not taken, many times in succession before possibly changing direction briefly. The branch has a bias to one behaviour. These kinds of branches can, in many cases, be seen to waste energy in the predictor since their predicted behaviour will be almost constantly the same [5] [8].

The principles of spatial and temporal locality intuitively tell us that biased branches account for a large proportion of the dynamic instruction stream. Identifying these branches in the static code and flagging them with an accurate static prediction would enable them to be executed without accessing the dynamic predictor. The profiler needs to read the static assembly code and log, for each each branch instruction during profiling, whether it was taken or not taken at each occurrence.

3.2   Difficult to Predict Branches (Anti Prediction)

Another class of branch instructions that would be useful to remove from dynamic branch predictor accesses are difficult to predict branches. In any static program there are branches which are difficult to predict and which are inherently data driven. When a prediction for a given branch is nearly always likely to be wrong, there is little point in consuming power to produce a prediction for it since a number of stalls will likely be incurred anyway [5] [8] [6].

Using profiling, it is possible to locate these branches at runtime using different data sets and by monitoring every branch. The accuracy of each dynamic prediction is required rather than just a given branch's behaviour. For every branch, the profiler needs to compare the predicted behaviour of the branch with the actual behaviour. In the case of those branch instructions where accuracy of the dynamic predictor is consistently poor, it is beneficial to flag the static branch as difficult to predict and avoid accessing the branch predictor at all, letting the processor assume the fallthrough path. Accordingly, filling the delay region with NOP instructions wastes significantly less power executing instructions that are unlikely to be committed.

4   Combined Approach Using Hint Bits

The main goal of the profiling techniques discussed previously can only be realised if there is a way of storing the results in the static code of a program, which can then be used dynamically by the processor to avoid accessing the branch prediction hardware [3].

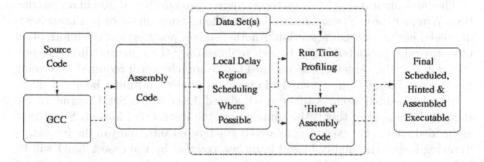

Fig. 3. Block diagram of the proposed scheduling and hinting algorithm. The dotted box indicates the new stages introduced by the algorithm into the creation of an executable program

The combined approach works as follows:

1. Compile the program, using GCC for instance, into assembly code.
2. The Scheduler parses the assembly code and decides for which branch instructions the local delay region can be used (see section 2.1).
3. The Profiler assembles a temporary version of the program and executes it using the specified data set(s). The behaviour of each branch instruction is logged (see section 3).
4. The output from the profiling stage is used to annotate the delay scheduled assembly code.
5. Finally, the resulting annotated assembly code is compiled and linked to form the new executable.

The exact number of branches that can be eliminated from runtime predictor access in the target program depends upon the tuning of the profiler and the number of branches where the local delay region can be used.

4.1 Hint Bits

So far we have described a process of annotating branch instructions in the static assembly code to reflect the use of the local delay region and of the profiling results. The way this is represented in the assembly/machine code is by using an existing method known as hint bits (though now with the new function of power saving).

The four mutually exclusive behaviour hints in our algorithm which need to be stored are:

1. Access the branch predictor for this instruction.
2. or Assume this branch is taken (don't access dynamic predictor logic).
3. or Assume this branch is not taken (don't access dynamic predictor logic).
4. or Use this branch's local delay region (don't access dynamic predictor logic).

The implementation of this method requires two additional bits in an instruction. Whether these bits are located in all of the instruction set or just branches is discussed in the proceeding section. Another salient point is that the information in a statically predicted taken branch replaces only the dynamic direction predictor in full; the target of the assumed taken branch is still required. Accessing the Branch Target Buffer is costly, in terms of power, and must be avoided.

Most embedded architectures are Reduced Instruction Set Computers [8]. Part of the benefit of this is the simplicity of the instruction format. Since most embedded system are executing relatively small programs, many of the frequently iterating loops (the highly biased branches, covered by the case 2 hint) will be PC relative branches. This means that the target address for a majority of these branches will be contained within a fixed position inside the format. This does not require that the instruction undergo any complex predecoding, only that it is offset from the current PC value to provide the target address. Branch instructions that have been marked by the profiler as having a heavy bias towards a taken path, but which do not fall into the PC relative fixed target position category have to be ignored and left for dynamic prediction.

The general 'hinting' algorithm:

1. Initially, set the hint bits of all instructions to: assume not taken (and do not access predictor).
2. Set hint bits to reflect use of the local delay region where the scheduler has used this method.
3. From profiling results, set hint bits to reflect taken biased branches where possible.
4. All remaining branch instructions have their hint bits set to use the dynamic predictor.

4.2   Hardware Requirements/Modifications

The two possible implementation strategies are:

Hardware Simplicity: Annotate every instruction with two hint bits. This is easy to implement in hardware and introduces little additional control logic. All non branch instructions will also be eliminated from branch predictor accesses. The disadvantages of this method are that it requires that the processor's clock frequency is low enough to permit an I-Cache access and branch predictor access in series in one cycle and that there are enough redundant bits in all instructions.

Hardware Complexity: Annotate only branch instructions with hint bits and use a hardware mechanism similar to a Prediction Probe Detector [8] to interpret hint bits. This has minimal effect on the instruction set. It also means there is no restriction to series access of the I-Cache then branch predictor. The main disadvantage is the newly introduced PPD and the need for instructions to pass through the pipeline once before the PPD will restrict predictor access.

The hardware simplicity model offers the greatest power savings and is particularly applicable for the embedded market where the clock frequency is generally relatively low, thus a series access is possible. It is for these reason we the use the hardware simplicity model. In order to save additional power, some minor modifications must be made to the Execution stage to stop the statically predicted instruction from expending power writing back their results to the predictor (since their results will never be used!).

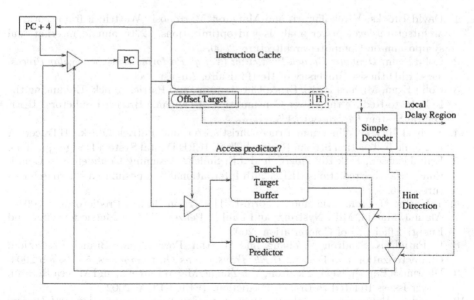

Fig. 4. Diagram of required hardware modifications. The block below the I-Cache represents a fetched example instruction (in this case a hinted taken branch).

It can be seen that after a given program has had its hint bits set, all of the branches assigned static predictions (of taken or not taken) have now essentially formed superblocks, with branch resolution acting as a possible exit point from the newly formed super block. When a hint bit prediction proves to be incorrect, it simply acts as a new source of a branch misprediction; it is left for the existing dynamic predictor logic to resolve.

5   Conclusion and Future Work

Branch predictors in modern processors are vital for performance. Their accuracy is also a great source of powersaving, through the reduction of energy spent on misspeculation [8]. However, branch predictors themselves are often comparable to the size of a small cache and dissipate a non trivial amount of power. The work outlined in this paper will help reduce the amount of power dissipated by the predictor hardware itself, whilst not significantly affecting the prediction accuracy. We have begun implementing these modifications in the Wattch [1] power analysis framework (based on the SimpleScalar processor simulator). To test the effectiveness of the modifications and algorithm, we can have chosen to use the EEMBC benchmark suite, which provides a range of task characterisations for embedded processors.

Future investigation includes the possibility of dynamically modifying the hinted predictions contained within instructions to reflect newly dynamically discovered biased branches.

References

1. David Brooks, Vivek Tiwari, and Margaret Martonosi. Wattch: a framework for architectural-level power analysis and optimizations. 27th annual international symposium on Computer architecture, 2000.
2. Colin Egan. *Dynamic Branch Prediction In High Performance Super Scalar Processors*. PhD thesis, University of Hertfordshire, August 2000.
3. Colin Egan, Michael Hicks, Bruce Christianson, and Patrick Quick. Enhancing the I-Cache to Reduce the Power Consumption of Dynamic Branch Predictors. IEEE Digital System Design, jul 2005.
4. Michael Hicks, Colin Egan, Bruce Christianson, and Patrick Quick. HTracer: A Dynamic Instruction Stream Research Tool. IEEE Digital System Design, jul 2005.
5. Erik Jacobsen, Erik Rotenberg, and J.E. Smith. Assigning Confidence to Conditional Branch Predictions. IEEE 29th International Symposium on Microarchitecture, 1996.
6. J. Karlin, D. Stefanovic, and S. Forrest. The Triton Branch Predictor, oct 2004.
7. Alain J. Martin, Mika Nystrom, and Paul L. Penzes. ET^2: A Metric for Time and Energy Efficiency of Computation. 2003.
8. D. Parikh, K. Skadron, Y. Zhang, and M. Stan. Power Aware Branch Prediction: Characterization and Design. *IEEE Transactions On Computers*, 53(2), feb 2004.
9. Dharmesh Parikh, Kevin Skadron, Yan Zhang, Marco Barcella, and Mircea R. Stan. Power Issues Related to Branch Prediction. IEEE HPCA, 2002.
10. David A. Patterson and John L. Hennessy. *Computer Organization and Design: The Hardware Software Interface*. Morgan Kaufmann, second edition, 1998.

Fault-Free Pairwise Independent Hamiltonian Paths on Faulty Hypercubes

Sun-Yuan Hsieh

Department of Computer Science and Information Engineering,
National Cheng Kung University,
No. 1, University Road, Tainan 70101, Taiwan
`hsiehsy@mail.ncku.edu.tw`

Abstract. A *Hamiltonian path* in G is a path which contains every vertex of G exactly once. Two Hamiltonian paths $P_1 = \langle u_1, u_2, \ldots, u_n \rangle$ and $P_2 = \langle v_1, v_2, \ldots, v_n \rangle$ of G are said to be *independent* if $u_1 = v_1$, $u_n = v_n$, and $u_i \neq v_i$ for all $1 < i < n$. A set of Hamiltonian paths $\{P_1, P_2, \ldots, P_k\}$ of G are *mutually independent* if any two different Hamiltonian paths in the set are independent. It is well-known that an n-dimensional hypercube Q_n is bipartite with two partite sets of equal-size. Let F be the set of faulty edges of Q_n such that $|F| \leq n - 2$. In this paper, we show that $Q_n - F$ contains $(n - |F| - 1)$-mutually independent Hamiltonian paths between any two vertices from different partite sets, where $n \geq 2$.

Keywords: Interconnection networks, hypercubes, Hamiltonian, pairwise independent Hamiltonian paths, fault-tolerant embedding.

1 Introduction

A *graph* $G = (V, E)$ is a pair of the *vertex set* V and the *edge set* E, where V is a finite set and E is a subset of $\{(u, v) \mid (u, v)$ is an unordered pair of $V\}$. We also use $V(G)$ and $E(G)$ to denote the vertex set and the edge set of G, respectively. Let n and m be the numbers of vertices and edges of G, respectively. *Interconnection network* (*network* for short) is usually represented by a graph where vertices represent processors and edges represent communication links between processors. There are several pairwise conflicting requirements in designing the topology for networks. The interested readers may refer to [1,11,16] for extensive references. Among them, the hypercube [2,12] has several excellent properties such as recursive structure, regularity, symmetry, small diameter, relatively short mean internode distance, low degree, and much small link (edge) complexity, which are very important for designing massively parallel or distributed systems. It is almost impossible to design a network which is optimal from all aspects. Specifically, fault-tolerance is highly desirable in massive parallel systems that have a relative high probability of failure. A number of fault-tolerant considerations for specific multiprocessor architectures have been discussed (for example, see [3,5,6,8,9,10,13,14,15]).

C. Jesshope and C. Egan (Eds.): ACSAC 2006, LNCS 4186, pp. 373–379, 2006.

Two vertices u and v are *adjacent* iff $(u, v) \in E(G)$. A *path* $P[v_0, v_k] = \langle v_0, v_1, \ldots, v_k \rangle$ in G is a sequence of distinct vertices such that any two consecutive vertices are adjacent. A path may contain other *subpath*, denoted as $\langle v_0, v_1, \ldots, v_i, P[v_i, v_j], v_j, v_{j+1}, \ldots, v_k \rangle$, where $P[v_i, v_j] = \langle v_i, v_{i+1}, \ldots, v_{j-1}, v_j \rangle$. A *cycle* is a path with $v_0 = v_k$ and $k \geq 3$. A path in G is called a *Hamiltonian path* if it contains every vertex of G exactly once. Two Hamiltonian paths in a graph G, $P_1 = \langle u_1, u_2, \ldots, u_n \rangle$ and $P_2 = \langle v_1, v_2, \ldots, v_n \rangle$, are *independent* if $u_1 = v_1$, $u_n = v_n$, and $u_i \neq v_i$ for every $1 < i < n$; and both are *full-independent* if $u_i \neq v_i$ for every $1 \leq i \leq n$. Moreover, P_1 and P_2, are *independent at* u_1 if $u_1 = v_1$ and $u_i \neq v_i$ for every $1 < i \leq n$. A set of Hamiltonian paths $\{P_1, P_2, \ldots, P_k\}$ of G, where $P_1 = \langle u_1, u_2, \ldots, u_n \rangle$, are *pairwise independent* (respectively, *pairwise full-independent*, *pairwise independent at* u_1) if any two different Hamiltonian paths in the set are independent (respectively, full-independent, independent at u_1). Broadcasting is the information dissemination problem that consists, for one node of a network, to send its pieces of information to all the other nodes of a network. Constructing a set of k pairwise independent Hamiltonian paths enable us to efficiently broadcast a message formed by k pieces on a graph G: one end-vertex of the paths works as the source to send the k pieces of the given message along the k parallel Hamiltonian paths. This broadcasting can be done in $O(n)$ time under the all-port model, where n is the number of vertices of G.

A graph $G = (V_0 \cup V_1, E)$ is *bipartite* if V is the union of two disjoint sets V_0 and V_1 such that every edge $(u, v) \in E$ implies either $u \in V_0$ and $v \in V_1$ or $u \in V_1$ and $v \in V_0$. It is well known that the hypercube is bipartite. Since edge failures may occur when a network is put into use, it is meaningful to consider networks with faulty edges. In this paper, we attempt to construct pairwise independent fault-free Hamiltonian paths in an n-dimensional hypercube $Q_n = (V_0 \cup V_1, E)$ with faulty edges, which is quite different from finding "exactly one" fault-free Hamiltonian cycle in the arrangement graph [6], longest path in the star graph [7,8,10], and arbitrary-length cycle in the Möbius cube [9]. Let F be the set of faulty edges of Q_n such that $|F| \leq n - 2$. We show the following three results:

1. $Q_n - F$, where $n \geq 2$, contains $(n - |F| - 1)$-pairwise full-independent Hamiltonian paths between two adjacent vertices.[1]
2. $Q_n - F$, where $n \geq 2$, contains $(n - |F| - 1)$-pairwise independent Hamiltonian paths starting at any vertex $v \in V_i$ to $n - |F| - 1$ distinct vertices belonging to V_{1-i}, where $i \in \{0, 1\}$.
3. $Q_n - F$, where $n \geq 2$, contains $(n - |F| - 1)$-pairwise independent Hamiltonian paths between any two vertices from different partite sets, where $n \geq 2$.

2   Preliminaries

A *subgraph* of $G = (V, E)$ is a graph (V', E') such that $V' \subseteq V$ and $E' \subseteq E$. Given a set $V' \subseteq V$, the subgraph of $G = (V, E)$ *induced* by V' is the graph

---

[1] Let F be a set of edges of a graph G. Throughout this paper, the notation $G - F$ represents the resulting graph obtained by deleting those edges in F from G.

$G' = (V', E')$, where $E' = \{(u, v) \in E \mid u, v \in V'\}$. For a vertex u in $G = (V, E)$, the *neighborhood* of u, denoted by $N_G(u)$, is the set $\{v \mid (u, v) \in E\}$. Moreover, $|N_G(u)|$ is the degree of u, denoted by $deg_G(u)$. For a path $P = \langle v_1, v_2, \ldots, v_k \rangle$ in G, let $P(i)$ denote the ith vertex of P, i.e., $P(i) = v_i$.

An *n-dimensional hypercube* (*n-cube* for short) Q_n is a graph with 2^n vertices in which each vertex u is labelled by an n-bit binary string $u = u_n u_{n-1} \ldots u_1$, where $u_i \in \{0, 1\}$. For $i \in \{1, 2, \ldots, n\}$, we use $u^i = v_n v_{n-1} \ldots v_1$ to denote the *ith neighbor of* u such that $v_i = 1 - u_i$ and $v_j = u_j$ for all $j \in \{1, 2, \ldots, n\}$ and $j \neq i$. Two vertices are adjacent if and only if their strings differ exactly in one bit position. An edge $e = (u, v) \in E(Q_n)$ is said to be of *dimension i* if $u = b_n b_{n-1} \ldots b_i \ldots b_1$ and $v = b_n b_{n-1} \ldots \overline{b_i} \ldots b_1$, where $b_j \in \{0, 1\}$ for $j = 1, 2, \ldots, n$, and $\overline{b_i}$ is the *one's complement of* b_i, i.e., $\overline{b_i} = 1 - b_i$. Note that there are 2^{n-1} edges in each dimension. The *Hamming weight* of $u = u_n u_{n-1} \ldots u_1$, denoted by $w(u)$, is the number of i such that $u_i = 1$. Since the degree of each vertex equals n, Q_n is an n-regular graph. Moreover, Q_n is a bipartite graph with bipartition $\{u \mid w(u) \text{ is odd}\}$ and $\{u \mid w(u) \text{ is even}\}$. For convenience, we use *black vertices* to denote those vertices of odd weight and *white vertices* to denote those vertices of even weight.

An n-cube Q_n can be represented by $\underbrace{* * \ldots *}_{n}$, where $* \in \{0, 1\}$ means the *"don't care"* symbol. An *i-partition on* $Q_n = \underbrace{* * \ldots *}_{n}$ is to partition Q_n along dimension i for some $i \in \{1, 2, \ldots, n\}$, into two *subcubes*, $Q_{n-1}^0 = \underbrace{* * \ldots *}_{n-i} 0 \underbrace{* * \ldots *}_{i-1}$ and $Q_{n-1}^1 = \underbrace{* * \ldots *}_{n-i} 1 \underbrace{* * \ldots *}_{i-1}$, where Q_{n-1}^0 and Q_{n-1}^1 are the subgraph of Q_n induced by $\{x_n x_{n-1} \ldots x_i \ldots x_1 \in V(Q_n) \mid x_i = 0\}$ and $\{x_n x_{n-1} \ldots x_i \ldots x_1 \in V(Q_n) \mid x_i = 1\}$, respectively. Note that each Q_{n-1}^j, $j \in \{0, 1\}$, is isomorphic to an $(n-1)$-cube. Assume that Q_{n-1}^0 and Q_{n-1}^1 are the subcubes after executing an *i-partition* on Q_n. The set of *crossing edges*, denoted by E_c, is $\{(u, v) \in E(Q_n) \mid u \in V(Q_{n-1}^0), v \in V(Q_{n-1}^1)\}$. Let F be the set of faulty edges of Q_n. Throughout this paper, we assume that $|F| \leq n - 2$. Let $F_0 = F \cap E(Q_{n-1}^0)$, $F_1 = F \cap E(Q_{n-1}^1)$, and $F_c = F \cap E_c$.

3   Fault-Free Pairwise Independent Hamiltonian Paths

We first provide a previous known property which is useful in our method.

Lemma 1. [14] *Let Q_n, $n \geq 2$, be an n-cube with $|F| \leq n - 2$. Then, $Q_n - F$ contains a fault-free Hamiltonian path between any two vertices from different partite sets.*

For convenience, we define $\delta = n - |F| - 1$ in the remainder of this paper.

Lemma 2 (Many-to-many). *Let Q_n, $n \geq 2$, be an n-cube with $|F| \leq n - 2$, and $\{(u_1, v_1), (u_2, v_2), \ldots, (u_\delta, v_\delta)\} \subset E(Q_n)$. Then, $Q_n - F$ contains δ-pairwise full-independent Hamiltonian paths $P_1[u_1, v_1], P_2[u_2, v_2], \ldots, P_\delta[u_\delta, v_\delta]$.*

Proof. The proof is by induction on n. The basis cases where $n = 2, 3$ clearly holds (the case where $n = 3$ can be easily verified by a computer program). We now consider an n-cube for $n \geq 4$. If $|F| = n - 2$, then $\delta = 1$. By Lemma 1, $Q_n - F$ contains a Hamiltonian path between any two vertices from different partite sets. Therefore, the result holds for $|F| = n - 2$. We next consider the situation in which the number of faulty edges is at most $n - 3$. For each $d \in \{1, 2, \ldots, n\}$, let c_d be the cardinality of the set $\{(u_i, v_i)|$ the dimension of (u_i, v_i) equals d, where $i \in \{1, 2, \ldots, \delta\}\}$. Without loss of generality, assume that $c_1 \geq c_2 \geq \cdots \geq c_n$. Obviously, $c_n = 0$ because $\delta = n - |F| - 1$. We then execute an n-partition on Q_n to obtain Q_{n-1}^0 and Q_{n-1}^1. Note that each (u_i, v_i) is in either Q_{n-1}^0 or Q_{n-1}^1. Let p be the cardinality of the set $\{(u_i, v_i) \in E(Q_{n-1}^0)|i \in \{1, 2, \ldots, \delta\}\}$ and let q be the cardinality of the set $\{(u_i, v_i) \in E(Q_{n-1}^1)|i \in \{1, 2, \ldots, \delta\}\}$. Clearly, $p + q = \delta$. Without loss of generality, assume that $\{(u_1, v_1), (u_2, v_2), \ldots, (u_p, v_p)\} \subset E(Q_{n-1}^0)$ and $\{(u_{p+1}, v_{p+1}), (u_{p+2}, v_{p+2}), \ldots, (u_\delta, v_\delta)\} \subset E(Q_{n-1}^1)$. Since $|F_0| \leq |F| - 1 \leq n - 3$ and $(n - 1) - |F_0| - 1 \geq (n - 1) - (|F| - 1) - 1 = n - |F| - 1 = \delta \geq p$, by the induction hypothesis, $Q_{n-1}^0 - F_0$ contains p-pairwise full-independent Hamiltonian paths $P_1[u_1, v_1], P_2[u_2, v_2], \ldots, P_p[u_p, v_p]$. On the other hand, since $|F_1| \leq |F| - 1 \leq n - 3$ and $(n - 1) - |F_1| - 1 \geq (n - 1) - (|F| - 1) - 1 = n - |F| - 1 = \delta \geq q$, $Q_{n-1}^1 - F_1$ contains q-pairwise full-independent Hamiltonian paths $P_{p+1}[u_{p+1}, v_{p+1}], P_{p+2}[u_{p+2}, v_{p+2}], \ldots, P_\delta[u_\delta, v_\delta]$. Then, there exist edges $(P_i(t), P_i(t + 1)) \in E(P_i[u_i, v_i])$ for all $i \in \{1, 2, \ldots, \delta\}$, where $t \in \{1, 2, \ldots, 2^{n-1} - 1\}$, such that the crossing edges $(P_i(t), P_i(t)^n)$ and $(P_i(t + 1), P_i(t + 1)^n)$ are both fault-free. (The reason is explained below: Since the number of edges in $P_i[u_i, v_i]$ equals $2^{n-1} - 1$, if these edges do not exist, then $|F| \geq |F_c| \geq \lceil \frac{2^{n-1}-1}{2} \rceil > n - 2$ for $n \geq 3$, which is a contradiction.) Each path $P_i[u_i, v_i]$ can thus be represented by $\langle u_i, P_i'[u_i, P_i(t)], P_i(t), P_i(t + 1), P_i''[P_i(t + 1), v_i], v_i \rangle$. Since $|F_1| \leq |F| - 1 \leq n - 3$ and $(n - 1) - |F_1| - 1 \geq (n - 1) - (|F| - 1) - 1 = n - |F| - 1 = \delta \geq q$, by the induction hypothesis, $Q_{n-1}^1 - F_1$ contains q-pairwise full-independent Hamiltonian paths $R_1[P_1(t)^n, P_1(t + 1)^n], R_2[P_2(t)^n, P_2(t+1)^n], \ldots, R_p[P_p(t)^n, P_p(t+1)^n]$. Similarly, $Q_{n-1}^0 - F_0$ also contains q-pairwise full-independent Hamiltonian paths $R_{p+1}[P_{p+1}(t)^n, P_{p+1}(t+1)^n], R_{p+2}[P_{p+2}(t)^n, P_{p+2}(t+1)^n], \ldots, R_\delta[P_\delta(t)^n, P_\delta(t+1)^n]$. Then, $\{\langle u_i, P_i'[u_i, P_i(t)], P_i(t), P_i(t)^n, R_i[P_i(t)^n, P_i(t+1)^n], P_i(t+1)^n, P_i(t+1), P_i''[P_i(t+1), v_i], v_i \rangle | 1 \leq i \leq \delta\}$ forms δ-pairwise full-independent fault-free Hamiltonian paths in Q_n. $\square$

Lemma 3 (One-to-many). *Let Q_n, $n \geq 2$, be an n-cube with $|F| \leq n - 2$. Let s be an arbitrary black (respectively, white) vertex in Q_n and $w_1, w_2, \ldots, w_\delta \subset V(Q_n)$ be δ distinct white (respectively, black) vertices. Then, $Q_n - F$ contains δ-pairwise independent Hamiltonian paths $P_1[s, w_1], P_2[s, w_2], \ldots, P_\delta[s, w_\delta]$ starting at s.*

Proof. Due to the space-limitation, the proof is omitted. $\square$

We next present another result regarding to pairwise independent Hamiltonian paths between two arbitrary vertices from different partite sets.

Theorem 1 (One-to-one). *Let Q_n, $n \geq 2$, be an n-cube with $|F| \leq n - 2$. Then, $Q_n - F$ contains δ-pairwise independent Hamiltonian paths between two arbitrary vertices from different partite sets.*

Proof. Let b and w be two arbitrary vertices from different partite sets. Without loss of generality, assume that b is a black vertex and w is a white vertex. In the following, we attempt to construct δ-pairwise independent Hamiltonian paths between b and w. The proof is by induction on n. The basis cases where $n = 2$ clearly holds. We now consider an n-cube for $n \geq 3$. If $|F| = n - 2$, then $\delta = 1$. By Lemma 1, $Q_n - F$ contains a Hamiltonian path between b and w. We next consider the situation in which the number of faulty edges is at most $n - 3$. Let $d \in \{1, 2, \ldots, n\} - \{k|$ there is a faulty edge of dimension $k\}$. A d-partition is executed on Q_n to obtain Q_{n-1}^0 and Q_{n-1}^1. Note that $F_c = \emptyset$ after this d-partition. Without loss of generality, assume that $b \in V(Q_{n-1}^0)$. There are the following two cases.

Case 1: Both b and w are in Q_{n-1}^0. Since $|F_0| \leq |F| - 1 \leq n - 3$ and $(n - 1) - |F_0| - 1 \geq (n - 1) - (|F| - 1) - 1 = n - |F| - 1 = \delta$, by the induction hypothesis, $Q_{n-1}^0 - F_0$ contains δ-pairwise independent Hamiltonian paths $P_1[b, w], P_2[b, w], \ldots, P_\delta[b, w]$. Note that $(P_i(t), P_i(t + 1))$ is an edge for all $i \in \{1, 2, \ldots, \delta\}$, where $t \in \{1, 2, \ldots, 2^{n-1} - 1\}$, and the crossing edges $(P_i(t), P_i(t)^d)$ and $(P_i(t + 1), P_i(t + 1)^d)$ are both fault-free because $F_c = \emptyset$. Note that $P_i[b, w] = \langle b, P_i'[b, P_i(t)], P_i(t), P_i(t + 1), P_i''[P_i(t + 1), w], w\rangle$. On the other hand, since $|F_1| \leq |F| - 1 \leq n - 3$ and $(n-1) - |F_1| - 1 \geq (n-1) - (|F| - 1) - 1 = n - |F| - 1 = \delta$, by Lemma 2, $Q_{n-1}^1 - F_1$ contains δ-pairwise full-independent Hamiltonian paths $R_1[P_1(t)^d, P_1(t + 1)^d], R_2[P_2(t)^d, P_2(t + 1)^d], \ldots, R_\delta[P_\delta(t)^d, P_\delta(t+1)^d]$. Then, $\{\langle b, P_i'[b, P_i(t)], P_i(t), P_i(t)^d, R_i[P_i(t)^d, P_i(t+1)^d], P_i(t+1)^d, P_i(t+1), P_i''[P_i(t+1), w], w\rangle| 1 \leq i \leq \delta\}$ forms δ-pairwise independent fault-free Hamiltonian paths in Q_n.

Case 2: $b \in V(Q_{n-1}^0)$ and $w \in V(Q_{n-1}^1)$. Let $w_1, w_2, \ldots, w_\delta$ be arbitrary δ white vertices in Q_{n-1}^0. Since $|F_0| \leq |F| - 1 \leq n - 3$ and $(n - 1) - |F_0| - 1 \geq (n - 1) - (|F| - 1) - 1 = n - |F| - 1 = \delta$, by Lemma 3, $Q_{n-1}^0 - F_0$ contains δ-pairwise independent Hamiltonian paths $P_1[b, w_1], P_2[b, w_2], \ldots, P_\delta[b, w_\delta]$ starting at b. Note that $w_1^d, w_2^d, \ldots, w_\delta^d$ are all black vertices in Q_{n-1}^1. Similarly, since $|F_1| \leq |F| - 1 \leq n - 3$ and $(n - 1) - |F_1| - 1 \geq (n - 1) - (|F| - 1) - 1 = n - |F| - 1 = \delta$, by Lemma 3, $Q_{n-1}^1 - F_1$ contains δ-pairwise independent Hamiltonian paths $R_1[w_1^d, w], R_2[w_2^d, w], \ldots, R_\delta[w_\delta^d, w]$. Then, $\{\langle b, P_i[b, w_i], w_i, w_i^d, R_i[w_i^d, w], w\rangle| 1 \leq i \leq \delta\}$ forms δ-pairwise independent fault-free Hamiltonian paths in Q_n.

By combing the above two cases, we complete the result.   □

4   Concluding Remarks

In this paper, we focus on fault-tolerant embedding, with the n-dimensional faulty hypercube Q_n being the host graph and Hamiltonian paths being the guest graph. We have shown the following results to demonstrate fault-tolerant embedding ability of pairwise independent Hamiltonian paths.

1. When $|F| \leq n - 2$, $Q_n - F$ contains $(n - |F| - 1)$-pairwise full-independent Hamiltonian paths between two adjacent vertices, where $n \geq 2$.
2. When $|F| \leq n - 2$, $Q_n - F$, contains $(n - |F| - 1)$-pairwise independent Hamiltonian paths starting at any vertex $v \in V_i$ to $n - |F| - 1$ distinct vertices belonging to V_{1-i}, where $i \in \{0, 1\}$ and $n \geq 2$.
3. When $|F| \leq n - 2$, $Q_n - F$ contains $(n - |F| - 1)$-pairwise independent Hamiltonian paths between any two vertices from different partite sets, where $n \geq 2$.

Since Q_n is regular of degree n, the number of tolerable faulty edges, the length of each fault-free paths, and the number of fault-free paths obtained are optimal with respect to a worse case where all faulty edges are incident to one common vertex.

References

1. J. C. Bermond, Ed., "Interconnection networks," a special issue of *Discrete Applied Mathematics*, vol. 37–38, 1992.
2. L. Bhuyan, and D. P. Agrawal, "Generalized hypercubes and hyperbus structure for a computer network," *IEEE Transactions on Computers*, c. 33, pp. 323–333, 1984.
3. J. Bruck, R. Cypher, and D. Soroker, "Embedding cube-connected-cycles graphs into faulty hypercubes," *IEEE Transactions on Computers*, vol. 43, no. 10, pp. 1210–1220, 1994.
4. M. Y. Chan and S. J. Lee, "Fault-tolerant embeddings of complete binary trees in hypercubes," *IEEE Transactions on Parallel and Distributed Systems*, vol. 4, no. 3, pp. 540–547, 1993.
5. Dajin Wang, "Embedding Hamiltonian cycles into folded hypercubes with faulty links," *Journal of Parallel and Distributed Computing*, vol. 61, no. 4, pp. 545–564, 2001.
6. S. Y. Hsieh, G. H. Chen, and C. W. Ho, "Fault-free Hamiltonian cycles in faulty arrangement graphs," *IEEE Transactions on Parallel Distributed Systems*, vol. 10, no. 32, pp. 223–237, 1999.
7. S. Y. Hsieh, G. H. Chen, and C. W. Ho, "Hamiltonian-laceability of star graphs," *Networks*, vol. 36, no. 4, pp. 225–232, 2000.
8. S. Y. Hsieh, Gen-Huey Chen, and Chin-Wen Ho, "Longest fault-free paths in star graphs with vertex faults," *Theoretical Computer Science*, vol. 262, issues. 1-2, pp. 215–227, 2001.
9. S. Y. Hsieh and Chun-Hua Chen, "Pancyclicity on Möbius Cubes with Maximal Edge Faults," *Parallel Computing*, vol. 30, no. 3, pp. 407–421, 2004.
10. S. Y. Hsieh, "Embedding longest fault-free paths onto star graphs with more vertex faults," *Theortical Computer Science*, vol. 337, issues 1–3, pp. 370–378, 2005.
11. D. F. Hsu, "Interconnection networks and algorithms," a special issue of *Networks*, vol. 23, no. 4, 1993.
12. F. T. Leighton, *Introduction to Parallel Algorithms and Architecture: Arrays · Trees · Hypercubes*, Morgan Kaufmann, San Mateo, CA, 1992.

13. R. A. Rowley and B. Bose, "Fault-tolerant ring embedding in deBruijn networks," *IEEE Transacions on Computers*, vol. 42, no. 12, pp. 1480–1486, 1993.
14. C. H. Tsai, J. M. Tan, T. Linag and L. H. Hsu, "Fault-tolerant Hamiltonain laceability of hypercubes", *Information Peocessing Letters*, vol. 83, pp. 301–306, 2002.
15. Yu-Chee Tseng, S. H. Chang, and J. P. Sheu, "Fault-tolerant ring embedding in star graphs with both link and node failures," *IEEE Transactions on Parallel and Distributed Systems*, vol. 8, no. 12, pp. 1185–1195, 1997.
16. Junming Xu, *Topological Structure and Analysis of Interconnection Networks*, Kluwer academic publishers, 2001.

Constructing Node-Disjoint Paths
in Enhanced Pyramid Networks

Hsien-Jone Hsieh[1] and Dyi-Rong Duh[2, *]

[1,2] Department of Computer Science and Information Engineering
National Chi Nan University, Puli, Nantou Hsien, Taiwan 54561
[1] s1321902@ncnu.edu.tw
[2] drduh@ncnu.edu.tw

Abstract. Chen et al. in 2004 proposed a new hierarchy structure, called the enhanced pyramid network (*EPM*, for short), by replacing each mesh in a pyramid network (*PM*, for short) with a torus. Recently, some topological properties and communication on the *EPM*s have been investigated or derived. Their results have revealed that an *EPM* is an attractive alternative to a *PM*. This study investigates the node-disjoint paths between any two distinct nodes and the upper bound of the ω-wide-diameter of an *EPM*. This result shows that the *EPM*s have smaller ω-wide-diameters than the *PM*s.

Keywords: Enhanced pyramid networks, pyramid networks, fault-tolerance, wide diameter, node-disjoint paths, container, interconnection networks.

1 Introduction

Pyramid networks (*PM*s, for short) have conventionally been adopted for image processing [6, 10], computer vision [6], parallel computing [5] and network computing [1]. A *PM* is a hierarchy structure based on meshes. Recently, there are many researches on the *PM*s, such as Hamiltonicity [2, 12, 16], pancyclicity [2, 16], fault tolerance [1], routing [7, 15], and broadcasting [8]. Note that the node degree of a *PM* is from 3 to 9, and both its node connectivity and edge connectivity are 3 [1, 16]. For establishing a *PM* in expandable VLSI chips, each of its nodes should be configured as a 9-port component or too many different components should be designed and fabricated. In other words, those nodes of degree less than 9 have unused ports. These ports can be used for further expansion or I/O communication. To modify a well-known network a little bit such that the resulting network has better topological properties. Chen et al. [4] in 2004 proposed a variant network of the *PM*, named the enhanced pyramid network, by reconnecting some of the unused ports.

An *enhanced pyramid network* (*EPM*, for short), suggested by Chen et al. [4], is a supergraph of a pyramid network with the same node set. In other words, a *PM* is a spanning subgraph of an *EPM*. The *EPM* can be constructed by replacing each mesh of the *PM* with a torus. Therefore, the hardware cost of the *EPM* would be slightly more expensive than the *PM* because some extra edges have to be added in the VLSI

---

* Corresponding author.

C. Jesshope and C. Egan (Eds.): ACSAC 2006, LNCS 4186, pp. 380–386, 2006.
© Springer-Verlag Berlin Heidelberg 2006

chips. Some topological properties and communication on the *EPM*s, including the number of nodes/edges, node connectivity, edge connectivity, diameter, routing algorithm, and a simple broadcasting algorithm, have been determined or derived [4]. Their results show that the *EPM* has better topological properties than the *PM* such as larger node/edge connectivity and better fault-tolerance ability.

The topological structure of an interconnection network (network, for short) can be modeled by a graph [3, 10, 12, 13, 17]. The vertices and edges of a graph respectively correspond to nodes and edges of an interconnection network. The *length* of a path is the number of edges, which the path passes through. Given two nodes s and t in a network G, the *distance* between them, denoted by $d_G(s, t)$, is the length of their shortest path. The *diameter* of a network G, denoted by $d(G)$, is defined as the maximum of $d_G(s, t)$ among all pairs of distinct nodes in G. A ω-*wide container*, denoted by $C_\omega(s, t)$, is a set of node-disjoint paths of width ω. The *length of* $C_\omega(s, t)$, denoted by $l(C_\omega(s, t))$, is the length of the longest path in $C_\omega(s, t)$. The *total length of* $C_\omega(s, t)$, denoted by $l_T(C_\omega(s, t))$, is the sum of the lengths of the ω paths in the $C_\omega(s, t)$. The ω-*wide distance* between s and t in G, denoted by $d_\omega(s, t)$, is minimum among all $l(C_\omega(s, t))$. The ω-*wide diameter* of G, written as $d_\omega(G)$, is the maximum of ω-wide distance among all pairs of distinct nodes in G. Obviously, $d_G(s, t) \leq d_\omega(s, t)$, $d(G) \leq d_\omega(G)$, and $d_\omega(s, t) \leq d_\omega(G)$. *Parallel transmission* is a one-to-one communication in G such that the message can be transmitted from the source node to the destination node via a container between them to enhance the transmission performance and/or improve fault tolerance ability of the communication. Notably, the parallel transmission delay is bounded above by $d_\omega(G)$. This work first constructs a ω-wide container between any two distinct nodes in an *EPM* and then based on the constructed containers the upper bound of the ω-*wide diameter* of the *EPM* can be determined.

The rest of this paper is organized as follows. Section 2 describes the structure and terms of an *EPM*, and some notations and definitions in graphs. Section 3 first constructs a ω-wide container between any two distinct nodes in an *EPM* and then determines the upper bound of the ω-wide diameter of the *EPM*. Finally, the conclusion is made in Section 4.

2 Preliminaries

This section first formally describes the structures of the *PM* and *EPM* and then defines some notations and definitions in graphs that are used in the rest of this paper.

The node set of a mesh $M(m, n)$ is $V(M(m, n)) = \{(x, y) \mid 0 \leq x < m, 0 \leq y < n\}$. Two nodes (x_1, y_1) and (x_2, y_2) are joined by an edge iff $|x_1 - x_2| + |y_1 - y_2| = 1$, where (x_1, y_1) and (x_2, y_2) belong to $V(M(m, n))$. The n-layer pyramid network, denoted by $PM[n]$, is a hierarchy structure based on meshes. The node set of $PM[n]$ is $V(PM[n]) = \{(k; x, y) \mid 0 \leq k \leq n, 0 \leq x, y < 2^k\}$, where $n \geq 0$. Note that the node $(0; 0, 0)$ is the $PM[0]$. A node $(k; x, y) \in V(PM[n])$ is said to be a node at layer k with the coordinate (x, y). The nodes at layer k are connected as a $M(2^k, 2^k)$.

The *EPM* is a conjunction of a quad tree and tori. The node set of a torus $T(m, n)$ is $V(T(m, n)) = \{(x, y) \mid 0 \leq x < m, 0 \leq y < n\}$. Let $\{u, v\}$ denote an edge connecting nodes u and v of a network. The edge set $E(T(m, n)) = E(M(m, n)) \cup \{\{(x, 0), (x, n-1)\}, \{(0, y), (m-1, y)\} \mid 0 \leq x < m, 0 \leq y < n\}$. In other words, an *EPM* can be constructed by replacing each mesh of a *PM* with a torus. The nodes at layer k are connected as a $T(2^k, 2^k)$. Notice that a $M(2, 2)$ is also a $T(2, 2)$ in some sense. An *EPM* of n layers is denoted by *EPM*[n]. The node set of *EPM*[n] is $V(EPM[n]) = \{(k; x, y) \mid 0 \leq k \leq n, 0 \leq x, y < 2^k\}$, where $n \geq 2$. In general, the node $(0; 0, 0)$ is called the *apex* of *EPM*[n] (apex, for short). For ease of discussion, we define some symbols in the following.

For a node $v = (k; x, y)$ at layer $1 \leq k \leq n$ in *EPM*[n], the coordinate of its *parent*, denoted by $P(v)$, is given by $(k-1; \lfloor x/2 \rfloor, \lfloor y/2 \rfloor)$. Conversely, v is a *child* of $P(v)$. Moreover, each node in *EPM*[n] has a parent (four children) except the apex (the nodes at layer n). More generally, we recursively define the hth *ancestor* of v, denoted by $P^h(v)$, as follows:

(1) $h=1$, $P^1(v) = P(v)$ is simply the parent of v.
(2) $h>1$, $P^h(v) = (k-h; \lfloor x/2^h \rfloor, \lfloor y/2^h \rfloor)$ is the parent of $P^{h-1}(v)$.

For a node $v = (k; x, y)$ at layer $0 \leq k < n$ in *EPM*[n], the coordinates of its four children are given by $(k+1; 2x, 2y)$, $(k+1; 2x+1, 2y)$, $(k+1; 2x, 2y+1)$, and $(k+1; 2x+1, 2y+1)$. Conversely, v is the parent of its children.

For simplicity, let $(a)_b$ denote a modulo b. For a node $v = (k; x, y)$ at layer $2 \leq k \leq n$ in *EPM*[n], $(k; (x+1)_{2^k}, y)$, $(k; x, (y+1)_{2^k})$, $(k; (x-1)_{2^k}, y)$, and $(k; x, (y-1)_{2^k})$ are the coordinates of its four *siblings*, and they are also denoted by $S_0(v)$, $S_1(v)$, $S_2(v)$, and $S_3(v)$, respectively.

3 Node-Disjoint Paths

Before describing how to construct ω node-disjoint paths between any pair of nodes in *EPM*[n], some lemmas are first presented. These lemmas related to how to routing paths in *EPM*[n] are stated in Subsection 3.1. By the aid of these lemmas, a shortest path between any pair of nodes is first constructed and then the other $\omega-1$ paths can be built based on the shortest path. Subsections 3.2 describes how to construct these ω paths, where $2 \leq \omega \leq 4$.

3.1 Routing in *EPM*[n]

Given two paths P_1 and P_2, let $P_1 \rightarrow P_2$ denote joining P_2 to the tail of P_1. Let $P_G(u, v)$ denote a path between two nodes u and v in a network G. Let $l(P)$ denote the length of a path P. Some results derived by Chen et al. [4] are described first.

Lemma 1 [4]. The node connectivity of *EPM*[n] is 4.

By Menger's theorem [17] and Lemma 1, there is a 4-wide container between any pair of nodes in *EPM*[n].

Lemma 2 [4]. If $d_{T(2^k, 2^k)}(u, v) < 2 + d_{T(2^{k-1}, 2^{k-1})}(P(u), P(v))$, $d_{T(2^k, 2^k)}(u, v) = d_{EPM[n]}(u, v)$.

Lemma 3 [4]. Given two nodes $u=(k_u k; x_u, y_u)$ and $v=(k_v k; x_v, y_v)$, $0 \leq k_v \leq k_u < n$, there is a shortest $P_{EPM[n]}(u, v)$ having the form as $P_{EPM[n]}(u, P^{k_u-k_v+i}(u)) \rightarrow P_{T(2^k, 2^k)}(P^{k_u-k_v+i}(u), P^i(v)) \rightarrow P_{EPM[n]}(P^i(v), v)$, where $0 \leq i < k_v$.

By Lemma 3, a shortest path $P_{EPM[n]}(u, v)$ can be constructed and it is the first constructed path when a container is built. Since a shortest path between any two nodes has been established, the diameter of $EPM[n]$ can be easily obtained and stated in the following lemma.

Lemma 4 [4]. $d(EPM[n]) = 2n$, where $n \geq 2$.

After constructing a ω-wide container between any pair of nodes in a network, the upper bound of the ω-wide diameter of the network can be determined as the maximum length among the constructed ω-wide containers.

The first path $P_1(s, t)$, constructed by Lemma 3, is shortest and its length is at most $d(EPM[n]) = 2n$. Then the other $\omega-1$ paths $P_2, ..., P_\omega$, can be constructed based on P_1, they disjoint to each other and also disjoint to P_1. Notably, the other $\omega-1$ paths are never shorter than P_1, and then a method is proposed to share P_1 with the others, in order to shorten the length of the ω-wide container.

Given two nodes u and v at layer k_u and k_v of $EPM[n]$, respectively. They have at most four siblings $S_i(u)$ and $S_j(v)$, respectively, where $0 \leq i, j \leq 3$. $P(u)$ $(P(v))$ also has at most four siblings $S_i(P(u))$ $(S_j(P(v)))$, $0 \leq i (j) \leq 3$. Let $Q_{ij}(u, v)$ denote a path from $S_i(u)$ to $S_j(v)$ along siblings of $P_1(u, v)$. We can recursively construct $Q_{ij}(u, v)$ as follows:

(1) v is $P(u)$: $Q_{ii}(u, P(u))$ is a shortest path from $S_i(u)$ to $S_i(P(u))$ excluding $P_1(u, P(u))$.

(2) v is $P^h(u)$, where $2 \leq h \leq k_u-2$: $Q_{ii}(u, P^h(u)) = Q_{ii}(u, P^{h-1}(u)) \rightarrow Q_{ii}(P^{h-1}(u)), P^h(u))$. Note that $Q_{ii}(u, P^h(u))$ might not be a shortest path from $S_i(u)$ to $S_i(P^h(u))$ in $EPM[n]$ excluding $P_1(u, P^h(u))$.

(3) Let $w=(k_w; x_w, y_w)=P^{k_u-k_w}(u)$, $z=(k_z; x_z, y_z)=P^{k_v-k_z}(v)$, if $2 \leq k_w=k_z \leq \min\{k_u, k_v\}$: $Q_{ij}(u, v) = Q_{ii}(u, w) \rightarrow P_{T(2^{k_w}, 2^{k_w})}(S_i(w), S_j(z)) \rightarrow Q_{jj}(v, z)$.

Obviously, there are 4 $Q_{ii}(u, P(u))$s can be constructed. For each $Q_{ii}(u, P(u))$, it is represented by π_1 (π_2) if $l(Q_{ii}(u, P(u))) = 1$ (2). $l(Q_{ii}(u, P(u)))+l(Q_{mm}(u, P(u))) = 3$, where m is $(i+2)_4$. Also, if $Q_{ii}(u, P^h(u))$ has h_1 π_1s and $h_2 = h-h_1$ π_2s, then $Q_{mm}(u, P^h(u))$ has h_2 π_1s and h_1 π_2s, where m is $(i+2)_4$. Therefore, $l(Q_{ii}(u, P^h(u)))=h+h_2$, $l(Q_{mm}(u, P^h(u)))=h+h_1$, and $l(Q_{ii}(u, P^h(u)))+l(Q_{mm}(u, P^h(u))) = 3h$. The shortest one of $Q_{ii}(u, P^h(u))$ and $Q_{mm}(u, P^h(u))$ is denoted by $Q_S(u, P^h(u))$. Otherwise, the longest of them is denoted by $Q_L(u, P^h(u))$. Therefore, $l(Q_S(u, P^h(u))) \leq \lfloor 3h/2 \rfloor = h+\lfloor h/2 \rfloor$, and $l(Q_L(u, P^h(u))) \leq 2h$. That is, there are at most $\lfloor h/2 \rfloor$ (h) π_2s in a $Q_S(u, P^h(u))$ $(Q_L(u, P^h(u)))$. Q_S is also denoted as Q_{SE} (Q_{SO}) if i is even (odd).

3.2 ω-Wide Container

This subsection constructs a ω-wide container between any pair of nodes in $EPM[n]$. For ease of discussion, let $s=(k_s; x_s, y_s)$, $t=(k_t; x_t, y_t)$, $w=(k_w; x_w, y_w)=P^{k_s-k_w}(s)$, $z=(k_z; x_z, y_z)=P^{k_t-k_z}(t)$ be four nodes in $EPM[n]$ for $n \geq 2$, where $2 \leq k_w=k_z \leq \min\{k_s, k_t\}$.

Lemma 5 [9]. $l(Q_S(s, w)+d_{T(2^2, 2^2)}(S_i(w), S_j(z))+l(Q_S(z, t) \leq 2n+2\lfloor n/2 \rfloor-4$, $l(Q_S(s, w)+d_{T(2^2, 2^2)}(S_i(w), S_j(z))+l(Q_L(z, t) \leq 3n+\lfloor n/2 \rfloor-5$, and $l(Q_L(s, w)+d_{T(2^2, 2^2)}(S_i(w), S_j(z))+l(Q_S(z, t) \leq 3n+\lfloor n/2 \rfloor-5$.

Lemma 6. $l(C_2(s, t))$ and $l(C_3(s, t)) \leq 2n+2\lfloor n/2 \rfloor - 2$, $l(C_4(s, t)) \leq 3n+\lfloor n/2 \rfloor - 3$, $l_T(C_2(s, t)) \leq 4n+2\lfloor n/2 \rfloor - 2$, $l_T(C_3(s, t)) \leq 6n+4\lfloor n/2 \rfloor - 4$, and $l_T(C_4(s, t)) \leq 10n+2\lfloor n/2 \rfloor - 6$.

Proof. For ω-wide container, $2 \leq \omega \leq 4$, by Lemma 3 and Lemma 4, a shortest path $P_1(s, t)$ can be first constructed and $l(P_1(s, t)) \leq 2n$. Second, a $Q_{ij}(s, t)$ is constructed as the second path $P_2(s, t) = \{s, S_i(s)\} \rightarrow Q_{SE}(s, w) \rightarrow P_{T(22, 22)}(S_i(w), S_j(z)) \rightarrow Q_{SE}(z, t) \rightarrow \{S_j(t), t\}$. By Lemma 5, $l(P_2(s, t)) \leq 2n+2\lfloor n/2 \rfloor - 2$. Thus, $l(C_2(s, t)) \leq 2n+2\lfloor n/2 \rfloor - 2$ and $l_T(C_2(s, t)) \leq 4n+2\lfloor n/2 \rfloor - 2$. A $C_3(s, t)$ can be constructed by adding the third path $P_3(s, t)=\{s, S_i(s)\} \rightarrow Q_{SO}(s, w) \rightarrow P_{T(22, 22)}(S_i(w), S_j(z)) \rightarrow Q_{SO}(z, t) \rightarrow \{S_j(t), t\}$ into the original $C_2(s, t)$. $l(P_3(s, t)) \leq 2n+2\lfloor n/2 \rfloor - 2$. Hence, $l(C_3(s, t)) \leq 2n+2\lfloor n/2 \rfloor - 2$ and $l_T(C_3(s, t)) \leq 6n+4\lfloor n/2 \rfloor - 4$. For constructing a $C_4(s, t)$, $P_3(s, t)=\{s, S_i(s)\} \rightarrow Q_{SO}(s, P^{n-2}(s)) \rightarrow P_{T(22, 22)}(S(P^{n-2}(s)), S(P^{n-2}(t))) \rightarrow Q_L(P^{n-2}(t), t) \rightarrow \{S_j(t), t\}$ and $P_4(s, t)=\{s, S(s)\} \rightarrow Q_L(s, P^{n-2}(s)) \rightarrow P_{T(22, 22)}(S(P^{n-2}(s)), S(P^{n-2}(t))) \rightarrow Q_{SO}(P^{n-2}(t), t) \rightarrow \{S_j(t), t\}$. By Lemma 5, both $l(P_3(s, t))$ and $l(P_4(s, t)) \leq 3n+\lfloor n/2 \rfloor - 3$, and $l_T(C_4(s, t)) \leq 10n+2\lfloor n/2 \rfloor - 6$ is maximum. Note that all $P_{T(22, 22)}$s disjoint to each other. ■

The $C_\omega(s, t)$ constructed in the proof of Lemma 6 is too long and $l(P_\omega(s, t))s - l(P_1(s, t))$ are too large, for $2 \leq \omega \leq 4$. A $C_\omega(s, t)$ can be shortened by rerouting its paths such that each path shares some part of the $P_1(s, t)$. The $X(P_{EPM[n]}(u, P^2(u)), Q_{ii}(u, P^2(u)))$ is an operation to reroute the two node-disjoint paths $P_{EPM[n]}(u, P^2(u))$ and $Q_{ii}(u, P^2(u))$ in $EPM[n]$ by using some nodes near to them, where $u \in V(P_1(s, P^{n-2}(s)))$. After rerouting, one path from u to $S_i(P^2(u))$ is denoted by R_1, the other path from $S_i(u)$ to $P^2(u)$ is denoted by R_2, and they are still disjoint to each other. The rerouting would little increase the sum of the lengths of the paths. $l(R_1) - l(P_{EPM[n]}(u, P^2(u)))$ and $l(R_2) - l(Q_{ii}(u, P^2(u)))$ are represented by c_1 and c_2, respectively. The main idea of rerouting is to share the shortest path of the original container with the other paths such that the longest path in $C_\omega(u, v)$ is only one longer than the shortest path and then $l(C_\omega(u, v))$ can be minimized.

Lemma 7. $X(P_{EPM[n]}(u, P^2(u))$ and $Q_{ii}(u, P^2(u)))$ can be completed within 2 layers, and $c_1=2$, $c_2=0$ or 1.

Proof. Given a node $u=(k; x, y)$, there are 4 $Q_{ii}(u, P^2(u)))$s. Without lost of generality, only $X(P_{EPM[n]}(u, P^2(u)), Q_{00}(S_i(u), S_i(P^2(u))))$ is discussed. Let $x=(x_{k-1}x_{k-2} \ldots x_2 0 x_0)_2$ in binary, and the bit 0 of y is y_0, $Q_{00}(P(u), P^2(u))$ is a π_2. Hence, $P(u)=(k-1; (x_{k-1}x_{k-2} \ldots x_2 0)_2, \lfloor y/2 \rfloor)$, $P^2(u)=(k-2; (x_{k-1}x_{k-2} \ldots x_2)_2, \lfloor y/4 \rfloor)$, $H_0(u)=(k; (x_{k-1}x_{k-2} \ldots x_2 10)_2, y)$, $H_0(P(u))=(k-1; (x_{k-1}x_{k-2} \ldots x_2 1)_2+1, \lfloor y/2 \rfloor)$, $S_0(P^2(u))=(k-2; (x_{k-1}x_{k-2} \ldots x_2)_2+1, \lfloor y/4 \rfloor)$, $a=(k; 2\lfloor x/2 \rfloor+2, 2\lfloor y/2 \rfloor+1)$, and $b=(k; 2\lfloor x/2 \rfloor+2, 2\lfloor y/2 \rfloor+2)$. Before rerouting, $l(P_1(u, P^2(u))) = 2$ and $l(Q_{00}(u, P^2(u))) = 4-x_0$. In order to keep disjoint to the other $Q_{ii}(u, P^2(u)))$s, after rerouting, R_2 must be $P_{T(2^k, 2^k)}(S_0(u), a) \rightarrow \{a, b\} \rightarrow P(b, P^2(u))$. $l(R_1) = 4$ and $l(R_2) = 5-x_0-y_0$. Hence, $c_1 = 4-2 = 2$, $c_2 = (5-x_0-y_0) - (4-x_0)=1-y_0 = 0$ or 1. ■

Theorem 8. $d_2(EPM[n]) \leq 2n+\lfloor n/2 \rfloor - 1$, for $n \geq 2$. $d_3(EPM[n]) \leq 2n+\lceil (2n+2)/3 \rceil$ $(2n+\lceil 2n/3 \rceil)$ if n is even (odd), for $n \geq 4$. $d_4(EPM[n]) \leq 2n+\lceil 3n/4 \rceil$ $(2n+\lceil (3n-1)/4 \rceil)$ if n is even (odd), for $n \geq 4$.

Proof. This theorem can be proved by rerouting the $C_\omega(s, t)$ constructed in the proof of Lemma 6.

Case 1. (for $C_2(s, t)$): Only the longest $C_2(s, t)$ should be considered. After reconstruction, the new paths are $P_1'(s, t) = P_{EPM[n]}(s, w) \rightarrow P_{T(2^2, 2^2)}(w, S_j(z)) \rightarrow Q_{jj}(z, t) \rightarrow \{S_j(t), t\}$ and $P_2'(s, t) = \{s, S_i(s)\} \rightarrow Q_{ii}(s, w) \rightarrow P_{T(2^2, 2^2)}(S_i(w), z) \rightarrow P_{EPM[n]}(z, t)$. The lengths of $P_1'(s, t)$ and $P_2'(s, t)$ are at most $2n + \lfloor n/2 \rfloor - 1$.

Case 2. (for $C_3(s, t)$): Assume there are h_s and h_t π_2s in $Q_{SE}(s, w)$ and $Q_{SO}(t, z)$, respectively, the lengths of h_s and h_t are at most $\lfloor (n-2)/2 \rfloor$. Let $h_{sx} = \lfloor 2 \times h_s/3 \rfloor - 1$, $h_{tx} = \lfloor 2 \times h_t/3 \rfloor - 1$. After applying $X(P_{EPM[n]}(P^{h_{sx}-2}(s), P^{h_{sx}}(s)), Q_{SE}(P^{h_{sx}-2}(s), P^{h_{sx}}(s)))$ and $X(P_{EPM[n]}(P^{h_{tx}-2}(t), P^{h_{tx}}(t)), Q_{SO}(P^{h_{tx}-2}(t), P^{h_{tx}}(t)))$, the new paths are $P_1'(s, t)$, $P_2'(s, t)$, and $P_3'(s, t)$ with lengths l_1', l_2', and l_3', respectively. By Lemma 6 and Lemma 7, l_1', l_3' $\leq 2n + \lceil (2n+2)/3 \rceil (2n + \lceil 2n/3 \rceil)$ and $l_2' \leq 2n + \lfloor (2n+2)/3 \rfloor (2n + \lfloor 2n/3 \rfloor)$ if n is even (odd), for $n \geq 4$.

Case 3. (for $C_4(s, t)$): After applying 3 times of rerouting, the new paths are $P_1'(s, t)$, $P_2'(s, t)$, $P_3'(s, t)$, and $P_4'(s, t)$ with lengths l_1', l_2', l_3', and l_4', respectively. Similarly, l_1', $l_4' \leq 2n + \lceil 3n/4 \rceil (2n + \lceil (3n-1)/4 \rceil)$, l_2', $l_3' \leq 2n + \lfloor 3n/4 \rfloor (2n + \lfloor (3n-1)/4 \rfloor)$ if n is even (odd), for $n \geq 4$.   ∎

It is easy to check that $d_2(EPM[1]) = d_3(EPM[1]) = 2$, $d_3(EPM[2]) = d_4(EPM[2]) = 4$, $d_3(EPM[3]) = 6$, and $d_4(EPM[3]) = 7$.

4 Concluding Remarks

This work has revealed that $d_2(EPM[n]) \leq 2n + \lfloor n/2 \rfloor - 1$, for $n \geq 2$, $d_3(EPM[n]) \leq 2n + \lceil (2n+2)/3 \rceil (2n + \lceil 2n/3 \rceil)$, n is even (odd), for $n \geq 4$, and $d_4(EPM[n]) \leq 2n + \lceil 3n/4 \rceil (2n + \lceil (3n-1)/4 \rceil)$, n is even (odd), for $n \geq 4$. In [1], $d_2(PM[n]) = 3n-1$, and $d_3(PM[n]) \leq 10n/3 + 6$. Therefore, an EPM has smaller ω-wide-diameter than the pertinent PM. The ω-path transmission delay of a network is bounded below by its ω-wide diameter. The lower bound of $d_\omega(EPM[n])$ is still unknown. We are going to determine the lower bound of $d_\omega(EPM[n])$ and we claim that it is equal to its upper bound. If this is true, $d_\omega(EPM[n])$ can be eventually obtained.

Acknowledgments. The authors would like to thank the National Science Council of the Republic of China for financially supporting this research under Contract No. NSC-93-2213-E-260-005-.

References

1. Cao, F., Du, D.-Z., Hsu, D. F., Teng, S.-H.: Fault tolerance properties of pyramid networks. IEEE Transactions on Computers 48 (1999) 88–93
2. Chen, Y.-C.: Pancycles and Hamiltonian connectedness of the pyramid network with one node or one edge fault. Master Report, Department of Computer Science and Information Engineering, National Chi Nan University (2003)
3. Chen, W.-M. Chen, G.-H. Hsu, D.-F.: Generalized diameters of the mesh of trees. Theory of Computing Systems 37 (2004) 547-556

4. Chen, Y.-C., Duh, D.-R., Hsieh, H.-J.: On the enhanced pyramid network. Proc. Int. Conf. on Parallel and Distributed Processing Techniques and Applications. Monte Carlo Resort, Las Vegas, Nevada, USA (2004) 1483–1489

5. Cinque, L., Bongiovanni, G.: Parallel prefix computation on a pyramid computer. Pattern Recognition Letter 16 (1995) 19–22

6. Cipher, R., Sanz, J. L. C.: SIMD architectures and algorithms for image processing and computer vision. IEEE Transactions on Acoustic, Speech, and Signal Processing 37 (1989) 2158–2174

7. Hsieh, H.-J., Duh, D.-R., Shiau, J.-S.: A constant time shortest-path routing algorithm for pyramid networks. Proc. Int. Conf. on Parallel and Distributed Computing and Systems. MIT Cambridge, MA, USA (2004) 71–75

8. Hsieh, H.-J., Duh, D.-R.: An Optimal Broadcasting Algorithm for Pyramid Networks. Proc. the 9th World Multiconference on Systemics, Cybernetics and Informatics. Orlando, Florida, USA (2005) 266-270

9. Hsieh, H.-J., Duh, D.-R.: Containers in Enhanced Pyramid Networks. Technical Report, http://tr.csie.ncnu.edu.tw/scripts/TR.asp?TRNo=NCNUCSIE-TR20060004 (2006)

10. Hsu, D. F.: Graph containers, information delay, and network vulnerability. Proc. Int. Conf. on Advanced Information Networking and Applications, Vol. 1. (2004) 16-21

11. Jenq, J. F., Sahni, S.: Image shrinking and expanding on a pyramid. IEEE Transactions on Parallel and Distributed Systems 4 (1993) 1291–1296

12. Omura, S., H. Zheng, Wada, K.: Neighborhood broadcasting in undirected de Bruijn and Kautz networks. IEICE Transactions on Information and Systems E-88-D (2005) 89-95

13. Park, J.-H.: Two-dimensional ring-banyan network: a high-performance fault-tolerant switching network, Electronics Letters 42 (2006) 249-251

14. Sarbazi-Azad, H., Ould-Khaoua, M., Mackenzie, L. M.: Algorithmic construction of Hamiltonians in pyramids. Information Processing Letters. Vol. 80. (2001) 75–79

15. Shen, Z.: A routing algorithm for pyramid structures, Proc. ACM Symposium on Applied Computing, Las Vegas, Nevada, USA (2001) 484–488

16. Wu, R.-Y.: Hamiltonicity of pyramid networks. Master Report, Department of Computer Science and Information Engineering, National Chi Nan University (2001)

17. Xu, J.: Topological structure and analysis of interconnection networks. Kluwer, Netherlands, (2002)

Striping Cache: A Global Cache for Striped Network File System

Sheng-Kai Hung and Yarsun Hsu

Department of Electrical Engineering,
National Tsing-Hua University, HsinChu 30055, Taiwan
{phinex, yshsu}@hpcc.ee.nthu.edu.tw

Abstract. Using caching to enhance performance has been widely used in the computer system. This is still true in the distributed paradigm. In the distributed environment, caches are distributed in each of the nodes and can be collected to form a global cache. However, the overall performance cannot benefit from the global cache without efficient cooperation of these global resources. The local file system in each node knows nothing about a stripe and thus can not benefit from the related blocks of a stripe. We propose a striping cache (SC) which knows the related blocks of a stripe and can use them to improve the performance of a striped network file system. This high level cache can benefit from previous reads and can aggregate small writes to improve the overall performance. We implement this mechanism in our reliable parallel file system (RPFS). The experimental results show that both read and write performance can be improved with SC support. The improvement comes from the fact that we can reduce the number of disk accesses by employing SC.

1 Introduction

I/O subsystem has been the bottleneck of a computer system[1] so far, both at space and bandwidth aspects. Network file systems[2,3] provide an unified naming space across network servers. Clients can utilize the centralized server model to extend their disk space in the network. Parallel file systems[4,5,6,7,8,9] use striping to add storage bandwidth which a single server could not offer. They alleviate the issue of concurrent accesses when serving many clients.

Caching is widely used in the computer system to enhance the performance. The client/server model of network file systems implies two possibilities for caching, either in the server or clients. Requested data hitting in the client's local cache can save the number of disk accesses. The benefit of caching in the server side comes from the fact that accessing remote memory is faster than accessing local disks. As the network technologies emerge[10,11], the potential advantage of remote caching becomes evident.

We proposed a modularized redundant parallel virtual file system[12] based on the original parallel virtual file system (PVFS)[13] to protect data from loss. We have demonstrated that using buffers to cache parity is beneficial when small write happens. We extend this prototype system and propose a striping cache

C. Jesshope and C. Egan (Eds.): ACSAC 2006, LNCS 4186, pp. 387–393, 2006.
© Springer-Verlag Berlin Heidelberg 2006

(SC) in our reliable parallel file system (RPFS). SC utilizes the concept of remote caching and can not only solve the problem of small write but also improve the performance of the original PVFS. The benefits come from the fact that we successfully reduce the number of disk accesses.

We organize this paper as follows. We first describe the related research topics in section 2. The system architecture of our RPFS along with SC are then presented in section 3. Finally, we show the evaluation of using SC in section 4, and section 5 concludes our work.

2   Related Work

Employing a cache to improve performance has been widely used either in hardware architecture or software infrastructure. xFS[7] is the first one to implement the concept of cooperative caching[14] in a distributed paradigm. Hint-based cooperative caching[15] reduced the communication overhead needed in a cooperative caching. Its hints decentralize the central coordination but still have high accuracy. NFS-cc[16] implements cooperative caching in NFS and can offer good concurrent accesses for many clients.

However, all of those mentioned before are client side cooperative caching schemes and have consistency problems. Our striping cache (SC) is a server side cache with each block having its home node. In other words, our SC suffers no duplicate problem and hence incurs no consistency problem. It is implemented in each of the I/O nodes without any kernel level modification. This global server-side cache has the knowledge of a stripe, knows how to collect related blocks to form a stripe and is aware of its corresponding parity. With our novel cache replacement algorithm, we can greatly reduce the number of disk accesses and thus enhance the overall performance. Besides, the penalty of parity updating can also be alleviated by employing SC.

3   System Architecture

First, we shortly describe the functionalities of PVFS. It has three main components: mgr, iod and libpvfs. The mgr daemon is executed in the management node and maintains the metadata of the system. There can be only one management node in the system. Iod runs on each of the I/O nodes, serving the requests from clients and feeding them with the requested data. Libpvfs provides native calls of PVFS, allowing applications to gain the maximal I/O performance that could offer. Besides, a kernel module implements POSIX-complaint interfaces which allow traditional applications to run without any modification.

Our RPFS has two functionalities which original PVFS does not provide. One is the redundancy mechanism, the other is the global striping cache (SC). These two functionalities are implemented without affecting the original striping structure of PVFS. We will describe both of them in more detail in the following subsections.

3.1   Striping Cache

The striping cache (SC) is implemented in each of the I/O nodes. It lies between iod daemon and local file system and is used both as a read ahead and a write behind buffer. Each node has 4096 cache blocks with each block (16K+32) bytes in size. These blocks are divided into 1024 sets, with each set contains 4 blocks. These buffers are pre-allocated within each I/O node when the iod daemon is executed. The 16 KB region is used to cache files, while the 32 *bytes* metadata contains many information used for cache replacement algorithm and parity updating. Fig. 1 shows this structure with detailed field names and their size.

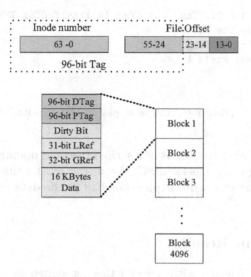

Fig. 1. Cache Blocks of an I/O Node: DTag is used to indicate whether this block contributes to a specific parity block described by PTag. If a write happens, the dirty bit would be set. LRef records the number of hits in this cache block. GRef indicates the number of related cache blocks being read or written within the same stripe.

DTag field describes the tag information which uniquely identifies the cache block itself. The identity of a data segment is its 64 *bits* inode number and its high 32 *bits* offset, shown in Fig. 1. Different data segments which hash to the same set have different DTag values. The dirty bit is set when the data block is a newly written one. Its value is cleared when the dirty block and its corresponding parity block have been written to disk. LRef field is used to record the number of hits in this cache block, which acts as the reference for cache replacement algorithm. GRef field monitors the related cache blocks (by the same DTag value) being read or written in SC.

3.2   Distributed Cache Replacement Algorithm

With SC support, we need a novel cache replacement algorithm. Fig 2 shows the pseudo code of our cache replacement algorithm. Each node runs its own thread

```
IF  PTag is null THEN
       IF Operation is READ THEN
              USE LRef Field & LRU
       ELSE
              IF Dirty bit is Set  THEN
                     Write the Parity Block and the replaced Block
              END IF
              Write Operation Proceed
              Update the PTag Field
       END IF
ELSE
       IF PTag == itself.DTag  and DTag != itself.DTag THEN
              Replace the block
       ELSE IF  PTag != DTag
              USE LRef Field & LRU
       END IF
END IF
```

Fig. 2. Distributed Cache Replacement Algorithm in SC

to periodically monitor the status of a stripe. It would update the GRef fields of the corresponding cache blocks in SC. Besides, it must write the PTag fields of cache blocks whenever a write happens or half of the data segments of a stripe are cached.

4   Experiment Results

Nine nodes are connected with a fast Ethernet switch to form a cluster, one metadata server and eight I/O servers. We perform three kinds of tests and would describe them separately in the following subsections.

4.1   Cache Hit Ratio Test

First, we measure the hit ratio in our SC by putting a hook in each of I/O nodes. We then count the number of hits in cache blocks within the measured time intervals ranging from 10 ms to 100 ms. Fig. 3 shows the hit ratio of our SC. The measurements are repeated several times and hit ratios within the same time interval are averaged.

4.2   Performance Test Using Native API

We use the pvfs_test.c utility accompanied with PVFS distribution to test the concurrent accesses. In this test, each I/O node acts as a client too. Fig. 4 shows the results of read when eight clients are used. The read performance of RPFS is better than PVFS because of the global server-side cache. Data segments are brought into cache blocks in the unit of 16 KB. This realizes the effect of prefetching.

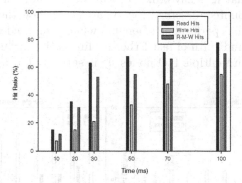

Fig. 3. Hit Ratio of SC: Measured in time intervals ranging from 10 *ms* to 100 *ms*. The measurements repeat several times and hit ratios within the same time interval are averaged.

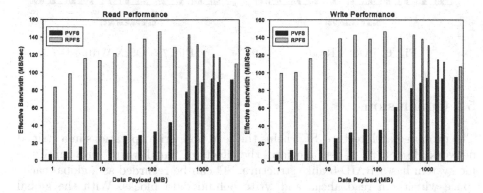

Fig. 4. Read - Native Call   **Fig. 5.** Write - Native Call

Fig. 5 shows the results when using pvfs_test.c to perform write tests. Updating parity blocks has significant impact on RPFS because small write still needs four operations : read the old striped blocks, read the old parity block, write the desired block and write the newly calculated parity block. Without a global cache, we cannot aggregate small writes to form a big write. A big write not only can reduce the number of parity writing. Besides, the global cache can shorten request time since data may be accessed directly from SC instead of disks. Compared with Fig. 4, the write performance of PVFS is better than that of read. As for the RPFS, parity writing has less impact due to the use of SC. Its write performance is only reduced by 3% when compared with its read performance.

4.3   Single Client Read/Write

We use Bonnie++[17] to test the traditional POSIX interfaces. In this test, a single client is used to run Bonnie++ program. We mount PVFS in the client's local directory so that it behaves like a local file system. All measurements are performed in the mounted directory. Fig. 6 and Fig. 7 show the results. Again, we observe that RPFS has performance benefits when compared with PVFS. In this test, the network bandwidth of fast Ethernet limits the throughput that a singe client could get from multiple I/O nodes. It is saturated at around 17 MB/sec.

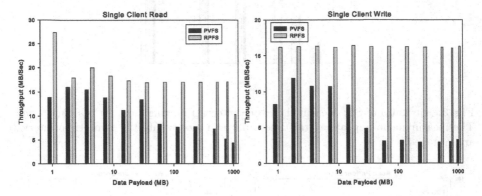

Fig. 6. POSIX Read   **Fig. 7.** POSIX Write

5   Conclusion

The proposed architecture, SC , helps the read and write operations in a striped network file system. It also alleviates the effects of "small-write" problem if the file system has a RAID-5 alike structure. SC can be regarded as a global cache space which can read ahead and write behind data blocks. With the global knowledge and our novel distributed cache replacement algorithm, it can efficiently utilize the cache both for reading and writing. SC is a high level global cache which does not need any kernel level modification. With this characteristic, it can be applied to any striped network file system with little effort.

References

1. Thakur, R., Lusk, E., Gropp, W.: I/O in parallel applications: The weakest link. The International Journal of High Performance Computing Applications **12**(4) (Winter 1998) 389–395
2. Sandberg, R., Goldberg, D., Kleiman, S., Walsh, D., Lyon, B.: Design and implementation of the Sun Network File System. In: Proceedings Summer 1985 USENIX Conference. (1985) 119–130
3. Howard, J.H., Kazar, M.L., Menees, S.G., Nichols, D.A., Satyanarayanan, M., Sidebotham, R.N., West, M.J.: Scale and performance in a distributed file system. ACM Transactions on Computer Systems **6**(1) (1998) 51–81
4. Pâris, J.F.: A disk architecture for large clusters of workstations. In: Cluster Computing Conference, GA (1997) 317–327

5. Corbett, P.F., Feitelson, D.G.: The Vesta parallel file system. In: High Performance Mass Storage and Parallel I/O: Technologies and Applications. IEEE Computer Society Press and Wiley, New York, NY (2001) 285–308
6. Hartman, J.H., Ousterhout, J.K.: The Zebra striped network file system. In: High Performance Mass Storage and Parallel I/O: Technologies and Applications. IEEE Computer Society Press and Wiley, New York, NY (2001) 309–329
7. Sweeney, A., Doucette, D., Hu, W., Anderson, C., Nishimoto, M., Peck, G.: Scalability in the xFS file system. In: Proceedings of the USENIX 1996 Technical Conference, San Diego, CA, USA (1996) 1–14
8. Soltis, S.R., Ruwart, T.M., O'Keefe, M.T.: The Global File System. In: Proceedings of the Fifth NASA Goddard Conference on Mass Storage Systems and Technologies, College Park, MD (1996) 319–342
9. Schmuck, F., Haskin, R.: GPFS: A shared-disk file system for large computing clusters. In: Proc. of the First Conference on File and Storage Technologies (FAST). (2002) 231–244
10. 10 Gigabit Ethernet Alliance: 10 gigabit ethernet whitepapers. (http://www.10gea.org/)
11. InfiniBand Trade Association: Infiniband architecture overview. (http://www.infinibandta.org/)
12. Hung, S.K., Hsu, Y.: Modularized redundant parallel virtual file system. In: Asia-Pacific Computer Systems Architecture Conference 2005, Singapore (2005) 186–199
13. Carns, P.H., Ligon III, W.B., Ross, R.B., Thakur, R.: PVFS: A parallel file system for linux clusters. In: Proceedings of the 4th Annual Linux Showcase and Conference, Atlanta, GA, USENIX Association (2000) 317–327
14. Dahlin, M., Wang, R., Anderson, T.E., Patterson, D.A.: Cooperative caching: Using remote client memory to improve file system performance. In: Operating Systems Design and Implementation. (1994) 267–280
15. Sarkar, P., Hartman, J.H.: Hint-based cooperative caching. ACM Transactions on Computer Systems 18(4) (2000) 387–419
16. Xu, Y., Fleisch, B.D.: NFS-cc: Tuning NFS for concurrent read sharing. The International Journal on High Performance Computing and Networking (IJHPCN) 1(4) (2004) 203–213
17. Coker, R.: Bonnie++ – file system benchmark. (http://www.coker.com.au/bonnie++/)

DTuplesHPC: Distributed Tuple Space for Desktop High Performance Computing

Yi Jiang, Guangtao Xue, Minglu Li, and Jinyuan You

Department of Computer Science and Engineering,
Shanghai Jiao Tong University, P.R. China
{jiangyi, xue-gt, li-ml, you-jy}@cs.sjtu.edu.cn

Abstract. This paper introduces a Linda [2] like peer-to-peer tuple space middleware build on top of distributed hash table – DTuplesHPC. This tuple space middleware is capable of being a high performance computing platform. And the decoupled style of tuple space [1] model is used instead of the message-passing model that is widely used in MPI based high performance computing. With the help of tuple space model, the distributed computing can be liberated from architectural consideration. First, the DTuples platform allows the dynamic organization of the computing resources. That is to say, the job can be submitted at any time, but the computation resources may be ready later. The time and space are all decoupled in DTuplesHPC. Second, it brings the simple tuple space programming model to the large-scale high performance computing at desktop. In our design, the *in()*, *rd()*, *out()*, *copy-collect()* and *eval()* primitives are supported. In this paper, we present the key design concepts of the DTuples.

1 Introduction

Since SETI@Home [12], the high performance computing has never been constrained in the laboratory and the expensive super computer. The peer-to-peer technology has been proven that it can explore the computation energies of the vast number of personal computers.

In the high performance computing area, the MPI is the de-facto standard. The P2P-MPI is a reasonable evolution in peer-to-peer to high performance computing, but the design and development of the program is not easy. The message-passing model only decoupled the processes from space, but not in time. Also, the MPI is a low level service, so it is a difficult to programming. To make MPI utilize the power of the all participants, the algorithm must be split into many pieces. The synchronization and message exchanging are controlled by the programmer itself. In this view, the MPI and P2P-MPI are primal solutions to the high performance computing. The primary difference between the message passing model and tuple space model is that the message passing model needs an end point to deliver the message, the P2P-MPI needs endpoint to deliver the message too, the tuple space model not. The tuple space model is look like a bulletin board system where some one post and some one read. The reader and

C. Jesshope and C. Egan (Eds.): ACSAC 2006, LNCS 4186, pp. 394–400, 2006.
© Springer-Verlag Berlin Heidelberg 2006

poster need not simultaneously online. The tuple space model can also been seen as topic-based system in which each tuple has a name. The tuple space can also be modeled to a hierarchy space where the tuple space is splited into spaces and sub spaces.

We think that the tuple space model is more suited to the distributed computing than the message-passing model. The main shortcoming of the tuple space model in high performance computing is that the tuple space model is a high level abstraction of the coordination language; it lacks the sorts to fine granularity control to the processes and resources. But fortunately, this shortcoming is not fatal in the notion of desktop high performance computing, such as SETI@Home. In this paper, we present the DTuples as a desktop high performance computing toolkit.

The remainder of the paper is structured as follows. Section 2 presents the primitives of the DTuples and the two level tuple space. Section 3 discusses some issues relating to the design and implementation of the DTuples. Finally, the last section concludes the paper with a brief summary.

2   DTuples Basics

Tuple space model is not conflicts with peer-to-peer model. But they have significant differences. First, the tuple-space model is a model to describe the communication between time and space decoupled process in local area network. Secondly, The tuple space model has well defined communication primitive to coordinate the processes. The tuple space model has the ability to decouple the processes in time and space. The peer-to-peer model is inability in this area. We have seen that the tuple space model is so similar to peer-to-peer model in the form of role of the nodes or agents in the view of application. This inspired us to build a kind of tuple space service on top of the distributed hash table.

2.1   DTuples

DTuples [8] is a tuple space middleware service build on top of the structured peer-to-peer network. The tuple space service on top of peer-to-peer network can benefits from the peer-to-peer in the scalability, fault-tolerance and self-organization. The underlying peer-to-peer network provides the DTuples storage and messaging service. The base of the DTuples is FreePastry [9], a free and open source DHT implementation. The DTuples support the following primitives: *rd()*, *in()*, *out()* and *coppy-collect()*.

2.2   Subject Tuplespace

DTuples provides a two level tuples space: the public space and the subject space. The subject space is owned by process and can be accessible by the other process under the permission of the owner. The subject tuple space can be used to partition the flat space. The unprefixed call to these primitives is on the public tuple space. For example, call to *out(t)* will output a tuple *t* to the public tuple space. Suppose *TS1* is the name of a subject tuple space, *TS1.out(t)* will output the tuple t into the subject space named *TS1*. The *eval()* primitive is supported in DTuplesHPC.

3   Design and Implementation

The DTuplesHPC system is composed of a set of distributed nodes in peer-to-peer mode. The centre node is the bootstrap node that initializes the computation and spawns some computation tasks that runs in the other nodes. After the computation tasks completed, the bootstrap node collects the intermediate results from tuple space and synthesis the final result.

DTuplesHPC is the prototyped as an extension of DTuples for the enabling of distributed computing. The main extension of the DTuplesHPC is to add support for the *eval()* primitive into DTuplesHPC.

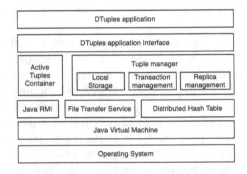

Fig. 1. Architecture of DTuples node. Every DTuplesHPC node has the same structure.

3.1   Design Requirements

To make the tuple service meaningful in usage, we require the design and implementation have the following requirements.

1. Task dispatched into appropriate peers. DTuplesHPC must have the ability to schedule the tasks to the processor that is willing to accept jobs.
   The task submitted to DTuples by the form of active tuple through *eval()* primitive.
2. Fault-tolerance. DTuples provides reliable tuples storage service through replication. DTuplesHPC programs use tuples to communicate and store intermediate result.
3. Scalable. The system will be higher performance when there are more computers joined in the system.

In the design of the DTuples, the tuple management function is build on top of replica management function. The tuples in DTuples space are replicated to make sure the fault-tolerance. The replica management function is complex and hard to implement because the replicas of tuple need to be maintained in consistency during lifetime.

3.2   Architecture

Fig.1 shows the overall architecture of the DTuplesHPC system. The Tuples in the tuple space is managed by tuple manager, which is a daemon process that runs in every peer that participants the work. The tuple manger maintains the tuples in local storage and cooperates with the other tuples through DHT based storage and routing protocol. The tuple manager manages the transaction and replication of the tuples. The DTuples API provides an event and message service on top of the DHT. In the left side of the tuple manager, there is an active tuple container. The code fragment in the active tuples is not complete program, but code fragment. The container is the execution context of those code fragments. The code can be locally executed or can be remotely executed through the RMI call to the Java remote object. All the codes, including the locally executed and remotely executed, are executed in container. In the architecture, the container is not a part of the tuple manager because the active tuple and the passive tuple are different.

The P2P nature of this architecture makes the DTuplesHPC system scalable and fault-tolerant. The system will continue running in case of node shutdown and benefits from the joining of extra nodes. The overlay network is distributed hash table based. In the help of this layer, the system is scalable and self organization. The local storage managed by the tuple manager is directly interact with the distributed hash table as the previous section stated. At the top of the architecture, the API layer provides five primitives to the application.

3.3   The *eval()* Primitive

Many tuple space implementation support only passive tuple, such as JavaSpaces [6]. In DTuplesHPC, active tuples is supported. *eval()* writes a tuple to tuple-space after arguments in the expression are evaluated by creating new processes which perform their tasks independently. When and where the new process is created is not specific. *eval()* taking an active tuple and placing it into the tuple space returning immediately. The process finishes by returning a passive tuple in tuple space. The active tuple cannot be retrieved from tuple space unlike passive tuples.

3.4   Active Tuples

The *eval()* primitive use formals in active tuples to specific the node that is suitable to accept the active tuple and run the tasks it carried on. This is a trade off to the requirements of the easy and efficiency. The active tuples in our system is modeled as the composition of passive tuple and code fragment (the code fragment is running in container). The active tuple is invisible in the tuple space to any operation. It will never be touched by any other processes until it has been evaluated. Once the active tuple has been evaluated, the code in the active tuple will be executed once. The evaluation of the active tuple is not the time the tuple is inserted into the tuple space, but the time the matching passive tuple was inserted. In DTuplesHPC, the *eval()* primitive is used to spawn the tasks that is parallel executed.

The active tuple is the used to create process in DTuplesHPC. The tasks the active tuple created are java object that implements the several specific interfaces. In DTuplesHPC, we call the object active object. The object must implements java.rmi.Remote, java.rmi.Serialable and java.lang.Runnable interface to enable it is callable from remote and it can be transferred between JVMs.

The task is executed in container, which is the context of the execution. The container provides the fault-detection and process management function. The process is executed in a thread in the container. Fig.2 shows the container. The container is composed of a thread pool and other components. The active tuples are executed in the context of a thread. The execution of the active tuples is coordinated by the dispatcher and security manager. The execution of the tasks in thread pool is monitored by activity monitor. The monitor detects the fault and restarts the faulty thread.

Each active tuple is composed of template and code fragment. The code fragment is a java object. The template is used to select the appropriate node that is suitable to execute the tasks carried by active tuple. Nodes that are ready to accept tasks perform *in()* primitive to wait tasks. The procedure of waiting tasks are hidden from the *eval()* primitive. It is done by the system. After the dispatcher daemon received a active tuple it places the corresponding active object in the container.

The active object produces a passive tuple in the tuple space, and then exit. The passive tuple produced by execution of the active object is the result of the computation. The bootstrap task collects those tuples and synthesis them into the final results of the algorithm.

3.5   Container for the Active Objects

The active tuples is resides in the tuple space in the view of the programmer. But in the internal view of DTuples, the tuple are resides in the local storage of the tuple manager. The active objects in the active tuples are resides in the active objects container. If the peer that the tuple reside isnt the peers that the code is executed, the code will executed remotely. The remote execution of the code is done by transfer the code from the home container to the execution container. The home container is the container where the code resides now. The execution container is the container the code will be executed in. The home container of active tuple may be the execution container, may be not. So the active tuple may be move from container to container.

The execution of the tasks need resources, the resources may not reside in the peers the code is executing. But the passive tuples in the tuple space is accessible in anywhere within the tuple space. So the resources the code in the active tuples needed can only be obtained in the form of tuples. In this way, the code can be migrate to any peers in tuple space and execute everywhere in the tuple space.

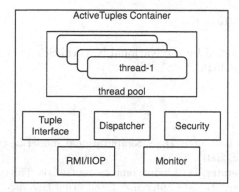

Fig. 2. The container in DTuplesHPC node. Tasks that spawned by *eval()* primitives are stored and exectued in container.

3.6 Data Items and Resources Needed by Computation

In DTuples, all the data are represented in the form of tuple, even the primitive data type, such as integer and float. So the data is referenced not by URL or address but by tuple. Tuple is shared data in shared space. Tuple are public accessible by any process running on the tuple space. In this meaning, the process can run on any of the nodes in the system. The process is executed transparently.

Data is represented by passive tuple. Data carried by tuples are shared. The tuples are not bounded into any specific node in the system. So the process can migrate among nodes. This is superior to the other system.

4 Conclusion

The main contribution of the DTuplesHPC is it extending the tuple space model to the area of peer-to-peer computing. It provides the ability of coordination that is lacked in the current peer-to-peer framework. This is needed in developing more sophisticated peer-to-peer applications. Second, it makes tuple space model an alternative for high performance computing area. Third, it is more scalable than the other tuple space implementation. The main drawback of DTuplesHPC is that the active tuple container use threads to execute the task. The different tasks are not isolated and may influence each other. In future, the DTuplesHPC will use separate JVM processes to execute the tasks.

In our opinion, the tuple space model is an ideal model for the peer-to-peer computing and grid computing for it provides the higher abstraction for the computation and data. And it decouples the participants in time and space which is more suitable than the other facilities that currently used in grid and peer-to-peer system. In the future, the load balancing and fine-granular tasks schedule will be researched.

Acknowledgment

This work was supported by the National Natural Science Foundation of China under Grant No.60503045.

References

1. Carriero, N. and Gelernter, D. A computational model of everything. Commun. ACM 44, 11 (Nov. 2001), 77-81.
2. Carriero, N.; Gelernter, D.; Linda: some current work, Thirty-Fourth IEEE Computer Society International Conference: Intellectual Leverage, Digest of Papers. 27 Feb.-3 March 1989 Page(s):98 - 101.
3. D. Gelernter, Domesticating Parallelism, IEEE Computer, 19(8):12-16, August 1986.
4. Sean Rhea, Brighten Godfrey, Brad Karp, John Kubiatowicz, Sylvia Ratnasamy, Scott Shenker, Ion Stoica, and Harlan Yu. OpenDHT: A Public DHT Service and Its Uses. Proceedings of ACM SIGCOMM 2005, August 2005.
5. Jini network technology, http://www.sun.com/software/jini/, 2005
6. Sun Microsystems. JavaSpaces Specification, http://www.sun.com/software/jini/specs/, March 2005.
7. Stphane Genaud and Choopan Rattanapoka, A Peer-to-Peer Framework for Robust Execution of Message Passing Parallel Programs, EuroPVM/MPI 2005, LNCS, vol. 3666, Springer-Verlag, pages 276–284, Ed. B. Di Martino et al., September 2005.
8. Yi Jiang, Guangtao Xue, Jinyuan You, DTuples: A Distributed Hash Table based Tuple Space Service for Distributed Coordination, To be appear in Proceedings of 5th International Conference on Grid and Cooperative Computing
9. FreePastry, http://freepastry.rice.edu/, 2006
10. A. Rowstron and A. Wood. Solving the Linda multiple rd problem using the copy-collect primitive. Science of Computer Programming, pages 335-358, Volume 31, Numbers 2-3, ISSN 0167-6423, July 1998.
11. http://jgrid.jini.org/, 2006
12. http://setiathome.berkeley.edu/, 2006

The Algorithm and Circuit Design of a 400MHz 16-Bit Hybrid Multiplier

Li Zhentao, Chen Shuming, Li Zhaoliang, and Lei Conghua

School of Computer Science and Technology, National University of Defense Technology,
410073 Changsha, China
lizhtao@nudt.edu.cn

Abstract. In this paper we present the algorithm of a 16-bit hybrid multiplier, which can work in two modes. In normal mode, it performs a 16-bit multiplication. In SIMD mode, it performs two parallel 8-bit multiplications. The proposed algorithm is based on the raix-4 modified Booth's algorithm. Our algorithm generates ten partial products and a modifier, which is five less than the other algorithms. We can get one 32-bit product or two 16-bit products by directly accumulating the ten partial products and the modifier, easing the design of the tree structures for compressing the partial products and the final adder. The proposed algorithm is adopted by YHFT-DSP/800, a high performance fixed-point DSP. The multiplier was full custom designed in 0.18um CMOS technology. We also designed a test chip. The test results show the multiplier works well at 400MHz in normal mode, 480MHz in SIMD mode. The simulated power is 35.8 mW at 400MHz, and 42.5 mW at 480MHz.

1 Introduction

The multiplier is an important kernel of the digital signal processors (DSP) because it typically determines the performance of the chips. Different digital signal processing algorithms need different data widths. 16-bit data is common for many applications. But some image and video processing tasks are well served by 8-bit data [1]. To enhance the performance of such multimedia applications, many DSPs provide SIMD instructions, in which the specified operation is executed on two (or more) operand sets to produce multiple outputs. In general purpose microprocessors, special SIMD units are designed to implement SIMD instructions, such as the MMX unit of Pentium II [2]. The multiplier often consumes a lot of layout area and power. So it is not economical to add a new unit to the embedded DSPs, which is power sensitive. For DSPs, a unit that supports both types of operations is more favorable.

Magnus Själander *et al.* proposed a twin-precision multiplier[3] which can perform one N-bit multiplication or two N/2-bit multiplications in parallel. Magnus's multiplier is based on simple array multiplier. For a 16-bit multiply, there will be 16 partial products. While the amount of hardware and delay depends on the number of partial products to be added. In this paper, we propose a novel hybrid multiplier algorithm which can work in two modes. In normal mode, it can perform a 16-bit multiplication. In SIMD mode, it can perform two 8-bit multiplications in parallel. Our multiplier is based on the radix-4 modified Booth's algorithm. For 16-bit hybrid multiplier, there

C. Jesshope and C. Egan (Eds.): ACSAC 2006, LNCS 4186, pp. 401–408, 2006.

are only ten partial products and a modifier. Our method generates only two more partial products than the ordinary 16-bit multiplier, but five less than the multiplier presented in [3]. So our algorithm is more efficient in performance, area and power.

We have organized this paper into three major sections. In Section 2, we introduce the algorithm of the 16-bit hybrid multiplier. In Section 3, we present the circuit design of YHFT-DSP/800's multiplier, which adopts the algorithm proposed in this paper. Section 4 depicts the design of the test chip and presents the test results.

2   The Algorithm of the 16-Bit Hybrid Multiplier

The methods of implementing integer multipliers can reduce to two steps—create a group of partial products, then add them to produce the final product. The speed and area of the multiplier are proportional to the number of partial products. Modified Booth's algorithm reduces the number of partial products by about a factor of two. Furthermore, only simple shifting and complementing are required to produce the partial products. So it is widely used in high speed multiplier. In radix-4 Booth's algorithm, the multipliers are divided into overlapping groups of 3 bits. Each group is decoded to select a single partial product from the set {-2M, -M, 0, M, 2M}, where M is the multiplicand. Fig. 1 shows the dot diagram for a 16×16 multiply using the radix-4 version of the algorithm (Booth 2) [4], where N_i refers to the *ith* bit of the multiplier N, S_N refers to the sign of N, S=1 indicates the partial product is inverted, E is used for sign extensions (Interested readers can refer to [4]). We should point out that the sign extensions of the first partial product are different with the others.

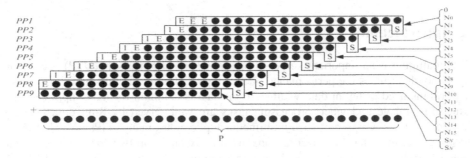

Fig. 1. 16 bit Booth 2 multiply

The algorithm of the 16-bit hybrid multiplier is based on the radix-4 modified Booth's algorithm. This multiplier can work in two modes. In normal mode, it operates as an ordinary 16-bit multiplier. The operation is

$$P[31:0] = M[15:0] \times N[15:0] \tag{1}$$

P is the output of the multiplier and it is 32-bit wide. When working in SIMD mode, it dose two 8-bit multiplications. The operations are

$$P[15:0] = M[7:0] \times N[7:0] \tag{2}$$

$$P[31:16] = M[15:8] \times N[15:8]$$

The lower 16 bits of P are used to hold the product of lower 8-bit SIMD multiply. The higher 16 bits of P are used to hold the product of higher 8-bit SIMD multiply.

The kernel of the hybrid multiplier is the method we used to generate the ten partial products and one modifier. No matter what mode the multiplier works in, if we accumulate the ten partial products and the modifier, we will get the correct results. Fig. 2 is the block diagram of the circuit that we use to generate the partial products and the modifier. M is a 16-bit multiplicand, and N is a 16-bit multiplier. The ten partial products are divided into two groups, each of which has a different multiplicand, M1 for partial products $PP1-PP5$, and M2 for $PP6-PP10$.

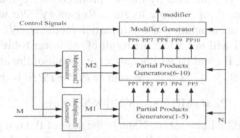

Fig. 2. Partial product generation circuit of the hybrid multiplier

The partial product generation process is illustrated by the use of a dot diagram, as shown in Fig.3. The values of S_{NL}, N_x, E_1, E_2, and E_3 in Fig. 3 depend on the multiplier's work mode. In the hybrid multiplier, we use the same algorithm to produce a partial product as in Fig. 1. If the multiplicand and the 3-bit multiplier group are the same, the generated partial products should be the same. We'll use this guideline to compare different partial products in the rest of this section.

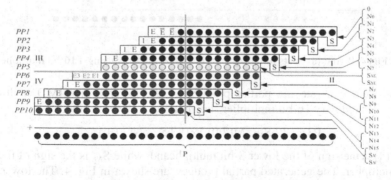

Fig. 3. Partial products of the hybrid multiplier

Now, let's see how the hybrid multiplier works in normal Mode. First, we assume the multiplicand and the multiplier in Fig. 1 are equal to those in Fig. 3. Second, we'll let $S_{NL} = N7$. So the multiplier group of $PP5$ is {N7, N7, N7}, and $PP5$ is 0. Next we will make M1 = M. Now *PP1—PP4* in Fig. 3 will be the same as *PP1—PP4* in Fig. 1. Then, we let M2 = M, Nx = N8, E1 = E, E2 = 1, E3=0. Now *PP6—PP10* in Fig. 3 will be equal to *PP5—PP9* in Fig. 1 respectively. If we add the ten partial products in Fig3, we will get the same result as in Fig. 1. Namely a 16-bit multiply is performed.

Next, we will show how this multiplier can perform two 8-bit multiplies. In SIMD mode, we'll initialize S_{NL} with the sign of the lower 8-bit multiplier. So *PP1—PP5* are the partial products of M1×N[7:0]. Then let Nx=0, E1 = $\overline{E}$, E2 = $\overline{E}$, E3=E. Now *PP6—PP10* are the partial products of M2×N[15:8]. Namely , the hybrid multiplier can be viewed as two 16×8 multipliers.

The dot products in Fig. 3 are divided into four regions. The effective result of the lower 8-bit multiply is generated by the dot products in Region I. The effective dot products of the higher 8-bit multiply locate in Region IV. We want to get two 16-bit products by simply accumulating the ten partial products. We must assure the dot products in Region II will not affect the result of the lower 8-bit multiply, and the dot products in Region I, II , and III will not affect the result of the higher 8-bit multiply.

If we set M2 = {M[15:8], 8'b0}, the sum of *PP6—PP10* is the product of

$$P2 = \{M[15:8], 8'b0\} \times N[15:8] \tag{3}$$

The lower 8 bits of P2 will be all 0s. Namely the sum of the dot products in Region II is 0. So the dot products in Region II don't affect the result of the lower 8-bit SIMD multiply. The higher 16-bit of P2 is the product of the higher 8-bit SIMD multiply.

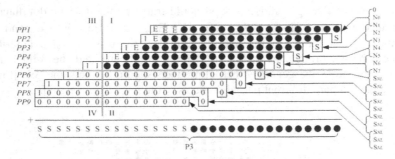

Fig. 4. Partial products of the lower 8-bit SIMD multiply using a 16-bit multiplier

Now we'll generate the partial products of the lower 8-bit SIMD multiply by means of an ordinary 16-bit multiplier shown in Fig. 1. The method is

$$P3 = \{8'bS_{ML}, M[7:0] \} \times \{8'bS_{NL}, N[7:0] \} \tag{4}$$

S_{ML} in (4) is the sign of the lower 8-bit multiplicand, while S_{NL} is the sign of the lower 8-bit multiplier. The generated partial products are shown in Fig. 4. The lower 16-bit of P3 are the product of the lower 8-bit multiply. While the higher 16-bit of P3 are all signs. S=0 if the product is positive. Otherwise S=1. Then we'll go back to *PP1-PP5*.

If we let M1={8'bS_{ML}, M[7:0] }, the sum of *PP1—PP5* will be equal to the sum of the dot products in Region I of Fig.4. Let P1 be the sum of *PP1—PP5*. The difference between P1 and P3 is 32'hfe00_0000. If we add 32'hfe00_0000 to P1 when the product of the lower 8-bit SIMD multiply is positive, or add 32'hfe01_0000 to P1 when the product of the lower 8-bit SIMD multiply is negative, the higher 16 bits of P1 will be all 0s. Namely the sum of $PP1-PP5$ will have no effect on the higher 16 bits of the result. Actually, we only need to add 16'hfe00 or 16'hfe01 to the higher 16 bits of the result. We call the value added a modifier. Now if we add the 10 partial products and the modifier together, we will get the products of two 8-bit multiplies.

We summarize the algorithm of the 16-bit hybrid multiplier in Table.1. In our algorithm, except the sign extensions of $PP6$, there is no modification to the Booth's algorithm. Our work focuses on changing the inputs to the Booth encoders and the circuits that produce a partial product. The modifier is the key to our algorithm. We can get one 32-bit or two 16-bit products by simply adding them together, easing the design of the tree structures for compressing the partial products and the final adder. Compared to the ordinary 16-bit multiplier, our algorithm produces one more partial product and one more modifier. Other penalties include the configuration circuits of the two multiplicands and several bits in the inputs to the Booth encoders.

Table 1. Summary of the 16-bit hybrid multiplier's algorithm

	Normal Mode	SIMD Mode
M1[15:0]	M[15:0]	{8'b S_{NL}, M[7:0]}
M2[15:0]	M[15:0]	{M[15:8], 8'b0}
S_{NL}	N8	the sign of the lower 8-bit multiplier
N_x	N8	0
{E3, E2, E1}	{0, 1, E}	{E, $\overline{E}$, $\overline{E}$ }
Modifier	0	16'hfe00 or 16'hfe01

The algorithm introduced in this section can also be extended to other word width. We have implemented a more complex 32-bit hybrid multiplier which can perform one 32-bit multiply, or two parallel 16-bit multiplies, or four parallel 8-bit multiplies.

3 Design Implementation

The algorithm presented in this paper is adopted by the multiplier unit of YHFT-DSP/800 [5]. YHFT-DSP/800 is designed in a cell based approach, and its maximum frequency is 250MHz. The test of the chip shows our algorithm is correct.

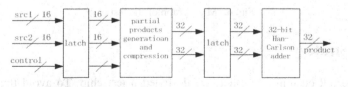

Fig. 5. Multiply pipeline of YHFT-DSP/800

To get higher performance, we redesigned the multiplier in 0.18um CMOS technology by full custom design. Multiply pipeline of YHFT-DSP/800 consists of two stages [6], as shown in Fig. 5. The first stage generates all partial products and the modifier, then compresses them into two 32-bit data. The second stage adds the two 32-bit data to produce the final product.

Only static complementary CMOS logic and pass transistor logic are used in the circuit. Tree structures for compressing the partial products are the most critical and complex part in the multiplier. We designed a tree consists of two stages of 4-2 compressor, one stage of 3-2 compressor [6]. All 8-bit operands of YHFT-DSP/800 are unsigned, so the modifier in SIMD mode is 16'hfe00. Only the higher 8 bits are effective. We spread them into the empty positions in the highest 8 columns of the dot products. So the partial products needed to be compressed in a column are no more than 10. In the layout design, all Booth encoders are located on one side of the tree structures, as shown in Fig. 6. The partial product generation circuits are near to their compressor to reduce the wire length and the needed route channels.

The adder in stage two is a 32-bit Han-Carlson adder [7, 8]. Han-Carlson adder is a parallel prefix adder with good balance between logic depth and fanout. 32-bit Han-Carlson adder consists of seven logic stages, one stage of P/G generation, 5 stages of carry propagation, and the final stage of sum. To reduce the input load, we insert one stage of inverter between the third and fourth stage of logic. The input load is reduced by 66% and the area is reduced by 30%, while the delay increase is 8% [9].

The multiplier consists of 13,444 transistors. The size of the multiplier is 400um×160um. The layout is shown in Fig. 6, with the test circuitry included.

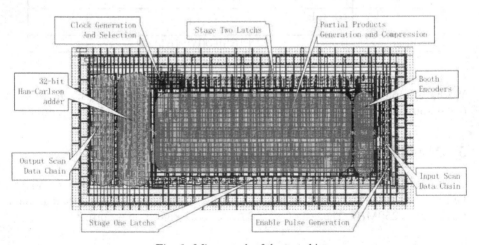

Fig. 6. Micrograph of the test chip

4   Test Strategy

To test the full custom multiplier, we designed a test chip. To avoid the expensive cost of high frequency package and test, we proposed a low cost, flexible test strategy. The basic idea of our test strategy is to use two scan chains to load the test vectors and scan out the results serially. The input scan chain has 37 registers, as much as the multiplier's input latches. The output scan chain consists of two levels of registers. The first level is used to capture the outputs of the multiplier, while the second level is used to scan out the result. The two scan chains worked at low speed. To capture the multiplier's high frequency characteristics, we preciously designed the enable pulse generation circuitry.

The multiplier's clock, *clk*, is generated by four on-chip ring oscillators. We can select *clk* from these four on-chip clocks and an external clock by three clock select pins. In order to know the real frequency of the multiplier, an output pin, *ClockOut*, is used to output the *clk* divided by 8.

Fig. 6 is the micrograph of the test chip. The package type is DIP24.We designed a test board to test the chip. The test condition is Vdd = 1.8V, room temperature. When we selected the external 27MHz clock as the multiplier's clock, the measured frequency of *ClockOut* was 3.45MHz. It showed the frequency-divide circuits worked well. Then we tested the chip in SIMD mode and normal mode respectively for each of the four on-chip clocks. In every mode, we tested 128 vectors. The test results are listed in Table 2. The multiplier can work at 400MHz in normal mode, 480MHz in SIMD mode. Because the period of the on-chip clock is fixed, we couldn't get more accurate frequencies. But we can say the real performance of the multiplier is better. The simulated power was 35.8 mW at 400 MHz, 42.5 mW at 480MHz.

Table 2. Test results of the test chip

ClockOut(MHz)	*clk*(MHz)	Normal Mode	SIMD Mode
37.2	300	succeeded	succeeded
43.8	350	succeeded	succeeded
50.6	400	succeeded	succeeded
59.4	480	failed	succeeded

5 Conclusion

This paper presents the algorithm of a 16-bit hybrid multiplier which can work in normal mode or SIMD mode. This algorithm generates ten partial products and a modifier. We can add them to produce the results of a 16-bit multiplication or two 8-bit multiplications. Compared to other similar researches, our algorithm produces less partial products. So it is more area and delay efficient. We implemented the algorithm by full custom design. The test results show our algorithm has the potential to achieve high frequency and low power. The proposed test strategy is very efficient to test hard macros. It avoids expensive packages and test equipments. What's more, we can locate the test vector that the chip fails. So it can help the designers to improve the design.

References

1. DSPs Adapt to New Challenges. A White Paper by Berkeley Design Technology, Inc (2003)
2. Michael, Kagan., *et al*: MMX™ Microarchitecture of Pentium® Processors With MMX Technology and Pentium®II Microprocessors. Intel Technology Journal, Q3'97 (1997)

3. Magnus, Själander., *et al*: An Efficient Twin-Precision Multiplier. In Proc. of the IEEE 22nd International Conference on Computer Design (ICCD 2004), San Jose, California (2004)
4. Bewick, G.W.: Fast Multiplications: Algorithms and Imlementation. PhD thesis, Stanford University (1994)
5. Chen, Shuming., Li, Zhentao., *et al*: Research and Development of High Performance YHFT Digital Signal Processor. Journal of Computer Research and Development, Vol. 43 (2006)
6. Li, Zhaoliang., Li, Zhentao,. Xing, Zuocheng.: The Full Custom Design of a 16-Bit Multiplier. NCCET'05, Jinan (2005)
7. Knowles, S.: A family of adders. The15th IEEE Symposium on Computer Arithmetic.(2001)
8. Kuo, Qi-Wei., *et al*: Substrate-Bias Optimized 0.18um 2.5GHz 32-bit Adder with Post-Manufacture Tunable Clock. The 2005 International Symposium on VLSI Technology, Systems, and Applications (2005 VLSI-TSA), Hsinchu, Taiwan (2005)
9. Lei, Conghua., Li, Zhentao,. Li, Shaoqing.: The Circuit Optimization of a 32-Bit static Adder. NCCET'05, Jinan (2005)

Live Range Aware Cache Architecture

Peng Li[1], Dongsheng Wang[2], Songliu Guo[3], Tao Tian[4], and Weimin Zheng[5]

Research Institute of Information Technology
National Laboratory for Information Science and Technology
Tsinghua University, Beijing, China
{p-li02[1], guosongliu01[3], tian00[4]}@mails.tsinghua.edu.cn
{wds[2], zwm-dcs[5]}@tsinghua.edu.cn

Abstract. Memory wall is always the focus of computer architecture research. In this paper, we observe that in computers with write-back cache, memory write operation actually lags behind write instruction commitment. By the time memory write operation executes, the data might already have gone out of its live range. Based on this observation, a novel Cache architecture called LIve Range Aware Cache (LIRAC) is proposed. LIRAC can significantly reduce the number of write operations with minimal hardware support. Performance benefits of LIRAC are evaluated by trace-based analysis using simplescalar simulator and SPEC CPU 2000 benchmarks. Our results show that LIRAC can eliminate 21% of write operations on average and up to 85% in the best case.

Keywords: Live Range, Cache, Memory Hierarchy.

1 Introduction

One of the most important problems in computer architecture discipline is Memory wall. While Processor follows the well-known Moore's law, doubling its performance every 18-24 months, the speed of memory access grows about 7% every year. Memory Access is the bottleneck of the whole computer system.

We notice that when scratch data is cached in write-back cache, it is unnecessary to write back cached data when the modified data is swapped out, since the modified data will no longer be read again. However, existing cache architectures cannot effectively take advantage of this observation. In this paper, we explicitly distinguish writes in processor domain and memory domain, and further propose LIve Range Aware Cache (LIRAC). LIRAC focuses on reducing the number of write-back operations, and does not affect read operations. With write operations decreased, LIRAC can reduce both execution time and energy.

The live range of register has been studied by previous research. In [1], Franklin and Sohi studied the lifetime of register instances and concluded that many registers were short-lived. Efforts have been made to reduce register commitments in superscalar processors to ease the pressure of register allocation and save energy [2],[3],[4],[5]. This paper studies the live range of memory address and focuses on reducing memory write operations. Compared with previous register

C. Jesshope and C. Egan (Eds.): ACSAC 2006, LNCS 4186, pp. 409–415, 2006.

live range analysis, memory optimization is more important because memory access is far more expensive than register access.

Trace-based simulation is used to evaluate the result of LIRAC. Simulation result shows that LIRAC can reduce 21% of write operations on the average and up to 85% in the best case.

The rest of this paper is organized as follows. Section 2 describes the architecture of LIRAC. Section 3 presents methodology and simulation results of LIRAC architecture. We conclude in Section 4.

2 Live Range Aware Cache Architecture

2.1 Write in Processor and Memory Domain

We observe that there are two types of writes in a computer system, writes in processor domain (Wp) and writes in memory domain (Wm). Wp refers to write instructions committed by processor and Wm refers to write operations performed to memory (e.g. cache write-back). In computers without buffering technology, Wp and Wm are exactly the same. However, in computers with buffering technology, both the occurrence and sequence of Wp and Wm may be different, as shown in Fig. 1.

Store R1, ADDR0   //Wp of ADDR0

Store R2, ADDR1   //Wp of ADDR1

Store R3, ADDR0   //Wp of ADDR0

Load R4,ADDR1'   //Wm of ADDR1

//ADDR1' and ADDR1 are mapped to the same cache line

Load R5,ADDR0'   //Wm of ADDR0

//ADDR0' and ADDR0 are mapped to the same cache line

Fig. 1. Writes in Processor and Memory Domain

Fig. 1 shows the assembly code of an example program. The first instruction writes R1 to memory address ADDR0. The value is temporally saved in cache and not written to memory. At this time, cache and memory are incoherent. Cache holds the current value while memory holds the stale value. The following two instructions write R2 to ADDR1 and R3 to ADDR0 respectively. Up till this time, all values are buffered in the write-back cache and no actual memory write operation has occurred. The fourth instruction reads memory address ADDR1, which is different from ADDR1 but mapped to the same cache location. The cache line containing ADDR1 is swapped out and replaced by the new line. At this time, the dirty cache line containing ADDR1 is written back to memory. Similar operation happens when the fifth instruction is executed.

Wp and Wm of ADDR0/ADDR1 are shown in the figure. From the figure, we can tell that both the occurrence and sequence of Wp and Wm are different.

For a given address, Wm always lags behind Wp. Wp is the inherent property of software. Given a program, the occurrence and sequence of Wp is fixed, so the number of Wp cannot be reduced. On the other hand, Wm is determined by both software and hardware. A program may generate different Wm sequences with different memory hierarchy. This paper focuses on how to reduce the number of Wm.

2.2 Live Range and Dead Range

To reduce Wm, the purpose of Wm is reexamined first. A write operation is useful only if the memory address might be read again. If a write operation is definitely followed by another write operation to the same memory address, then the first write becomes useless.

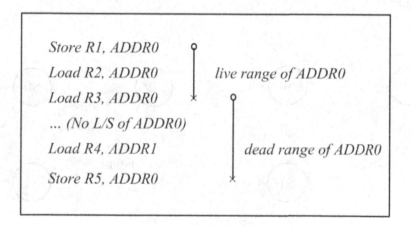

Fig. 2. Live Range and Dead Range

Fig. 2 shows a sequence of instructions. The first instruction writes R1 to ADDR0. If it is executed on a computer with no write-back caches, the value must be written to memory to ensure correctness. If the program is executed on a computer with write-back cache, the value can be buffered in cache temporally. Thereafter the second instruction reads the value from cache. In conventional write-back cache, when the fourth instruction is executed, the dirty cache line containing ADDR0 will be swapped out and written back to memory. Nonetheless, if we can know in advance that the next memory access to ADDR0 is definitely write, as shown in the figure, we can discard the dirty line without writing it back to memory. This observation can be used to reduce Wm.

To achieve this, the live range and dead range of a memory address are defined. The word "Live Range" is borrowed from compiler technology. Here we define the live range and dead range of a memory address. The live range of a memory address is from a write of the memory address to the last read of the address before another write of the same address. Similarly, the dead range of a memory address is from the last read of the memory address to the next write of the address. The definitions are also illustrated in Fig. 2.

2.3   Architecture of LIRAC

In conventional write-back cache, a cache line will be written back to memory if the data has been modified. But, in our proposed LIRAC architecture, a cache line is written back to memory if the data has been modified AND the modified address is in its live range. In other words, when the data is in its dead range at eviction, nothing will be written back regardless of the dirty flag. LIRAC architecture does not change the replacement policy of cache, nor does it change read operations. Compared with conventional write-back cache, LIRAC can significantly reduce the number of write operations with minimal hardware support.

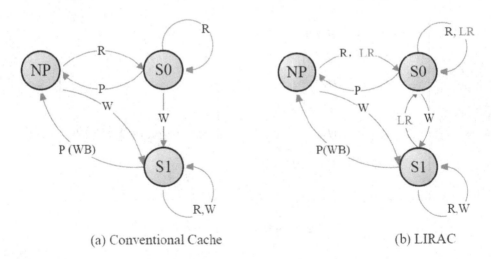

(a) Conventional Cache   (b) LIRAC

Fig. 3. Cache State Transition Graph

Fig. 3(a) shows the state transition graph of a cache line in conventional write-back cache. There are three states: NP, S0 and S1. NP stands for "Not Present", indicating that the address is not located in cache. S0 indicates that the address is in cache and it is clean. S1 indicates that the address is in cache and it is dirty. Three operations, R, W and P, can act on these states. R, W and P stands for read, write and replace operation to the address respectively. If operation P acts on the state S0, the cache line is just replaced and not written back to memory. If P acts on the S1, the cache line is written back to memory before replaced by another cache line.

Fig. 3(b)shows the state transition of a cache line in a LIRAC system. A new operation, LR, is added to indicate the LastRead instruction mentioned above. LR acts similarly to normal read operation except on state M. If LR acts on M, the next state is S because the live range of the given address ends. In other words, if a cache line in dead range is replaced by others, it is simply thrown away rather than written back to main memory. With the additional transition, the number of Wm can be reduced.

3   Performance Evaluation

In this paper, we use memory tracing to evaluate the benefit of LIRAC. First run the program and record all memory access information, then, analyze the traces to find the live range of each memory address. Tracing is fairly simple to implement, but it is not a realistic approach. Trace studies depend on many factors such as program input and thus is unreliable. Moreover, trace analysis is an oracle heuristics approach (i.e. perfect branch prediction, perfect memory disambiguation, etc.) and thus the result can only be used as an upper bound of practical approach (e.g. compiler analysis or binary transformation). However, the result of trace analysis can be helpful to compiler analysis and binary transformation. Since trace analysis is simple, we use this method in this paper to evaluate the performance of LIRAC architecture.

Memory trace simulation contains three steps: trace generation, trace analysis and trace execution. 3 multimedia applications(MPEG Decode, MPEG Encode and H.264 Decode) and 10 SPEC 2000 applications are selected to evaluate the performance of LIRAC architecture. All benchmarks are compiled with "-O2" option.

Simplescalar simulator [6] is used to generate traces. Trace generation is to get memory access sequence in processor domain, so sim-fast mode is selected because no detailed hardware implementation is necessary. Each trace item contains three fields: memory access type, memory access address and instruction address. The size of the generated trace files are huge. For example, running gcc in test mode will generate a trace file larger than 5GB. To save disk space and simulation time, scaled inputs instead of standard inputs are used in some benchmarks including gcc, gzip, and bzip2. Sampling technique is not used because accurate live range information is not available in sampled traces.

Trace analysis is used to find live range of every memory address. The algorithm is sketched in Fig. 4. Live structure is a hash map with address as key and trace number as value. It is used to track the last live read. Trace file is fed to trace analyzer sequentially. For a read trace item, Live structure is updated; for a write item, trace analyzer will look up Live structure and mark previously recoded read as LastRead.

```
map< int, int> Live;
while(!trace_end)
{
    traceno++;
    fetch_trace();
    if (tracetype == READ)
        Live[addr]=traceno;
    else //Write
        if (find(Live, addr))
        {
            LastRead.insert(index->traceno);
            Live.erase(index);
        }
}
For_each_traceitem()
    LastRead.insert(index->traceno);
```

Fig. 4. Algorithm for Trace Analysis

In trace execution, both the original trace and optimized trace are run on a trace simulator to evaluate the effect of LIRAC architecture. Dinero IV simulator [7] is a fast, highly configurable trace-driven cache simulator developed by Wisconsin University. It supports multi-level cache, different replacement policy and sub-block organization. Less than 10 lines are modified to support LIRAC architecture in Dinero IV simulator.

Baseline structure in our experiment is 4-way associative, write-back, write-alloc data cache. The replacement policy is LRU.

Fig. 5. Reduction of Wm using LIRAC architecture

Simulation results are shown in Fig. 5. For each benchmark, there are 6 bars, respectively for cache sizes 1KB, 4KB, 16KB, 64KB, 256KB and 1MB. The height of each bar shows the ratio of writes in LIRAC to writes in baseline conventional cache(i.e. the shorter the better). From the figure, we can see that LIRAC can reduce 21% memory writes on average and up to 85% in the best case.

4   Conclusion

In this paper, we explicitly distinguished two kinds of writes: write in processor domain (Wp) and writes in memory domain (Wm) and defined live range and dead range of a memory location. Based on this we proposed the architecture of LIve Range Aware Cache (LIRAC) Simulation results show that the potential benefit of LIRAC can be great. This is only an initial result for Live Range Aware Memory Hierarchy study. While the initial results are promising, a lot more work needs to be done. In the future, we plan to modify compiler implementation to support LIRAC architecture.

Acknowledgments. We would like to thank the anonymous reviewers for their valuable feedback. This material is based on work supported by Funded by Basic Research Foundation of Tsinghua National Laboratory for Information Science and Technology (TNList) and Intel China Research Center.

References

1. Manoj Franklin and Gurindar S. Sohi, "Register Traffic Analysis for Streamlining Inter-Operation Communication in Fine-Grain Parallel Processors", Proceedings of 25th International Symposium on Microarchitecture, 1992, 236–245.
2. Luis A. Lozano C. and Guang R. Gao, "Exploiting Short-Lived Variables in Superscalar Processors", Proceedings of 28th International Symposium on Microarchitecture, 1995, 292–302.
3. Guillermo Savransky, Ronny Ronen and Antonio Gonzalez, "A Power Aware Register Management Mechanism". International Journal of Parallel Programming, Volume 31, Issue 6, December 2003, 451–467.
4. Dmitry Ponomarev, Gurhan Kucuk, Ponomarev, Oguz Ergin and Kanad Ghose, "Isolating Short-Lived Operands for Energy Reduction", IEEE Transaction on Computers, Vol. 53, No. 6, June 2004, 697–709.
5. Milo M. Martin, Amir Roth, and Charles N. Fischer, "Exploiting Dead Value Information". Proceedings of 30th International Symposium on Microarchitecture, 1997, 125–135.
6. Todd Austin, Eric Larson and Dan Ernst, "SimpleScalar: An Infrastructure for Computer System Modeling", IEEE Computer 35(2), 2002, 59–67.
7. Jan Edler and Mark D. Hill, "Dinero IV Trace-Driven Uniprocessor Cache Simulator", http://www.cs.wisc.edu/ markhill/DineroIV, 2003.

The Challenges of Efficient Code-Generation for Massively Parallel Architectures

Jason M McGuiness[1], Colin Egan[1], Bruce Christianson[1], and Guang Gao[2]

[1] Department of Compiler Technology and Computer Architecture, University of
Hertfordshire, Hatfield, Hertfordshire, U.K. AL10 9AB
c.egan@herts.ac.uk
[2] CAPSL, University of Delaware, Delaware, U.S.A.
g.gao@capsl.udel.edu

Abstract. Overcoming the memory wall [15] may be achieved by increasing the bandwidth and reducing the latency of the processor to
memory connection, for example by implementing Cellular architectures,
such as the IBM Cyclops. Such massively parallel architectures have sophisticated memory models. In this paper we used DIMES (the Delaware
Iterative Multiprocessor Emulation System), developed by CAPSL at
the University of Delaware, as a hardware evaluation tool for cellular
architectures. The authors contend that there is an open question regarding the potential, ideal approach to parallelism from the programmer's perspective. For example, at language-level such as UPC or HPF,
or using trace-scheduling, or at a library-level, for example OpenMP or
POSIX-threads. To investigate this, we have chosen to use a threaded
Mandelbrot-set generator with a work-stealing algorithm to evaluate the
DIMES *cthread* programming model for writing a simple multi-threaded
program.

1   Introduction

Integrating the processing logic and memory [2], termed PIM, is an approach
to overcome the memory wall [15]. PIM architectures may improve both data-
processing and data-access times, but the combined processor speed and the
amount of memory may be reduced [2]. This may be overcome by connecting
multiple, independent PIM cells, giving a *cellular architecture*. In this organisation, every thread unit is an independent single-issue, in-order processor, thus
able to potentially access memory independently. Moreover, the different memory hierarchies may have different access timings and consistency models such as
location consistency [7]. This gives rise to a number of code-generation problems,
centred around the fact that to provide computational power, these systems are
not only massively parallel, but have complex memory hierarchies.

Research also proceeded towards thread-generating compilers, for example,
HPF and UPC [9], IBM XL Fortran and Visual Age C/C++, largely based
upon OpenMP, all of which have their compromises. Some of these also have
support for the various memory models.

C. Jesshope and C. Egan (Eds.): ACSAC 2006, LNCS 4186, pp. 416–422, 2006.
© Springer-Verlag Berlin Heidelberg 2006

Unfortunately general-purpose languages have been slow to adopt a sophisticated abstraction of the machine model, library-based approaches have developed, for example, the various implementations of OpenMP. But, the authors contend that library-based solutions to threading are too dependent upon the programmer to use effectively. For example, the explicit use of locks in programs is prone to error, with deadlocks and race-conditions that are hard to track down easily, introduced, even on systems with only a few processors. The development of suitable tools to debug multi-threaded applications has also been slow. Debuggers are in development, for example for Cyclops [8], but there have been too few, with limited functionality.

As identifying parallelism both correctly and efficiently is very hard for the programmer to do, the authors contend that they should not do it. The compiler, equipped via these libraries with a detailed machine-model, could be able to use the programmer-identified parallelize-able variables and functions, to generate more efficient code. The authors identified little work investigating the software aspect of the code-generation problem for massively-parallel architectures. Unfortunately, if this case would continue, this shortcoming could adversely affect the popularity of such systems and maintain the perception that massively parallel architectures are too specialised and thus too expensive to be of more general use. Given the popularity of introducing multi-core processors, this position is set to become even more untenable.

2   Related Work

2.1   The Programming Models: From Compiler to Libraries

With such compute bandwidth, and parallelism, a number of problems for the programmer have been raised, primarily these are focused on the problems of memory reads and writes. Super-scalar chips have had mechanisms to hide these problems from the programmer, but the cellular architectures of such chips as picoChip [6] and IBM BlueGene/C [1] do not. Thus the programmer needs to know how memory reads and writes interact with:

- the software-controlled data-cache attached to that pipeline,
- the software-controlled data-cache of other on-chip pipelines,
- any global on-chip memory,
- the software controlled data-caches of other off-chip pipelines,
- the global on-chip memory that is on any other chips,
- any global memory that is not on any chip
- and finally, given the massive parallelism available, how to make efficient use of it.

For a programmer, the memory access models are important to understand, or to have a library or compiler that hides the details from the applications programmer. In the remainder of the paper the authors will focus on the IBM BlueGene/C architecture, and a prototype implementation of it called Cyclops

[2,4], that was implemented at CAPSL at the University of Delaware in collaboration with the University of Hertfordshire. The Cyclops architecture was prototyped in hardware, called DIMES/P, [14] which was used as the platform for executing the programming example, described later in this paper. In the following sections the memory access models will be discussed, leading on to a presentation of the authors' experience in developing a program for such an architecture. The experience gained from this will allow the authors to discuss the major problems that were faced, how, if at all, they were overcome, and the outstanding problem domains that, in the authors' experience, would hinder the acceptance of multi-core chips and, moreover such massively parallel designs as IBM BlueGene/C.

2.2   Programming Models on Cellular Architectures

The hardware differences between cellular and super-scalar architectures indicate that different programming models, to those used for super-scalar architectures, are required to make effective use of the cellular architectures [7,8]. In the first two of those three papers, their authors propose the use of a combination of execution models and memory models, as already noted in this paper.

The primary concerns when programming DIMES/P, and thus any Cyclops-based architecture, were:

- How to manage the potentially large numbers of threads.
- How to easily express any parallelism within the input source-code.
- How to make correct, and most effective use, of the memory consistency models.

Some research has already been done regarding programming models for the threading, such as using thread percolation as a technique to perform dynamic load-balancing [10]. Another piece of research [3] investigated using multi-level scheduling-schemes: a work-stealing algorithm at the higher-level and a multi-threading technique at the lower-level to hide communication latencies. Alternatively there is research [13] into how to implement OpenMP efficiently on cellular architectures such as IBM BlueGene/C.

3   Programming for Cyclops - *cthreads*

This section will very briefly describe the *cthread* programming model, which is an early version of TNT [5,8], then how it was used to implement the programming example, followed by a discussion of the implementation.

The implementation of the memory consistency models was relatively simple: earlier, unpublished, work on the GCC-based compiler had implemented a simple algorithm: all static variables were stored in on-chip memory, and the function call stack, including all automatic variables was placed in the scratch-pad memory.

As there was no language-level support for thread management, a library had to be implemented to support the thread management instructions in the Cyclops ISA, which was used as the basis for creating a higher-level C++ abstraction. This was because the cthread implementation, that closely followed a POSIX-Threads API, was considered far too primitive by the authors to be effectively used for programming Cyclops. This C++ API also included critical-section, mutex and event objects to allow for easier management of the lower-level objects.

To test these ideas, and the Cyclops architecture, a small, simple and embarrassingly parallel program to generate Mandelbrot sets [12] was created. In the following sections a brief overview of how this how this program may be implementation for DIMES/P.

3.1 Threading and the Mandelbrot Set

Due to the properties of DIMES/P, alternative techniques were not possible, as there are only 8 thread units between two processors. In this implementation, the complex plane was divided into a series of horizontal strips. Those strips may be calculated independently of each other, using separate threads, implemented as algorithm 1.

Algorithm 1. The render-thread algorithm.

1. Set the value of m, the maximum iterations, greater than zero. Set the estimated completion-time, t, to ∞.
2. Set $c = x$, where x is the top-left of the strip to be rendered.
3. Initialise $n = 0$, $z_0 = 0$.
   (a) Execute $z_{n+1} = z_n^2 + c$.
   (b) Increment n.
   (c) If $\mid z_n \mid \geq 2$ then that c is not in the set of points which comprise the Mandelbrot set. Go to 4.
   (d) If $n > m$ then that c is in the Mandelbrot set, i.e. $c \subset M$. Go to 4.
   (e) Go to 3a.
4. Increment the real part of c. If the real part of c is less than the width of the strip to be rendered, go to 3.
5. Calculate the average of t and the time it took to render that line.
6. Set the real part of c to the left-hand of the strip. Increment the complex part of c. If the complex part of c is less than the height of the strip, go to 3.
7. Signal work completed, set $t = 0$ (thus this thread is guaranteed not to be selected by the work-stealing algorithm 2).
8. Suspend.

However, each strip will, in general, take a different amount of time to complete, thus the threads would have completed their assigned portion of work at different times. Thus a work-stealing algorithm 2 performed the load-balancing between the threads.

The bandwidth of the work-stealing thread, algorithm 2, limited scaling to more worker threads, algorithm 1. But algorithm 2 would able to tolerate failures: if a worker thread stopped responding, its work would have been eventually stolen.

Algorithm 2. The work-stealing algorithm.

1. Monitor render threads for a work-completed signal. That thread that completes we shall denote as T_c.
2. Find that render thread with the longest estimated completion-time, t, note that each render thread updates this time upon completion of a line. Call this thread T_l.
3. Stop T_l when it completes the current line it is rendering.
4. Split the remaining work to be done in the strip equally between the two render threads T_c and T_l.
5. Restart the render threads T_c and T_l.
6. Go to 1.

If robustness is not required, then the image generated may be viewed as an array values. Each of these values would be the classification of c. Thus if one has $p_{0...q}$ threads, each p_n thread initially classifies a point in the array offset by n, and once completed, would move along the array using a stride of q. This would allow the use of a number of threads that is bounded by the number of points within the image.

3.2   DIMES/P Implementation of the Mandelbrot-Set Application

In cthreads, each software thread was statically allocated to one of the 8 hardware thread-units in DIMES/P at program start-up. The software threads were:

1. The a thread was required for cthreads support and the debugger [8], if it were to be run.
2. The main loop of the Mandelbrot-set application.
3. The thread that executed the work-stealing algorithm 2. In principle, a worker thread could also run on this thread unit, but cthreads did not support virtual threads.
4. The remaining 5 threads were worker threads that executed algorithm 1.

Further details regarding the implementation may be found in [11].

4   Discussion

The limitations of DIMES/P prevented further study of the properties of this program: scalability and timings were not done because of the limited number of thread units (8) and memory capacity.

The memory model support, using the C/C++ keyword *static* by the compiler, made natural use of language-level syntax to map data into scratch-pad and on-chip memory made using these different memory models. The atomic, word-sized, memory-operations on Cyclops were not used for this problem, because of the multiple, read-modify-write operations that had to be maintained as an atomic unit. If the manual locking had been implemented within the compiler, then it may have been possible for the compiler to perform optimization on the locking of access to the data.

With regards to the thread library: in the opinion of the author's, the complexity of POSIX-Threads has been a hindrance to successful multi-thread program creation. Abstracting the algorithms that expressed the parallelism within the Mandelbrot program, for example the work-stealing algorithm, was not implemented for this paper, as this was considered to be potentially too closely coupled to the actual program in question. Ultimately this decision, in the authors' opinion, was flawed, and by extracting and abstracting the work-stealing algorithm from both the program and Cyclops, would have allowed a programmer to reuse that algorithm with other programs, thus separating the design of the parallelism from the details of the program that would wish to use it.

It is still an open question regarding what may be the ideal approach to parallelism: language-level support such as UPC, HPF or other language extensions, or within the compiler using trace-scheduling, or should it be at a library-level using, for example OpenMP or POSIX-Threads, or should it be within the architecture, such as the data-flow design. If programs more sophisticated than the one described in this paper are to be successfully written for these cellular architectures, then based upon this brief examination, it is the authors' contention that it would be highly advantageous to have:

- Compiler support for making use of any available the memory model of the architecture.
- Compiler support for locking, which would aid the programmer with writing code that avoids race-conditions.
- Reusable abstractions of techniques of implementing parallelism, such as work-stealing, or master-slave models. These abstractions could make use of both data and code locality to ensure that a thread unit re-executes the same code, if desirable.

Acknowledgement. The research presented in this paper is supported by the Engineering and Physical Research Council (EPSRC) grant number: GR/S58492/01.

References

1. Almásil, G., Cascaval, C., Castaños, J.G., Denneau, M., Lieber, D., Moreira, J.E. and Warren, H.S., "Dissecting Cyclops: Detailed Analysis of a Multithreaded Architecture.", ACM SIGARCH Computer Architecture News, Vol. 31, March 2003.
2. Cascaval, C., Castaños, J.G., Ceze, L., Denneau, M., Gupta, M., Lieber, D., Moreira, J.E., Strauss, K. and Warren, H.S., "Evaluation of a Multithreaded Architecture for Cellular Computing.", 8th International Symposium on High-Performance Computer Architecture (HPCA), February 2002.
3. Cavalherio, G.G.H., Doreille, M., Galilée, F., Gautier, T., Roch, J-L., "Scheduling Parallel Programs on Non-Uniform Memory Architectures.", HPCA Conference – Workshop on Parallel Computing for Irregular Applications WPCIA1, Orlando, USA, January 1999.
4. del Cuvillo, J.B., Zhu, W., Hu, Z. and Gao, G.R., "FAST: A Functionally Accurate Simulation Toolset for the Cyclops-64 Cellular Architecture.", Workshop on Modeling, Benchmarking and Simulation (MoBS), held in conjunction with the 32nd Annual International Symposium on Computer Architecture (ISCA'05), Madison, Wisconsin, June 4, 2005.

5. del Cuvillo, J.B., Zhu, W., Hu, Z. and Gao, G.R., "TiNy Threads: a Thread Virtual Machine for the Cyclops64 Cellular Architecture.", Fifth Workshop on Massively Parallel Processing (WMPP), held in conjunction with the 19th International Parallel and Distributed Processing System, Denver, Colorado, April 3 - 8, 2005.

6. Duller, A., Towner, D., Panesar, G., Gray, A. and Robbins, W., "picoArray technology: the tool's story.", Proceedings of the Design, Automation and Test in Europe Conference and Exhibition, IEEE, 2005.

7. Gao, G.R. and Sarkar, V., "Location Consistency - a New Memory Model and Cache Consistency Protocol.", IEEE Transactions on Computers, Vol. 49, No. 8, August 2000.

8. Gao, G.R., Theobald, K.B., Govindarajan, R., Leung, C., Hu, Z., Wu, H., Lu, J., del Cuvillo, J., Jacquet, A., Janot, V. and Sterling, T.L., "Programming Models and System Software for Future High-End Computing Systems: Work-in-Progress.", International Parallel and Distributed Processing Symposium (IPDPS'03) April 22 - 26, 2003 Nice, France.

9. El-Ghazawi, T.A., Carlson, W.W., Draper, J.M., "UPC Language Specifications V1.1.1", October 2003.

10. Kakulavarapu, P., Morrone, C.J., Theobald, K., Amaral J.N. and Gao, G.R., "A Comparative Performance Study of Fine-Grain Multi-threading on Distributed Memory Machines.", 19th IEEE International Performance, Computing and Communication Conference-IPCCC2000, Phoenix, Arizona, USA, Feb. 20-22, 2000.

11. M^{C}Guiness, J.M., "A DIMES Demonstration Application: Mandelbrot-Set Generation Using a Work-Stealing Algorithm.", CAPSL Technical Note 11, Department of Electrical and Computer Engineering, University of Delaware, Newark, Delaware, June 2003, ftp://ftp.capsl.udel.edu/pub/doc/notes/.

12. Mandelbrot, B.B., "The Fractal Geometry of Nature.", W.H.Freeman & Co., Sept., 1982.

13. Rodenas, D., Martorell, X., Ayguade, E., Labarta, J., Almasi, G., Cascaval, C., Castanos, J. and Moreira, J., "Optimizing NANOS OpenMP for the IBM Cyclops Multithreaded Architecture.", 19th IEEE International Parallel and Distributed Processing Symposium, Vol. 1, pp. 110, 2005.

14. Sakane, H., Yakay, L., Karna, V., Leung, C. and Gao, G.R., "DIMES: An Iterative Emulation Platform for Multiprocessor-System-on-Chip Designs.", IEEE International Conference on Field-Programmable Technology, December 15-17, 2003, Tokyo, Japan.

15. Wulf, W. and McKee, S., "Hitting the memory wall: Implications of the obvious.", Computer Architecture News, 23(1), pp. 20-24, 1995.

16. Zhang, Y., Zhu. W., Chen, F., Hu, Z. and Gao, G.R, "Sequential Consistency Revisited: The Sufficient Conditions and Method to Reason Consistency Model of a Multiprocessor-on-a chip Architecture.", The IASTED International Conference on Parallel and Distributed Computing and Networks (PDCN2005), February 15 - 17, 2005, Innsbruck, Austria.

Reliable Systolic Computing Through Redundancy*

Kunio Okuda[1], Siang Wun Song[1], and Marcos Tatsuo Yamamoto[1]

Universidade de São Paulo, Brazil
{kunio, song, mty}@ime.usp.br,
http://www.ime.usp.br/~song/

Abstract. The systolic array paradigm has low communication demand
because it does not use costly global communication and each processor
communicates with few other processors. It is thus suitable to be used
in cluster computing. The systolic approach, however, is vulnerable in a
heterogeneous environment where machines perform differently. In this
paper we propose a redundant systolic solution with high-availability to
deal with this problem. We analyze the overhead that results from the
need to coordinate the actions of the redundant processors and show that
this overhead is worth the performance improvement it provides.

Keywords: cluster computing, heterogeneity, redundancy, high-availability.

1 Introduction

Since the early eighties, systolic arrays have been proposed to implement numerically intensive applications, e.g. image and signal processing operations such as
the discrete Fourier transform, product of matrices, matrix inversion, etc. for
VLSI implementation on silicon chips [3]. Given a sequential algorithm specified
as nested loops, more formally as a system of uniform recurrence equations, dependence transformation methods [4,5,6] map the specified computation into a
time-processor space domain that can be mapped onto a systolic array.

One nice property of a systolic algorithm is that each processor communicates only with a few other processors. It is thus suitable for implementation on
a cluster of computers in which we wish to avoid costly global communication
operations. A recent work [2] explores the systolic array paradigm in cluster
computing. This approach, however, is not adequate in a heterogeneous environment where the performance of the computers may vary along time. Since the
systolic structure is based on tightly-coupled connections, the existence of one
single slow processor can compromise and degrade the overall performance. In
this paper we propose a solution based on redundancy to deal with this problem.
There are many techniques for dependable computing based on check-pointing

---

* Partially supported by CNPq Proc. No. 55.0094/2005-9 and 30.5218/03-4. The authors wish to thank the anonymous referees for their helpful comments.

C. Jesshope and C. Egan (Eds.): ACSAC 2006, LNCS 4186, pp. 423–429, 2006.

and roll-back recovery [7]. The redundant approach is simple but we introduce some overhead to coordinate the actions of the redundant processors. We show that this overhead is worth the performance improvement it provides. The experimental results show that the incurred overhead is small compared to the overall performance we get over the non-redundant solution.

2   Matrix Multiplication Example

In [2] we use the systolic array structure to solve two basic problems: matrix product and alignment of two strings. We now use the matrix product example to illustrate the redundancy method. Given two $n \times n$ input matrices A and B, we wish to compute matrix $C = AB$. The basic systolic matrix multiplication algorithm is shown in Figure 1. For matrices of size $n \times n$, the number of processors p used is n^2. The input elements of A and B enter the systolic array and move across the array while elements of the product C remain in the processors.

To implement this systolic algorithm on a cluster, synchronization can be implemented by using non-blocking sends and blocking receives. However, as observed in [2], the basic systolic algorithm is not suitable for cluster computing because of the fine granularity and the large number of processors required. To make the granularity coarser we consider sub-matrices instead of single elements in the basic algorithm. Assume the number of processors is $P = p \times p$ and assume also n divides p. We can view the product of two $n \times n$ matrices as multiplying two $p \times p$ matrices whose elements are $n/p \times n/p$ sub-matrices.

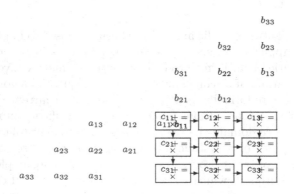

Fig. 1. Basic systolic matrix multiplication algorithm

3   Use of Redundancy

The redundancy approach to deal with heterogeneity is relatively straightforward but nonetheless promising in terms of the results obtained. For this approach to be feasible, we rely on the abundance of computing resources in the cluster. One

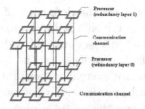

Fig. 2. Redundant systolic structure with degree of redundancy = 2

issue that needs to be addressed is how we employ redundancy. Another issue is that the use of redundancy may incur in overhead and we need to investigate the influence of this overhead on the overall performance.

Assume we want to implement a parallel systolic algorithm that requires p processors. To implement this algorithm, we use kp processors, where k is a small integer. To facilitate the presentation, we use $k = 2$. We first define a few terms. A *redundancy group* is a collection of processors that execute the same computation, with the same input data and produce the same output. The number of processors in each redundancy group is called the *degree of redundancy*. For simplicity, we assume the same degree of redundancy for all the redundancy groups. For each redundancy group of degree k, identify each processor of the group by the label h, where $0 \leq h < k$. With this, we denote by *redundancy layer h* the collection of processors with label h. We use the term *bad processor* to denote a processor that out-stands negatively in terms of available capability to process the given application. Similarly, we denote by *good processor* the processor that out-stands in the group positively in performance.

The proposed redundant structure will be composed by copies of the original systolic array by adding, if necessary, communication channels among the redundancy layers, as shown in Figure 2.

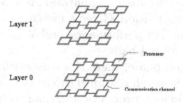

Fig. 3. Replicated independent systolic arrays

A straightforward way to employ redundancy is merely to have k copies of the original systolic structure and perform computation in each redundancy layer independently (see Figure 3). Whichever redundancy layer finishes first would report the desired result. There is practically no overhead incurred. Note, however, the existence of one bad processor in a redundancy layer determines the bad performance of the entire layer.

The above discussion motivates the definition of the *bad performance proba-bility* of the redundant system. Given a redundant systolic structure of degree of redundancy k and total of kp processors in each redundant layer of p processors, and given the existence of m bad processors, the *bad performance probability* is the probability of the redundant system to perform poorly due to the influence of at least one of the m bad processor. To compute this probability, consider k urns each with p balls. Given that a total of m balls are red (bad), it is the probability of all the urns having at least one red ball.

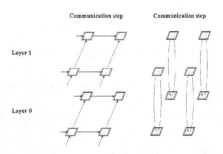

Fig. 4. Communication phase in the redundancy layers (left) and computation phase in the redundancy groups (right)

Alternatively, we can employ redundancy in each of the processors of the original systolic array (see Figure 4). In the original systolic algorithm each processor repeats three phases: *data input* from neighbor processors, *computation* of the received data, and *output* of computed data to neighbor processors. On the right of Figure 4 we show that each individual processor of the original systolic algorithm defines a redundant group, in which all its processors execute the same computation of the computation phase in parallel. The running time of the redundancy group to execute a computation is given by the processor that finishes first the given computation. Given k urns each with p balls, and knowing that m balls are red, the bad performance probability is the probability of at least one urn containing all red balls.

During the computation phase, there is a competition among the redundant processors, so that only the result obtained by the fastest processor is considered. We create two processes in each processor: the *computation process* computes the product of the sub-matrices of A and B, and the *control process* coordinates the processors of the redundancy group to determine the winner. The two processes share the same memory and mutual exclusion is enforced so that only one process can access shared data at a time. The control process needs to be informed when the computation process has finished the computation. The computation, on the other hand, needs to be informed by the control process when to abort its computation.

To guarantee that only one processor is the declared winner within a redun-dancy group, we use the token ring algorithm [1]. The processors of the group

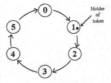

Fig. 5. The ring topology used by the token ring algorithm to ensure mutual exclusion

have the ring topology and each processor is identified by an integer *label* from
0 to $k - 1$. A *token* circulates from processor to processor in the ring. When the
token reaches processor $k - 1$, it returns to processor 0 and the cycle repeats.
The processor that holds the token at any moment has the priority to enter a
critical region and thus can execute the necessary tasks exclusively. If a processor
holding the token does not want to enter the critical region, it simply passes the
token forward to the next processor in the ring. See Figure 5. The token carries
a token value, initially defined to be -1. The processor that finishes its computation and that currently holds the token assigns its label as the new token value
and then passes it forward, declaring itself to be the winner. The new token
circulates in the ring to signal all the participants to abort their computation.

4   Experimental Results

We ran experiments on a cluster of 16 microcomputers with a Switch 3COM
3300 and Fast Ethernet 100Mbit/s. Each microcomputer consists of a 1.2GHz
Athlon Thunderbird processor with 256 KB L2 cache, 768 MB PC133 SDRAM
and a 30 GB ATA100 hard disk. The operating system is Debian Linux 2.2.19.
We use ANSI C, compiled under version GNU gcc 2.95.2-13, POSIX Threads
package for the local threads and LAM-MPI for the message exchanges. The test
consists of running a sequence of 50 problems of matrix products. Figure 6 shows
results in a homogeneous environment, with no *slow* machines. The matrix sizes
tested were 180×180 up to 420×420.

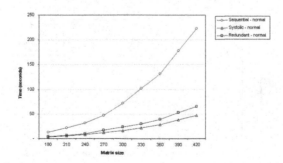

Fig. 6. Running times in a homogeneous environment

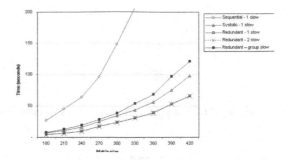

Fig. 7. Heterogeneous environment - "redundant - 2 slow": each group has a slow machine, and "redundant - group slow": all the machines of a group are slow

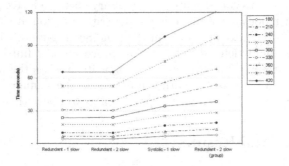

Fig. 8. Running times in a heterogeneous environment for different matrix sizes

To simulate a heterogeneous environment, we made one or more machines to act as *slow* machines, by running another process simultaneously. In Figure 7 we assume there is at least one *slow* machine in a redundancy group. Figure 8 shows the same results for several matrix sizes and slow machines with different degrees of *slowness*. Figure 9 shows the running times of the normal systolic algorithm

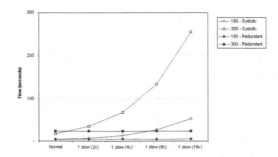

Fig. 9. The effect of one slow machine on the performance

without redundancy and the redundant systolic algorithm, for two matrix sizes and different degrees of slowness of the bad machine.

The experiment shows clearly the benefit of the redundant approach. The most interesting fact we observe in this experiment is that the redundant solution does not depend on the degree of slowness of the bad machine.

5   Conclusion

The systolic array paradigm has less demand on communication because they do not use the global communication primitives. The tightly coupled nature of its processors, however, show the vulnerability to the presence of even one single slow machine in the system. This paper proposes a way to use the abundant computing resources to deal with this problem. The use of redundancy do incur in additional cost, due to the overhead to implement the redundancy control mechanism. We compared the behavior of the sequential algorithm, the systolic algorithm without redundancy, and the redundant systolic algorithm, in homogeneous environment and also in a heterogeneous environment where one or more machines are forced to act as slow machines. Our experiment shows the benefit of the redundant approach. Despite the overhead, the redundant solutions outperform the non-redundant one. We note also that the redundant solution does not depend on the degree of slowness of the bad machine.

References

1. D. Bird. *Token Ring Network Design*. Addison-Wesley, 1994.
2. U. K. Hayashida, K. Okuda, J. Panneta, and S. W. Song. Generating parallel algorithms for cluster and grid computing. In *The 2005 International Conference on Computational Science - ICCS 2005*, volume 3514 of *Lecture Notes in Computer Science*, pages 509–516. Springer Verlag, 2005.
3. H. T. Kung. Why systolic architectures. *IEEE Transactions on Computers*, 15:37–46, 1982.
4. D. I. Moldovan. *Parallel Processing: from Applications to Systems*. Morgan Kaufmann Publishers, 1993.
5. K. Okuda. Cycle shrinking by dependence reduction. In *Proceedings 2nd International Euro-Par Conference*, volume 1123 of *Lecture Notes in Computer Science*, pages 398–401. Springer Verlag, 1996.
6. P. Quinton and Y. Robert. *Algorithmes et architectures systoliques*. Masson, 1989.
7. M. Treaster. A survey of fault-tolerant and fault-recovery techniques in parallel systems. *ArXiv Computer Science e-prints*, pages 1–11, January 2005.

A Diversity-Controllable Genetic Algorithm for Optimal Fused Traffic Planning on Sensor Networks

Yantao Pan, Xicheng Lu, Peidong Zhu, and Shen Ma

School of Computer, National University of Defense Technology, Changsha, P.R. China
pytmail@126.com

Abstract. In some sensor network applications e.g. target tracing, multi-profile data about an event are fused at intermediate nodes. The optimal planning of such fused traffic is important for prolonging the network lifetime, because data communications consume the most energy of sensor networks. As a general method for such optimization problems, genetic algorithms suffer from tremendous communication diversities that increase greatly with the network size. In this paper, we propose a diversity-controllable genetic algorithm for optimizing fused traffic planning. Simulation shows that it gains remarkable improvements.

Keywords: Sensor Networks, Lifetime Optimization, and Data Fusion.

1 Introduction

Consider a number of wireless static sensor nodes randomly distributed in a region for target tracing. Each node has a limited battery energy supply which is mainly used for data communications, and the nodes' throughputs are limited too. When a target enters in the sensing field of a node, a report is generated to describe this event. Other nodes maybe detect the same target and these reports are usually temporal or spatial related. These raw data are fused at intermediate nodes to achieve deep knowledge about the position and the speed of a target. We call such data flow fused traffic.

The energy storage of a sensor node is greatly constrained and it is almost infeasible to replace a large amount of nodes' batteries. Therefore, one of the key challenges of sensor networks is to maximize the lifetime. Since data communications consume the most energy, it is reasonable and efficient to optimize fused traffic planning to prolong a network's lifetime. The lifetime is usually regarded as a period from a network's deployment to its partition when there is a node that cannot send its report to the sink.

Some existing works focus on this problem. The literatures [1-4] investigate the upper bound or the expectation of the maximum lifetime. In [5] and [6], Chang et al. provide a heuristic algorithm. But it performs arbitrarily badly in the worst case [7]. In the literature [8], another heuristic approach is presented, but the running time of it has a bad scalability to the network size [9]. In [10], a tree-based approximate algorithm is presented to reduce the running time and achieve better scalability in terms of network size. These works [5-10] present heuristic algorithms to maximize the lifetimes approximately. However, these works do not take energy consumed by

C. Jesshope and C. Egan (Eds.): ACSAC 2006, LNCS 4186, pp. 430–436, 2006.

receiving data, throughput constraints, and data fusion into account. Actually, the energy consumed by receiving data should not be ignored in most cases. In literature [11-13], the powers of RX and TX units are reported as in the same order of magnitude. The energies consumed by Mote [14] to send and receive a unit packet are 20 nAh and 8 nAh. Furthermore, Throughput constraints and the influence of data fusion should be considered too.

In this paper, we investigate the fused traffic planning optimization problem with considering energy and throughput constraints. We propose a diversity-controllable genetic algorithm to solve it. The rest of this paper is organized as follows. In section 2, the problem is formulated. In section 3, our approach is described. In section 4, simulations are given. Finally in section 5, some concluding remarks are made.

2 Problem Formulation

A sensor network in consideration is modeled as $N^s = (G, p, q, w, o, X, Y)$. $G(V, A)$ is a connected directed graph, where V is the set of nodes and A is the set of directed links. Each node u has initial energy E_u. Let $p(u)$ be the residual energy of node u. Let $q(u, v)_s$ and $q(u, v)_r$ denote the energies required by node u to send and receive an information unit to and from v. According to the probability distribution of events, each node u has a data-generating rate $w(u)$. Let $o(u)$ denote the limited data throughput at node u. In addition, we denote the sets of sources and sinks as X and Y.

A virtual traffic planning is defined to be $\delta_a^x : (X, A) \mapsto \overline{R^-}$, if

$$\sum_{v \in V} \delta_{(x,v)}^x - \sum_{v \in V} \delta_{(v,x)}^x = w(x) \text{ for } \forall x \in X , \quad (1)$$

$$\sum_{y \in Y} \left(\sum_{v \in V} \delta_{(v,y)}^x - \sum_{v \in V} \delta_{(y,v)}^x \right) = w(x) \text{ for } \forall x \in X , \quad (2)$$

$$\sum_{u \in V} \delta_{(v,u)}^x = \sum_{u \in V} \delta_{(u,v)}^x \text{ for } \forall x \in X , \forall v \in V \setminus (X \bigcup Y) , \quad (3)$$

$$\sum_{v \in V} \max_{x \in X} \delta_{(v,u)}^x + \sum_{v \in V} \max_{x \in X} \delta_{(u,v)}^x \leq o(u) \text{ for } \forall u \in V . \quad (4)$$

The lifetime of N^s under the virtual traffic planning δ_a^x is defined as formula (5). If there are no $\delta_a^{x'}$ and its corresponding lifetime T' so as to $T' > T$, δ_a^x is an optimal virtual traffic planning and T is the maximum lifetime. It is obvious that an optimal fused traffic planning can be deduced from an optimal virtual traffic planning easily. Therefore, the problem can be stated as follows. Given a sensor network $N^s = (G, p, q, w, o, X, Y)$, ask for an optimal virtual traffic planning $\delta_a^{x^*}$ and the maximum lifetime T^*.

$$T \triangleq \min_{u \in V} \left(p(u) \middle/ \left(\sum_{v \in V} q(v,u)_r \cdot \max_{x \in X} \delta_{(v,u)}^x + \sum_{v \in V} q(u,v)_s \cdot \max_{x \in X} \delta_{(u,v)}^x \right) \right) . \quad (5)$$

3 A Diversity-Controllable Genetic Algorithm

3.1 Basic Approach

Since the fused traffic planning optimization problem can be modeled as a virtual flow velocity assignment optimization problem, we take paths with unit flow velocities as coding objects.

Consider a sensor network with a maximum lifetime T^*. In the period of the maximum lifetime, node u generates $w(u) \cdot T^*$ units flow, and could take $w(u) \cdot T^*$ paths at most to balance its original data flow. An individual is defined to be a set of chromosomes. The number of chromosomes depends on the number of sources in the network. A chromosome contains a set of unit paths as genes. Each path takes a unit virtual flow velocity from a source to the sink. We define a parameter *PREC* to control the number of paths that a source can take. The number is determined by $\lfloor w(u) \cdot PREC \rfloor$, where $\lfloor \cdot \rfloor$ is the greatest integer no more than a number. While *PREC* increases, a node can balance its original data flow to more paths, and the network is expected to live for a longer time.

The crossover operation includes two steps. The first step is to choose individuals according to parameter *CP* and individuals' fitness. We use *CP* to control the total number of individuals that will take part in the crossover operation. However, the opportunity of each individual depends on its fitness. The second step is to crossover two individuals in each chromosome. Here, we use parameter *CN* to control the number of points that two chromosomes will take crossover in. The mutation operation is similar. The first step is to choose individuals according to *MPROB* and fitness. The second step is to choose random genes according to *MPER* and replace them with new generated ones. From numeric experiments, we get a set of parameter values: $MPER = 0.15$; $MPROB = 0.95$; $CP = 0.40$; $CN = 4$.

In order to evaluate the fitness of an individual, we calculate its lifetime and punishment. The actual flow velocity on each link depends on the maximum virtual traffic. The lifetime depends on the most short-lived node and is calculated by formula (5). Additionally, a punishment function is defined as formula (6) to support throughput constraints.

$$P \triangleq \sum_{u \in V} \varphi(u), \text{ where } \varphi(u) = \begin{cases} 0, o(u) \geq \left(\sum_{v \in V} \max_{x \in X} \delta^x_{(v,u)} + \sum_{v \in V} \max_{x \in X} \delta^x_{(u,v)} \right), \\ o(u) - \left(\sum_{v \in V} \max_{x \in X} \delta^x_{(v,u)} + \sum_{v \in V} \max_{x \in X} \delta^x_{(u,v)} \right), otherwise. \end{cases} \qquad (6)$$

Since the lifetime and the punishment have different units, it is reasonable to standardize them to values between 0 and 1 according to the average lifetime and the average punishment of a population. We denote standardized lifetime and punishment as T' and P'. The fitness of an individual is calculated by $F = \alpha \cdot T' + (1-\alpha) \cdot P'$, where α is set to balance the influences of the lifetime and the punishment.

3.2 Diversity Control

The performance of a genetic algorithm greatly depends on the fitness of initial population. However, the basic way to generate initial populations is the random method which takes random unit paths as genes. Therefore, the average fitness of a random generated population greatly depends on the population size and the individual diversity. With the increase of individual diversity, greater population size is necessary to ensure that there are good individuals in a random generated population.

In the worst case, the type of paths is in the same order of the network size's factorial. Since unit paths are taken as genes, the type of genes, and consequently the individual diversity, increases greatly with the network size. If individual diversity is not controlled efficiently, the basic genetic algorithm will have a bad scalability.

We use two methods to control the individual diversity. The first is to control the number of genes in a chromosome by using parameter *PREC*. The second is to control the type of genes by limit the hop counts of unit paths.

However, when we set limits to the number and the type of genes in chromosomes, we also set a limit to the algorithm's approximation. In order to achieve better results, we use a method called incremental diversity. The basic idea is to use a final population under a small *PREC* and a tight hop count constraint to generate an initial population under a large *PREC* and a loose hop constraint. At beginning, we set a tight limit to the number and the type of genes. The individual diversity is low and a small population size is enough to offer sufficient population average fitness. Then, we loose the constraints step by step and construct a newer initial population based on an older finial population. While the constraints are loosen gradational, nodes might divide their original flow velocities into more pieces and distribute them to more paths basing on their earlier assignments. In this way, we will get an initial population with high fitness and a small population size works well even under a high individual diversity.

4 Simulations

Firstly, let's consider a sensor network shown in Fig. 1.1. Node 0, 1 and 2 take node 6 as their sink. Node 3 and 4 take node 7 as their sink. An ideal solution is plotted in Fig.1.2. The lifetime of each node is shown in Table 1. The maximum lifetime of the network is 1.113468.

Table 1. The lifetime of nodes in the ideal solution

Node	0	1	2	3
Lifetime	1.338458	1.113468	1.113468	1.397984
Node	4	5	6	7
Lifetime	1.113468	1.236226	1.724138	6.666667

At beginning, we use GA (Genetic Algorithm) without diversity control. We set *PREC* = 10 and increase *PS*. The results are shown in Table 2. The parameter *GENERATION_NUM* denotes the time of genetic manipulations.

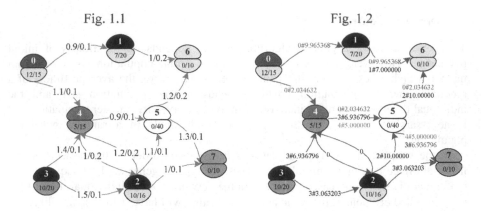

Fig. 1. An 8-node 2-sink sensor network and one of its ideal solutions

Table 2. The lifetime as a function of *PS* (*GENERATION_NUM*=100)

PS	100	150	200	250	300
Lifetime	1.078167	1.102688	1.101322	1.109570	1.111111
PS	400	450	500	550	600
Lifetime	1.111111	1.104362	1.111111	1.111111	1.111111

We find that the lifetime increases scarcely while *PS* rises from 100 to 600. Then, we set *PREC* to a greater value to get a better result. Table 3 shows the lifetime as a function of *PREC*, which increases from 10 to 80. We set *PS* = 600 and *GENERATION_NUM* = 100. Note that the lifetime decreases while *PREC* increases. The reason is that such population size can not offer sufficient average fitness while individual diversity has increased with *PREC*.

Table 3. Lifetime as a function of *PREC* (*PS*=600)

PREC	10	30	50	60	70	80
Lifetime	1.111111	1.038287	0.914599	0.894988	0.853593	0.847009

Table 4 shows the result of an improved algorithm, where the number of genes are controlled by *PREC* and *PS* = 400. This improved algorithm achieves 1.113173. The flow velocity assignments are very close to those shown in the ideal solution.

Table 4. The lifetime under each value of the *PREC* vector

PREC	5	10	20	40	80
GENERATION_NUM	100	50	50	50	100
Lifetime	1.111111	1.111111	1.111111	1.112811	1.113173

Additional, we use random generated networks to compare GAs with and without diversity control. We generate three sensor networks, which have 20, 50, 100 nodes being distributed randomly in a 10×10 square area. To each network, 2~8 nodes are selected to be sinks. An initial energy (chosen from 200 to 500 randomly) and a data-generating rate (chosen from 5 to 12 randomly) are assigned to each node. The energy needed to receiving or sending an information unit is assigned to each link according to its length. The maximum *PREC* is set to be 3.2. The maximum hop count is set to the network size.

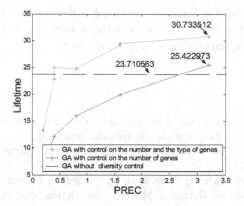

Fig. 2. Performance comparison of GAs with and without diversity control on a 20 node sensor network

Fig. 3. The evolution of results on a 20 node sensor network with hop count constraint increasing from 4 to 20

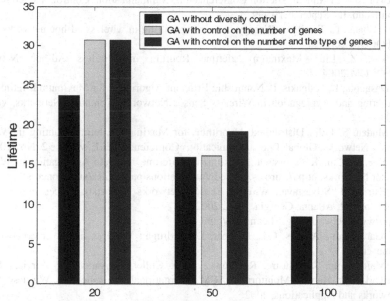

Fig. 4. Performance comparison of GAs with and without diversity control

We could observe that GA with diversity control gains remarkable improvements.

5 Conclusion

In this paper, we propose a diversity-controllable genetic algorithm to solve the fused traffic planning optimization problem in sensor networks. Different from previous works, we take the number and the type of genes as controllers of individual diversity and achieve good scalability to the network size.

The time complexity of the basic approach is $PANSMG$, where P is the maximum $PREC$, A is the maximum data-generating rate, N is the population size, S is the sources' number, M is the number of arcs, and G is the generation number.

References

1. M. Bhardwaj, A. Chandrakasan, T. Garnett.: Upper Bounds on the Lifetime of Sensor Networks. IEEE International Conference on Communications, Helsinki, June 2001
2. M. Bhardwaj, A. Chandrakasan.: Bounding the Lifetime of Sensor Networks Via Optimal Role Assignments. IEEE INFOCOM'2002
3. E. J. Duarte-Melo, M. Liu, A. Misra.: A Modeling Framework for Computing Lifetime and Information Capacity in Wireless Sensor Networks. Modeling and Optimization in Mobile, Ad Hoc and Wireless Networks, Cambridge, UK, March 2004
4. Vivek Rai, Rabi N. Mahapatra.: Lifetime Modeling of a Sensor Network. Design, Automation and Test in Europe, Munich, Germany, March 2005
5. J.-H. Chang, L. Tassiulas.: Routing for Maximum System Lifetime in Wireless Ad-hoc Networks. 37th Annual Allerton Conference on Communication, Control, and Computing, Monticello, IL, September 1999
6. J.-H. Chang, L. Tassiulas.: Energy conserving routing in wireless ad-hoc networks. IEEE INFOCOM'2000
7. Sankar, Z. Liu.: Maximum Lifetime Routing in Wireless Ad-hoc Networks. INFOCOM'2004
8. K. Dasgupta, K. Kalpakis, P. Namjoshi.: Efficient Algorithms for Maximum Lifetime Data Gathering and Aggregation in Wireless Sensor Networks. Computer Networks, vol. 42, 2003
9. R. Madan, S. Lall.: Distributed Algorithms for Maximum Lifetime Routing in Wireless Sensor Networks. Global Telecommunications Conference, IEEE, volume 2, Nov 2004
10. Y. Xue, Y, Cui, K. Nahrstedt.: Maximizing Lifetime for Data Aggregation in Wireless Sensor Networks. http://cairo.cs.uiuc.edu/publications/paper-files/xue-monet.pdf
11. D. Estrin, M. Srivastava.: Wireless Sensor Networks (Tutorial). Proceedings of ACM MobiCom'02, Atlanta, Georgia, USA, 2002
12. http://www.networks.digital.com/npb/html
13. J.J. Garcia-Luna-Aceves, C.L. Fullmer, E. Madruga.: Wireless mobile internetworking. Manuscript
14. A. Mainwaring, J. Polastre, R. Szewczyk, D. Culler, J. Anderson.: Wireless Sensor Networks for Habitat Monitoring. ACM International Workshop on Wireless Sensor Networks and Applications, 2002
15. G. Winter, J. Periaux, M. Galan.: Genetic Algorithms in Engineering and Computer Science. Published by JOHN WILEY & SON Ltd, 1995
16. L. Darrell Whitley, Michael D. Vose.: Foundations of Genetic Algorithms Volume 3. Published by Morgan Kaufmann Publishers Inc, 1995

A Context-Switch Reduction Heuristic for Power-Aware Off-Line Scheduling

Biju Raveendran[1], Sundar Balasubramaniam[1],
K Durga Prasad[1], and S. Gurunarayanan[2]

[1] Computer Science Group,
[2] Electronics & Instrumentation Group,
BITS, Pilani, Rajasthan, India - 333031
{biju, sundarb, f2001287, sguru}@bits-pilani.ac.in

Abstract. Scheduling algorithms significantly affect the performance of a real-time system. In systems with power constraints, context switches in a schedule result in wasted power consumption. We present a scheduling algorithm and a heuristic for reducing the number of context switches. The algorithm executes in near linear time in terms of the number of jobs, finds a feasible schedule in most cases if it exists, and reasonably reduces the number of context switches. Thus it is a power-aware scheduling algorithm.

1 Introduction

Task Scheduling for real-time systems is a well understood and widely studied issue in literature. The primary focus of most task scheduling algorithms is to generate a feasible schedule. In some real-time systems additional constraints like availability of power, size of memory and speed of processor among others may affect the scheduling policies and algorithms with feasibility ([1-3]). Scheduling algorithms may be online or offline. In online scheduling, the scheduling algorithm competes for processor time along with the tasks being scheduled. In offline scheduling, all task related information required for scheduling must be available for the scheduling algorithm[4].

Due to limited battery life of many mobile and embedded systems, power consumption is an important factor for any processing in these systems. This issue has been addressed at various levels – at the architectural level (e.g. DVS, DFS), at the systems level (e.g. scheduling, caching techniques, compilation techniques [5 - 8]), at the applications level (e.g. data structures and algorithm design).

Most of the power-aware scheduling techniques in the literature are dependent of specific platform features such as clocks, device characteristics, or memory technologies. It is also possible to consider the impact of generic factors – such as process-idle time, and context-switch time, in power-aware scheduling.

Our approach to power-aware scheduling is to consider the time spent on context switches and reduce it as much as possible. We discuss the impact of context switching on task schedules in Section 2. In Section 3, we describe a static scheduling algorithm that attempts to minimize the number of context switches in a schedule. We

C. Jesshope and C. Egan (Eds.): ACSAC 2006, LNCS 4186, pp. 437–444, 2006.
© Springer-Verlag Berlin Heidelberg 2006

analyze the algorithm in Section 4. The experimental results of the static scheduling algorithm are described in Section 5. We discuss some limitations of the algorithm as well as improvements and alternatives in Section 6.

2 Context Switching

Context switch time is the time taken to switch between two processes or threads in a schedule. The context switch duration includes the time taken for saving the context of the current process / thread and loading the context of the next process / thread. This implies that when a process finishes or a new process starts a context switch is not counted. There are various factors that impact the context switch duration. Most of them are architecture or operating system related [9], [10].

Available analyses or evaluations of scheduling algorithms in literature do not account for context switch time. In particular, they use a simplistic model where context switch duration is assumed to be 0. This affects the evaluations in two ways: (a) actual execution times may not match scheduled times and in particular, hard real time tasks may miss deadlines;   (b) the context switch is unproductive and the energy consumed for the operation is a waste and in particular, this may critically impact the performance of a low-power system. An indirect but more significant impact of context switches could be due to cache flushes. In fact, the additional energy consumption due to this indirect impact has been reported to be significantly higher [11]. A power-aware operating system and scheduling algorithm should account for the impact of context switches on power consumption. We partially address this issue through a scheduling algorithm that reduces the number of context switches in a schedule.

3 Algorithms

Our objective is to design an off-line scheduling algorithm for hard real-time systems such that the generated schedule has the minimum possible number of context switches. Toward this we make some simplifying assumptions for each task type t:

All t are periodic and preemptible in nature. For each job j of task type t, the deadline d(j) is equal to Arri. Time(j) + period p(t). For all t, the arrival time for the first job is time 0 and for all t, the worst case execution time e(t) is known.

Under these assumptions, given a list of task types L ordered by their periods, one can pre-compute the Hyper-period H and a list of job records Jobs, lexicographically ordered by the key (p(t(j)), t(j)), where each record has a job identifier j, task type t(j), deadline d(j), arrival time a(j) and execution time e(j).

A brute force scheduling algorithm can now be easily arrived at:

3.1 Algorithm Brute-Force

Inputs: hyper-period H, a list of job records Jobs (ordered as above)
Output: A feasible schedule if it exists, the number of context switches.
Steps:
1. Generate all schedules P of Jobs i.e. divide each job into sub-jobs of unit execution time and compute all permutations of the list of sub-jobs.

2. m=H; cur=first schedule in P.
3. for each permutation pi in P,
    a. check if pi is feasible
    b. if yes, then count the number of context switches, say m'; if (m' < m) ,
        then m=m'; cur=pi.
4. if (m=H) then output 'infeasible'
5. else output cur and m.
Fact: Algorithm *Brute-Force* computes a feasible schedule if it exists and the computed feasible schedule has the minimum possible number of context switches.

But Algorithm *Brute-Force* is exponential (it requires O(H!) steps). This is impractical to compute when H is large. We need an algorithm which can compute a feasible schedule (if one exists) in polynomial time such that the number of context switches in the schedule is low.

3.2 Heuristic Algorithm

Our heuristic is to minimize the fragmentation of *schedulable intervals*. Consider the input from the table 1.

<table>
<tr><td colspan="4">**Table 1.** Task list for the schedule</td><td colspan="4">**Table 2.** Job list derived from table1</td></tr>
</table>

Task	Arri. Time	Period	Exec. Time
A	0	2	1
B	0	8	4

Job	Arri.Time	Deadline	Exec. Time
A1	0	2	1
A2	2	4	1
A3	4	6	1
A4	6	8	1
B	0	8	4

Table 2 provides arrival time, deadline and execution time of all the jobs corresponding to each of the tasks in the table 1.

In this case our heuristic gets applied as follows.

1. Schedule A1 in the first feasible slot and A4 in the last feasible slot (see Figure 1).
2. Schedule A2 in the last feasible slot and A3 in the first feasible slot (see Figure 1).
3. Schedule B in the first feasible slot. At the end of time slot 3 it has to be switched out and rescheduled at the end of time slot 5 (see Figure 1).

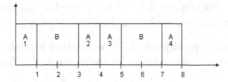

Fig. 1. Gantt chart after step-3

Algorithm 2 uses this heuristic to generate a feasible schedule if it exists. The schedule is likely to reduce context switches as it reduces fragmentation of intervals thereby allowing jobs to fit into these intervals without switching. Assume that H and the list of jobs is pre-computed as it was done for Algorithm BruteForce.

Algorithm IntFragment

Inputs: hyper-period H, a list of job records J (ordered as above)

Output: A feasible schedule if it exists, the number of context switches.

Steps:

1. odd = true
2. let J_i, J_{i+1}, ... J_k be all the jobs of task t
   a. if (odd) then schedule J_i, J_k in the first and last feasible slots respectively
   b. else schedule J_i, J_k in the last and first feasible slots respectively.
   c. odd = !odd; i=i+1; k=k-1;
   d. repeat steps 2.a to 2.d until k<=i
   e. if (k==i) then schedule J_i in the first feasible slot.
3. repeat steps 1 and 2 until no more tasks left.
4. output the schedule and the number of context switches in the schedule

3.3 Correctness Arguments

Algorithm IntFragment may fail to find a feasible schedule for some inputs that admit feasible schedules. For instance, consider the input from the table 3. Job list can be derived out of the task list like in the previous example.

Table 3. Task list for which IntFragment algorithm fails to find a valid schedule

Task	Arri. Time	Period	Exec. Time
A	0	3	1
B	0	5	3

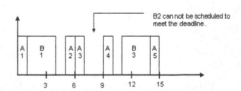

Fig. 2. Gantt chart after step-5

In this case our heuristic gets applied as follows.

1. Schedule A1 in the first feasible slot and A5 in the last feasible slot (see Figure 2).
2. Schedule A2 in the last feasible slot and A4 in the first feasible slot (see Figure 2).
3. Schedule A3 in the first feasible slot (see Figure 2)
4. Schedule B1 in the first feasible slot and B3 in the last feasible slot (see figure 2).
5. B2 can not be scheduled to meet its deadline (see Figure 2).

Such failures happen typically when the utilization is high. The following schedulability test states a sufficient condition for the algorithm to find a feasible schedule:

3.3.1 Schedulability Test

Given a set of N independent, pre-emptible and periodic tasks on a uniprocessor such that their relative deadlines are equal to their respective periods, if for each task i,

$$(p(i) - \Sigma_{j < i} (\lceil p(i) / p(j) \rceil * e(j))) <= e(i) \tag{1}$$

where $p(i)$ is the period of task i and $e(i)$ is the execution time of task i, then this is a sufficient condition to obtain a feasible schedule through Algorithm IntFragment.

3.3.2 Correctness

Given a set of N independent, pre-emptible and periodic tasks on a uniprocessor such that their relative deadlines are equal to their respective periods, Algorithm IntFragment generates a feasible schedule if one exists and if the schedulability test is satisfied.

Proof: Omitted because of space limit.

4 Analysis of Algorithm IntFragment

4.1 Complexity of the Algorithm

Claim: The worst case time complexity of Algorithm IntFragment is

$$p_{max} * \Sigma_{t \in Tasks} H/p (t) \tag{2}$$

where p_{max} is the maximum among the periods of all tasks, H is the hyper-period, and $p(t)$ is the period of task t.

Proof: Omitted because of space limit.

4.2 Quality of the Schedule

Since our objective was to minimize the number of context switches we evaluate our algorithm by this metric (applied on the generated schedule) and compare it with the other algorithms.

Consider the example used in Section 3.2. Algorithm Intfragment produces a schedule with 1 context switch (see Figure 1 in Section 3.2). In comparison, for the same input, both the Rate Monotonic algorithm and the Earliest Deadline First algorithm will produce a schedule with 3 context switches (see Figure 3).

Fig. 3. Schedule obtained by Rate Monotonic and Earliest Deadline First Algorithms

Although Algorithm IntFragment typically fares better than other scheduling algorithms in reducing context switches, it does not necessarily produce a schedule with the minimum number of context switches. For instance, consider the input from the table 4.

Table 4. Task list for which IntFragment algorithm performs better than the other scheduling algorithms like rate monotonic and EDF

Task	Arri.Time	Period	Exec. Time
A	0	2	1
B	0	10	4

For this input, Algorithm IntFragment produces a schedule with 2 context switches (see Figure 4) whereas there is a feasible schedule with 1 context switch (see Figure 5). Thus Algorithm IntFragment is an approximation algorithm.

Fig. 4. Schedule obtained by the IntFragment algorithm

Fig. 5. Schedule obtained by the Brute-Force Technique.

Worst-case Approximation Claim

Let I be an input of t tasks. If I admits a feasible schedule and satisfies the Schedulability Test 3.3.1, then Algorithm IntFragment will produce a feasible schedule, with at most $O(t^2)$ context switches.

Proof: (Omitted).

Although this may imply that a schedule produced by Algorithm IntFragment is infinitely worse compared to a minimal context-switch schedule, in practice, it produces far fewer number of context switches than the worst possible case, which is $O(H)$, where H is the hyper-period.

5   Experimental Results

We performed energy characterization by running eCos Operating System on StrongARM 1100, the processor core of the SmartBadge at a speed of 59MHz. The period and execution time of periodic tasks in the experiment are listed in the table 5. Task list for each of the experiments are presented in the table 6.

The experimentation is carried out with standard algorithms like EDF, LSTF and the proposed IntFragment algorithm extensively. The saving of context switches and energy per unit time (one second) for IntFragment with respect to EDF and LST algorithms are presented in table 7.

Experimentation results show that the indirect impact because of cache miss increases the energy consumption thus reduces the performance. The detailed discussion supporting the secondary impact with minimum and maximum energy consumption for context switching is described in [11]. The base value of the minimum and the maximum energy consumption for a context switch is borrowed from [11].

Table 5. List of all the periodic tasks involved in the energy characterization experiment

Task No	Period(ms)	Exe. Time(ms)
T1	3.39	1.695
T2	5.085	1.695
T3	10.17	3.39
T4	13.56	5.085
T5	16.95	3.39
T6	33.9	3.39
T7	33.9	6.78
T8	45.765	5.085
T9	50.85	16.95
T10	67.8	8.475
T11	81.36	13.56
T12	91.53	15.255
T13	101.7	8.475
T14	101.7	15.255
T15	162.72	6.78
T16	162.72	27.12
T17	203.4	33.9
T18	203.4	101.7
T19	406.8	37.29

Table 6. Task set corresponding to each of the experiments

Exp. No	Task Set
Exp 1	T1, T3, T16
Exp 2	T1, T4, T15
Exp 3	T1, T3, T11
Exp 4	T1, T3, T8
Exp 5	T1, T6, T12
Exp 6	T1, T18
Exp 7	T1, T3, T17
Exp 8	T2, T9, T14, T13, T19
Exp 9	T1, T7, T10, T13, T19
Exp10	T1, T5, T6, T13, T19

Table 7. Context Switches and Energy saved by IntFragment algorithm compared to Earliest Deadline First algorithm

Exp No	CS Saved w.r.t. EDF	MinEnergy saved w.r.t. EDF (uJ)	MaxEnergy Saved w.r.t. EDF (mJ)	CS Saved w.r.t. LSTF	MinEnergy saved w.r.t. LSTF (uJ)	MaxEnergy Saved w.r.t. LSTF (mJ)
Exp 1	141	482.22	3.584	147	502.74	3.736
Exp 2	110	376.2	2.796	110	376.2	2.796
Exp 3	135	461.7	3.431	147	502.74	3.736
Exp 4	109	372.78	2.77	109	372.78	2.77
Exp 5	90	307.8	2.287	90	307.8	2.287
Exp 6	142	485.64	3.609	142	485.64	3.609
Exp 7	142	485.64	3.609	148	506.16	3.762
Exp 8	140	478.8	3.558	140	478.8	3.558
Exp 9	159	543.78	4.041	159	543.78	4.041
Exp 10	140	478.8	3.558	140	478.8	3.558

6 Conclusions

We have shown an approximation algorithm for offline scheduling called IntFragment which will reduce the number of context switches and energy consumption. The schedulability test and detailed experimentation results for the same are addressed. Future work would include extension of this approach to reduce the time taken for an average context switch as well as the number of context switches. Also, this algorithm could be adapted for online scheduling. Experimental evaluation may substantiate our claims regarding the implied energy savings.

References

1. M. Kandemir, G. Chen, W. Zhang, and I. Kolcu, "Data Space Oriented Scheduling in Embedded Systems", Proceedings of the conference on Design, Automation and Test in Europe - Vol. 1, 2003. Page: 10416
2. Padmanabhan Pillai, and King G. Shin, "Real-Time dynamic voltage scaling for Low-power embedded operating systems", In Greg Ganger, editor, Proceedings of the 18th ACM Symposium on Operating Systems Principles (SOSP – 01), Volume 35, 5th ACM SIGOPS Operating Systems Review, Pages 89 – 102, New York, October 21 – 24 2001. ACM Press.
3. J. Pouwelse, K. Langendoen, H. Sips, "Dynamic Voltage Scaling on a Low-Power Microprocessor", UbiCom Technical Report 2000/3, Delft University of Technology.
4. Jane Liu. "Real-Time Systems", Prenctice Hall. 2000.
5. Yu-Ting Hung , "Power-Aware Compilation with Architectural Support and. Instruction Scheduling", In proceedings of Eleventh Workshop on Compiler Techniques for High Performance Computing, Taiwan, 2005.
6. J. L. Ayala, and A. Veidenbaum, "Reducing Register File Energy Consumption Using Compiler Support", Workshop on Application Specific Processors (*in conjunction with IEEE International Symposium on Microarchitecture*), Istanbul (Turkey), November 2002.
7. Hongbo Yang, "Power-Aware Compilation Techniques for High Performance Processors", Ph.D. Thesis. Department of Electrical and Computer Engineering, University. of Delaware, Delaware, USA, 2004.
8. D. Mosse, H. Aydin, B. Childers and R. Melhem, "Compiler-assisted dynamic power aware scheduling for real-time applications", In Workshop on Compilers and Operating Systems for Low Power, October 2000.
9. Bill Dittman "Strategied for Minimizing Context Switch Times in Large Register set Environment with Primary Focus on the PowerPC Architecture with Floating Point and AltiVec Extensions",QuadrosSystems. http://www.rtxc.com/pdf/article_esd-conference_05-08-2004.pdf
10. Richard Gooch, "Linux Scheduler Benchmark Results",
11. http://www.atnf.csiro.au/people/rgooch/benchmarks/linux-scheduler.html
12. A. Acquaviva, L. Benini, B. Ricco', "Energy Characterization of Embedded Real-Time Operating Systems," *ACM Computer Architecture News*, vol. 29, no. 5 pp. 13--18, December 2001.

On the Reliability of Drowsy Instruction Caches*

Soong Hyun Shin[1], Sung Woo Chung[2], and Chu Shik Jhon[1]

[1] School of Electrical Engineering and Computer Sciences,
Seoul National University, Seoul 151-742, Korea
{shordan, csjhon}@panda.snu.ac.kr
[2] Corresponding Author
Division of Computer and Communication Engineering,
Korea University, Seoul 136-713, Korea
swchung@korea.ac.kr

Abstract. As technology scales down, the leakage energy accounts for
more portion of total energy in a cache. Applying the Dynamic Voltage
Scaling(DVS) to a cache, which is called a drowsy cache, is known as one
of the most efficient techniques for reducing leakage energy in a cache.
However, it increases the Soft Error Rate(SER) and many researchers
began to doubt the reliability of a drowsy cache. In this paper, we show
that the instruction cache(I-cache) can adopt the DVS without reliability
problems for several reasons. First, an I-cache always stores read-only
data, rarely incurring unrecoverable errors. In the I-cache, the soft error
can be recovered by re-fetching from the lower level memory. Second,
the effect of soft errors on performance is negligible, because the SER is
extremely low. Additional, considerable percentage of soft errors do not
harm the performance. In this paper, the evaluation results show that
the drowsy I-cache rarely increases unrecoverable errors and negligibly
degrades the performance.

1 Introduction

Reliability is one of the most crucial considerations for computer systems. As
technology shrinks and the supply voltage is lowered, the reliability of memory systems including caches is threatened[1]. In addition, the dependability
is more weakened, when the DVS is used. Many researchers have investigated
the wide range of soft error issues, such as physical phenomena of soft errors,
soft error models, calculating the Soft Error Rate(SER) according to technology
scaling[2][3][4]. Moreover, a number of methods for protecting circuits from soft
errors, detecting soft errors, and correcting data have been proposed[5].

The soft errors occur in the drowsy cache[6] ten times frequently as many as
in the conventional cache. Moreover, as the probability that two or more cells in
a cache line is defected by a soft error is increased, the necessity of a design for
reliability becomes serious. The reliability of a cache is important because the
error may induce system malfunction.

---

* This work was supported by the Brain Korea 21 Project.

C. Jesshope and C. Egan (Eds.): ACSAC 2006, LNCS 4186, pp. 445–451, 2006.

Fortunately, the soft error problem in an I-cache, which is concerned in this paper, is mitigated because of its read-only feature. As the data in an I-cache always exist in the lower level cache, they do not need to correct the errors with error correction techniques, but just to re-fetch the erroneous data from the lower level memory. Complicated recovery circuits are not cost-effective under the current SER. The re-fetching recovery has another merit that the conventional cache architecture is hardly changed because the recovery policy needs only parity bits and the bit interleaving method. The bit interleaving makes physically adjacent bits belong to different logic words, which is commonly used to reduce multi-bit errors[1].

In this paper, we evaluate the performance and reliability effects of soft errors on the drowsy I-cache. The rest of this paper is organized as follows. Section 2 introduces our soft error model, error correction codes, and the soft error effect on a drowsy I-cache. Section 3 simulates the soft error effects on the drowsy I-cache. Lastly, section 4 concludes this paper.

2   Soft Error

2.1   Soft Error Model

Soft errors, different from hard errors incurred by a bad electronic circuit, are temporal upsets caused by alpha particles or neutrons from cosmic radiation[4]. The soft error threatens a circuit more aggressively according as the supply voltage is lowered to reduce power consumption[3]. There are many factors which influence the probability of soft error occurrences: technologies, doing and packaging materials, altitude and so on. All of other parameters, except supply voltage, are assumed to be fixed in order to investigate the relation between the supply voltage and the SER. Based on [3], the SER at sea level is calculated as

$$SER \propto A \times exp(-\frac{Q_{crit}}{Q_s}) \tag{1}$$

where,
A: the drain area,
Q_{crit}: the critical charge,
Q_s: the collection slope.

A soft error occurs if collected charges of a cell exceed the Q_{crit} of that cell. Because the Q_{crit} is proportional to the supply voltage, the SER increases at exponential rate as the supply voltage is decreased. In the 70 nm technology, an SRAM cell operates normally at 1.0V and retains data at 0.3V(the drowsy state). Thus, the SER in the drowsy state is ten times higher than the SER in the normal state. Besides, the SER during read or write is five times higher than that of normal state[1]. Based on[1], the SER of a 6T SRAM(70-nm technology) cell is 2.7e-14 per cycle(1ns cycle).

Generally, almost every soft error is single bit error. However, as the Q_{crit} decreases these days, the collected charge exceeds two or more times of Q_{crit}

more frequently than before and two or more adjacent cells are infected together at an event more often. Thus, consideration for double bit errors(DBEs) and multi bit errors(MBEs) becomes important. DBEs and MBEs differ from a multi-SBE which originates from single upset event. Contrary to DBEs or MBEs, the multi-SBE means that two or more SBEs occur in the same cache line by chance. The position pattern of multi-SBE cells cannot be specified

The probability of SER is estimated at 7.e-12, based on[1], and the DBE found to be 1/100 of SBE at 1.0 supply voltage. The possibility of the multi-SBE is quite low because two or more errors occur in the same cache line without any memory references between the errors.

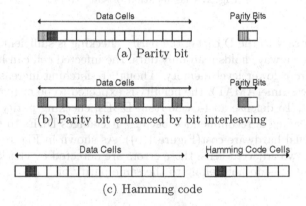

(a) Parity bit

(b) Parity bit enhanced by bit interleaving

(c) Hamming code

Fig. 1. Examples of error detectioin/correction code

2.2   Error Correction Codes

Until now, many error correcting codes(ECCs) have been introduced. Almost every ECCs are hardware redundancies which need additional hardware. The additional amount of hardware is highly dependant on the ability to detect and correct errors. The most widely known ECCs are parity bits and the hamming code. Figure 1 shows the parity bits and the hamming code. Gray cells and white cells indicate two cache lines. Figure 1(a) depicts parity bits which are commonly used in I-caches. It is very simple and takes low hardware cost; however, it is not able to recover original value and to detect two or more errors. Figure 1(c) depicts the hamming code[7], which corrects single-bit errors and detect double-bit errors(SEC-DED). Its hardware overhead is 50% when the number of data bits is 8. This policy is fit for an architecture which has responsibility to recover.

2.3   Soft Error Recovery in Caches

Characteristics of the target structure have to be studied to find an appropriate ECC, because the reliability and the cost of ECC should be considered together. A data cache(D-cache) should recover a cell infected by a soft error if the cell holds modified data because the data is the only valid copy in the

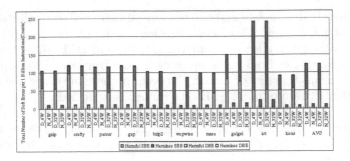

Fig. 2. Classification of soft errors

system. Contrary to the D-cache, the parity checking is sufficient for an I-cache. As the I-cache always holds read-only data, the infected cell can be recovered by re-fetching from lower level memory. Though re-fetching increases the average memory access time(AMAT), the penalty is expected to be negligible because of the low SER. To defense an I-cache from DBEs, checking parity bits enhanced by bit interleaving is recommended because it changes DBEs to two SBEs with little additional hardware cost(Figure 1(b)). As shown in Figure 1(b), even if a DBE infects two adjacent cells, these errors are detected by checking parity bits because these cells do not belong to the same parity bit.

2.4   Soft Error Effects on Performance

Soft errors of an I-cache disappear without any damages when the erroneous cache line is evicted without following read operation. Thus, the cache execution time can be divided into harmful periods or harmless periods according to whether the following reference exists or not. As an I-cache handles harmful soft errors as cache misses in the proposed technique, the recovery is simple, but the cache miss rate and the AMAT would increase.

3   Simulation

We implemented a soft error generator in the simulator SimpleScalar 3.0 for simulations[8]. The default simulator configuration is a 32KB, 32byte, 32-way L1 I-cache with parity bits and bit interleaving, a 32KB, 32byte, 4-way L1 D-cache and a unified 256KB, 64byte, 4-way L2 cache. To observe a soft error effect on the other configuration, we simulated a 32KB, 32 byte, 4-way L1 I-cache as well. The access times to the L1, L2, and memory are 1, 8, and 40, respectively. In the drowsy I-cache, cache lines are put into the drowsy mode every 2000 cycles. The benchmarks are selected from SPEC2000[9] and each benchmark is fast forwarded 300 million instruction and then simulated 1 billion instructions.

Figure 2 shows a classification of soft error. In every benchmark, the number of DBEs and MBEs occupies is less than 1%. Every DBE is detected as two SBEs

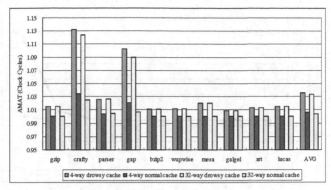

(a) The AMAT including wakeup penalties

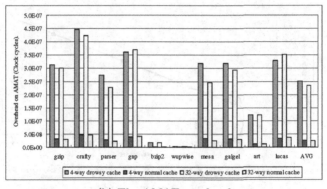

(b) The AMAT overhead

Fig. 3. The AMAT and AMAT overhead with current soft error rates

by bit interleaving and corrected. A multi-SBE, or an unrecoverable soft error, does not appear in all benchmarks because of its extremely low probability.

Though the total soft error of the drowsy cache is about 9.8 times higher than that of the normal cache, the number of total soft errors of the drowsy cache is 117, on average(average error per 1 billion inst. = 1.17e-7). Moreover 49 - 52% of the soft errors in drowsy cache are harmless. Thus, the I-cache has only 56 - 60 erroneous cells while executing 1 billion instructions. Difference between the 4-way cache and the 32-way cache is not shown.

To evaluate the soft error damage to the I-cache, we examined the AMAT. Shown in Figure 3(a), the AMATs of the 4-way and 32-way drowsy cache are 1.035 and 1.033, respectively and those of the normal cache are 1.006 and 1.004, respectively; the AMAT of the drowsy cache is about 3% longer, relatively small, than that of the conventional cache. Moreover, the AMAT overhead caused by soft errors are almost invisible because its probability is 2.66E-7 in the 4-way

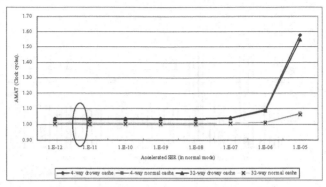

(a) The AMAT including wakeup penalties

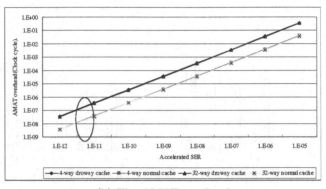

(b) The AMAT overhead

Fig. 4. The AMAT and AMAT overhead with various soft error rates. The circle represents the SER of the current technology.

drowsy cache(Figure 3(b)). Most of the AMAT overhead is caused by the wake-up penalties. Hence, the SER does not affect the reliability significantly at present. Though the soft error ovehead is negligible with current technology, the SER is expected to increase in the future. To evaluate the SER in future technology, we simulated the AMAT with accelerated SERs from 1.E-12 to 1.E-4(for a cache line). Figure 4(a) depicts the AMATs with the accelerated SERs including wake-up penalties and Figure 4(b) shows the AMAT overheads of soft errors, excluding the wake-up penalties. In Figure 4(a), AMATs of the 32-way drowsy cache are 2.79%, 2.84%, and 32.32% longer at 1.E-11, 1.E-8, and 1.E-5, respectively. Except the cases of 1.E-5 or 1.E-6, there are no significant differences between the drowsy cache and the normal cache. As shown in Figure 4(b), the AMAT overhead increases linearly and the overhead is less then 0.01 clock cycles if the SER is 1.E-7 or less. Consequently, when the SER of a cache line is below 1.E-6, the drowsy I-cache is reliable enough even with the re-fetch penalty.

4   Conclusion

It has been widely considered that the drowsy cache is inefficient to use in the future because the SER is increased exponentially by suppressing supply voltage. The key observation is that I-caches store only read-only data. Thus, the drowsy I-cache overcomes the soft error problems by re-fetching the corresponding data. Though the SER is expected to be increased in the future, it may not hurt the performance noticeably. It is reasonable to apply drowsy technique to an I-cache. The multi-SBE threatens the system reliability because it is not detected by parity bits and cannot be resolved with bit interleaving. Fortunately, it is not so serious, since the error rate of multi-SBE is very low. This paper investigates reliability of the drowsy I-cache that dramatically reduces the leakage energy.

References

1. Degalahal, V., Li, L., Vijaykrishnan, N., Kandemir, M.T., Irwin, M.J.: Soft errors issues in low-power caches. In: VLSI. (2005) 1157–1166
2. Nguyen, H.T., Yagil, Y., Seifert, N., Reitsma, M.: Chip-level soft error estimation method. In: IEEE Transaction on Device and Materials Reliability. (2005) 365–381
3. Hazucha, P., Svensson, C.: Impact of cmos technology scaling on the atmospheric neutron soft error rate. In: IEEE Transcation on Nuclear Science. (2000) 2586–2594
4. Baumann, R.: Soft errors in advanced computer systems. In: IEEE Design and Test of Computers. (2005) 258–266
5. Slayman, C.W.: Cache and memory error detection, correction, and reduction techniques for terrestrial servers and workstations. In: IEEE Trans. on Device and Materials Reliability. Volume 5. (2005) 397–404
6. Kim, N.S., Flautner, K., Blaauw, D., Mudge, T.N.: Drowsy instruction caches: leakage power reduction using dynamic voltage scaling and cache sub-bank prediction. In: MICRO. (2002) 219–230
7. Chen, C.L., Hsiao, M.Y.: Error-correcting codes for semiconductor memory applications: A state-of-the-art review. IBM Journal of Research and Development **28**(2) (1984) 124–134
8. Burger, D., Austin, T.M., Bennett, S.: Evaluating future microprocessors: the simplescalar tool set. Technical Report TR-1308, Univ. of Wisconsin-Madison Computer Sciences Dept. (1997)
9. SPEC: (SPEC CPU2000 Benchmarks.) http://www.specbench.org.

Design of a Reconfigurable Cryptographic Engine*

Kang Sun, Lingdi Ping, Jiebing Wang, Zugen Liu, and Xuezeng Pan

College of Computer Science and Technology, Zhejiang University, Hangzhou 310027,
China
ksun@zju.edu.cn

Abstract. Cryptographic algorithms are usually compute-intensive and
more efficiently implemented in hardware than in software. By taking
advantage of FPGA technology, some work offers high performance and
flexible solutions for cryptographic algorithms. But FPGAs still have
some drawbacks. To overcome inherent shortages of FPGA, a novel asynchronous reconfigurable cryptographic engine (ARCEN) is introduced.
In this architecture, reconfigurable cryptographic array is the kernel. It
routes signals asynchronously between adjacent cells through Neighbor-
to-Neighbor wires with 4-phase handshaking protocol. Computation circuit for reconfigurable cell is developed with modified DSDCVS logic.
Experiment results show that the architecture has a better performance
than FPGA.

1 Introduction

Cryptographic algorithms can be implemented in hardware by ASICs (Application Specific Integrated Circuits) or in software by software-programmed processors. Due to the diversity of applications, cryptographic machines have to meet
the enormous computing demands of the algorithms. Such flexibility is also crucial for adapting to the evolving requirements of state-of-the-art algorithms
and standards. ASIC-based solutions, lacking flexibility, provide effective performance but they can only offer a fixed number of algorithms to designers.
Software solutions can provide the required flexibility but they are inadequate
for high speed encryption applications.

Reconfigurable hardware is a general term that applies to any device which
can be configured, at run-time, to implement a function as a hardware circuit.
It typically consists of a set of computing elements connected by communication medium. Both the computing elements and the communication medium are
programmable. The computing elements can be either fine-grained or coarse-
grained, which can exploit fine grain and coarse grain parallelism available in
the application.

* This work is supported by Natural Science Foundation of Zhejiang Province, China
(Grant No. Y105355).

C. Jesshope and C. Egan (Eds.): ACSAC 2006, LNCS 4186, pp. 452–458, 2006.

In the past several years, there has been a growing body of work on using reconfigurable devices to implement cryptographic algorithms. Some early studies have shown that reconfigurable implementations of DES and RSA have both achieved significant speedups over general-purpose processors[1][2]. In some recent research work, reconfigurable hardwares have been integrated into System-on-a-Chip (SoC) as cryptographic engines. In [3], a reconfigurable elliptic curve cryptosystems on a chip has been designed and the experiment results show over 2000 times speedup when compared with general-purpose processor solutions. The SHA-2 hash algorithm family has also been implemented successfully on reconfigurable hardware[4]. However, all the work mentioned above employs FPGAs (Field-Programmable Gate Arrays) as reconfigurable cryptographic engine. Although FPGAs can provide good performance and flexibility, they still have some drawbacks. Firstly, as fine-grained reconfigurable device, FPGAs usually need a large amount of configuration data, which will lengthen the configuration time. Secondly, as general-purpose reconfigurable device, FPGAs require abundant routing resources in order to adapt to various applications, which will increase the chip area and power consumption[5].

In this paper, we introduce a novel adaptive cryptographic engine. Different from the stated preceding work, we develop a coarse-grained asynchronous reconfigurable array with high-performance for cryptographic applications. Without global clocks, asynchronous circuits can be totally prevented from the inferiority of clock-skew. And the problem of clock tree power consumption has been eased off. Moreover, in asynchronous circuits, there is no global timing signal which can be used as a reference clock, thus timing and power analysis attack are consequently expected to be more difficult[6]. The architecture we developed is called ARCEN (Asynchronous Reconfigurable Cryptographic ENgine).

The rest of this paper is organized as follows. Section 2 describes the architecture of our cryptographic engine. Section 3 presents the implementation details of this device. Section 4 analyzes the performance of this architecture and provides the experiment results. At last, Section 5 is the conclusion.

2   System Architecture

The proposed asynchronous cryptographic engine (ARCEN) is shown in figure 1. It consists of five main components:

- A random number generator, which is mainly used for generating secret keys.
- A data packets dispatcher, which is responsible for data moving between reconfigurable array and the outside.
- A cryptographic control unit, which is the main controller of the system. In this unit, there's an address generator which is responsible for generating memory addresses for data input/output.
- A reconfigurable cryptographic array, which is the computation core of the whole system.
- A cryptographic library, which stores the ARCEN configuration of cryptographic algorithms.

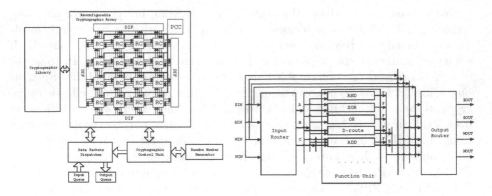

Fig. 1. Architecture of ARCEN   **Fig. 2.** The structure of logic cell

The reconfigurable cryptographic array (RCA) is the core component of this system. With this component, ARCEN can be dynamically adapted to cryptographic algorithms of different secret keys.

The RCA is SRAM-based, asynchronous reconfigurable computing device and consists of logic cells surrounded by NN (Nearest Neighboring) channels. It consists of a parallel configuration controller (PCC), four data input interfaces (DIF) and a set of reconfigurable logic cells (RC). PCC is used for configuring the reconfigurable cells. DIFs are responsible for data transferring. Because of the regularity of cryptographic algorithms, the routing resources are the NN connections between the logic cells. The routing requirement can be satisfied by NN connections in most cryptographic applications. Even a small amount of long wires exist, they can be substituted with several NN connections. Compared with FPGA, this architecture can save more routing area. The datapath of the logic cells is 8-bit wide and the cells communicate with the nearest neighboring cells from ESWN (East, South, West, North) directions through a pair of data-wires which are 8-bit wide, dual-rail encoded. Since there is no clock in RCA design, logic cells have to use asynchronous hand-shaking protocol when communicating.

The structure of RCA logic cell is shown in figure 2. Each logic cell is composed of input router, function unit and output router. Input router channels from physical input ports of four nearest neighboring directions (EIN, SIN, WIN, NIN) to three internal logical channels (A, B, C) as the inputs of the function unit. The input router is implemented by several MUXs.

Output router is the part that channels data from inside to the physical output port of logic cell (EOUT, SOUT, WOUT, NOUT). Besides being outputted through function unit (F, Z), input data from the four nearest neighboring input ports of logic cell (EIN, SIN, WIN, NIN) can also be channeled to the output ports directly through output router.

The function unit of logic cell is designed to support up to 10 operations. Among these 10 operations, "and", "or" "xor" "shift" operations are used for basic logical functions; "add" and "sub" operations take charge of fundamental arithmetic functions; "zero", "one", "2-1mux" and "d-router"(dynamic router) are supposed to provide some control logic resources in some special applications.

3 Implementation

3.1 Asynchronous Handshake Protocol

Since there is no clock in RCA, logic cells have to use handshake protocol to send and receive data on NN channels. In our design, we choose 4-phase handshake protocol (see in figure 3). In 4-phase handshake protocol, only the rising of "Req" signal can inspire the transfer process, but its control circuit is simple, and this protocol is well suited for DCVSL (Differential Cascode Voltage Swing Logic)[7].

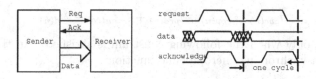

Fig. 3. 4-phase asynchronous handshake protocol

We adopt dual-rail encoding technology to implement 4-phase handshake protocol with simple control circuit. In dual-rail encoding, each bit of data is implemented by two wires, of which one is the original data, and the other is the complement of it. Both "01" and "10" represent valid data and inspire the "Req" signal rising, while the state of "00" means invalid data and set the "Req" signal falling. "11" is an illegal state, which is not supposed to appear.

3.2 Control Circuit Design

In short, the role that control circuit plays is to implement dual-rail encoding 4-phase handshake protocol. After configuration, logic cells in RCA form the structure of asynchronous mircopipeline, which is indicated in figure 4. In each logic cell, there are three main parts, namely, OP, CD and RE. OP is the operation circuit taking charge of computation logic, which is implemented by DCVSL and will be discussed later, and the other two parts constitute the control circuit. RE (Request Enabler) is used for generating req signal, whose active falling edge can make the operation circuit pre-charged (reset). Meanwhile, CD (Completion Detector) is used for detecting the state of operation circuit and generating ack signal, which is asserted high when operation circuit has finished an evaluation or low when it has finished a pre-charge phase. The functioning process of the synchronous micropipeline will be analyzed in detail in section 4. The following terms are used in the discussion of latency issues:

- $t_{op(n)}$: evaluation time of a computation of operation circuit in logic cell n.
- t_{cd}: processing time of CD (Completion Detector).
- t_{re}: processing time of RE (Request Enabler).
- $t_{pre(n)}$: pre-charge time of operation circuit in logic cell n.
- $t_{d(n)}$: delay of signal transition on wires between logic cell n and logic cell n+1.
- $t_{cyc(n)}$: the time interval which logic cell n should be ready for evaluating a new data after it has started to evaluate the previous one.

Since $t_{op(n)}$ and $t_{pre(n)}$ are specified by operation circuits, and $t_{d(n)}$ is determined by the routing resources of RCA, the factors which can reduce $t_{cyc(n)}$ are t_{re} and t_{cd}. We place the CD part before operation circuit, and parallel the parts of RE and CD, which can merge t_{re} and t_{cd} into the same time interval. In this case, both t_{re} and t_{cd} are replaced by $t_{control}$, then the $t_{cyc(n)}$ can be described as equation (1):

$$t_{cyc(n)} = t_{op(n)} + t_{pre(n)} + 2t_{control} + 2t_{d(n)} \tag{1}$$

Obviously, only when the following constrain is satisfied, can this improved structure of asynchronous micropipeline function.

$$t_{cd} + t_{d(n)} > t_{op(n)} \tag{2}$$

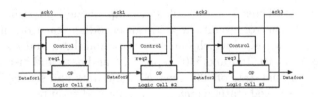

Fig. 4. Asynchronous micropipeline with improved control circuit

3.3   Operation Circuit Design

Since well suited for dual-rail encoding, DCVSL is taken into consideration for implementing operation circuit in RCA. We propose a new DSDCVSL (Data-Driven DCVSL) for synchronous pipeline with the advantages of high-speed, simple-control and low-cost[8]. The usage of DSDCVSL structure for operation circuit is shown in figure 5. There must be a series of circuits in a logic cell to support various operations. They can be implemented by NMOS tree with different logic functions. In figure 5, the ack and req signals are responsible for setting the state of operation circuit.

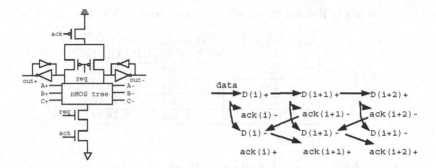

Fig. 5. DSDCVSL operation circuit   **Fig. 6.** STG of asynchronous micropipeline

4   Evaluation and Results

4.1   Performance Evaluation

The functioning process of asynchronous micropipeline formed by logic cells in RCA is shown in figure 6 by signal transition graph (STG). In figure 6, the transition of ack is represented by ack+ and ack-, of which "+" means the transition from low to high and "-" means high to low. D+ and D- represent the state of operation circuit, of which "+" means evaluation and "-" means pre-charging. (i) represents the Logic Cell of stage i in asynchronous pipeline, while (i+1) and (i+2) represent its successive two logic cells. The arrows dedicate the constrain relationships of signals of neighboring logic cells. For instance, the arrow between ack(i+1)- and D(i)- means that before the operation circuit of logic cell i being pre-charged, the signal of ack from logic cell (i+1) to logic cell i must be inspired from high to low. The minimum cycle of one logic cell from the asynchronous micropipeline has been stated in equation (1). The latency of total asynchronous micropipeline, which is the main measurement of RCA, can be described as equation (3).

$$T = \sum_{i=1}^{n} \left(t_{op(i)} + t_{d(i)} \right) \tag{3}$$

4.2   Experiment Results

To show the effectiveness of our cryptographic engine, we have conducted several tests of simulation, which are based on the technology library of SMIC in 0.18 CMOS process. We have implemented the modulo multiplication on FPGA and compared the performance with our design (ARCEN). The comparison results are listed in table 1, and the target FPGA device is Xilinx Virtex-E. The results of ARCEN is generated by analyzing Synopsys HSPICE report.

Table 1. Estimated throughput comparisons of ARCEN and FPGA

Key Length (bit)	Throughput (Mbit/s)	
	FPGA (Virtex-E)	ARCEN
128	14.455	78.278
256	7.926	78.201
512	4.383	78.163
1024	2.486	78.144

5   Conclusions and Future Work

We introduce a novel asynchronous reconfigurable cryptographic engine (ARCEN) and discuss the design of ARCEN to achieve high performance. The analysis and experiment results have proven that ARCEN functions well with high-performance.

Future work includes designing a dynamic partial reconfigurable architecture to achieve further savings in area and to reduce the reconfigure time of the device. And we will go deeper into the research of using asynchronous circuits to defend timing analysis and power analysis attack, thus to enhance chip security.

References

1. K. W. Tse, T. I. Yuk, and S. S. Chan. Implementation of the data encryption standard algorithm with FPGAs. Proceedings of the 3th International Workshop on Field-programmable Logic and Applications, Oxford, England, September 1993. p.412-419.
2. M. Shand, J. Vuillemin. Fast implementations of RSA cryptography. Proceedings of the 11th Symposium on Computer Arithmetic, Windsor, ONT, Canada, 29 June-2 July 1993. p.252-259.
3. Ray C.C. Cheung, Wayne Luk, Peter Y. K. Cheung. Reconfigurable Elliptic Curve Cryptosystems on a Chip. Proceedings of the conference on Design, Automation and Test in Europe, Vol. 1, Munich, Germany, March 07-11, 2005. p.24-29.
4. N. Sklavos, O. Koufopavlou. Implementation of the SHA-2 Hash Family Standard Using FPGAs. The Journal of Supercomputing, Vol. 31, No. 3 March 2005. p.227-248.
5. R. W. Hartenstein, T. Hoffmann, U. Nadeldinger. Design-Space Exploration of Low Power Coarse Grained Reconfigurable Datapath Array Architectures. Proceedings of the 10th International Workshop on Integrated Circuit Design, Power and Timing Modeling, Optimization and Simulation, Gottingen, Germany, September 13-15, 2000. p.118-128.
6. Z. C. Yu, S. B. Furber, L. A. Plana. An investigation into the security of self-timed circuits. Proceedings of the 9th International Symposium on Asynchronous Circuits and Systems. IEEE Computer Society, 2003. p.206-215.
7. C. S. Choy, J. Butas, J. Povazanec et al. A New Control Circuit for Asynchronous Micropipelines. IEEE Transaction on Computer, vol. 50, No. 9, 2001. p.992-997.
8. S. Mathew, R. Sridhar. A data-driven micropipeline structure using DSDCVSL. Proceedings of the IEEE 1999 Custom Integrated Circuits Conference, San Diego, CA, USA, May 16-19, 1999. p.295-298.

Enhancing ICOUNT2.8 Fetch Policy with Better Fairness for SMT Processors*

Caixia Sun[1], Hongwei Tang[2], and Minxuan Zhang[2]

College of Computer, National University of Defense Technology,
Changsha 410073, Hunan, P.R.China
[1] cxsun1979@163.com
[2] {hwtang, mxzhang}@nudt.edu.cn

Abstract. In Simultaneous Multithreading (SMT) processors, the instruction fetch policy implicitly determines shared resources allocation among all the co-scheduled threads, and consequently affects throughput and fairness. However, prior work on fetch policies almost focuses on throughput optimization. The issue of fairness between threads in progress rates is studied rarely.

In this paper, we take fairness as the optimization goal and propose an enhanced version of ICOUNT2.8 with better fairness called ICOUNT2.8-fairness. Results show that using ICOUNT2.8-fairness, RPRrange (a fairness metric defined in this paper) is less than 5% for all types of workloads, and the degradation of overall throughput is not more than 7%. Especially, for two-thread MIX workload, ICOUNT2.8-fairness outperforms ICOUNT2.8 in throughput at the same time of achieving better fairness.

Keywords: SMT, Instruction Fetch Policy, Throughput, Fairness.

1 Introduction

Simultaneous Multithreading (SMT) processors [1,2] improve performance by running instructions from several threads at a single cycle. Co-scheduled threads share some resources, such as issue queues, physical registers, and functional units. The way of allocating shared resources among the threads will affect throughput and fairness. Throughput measures the combined progress rate of all the co-scheduled threads, whereas fairness measures how uniformly the threads are slowed down due to resource sharing [3]. Currently, shared resources allocation is mainly decided by the instruction fetch policy. However, Prior work on fetch policies has ignored fairness and almost focused on throughput optimization, such as ICOUNT2.8 [2], STALL, FLUSH [4], DG, PDG [5, and so on. In order to achieve higher throughput, these policies tend to favor threads that naturally have high IPC [6], hence sacrificing fairness.

In fact, fairness in progress rates is very critical because the Operating System (OS) thread scheduler assumes that in a given timeslice, the resource sharing uniformly impacts the progress rates of all co-scheduled threads in SMT processors. Based on this assumption, an OS assigns more timeslices to threads with higher

---

* This work was supported by Chinese NSF under the grant No.60376018.

C. Jesshope and C. Egan (Eds.): ACSAC 2006, LNCS 4186, pp. 459–465, 2006.

priority, thus priority-based timeslice assignment can work in a SMT processor system as effectively as in a time-shared single-thread processor system. On the contrary, if this consumption can not be met, priority inversion may arise. It is worse that OS is not aware of this problem, and cannot correct this situation. Therefore, in order to ensure the OS scheduler's effectiveness, the hardware in SMT processors should provide fair progress rates to all the co-scheduled threads.

In this paper, we take fairness as the main optimization goal and propose an enhanced version of ICOUNT2.8 with better fairness, which is called ICOUNT2.8-fairness. In our new policy, relative progress rates of all co-scheduled threads are recorded and detected each cycle. If the range of relative progress rates is lower than a threshold, fairness is met approximately and ICOUNT2.8 is used as the fetch policy. Thus throughput would not be degraded significantly. Otherwise, relative progress rates are used to decide fetch priorities. The lower a thread's relative progress rate is, the higher its fetch priority is. Unfair situation is corrected by this way.

The rest of the paper is organized as follows. Section 2 presents the methodology and gives the definition of a new fairness metric RPRrange. In Section 3, we analyze the fairness of ICOUNT2.8 fetch policy. Section 4 details how to enhance ICOUNT2.8 with better fairness and Section 5 illustrates the results. Finally, concluding remarks are given in Section 6.

2   Methodology

Execution is simulated on an out-of-order superscalar processor model derived from SMTSIM [7]. The simulator models all typical sources of latency, including caches, branch mispredictions, TLB misses, etc. The baseline configuration of our simulator is shown in Table 1.

Table 1. Baseline configuration of the simulator

Parameter	Value
Fetch Width	8 instructions per cycle
Instruction Queues	64 int, 64 fp
Functional Units	6 int (4 load/store), 3 fp
Renaming Registers	100 int, 100 fp
Branch Predictor	2K gshare
Branch Target Buffer	256 entries, 4-way associative
L1I cache, L1D cache	64KB, 2-way, 64-bytes lines, 1 cycle access
L2 cache	512KB, 2-way, 64-bytes lines, 10 cycles latency
L3 cache	4MB, 2-way, 64-bytes lines, 20 cycles latency
Main Memory Latency	100 cycles

All benchmarks used in our simulations are taken from the SPEC2000 suite [8] and are executed using the reference input set. We follow the idea proposed in [9] to run the most representative 300 million instruction segment of each benchmark. Benchmarks can be divided into two groups based on their cache behaviors: MEM and ILP. MEM benchmarks used in our simulations include parser, twolf, lucas, art, swim and applu. ILP benchmarks include gzip, eon, gap, crafty, fma3d and mesa. Table 2 lists the multithreaded workloads used in our simulations. These workloads either contain benchmarks all from MEM type (the MEM workloads in Table 2), or all from ILP type (ILP), or an equal mix from MEM type and ILP type (MIX).

Table 2. Multithreaded Workloads

Size	Type	Workloads
2	ILP	{gzip, crafty}, {gzip, fma3d}, {gap, mesa}, {fma3d, mesa}
	MIX	{gzip, parser}, {gzip, lucas}, {fma3d, twolf}, {fma3d, swim} {parser, eon}, {parser, mesa}, {art, fma3d}, {applu, mesa}
	MEM	{parser, twolf}, {parser, lucas}, {twolf, applu}, {art, swim}
4	ILP	{gzip, eon, gap, crafty}, {gzip, crafty, fma3d, mesa}
	MIX	{gzip, gap, parser, twolf}, {gzip, crafty, art, swim} {parser, twolf, fma3d, mesa}, {applu, lucas, fma3d, mesa}
	MEM	{lucas, art, swim, applu}, {parser, twolf, lucas, art},
6	ILP	{gzip, eon, gap, crafty, fma3d, mesa}
	MIX	{gzip, gap, mesa, parser, twolf, lucas}, {gap, famed, mesa, parser, twolf, lucas}
	MEM	{parser, twolf, lucas, art, swim, applu}
8	ILP	{gzip, eon, gap, crafty, fma3d, mesa, gzip, crafty}
	MIX	{gzip, gap, fma3d, mesa, parser, twolf, art, applu} {gzip, eon, gap, crafty, lucas, art, swim, applu}
	MEM	{parser, twolf, lucas, art, swim, applu, art, parser }

We use IPC to measure throughput and also define a new metric to measure fairness. Let $IPCalone_i$ denote IPC of thread i when it runs alone in a SMT processor and $IPCsmt_i$ denote IPC of thread i when it runs with other threads. The relative progress rate of thread i (RPR_i) is defined as Equation (1):

$$RPR_i = \frac{IPCsmt_i}{IPCalone_i} \times 100\% \tag{1}$$

Assume the number of co-scheduled threads is n. We define a fairness metric RPRrange, which is the range of relative progress rates of all co-scheduled threads and given by equation (2):

$$RPRrange = MAX(RPR_1, RPR_2, ..., RPR_n) - MIN(RPR_1, RPR_2, ..., RPR_n) \tag{2}$$

RPRrange is always between zero and one. The smaller RPRrange is, the better fairness is. We say that an ideal fairness is achieved when RPRrange is zero, that is, the relative progress rates of all co-scheduled threads are equal.

3 Fairness of ICOUNT2.8 Fetch Policy

ICOUNT2.8 is used widely in SMT processors. ICOUNT presents that the threads with few instructions in decode, rename, and the instruction queues are prioritized to fetch instructions; 2.8 presents that the number of threads that can fetch in one cycle is 2, and the maximum number of instructions fetched per thread in one cycle is 8.

To get how uniformly the co-scheduled threads are slowed down when using ICOUNT2.8 fetch policy, we choose some workloads from Table 2 to simulate.

Figure 1 shows the RPRrange results. We can see that for most of workloads, unfairness arises. Especially for {fma3d, swim}, RPRrange reaches 0.71, where the relative progress rate of fma3d is 0.26 and that of swim is 0.97.

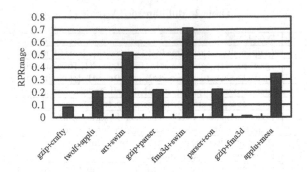

Fig. 1. Fairness of ICOUNT2.8

Under this unfair situation, problems may occur. Assume that fma3d and swim are ready threads waiting to be scheduled by the OS scheduler and fma3d has a higher priority. To make fma3d achieve a faster forward progress, the OS scheduler can assign more timeslices to it. However, in the timeslices in which fma3d and swim are co-scheduled, swim makes faster forward progress. The OS scheduler is not aware of this problem, so it will not assign further more timeslices to fma3d. Finally, swim may achieve a faster forward progress, which makes the OS scheduler ineffective.

4   Enhancing ICOUNT2.8 Fetch Policy with Better Fairness

The basic idea behind ICOUNT2.8-fairness is: when fairness is met, use ICOUNT2.8 as fetch policy; otherwise, correct unfairness by other method. So two things must be resolved. First is to detect when unfairness happens. Second is to correct unfairness.

For the first thing, we use RPRrange to determine if fairness is met. Therefore, *IPCsmt* and *IPCalone* of all threads are needed. *IPCsmt* can be gotten easily. To get *IPCalone* dynamically, we employ two phases: sample phase and statistic phase.

During the sample phase, the processor runs in single-thread mode. Each thread runs alone for a certain interval respectively.

During the statistic phase, the processor runs in multi-thread mode and all threads are co-scheduled. Each cycle, *IPCsmt* and RPRrange are re-calculated. If RPRrange is more than a threshold, we say that unfairness happens.

A key point must be considered. Programs experience different phases in their execution in which their IPC varies significantly [10]. Hence, if we want to get more accurate progress rates, we need take into account this variable IPC. Our solution is to execute sample phase and statistic phase in an alternate fashion.

For the second thing, it is obvious that we can use relative progress rates to correct unfairness. That is, make the thread with lower progress rate run faster by assigning higher fetch priority to it. However, when there are only two threads co-scheduled, this method may not correct unfairness. The reason is that instructions are fetched from two threads each cycle. Although the thread with lower relative progress rate has higher fetch priority, if it can not fill the fetch bandwidth, instructions from the other thread with higher relative progress rate can be fetched still. In order to address this problem, when fairness is not met and the number of threads co-scheduled is two, only one thread can fetch instructions in one cycle.

Now three parameters are needed to be defined for ICOUNT2.8-fairness policy.

$Length_{statistic}$: the length of the statistic phase.

$Length_{sample}$: the length of interval in which each thread runs alone during the sample phase. So the total length of a sample phase is $Length_{sample}$ multiplied by n, where n is the number of co-scheduled threads.

$Threshold_{fairness}$: a threshold to detect unfair situation. If RPRrange is more than $Threshold_{fairness}$, we say that unfairness arises. Otherwise, fairness is met.

5 Results

5.1 Choosing Parameters for ICOUNT2.8-Fairness

To simulate the impact of $Length_{statistic}$ on throughput, only ICOUNT2.8 is used during the statistic phase. Figure 2 shows the results. Y-axis denotes the average degradation of throughput per thread compared to ICOUNT2.8. We can see that 2^{24} is an inflexion point. So we choose 2^{24} as the value of $Length_{statistic}$.

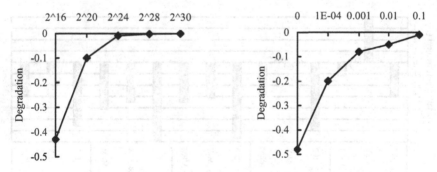

Fig. 2. Impact of $Length_{statistic}$ on throughput   **Fig. 3.** Impact of $Threshold_{fairness}$ on throughput

In our simulations, $Length_{sample}$ is smaller than $Length_{statistic}$ greatly and the impact of $Length_{sample}$ on throughput is very limited. Therefore, we choose 2^{16} as the value of $Length_{sample}$ without simulation.

Now we measure the impact of $Threshold_{fairness}$ on throughput. Figure 3 shows the results. Y-axis denotes the degradation of overall throughput compared to ICOUNT2.8. Similarly, we can see that 0.001 is an inflexion point, so we choose 0.001 as the value of $Threshold_{fairness}$.

5.2   ICOUNT2.8-Fairness vs. ICOUNT2.8

In this section, we compare ICOUNT2.8-fairness to ICOUNT2.8 with chosen para-meters.

Figure 4 depicts fairness results of ICOUNT2.8 and ICOUNT2.8-fairness. The av-erage RPRrange of ICOUNT2.8 for ILP, MIX and MEM workloads are 8.8%, 21.0% and 14.3%, respectively. For ICOUNT.28- fairness-2^{24}-2^{16}-0.001, the respective val-ues are 4.4%, 2.8% and 3.0%. Fairness is improved greatly. We can also see that for all types of workloads, RPRrange of ICOUNT2.8-fairness is less than 5%. So we can say that ICOUNT2.8-fairness is very stable in fairness.

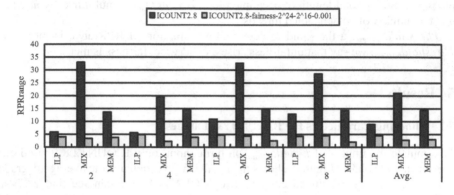

Fig. 4. Fairness results

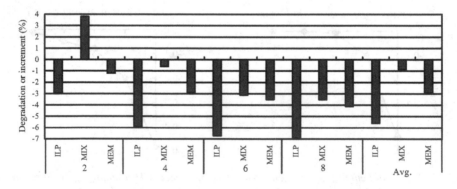

Fig. 5. Throughput of ICOUNT2.8-fairness relative to ICOUNT2.8

Figure 5 shows throughput increment or degradation of ICOUNT2.8-fairness com-pared to ICOUNT2.8. We can see that the degradation is 6.9% in worst. For two-thread MIX workload, throughput is improved when better fairness is achieved. The key point is ICOUNT2.8 fetches instructions from two threads in one cycle, and the thread with cache misses can fetch instructions still if there are only two threads co-scheduled. After a certain number of cycles, shared resources clogging may happen. Two-thread MIX workloads contains an MEM-thread with low IPC and an ILP-thread with high IPC. Therefore, it is easier that shared resources are clogged by MEM-thread, which causes ILP-thread cannot make forward progress because of lack of resources. However, in ICOUNT2.8-fairness, when the number of co-scheduled threads is two, only one thread can fetch instructions if unfairness arises. Thus, resources can be occupied fairly by two threads according to their IPC, and the ILP-thread can acquire enough resources to make forward progress.

6 Conclusions

Our contribution is that we propose an enhanced version of ICOUNT2.8, called ICOUNT2.8-fairness. When fairness is met, ICOUNT2.8 is used to ensure throughput. Otherwise, fetch priorities of threads are determined by relative progress rates to correct unfair situation. Results show that compared to ICOUNT2.8, ICOUNT2.8-fairness achieves better fairness, and throughput is only affected slightly. For all types of workloads, RPRrange is less than 5% and the degradation of throughput is not more than 7%. Especially for two-thread MIX workload, ICOUNT2.8-fairness outperforms ICOUNT2.8 in throughput at the same time of achieving better fairness.

References

1. D. Tullsen, S. Eggers and H. Levy: Simultaneous multithreading: Maximizing on-chip parallelism. In Proc. ISCA-22 (1995)
2. D. Tullsen, S. Eggers, J. Emer, H. Levy, J. Lo and R. Stamm: Exploiting choice: Instruction fetch and issue on an implementable simultaneous multithreading processor. In Proc. ISCA-23 (1996)
3. S. Kim, D. Chandra and Y. Solihin: Fair cache sharing and partitioning in a chip multiprocessor architecture. In Proc. PACT-13 (2004)
4. D. Tullsen and J. Brown: Handling long-latency loads in a simultaneous multithreaded processor. In Proc. MICRO-34 (2001)
5. A. El-Moursy and D. Albonesi: Front-end policies for improved issue efficiency in SMT processors. In Proc. HPCA-9 (2003)
6. A. Snavely and D. Tullsen: Symbiotic jobscheduling for a simultaneous multithreading architecture. In Proc. ASPLOS-9 (2000)
7. 7 D. Tullsen: Simulation and modeling of a simultaneous multithreading processor. In Proceedings of 22nd Annual Computer Measurement Group Conference (1996)
8. The standard performance evaluation corporation. WWW site. http://www.specbench.org
9. T. Sherwood, E. Perelman and B. Calder: Basic block distribution analysis to find periodic behavior and simulation points in applications. In Proc. of PACT-10 (2001)
10. T. Sherwood and B. Calder: Time varying behavior of programs. Tech. Report UCSDCS99 -630, Univ. of Calif. (1999)

The New BCD Subtractor and Its Reversible Logic Implementation

Himanshu Thapliyal and M.B Srinivas

Center for VLSI and Embedded System Technologies
International Institute of Information Technology, Hyderabad-500032, India
{thapliyalhimanshu@yahoo.com, srinivas@iiit.net}

Abstract. IEEE 754r is the ongoing revision to the IEEE 754 floating point standard and a major enhancement to the standard is the addition of decimal format. Thus in this paper we propose a novel BCD subtractor called carry skip BCD subtractor. We also propose the reversible logic implementation of the proposed carry skip BCD subtractor. Reversible logic is emerging as a promising computing paradigm having its applications in low power CMOS, quantum computing, nanotechnology, and optical computing. It is not possible to realize quantum computing without reversible logic. It is being tried to design the BCD subtractor optimal in terms of number of reversible gates and garbage outputs.

1 Introduction

The decimal arithmetic is receiving significant attention as the financial, commercial, and Internet-based applications cannot tolerate errors generated by conversion between decimal and binary formats. A number of decimal numbers, such as 0.110, cannot be exactly represented in binary, thus, these applications often store data in decimal format and process data using decimal arithmetic software [1]. The advantage of decimal arithmetic in eliminating conversion errors also comes with a drawback; it is typically 100 to 1,000 times slower than binary arithmetic implemented in hardware. Since, the decimal arithmetic is getting significant attention; specifications for it have recently been added to the draft revision of the IEEE 754 standard for Floating-Point Arithmetic. IEEE 754r is an ongoing revision to the IEEE 754 floating point standard [2,3]. Some of the major enhancements so far incorporated are the addition of 128-bit and decimal formats. It is anticipated that once the IEEE 754r Standard is finally approved, hardware support for decimal floating-point arithmetic on the processors will come into existence for financial, commercial, and Internet-based applications. Still, the major consideration while implementing BCD arithmetic will be to enhance its speed as much as possible.

Reversible logic is also emerging as a promising computing paradigm. Researchers like Landauer have shown that for irreversible logic computations, each bit of information lost, generates kTln2 joules of heat energy, where k is Boltzmann's constant and T the absolute temperature at which computation is performed [4]. Bennett showed that kTln2 energy dissipation would not occur, if a computation is carried out in a reversible way [5], since the amount of energy dissipated in a system bears a direct relationship to the number of bits erased during computation. Reversible

C. Jesshope and C. Egan (Eds.): ACSAC 2006, LNCS 4186, pp. 466–472, 2006.
© Springer-Verlag Berlin Heidelberg 2006

circuits are those circuits that do not lose information and reversible computation in a system can be performed only when the system comprises of reversible gates. These circuits can generate unique output vector from each input vector, and vice versa, that is, there is a one-to-one mapping between input and output vectors.

Reversible circuits are of high interest in low-power CMOS design, optical computing, nanotechnology and quantum computing. The most prominent application of reversible logic lies in quantum computers [6]. A quantum computer performs an elementary unitary operation on one, two or more two–state quantum systems called qubits. Each qubit represents an elementary unit of information; corresponding to the classical bit values 0 and 1. Any unitary operation is reversible and hence quantum arithmetic must be built from reversible logical components.

The major constraint while designing reversible logic circuits is to minimize the reversible gate used and garbage output produced(outputs which may not be used but are provided to maintain reversibility). In this paper we introduce a novel BCD subtractor called Carry Skip BCD subtractor. The proposed BCD architecture is designed especially, to improve the speed of the BCD subtraction. The BCD subtractor internally consists of nine's complementer, BCD adder and parallel adder. Thus special emphasize has been laid on their architecture, to make them carry skip, to overall improve the efficiency of the subtractor. We also propose a novel reversible implementation of the carry skip BCD subtractor, using the recently proposed TSG gate [7] and the other existing gates in literature. The TSG gate has the advantage that it can work singly as a reversible Full adder with only two garbage outputs. The reversible implementation of the proposed BCD subtractor is being tried to be optimal, in terms of number of reversible gates and garbage outputs. Thus an attempt has been tried to design the fast BCD adder, as well as, to provide the platform for building decimal ALU of a Quantum CPU.

2 BCD Subtractor

In the BCD subtraction, nine's complement of the subtrahend is added to the minuend. In the BCD arithmetic, the nine's complement is computed by nine minus the number whose nine's complement is to be computed. This can be illustrated as the nine's complement of 5 will be 9-5= 4 which can be represented in BCD code as 0100.

In BCD subtraction, there can be two possible possibilities:

- The sum after the addition of minuend and the nine's complement of subtrahend is an invalid BCD Code or a carry is produced from the MSB. In this case decimal 6 (binary 0110) and the end around carry (EAC) is added to the sum. The final result will be the positive number represented by the sum.
- The sum of the minuend and the nine's complement of the subtrahend is a valid BCD code which means that the result is negative and is in the nine's complement.

In BCD arithmetic, instead of subtracting the number from nine, the Nine's complement of a number is determined by adding 1010(Decimal 10) to the one's complement of the number. The nine's complementer circuit using a 4-bit adder and XOR gates is shown in Fig. 1 and the one-digit BCD subtractor, using the nine's complementer circuit is shown in Fig. 2.

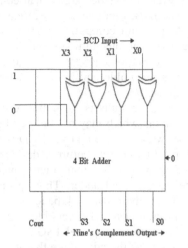

Fig. 1. Nine's Complementer

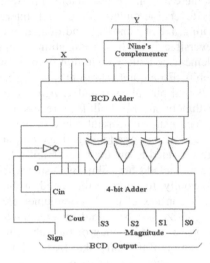

Fig. 2. BCD Subtractor

3 Proposed Carry Skip BCD Subtractor

In order to design the carry skip equivalent of the BCD subtractor, the authors propose the carry skip equivalent of its individual components.

3.1 Carry Skip BCD Adder

Recently, the Carry Skip BCD Adder is constructed in such a way that, the first full adder block consisting of 4 full adders can generate the output carry 'Cout' instantaneously, depending on the input signal and 'Cin', without waiting for the carry to be propagated in the ripple carry fashion [8]. Fig. 3 shows the Carry Skip BCD adder. The working of the Carry Skip BCD Adder (CS BCD Adder) can be explained as follows.

In the single bit full adder operation, if either input is a logical one, the cell will propagate the carry input to its carry output. Hence, the ith full adder carry input C_i, will propagate to its carry output, C_{i+1}, when $P_i = X_i \oplus Y_i$ where X_i and Y_i represents the input signal to the ith full adder. In addition, the four full adders at the first level making a block can generate a "block" propagate signal 'P'. When 'P' is one, it will make the block carry input 'Cin', to propagate as the carry output 'Cout' of the BCD adder, without waiting for the actual propagation of carry in the ripple carry fashion. An AND4 gate is used to generate a block propagate signal 'P'. Furthermore, depending on the value of 'Cout', appropriate action is taken. When it is equal to one, binary

0110 is added to the binary sum using another 4-bit binary adder (Second level or bottom binary adder). The output carry generated from the bottom binary adder is ignored, since it supplies information already available at the output carry terminal.

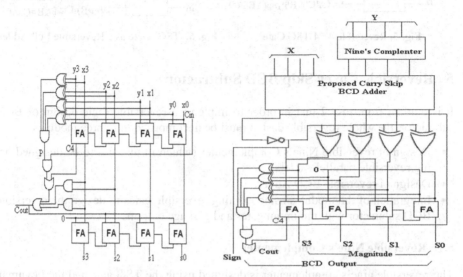

Fig. 3. Carry Skip BCD Adder   **Fig. 4.** Proposed Carry Skip BCD Subtractor

3.2 Carry Skip BCD Subtractor

Figure 4 shows the proposed carry skip BCD subtractor consisting of nine's complementer and carry skip BCD adder. It is to be noted that the carry skip implementation of the nine's complementer will not be beneficial. The reason for this lies in the fact that we are concerned only with generating the complementing output in nine's complementer not with 'Cout'. In Fig. 4, the last block (bottom 4-bit adder) is being designed in the carry skip fashion, to quickly generate the 'Cout'. The proposed circuit in Fig.4 is the maiden attempt to provide the carry skip equivalent of the conventional BCD subtractor.

4 Basic Reversible Gates

There are number of a existing reversible gates in literature such as Fredkin gate, Feynman Gate and Toffoli Gate (TG) [9,10]. Since, the major reversible gate used in designing the BCD subtractor is TSG gate, hence only the TSG gate is discussed in this section. The TSG gate is a 4 * 4 one through reversible gate [7] as shown in Fig.5. One of the prominent functionality of the TSG gate is that it can work singly as a reversible Full adder unit with bare minimum of two garbage outputs (lower bound for reversible full adder). Fig. 6 shows the implementation of the TSG gate as a reversible Full adder. It was shown in [7] that the reversible full adder design using TSG gate, is better than the reversible full-adder designs existing in literature.

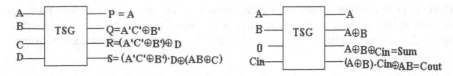

Fig. 5. Reversible 4 *4 TSG Gate   **Fig. 6.** TSG Gate as a Reversible Full Adder

5 Reversible Carry Skip BCD Subtractor

It is evident from Fig. 2 that in order to implement reversible logic design of BCD subtractor, the whole reversible design must be decomposed into three modules

- Design of reversible Nine's Complementer (which in turn has to be designed using reversible parallel Adders).
- Design of reversible BCD Adder.
- Integration of the modules using existing reversible gates to design the reversible BCD subtractor with minimum gates and garbage outputs.

5.1 Reversible Nine's Complementer

The reversible nine's complementer is designed using the TSG gate and the Feynman Gate (FG). FG is used to design the reversible XOR function, as it can implement the XOR function with bare minimum of one garbage output. The 4-bit reversible adder used in the nine's complementer can be further improved for efficiency by employing reversible parallel adders proposed by us in [7]. Fig. 7 shows one of the possible ways of realizing reversible nine's complementer.

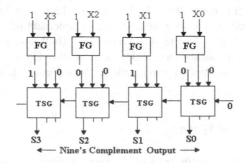

Fig. 7. Reversible Nine's Complementer

5.2 Reversible Carry Skip BCD Subtractor

The design of reversible carry skip BCD adder is presented by us in [8], thus its design is not discussed in this paper. Fig. 8 shows the reversible implementation of the proposed carry skip BCD subtractor. In order to simplify the explanation of the design, the design is labeled as part 1 and part 2. It is to be noted that we have carefully examined the architecture of BCD subtractor to design it optimal, in terms of number of reversible gates and garbage outputs. In Fig.8 (Part 1), we have used the Feynman gates as chains for generating the XOR, copying, and NOT functions with zero garbage. If the architecture is not deeply examined, it can lead to increase in the garbage. The reason for this stems from the fact that when Feynman gate is used for generating the XOR and NOT functions, it produces atleast one garbage output in both cases but the careful examination by us has produced the zero garbage. Fig.8 (Part 2) shows the reversible implementation of the bottom 4-bit carry skip adder block. The TSG and the Fredkin gates (F) are used for designing this block. In the proposed design, three outputs of the TSG gate are utilized (as propagate $Pi = Xi \oplus Yi$ is also required), thus reducing the garbage of reversible full adder from two to one. The three Fredkin in the middle of Fig.8 (part 2) are used to perform the AND4 operation. The single Fredkin in the left side of Fig.8 (part 2) performs the AND-OR function to create the carry skip logic and generate the block carry out signal 'Cout'. Fan-out is avoided by using the Feynman gate. Since, the proposed reversible Carry skip BCD adder is designed using optimal modules; hence overall it will be optimal in terms of number of reversible gates and garbage outputs.

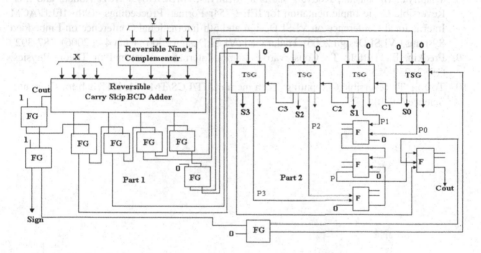

Fig. 8. Reversible Carry Skip BCD Subtractor

6 Conclusions

The focus of this paper is the IEEE 754r (the ongoing revision to the IEEE 754 floating point standard considering decimal arithmetic) and the design of reversible BCD arithmetic units. Thus, this paper proposes novel Carry Skip BCD subtractor along with its reversible logic implementation. It is being tried to design the BCD subtractor optimal both in terms of number of reversible gates and garbage outputs. This is done by choosing the appropriate reversible gates for realizing the Boolean functions. The reversible circuits designed and proposed here, form the basis of the BCD ALU of a primitive quantum CPU.

References

1. Cowlishaw, M.F.: Decimal Floating-Point: Algorithm for Computers. Proceedings 16th IEEE Symposium on Computer Arithmetic. (June 2003) 104-111.
2. http://en.wikipedia.org/wiki/IEEE_754r
3. http://www2.hursley.ibm.com/decimal/754r-status.html
4. Landauer, R.: Irreversibility and Heat Generation in the Computational Process. IBM Journal of Research and Development, 5,(1961) 183-191
5. Bennett, C.H.: Logical Reversibility of Computation. IBM J. Research and Development. (Nov 1973) 525-532
6. Vedral, Vlatko.,Bareno, Adriano., Artur, Ekert.: Quantum Networks for Elementary Arithmetic Operations. arXiv:quant-ph/9511018 v1. (nov 1995)
7. Thapliyal, Himanshu., Srinivas, MB.: Novel Reversible TSG Gate and Its Application for Designing Reversible Carry Look Ahead Adder and Other Adder Architectures. Proceedings 10th Asia-Pacific Computer Systems Architecture Conference (ACSAC 05). Lecture Notes of Computer Science, vol. 3740, Springer-Verlag (Oct 2005) 775-786.
8. Thapliyal, Himanshu., Kotiyal, Saurabh., Srinivas, MB.: Novel BCD Adders and their Reversible Logic Implementation for IEEE 754r Format. Proceedings 19th IEEE/ACM International Conference on VLSI Design and 5th International Conference on Embedded Systems (VLSI Design 2006), Hyderabad (VLSI Design 2006). (Jan 4-7, 2006) 387-392
9. Fredkin, E., Toffoli, T.: Conservative Logic. International Journal of Theor. Physics. (1982) 219-253
10. Toffoli, T.:Reversible Computing. Tech memo MIT/LCS/TM-151. MIT Lab for Computer Science (1980).

Power-Efficient Microkernel of Embedded Operating System on Chip

Tianzhou Chen, Wei Hu, and Yi Lian

College of Computer Science, Zhejiang University, Hangzhou, Zhejiang, 310027, China
{tzchen, ehu, yl}@zju.edu.cn

Abstract. Because the absence of hardware support, almost all of embedded operating system are based on SDRAM in past time. With progress of embedded system hardware, embedded system can provide more substrative supports for embedded operating systems. In this paper we present an operating system microkernel for embedded system which can reside in the SRAM on chip. With progress of embedded system hardware, embedded system can provide more substrative supports for embedded operating systems. In this paper we present an operating system microkernel named SRAMOS for embedded system which can reside in the SRAM on chip. This microkernel can make the most of low power consumption of SRAM. The experiment results show that this microkernel performs better than the traditional embedded operating systems.

Keywords: power-efficient, microkernel, embedded operating system.

1 Introduction

In recent years, wireless networks are employed everywhere and mobile devices are used more and more popularly. Most mobile devices have limited hardware support compared to PCs. And embedded operating systems for mobile devices have to base on this hardware.

According to the operating system design concept which comes from the desktop operating system and limited by the hardware, current embedded operating systems such as Embedded Linux [1], Symbian [2], Plam [3], Pocket PC [4] and the proprietary system all reside in SDRAM. There are many constraints exist if they are in SDRAM such as real-time response.

With the evolution of embedded hardware and software, some new techniques have appeared, such as cache programmable. Programmable cache is one of the main features of Intel 27x family [5] based on ARM 10 architecture. To enhance the efficiency of embedded operating system, we present the microkernel in SRAM (the programmable cache). This a new concept for embedded operating system designs.

The remainder of this paper is organized as follows. Section 2 introduces the architecture of Intel 27x family; section 3 describes architecture of the SRAMOS; Experimental results will be given in section 4. Finally, section 5 provides conclusion and future work.

C. Jesshope and C. Egan (Eds.): ACSAC 2006, LNCS 4186, pp. 473–479, 2006.
© Springer-Verlag Berlin Heidelberg 2006

2 SRAM on Chip of Intel 27x Family

Intel 27x processor is owned by Intel Company and it is an integrated system-on-a-chip microprocessor designed for mobile devices.

High-performance and low-power is the main target for this processor. The architecture is in accordance with ARM 10 but it does not support all of ARM Instructions (V5TE) in which floating point instructions are excluded. The ARM programmer's model is complied by the Intel PXA27x processors. In additional, Intel provides extra supports to PXA27x family which is added by Intel techniques: Intel® Wireless MMX™ integer instructions in applications such as those that accelerate audio and video processing.

PXA27x provides extra 256K cache which is considered as internal memory. This cache is internal memory-mapped SRAM which consists of four banks in which then capacity is 64K. The SRAM array module consists of four banks of 8-K x 64-bit memory arrays. Each memory bank has a dedicated single-entry queue and 8 K x 64 bits for data storage. If a memory bank is in standby mode, the access request is stored in the queue while the memory bank is placed in run mode. The access is completed when the memory bank has entered run mode. If a memory bank is in run mode and the queue does not contain any pending access requests, the queue is bypassed and the memory is accessed normally.

This piece of SRAM is placed on chip and thus PXA27x can provide extra power management which is bank-by-bank management for this cache and thus can reduce the power consumption. In addition, this cache can support Byte Write Operation and are not associated with any I/O signals. Figure 1 shows the block diagram of this cache.

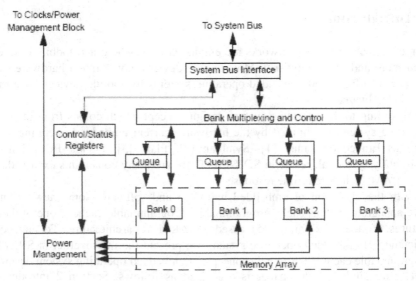

Fig. 1. Internal memory block diagram [5]

As we can see from Figure 1, six parts are consisted of this cache: the four SRAM banks, queues, the system-bus interface, control and status registers, power management block, and memory-bank multiplexing and control.

Table 1 shows the internal memory banks how to be mapped to registers.

Table 1. Extra cache mapped to registers [5]

Address	Name	Description	Page
0x5800_0000– 0x5BFF_FFFC	—	reserved	—
0x5C00_0000– 0x5C00_FFFC	Memory Bank 0	64-Kbyte SRAM	—
0x5C01_0000– 0x5C01_FFFC	Memory Bank 1	64-Kbyte SRAM	—
0x5C02_0000– 0x5C02_FFFC	Memory Bank 2	64-Kbyte SRAM	—
0x5C03_0000– 0x5C03_FFFC	Memory Bank 3	64-Kbyte SRAM	—
0x5C04_0000– 0x5C7F_FFFC	—	reserved	—
0x5C80_0000– 0x5FFF_FFFC	—	reserved	—

3 Architecture of SRAMOS

Commonly embedded operating systems are stored in Flash or some other external storage. And these traditional embedded operating systems have many functions integrated together even if it is an embedded operating system with a microkernel because there are much memory can be used for this kernel.

But as we can see from section 2, the size of SRAM on chip is only 256KB and it's too small to place so many data and instructions in SRAM. Thus we design a microkernel fro SRAM which we name it after SRAMOS. In the following part of this section, we will illustrate this SRAMOS in details.

SRAMOS must ensure that this microkernel can run in SRAM. Because of the size limitation of SRAM, the microkernel has to be designed as small as possible. Thus some parts in traditional embedded operating system must be taken from the kernel and the remainders have to be cut down or modified in order to make all parts of SRAMOS be able to be contained in the microkernel. The most design principle is minimum and optimal.

According to the foregoing design principle, we design three parts in the microkernel of SRAMOS: Task Management, SRAM Management and Security. The architecture is shown in Figure 2.

Commonly microkernel is stored in flash on chip. When system starts, microkernel is loaded from flash on chip.

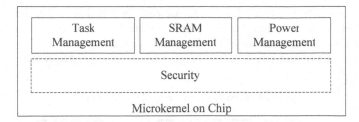

Fig. 2. Architecture of microkernel

3.1 Task Management

Processes and threads scheduling is the mainly work of this part. Task Management is designed to be able to scheduling tasks by different policies which are used mixedly in the microkernel.

The most important policy is to support real-time response. Because of the gap between main memory and CPU, embedded operating systems for real-time are difficult to design and implement. With the evolution of CPU, this gap will be more and broader. In memory hierarchy, cache which is mainly based on SRAM memory is used to reduce the speed gap between CPU and main memory and other external storage. The same policy is used by SRAMOS to reduce the gap. Scheduling in SRAM will obtain faster response to the real-time tasks.

The traditional embedded systems like to place more tasks in memory for scheduler. But not same to the traditional embedded systems, SRAMOS only places enough tasks into SRAM to ensure the efficiency of scheduling. The relative security mechanisms can be added into this part if necessary.

3.2 SRAM Management

Now there are only 256KB SRAM provided by the processors. Thus SRAM Management must provide finely management for SRAMOS.

Different from common memory management, we divide SRAM into different District which is allocated to different processes and threads. Three Districts are divided: Kernel District, Real-Time District and User District as shown in Figure 3. Kernel District is allocated to the microkernel of SRAMOS. Microkernel runs in this part of SRAM to ensure the security of kernel data and instructions.

Real-Time District is allocated to the Real-Time tasks. User District is allocated to the common tasks. Kernel District and Real-Time District can use the space of the User District if necessary. But User District can not use the space of Kernel District and Real-Time District. Further, different Memory Banks of SRAM are divided into pages to manage.

3.3 Power Management

This part takes charge of power-efficient management. A large number of embedded systems are driven by batteries, not by wired power supply. Efficient power usage is

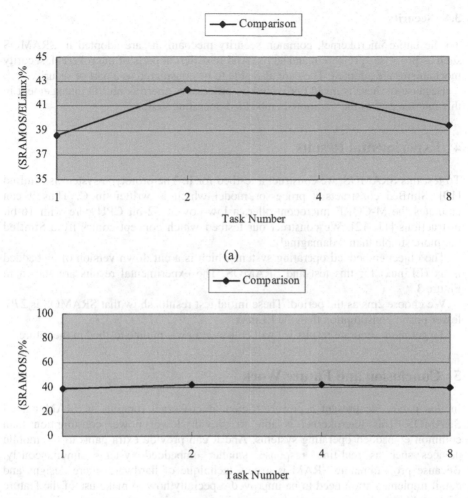

Fig. 3. Experimental results

required to increase utilization time. Normal embedded OS makes use of DPM [6, 7, 8] or other optimized algorithm to reduce power consumption. But previous platform architecture must use SDRAM on board as memory. And SDRAM costs power very much. SRAMOS run in SRAM on chip. The ratio of power consumption for SRAM is expected to be 10% of SDRAM [9]. So power efficiency of new architecture will be more excellent than previous architecture.

Table 2. Power comparison of SDRAM and SRAM [5]

Memory	Idle (mA)	Active (mA)	Read (16 bit)	Erase (16bit)	Write (16 bit)
Mobile SDRAM	0.5	75	90ns	N/A	90ns
Low Power SRAM	0.005	3	55ns	N/A	55ns

3.4 Security

To the entire microkernel, common security mechanisms are adopted in SRAMOS such as processes protection and so on. And In different parts of microkernel, security mechanisms are adopted. They are also able to be considered as a part of security.

Because of there is no I/O provided by processors, there is no I/O management in this microkernel as the traditional embedded operating system.

4 Experimental Results

To test this SRAMOS, we construct a testbed for it. The prototype system is SimBed [10]. SimBed constructs a processor model which is written in C. Thus it can emulates the M-CORE microcontroller, a low-power, 32-bit CPU core with 16-bit instructions [11, 12]. We construct our testbed which concept comes from SimBed but more simple than it damagingly.

The object embedded operating system which is a cut down version of embedded linux (ELinux) for this test and SRAMOS. The experimental results are shown in Figure 3.

We choose 2ms as the period. These initial test results show that SRAMOS is 27% lower power consumption than the ELinux.

To get more accurate results we will construct new simulate testbed in the future.

5 Conclusion and Future Work

In this paper, we present a power-efficient microkernel running in SRAM named SRAMOS. This microkernel is able to provide lower power consumption than common embedded operating systems. And it can provide extra gains to the mobile devices such as real-time response, smaller embedded systems simultaneously. Because programmable SRAM is a new technique of hardware, more designs and detail implementation need to be improved especially how to make use of the feature of SRAM which can provide low power consumption. At the same time, more accurate test methods and tools should be proposed to test the energy and power consumption of this microkernel.

References

1. Joel R. Williams. Embedding Linux in a Commercial Product: A look at embedded systems and what it takes to build one. Linux Journal, Volume 1999 , Issue 66es (October 1999), Article No. 3
2. Seizen, S. 2005. Symbian OS v9.1 functional description. Revision 1.1, Feb. 2005. www.symbian.com/technology.
3. Eddie Harari. Palm Pilot Development Tools. Linux Journal, Volume 2000 , Issue 73es (May 2000), Article No. 8
4. Bruce E.Krell. Pocket PC Developer's Guide, Osborne/McGraw-Hill, 2002

5. Intel, Intel® PXA27x Processor Family Developer's Manual, http://www.intel.com/design/pca/prodbref/253820.htm
6. IBM and MontaVista Software: Dynamic Power Management for Embedded Systems, 2003
7. Le Cai and Yung-Hsiang Lu : Dynamic Power Management Using Data Buffers, School of Electrical and Computer Engineering, Purdue University
8. G. A. Paleologo, L. Benini, et.al, "Policy Optimization for DynamicPower Management", Proceedings of Design Automation Conference, pp.182-187, Jun. 1998
9. Hojun Shim, Yongsoo Joo, Yongseok Choi and Hyung Gyu Lee, et al. Low-energy off-chip SDRAM memory systems for embedded applications, ACM Transactions on Embedded Computing Systems (TECS), Volume 2 , Issue 1 (February 2003), Pages: 98 - 130
10. Kathleen Baynes, Chris Collins and et al. The performance and energy consumption of three embedded real-time operating systems, Proceedings of the 2001 international conference on Compilers, architecture, and synthesis for embedded systems, Pages: 203 – 210, Atlanta, Georgia, USA, 2001
11. J. Turley. "M.Core shrinks code, power budgets." Microprocessor Report, vol. 11, no. 14, pp. 12–15, October 1997.
12. J. Turley. "M.Core for the portable millenium." Microprocessor Report, vol. 12, no. 2, pp. 15–18, February 1998.

Understanding Prediction Limits
Through Unbiased Branches

Lucian Vintan[1], Arpad Gellert[1], Adrian Florea[1], Marius Oancea[1], and Colin Egan[2]

[1] "Lucian Blaga" University of Sibiu, Computer Science Department,
Emil Cioran Street, No. 4, 550025 Sibiu, Romania,
{lucian.vintan, arpad.gellert, adrian.florea,
marius oncea}@ulbsibiu.ro
[2] University of Hertfordshire, School of Computer Science, Hatfield,
College Lane, AL10 9AB UK
c.egan@herts.ac.uk

Abstract. The majority of currently available branch predictors base their prediction accuracy on the previous k branch outcomes. Such predictors sustain high prediction accuracy but they do not consider the impact of unbiased branches which are difficult-to-predict. In this paper, we quantify and evaluate the impact of unbiased branches and show that any gain in prediction accuracy is proportional to the frequency of unbiased branches. By using the SPECcpu2000 integer benchmarks we show that there are a significant proportion of unbiased branches which severely impact on prediction accuracy (averaging between 6% and 24% depending on the prediction context used).

1 Introduction

Branch instructions are a major bottleneck in the exploitation of instruction level parallelism (ILP) since (in general-purpose code) conditional branches occur approximately every 5 – 8 instructions [5]. With increasing instruction issue rate and depth of the pipeline, accurate dynamic branch prediction becomes more essential. Very high prediction accuracy is required because an increasing number of instructions are lost before a branch misprediction can be corrected. Even a 3% misprediction rate can have a severe impact on MII processor performance [1, 10].

Chang [2] introduced the idea of grouping branches by their bias in an attempt to reduce the impact of aliasing. By profiling, branches were classified between 6 static classes and were then guided to the most appropriate dynamic predictor. Chappell [3] investigated difficult-to-predict branches in a Simultaneous Subordinate Micro-Threading (SSMT) architecture. Chappell constrained microthreading to only difficult-to-predict branches which were identified as those being reached along a 'difficult-path'. We believe that such branches are unbiased. More recently, Desmet [4] applied the concept of *Gini-index* to construct a decision tree based on a number of dynamic and static branch features. In line with our thoughts, Desmet concluded that accurate branch predictors require more than just the type of predictor and history register length to achieve accurate branch prediction.

Alternative methods of dynamic branch prediction are available such as neural branch prediction [6, 15]. Despite a neural branch predictor's ability to achieve a very

C. Jesshope and C. Egan (Eds.): ACSAC 2006, LNCS 4186, pp. 480–487, 2006.
© Springer-Verlag Berlin Heidelberg 2006

high prediction rate and the ability to exploit deeper correlations at linear costs, the associated design complexity due to latency, large quantity of adder circuits, area and power are still obstacles to industrial adoption. As such we therefore consider neural prediction techniques to be outside the scope of this paper.

The main objective of this paper is to highlight the impact of unbiased branches so that they can be considered in the design of two-level predictors. In remainder of this paper we evaluate the impact of unbiased branches, and therefore difficult-to-predict branches, on three commonly used prediction contexts (local, global and global XOR branch address) and their corresponding two-level predictors [8, 9, 10, 13].

2 Identifying Difficult-to-Predict Branches

The majority of branches demonstrate a bias to either the taken or the not-taken path which means branches are highly polarised towards a specific prediction context (a local prediction context, a global prediction context or a path-based prediction context) and such polarised branches are relatively easy-to-predict. However, a minority of branches show a low degree of polarisation since they tend to shuffle between taken and not-taken and are therefore unbiased and difficult-to-predict.

In this study, we identify unbiased branches by cascading branches through the three different prediction contexts and their respective predictors: a PAg, a GAg and a Gshare predictor. We also increase the history register lengths in units of 4-bits from 16-bits to 28-bits as shown in Figure 1. Within our prediction contexts, a feature is the binary context on p bits of prediction information. Finally, each static branch has associated k dynamic contexts in which it can appear ($k \leq 2^P$). We define the polarisation index (P) of a certain dynamic branch context as equation (1):

$$P(S_i) = \max(f_0, f_1) = \begin{cases} f_0, & f_0 \geq 0.5 \\ f_1, & f_0 < 0.5 \end{cases} \tag{1}$$

where:

- $S = \{S_1, S_2, ..., S_k\}$ = the set of prediction contexts that appear during all branches instances;
- k = the number of distinct prediction contexts that appear during the branch's execution instances, $k \leq 2^P$, and p is the history register length;
- $f_0 = \dfrac{T}{T+NT}$, $f_1 = \dfrac{NT}{T+NT}$, NT = the number of "not-taken" branch instances corresponding to context S_i, T = the number of "taken" branch instances corresponding to context S_i, $(\forall)i = 1, 2, ..., k$, and therefore $f_0 + f_1 = 1$;
- if $P(S_i) = 1$, $(\forall)i = 1, 2, ..., k$, then the context S_i is completely biased (100%) and the branch is highly predictable;
- if $P(S_i) = 0.5$, $(\forall)i = 1, 2, ..., k$, then the context S_i is totally unbiased and the branch might be difficult to predict.

Consider the following trivial examples, a branch in a certain dynamic context shows the following behaviour: TTTTTT... or NNNNNN... in which case the transitions are always taken or always not-taken, and would be biased and easy-to-predict. However, a branch in a certain context that is stochastic will show a highly shuffled behaviour, which would result in the branch being unbiased and difficult-to-predict with its transitions toggling between T and N. We therefore consider that the rate of transition between branch outcomes is an important feature that can be applied to branch prediction. We introduce the distribution index which is the based on the rate of transitions as shown by equation (2):

$$D(S_i) = \begin{cases} 0, \ n_t = 0 \\ \dfrac{n_t}{2 \cdot \min(NT, T)}, \ n_t > 0 \end{cases} \quad (2)$$

where:

- n_t = the number of branch outcome transitions in context S_i;
- $2 \cdot \min(NT, T)$ = the maximum number of possible transitions;

- k = the number of distinct dynamic contexts, $k \le 2^p$, and p is the history register length;
- if $D(S_i) = 1$, $(\forall)i = 1, 2, ..., k$, then the behaviour of the branch in context S_i is "contradictory" (the most unfavourable case), and the predictor cannot learn it;
- if $D(S_i) = 0$, $(\forall)i = 1, 2, ..., k$, then the behaviour of the branch in context S_i is constant (the most favourable case), and the predictor can be learned.

A branch with a low distribution index (tending to 0) will show a repeating pattern and there will be few transitional changes. In contrast, a branch that exhibits many transitional changes will show a shuffled pattern and will have a high distribution index (tending to 1). Hence, the greater the distribution index means that the branch becomes more difficult-to-predict in a given predictor. We consider any branch for a given prediction context that has a distribution index of ≤ 0.2 to be easy-to-predict and define a difficult-to-predict branch for a given prediction context to be a branch with a low polarisation index (P<0.95 as derived from equation 1 (an unbiased branch)) and with a distribution index of >0.2. We chose this value because for a given branch context with a polarisation index >0.95 will be easy-to-predict and will achieve a high prediction accuracy. Consequently branches with a polarisation index of <0.95 will be difficult-to-predict.

We identify and reduce the number of unbiased branches (Figure 1) by passing unbiased branches through successive cascades of different prediction contexts with increasing history information (from 16- to 28-bits).

The number of unbiased branches is reduced from one prediction context to the next because an unbiased branch in one prediction context is not necessarily unbiased in a different prediction context. By the time our final prediction context (28-global history bits XORed with 28-bits of the branch address) is iterated the only remaining unbiased branches are those that have been unbiased throughout all iterations of all of the previous prediction contexts and these remaining unbiased branches are therefore identified as difficult-to-predict. We therefore predict with a short history prediction context before a long history prediction context to remove biased branches (those that are easy-to-predict) as early as possible.

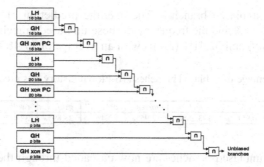

Fig. 1. Unbiased branches cascading through the prediction contexts

3 Simulations

In this study we identify unbiased branches in the SPEC2000 benchmark suite [12] by cascading branches through the three different prediction contexts and their respective predictors: a PAg predictor, a GAg predictor and a Gshare predictor. We use the SimpleScalar simulator [11] and all results are reported on 1 billion dynamically executed instructions, skipping the first 300 million instructions.

Figure 2 shows the prediction accuracy achieved by the 16-local history bit prediction context using the PAg predictor. The average prediction accuracy of this local prediction context is around 91%, which is limited by the impact of the unbiased branches which have an average prediction accuracy of around 76%. The frequency of unbiased branches (Table 1) varies between 5.76% (*mcf*) and 44.98% (*twolf*) with an average of 24.55%.

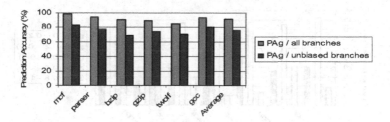

Fig. 2. PAg prediction accuracy with the 16-local history bits prediction context

Table 1. Percentage of unbiased branches (16-local history bits prediction context)

Benchmark	*mcf*	*parser*	*bzip*	*gzip*	*twolf*	*gcc*	Avg.
Unbiased branches (P<0.95)	5.76%	20.60%	26.42%	38.73%	44.98%	10.80%	24.55%

The unbiased branches are now cascaded through the 16-global history bit prediction context and its corresponding GAg predictor. The average prediction accuracy of this global prediction context is around 93%, which again is limited by the impact of the unbiased branches. The average prediction of accuracy unbiased branches is around 72% and the frequency of these unbiased branches (Table 2) varies between 3.28% (*mcf*) and 32.41% (*twolf*) with an average of 17.48%.

Table 2. Percentage of unbiased branches (16-global history bits prediction context)

Benchmarks	*mcf*	*parser*	*bzip*	*gzip*	*twolf*	*gcc*	Avg.
Unbiased branches (P<0.95)	3.28%	12.95%	23.4%	28.89%	32.41%	3.92%	17.48%

The remaining unbiased branches are now cascaded through the 16-global history prediction context XORed with 16-bits of the branch address and its associated Gshare predictor. The prediction accuracy of the 16-history bit Gshare predictor improved by around 1% in comparison with the 16-history bit GAg predictor. However, the number of unbiased branches remained the same as those of the GAg predictor apert from *gcc* which showed a marginal reduction to 3.91%.

The history register length was increased by 4-bits to 20-bits and then the remaining unbiased branches were cascaded through the 20-local history bit prediction context and its associated PAg predictor. We continued to cascade through our remaining prediction contexts (local, global, global XOR branch address), increasing the amount of history information by 4-bits at a time (to a maximum of 28-history bits) as shown by Figure 1 thereby gradually reducing the number of unbiased branches through each context and decreasing the number of unbiased branches.

A distribution index tends to 0 for a branch that is not shuffled (and is easy-to-predict) and tends to 1 (and is difficult-to-predict) for a shuffled branch. We partitioned the percentage of branches into 5 distribution index intervals: (0.0 - 0.2), (0.2 - 0.4), (0.4 - 0.6), (0.6 - 0.8) and (0.8 - 1.0).

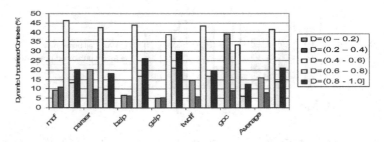

Fig. 3. Distribution rates of the 16-local history bit prediction context

Figure 3 shows the intervals for the 16-local history bit context and that around 41% of the unbiased branches have a distribution index interval (0.4 - 0.6), making their branch behaviour relatively shuffled and around 21% of the branches have a distribution index between (0.8 - 1.0), making their behaviour highly shuffled and therefore difficult-to-predict. Using the cut-off distribution index of <0.2, our simulations show that only around 16% of the unbiased branches are easy-to-predict with the 16-history bit local prediction context. *Gcc* has the greatest percentage of unbiased and easy-to-predict branches (around 39%) and *gzip* the greatest percentage of unbiased and difficult-to-predict branches (around 30%).

Similarly, we determined the intervals for the 16-global history bit prediction context and the intervals for the 16-global history bit XORed with 16-bits of the branch address prediction context (intervals were the same for both contexts). Since both of these are global prediction contexts, it is not surprising that their distribution indices are similar. With the 16-history bit global prediction contexts only around 3% of the unbiased branches have a distribution index <0.2, around 33% have a distribution index of (0.4 - 0.6), and around 28% have a distribution index of (0.8 – 1). As with the local prediction context, *gcc* has the greatest percentage of unbiased but easy-to-predict branches (around 8%), but *twolf* has the greatest percentage of unbiased and difficult-to-predict branches (around 39%).

Figure 4 shows the reduction in the number of unbiased branches as they cascade through the three prediction contexts. The percentage reduction in the number of unbiased branches decreases from around 25% to around 6%. We consider that this value of 6% is still too high and further investigations are required.

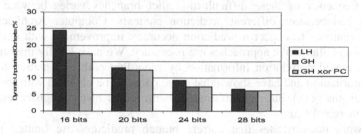

Fig. 4. Reducing the number of unbiased branches with increasing history register length

In an earlier paper [14], we explored the benefits of adding sufficient information, in the form of successive branch addresses, to uniquely identify each program path. We continue that work in this study evaluating, on all branches, paths of different lengths (p branches) used together with global histories of the same length (p bits). The results are presented in Figure 5, where they are compared with the results obtained using only global history prediction context.

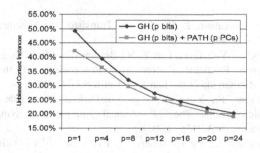

Fig. 5. The gain introduced by the path for different context lengths

Our simulations show that the best gain is achieved with short history lengths ($p<16$) and there is only marginal gain with longer history lengths, meaning that long global history (p bits) approximates very well the longer path information (p branches).

We have also undertaken similar simulations with neural predictors [6, 15] and in addition to the SPEC benchmarks we have used the Championship Branch Prediction benchmarks [7, 16]. However, due to space limitations we have not shown the results of these simulations in this paper.

4   Conclusions and Further Work

In this paper, we have shown that the design of branch predictors should consider the identification of difficult-to-predict branches. Different branches exhibit different behaviours for given prediction contexts and predictors, and the amount of shuffling impacts on prediction accuracy. Even after cascading branches through a series of prediction contexts there remains a significant number of difficult-to-predict branches and the frequency of these difficult-to-predict branches varies between different programs and between different prediction contexts. Computer Architects cannot therefore continue to expect a prediction accuracy improvement with conventional predictors and alternative approaches are necessary. We have briefly investigated the use of increased correlation information by recording path information as well as history information and have shown that some gain can be obtained with short history register lengths (<16), but path information with longer history register lengths only achieves marginal gain.

This work demonstrates that current branch predictors use limited prediction contexts (local, global correlation and path information) due to the degree of polarisation. We have therefore shown that the use of more prediction contexts is required to further improve prediction accuracies. Our current thoughts are to use a particularly relevant "piece" of the dynamic CPU context or alternatively some HLL code information. In order to efficiently use such information we consider it will be necessary to have a significant amount of compiler support.

References

1. Burger, D. and Goodman, J. R.: Billion Transistor Architectures. IEEE Computer. September 1997, 46 – 49.
2. Chang P.-Y., Hao E., Yeh T.-Y., Patt Y. N.: Branch Classification: a New Mechanism for Improving Branch Predictor Performance, Proceedings of the 27th International Symposium on Microarchitecture, San Jose, California, (1994).
3. Chappell R., Tseng F., Yoaz A., Patt Y.: Difficult-Path Branch Prediction Using Subordinate Microthreads, The 29th Annual International Symposia on Computer Architecture, Alaska, USA, (May 2002).
4. Desmet V., Eeckhout L., De Bosschere K.: Evaluation of the Gini-index for Studying Branch Prediction Features. Proceedings of the 6th International Conference on Computing Anticipatory Systems (CASYS). AIP Conference Proceedings. Vol. 718. (2004) 376-384.

5. Hennessy J. and Patterson D.: Computer Architecture: A Quantitative Approach, Third Edition, Morgan Kaufmann Publishers, (2003).
6. Jiménez D. A., Lin C.: Dynamic Branch Prediction with Perceptrons, Proceedings of the 7th International Symposium on High Performance Computer Architecture, (January 2001).
7. Loh G. H.: Simulation Differences Between Academia and Industry: A Branch Prediction Case Study, International Symposium on Performance Analysis of Software and Systems (ISPASS), pp.21-31, Austin, TX, USA, March 2005.
8. McFarling S.: Combining Branch Predictors, WRL Technical Note TN-36, Digital Equipment Corporation, (June 1993).
9. Pan S. T., So K. and Rahmeh J. T.: Improving the accuracy of dynamic branch prediction using branch correlation. Proceedings of ASPLOS V, Boston, MA, October (1992) 76-84.
10. Patt, Y. N., Patel, S. J., Friendly, D. H. and Stark, J.: One Billion Transistors, One Uniprocessor, One Chip. IEEE Computer 1 (September 1997) 51–57.
11. Simplescalar The SimpleSim Tool Set, ftp://ftp.cs.wisc.edu/pub/sohi/Code/simplescalar.
12. SPEC, The SPEC benchmark programs, http://www.spec.org.
13. Yeh T. Y. and Patt Y. N.: Two-level adaptive branch prediction. In Proceedings of the 24-the ACM/IEEE International Symposium on Microarchitecture, (November 1991).
14. Vintan L. and Egan C.: Extending Correlation in Branch Prediction Schemes, International Euromicro'99 Conference, Italy, (September 1999).
15. Vintan L., Iridon M.: Towards a High Performance Neural Branch Predictor, International Joint Conference on Neural Networks, Washington DC, USA, July 1999.
16. The 1st JILP Championship Branch Prediction Competition (CBP-1). http://www.jilp.org/cbp, 2004.

Bandwidth Optimization of the EMCI for a High Performance 32-bit DSP*

Dong Wang, Xiao Hu, Shuming Chen, and Yang Guo

Microelectronics Institute, School of Computer Science,
National University of Defense Technology
410073, Changsha, Hunan Province, China
nudtjum@163.com

Abstract. Memory bandwidth and interface flexibility are often bottlenecks of embedded processors. The research about memory bandwidth optimization has become a hot topic. This paper introduces four new bandwidth optimization methods for External Memory Control Interface (EMCI) integrated in high performance digit signal processors (DSP), and aims at realization of the maximum throughput of data transmission and architecture flexibility, i.e. programmable and decoupled structure, pipelined transmission of burst mode, programmable priority for arbitration, and preferential reading based on cache-line offset. The experiment results show that the performance improvement is remarkable, but different for synchronous and asynchronous memories, and depends on the application behavior. The decoupled structure proves to be of great benefit to the architectural exploration and optimization for DSPs.

1 Introduction

External Memory Control Interface (EMCI) is a memory management unit used in embedded microprocessors for transmitting data with external memories. The advantage of integrated EMCI includes high transmission bandwidth, low power consumption and high reliability. In DSP application systems, DSP often need to connect various memories through the integrated EMCI unit. How to increase the data throughput and maximum the flexibility of memory interface architecture is the biggest design challenge of EMCI for high performance DSPs.

Many related works have been presented about the design methodology of memory interface. The paper [1] presents a design of memory interface logic of FPGA core. The authors in [2] decouple the application specific datapath design with the development and synthesis of the external memory interfaces. The memory interface design in [8] decouples the target architecture dependent characteristics from the datapath that implements the application. The authors in [3] present the design of memory sequencers that can be automatically generated from a behavioral synthesis tool and which can efficiently handle predictable address patterns. Paper [9, 10] also gives the exploration of the memory interface design techniques.

* Funded by"863"High Tech Project of China （No. 2004AA1Z1040） and the project from National Science Foundation of China (No. 60473079).

C. Jesshope and C. Egan (Eds.): ACSAC 2006, LNCS 4186, pp. 488–494, 2006.
© Springer-Verlag Berlin Heidelberg 2006

In our previous work [6] [7], we presented an EMCI design which transmitted data for L2 cache and DMA. We will give the optimization of previous EMIC design taking into account the real-time consideration in this paper.

2 Architecture Profile

The EMCI presented in this paper can handle L2 cache requests and DMA requests according to certain priority, totally support four subspaces of memory address sized 512MB, support pipelined synchronous burst SRAM (SBSRAM), synchronous dynamic RAM (SDRAM) and typical asynchronous memories (such as ROM, FIFO and Flash) with width of 8-bit, 16-bit and 32-bit respectively.

EMCI uses a set of external buses to access external memories in time share mode. EMCI unit consists of L2 read/write buffers, DMA read/write buffers, arbitration unit, decoder unit, control register group, memory controllers and bus switch, as shown in Fig. 1. The L2 cache/DMA reading requests are queued in the buffers and then dispatched to the memory controller to be processed. Data returned from memories is stored in buffers temporarily and transmitted to L2 cache or DMA.

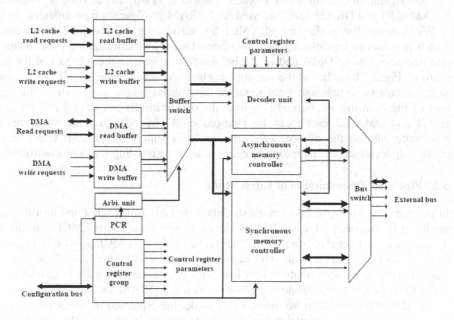

Fig. 1. The block diagram of EMCI

The arbitration unit makes arbitration between L2 cache requests and DMA requests. The buffer that wins in arbitration will get a token flag, and then dispatch requests to the memory controllers, and won't lose the token flag until its requests are processed completely. The data coherency between L2 and DMA is not the design consideration of EMCI. The control register group consists of six registers, and can be configured by CPU through configuration bus. The decoder unit decodes the read/ write addresses and provides decoding results to memory controllers. The memory controller consists of a synchronous memory controller and an asynchronous memory controller. The synchronous memory controller processes accesses of SDRAM and SBRAM. The asynchronous one processes the accesses of asynchronous SRAM, ROM, FIFO, and Flash. The bus switch selects a group bus signals generated by the memory controllers and sends them onto the external bus. Thus only one memory of the four subspaces is accessed at any given time.

3   Design Methodology of Bandwidth Optimization

3.1   Programmable and Decoupled Structure

Programmability is an important design methodology of embedded processors. The programmable parameters of our optimized EMCI include the memories type, width, and access latency, etc. EMCI uses a global control register EMCI_GLB to hold the general configuration information, and uses a 32-bit control register SS_CR to hold the configuration parameter for each subspace. Two extra control registers, DRAM_CR1 and DRAM_CR2 are used for SDRAM configuration parameters.

We improve the scalability of EMCI by introducing a decoupled architecture, which is achieved by defining two interfaces. One communicates with the datapath and transmits data to DMA and L2 cache, which is shown as the left part of the diagram of Fig.2. The other is the memory controllers, which generate all the external memory control signals and implement the assembly of data, as shown as the right part of Fig.2. In this decoupled structure, the data transmission granularity between EMCI and DMA/L2 cache can be changed easily by changing the structures of read/write buffers; the number of memories types supported by EMCI can be increased or decreased by increasing or decreasing corresponding memory controllers.

3.2   Pipelined Transmission of Burst Mode

In our previous work [6], DMA requests data from EMCI in single burst transmission mode. In this mode, DMA won't issue the next burst requests to EMCI until all the data of last burst returns from EMCI. The read buffer of EMCI holds one burst request at most at a time. It is shown that the transmission efficiency and throughput of single burst transmission mode is very low. This performance penalty is serious especially for high-speed synchronous memories, such as SDRAM and SBSRAM.

To address this problem, we use a novel mode, the pipelined transmission of burst mode, to improve the throughput of EMCI. As shown in Fig. 2, DMA first issues burst request 1∼N to EMCI successively before any data returns. After the data of the first burst request returns from EMCI, DMA issues the burst request N+1 to EMCI. After the data of the second burst request returns DMA from EMCI, DMA issues the burst request N+2 to EMCI, and so on. The depth of EMCI read buffers for DMA must not less than N. Once the pipelined transmission starts, the EMCI read buffers will not get idle, and the usage of external bus and data throughput is

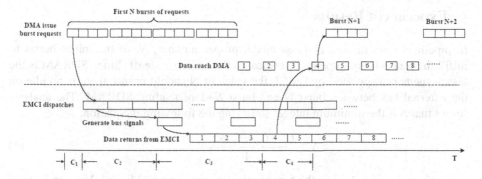

Fig. 2. The procedure of the pipelined transmission of burst mode between DMA and EMCI

improved significantly. Fig. 2 presents the procedure of this mode. The frequency of DMA operation clock, CLK_I, is higher than that of EMCI operation clock CLK_E.

3.3 Access Bypass and Preferential Reading Based on Cache-line Offset

In typical processors' design, L2 cache read data from external memories through DMA, and has no direct data-path to memory interfaces. This structure is simple for the implementation, but increases the stall time of L2 cache read miss. We add an access bypass from L2 cache to EMCI in our DSP to reduce the access latency.

The data replacement strategy of L2 cache is LRU (Least Recently Used). In our previous design, when a read miss of L2 cache occurs, L2 cache only sends the start address of the cache line to EMCI to request a cache-line. Then EMCI reads the words of this cache-line sequentially from memories. To reduce the stall time of CPU pipeline when L2 cache miss occurs, we use the preferential reading method based on cache-line offset. In this method, each cache line is divided into four blocks, and 8 words in each block. When a cache line miss occurs, L2 cache uses two signals to indicate the offset value of the block including the missing word. Then EMCI first reads the block indicated by the cache-line offset, and then reads other blocks.

3.4 Programmable Arbitration Priority

In our previous work [6], EMCI used the token spin method based on fixed priority to handle the L2 requests and DMA requests. However, this token spin method can't achieve bounded delays and lacks of consideration of real-time transmission. In this paper we revise this arbitration strategy to programmable priority. We add a priority control register (PCR) to the arbitration unit. PCR can be configured through the configuration bus, and indicates the priority order of L2 cache and DMA requests. This method of programmable priority is very useful for users to process data transmission with real-time constraint through the EMCI to DMA datapath. Users can set the value of PCR at the headline of the interrupt service procedure of a DMA transmission, and recover its value at the end of the procedure. Real-time data transmission through DMA won't be starved by L2 cache requests.

4 Experiment Results

In pipelined transmission of burst mode, proper number, N, of the initial bursts to fulfill the transmission pipeline is critical in the design tradeoff. Since SDRAM is the fastest memory supported by EMCI, the value of N should ensure there is no idle on the external bus between burst N and burst N+1 of reading SDRAM. The analysis shows that N is the minimum integer satisfying the following inequation.

$$N > \frac{C_1 + C_2 + C_3 + C_4}{4} \tag{1}$$

As shown in Fig. 2, C_1 is the synchronization time (cycles) from DMA sending out to EMCI starting decoding the first address. C_2 is the time from the end of C_1 to EMCI activating the external bus. C_3 is the time from the end of C_2 to the fourth word of the first burst appearing on the bus. C_4 is the time from the end of C_3 to returning DMA. The value of C_1 and C_4 is related with the clock synchronization scheme used between CLK_I and CLK_E. C_3 is related to the specific SDRAM module. In our design, $C_1 \approx 2.5$, $C_2 = 3$, $C_3 = 6$, $C_4 \approx 3$, so $N=4$. To validate the efficiency of the pipelined method, we carry out some comparison experiments. We use EMCI to read 4KB data from external memories, i.e. SDRAM, SBSRAM and ASRAM, respectively. Fig. 3 gives the cycles needed by EMCI to transmit 32 words from the three memories in two transmission modes respectively. This experiment shows that the performance improvement for accessing SDRAM and SBSRAM is 58%~63%, and for asynchronous SRAM (ASRAM) is 8%~12% compared with our previous design. It implies that continuous transmission is critical to exploit the maximum performance of high-speed synchronous memories.

As mentioned above, we use the preferential reading method to handle read miss of L2 cache. Experiment show that this method is more efficient than sequential read starting from the first address of a cache line. One block of L2 cache line consists of eight words. If the missing word locates at block 1, block 2, block 3 and block 4 of L2 cache line, EMCI reading the missing block sequentially needs 18, 26, 34, and 42 cycles respectively, while the preferential reading always needs 18 cycles. The improvement is 45% on average.

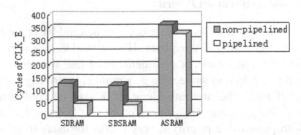

Fig. 3. The performance improvement of pipelined burst transmission compared with non-pipelined mode of reading 32 words. The synchronous memories SDRAM and SBSRAM benefit more than asynchronous memory ASRAM.

There are two levels of cache in our DSP. If there is only one level cache, it needn't wait the whole block of data returning from EMCI. Once the requested word returns from EMCI, CPU pipeline can be released. In this case, the offset of the preferential reading method could be selected as the location of the missing word in the cache line.

The programmability of timing parameters of our design provides a great deal of flexibility for memories connection. The simulation results show that all supported memories can be connected with EMCI smoothly. Moreover, the programmability of timing parameters can achieve a smooth connection of two DSPs by EMCI of one DSP and HPCI (Host Port Control Interface) of the other DSP as shown in Fig. 4. By programming the timing parameters of EMCI in DSP-1 in terms of the timing requirement of HPCI in DSP-2, we can realize 16-bit data transmission between them, which is very useful for building a multiprocessor system.

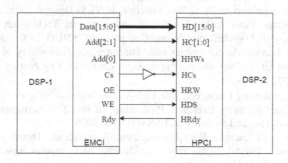

Fig. 4. The smooth direct data-path of two DSPs connected by EMCI and HPCI of two DSPs

The decoupled architecture of our EMCI design proves to be of great benefit to the architectural exploration and optimization of the whole DSP. It takes only a week to revise the first design version of our processor to the new one and complete the verification work, which saves a great deal of the time to market of the whole chip.

To verify the efficiency of the programmable priority strategy, we use nine typical benchmarks of DSP applications to make this comparison experiment. First, we set the priority order as L2 cache write > L2 cache read > DMA write > DMA read, then change the priority to the reverse order, and record the CPU cycles needed by each benchmark. The result shows that that the benefit of programmable priority technique heavily depends on the application behavior. The priority has no effect on the applications that have no use of DMA transmissions, and provides maximum 4.1% speedup for the applications using DMA transmissions.

5 Conclusion

The throughput of data transmission and real-time performance is critical to DSP and embedded processors. The memory controller interface integrated in these processors is the first stage of the datapath and must be optimized for embedded applications. The programmability is another important architecture feature of embedded systems and can enlarge the adoption of embedded processors by users. However, the efficiency of programmability depends on applications. The architects must make some trade-off between flexibility and cost of the implementation of programmability.

References

1. Francis Crowe, Alan Daly, etc, Design of an Efficient Interface between an FPGA and External Memory, Proceedings of the International Symposium of Solid-state Circuit 2004 (ISSC'04), Belfast, June 30–July 2, 2004.
2. Joonseok Park and Pedro C. Diniz, Synthesis and Estimation of Memory Interfaces for FPGA-based Reconfigurable Computing Engines, Proceedings of the 11th Annual IEEE Symposium on Field-Programmable Custom Computing Machines, April 08-11, 2003.
3. Bertrand Le Gal, Emmanuel Casseau, etc., Pipelined Memory Controllers for DSP Applications Handling Unpredictable Data Accesses, Proceedings of the IEEE Computer Society Annual Symposium on VLSI New Frontiers in VLSI Design, 2005
4. C. E. Cummings, Peter Alfke, Simulation and Synthesis Techniques for Asynchronous FIFO Design with Asynchronous Pointer Comparisons, SNUG-2002, San Jose, CA.
5. Dong Wang, Jianwu Ma, Shuming Chen, The Interface Technology of Asynchronous FIFOs Based on Gray Code and its Application, Computer Engineering and Science (Chinese), Vol.27, 2005 No.1
6. Dong Wang, Shuming Chen, etc. The Design and Analysis of a High Performance Embedded External Memory Interface, Proceeding of the 2nd International Conference on Embedded Software and Systems (ICESS-05), Dec.2005
7. Shuming Chen, Li Zhentao, Wan Jianghua, etc. Research and Development of High Performance YHFT Digital Signal Processor, Journal of Computer Research and Development (Chinese), Vol. 43
8. Joonseok Park and Pedro Diniz, An External Memory Interface for FPGA-Based Computing Engines, Proceedings of the 9th Annual IEEE Symposium on Field-Programmable Custom Computing Machines (FCCM'01), 2001
9. Mohamed Schalan, Vincent J. Mooney, Hardware Support for Real-Time Embedded Multiprocessor System-on-a-Chip Memory Management, CODES'02, May 6-8, 2002, Estes Park, Colorado, USA
10. Jürgen Becker, Martin Vorbach, Architecture, Memory and Interface Technology Integration of an Industrial/Academic Configurable System-on-Chip (CSoC), Proceedings of the IEEE Computer Society Annual Symposium on VLSI (ISVLSI'03), 2003

Research on Petersen Graphs and Hyper-cubes Connected Interconnection Networks

Wang Lei and Chen Zhiping

Department of Computer and Information Science,
Fujian University of Technology, Fuzhou, Fujian, RP China, 350014
wanglei_hn@hn165.com

Abstract. On the basis of the short diameter of Petersen graph, and high connectivity of Hypercube, an innovative interconnection network named HRP(n) (Hyper-cubes and Rings connected Petersen Graph), is proposed, and whose characteristics are studied simultaneously. It is proved that HRP(n) has not only regularity and good extensibility, but also has shorter diameter and better connectivity than those interconnection networks such as Q_n, TQ_n, CQ_n, and HP(n). In addition, the unicasting, broadcasting, and fault-tolerant routing algorithms are designed for HRP(n), analyses show that those routing algorithms have good communication efficiency.

Keywords: Petersen graph; Interconnection network; Routing algorithm.

1 Introduction

Parallel computer interconnection networks have been a hot spot in the researching fields of parallel and distributed systems for a long time. Researchers have studied all of the topologies of Parallel computer interconnection networks such as *Ring, Tree, Star, Mesh, Torus, Hypercube* and *Petersen Graph* etc. Since their topologies are both of the characteristics such as regularity, high fault-tolerance, short diameter and embeddable ability, *Hypercube* and *Petersen Graph* are welcomed and well studied by most of the researchers and scientists, and are two kinds of important and attractive topologies of Parallel computer interconnection networks [1-3].

In 1987, *Hibers* [4] etc studied the topologies of hypercube interconnection networks, and proposed a kind of new hypercube network named TQ_n (Twisted Cubes). In 2000, *Chang* [5] etc studied the problem of edge congestion in TQ_n, and presented a new shortest path algorithm with time complexity of $O(n)$ and the edge congestion of $2n$. In 2002, *Huang* [6] etc studied the Hamilton path in fault-tolerant TQ_n, and proved that in TQ_n with both faulty nodes and links, when $|F|<n-4$, there exists a Hamilton path between any two nodes u, v in $V(TQ_n)-F$, which belongs to TQ_n-F, where F represents the set of faulty nodes in TQ_n. In 2000, *Chang* [7] etc studied another novel hypercube network CQ_n (Crossed Cubes), and proved that CQ_n is of shorter diameter than that of hypercube network Q_n. In 2003, *Yang* [8] etc studied the fault-tolerant ability of CQ_n with both faulty nodes and links, and proved that rings with length $l(4 \le l \le |V(CQ_n)|-f_v)$ can be embedded into CQ_n, when the number of faulty nodes f_v and the number of faulty links f_e satisfy $f_v+f_e \le (n-2)$ where $V(CQ_n)$ is the number of nodes in CQ_n. In 2004, *Wang* and

C. Jesshope and C. Egan (Eds.): ACSAC 2006, LNCS 4186, pp. 495–501, 2006.

Lin [9,10] studied the fault-tolerant characteristics of hypercube networks, and proposed two kinds of innovative fault-tolerant models and routing algorithms based on the concepts of Maximum Safety-Path Vectors and Maximum Safety-Path Matrix, which solved the problems of how to record the most of optimal paths in n dimensional hypercube networks by using vectors or matrices through n-1 rounds of information exchanges between neighboring nodes only.

In 1992, Das [11] etc studied Petersen Graph interconnection networks, and constructed a new Petersen Graph network *HP* (Hyper Petersen Network) by embedding Petersen Graph into Hypercube networks, which is proved to have shorter diameter and better fault-tolerant ability than that of Q_n. In 2001, Liu [12] etc proposed an innovative extension of Petersen Graph network on the basis of ring, and constructed a new Petersen Graph interconnection network *RP* (Ringed Petersen),which has $10 \times n$ nodes, and in which the node connection degree and network diameter are 5 and $[n/2]+2$ separately. In 2004, *Wang* and *Lin* [13] proposed two kinds of novel interconnection networks such as *DCP(n)* (Double-loops Connected Petersen graph) and *TCP(n)* (Torus Connected Petersen graph) by combining the topological characteristics of Petersen graph with Double-loops and Torus respectively. And it is prove that both *DCP(n)* and *TCP(n)* networks have better communication performances than those previous well-known interconnection networks such as *RP* and Torus etc.

By combining the characteristics of short diameter of Petersen Graph and the high connectivity of Hypercube networks, an innovative interconnection networks *HRP(n)* (Hyper-cubes and Rings connected Petersen Graph) is proposed in this paper. It is proved that *HRP(n)* has characteristics such as regularity and good extensibility. And in addition, *HRP(n)* network has 1.5625×2^n nodes, and it is proved that the diameter and node connection degree of *HRP(n)* are $(n-1)$ and n separately, so *HRP(n)* network has shorter diameter and better connectivity than those previous well-known Q_n, TQ_n, CQ_n and *HP(n)* networks. Finally, unicasting, broadcasting and fault-tolerant routing algorithms are designed for *HRP(n)* respectively, which are proved to be of good communication efficiency.

2 Notations And Terminology

In this section we briefly review some notations and definitions commonly used in interconnection networks, which are closely followed by this paper.

An interconnection network can be represented by a undirected graph $G=(V, E)$ where V is the node set and edge set E represents the set of bidirectional communication links among the nodes.

The *connection degree* of a node $u \in V$ denotes the number of neighboring nodes of u. Equivalently, connection degree is the number of links incident on the node.

The *distance* between two nodes u and v in G represents the length of the shortest path between them. The maximum distance between any two nodes in G is called the *diameter* of network G.

A node can be labeled with a binary string $(b_1 b_2 ... b_n)$. Without otherwise specified, any node in G process distinct labels.

An n dimensional *Hypercube Interconnection Network* Q_n (n-cube) is consisted of 2^n nodes and $n2^{n-1}$ links. There exists a link between two nodes u and v if and only if they are labeled with binary strings of length n differing in one bit. In other words, any pair of neighboring nodes differs exactly in one bit. Fig. 1 illustrates the topology of the 4 dimensional Hypercube network.

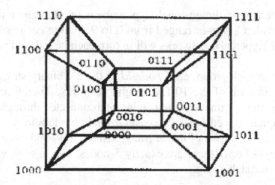

Fig. 1. A 4 dimensional Hypercube network

The well known *Petersen Graph* is composed of 10 nodes denoted by $V = \{u_0, u_1, ..., u_4, v_0, v_1, ..., v_4\}$. The 10 nodes can be grouped into inner and outer groups which in turn are connected by the edge set $E = \{u_i v_i\} \cup \{u_{i+1} u_i\} \cup \{v_i v_{(i+k) \bmod 5}\}$. Fig 2 illustrates the topology of the Petersen Graph interconnection network.

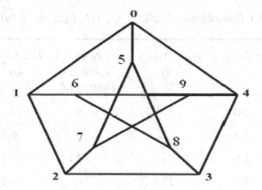

Fig. 2. A Petersen Graph network

In Fig. 2, it is obvious that $u_0=0$, $u_1=1$, $u_2=2$, $u_3=3$, $u_4=4$, $v_0=5$, $v_1=6$, $v_2=7$, $v_3=8$, $v_4=9$, and so that the edges set E of which is $\{ u_i v_i \} \cup \{ u_{i+1} u_i \} \cup \{ v_i v_{(i+ 2) \bmod 5} \}$, where $i=0,1,2,3,4$.

3 Construction And Analysis Of *HRP(n)* Network

Let there are $N=1.5625 \times 2^n$ nodes totally, then a *Hypercubes and Rings connected Petersen Graph (HRP)* can be constructed as follows:

1) The 1.5625×2^n nodes can be assembled into 50 groups each containing 2^{n-5} nodes. Within each group, nodes will then be connected via a $(n-5)$ dimensional Hypercube network and each node is identified with a *node-id* of binary string $(b_1 b_2 \cdots b_{n-5})$.

2) The 50 different n-5 dimensional Hypercube networks can be further divided into 10 groups, each with a *group-id* ranged from 0 to 9. Within each group, the 5 different $(n-5)$ dimensional Hypercube networks will in turn each be indexed with a *net-id* from 0 to 4.

3) Notice that in each group, each *node-id* in the 2^{n-5} binary string space is attached to 10 nodes, one in each of the 10 Hypercube networks. Therefore, nodes within the same group and with the same *node-id* can be interconnected through a Petersen Graph. This Petersen graph is termed *Inner Petersen Graph* in our topology.

4) Notice that for each pair of *net-id* (range from 0 to 9) and *node-id* (in the space of binary string $(b_1 b_2 \cdots b_{n-5})$) there are exactly 5 nodes, one in each group. These nodes will be connected through a ring.

Consequently, each node in the $HRP(n)$ constructed above can be identified by a 3-tuple (r, s, t), where r $(0 \le r \le 4)$ is the node's *group-id*, s $(0 \le s \le 9)$ is the node's *net-id*, and t, in the form of binary string $(b_1 b_2 \cdots b_{n-5})$, is the node's *node-id*.

Table I summarizes the key properties of *HRP* in parallel with several other well-known topologies. Compared to Q_n, TQ_n, CQ_n, or $HP(n)$, *HRP* demonstrates same or shorter diameter but with much lager number of nodes. At the same time, *HRP* furnishes the networks with higher degree of connection.

Table 1. Comparisons of $HRP(n)$, Q_n, TQ_n, CQ_n, and $HP(n)$ networks

Topology	Regularity	Total Nodes (N)	Node Connection Degree (d)	Diameter (D)	Construction Costs (d×D)
Q_n	Yes	2^n	n	n	n^2
TQ_n	Yes	2^n	n	$n-1$	n^2-n
CQ_n	Yes	2^n	$n+1$	$n-1$	n^2-1
$HP(n)$	Yes	1.25×2^n	n	$n-1$	n^2-n
$HRP(n)$	Yes	1.5625×2^n	n	$n-1$	n^2-n

From table 1, we can prove that *HRP* has the following properties:

Lemma 1: $HRP(n)$ is composed of 1.5625×2^n nodes.
Lemma 2: The node connection degree of $HRP(n)$ is n.
Lemma 3: The diameter of $HRP(n)$ is n-1.
Lemma 4: $HRP(n)$ is regular.
Theorem 1: The construction cost of $HRP(n)$ is $n^2 - n$, where the construction cost of a network is defined as the product of its diameter and node connection degree.

4 Routing Algorithms for $HRP(n)$ Network

4.1 Unicast Routing Algorithm for HRP(n)

Assume that a message needs to be routed from node $A = (r_1, s_1, t_1)$ to node $B = (r_2, s_2, t_2)$:

Step 1: If $r_1 = r_2$ and $s_1 = s_2$, then A and B are in the same Hypercube. Assume the *Hamming* distance between t_1 and t_2 is t. If $t = 1$, A will send the messages to B directly. Otherwise, A will send the messages to its neighboring node C with *Hamming* distance t-1 to B at first, and C will send the messages to its neighboring node D with *Hamming* distance t-2 to B. This pattern will continue until the message reaches B.

Step 2: If $r_1 = r_2$ but $s_1 <> s_2$, then A and B are not in the same Hypercube, but in the same group. A shall send the message to node C identified by 3-tuple (r_1, s_1, t_2) according to Case 1. Since C and B are within the same group and with the same *node-id*, and are connected by a Petersen Graph. So the routing can be done through standard algorithms for Petersen graph.

Step 3: If $r_1 <> r_2$, then A and B are not in a same group. A shall first send the message to node C (r_2, s_1, t_1). Notice that C posses the same *node-id* and *net-id* as A and hence is connected to A via a ring. C, residing in the same group as B, can then use Case 1 and Case 2 to route the message to B.

Since the diameter of HRP is $(n$-1), in the worst condition, the message needs to be routed $(n$-1) times before reaching is destination.

4.2 Broadcasting Routing Algorithm for HRP(n)

To broadcast a message to all the nodes within HRP, node A can follow the steps below:

Step 1: A shall send messages to all the nodes on the same Petersen Graph and ring as itself.

Step 2: These nodes (including A itself) shall broadcast the message its own Hypercube network.

According to the above broadcasting routing algorithm, it is obvious that the step (1) needs 2 rounds of information exchanges, and the step (2) needs n-5 rounds of information exchanges, so the whole broadcasting needs $2+n$-5=n-3 rounds of information exchanges totally.

4.3 Fault-Tolerant Routing Algorithm for HRP(n)

For any node A in the n dimensional HRP(n) network, we define the n-1 dimensional vector $SPV_A[k]$ $(1 \le k \le n$-1) as follows:

$$SPV_A[1] = \begin{cases} 1 : \text{If the links between } A \text{ and its all neighbors are not fault} \\ 0 : \text{Otherwise} \end{cases}$$

$$SPV_A[k] = \begin{cases} 1: If \ \sum SPV_{nei(A)}[k-1] = n \\ 0: Otherwise \end{cases}$$,where $1 < k \leq 6$ and $nei(A)$ represents A's neighboring nodes.

$$SPV_A[k] = \begin{cases} 1: If \ \sum SPV_{nei(A)}[k-1] > n-k \\ 0: Otherwise \end{cases}$$,where $k > 6$ and $nei(A)$ represents A's neighboring nodes.

It is easy to prove that the following theorem stands:

Theorem 2: For any given node A in HRP(n), $SPV_A[k] = 1 (1 \leq k \leq n-1) \Rightarrow$ For any node B other than A in HRP(n), .if the distance between A and B is k, then there exists a fault-free path between A and B, and in addition, the length of the path is k.

According to the description of theorem 2, it is obvious that the routing based on $SPV_A[k]$ ($1 \leq k \leq n-1$) is fault-tolerant.

5 Conclusions

By combining the characteristics of the short diameter of Petersen Graph and the high connectivity of Hypercube networks, a novel interconnection networks $HRP(n)$ is proposed. It is proved that $HRP(n)$ has good characteristics of both Petersen Graph and Hypercube networks such as regularity, short diameter and high node connection degree etc, and in addition, $HRP(n)$ is of the same or shorter diameter, more nodes and higher node connection degree than Q_n, TQ_n, CQ_n and $HP(n)$ networks. So, $HRP(n)$ has better communication performances than Q_n, TQ_n, CQ_n and $HP(n)$ networks, and is a kind of interconnection network with good characteristics.

Acknowledgements

The authors' research supported in part by Programme of Young Scientists and Technicians of Fujian Province with Grant 2005J051.

References

[1] Laurence E. LaForge, Kirk F. Korver, M. Sami Fadali, What Designers of Bus and Network Architectures Should Know about Hypercubes. IEEE Transactions on Computers,4 (2003) 525-544.
[2] P.C. Saxena, Sangita Gupta, and Jagmo han Rai, A delay optimal coterie on the k dimensional folded Petersen graph, Journal of Parallel Distributed Computing. 63(2003) 1026-1035.
[3] Naserasr, Reza Skrekovski, Riste, The Petersen Grapg is not 3-Edge-Colorable: A New Proof. Discrete Mathmatics, 1(2003)325-326.
[4] P. A. J. Hibers, M. R. J. Koopman, and J. L. A. van de Snepscheut, The twisted cube, Lecture Notes in Computer Science, 2809(1987)152-159.

[5] Chien-Ping Chang, Jyh-Nan Wang, Lih-Hsing Hsu: Topological Properties of Twisted Cube. Information Science, 1(1999) 147-167.

[6] Wen-Tzeng Huang, Jimmy J. M. Tan, Chun-Nan Hung, and Lih-Hsing Hsu. Fault Tolerant Hamiltonicity of Twisted Cubes. Journal of Parallel and Distributed Computing, 4(2002) 591-604.

[7] Chang, Chien-Ping, Ting-Yi Sung and Lih Hsing Hsu. Edge congestion and topological properties of crossed cubes, IEEE Transactions on Parallel and Distributed Systems, 1(2000) 64-80.

[8] Ming-Chien Yang, Tseng-Kuei Li, Jimmy J.M.Tan, Lih-Hsing Hsu. Fault-tolerant cycle embedding of crossed cubes. Information Processing Letters, 4(2003) 149-154.

[9] Wang Lei, Lin Yaping, A Fault-tolerant Routing Strategy Based on Maximum Safety-Path Vectors for Hypercube Multicomputers, Journal of China Institute of Communications, 4(2004) 130-137.

[10] Wang Lei, Lin Yaping, Fault-tolerant Routing for Hypercube Multicomputers Based on Maximum Safety-Path Matrix, Journal of Software, 7(2004) 994-1004.

[11] Das, S.K.; Banerjee, A.K.; Hyper Petersen network: yet another hypercube-like topology, In Proceedings of Fourth Symposium on the Frontiers of Massively Parallel Computation, IEEE Computer Society, San Francisco, USA, (1992) 270-278.

[12] Liu Fang-Ai, Liu Zhi-Yong, Qiao Xiang Zhen, A practical interconnection network RP(k) and its routing algorithms. Science in China (Serial F), 6(2001) 461-473.

[13] Wang Lei, Lin Yaping, Topology and Routing Algorithms of 2-D Torus/Double-Loops connected Petersen Graph Networks. Chinese Journal of Computers, 9(2004) 1290-1296.

Cycle Period Analysis and Optimization of Timed Circuits*

Lei Wang, Zhi-ying Wang, and Kui Dai

School of Computer, National University of Defense Technology,
Changsha, Hunan province, China
leiwang@nudt.edu.cn

Abstract. In this paper, a method is proposed to analyze the minimum average cycle period of the timed circuits. Timed Petri net is used to model timed circuits. Our method is focus on structural analysis of the Petri net model of the timed circuits, which is another way to reduce the state space of the analyzed model. Then an algorithm is proposed to optimize the performance of timed circuit by asynchronous retiming technique. The algorithm balances the asynchronous pipelines to gain the target cycle period while minimize the area at the same time. Experimental results demonstrate the computational feasibility and effectiveness of both approaches.

1 Introduction

Timed circuits[1][2][3] are asynchronous circuits considering timing information during synthesis. Compared to delay-insensitive circuits, speed-independent circuits and quasi-delay insensitive circuits, timed circuits are more efficient with speed and cost. But traditional analysis and optimization method can not be used for timed circuit. In this paper, a systematic approach for evaluating and optimizing the cycle period of timed circuits is presented.

The outline of the rest of this paper is as follows. In the next section the mathematical preliminary of timed Petri net and basic concept of retiming are given. The following section is dedicated to cycle period analysis of timed circuits. In section 4, timed circuit optimization techniques are presented. Section 5 shows the comparison with other methods. We concluded the paper with a discussion of our future work.

2 Preliminary

2.1 Timed Petri Net

The timed Petri net model used in this paper is defined as:

---

* This work has been supported by the National Natural Science Foundation of China (Grant 90407022).

C. Jesshope and C. Egan (Eds.): ACSAC 2006, LNCS 4186, pp. 502–508, 2006.

Definition 1. *A timed Petri Net is a five-tuple* $N = < P, T, F, \Delta, M_0 >$. $P = \{p_1, \ldots, p_m\}$ *is a finite nonempty set of places.* $T = \{t_1, \ldots, t_n\}$ *is finite set of transitions.* $F \in (P{\times}T) \cup (T{\times}P)$ *is the flow relation.* $\Delta := T \rightarrow Q^+ \times (Q^+ \cup \{\infty\})$ *is a function mapping each* $t \in T$ *to a possibly unbounded delay, where* Q^+ *is the set of non-negative rational numbers.* $M_0 \subseteq P$ *is the initial marking of the net.*

For convenience, $\Delta(t) = (l, u)$ where $l < u$; $\Delta_l(t) = l$ and $\Delta_u(t) = u$ return the lower and upper bound of delay of transition t.

The incidence matrix C of a PN with n transitions and m places is an $n \times m$ matrix $C = [c_{ij}]$ whose entries are defined as $c_{ij} = c_{ij}^+ - c_{ij}^-$. where $c_{ij}^+ = w(i, j)$ is the weight of the arc from transition i to its output places j and $c_{ij}^- = w(j, i)$ is the weight of the arc to transition i from the place j.

A P-invariant (place invariant) of a PN is any integer positive (column) vector I which is solution of the matrix equation: $C \times I = 0$. Finding basic invariants is a classical problem of linear algebra, and there are known algorithms to solve this problem efficiently.

2.2 Retiming

Asynchronous circuits differ from synchronous circuits in the way clock signal generated. Clock trees are used in synchronous circuits to drive the clocks of registers and latches. However, local handshake circuits are used to generated clocks of registers and latches in asynchronous circuits. Retiming is a powerful technique for synchronous sequential circuits optimization, can this technique be used for asynchronous circuits optimization? The answer is 'Yes'.

Suppose that the handshake logic of asynchronous circuits is ignored during optimizing stage, asynchronous circuits can be viewed as an interconnection of logic gates and memory elements (registers and latches) controlled by handshake circuits, which can be modeled as a directed graph $G = (V, E, d, w)$. The vertex set V of the graph models the functional elements of the circuit, and each vertex v has an attribute d(v) that denotes the propagation delay of the corresponding functional element. The directed edges E of the graph models the interconnections between functional elements. Each edge $e \in E$ has a weight (number of memory elements) $w(e)$. The timed Petri net model and the digraph model of the timed circuit can transformed into each other.

For any path $p = v_0 \xrightarrow{e_0} v_1 \xrightarrow{e_1} \ldots \xrightarrow{e_{k-1}} v_k$, the path weight can be defined as: $w(p) = \sum_{i=0}^{k-1} w(e_i)$. The path delay can be defined as: $d(p) = \sum_{i=0}^{k} d(v_i)$. A retiming of a circuit $G = < V, E, d, w >$ is an integer-valued vertex-labeling $r : V \rightarrow Z$. The retiming specifies a transformation of the original circuit in which memory elements are added or removed or moved so as to change the graph G into a new graph $G_r = (V, E, d, w_r)$ so as to minimize the cycle period and area at the same time. For timed circuits, cycle period means average time separation between events, which is reciprocal with throughput of the timed circuit.

The number of flip-flops on a given edge (u, v) after retiming is given by

$$w_r(u, v) = w(u, v) + r(v) - r(u) \tag{1}$$

In order to characterize the clock period of a retimed circuits, we define two quantities:

$$W(u, v) = \min\{w(p) : p : u \rightsquigarrow v\} \tag{2}$$
$$D(u, v) = \max\{d(p) : p : u \rightsquigarrow v \text{ and } w(p) = W(u, v)\} \tag{3}$$

The quantity $W(u, v)$ is the minimum number of registers on any path from vertex u to vertex v. Path $w(p) = W(u, v)$ is called a *critical path* from u to v. The quantity $D(u, v)$ is the maximum total propagation delay on any critical path from u to v.

3   Cycle Period Analysis

It is assumed that the timed Petri net is consistent, ie., $\exists x > 0$, $C^T x = 0$. Suppose there is a delay of at least $l_i = \Delta_l(t_i)$ associated with transition $t_i, i = 1, \ldots, n$. This means when t_i is enabled, c_{ij}^- tokens will be reserved in place p_j for at least l_i before their removal by firing t_i. We define *resource-time product(RTP)* as the product of the number of tokens (resources) and length of time that these tokens reside in a place. Thus, the RTP is given by $c_{ij}^- l_i x_i$, which can be rewritten in matrix form:

$$(C^-)^T Dx \tag{4}$$

Where $C^- = [c_{ij}^-]_{n \times m}$ and D is the diagonal matrix of l_i, $i = 1, \ldots, n$. $(C^-)^T Dx$ represents of the vector of m RTP's for m places, and each RTP considers only reserved tokens. Now suppose there are on the average $\bar{M}(p_j)$ tokens in the place p_j during one cycle τ. Then the RTP in the vector is given by $\bar{M}\tau$. Since RTP obtained by this way of measure includes both reserved token and nonreserved tokens, we have the following inequality:

$$\bar{M}\tau \geq (C^-)^T Dx \tag{5}$$

Taking the inner product of equation (5) with a nonnegative P-invariant y and using the invariance, $y_i^T \bar{M} = y_i^T M_0$, we have

$$y_i^T M_0 \tau \geq y_i^T (C^-)^T Dx$$

and

$$\tau \geq \frac{y_i^T (C^-)^T Dx}{y_i^T M_0} \tag{6}$$

Therefore, a lower bound of the cycle τ or the minimum average cycle time is given by

$$\tau_{min} = \max_i \{\frac{y_i^T (C^-)^T Dx}{y_i^T M_0}\} \tag{7}$$

Where the maximum is taken over all independent minimal-support of P-invariant, $y_i \geq 0$ [5]. This is the minimum cycle period of the best case.

We substitute the diagonal element of matrix D to u_i where $u_i = \Delta_u(t_i)$ is the upper bound of the delay of transition t_i. Using equation (7) we can get the worst case minimum average cycle period of the timed Petri net.

4   Cycle Period Optimization

4.1   Algorithm

In this section, we give an algorithm to solve the timed circuit minimum cycle period retiming problems. Our algorithm is based on Leiserson and Saxe's algorithm [4], changed the searching range of feasible clock periods, reduced the computation complexity, and optimization objective is minimum area at the same time of minimizing clock period. The feasible clock period test can be done by solve a MILP problem[4].

Theorem 1. *Let* $G = < V, E, d, w >$ *be a timed circuit, let c be an arbitrary positive real number, and let r be a function from V to integers. Then r is a legal retiming of G such that* $\Phi(G_r) \leq c$ *if and only if:*

$$r(u) - r(v) \leq w(e), \text{for every edge } u \to v \text{ of } G \qquad (8)$$
$$r(u) - r(v) \leq W(u, v) - 1, \text{for all vertex } u, v \in V, \text{such that } D(u, v) > c \qquad (9)$$

Proof can be referenced at [4]. Equation (8) is called *non-negativity constraints*, equation (9) is called *long path constraints*.

Definition 2. *Let c be an arbitrary positive real number, c is a feasible clock period of an asynchronous circuits if and only retiming r with* $\Phi(G_r)$ *is a legal retiming.*

If condition (8) and (9) is satisfied, the clock period c is feasible. The feasible clock period test can be reduced to the following mixed-integer linear programming problem below.

Problem 1 (MILP). Let S be a set of m linear inequalities of the form $x_j - x_i \leq a_{ij}$ on the unknown $x_1, x_2, \ldots, x_n$, where the a_{ij} are given real constants, and let k be given. Determine feasible values for unknown x_i subject to the constraint that x_i is integer for $i = 1, 2, \ldots, k$, x_i is real for $i = k + 1, k + 2, \ldots, n$, or determine no such value exist.

For a graph $G = < V, E, d, w >$, it can be proved that if there exist a function $s : V \to [0, c]$, satisfy $s(v) \geq d(v), \forall v \in V$ and $s(v) \geq \Delta(v) + d(v)$, for zero weight edge $u \to v$, then the cycle period of the graph $\Phi(G) \leq c$. So if r is a feasible retiming of graph G, and $\Phi(G_r) \leq c$, then the following inequalities must be satisfied:

1) $-s(v) \leq -d(v)$, for every vertex $v \in V$,

2) $s(v) \leq c$, for every vertex $v \in V$,
3) $r(u) - r(v) \leq w(e)$, for every edge $u \xrightarrow{e} v$,
4) $s(u) - s(v) \leq -d(v)$, for every edge $u \xrightarrow{e} v$ such that $r(u) - r(v) = w(e)$.

We substituted $s(v) = c(R(v) - r(v)), \forall v \in V$, we got:

Theorem 2. *Let* $G = < V, E, d, w >$ *be a asynchronous circuit, and let c be a positive real number. Then there is a retiming r of G such that* $\Phi(G_r) \leq c$ *if and only if there exist an assignment of a real value $R(v)$ and an integer value $r(v)$ to each vertex $v \in V$ such that the following conditions are satisfied:*

> *1) $r(v) - R(v) \leq -d(v)/c$ for every vertex $v \in V$,*
> *2) $R(v) - r(v) \leq 1$ for every vertex $v \in V$*
> *3) $r(u) - r(v) \leq w(e)$ wherever $u \rightarrow v$, and*
> *4) $R(u) - R(v) \leq w(e) - d(v)/c$ wherever $u \rightarrow v$*

Theorem.2 reduces the clock period feasible test to a MILP. The algorithm is given below:

Algorithm retiming timed circuit
Description Give an asynchronous circuit $G = < V, E, d, w >$, this algorithm
    determines a retiming r such that $\Phi(G_r)$ is as small as possible.
Input A graph representation $G = < V, E, d, w >$ of the circuit.
Output A retiming for minimum clock period, minimize area at each clock
    period.
Begin
s1 Compute cycle period T_l with the method presented in section 3.
    Set $T_u = \max\{\Delta(v), \forall v \in V\}$. T_l and T_u are the lower bound and upper
    bound of cycle period of graph $G = < V, E, d, w >$.
s2 Set $T = \frac{T_u + T_l}{2}$.
    To test whether a potential clock period T is feasible, solve problem MILP
    to determined whether conditions in Theorem 2 can be satisfied.
    if T is feasible, then record $r(v), \forall v \in V$, set $T_u = T$; Else, set $T_l = T$.
    If $T_u - T_l > \varepsilon$ goto s2
s3 For the minimum clock period find in step 3, use the value for r found by
    the algorithm that solves Problem MILP as the optimal retiming.
End

The cycle period analysis method in section 3 gives the lower bound of feasible cycle period with $\sum_{e \in E} w(e)$ registers. In step 2 of algorithm, $\Delta(v), \forall v \in V$ is computed by construct the subgraph G_0 of G, the subgraph contains precisely those edges e with register count $w(e) = 0$, G_0 should be acyclic to insure no combinational loop exist. Perform a topological sort on G_0, go through the vertices in the order defined by the topological sort. On visiting each vertex, compute the quantity $\Delta(v)$ as follows:

1) If there are no incoming edge to v, set $\Delta(v) = d(v)$,
2) Otherwise, set $\Delta(v) = d(v) + \max\{\Delta(u), u \rightarrow v \text{ and } w(e) = 0\}$

The minimum clock period computation algorithm is implemented in Matlab. The asynchronous circuits retiming algorithm is implemented in C. The MILP problem is solved by *glosol*, a freely available MILP solver. In the next section, an example is given to prove the feasibility and effectiveness of this method.

4.2 Example

The left of figure.1 gives an example of the digraph of a simple RISC processor design. This processor is a simple Von Neumann computer which performs an instruction fetch, decode, operand read, ALU operation and operand write to execute each instruction. The black dash on the edge of digraph means the register in the circuit.

The timed Petri net model of the graph is shown in figure.2. The token represent the registers in the circuit. The model has 3 minimal-support P-invariants, the cycle period can be computed by equation (7). Thus cycle period lower bound is $T_l = 59ns$. Then the upper bound is computed, $T_u = \max\{\Delta(v), v \in V\} = 71ns$.

Once the upper bound and lower bound of cycle period of the circuit is computed, our algorithm is applied to computer the minimum cost retiming. Suppose $\varepsilon = 0.1$, then after 7 times iteration of MILP solve procedure, the minimum cost retiming of the circuit is shown in figure.1 right.

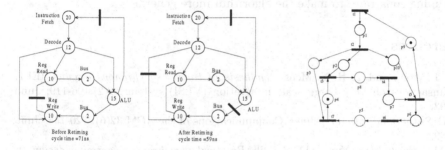

Fig. 1. A simple RISC processor model: Before retiming and after retiming   **Fig. 2.** Timed Petri net model for cycle period analysis

5 Prior Work

In [6] the author formulate the cycle time computation as a *minimal cost-to-time ratio cycle problem* and used the *Lawler's* algorithm[7]. The algorithm requires $\Theta(n^3)$ steps to compute the shortest distance between all pairs of places, using the *Floyd-Warshall* algorithm. The overall computation requires $\Theta(n^3 \log_2 n)$ steps. Where n is the number of places in the Petri net model. The total complexity of our method is $\Theta(M|P_{ST}|^3)$, which is better than the algorithm in [6]. where M is the number of siphons that are traps of the Petri net model, $|P_{ST}|$ is the number of places in siphon P_{ST}.

The major difference between our asynchronous retiming algorithm and Leiserson and Saxe's algorithm is the way to search possible feasible minimum clock period. Leiserson and Saxe's algorithm computed $d(u, v)$ matrix and sort the elements of $d(u, v)$, binary search is used to find feasible minimum clock period, which is very time-consuming. Our algorithm used the lower bound and upper bound and binary search in an constant interval $[T_l, T_u]$, which reduced the iteration times efficiently. The second difference is that when solving the MILP to test whether a clock period is feasible, the optimization objective is to minimize the area represented by $\sum_{\forall e:u \to v} w(e) + r(v) - r(u)$. This method minimize area at the same time of minimizing clock period.

6   Conclusion and Future Work

This paper first presented an algorithm for cycle period analysis of the timed circuits. The timed circuits is modeled as a consistent timed Petri net model. Then based on the cycle period analysis method, we proposed an algorithm to optimize the performance of timed circuits, including cycle period minimization and area minimization. This algorithm can be used to balance the pipeline stage of asynchronous circuits to achieve better performance.

The further research will focus on extensions on retiming algorithm to take into account the delay variation of asynchronous unit and take into account the min timing constraint to make the algorithm more general.

References

1. C. J. Myers and T. H.-Y. Meng. *Synthesis of timed asynchronous circuits.* IEEE Transactions on Very Large Scale Integration (VLSI) systems, 1(2):106-119, June 1993.
2. I. E. Sutherland. *Micropipelines.* Communications of the ACM 32(6): 720-738, June 1989.
3. S. M. Nowick, K. Y. Yun and D. L. Dill, *Practical asynchronous controller design.* In Proc. International Conf. Computer Design (ICCD), pages 341-345. IEEE Computer Society Press, October 1992
4. Leiserson C, Saxe J. Optimizing synchronous systems. Journal of VLSI and Computer Systems, 1983, 1(1): 41-67.
5. Murata T. *Petri net: properties, analysis and applications.* Proceedings of the IEEE, vl. 77, no. 4, pp. 541-579, 1989.
6. Y. Yaw, Belle W. Y. Wei, C. V. Ramamoorthy et. al., *Extension on Performance Evaluation Techniques for Concurrent Systems.* Computer Software and Applications Conference, 1988. COMPSAC 88. Proceedings., Twelfth International 5-7 Oct. 1988 Page(s):480 - 484.
7. Lawler, E. L., *Combinatorial Optimization: Networks and Matroids.* Holt, Reinhart, and Winston, New York, NY, USA, 1976.

Acceleration Techniques for Chip-Multiprocessor Simulator Debug

Haixia Wang, Dongsheng Wang, and Peng Li

Research Institute of Information Technology,
National Laboratory for Information Science and Technology,
Tsinghua University, Beijing, 100084, P.R. China
{hx-wang, wds}@tsinghua.edu.cn, p-li02@mails.tsinghua.edu.cn

Abstract. By exploring thread-level parallelism, chip multiprocessor (CMP) can dramatically improve the performance of server and commercial applications. However, complex CMP chip architecture made debugging work time-consuming and rather hard. In this paper, based on the experience of debugging CMP simulator ThumpCMP, we present a set of acceleration techniques, including automatic cache-coherence check, fast error location, and workload rerun times reducing technique. The set of techniques have been demonstrated to be able to make CMP chip debugging work much easier and much faster.

1 Introduction

Integrated circuit processing technology offers increasing integration density, which fuels microprocessor performance growth. In coming 10 years, to integrate a billion transistors on reasonably sized silicon chip is not a dream. However, traditional processor performance will not always scale while the transistor counts increases. Many researchers deemed multiprocessor architecture ideal to utilize more and more dense transistor integration. One of the promising multiprocessor architecture is chip multiprocessors (CMP) [1,2,3].

Before designing a physical CMP system, developing a simulator is well-suitable for fast and initial performance evaluation and correctness verification. There are a few open source CMP simulator research projects, such as GEMS [4] by university of Wisconsin Madison, M5 [5] by university of Michigan, Liberty [6] by Princeton and SimFlex [7] by CMU. GEMS focus on memory hierarchy, cache coherence protocol, and interconnection topology, enabling fast performance evaluation different CMP architectures. M5 allows flexible configuration of multi-system networks on chip. Liberty introduces structural modeling methodologies into simulation. SimFlex specializes in fast, accurate and flexible full-system simulation by sampling simulation method.

These open source simulators are flexible to configure different CMP structures. However, CMP simulation usually needs to take much longer time than single-core processor. This is not only because CMP chip integrates many more cores, on chip inter-connect network and cache-consistency protocols complicated the whole system and lengthen system simulation time.

C. Jesshope and C. Egan (Eds.): ACSAC 2006, LNCS 4186, pp. 509–515, 2006.

Many simulation acceleration techniques are explored and applied in CMP system simulation, including trace-driven and sampling method. However, simulation is still rather time-consuming. [7] reports that CMP Simulation is much slower than real hardware platforms, especially when CMP is composed of out-of-order processor cores. This paper figures out that an out-of-order simulation system needs 150 years to run audited TPC-C to the end.

The time-consuming simulation made CMP design debugging work even harder, since it need much long time to re-run the workload to fix bugs. So it is quite important to speedup the CMP debugging in the early development cycle. In this paper, we propose several CMP debugging acceleration techniques, automatic cache coherence check and fast bug positioning, which have been proven useful in acceleration the debugging work of a dual-core CMP, ThumpCMP by Tsinghua Univ. China.

The remainder of the paper is organized as followings: Section 2 gives an overview of ThumpCMP, and then Section 3 describe debug acceleration techniques, such as automatically cache coherence checking, Section 4 discusses fast bug positioning. Finally, Section 6 draws conclusion.

2   ThumpCMP Simulator

ThumpCMP is a full system cycle-accurate dual-core simulator. Each core of ThumpCMP simulates a Thump processor, a 32-bit MIPS-like microprocessor. The typical frequency of Thump is 400MHz. Each core owns private L1 instruction and data cache. Two cores share the unified L2 Cache. L1 cache uses write-through policy and L2 Cache takes write-back policy. ThumpCMP uses snooping protocol to maintain cache coherence, and adopts write-invalidate strategy to keep only one copy available in all caches once writing new data.

The software architecture of thumpCMP simulator itself is component-based. All components are grouped and ordered automatically based on the relations of their inputs and outputs. Only when inputs change, a component is activated and whose state transitions are simulated, which avoids unnecessary operation simulation and accelerates simulation.

Compared with debugging on single-core simulator, ThumpCMP debugging is much harder and slower. During the Linux 2.6 kernel boot process debugging on ThumpCMP simulator, we explored several effective multiprocessor debugging acceleration techniques.

3   Automatic Cache Coherence Check

Principle. Errors in multiprocessor architecture design or in program running in CMP simulator usually incur cache incoherence. However, it is often far from the spot where coherence violation happened while people catch the incoherence bugs. In normal cases, people have to re-run the workload from the start step by step to find the spot where multiple cache copies are different. This process is quite time-consuming.

Automatic cache-coherence check is proposed to avoid the step-by-step re-run process. The basic idea of automatic cache-coherence check is to check all cache copies while the usual simulation is going on. Once cache-coherence violation is detected, system will notify designer immediately, so the re-run time to find the cache-coherence violation spot is saved.

In fact, only memory load/store instructions can incur cache incoherence problems. Thus cache-coherence check can be conducted only at the time of processor core performing data load or store operations instead of at each target clock cycle. Fig. 1 illustrates cache-coherence check mechanism that performed at each data loading. In detail, if a processor core needs to load data at address A, after data is returned to processor, the data is compared with all other valid cache copies of address A. If same, cache is coherent. Otherwise,cache is incoherent at address A.

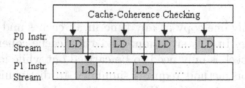

Fig. 1. Automatic Cache-coherence Check at the Time of Data Loading

In shared L2 cache CMP structure, when all data load and store operations visit cache, the above cache-coherence check is able to find all cache-coherence defects. But in the case that L2 cache uses write-back policy and some processor cores bypass cache and visit memory directly, there may be incoherence between cache and memory copies.

For example, as shown in Fig. 2, processor core 0 stored data x at address A, that operation invalidated original cache data y in core 1 and wrote new data x to L2 cache. L2 cache uses write-back policy and not write data back into memory immediately. If processor core 1 directly visits memory address A now, stale data y is returned from memory to core 1, and incoherence occurs.

Thus, if a processor core performs data load/store operation with cache bypassed, the address copies in memory should be checked to be consistent with all cache copies.

For each load instruction simulation, cache-coherence check incurs additional latency for data comparison of all valid cache copies corresponding to the load address. The time complexity of each cache-coherence check is linear with cache numbers. Compared with thousands of host instructions in simulating a load instruction of target CMP system, overhead of cache-coherence check can be basically neglected or fully tolerated for current CMP system (mostly core numbers are no more than 32).

Optimization. In CMP system, not all load operations would introduce cache incoherence problems. If the data to be loaded is private for a processor core, the

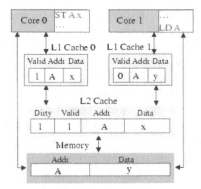

Fig. 2. Cache and Memory Incoherent Case

data must have only one copy at any time in all caches and the load operation can't pollute cache. In this situation, load time cache-coherence check can be avoided and the check is only need to be carried out while loading shared data.

The optimization method requires simulator to distinguish between private and shared load operations. If CMP system shares L2 cache, and MESI protocol is used to maintain L1 cache coherence, the state of cache block (E (exclusive) and S (shared)), can be used to determine whether data to be loaded is private or shared.

Besides, cache bypass operations need also be pay attention to. To detect whether data is private or not in this case, memory should provide support for times data have been read. As an alternative method, cache coherence check is performed on all load operation in the case of cache bypass, and only on shared data load operation if not cache bypass.

4   Fast Bug Positioning

Save Checkpoint Periodically. ThumpCMP Simulator provides breakpoint function so that designer can use it to set the conditions of triggering breakpoint, e.g., the number of instructions before simulator pauses. It's helpful when debug long-piece software code on ThumpCMP. However, in some time, before the pre-set breakpoint triggering condition meets, some system errors may occur. In this situation, system usually asked for re-run from scratch. For an error occurred a bit later, the re-run is rather time-consuming.

To avoid overleaping and re-running, checkpoint is used to save spot and recover later. Because nobody know when and where an error will appear, it is reasonable to let simulator save checkpoints automatically in a given time-interval.

Fast Error Positioning using calling chain. When an error occurred and simulation halted, it's fairly easy to know which function was being executed according to program counter register, but the information is usually not enough. The current resided function may be some widely and frequently used subroutine, and shows nothing information on what is wrong with the simulation.

Anyway, it must be some statements in the previous function calling chains caused the final fatal error. So it's useful to record the whole function calling chains and analyze the function calling chains when error occurred. Usually, by this way, the bugs are much easy to find. In ThumpCMP simulator, there exists such a function calling stack to record the function calling chain for each processor core.

ThumpCMP uses MIPS compatible instruction set. The caller function uses JAL/JALR jump instruction to transfer control to other function. At the same time, the return address is stored in general purpose register r31. After callee function finishs its work, it uses JR AR instruction to return to the address saved in r31 and return control to the caller function.

In ThumpCMP implementation, when processor core encounters a jump instruction, including J, JR, JAL, JALR instructions, the jump destination address is push into the function calling stack. Whenever a processor encounters a JR AR instruction, ThumpCMP will pop the top record from function calling stack. In this way, the function calling stack records all previous function calls by now.

5   Reducing Workload Rerun Times

For a new CMP design, bugs lies not only in hardware (simulator) but also in software (workload running on simulator, such as Linux Operating System in ThumpCMP). If each bug correction brings simulation from scratch, to fix all bugs is very time-consuming. In fact, after hardware or software modification, it is possible for most cases that workload need not to be run newly from beginning, but just run from a previous checkpoint or modify a register value by hand. This section will find these cases and propose how to avoid rerunning.

First, this section analyzes what system state variables and checkpoint contents are composed of. Second, this section gives an analysis on how to avoid rerunning in the simple case that only a few of state variable are needed to modify. At Last, we discuss how to avoid rerunning in two cases of modification respectively, hardware and software modification.

Checkpoint Contents. An integrated circuit mainly consists of memory (including registers, caches and memory), data-path (combinational circuit and pipeline registers), and control logic (combinational circuit), as shown in Fig. 3. System status is defined by all register variables, including registers (general purpose or CP0), caches (L1 instruction cache, L1 data cache, L2 Cache), TLBs (instruction TLB, data TLB), memory and pipeline registers (registers to save data for next clock cycle use between pipelines).

To recovery simulation later, checkpoint should record total system status accurately. Besides that, for full-system simulation, checkpoint should also record IO information (for example, record console information to recovery all printed information on console).

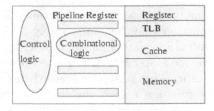

Fig. 3. Integrated Circuit Component Sketch

Simple Modification Case. If errors are found in design, but only a few of state variables have to change their values in correct simulation, the modification can be made by hand on the basis of previous simulation. In ThumpCMP, we provide modification function on all state variables.

In the course of debug Linux operating system in ThumpCMP, we tried and succeeded in modifying general purpose register value to correct data, modifying PC to jump over some function and go on from a new position, and modifying word value in cache or memory to maintain consistent state.

Though modification by hand in the process of workload running has risk of correctness and requires more attention, it does great help in the debug of complicated and slow simulation system.

Complex Modification Case. In the case that simulator is modified, if all register variables are kept same, to reuse checkpoint is to find a previous available checkpoint that has the same system status at a specific time point with new simulation after modification. Otherwise, if added or removed registers are independent with other registers at the time point of previous checkpoint saved, previous checkpoint can still be used.

In ThumpCMP, we define a unique id for each pipeline register. Id is reserved even if the register is discarded after some modification. In this method, even if pipeline registers are added or removed, values in previous checkpoint can be set on variables in new design. When new pipeline registers are added into design, the new registers are set zero by default or assigned by user.

In the other case that software is modified, virtual address of code and data after recompilation is changed even if there is a checkpoint in that codes executed are kept same as newly correct simulation. To reuse checkpoint, one way is to use compiler to keep virtual address of previous preformed code and data unchanged by the time point of checkpoint saved, or an alternative way is to build map function between different virtual address of same code or data, and replace all of them to new value in previous checkpoint. Both methods are difficult to implementation and being researched on ThumpCMP.

6   Debug Results on ThumpCMP

In the debug of ThumpCMP, above introduced techniques make great contribution on reducing debug time and making debug easier. Using automatic cache-coherence check mechanism, we found two cache bypass errors. One error is due to simulator design bug on Hit_invalidate_writeback L2 cache instruction, which make cache flush did not write correct values back to memory so that other processor fetch wrong data from memory into its cache. Another error came from that a cache flush is forgotten in operating system design. Furthermore, fast bug positioning methods and workload rerun times reducing techniques together accelerate ThumpCMP debug.

7 Conclusions and Future Work

Based on the debug work in ThumpCMP, this paper presents several debug accelerate techniques from the aspect of automatic cache-coherence check, fast bug positioning and workload rerun times reducing techniques. These techniques make it easy and fast to debug large-scale multiprocessor system.

Next, we will go further in research on how to avoid rerunning in the case of software modification, and try to re-use previous checkpoint as more as possible.

References

1. Hammond, L., Nayfeh, B., Olukotun K.: A single-chip multiprocessor. IEEE Computer **30**(1997)79–85
2. Olukotun, K., Nayfeh, B., Hammond, L., Wilson, K. , Chung, K.: The case for a single-chip multiprocessor. Int'l Conf. on Arch. Supp. for Prog. Lang. and Oper. Syst. (1996) 2–11
3. Krishnan, V., Torrellas, J.: A chip-multiprocessor architecture with speculative multithreading. IEEE Tran. of Comp. 48 (1999) 866–880
4. Martin, M., Sorin, D., Beckmann, B., Marty, M., Xu, M., Alameldeen, A., Moore, K., Hill, M., Wood, D.: Multifacet's General Execution-driven Multiprocessor Simulator (GEMS) Toolset. Comp. Arch. News **33** (2005) 92–99
5. Binkert, N., Hallnor, E., Reinhardt, S.: Network-oriented full-system simulation using M5. Workshop on Computer Architecture Evaluation using Commercial Workloads (2003) 36–43
6. Vachharajani, M., Vachharajani, N., Penry, D., Blome, J., Malik, S., August, D.: The Liberty Simulation Environment: A Deliberate Approach to High-Level System Modeling. ACM Trans. on Computer Systems (Accepted).
7. Wenisch, T., Wunderlich, R.: SimFlex: Fast, Accurate and Flexible Simulation of Computer Systems. Tutorial in the Int'l Symp. on Microarchitecture (2005)

A DDL–Based Software Architecture Model*

Meiling Wang, and Lei Liu**

Key Laboratory of Symbolic Computation and Knowledge Engineering of Ministry
of Education of P.R. China, College of Computer Science and Technology,
Jilin University, Changchun, 130012, P.R. China
liulei@jlu.edu.cn

Abstract. Dynamic Description Logic (DDL) can support both the static and dynamic knowledge representation, thus this paper introduces a kind of Software Architecture (SA) Model based on DDL, the purpose of which is to facilitate the description of each part of SA as well as the constraints between them. In addition, the model also supports the detection of the consistency problems existed in dynamic architecture. In the end, the mapping from SA to DLL is discussed, and an example of a complete architecture model of Pipeline-Filter style is described.

1 Introduction

Software Architecture (SA) is significant for software system design, and has important effects to the development of large-scale software as well. SA defines the structure of components, their interrelationships, composing pattern and satisfied constraints, and principles and guidelines governing their design [1][2].

Description Logic (DL) is one of effective tools for knowledge representation, supporting domain-level abstraction [3], while Dynamic Description Logic (DDL) supports static and dynamic knowledge representation at the same time [4][5]. This paper applies DDL to the modeling of SA: Section 2 gives a brief introduction to DDL; Section 3 presents the mapping from SA to DDL and a complete architecture model of Pipeline-Filter style; Section 4 discusses its application on consistency detection; Section 5 introduces some related work; the final section concludes the paper and discusses some further work.

2 Dynamic Description Logic DDL

DL is a decidable fragment of First-Order Logic (FOL), providing better expressing ability and decidable reasoning. DDL is the extension of DL: the representation and reasoning of static and dynamic knowledge are integrated, and the description and semantic interpretation of actions are presented, dealing with static and dynamic knowledge synchronously.

---

* This paper is sponsored by European Commission under grant No.TH/Asia Link/010
  (111084) and Jilin province science development plain project of China under grant
  No. 20050527.
** Corresponding author.

C. Jesshope and C. Egan (Eds.): ACSAC 2006, LNCS 4186, pp. 516–522, 2006.

DDL of this paper is based on the *ALCN* and the details can refer to [5], especially an action constructors ‖(*parallel composition*) is introduced, where

$$\alpha\|\beta \equiv \begin{cases} \alpha;\beta \cup \beta;\alpha, & \text{if } \alpha \text{ and } \beta \text{ are atom actions;} \\ \alpha_1;\alpha_2;\beta \cup \alpha_1;\beta;\alpha_2 \cup \beta;\alpha_1;\alpha_2, \text{if } \alpha \equiv \alpha_1;\alpha_2, \text{ and } \beta \text{ is an atom action} \\ \alpha_1;\alpha_2;\beta_1;\beta_2 \cup \alpha_1;\beta_1;\beta_2;\alpha_2 \cup \alpha_1;\beta_1;\alpha_2;\beta_2 \cup \beta_1;\beta_2;\alpha_1;\alpha_2 \\ \cup \beta_1;\alpha_1;\beta_2;\alpha_2 \cup \beta_1;\alpha_1;\alpha_2;\beta_2, & \text{if } \alpha \equiv \alpha_1;\alpha_2, \text{ and } \beta \equiv \beta_1;\beta_2; \\ \cdots, & \text{and all that} \end{cases}$$

3 Description of SA Model

SA describes the structures of program or computing system, including components, connectors, their outside-accessible attributes, and interrelations. Component is a kind of logic unit featuring particular functions, two sorts of which are simple component and composite component. Connector presents the manners and rules of components' cooperation, and provides a kind of glue [6] that integrates the components. The configuration of SA is described by compounding some components and connectors to be larger complex component. A subsystem is a kind of composite component, whose configuration is its overall arrangement.

Section 3.1 presents the mapping from SA to DDL, and Section 3.2 describes a complete architecture model of Pipeline-Filter style based on DDL.

3.1 Mapping from SA to DDL

3.1.1 Component. Concept *Component* describes component, and concrete simple and composite components are described as the subconcepts of *Component*. Concept *Connector* describes connector, and concrete connectors are described as the subconcepts of *Connector*. The connective relation between *Component* and *Connector* is denoted as relation *linkto*. Relation *havepart* denotes the comprising relation between *Component* and its subcomponents and their connectors; especially simple component has no subcomponent. *Component* does some cooperation such as providing service to and requiring service from outside-environment. Cooperation is realized by Concept *Gate*, two subconcepts of which are *InGate* for requiring service and *OutGate* for providing service. Relation *provide* denotes providing service that is output, and *require* denotes requiring service that is input. The axiomatization of *Component* is:

$$Component \equiv (\exists provide.OutGate \cup \exists require.InGate) \cap \geq 0linkto.Connector \cap \geq$$
$$0havatype.\top \quad (\top \text{ denotes universal concept})$$

Each *Component* has a certain function, which is realized as a concrete *action*. *Component* is *BeforeCompute* before the *action* and is *AfterCompute* after the *action*. If an *action* is *compute* and the processed datum is x, then:

$BeforeCompute \equiv Component \cap [compute(x)]AfterCompute$
$AfterCompute \subseteq Component$

3.1.2 Gate. Each *Gate* has a certain type character, denoted by concept *Type*, and the relation is described as *havetype*. The actions on *Gate* are *input* and *output*. The *Gate* is *BeforeIO* before *input* or *output*, and is *AfterIO* after *input* or *output*. In the following axioms, *in* and *out* are the instances of *InGate* and *OutGate* respectively, and x and v are the instances of a certain type.

$Gate \equiv (InGate \bigcup OutGate) \bigcap = 1havetype.Type$

$BeforeIO \equiv Gate \bigcap [input(in, x) \bigcup output(out, v)]AfterIO \qquad AfterIO \subseteq Gate$

3.1.3   Type.

The subconcepts of *Type* are some concrete data types characterizing all their instances. For example, *Int* characterizes all its instances as integer. *Type* is *FullData* after completely *input* and before *output*, otherwise is *EmptyData*. After *input* or *output* is completed, the current value is *Eof*.

$EmptyData \equiv Type \bigcap [input(in, x)]FullData$

$FullData \equiv Type \bigcap [output(out, v)]EmptyData \qquad Eof \subseteq Type$

3.1.4   Connector.

Connector describes the common character of certain cooperation and consists of two *Gates* to connect with a *Component* by each to indicate the outside-behavior of the components taking part in the cooperation. A protocol for cooperation connects the gates to compound the functions of the components as a complex function. Relation *receive* denotes *input* from *OutGate*, and *send* denotes *output* along *InGate*. *Connector* is axiomatized as:

$Connector \equiv\equiv 1receive.OutGate \bigcap = 1send.InGate \bigcap = 1linkto.Component$

Component and *Connector* should be connected by the same-type *Gate* and the behavior on the *Gates* is complementary for the protocol, that is if *Component* is *output* along the *Gate*, then the protocol *input* from it, vice versa. The cooperation is described as action *glue*, which is the composition of *actions* on connector's gate and is parallel to the *actions* on component's gate connected to the connector. *Connector* is *BeforeGlue* before *gule* and is *AfterGlue* after *glue*.

$BeforeGlue \equiv Connector \bigcap [glue(in, out, x)]AfterGlue \qquad AfterGlue \subseteq Connector$

3.1.5   Composite Component.

Relation *attach* realizes the same-type connecting between the *Gates* of *Connector* and *Component*, substituting the connector's gate by the gate of concrete component. Relation *bind* designates the subcomponent'gate as the same-type gate of the composite component. The function of composite component is described as the parallel composition of all the subcomponents'actions and the connectors' *glue* action.

$InGate \equiv Gate \bigcap (\leq 1attach.InGate \bigcup \leq 1bind.InGate)$

$OutGate \equiv Gate \bigcap (\leq 1attach.OutGate \bigcup \leq 1bind.OutGate)$

3.2   An Architecture Example of Pipeline-Filter Style

In this section, a complete SA model of Pipeline-Filter Style is introduced based on DDL. Fig.1 presents an instance *compositefilter* of composite component *CompositeFilter*, consisting of an instance *pipe* of connector *Pipe* and two instances $filter_1$ and $filter_2$ of simple component *Filter*. Suppose that all the types of gates in the system are *Int*.

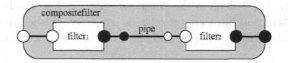

Fig. 1. compositefilter

3.2.1   DDL Description Language

Concept:Component,Connector,Gate,InGate,OutGate,Type,Int,Filter,CompositeFilter,Pipe,BeforeIO,AfterIO,FullData,EmptyData,BeforeCompute,AfterCompute,BeforeGlue,AfterGlue,Eof;

Relation:havepart,provide,require,linkto,havetype,attach,bind,receive, send;

Instances: in:InGate,out:OutGate,x:Int,v:Int;

Concept constructors: $\cap, \cup, \neg, \exists, \forall, \geq n, \leq n, = n$

Action definition:

$\alpha(in, x) \equiv (\{InGate(in), Int(x), havetype(in,x), BeforeIO(in), EmptyData(x)\},$
$\qquad \{\phi/FullData(x), \{Eof(x)\}/AfterIO(in), \{\neg Eof(x)\}/BeforeIO(in)\})$

$\beta(out, v) \equiv (\{OutGate(out), Int(v), havetype(out,v), BeforeIO(out), FullData(v)\},$
$\qquad \{\phi/EmptyData(v), \{Eof(v)\}/AfterIO(out), \{\neg Eof(v)\}/BeforeIO(out)\})$

$input(in, x) \equiv (\alpha(in, x))^* \qquad\qquad output(out, v) \equiv (\beta(out, v))^*$

$glue(in, out, x) \equiv (\alpha(in, x); \beta(out, x))^*$

$compute_i$ realizes a certain computing function, and the details are ignored. State definition:

$w_1 = \{InGate(in), Int(x), havetype(in,x), BeforeIO(in), EmptyData(x), \neg Eof(x)\}$

$w_2 = \{InGate(in), Int(x), havetype(in,x), FullData(x), BeforeIO(in)\}$

$w_3 = \{InGate(in), Int(x), havetype(in,x), BeforeIO(in), EmptyData(x), Eof(x)\}$

$w_4 = \{InGate(in), Int(x), havetype(in,x), FullData(x), AfterIO(in)\}$

$w_5 = \{OutGate(out), Int(v), havetype(out,v), BeforeIO(out), FullData(v), \neg Eof(v)\}$

$w_6 = \{OutGate(out), Int(v), havetype(out,v), EmptyData(v), BeforeIO(out)\}$

$w_7 = \{OutGate(out), Int(v), havetype(out,v), BeforeIO(out), FullData(v), Eof(v)\}$

$w_8 = \{OutGate(out), Int(v), havetype(out,v), EmptyData(v), AfterIO(out)\}$

and then $\qquad T\alpha(in, x) = \{(w_1, w_2), (w_3, w_4)\} \qquad T\beta(out, v) = \{(w_5, w_6), (w_7, w_8)\}$
$\qquad\qquad Tinput(in, x) = (T\alpha(in, x))^* \qquad Toutput(out, v) = (T\beta(out, v))^*$
$\qquad\qquad Tglue(in, out, x) = (T\alpha(in, x) \circ T\beta(out, v))^*$

3.2.2   TBox.

Some new axioms are added to describe some constraints of the Pipeline-Filter styled SA based on the general description in Section 3.1.

$CompositeFitler \equiv Component \cap \geq 1havepart.CompositeFilter \cap \geq 0havapart.Pipe$
$\qquad\qquad \cap \geq 0linkto.Pipe$

$Filter \equiv CompositeFilter \cap \forall havepart.\bot \qquad$ ($\bot$ denotes bottom concept)

$Int \subseteq Type \qquad Eof \subseteq Int \qquad Gate \equiv (InGate \cup OutGate) \cap = 1havapart.Int$

$EmptyData \equiv Int \cap [input(in, x)]FullData$

$FullData \equiv Int \cap [output(out, v)]EmptyData$

$BeforeCompute \equiv CompositeFilter \cap [compute_i(x)]AfterCompute$

$AfterCompute \subseteq CompositeFilter \quad Pipe \equiv Connector \cap = 1linkto.CompositeFilter$

$BeforeGlue \equiv Pipe \cap [glue(in, out, x)]AfterGlue \qquad AfterGlue \subseteq Pipe$

3.2.3   ABox. Fig.2 depicts the *compositefilter* in Fig.1, where dot denotes instances, directive real line denotes relation, directive dashed denotes the cooperating relation between concepts, and the word below is action name.

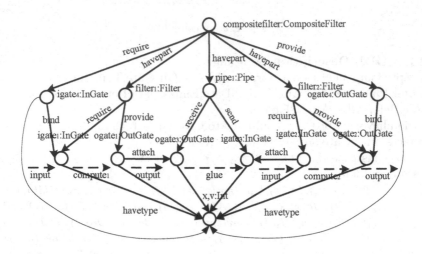

Fig. 2. An Instance in ABox

4   Application in Consistency Detection Aspect

Dynamic SA reconfigures during executing time, thus change and evolution arise and consistency detection is necessary. The decidable reasoning and mature tools of DDL support the consistency detection of dynamic SA very well, such as Loom [7] and Racer [8]. The corresponding relation between the reasoning mechanism of DDL and the consistency detection of dynamic SA is depicted as Table 1.

Table 1. Detecting Consistency Problem

Consistency problem of SA	Detecting support of DDL reasoning	Example of inconsistency problems
Consistency problem of SA description	Satisfiability detection of TBox concept	$Com_2 \equiv \neg Com_1 \cap \ldots$ $Com_2 \subseteq Com_1$
Consistency problem between SA description and instances	Consistency detection of DDL Knowledge base	$Com_2 \subseteq \neg Com_1$ $Com_2(a_1)$ $Com_1(a_1)$
Consistency problem among SA instances	Consistency detection of ABox assertion	$Com_1(a)$ $Con_1(p)$ $Int(x)$ $Double(y)$ $OutGate(og_1)$ $OutGate(og_2)$ $provide(a, og_1)$ $havetype(og_1, x)$ $receive(p, og_2)$ $havetype(og_2, y)$ $attach(og_1, og_2)$
Consistency problem within an instance of SA	Instance detection of ABox	$BeforeIO(in)$ $AfterIO(in)$

Taking the consistency problem among SA instances as an example, if there is $Double \subseteq \neg Int \cap \ldots$ in Tbox, that is type $Double$ and Int are inconsistent, and for an assertion set $A_0 = \{OutGate(og_1), OutGate(og_2), havetype(og_1, x), havetype(og_2, y), Int(x), Double(y)\}$, according to the $ALCN\text{-}Tableau$ arithmetic, extend $OutGate(og_2)$ using $\cap -rule$ and get another assertion set $A_1 = \{OutGate(og_1), OutGate(og_2), havetype(og_1, x), havetype(og_2, y), Int(x), Double(y), Int(y)\}$, finally detect the inconsistency $\{Double(y), Int(y)\}$.

"trace concept" and "trace relation" [9] can be explicitly added into the model and the querying function of Loom and Racer can assist the detection.

5   Related Work

DL is a kind of Object-Oriented formalization for knowledge representation. In 1991, Schmidt-Schauß and Smolka proposed the minimal DL language of practice AL [10]. Wolter presented a kind of dynamic DL theory [4], in which action is seen as a modal operator and enhances the expressing ability of DL. According to the character and requirement of Semantic Web, Zhongzhi Shi etc. proposed a kind of new DDL [5], integrating the static and dynamic knowledge and providing the legible semantic and decidable reasoning service.

At present, many Architecture Description Language (ADL) have been realized: XYZ/ADL [11] supports the stepwise transition from higher-level architectures to lower-level architectures; based on the Pi-calculus, Darwin [12] is used to describe distributing architecture; π-ADL [13] specifies the dynamic and mobile architecture; etc. Considering the better expressing ability and decidable reasoning, this paper presents a kind of SA model based on the DDL.

6   Conclusion

DL is one of effective tools for knowledge representation, while DDL supports the representation of static and dynamic knowledge at the same time, providing better expressing ability and decidable reasoning. This paper presents a kind of SA model based on the DDL: the expressing ability facilitates the description of constraints satisfied by each part of SA, the decidable reasoning can efficiently detect some consistency problems existed in dynamic SA, and DDL classifies the components and supports the incremental specification and modularity.

There is a lot of work need to do, for example, based on the fruits of research on DDL, to perfect the SA model, and then to define the ADL and to develop the corresponding system supporting it. On the other hand, the research on resolving the consistency problem of dynamic SA becomes the emphasis of next-step work.

References

1. Bass, L., Clements, P., Kazman, R.: Software Architecture in Practice. Addison-Wesley (1998)
2. Liu, X., Li, M., Wang, Q., Zhou, J.: Review of software architecture analysis and evaluation methods. Jounal of Computer Research and Development **42**(7) (2005)

3. Baader, F., Nutt, W.: Basic Description Logics. In Baader, F., Calvanese, D., McGuinness, D., Nardi, D., Patel-Schneider, P.F., eds.: The Description Logic Handbook: Theory, Implementation, and Applications. Cambridge University Press (2003) 43–95

4. Wolter, F., Zakharyaschev, M.: Dynamic Description Logic. In Zakharyaschev, M., Segerberg, K., de Rijke, M., Wansing, H., eds.: Advances in Modal Logic II. CSLI Publications, Stanford (2001) 431–445

5. Shi, Z., Dong, M., Jiang, Y., Zhang, H.: Logic foundation for the Semantic Web. SCIENCE IN CHINA Ser.E Information Sciences **34**(10) (2004) 1123–1138

6. M. Shaw, D.G.: An Introduction to Software Architecture. Advances in Software Engineering and Knowledge Engineering **1** (1993)

7. MacGregor, R.M.: Inside the LOOM description classifier. SIGART Bulletin **2**(3) (1991) 88–92

8. Haarslev, V., Möller, R.: Racer: A core inference engine for the Semantic Web. In: Proceedings of the 2nd International Workshop on Evaluation of Ontology-based Tools (EON2003), located at the 2nd International Semantic Web Conference ISWC 2003, Sanibel Island, Florida, USA, October 20. (2003) 27–36

9. Straeten, R.V.D., Mens, T., Simmonds, J., Jonckers, V.: Using Description Logic to maintain consistency between UML models. In Stevens, P., Whittle, J., Booch, G., eds.: UML 2003 - The Unified Modeling Language. Model Languages and Applications. 6th International Conference, San Francisco, CA, USA, October 2003, Proceedings. Volume 2863 of LNCS., Springer (2003) 326–340

10. Schmidt-Schauβ, M., Smolka, G.: Attributive concept descriptions with complements. Artif. Intell. **48**(1) (1991) 1–26

11. Zhu, X., Tang, Z.: A temporal logic-based software architecture description language XYZ/ADL. Journal of Software **14**(4) (2003) 713–720

12. Magee, J., Dulay, N., Eisenbach, S., Kramer, J.: Specifying distributed software architectures. In: ESEC. (1995) 137–153

13. Oquendo, F.: π-ADL: an architecture description language based on the higher-order typed π-Calculus for specifying dynamic and mobile software architectures. SIGSOFT Softw. Eng. Notes **29**(3) (2004) 1–14

Branch Behavior Characterization for Multimedia Applications

Chia-Lin Yang, Shun-Ying Wang, and Yi-Jung Chen

Department of Computer Science and Information Engineering
National Taiwan University
No. 1, Rooselevet Rd., Sec 4 Taipei, Taiwan 106, R.O.C
{r93104, yangc, d91015}@csie.ntu.edu.tw

Abstract. Modern embedded processors employ dynamic branch prediction to reduce performance penalty caused by branch instructions. Existing branch predictor designs are all based on the behavior of applications on a GPP (general purpose processor). However, for an embedded system, such as smart phone, multimedia applications are the main workload. Therefore, in this paper, we perform detailed analysis on the branch behavior of multimedia applications. We believe that identifying important characteristics of the branch behavior of multimedia applications is important for designing a branch predictor for embedded processors.

1 Introduction

The design of embedded processors is getting complicated to meet the performance demand of multimedia and communication applications. Deeper pipelining is commonly used to improve performance. For example, the Intel Xscale processor [1] has 7 stage pipelines. Therefore, a dynamic branch predictor is usually employed to reduce the performance degradation caused by instructions that alter the execution flow (branch instructions). The branch prediction accuracy is not only critical for performance; it also affects power consumption since mis-predicted branches incur energy wastes.

Existing branch predictor designs are based the branch behavior of applications running on a GPP (general purpose processor). However, the workloads for embedded system are mainly multimedia applications. We found that with a commonly used bi-modal branch predictor [2], multimedia workloads have an average 7.73% mis-prediction rate. This observation confirms with the findings in the work by Bishop et al.[3]. They also found that branch prediction accuracy of multimedia applications is poor due to unpredictable data dependent branches. Therefore, it is important to understand the branch behavior of multimedia applications.

Previous works on workload characterization of multimedia applications focus the memory subsystem [4][5]. Bishop et al.[3] looked at the branch prediction accuracy of multimedia application but they did not analyze the branch behavior

C. Jesshope and C. Egan (Eds.): ACSAC 2006, LNCS 4186, pp. 523–530, 2006.
© Springer-Verlag Berlin Heidelberg 2006

in detail. There are works on characterizing branch behavior, but they focus on the workloads on GPP (e.g., SPEC2000 benchmark)[6]. In this paper, we analyze the branch behavior of multimedia applications through the simulation-based methodology. We assume an ARM-like branch prediction unit: bi-modal branch predictor, return stack. We make the following important observations:

1. Although loops are easier to predict than if-branches, we observe that loops account for 50% of mis-predicted branches. That is because the multimedia applications contain tight loops. The loop iteration count ranges from 3 to 19 on the average for most of the applications tested in this paper.
2. About 90% of loops are counted loops,70% of them are nested loops. If counted loops can be correctly predicted, the branch prediction accuracy can increase up to 8%.
3. The correlation degree between branches varies among applications tested. The percentage of correlation branches in mis-predicted forward branches ranges from 2% to 99.04%. Our experimental results show that if correlation branches can be correctly predicted, the branch prediction accuracy can increase up to 6%.
4. We find only 20% of mis-predicted if-branches shows regularity in control variable values. This indicates that a value-based branch predictor [7] may not be effective for multimedia applications.

The rest of this paper is organized as following. Section 2 presents the simulation methodology. In Section 3, we characterize mis-predicted branches. Section 4 discusses possible enhancements to the branch predictor design. Finally, Section 5 concludes.

2   Evaluation Methodology

We adopt the simulation-based approach for the branch behavior characterization of multimedia applications. We use the SimpleScalar tool set [8] as our simulator. We use the MediaBench suit [9] as our target applications. The MediaBench contains a set of multimedia applications: adpcm encoder/decoder, g721 encoder/decoder, jpeg encoder/decoder, epic/unepic, lame, and mpeg encoder/decoder. We assume an ARM-like architecture. The branch prediction unit contains a bi-modal branch predictor, and return stack. The arm instruction set contains predicted instructions to eliminate branch instructions. Figure 1 shows the branch prediction accuracy of multimedia applications for an ARM-like architecture. We can see that most of the multimedia applications have only about 90% of prediction accuracy. To understand the behavior of mispredicted branches, we look into both the backward and forward branches. For mis-predicted backward branches, we quantify the distribution of counted loop, general loops, and nested loops. For mis-predicted forward branches, we analyze three properties: correlation between branches, regularity of control variable values of if-branches, and how the control variable values are generated. Note that some of the mis-predicted branches are located in the pre-built libraries which

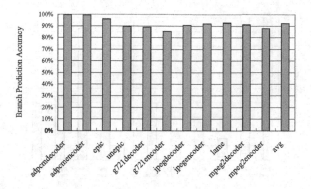

Fig. 1. Branch prediction accuracy of MediaBench Benchmarks on ARM architecture

do not have source codes. Therefore, the results presented below only cover the branches in the user codes.

3   Characteristics of Mispredicted Branches

Figure 2 shows that distribution of forward and backward branches in mispredicted branches. We can see that even though backward branches are easy to predict, they still account for a significant number of mis-predicted branches. With a bi-modal branch predictor, a loop branch is mis-predicted in the last iteration. Therefore, a tighter loop would result in higher mis-prediction rate. Figure 3 shows the loop iteration on the average for each application. We can see that, except for the adpcm encoder/decoder, the average iteration counts range from 3 to 19. Therefore, we will look into both the forward and backward branches carefully in the sections below.

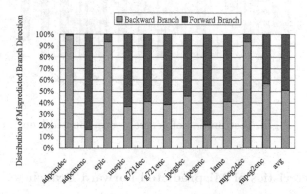

Fig. 2. Backward and forward branch distribution in mis-predicted branches

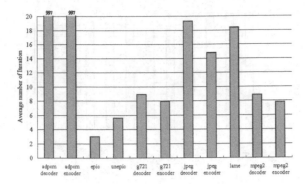

Fig. 3. Distribution of Loop Iteration

3.1   Characteristics of Mispredicted Backward Branches

There are two forms of loops, general loops vs. counted loops. We further divide counted loops into two categories: loop iteration count can be determined at compile time vs. run time. Figure 4 shows the distribution. We can see that most of backward branches are counted loops, 90% on average. Roughly half of counted loops have statically determined iteration counts. We also find most of counted loops are nested loops, 70% on average. Since counted loops have predictable looping behavior, it presents opportunity for improving branch predictordesign.

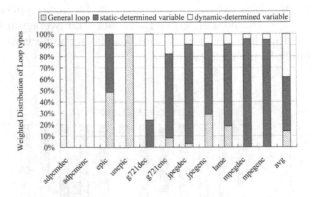

Fig. 4. Distribution of general loops, counted loops

3.2   Characteristics of Mispredicted Forward Branches

To understand the behavior of mispredicted forward branches, we classify the forward branches in three aspects. We first analyze correlation between branches. We then identify the regularity of control variable value of if-branches. This gives

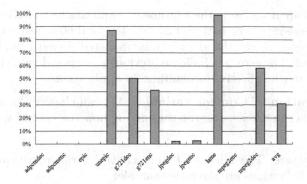

Fig. 5. Distribution of correlation branches in mis-predicted forward branches

us an insight on the effectiveness of the previously proposed value-based branch predictor [10]. Finally, we analyze the sources of if-branch control variables.

Correlation between Branches. We identify the correlation between branches by examining the source codes. Figure 5 shows the percentage of correlation branches among mis-predicted forward branches. We see the distribution of correlation branches varies among applications. For lame, almost 100% of mis-predicted branches exhibit correlation property. However, for the jpeg encoder/ decoder, we only see 2 to 3% of mis-predicted branches are correlation branches. On average, about 31% of mis-predicted forward branches are correlation branches.

Regularity of Control Variable Values. Some of the control variable values actually present regularity: stride and repeating patterns. Figure 6 shows the distribution of mispredicted forward branches in terms of the value pattern of control variables: stride, repeating and irregular. Note that there are no mispredicted forward branches in the adpcm decoder. We can see that most of control

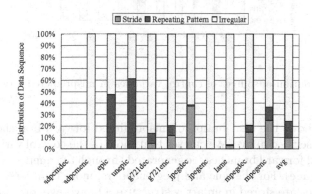

Fig. 6. Distribution of control variable value pattern in mispredicted forward branches

variable values are irregular in the multimedia applications tested except for epic and unepic where repeating pattern takes up 45% and 60%, respectively. On average, 22% of control variable data in mis-predicted forward branches exhibit regular patterns. These results indicate previously proposed value-based branch predictor may not be effective for multimedia applications.

Value Generation of Control Variables. We can classify the mis-predicted forward branches in three categories considering how the control variable values are generated:

1. Array structure. The values of branch control variable are stored in array structure. Followings are the code example:

$$for\ (\ i\ =\ 0;\ i\ <\ n;\ i++\ )\{$$
$$if\ (im[i]\ ==\ 0)$$
$$\{\ statement;\ \}$$
$$\}$$

For this type of branches, the branches can actually be resolved earlier if we can compare the array with the branching conditions in parallel.

2. Calculation. The value of branch control variable is produced by a sequence of operations like add, sub, shift, etc.

3. Function parameters/return values. The value of branch control variable could come from either function parameters or return value of a function call.

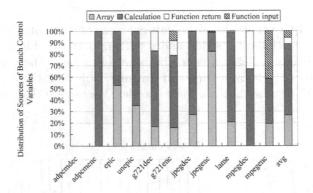

Fig. 7. Distribution of sources of control variables in mispredicted forward branches

Figure 7 shows the distribution of mispredicted forward branches in the four categories described above. We can see that most of the control variable values of mis-predicted forward branches are generated through a sequence of computation (62% on average). For the epic and jpeg encoders, more than 50% of the control variable values are stored in an array structure. On average, only 10% of control variable values are from function parameters or return value.

4   Discussion

In this section, we discuss possible branch predictor enhancements based on the analysis presented in the above. Figure 8 shows the distribution of 5 categories of mis-predicted instructions in the dynamic branch instruction stream: counted loops, predictable control variable values of if branches, correlation branches, the value of branch control variable are stored in array structure or through a sequence of calculation. We can see that counted loop and correlation branches are two main types that are worth paying attention. For example, in the mpeg2 encoder, if the counted loops can be predicted correctly, the branch prediction accuracy can increase 8%. Several applications could benefit from correlation branch predictor, such as the g721 encoder and decoder. The results also show that value-based branch predictor is not effective for multimedia applications.

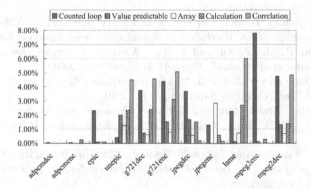

Fig. 8. Distribution of 5 branching types in dynamic branch instructions

To solve the counted loop problem, we can adopt the approach of the Itanium architecture which provides a special counted loop branch instruction (the br.cloop instruction) and the Loop Counting application register (LC) [11]. The challenge of adopting this approach is to handle the nested loops which are commonly seen in multimedia applications. To increase the predictability of correlation branches, we could adopt the correlation branch predictor commonly seen in a modern GPP. However, the higher design complexity of the correlation branch predictor would lead to more energy consumption compared to the bi-modal branch predictor used in most of current embedded processors. Since low power is a critical design issue of an embedded processor, the energy/performance tradeoff by adopting correlation branch predictor needs to be carefully evaluated.

5   Conclusion

In this paper, we characterize the branch behavior of multimedia applications. We find that the forward and backward branches account for 50% of mis-predicted branches, respectively. 90% of mis-predicted backward branches are counted loops, and 31% of mis-predicted forward branches are correlation branches. Therefore, to increase branch prediction accuracy, we should target at both correlation branches and counted loops. We are currently investigating techniques to improve the prediction accuracy of these two types of branches.

Acknowledgements. This work is supported in part by research grants from ROC Industrial Technology Research Institute 95-S-B43.

References

1. *Intel XScale Microarchitecture*, 2000.
2. J.E. Smith, "A study of branch prediction strategies," *8th International Symposium on Computer Architecture*, 1981.
3. Benjamin Bishop, Thomas P. Kelliher, and Mary Jane Irwin, "A detailed analysis of mediabench," *IEEE Workshop on Signal Processing Systems*, November 1999.
4. HS. Sohoni, R. Min Z. Xu, and Y. Hu, "A study of memory system performance of multimedia applications," *Proc. ACM Sigmetrics*, 2001.
5. N. Slingerland and A. J. Smith, "Cache performance for multimedia applications," *Proc. ACM Intl. Conf. on Supercomputing*, 2001.
6. Jason Fritts, *Architecture and Compiler Design Issues in Programmable Media Processors*, Ph.D. thesis, Dept. of Electrical Engineering, Princeton University, 2000.
7. Yiannakis Sazeides and James E. Smith, "The predictability of data values," *Proceedings of the 30th Annual ACM/IEEE International Symposium on Microarchitecture*, December 1997.
8. Doug Burger, Todd M. Austin, and Steve Bennett, "Evaluating future microprocessors: The simplescalar tool set," Tech. Rep. CS-TR-96-1308, University of Wisconsin-Madison, July 1996, http://www.simplescalar.com.
9. Chunho Lee, Miodrag Potkonjak, and William H. Mangione-Smithg, "Mediabench: A tool for evaluating and synthesizing multimedia and communications systems," *Proc. 30th Annual International Symposium on Microarchitecture*, pp. 330–335, December 1997.
10. Bohuslav Rychlik, John Faistl, Bryon Krug, and John P. Shen, "Efficacy and performance impact of value prediction," *Intl. Conf. on Parallel Arch. and Comp*, 1998.
11. *Intel Itanium Architecture Software Developer's Manual*, 2002.

Optimization and Evaluating of StreamYGX2 on MASA Stream Processor

Mei Wen, Nan Wu, Changqing Xun, Wei Wu, and Chunyuan Zhang

Computer School, National University of Defense Technology
Chang Sha, Hu Nan, P.R. of China, 410073
meiwen@nudt.edu.cn

Abstract. The characteristics of the stream architectures--stress locality, parallelism, decoupling of memory operations and computation--matches the capabilities of modern semiconductor technology with computer-intensive parallel applications and allow for high performance of compiler optimized code. This paper presents a detailed study of porting the fluid dynamics calculation with 2D Lagrange and Euler Method to a stream processor---- MASA.

Keywords: stream processor, scientific computing, Ygx2, 2D Lagrange-Euler Method.

1 Introduction

YGX2 combines Lagrange method and Euler method to calculate 2D detonation hydrodynamics problems. There are mainly three reasons that StreamYGX2 was chose as our study of application development on MASA [1]. Firstly, YGX2 is one of IAPCM (Beijing Institute of Application Physics and Computing Mathematics) Benchmarks, which shares many characteristics with other scientific codes. Secondly, the program is fairly straightforward to understand, and the amount of experiments and data analysis required is reasonable. Finally, several versions of conventional processors are available now for comparison and reference of our study. These problems are also commonly found in other scientific codes. The techniques we developed for StreamYGX2 are generally applicable to scientific codes on MASA and other stream processors, and are not limited to fluid dynamics. Our research in StreamYGX2 covers extensive experiments in the MASA hardware design and software systems. Moreover, we will be honored to provide feedback to the MASA architecture and compilation teams, if needed.

Since this paper mainly studies the performance of single chips, of which the size of the mesh grid is about 40000 particles. YGX2 calculates partial differential equation by finite difference approach, in order to obtain density, velocity, pressure and energy of particles in 2D mesh grid. In this case, the calculation of every particle needs relative values of up to 8 neighbors. We discussed the algorithm on MASA in [6].

C. Jesshope and C. Egan (Eds.): ACSAC 2006, LNCS 4186, pp. 531–537, 2006.
© Springer-Verlag Berlin Heidelberg 2006

2 Optimization of StreamYGX2

We developed StreamYGX2 to perform the fluid computing of YGX2, using highly parallel hardware of MASA. StreamYGX2 performs special processing on original bounds that has short parallelism. At the same time strip-mining creates new boundary particles. Since values of the first row and the last row in each batch can not be calculated correctly, these new boundary particles need to be computed repeatedly in neighboring batches. Correct values must replace wrong values. Batches of long stream need redundant boundary rows other than simply striped. This process needs data reorganization. However, a row of particles is not sequential records in stream. Since kernel cannot operate on irregular records very well, data reorganization is completed in scalar core rather than stream core. This can be briefly illustrated in the pseudo-code (Kernel uvxrlUv) below:

```
...... //other kernel
for(int i=0;i<NUM;i++)// strip-mining incurs loop (in the case, NUM=12)
        {
               streamLoad(p[NUM], 3600 ,ysp); //non-block transfer
          im_stream<im_float> pin = ysp(0,3600); //repair stream
          uvxrlUv(pin,pout); //invoke kernel uvxrlUv, StreamYGX2 consists of 18
     kernels
          streamSave(pout, 3600 ,ysp) // non-block transfer
          ...... // scalar operations of data reorganizing between batches
        }
....... // scalar operation between Kernels
```

Since there is no data dependency between several invocations of the same kernel while processing different batches, this loop can be software pipelined in order to hide memory latency and scalar operation latency. In our implementation, scalar operations have little detrimental effect on the overall performance (only 18% of the total run time). The other advantage of running the same kernel in series is that the kernel's microcode is only loaded once every 12 kernel invocations, which expresses time locality.

To attain high performance on MASA, we must ensure program latency tolerance, parallelism, and locality. Share memory and non-block transfer allow executing scalar operations, memory operations and kernel computations concurrently and frequently. StreamYGX2 has abundant parallelism, not only because each particle can be calculated independently from any other particles, but also different properties can be computed in a separate step. This parallelism is used to operate MASA's 8 cluster in SIMD fashion. Multiple memory hierarchies capture locality that is expressed by stream model. This section explains what optimizations are available on MASA.Several optimizations are effective at improving the performance of application on MASA. This paper presents two important software optimizations for scientific computing: 1. how loop unrolling at kernel level improves inner-loop IPC, 2. how software-pipelining at stream level hides memory latency.

A kernel is a computation intensive function that operates on streams. It usually consists of a single, computation-intensive loop, thus loop unrolling highly increases functional unit utility. The effectiveness of optimization is more evident for MASA with several symmetrical multiply-add units than without these units.

Figures 1a and 1b show the effect of applying loop unrolling to the kernel Roqpp. In each figure, the 6 columns represent the cluster's 6 functional units, and the box represents an instruction that starts execution at a particular cycle. The optimized kernel is unrolled 4 times to achieve an execution rate that is 3.45 time of the original kernel. It takes 220 cycles for each loop iteration, each cycle achieve four original independent interactions with unrolled loop. However, loop unrolling is not effective for the kernel with heavy workload, because IPC is high enough to support functional units to achieve almost peak arithmetic rate.

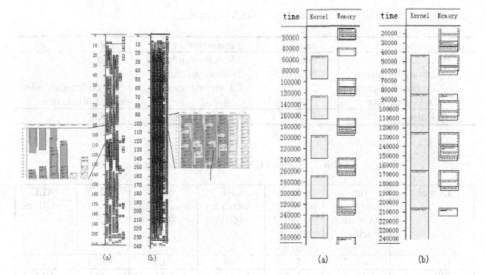

Fig. 1. (left) Schedules of the kernel Roqpp, before, and after loop unrolling is applied – (a) and (b) respectively[1]

Fig. 2. (right) Snippet of execution of Kernel uvxrlUv showing the improvement in overlap of memory and kernel operations. Left column of both (a) and (b) represents a kernel being executed, and the right columns are for memory operations.

Kernels of StreamYGX2 process long streams in smaller batches. There is no data dependency between different batches. Software pipelining the loop so that kernels from one stage can be executed at the same time as serial memory accesses between kernels of other stages. Figure 2 shows a snippet of execution of Kernel uvxrlUv. Figure 2a and 2b represent both before and after the application of software pipelining respectively. The next kernel invocation cannot start immediately after the last invocation finishes, and it must wait for the intervening memory load to complete as shown in Figure 2a. Figure 2b shows a perfect overlap of memory and computation. Scalar operation between batches is also executed at the same time as memory operation.

---

[1] All results of compiler and running are obtained from MASA compiler and MASA cycle-accurate simulator which can be downloaded from our academic website http:// masa. nudt.edu.cn.

3 Performance Evaluating

We developed both the C++ cycle accurate simulator [2] of MASA and the hardware emulator on Xilinx Vertex4 FPGA based on ISIM[2]. The parameters of the MASA system are summarized in Table 1. The C++ cycle accurate simulator simulates the MASA's behavior cycle-accurately. Experiments were carried out for the run of the fluid system of StreamYGX2.

Table 1. MASA parameters

Parameter	value	Parameter	value
Word length	64bit	Memory bandwidth	5.3GB/s
Operating frequency	500MHz	Number of clusters	8
Number of streams address generators	2	Cluster component	4 adder-multiplier units, 1 divide unit
SRF size	512KB	Peak performance	36GFlops

Table 2. StreamYGX2 kernels Performance

Kernel	run time every invocation (cycle)	float-point operates/ SRF reference	LRF bandwidth (GB/s)	SRF bandwidth (GB/s)	IPC[3]	ALU Gflops
Ell	4187	5	304	20.5	20.4	12
Ell2	100212	112	351	1.15	23	19.1
Meuvef	7174	4	219	20	15.3	10.5
Meuvfue	4872	9	443	18	24.2	19.5
Meuvm1	3960	2	141	14.5	11.8	3.1
Meuvmead	3743	5	531	34.5	39.2	20.1
Meuvuv1	3910	6	468	21.3	36.2	16.8
Meuvuv2	3040	6	411	25.3	24.4	17.9
Meuvxr41	2101	4	325	27.4	22.3	13.7
Roqpden	4080	14	526	14.1	34.3	24
Roqpp	50475	51	273	1.71	17.6	10.9
Roqpq1	9169	21	619	9.5	36.7	25.3
Roqpq2	3566	10	466	16.08	27.5	19.1
Uvxrlden	3788	13	524	15.1	31.3	25.1
Uvxrluv	54686	88	517	2.37	29.5	25.9
Uvxrluv0	1118	71	131	0.7	6.9	6.2
Xrwxlrl1	25699	29	371	4.41	22.4	16
Xrwxlrl2	21556	56	417	2.63	27.1	18.5
weighted average		68.8	385	4.8	24.2	18.4

---

[2] Cycle Accurate Simulator of Imagine.
[3] Including non-arithmetic instruction.

The arithmetic intensity and locality are tightly related. In most cases, the higher arithmetic intensity, the more stress is the locality. Arithmetic intensity of application refers to the ratio of arithmetic to global bandwidth, while arithmetic intensity of kernel refers to the ratio of arithmetic to SRF bandwidth. Table 2 summarizes the statistics of all kernels. The last row of Table 2 shows the weighted average of StreamYGX2. The ratio used in calculation of weighted average is the run time of one kernel to the run time of total kernels. The second column of Table 2 shows the run time of each Kernel invocation. The third column of Table 2 shows arithmetic to memory bandwidth ratio at floating point in each Kernel. The weighted average is 68.8 (perform over 68.8 floating point operations for each 64-bit word transferred over the SRF interface), which allows ALU array executes with full loads. The cluster stalls, which were caused by SRF data supply delay, are less than 1% of the kernel's run time.

LRF bandwidth and SRF bandwidth (only account bandwidth between cluster and SRF, other SRF client includes net interface, DRAM and scalar core) during Kernel execution are shown in the fourth column and fifth column of Table 2. More than 90% of references are made to the LRF due to the large mounts of kernel locality available in this application. SRF bandwidth which is no more than 65% of the peak (51.2GB/s) shows SRF bandwidth can satisfy client requirements, including bursty SRF bandwidth requirements.

Instructions per cycle (IPC) and performance result (Gflops) of each Kernel are shown in the sixth and seventh column. As shown in the Table, MASA demonstrates potential to deliver high performance.

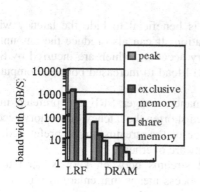

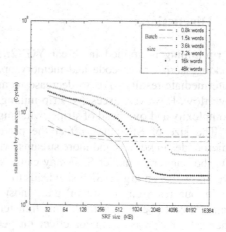

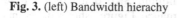

Fig. 3. (left) Bandwidth hierachy   **Fig. 5.** (right) Stall caused by data access affected by varied sizes of SRF and various strips

Figure3 illustrates the bandwidth of the memory hierarchy, in three levels. The access ratio of the three levels of the memory hierarchy (DRAM, SRF, LRF) in the whole application is 1:2.5:114, and the actual bandwidth needs are 2.1GB/s, 7.3GB/s, 386GB/s respectively. Bounds processing requires streams in SRF to be transferred to

DRAM. SRF is mainly used as a buffer between clusters and memory. It is unable to capture the producer-consumer locality between kernels. Nevertheless, locality within kernels is fully captured. Shared memory can dramatically reduce the access of DRAM and SRF, compared to exclusive memory.

StreamYGX2 has abundant Data Level Parallelism (DLP) and Instruction Level Parallelism (ILP), and it is compute-intensive, too. The total runtime of StreamYGX2[4] is 11.8s, while IPC is 24.2. The performance that can be achieved for StreamYGX2, in our experiment, is 18.4Gflops (double-precision). Figure4 shows speedup of Ygx2 running on Alpha21264 (500MHz) versus a number of other processors. The numbers above the bars are the runtime [3]. MASA is approximately 4 times faster than Itanium2 (1.6GHz, optimization flag -o3 -fast).

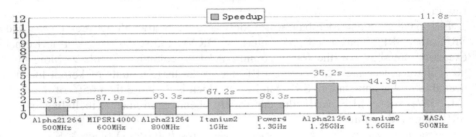

Fig. 4. Speedup of Ygx2 running on various processors, the number above the bars declares the runtime of YGX2 application

4 Discussions

Strip-mining is applied in StreamYGX2. It is beneficial to hide the latency when loading kernel microcode and memory operation. It can also reduce the amount of intermediate results so as to decrease memory accesses, which are incurred by SRF overflow. However, excessive strip-mining will lead to increased bounds, computing complexity and overhead of strips switching.

The size of SRF may affect the performance. Larger SRF can prefetch more microcodes in kernels and more streams, which shorten the latency of memory access. On the contrary, smaller SRF may cause some of the streams not be prefetched. As we know that enlarging SRF size leads to hardware overhead.

In our research in SreamYgx2, most of streams between kernels need to be transferred to be reorganized. This transfer process means that enlarging SRF (more than 512 KB) has no major effect on performance. Our experiments attempted to optimize size and number strips to achieve minimum SRF demands, in order to improve effectiveness and efficiency of the performance. Figure5 shows different data access stalls (memory stall + SRF stall[5]) caused by various sizes of SRF and various strips. The result shows that 3600-words batch with 512KB SRF can achieve the best performance so far. Continuing enlarging SRF can barely reduce the stall and

---

[4] 537 time-steps.

[5] Cluster stalls refers stall when the SRF is not ready to accept stream read or write requests from the clusters. Memory stalls refers stall waiting for a stream load or store to complete.

changing batch sizes will not improve the performance at all. Therefore, it is vital to consider the characteristics of applications when deciding SFR sizes. And the size of SRF determines batch size.

StreamYGX2 shares characteristics with other scientific applications, such as streamFEM-3D, streamFLO and streamMD[4]. The ratio of memory access, SRF access and LRF access of scientific applications shown in table3 is about 1:3:100, and of media process is about 1:10:200[5].

Table 3. References in scientific applications (data of streamYGX2 is one time-step)

Application	LRF Refs	SRF Refs	memory Refs
StreamFEM3D	153.0M	6.3M	1.8M
StreamMD	90.2M	1.6M	0.7M
StreamFLO	234.3M	7.2M	3.4M
StreamYGX2	206.5G	4.6G	1.8G

Furthermore, the application-level access patterns of scientific computing may be irregular. For instance, the scientific applications exhibit large amounts of *irregular producer-consumer locality*, which results from the prevalence of irregular intermediate streams (need to be reorganized). Irregular producer-consumer locality refers to the consumption of the stream occurs in a different sequence than the one it was generated in. Consequently, SRF only captures limited producer-consumer locality.To keep up with the new characteristics of scientific applications, MASA SIMD architecture has to be constantly improved and updated. In terms of hardware, multiple flexible SRF accesses needs to be supported. When irregular producer-consumer locality is captured, the performance will be improved noticeably. In terms of software design, vectorlized stream programming language plays the vital role since it makes coding much easier. Our future task is to try our best to develop StreamYGX2 in other parallel execution modes.

Acknowledgments. This research was supported by NSFC (60473080, 60573103), high performance computing creative team fund (IRT0446).

References

1. Mei Wen, Nan Wu, Haiyan Li, Chunyuan Zhang, Multiple-Morphs Adaptive Stream Architecture, JCST vol.20 No.5, 2005.9.
2. http://masa.nudt.edu.cn
3. Yuan Guoxing, Shao jingyun, Evaluating performance of scientific applications on several high performance processors, Beijing Institute of Application Physics and Computing Mathematics, www.ccw.com.cn, 2003.4
4. Nuwan S. Jayasena, Memory Hierarchy Design for System Computing, Stanford Ph.D. Thesis, 2005
5. Scott Rixner, stream processor architecture , Kluwer Acedemic Publishers,2002
6. Mei Wen, Nan Wu, Changqing Xun, Wei Wu, Chunyuan Zhang, Analysis and Performance Results of a fluid dynamics Application on MASA Stream Processor, ICIS2006, IEEE computer press, Hawaii , 2006

SecureTorrent: A Security Framework for File Swarming

Kenneth Wilson[1] and Philip Machanick[2]

[1] School of ITEE, University of Queensland, St Lucia, Qld 4072, Australia
kenneth.wilson@gmail.com
[2] National ICT Australia and School of ITEE, University of Queensland, St Lucia,
Qld 4072, Australia
philip@itee.uq.edu.au

Abstract. SecureTorrent is a secure file swarming system based on Bit-Torrent. It provides access control, end-to-end confidentiality, and auditability, while maintaining advantages of file swarming. This paper presents an initial performance evaluation. As compared with BitTorrent, the performance overhead of encryption in most cases is negligible, at worst 15%. In a real-world higher latency network, the extra overhead of encryption would be significantly lower.

1 Introduction

File swarming is a peer-to-peer mechanism for distributing content on the Internet. By distributing workload and bandwidth requirements as widely as possible, it aims to eliminate bottlenecks and hot spots. File swarming evolved initially for free content, with no concern for security. Security can be added by e.g. by password-protecting content, but changes to content are a stop-gap solution.

The approach explored in this paper is to add encryption to file swarming. Specifically, encryption has been added to BitTorrent [1]; the resulting system is called *SecureTorrent*. BitTorrent was chosen as a typical, popular example, with source code amenable to the required changes.

A major motivation for file swarming is to speed up file downloads, so the focus in our evaluation is on showing that our implementation has no significant performance cost. Work reported on here is a proof of concept, so SecureTorrent does not include a convenient user interface or set up tools.

Section 2 relates this work to previous work. Section 3 provides an overview of SecureTorrent, starting from a brief description of BitTorrent. Section 4 contains performance measures, followed by conclusions.

2 Related Work

There has not been much previous work on secure file swarming, but it is useful to review some of the alternative approaches to content distribution and to security, as a basis for understanding the design decisions in SecureTorrent. The remainder of this section explores these issues in turn, followed by tying the ideas together as a basis for the design decisions in SecureTorrent.

C. Jesshope and C. Egan (Eds.): ACSAC 2006, LNCS 4186, pp. 538–544, 2006.

2.1   Content Distribution

Two fundamental difficulties in content distribution arise from unpredictable demand and dynamic content (not addressed in this paper), otherwise it would be simple to minimize latency by caching. Studies have shown that the amount of Web traffic that cannot be cached is as high as 20% [2]; even with an infinite cache size, the upper bound for the hit rate is 30-50% [2].

A simple approach to load balancing content distribution is round robin DNS, where a domain name server has multiple addresses for the same name, an approach is in wide use for web sites, with various variations [3]. Round robin DNS only addresses server load, not network congestion. A more sophisticated approach is to use distributed servers, redirecting traffic to the nearest server, as is done by Akamai's *edge* delivery service [4].

Another approach to distribution of like content to multiple users is multicasting (in the network layer: single packet to multiple hosts [5]). We have elsewhere reviewed difficulties with scalability and internet-wide use of multicasting [6].

There are three main types of P2P system. *Purely decentralised* systems (e.g., Chord [7], Gnutella [8], FreeNet [9]) rely on peers finding each other by broadcast messages. *Partially decentralised* systems have dynamically selected "supernodes" with fast network connections to provide searching and routing for parts of the network (modified Gnutella protocol [8] and KaZaA[1]). *Hybrid systems* eschew fault tolerance of no single point of failure for improved performance with static servers for peer discovery and searching (Napster[2], BitTorrent [1]).

The main benefit of peer-to-peer approaches over the other surveyed approaches is their potential to adapt to unpredictable demands.

2.2   Secure P2P Content Distribution

Secure distribution using peer-to-peer file sharing may have some novely, but basic precepts remain the same as in current secure content distribution systems. Two main ideas that have to be implemented: access control and encryption. Authentication may also be an issue, if users have to be identified.

A system has to control who has access to it, and stop a third party from listening in on any transactions. At time of writing, only a few P2P networks implement access control, e.g., KaZaA and Napster, which only use it for accounting. Both use at least one central server, which they can use to authenticate against. Without a central server, access control using authentication would be possible if a Kerberos [10] or LDAP style authentication system is used. This functionality can be handled by the tracker (the server which coordinates file transfers), but it introduces another point of failure. Another option is a distributed Byzantine agreement protocol [11], at the cost of extra broadcasts.

In a purely decentralised P2P network, it is difficult to implement access control without a central server to authenticate against. These networks also

---

[1] http://kazaa.com
[2] http://www.napster.com

make it hard to implement economical peer to peer encryption. Using SSL it can be done very easily, but this raises other issues, such as trust and high computational expense. If a shared key can be agreed on, encryption becomes much less expensive, as most of the computationally expensive operations (in SSL: prime number generation) are not needed. Without a central server, it is unclear how to share the key securely.

The only application using peer-to-peer encryption is Skype[3], using the same underlying partially decentralised network as KaZaA to route phone calls.

2.3   Putting It All Together

If the level of security is no worse than any packet eavesdropping, a secure P2P approach would not offer serious drawbacks compared with a web site download.

The approach in the work reported on here is based on encryption of the data stream, with design compromises based on points in this section. Technologies used are not novel in themselves, so the focus in evaluation is on performance.

3   Overview of SecureTorrent

SecureTorrent is based on BitTorrent, a popular P2P file swarming system. It aims to add access control, end-to-end confidentiality, and auditability to file swarming. The system also stops attackers from intercepting content in transit.

The remainder of this section provides a little more detail of BitTorrent, an overview of details of how SecureTorrent adds security to BitTorrent, and concludes with a brief report on the status of SecureTorrent.

3.1   BitTorrent and SecureTorrent

BitTorrent is a hybrid peer-to-peer system [12]: clients (*peers*) use to a central server (*tracker*) to discover peers. BitTorrent does not support searching; instead, .torrent files containing metadata about content being distributed, including the address of the tracker, and hashes of the content, are used. A BitTorrent peer process loads these metadata files, and contacts the tracker for a list of peers. It then communicates with the other peers in the swarm, trading small chunks (know as pieces) of the content. In this way, the content is distributed across the swarm. Each peer aims to maximise its download rate, and uses strategems such as favouring peers with higher upload rates, and ignoring peers without many pieces of the content [1,13]. File integrity is checked from a hash (stored in the .torrent file) of each piece (usually 256 KB) of the content.

SecureTorrent consists of two pieces of software: the peer and the tracker, each based on BitTorrent versions. They differ from the originals in providing the confidentiality, access control, and auditability required to add security.

Confidentiality and *access control* are achieved in two ways. Confidentiality of transmitted data is ensured by encrypting all peer-to-peer traffic, and peers to

---

[3] http://www.skype.com

the tracker, while access control is implemented by forcing peers to authenticate with the tracker, when they first join the swarm. If the peers do not authenticate, they will not receive a list of other peers, or any encryption keys.

For simplicity of implementation, traffic between the peers and the tracker is encrypted using SSL. SSL encryption is not used for peer-to-peer traffic, mainly because of the need for certificates. SSL is a public key encryption system, which means that two systems can negotiate a secret key over an insecure channel. However, to verify identity of the system, a certificate is used. Providing certification for each peer in the swarm would seriously degrade tracker performance, and also increase data transfers. Consequently, a shared-key system is used.

The shared-key system is uses 128-bit keys (AES encryption standard). When peers authenticate with the tracker, they receive a serialised list of keys, unique to that content. When two peers start their handshake, each randomly selects a key from the list, and then randomly generates an initialisation vector (IV). The key number and IV are then transmitted unencrypted to the other peer, and all traffic after that is encrypted with the key and initialisation vector specified. The keys are never transmitted in clear, and as a random initialisation vector is used each time, the encrypted traffic is no more vunerable than usual.

The shared-key system also implements key swapping. After a random amount of time, each peer will generate a new IV, and pick another key number. The peer then sends these details over the encrypted link, and sends the next packet encrypted with the new parameters. This is done so that if one key becomes compromised, only a segment of the communication is compromised.

Authentication is the weakest link: a peer can give away its copy of the keys.

SecureTorrent provides *auditability* by logging when a peer logs on, and logging event messages from users. Event messages (`started`, `stalled`, `finished`, and `disconnecting`) let the tracker know the current status of the peer. These messages can suggest possible intrusions: e.g., if a single user logs on from multiple IP addresses, and sends lots of `started` and `finished` messages, it would be probable that the account has been compromised. It would also be possible in principle to detect a peer who has not been given the keys by a tracker.

3.2 SecureTorrent Progress

SecureTorrent is a working beta. The encrypted socket code could more efficient, but it is testable, permitting performance evaluation against BitTorrent. It has been verified that SecureTorrent exhibits the same behaviour as BitTorrent in a range of scenarios, including those reported here. If, despite minor implementation inefficiencies, SecureTorrent performs comparably to BitTorrent, with no more difference than reasonable experimental variation, the performance would be acceptable. SecureTorrent could be deployed after additional testing covering a wider variety of conditions (load, different platforms, etc.).

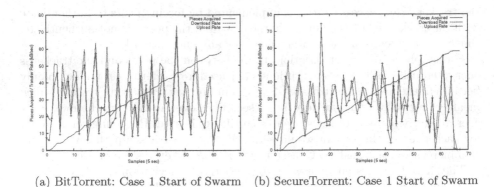

(a) BitTorrent: Case 1 Start of Swarm   (b) SecureTorrent: Case 1 Start of Swarm

Fig. 1. BitTorrent *vs.* SecureTorrent Behaviour

4   SecureTorrent Performance

The overhead of encrypting all traffic should make SecureTorrent slower than
BitTorrent in a CPU-limited situation, which may happen on a fast, lightly
loaded LAN – not the scenario for which file swarming was designed.

To evaluate performance, Internet connections were simulated via bandwidth
shaping on a single ethernet. In a more realistic scenario with longer latencies
for transactions, additional overheards of SecureTorrent should be less significant. The experiment was run on Pentium 4 systems, five running Linux Fedora
Core 2 (SecureTorrent clients), and one Windows XP (tracker). For bandwidth
shaping, the Linux machines used `trickle`[4]. Incoming bandwidth was limited to
800 kb/s, outgoing to 160kb/s, to simulate a typical home internet connection.
Three experimental scenarios simulated different stages of the swarm.

The remainder of this section presents results from each scenario, followed by
an overall summary.

The first experimental case simulated the start of the swarm: one peer (the
seed) had a complete copy of the content. The other four all initially had to
receive pieces from the seed. Only one machine was incurring all the encryption overhead, but the lack of distribution of network overheads should be a
bigger bottleneck; a best-case scenario for SecureTorrent. Figure 1 shows average transfer and piece acquisition rates across the swarm for BitTorrent and
SecureTorrent. Both reach a stable state quickly, with a constant rate of piece
acquisition.

The next two cases simulate operations after the swarm has started. The first
case has two peers as seeds, and the second has three, representing respectively
a middle and a late phase of the swarm. There should be a faster acquisition rate
in these two cases, as there is more aggregate bandwidth available for uploading
pieces. As the number of peers grows, we expect the effect of encryption to be
more significant: the rate of piece acquisition will depend less on network speed.

---

[4] http://monkey.org/~marius/pages/?page=trickle

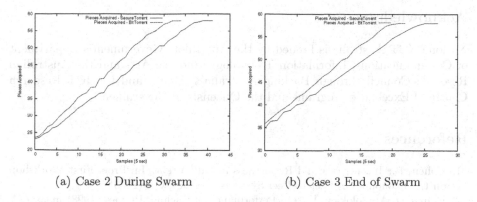

(a) Case 2 During Swarm   (b) Case 3 End of Swarm

Fig. 2. SecureTorrent vs BitTorrent Concluded

Figure 2 compares SecureTorrent and BitTorrent with two and three seeds. The acquisition rate for BitTorrent is slightly higher in all cases, most likely because of inefficiencies in the encrypted sockets library. The biggest difference in any piece acquisition time is 15%, the largest seen in any of our measurements. The two and three seed cases are not significantly different.

In summary: when the most effective bandwidth distribution is taking place, the difference between BitTorrent and SecureTorrent is largest, but the difference in piece acquisition rate was never above 15% in measured examples. BitTorrent and SecureTorrent exhibit the same trends, with both going into a steady state as all of the peers start to exchange pieces.

5 Conclusions

This paper has described an evaluation of a preliminary framework for secure file swarming. The emphasis has been on comparing performance with a standard implementation of file swarming. As expected, the performance impact of encryption is most significant when the network is not a bottleneck.

In a real-world scenario with other traffic on the Internet and long-haul connections, the worst-case scenario is improbable: network latency would be more significant than on our testbed network. Further, as processor speeds improve, overheads of encryption reduce. So we expect larger topologies on a real network with relatively high latencies to perform at least as well as our test bed.

In future work, it would be useful to extend the model to include more aspects of security. Areas to consider include authentication and key distribution. It would also be useful to investigate a wider range of traffic conditions.

We have demonstrated feasibility of adding encryption to file swarming. The approach is relatively simple, and is at least as good a level of protection against eavesdropping as downloading from a web site. Giving an unauthorised third party the keys is possible, but so is giving away log in details; auditability of SecureTorrent creates potential to trap such unauthorized use. Data encryption means that intercepting packets will not make content immediately accessible.

Acknowledgments

National ICT Australia is funded by the Australian Government's Department of Communications, Information Technology, and the Arts and the Australian Research Council through Backing Australia's Ability and the ICT Research Centre of Excellence programs and the Queensland Government.

References

1. Cohen, B.: Incentives Build Robustness in BitTorrent. In: Proc. First Workshop on the Economics of Peer-to-Peer Systems, Berkley, CA (2003)
2. Rousskov, A., Solokiev, V.: On Performance of Caching Proxies (1998) `http:// www.cs.ndsu.nodak.edu/ rousskov/research/cache/squid/profiling/papers`.
3. Colajanni, M., Yu, P.S.: Adaptive TTL schemes for load balancing of distributed web servers. SIGMETRICS Perform. Eval. Rev. **25** (1997) 36–42
4. Akamai: Internet bottlenecks: the case for edge delivery services (2000) `http://www.akamai.com/en/resources/pdf/whitepapers/Akamai_Internet_ Bottlenecks_Whitepaper.pdf`.
5. Thyagarajan, A.S., Casner, S.L., Deering, S.E.: Making the MBone real. In: Proc. INET'95, Hawaii (1995)
6. Machanick, P.and Andrew, B.: Latency improvement in virtual multicasting. In Omondi, A., Sedukhin, S., eds.: Advances in Computer Systems Archietcture (AC-SAC 2003), Aizu-Wakamatsu, Japan (2003) 380–394
7. Stoica, I., Morris, R., Karger, D., Kaashoek, F., Balakrishnan, H.: Chord: A scalable Peer-To-Peer lookup service for internet applications. In: Proc. 2001 ACM SIGCOMM Conference, San Diego, CA (2001) 149–160
8. Ripeanu, M.: Peer-to-peer architecture case study: Gnutella network. In: Proc. Int. Conf. on Peer-to-peer Computing. (2001) 99–100
9. Clarke, I., Sandberg, O., Wiley, B., Hong, T.W.: Freenet: A distributed anonymous information storage and retrieval system. In: In Proc. ICSI Workshop on Design Issues in Anonymity and Unobservability, Berkeley, CA (2000) 46–66
10. Kohl, J., Neuman, B.: RFC1510 The Kerberos Network Authentication Service (1993) `http://www.faqs.org/rfcs/rfc1510.html`.
11. Cachin, C.: Distributing trust on the Internet. In: Proc. Conf. on Dependable Systems and Networks (DSN-2001), Gothenborg, Sweden (2001) 183–192
12. Androutsellis-Theotokis, S., Spinellis, D.: A survey of peer-to-peer content distribution technologies. ACM Comput. Surv. **36** (2004) 335–371
13. Izal, M., Urvoy-Keller, G., Biersack, E.W., Felber, P.A., Al Hamra, A., Garces-Erice, L.: Dissecting BitTorrent: five months in a torrent's lifetime. In: PAM'2004, 5th annual Passive & Active Measurement Workshop. (2004)

Register Allocation on Stream Processor
with Local Register File

Nan Wu, Mei Wen, Ju Ren, Yi He, and Chunyuan Zhang

Computer School, National University of Defense Technology
Chang Sha, Hu Nan, P.R. of China, 410073
nanwu@nudt.edu.cn

Abstract. Emerging stream processors for intensive computing use local register file to support ALUs array and use VLIW to explore instruction level parallelism. The current VLIW compilers for local register file such as ISCD work well on moderate media application without considering register allocation pressure. However, more complicated applications and optimizations that increase the size of the working set such as software pipelining make consideration of register pressure during the scheduling process. Based on ISCD complier, this paper presents two new techniques: spilling schedule and basic block repartition that compose a new schedule algorithm to alleviate register pressure. Experimental results show that it can deal with heavy workload application very well. The algorithm can also be applied to other microprocessors with the similar register architecture.

Keywords: stream processor, VLIW, register allocation, local register file, spilling.

1 Introduction

Along with the requirement to computation performance increasing in entertainment, national defense, commerce, computation intensive application is becoming the main workload of microprocessor. Computation intensive application demands high performance processor (10~100Gflops/s). As a result some emerging programmable processors for intensive computation, such as Imagine[1], Merrimac[2], MASA[3], are noticeable. They are all called *stream processor* that achieve high performance by using a large amount of ALUs, the requirement for the register file's size and bandwidth is very high. Since conventional central register file, cannot satisfy the requirement [4], stream processors all use distributed register file with shared bus connected.

In the mid-1990's, Scott Rixner and Peter Mattson first introduced the concept of distributed register file in stream architecture [4] which is called local register file (LRF), and developed compiler ISCD for it. Till now, ISCD has been improved continually. ISCD deals with VLIW schedule for distributed register file, which is employed in Imagine stream media processor and Merrimac. However, since the ISCD compiler does not consider registers during the scheduling process, it is possible for more registers to be required than are available in a register file. Register pressure is not as important for a media processor because the working set of most media processing

C. Jesshope and C. Egan (Eds.): ACSAC 2006, LNCS 4186, pp. 545–551, 2006.
© Springer-Verlag Berlin Heidelberg 2006

functions is relatively small and distributed register file architecture supports a large number of registers. As implemented, the ISCD compiler does not incorporate any mechanism to alleviate register pressure. However, more complicated application (e.g. science computing) and optimizations that increase the size of the working set such as software pipelining make consideration of register pressure during the scheduling process. If we use ISCD to compile these heavy workload programs, the ISCD will get a register allocation spilling failed and terminate. Peter Mattson the designer of ISCD agrees that this problem will limit the distributed register file architecture to extend to more application domains [1].This paper presents two new techniques as follows to alleviate register pressure.

2   VLIW Compiler for Distributed Register File

Since distributed register file processor owns a number of ALUs, VLIW is often used to exploit instruction level parallelism (ILP). Functional units array usually is divided into multiple clusters, while each cluster consists of several functional units including ALUs and other functional units. In stream processor, one VLIW is issued at every cycle, while multiple VLIWs can be pipelined.

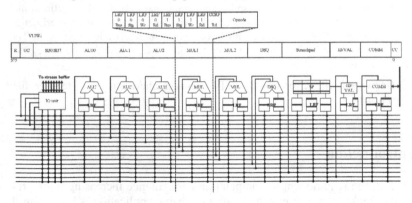

Fig. 1. VLIW format and functional units of Imagine stream processor

Communication scheduling and basic block partition [1], which has been never used in compilation for conventional central register file, are employed in the step, especially for distributed register file. Communication scheduling is responsible for data transfer between local register files. In the register allocation of scalar processor with single central register file, if any nodes are marked as actual spills, we generate spill code store/load to temporarily pop the variable to memory. However, in stream architecture the random memory accessing is limited, while only the stream memory accessing is permitted. It's impossible for complier to construct a stream for the variable that spills in a LRF, because the number of streams is fixed before schedule. Furthermore, since the other LRFs may have idle registers, it's wasteful of popping this variable to memory.

The original ISCD schedule strategy allocates the register at the last step and does not consider it before. In fact, the failure is not caused by the register allocation algorithm itself, because after instruction schedule and communication schedule, every variable is in a fixed LRF at a certain cycle. It is the main reason of register allocation failure that the register allocation algorithm at the last step can not allocate registers among LRFs if some LRFs spill.

An algorithm predicting the LRFs usage when choosing LRF during instruction and communication schedule could avoid the LRF spilling. But the scheduling process for a VLIW architecture is already NP-complete and shared interconnect introduces additional, non-orthogonal resources to the allocation problem so an exact approach is difficult [1]. We try other two naïve method: *spilling schedule* which deals with register pressure after the schedule and *basic block repartition* which deals with register pressure before the schedule.

3 Spilling Schedule

The ISCD compiler allocates registers for each register file separately using conventional techniques. Once the ISCD compiler has constructed the webs for a given register file, it assigns webs to registers using a standard interference graph and graph coloring [5]. The flow of a traditional graph coloring algorithm is shown in figure 2. Because of low register pressure and strict memory access limitation, ISCD cut off the spill procedure of the algorithm (shown as dashed in figure 2). So when it failed to finding a k-coloring of interference graph, the compiling will stop immediately.

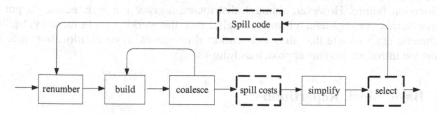

Fig. 2. The flow of a traditional register allocation algorithm

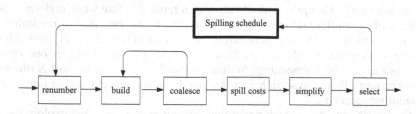

Fig. 3. The flow of the improved register allocation algorithm

This paper improves the traditional register allocation algorithm for distributed register file, by introducing a new approach called *spilling schedule*, which synthesized techniques of communication schedule and traditional spilling process. In the improved algorithm shown in figure 3, the nodes marked as actual spills are popped to other LRFs instead of memory. Basic principles of spilling schedule is: adding copy operations to allow a value to be stored in another register file until just before it is used, and moving operations from functional units with high register pressure to that with relatively low register pressure. Spilling schedule shorten the live ranges of some nodes in interference graph that will alleviate register allocation pressure of the spilled LRF.

In spilling schedule, the resources used by copy operations should not conflict with that used by previous VLIW and communication schedule. These resources include buses, function units and registers. As referred before, VLIW communication schedule are already NP-complete. Any conflict may result in all schedules being invalid. The same is true for the register allocation. Thus spilling schedule construct a *residual networks*, which composed by all the idle data paths (bus, units) and registers. It's easy to construct the residual networks by marking used resources as "busy" at each cycle based on the result of previous schedules. Then the copy operation can be scheduled directly on residual networks by original communication scheduling of ISCD. The residual network must be updated after spilling schedule for the next spilling process.

Spilling schedule need to pre-allocate all the LRFs before schedule copy operations. Set all the LRFs's size to be infinite before pre-allocate, so the pre-allocate will not failed by spilling. Then, allocate LRFs on previous schedule result to get exact usages of each register file. The popped variable will be stored in the LRF with lowest usage to avoid another spilling. Follows describes the procedure of spilling schedule:Spilling schedule will not increase the schedule length of program, because the Copy operation is always inserted before the consumer operation of the spilling node. It's a most efficient approach to solve the register allocation failure. However, although distributed register file architecture supports a large number of registers, it is much smaller than the working set in memory. Spilling schedule can't ensure that all heavy workload programs' register allocation succeed, thus we introduce another approach as follows.

4   Basic Block Repartition

We present a new basic block partition algorithm. The main idea is that, before instruction scheduling, register workload are considered according the last register allocation result.. Compiler with old algorithm reports failure when register allocation fails, while compiler with new algorithm returns to the first step to repartition basic block according to the last scheduling result and schedule again until allocation succeeds. Continually adding new basic blocks which even includes one operation, can ensure successful scheduling. So times of backtracking are at most N (the number of operations). Result in section 5 shows that the average backtracking time is 2 when scheduling succeeds.

To describe the basic block repartition procedure, we must first explore the notion of a cut of a DAG, which is similar to the definition of "cut" used in Ford-Fulkerson method for solving the maximum-flow problem[6], except that here we enhances constraint on cut. Let $G=<V, E, >$ be a directed acyclic graph, in which V is the set of vertices and E is the set of edges. We distinguish two kinds of vertices in a DAG: a source vertices set S and a sink vertices set T. A cut (V1, V-V1) of a directed acyclic graph G is a partition of V. We says that an edge crosses the cut (V1, V-V1) if one of its endpoints is in V1 and the other is in V-V1. All the edges crossing the cut have to be the same direction (from S to T or from T to S, this constraint is required to ensure repartition against bringing nested basic blocks) .Let Eg be the set of edges crossing a cut. A minimum cut of a DAG is a cut whose |Eg| is minimum over all cuts of the DAG, and a maximum cut otherwise. And if |V1|=|~V1| we call it an equal cut, else w call it an unequal cut. Equal cut may both be a minimum cut or a maximum cut, and similarly for an unequal cut as well.

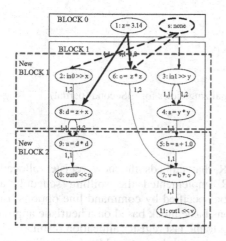

Fig. 4. Equal cut by BFS algorithm   **Fig. 5.** Equal cut by DFS algorithm

   Different graph searching algorithms may used to cut DAG, which will also result in the different characteristics of cut. Figure 4 and figure 5 show two cut algorithms both for equal cut respectively using breadth-first search (BFS) or depth-first search (DFS) algorithm. Cut results shown in figure 4 and figure 5 demonstrate that DFS cut algorithm may badly break the parallelism among weak-connected components, as it preferentially separates independent operations in two new blocks but keeps the length of crucial paths, while BFS cut may do rather lightly, as it preferentially separates dependent operations in two new blocks but shortens the length of crucial paths. So the schedule lengths of new blocks that cut by BFS are better than DFS, at the cost of more interferential node in coloring graph.

   Basic block partition based on cut considers global operation distribution of program. The time to cut a DAG by BFS or DFS algorithm is O(|E|) [6]. When register allocation fails, basic block repartition is started. The backtracking ensures the new algorithm can completely avoid register allocation failure. The performance and the probability of successful scheduling present a wide range of algorithmic trade-offs, which is determined by different cut algorithms. Figure 6 shows VLIW schedules for ElSecond (An IAPCM [9] benchmark) using two algorithms respectively. Register allocation fails using the old strategy. Purple block denotes operation, whose register allocation fails. The compiler with new strategy schedules successfully. A suitable algorithm results in minimal times of backtracking and lowest lost of compiling efficiency. It can be seen in section 5.

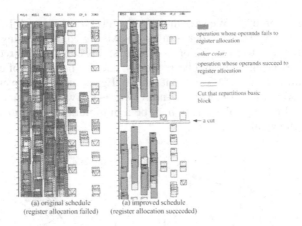

(a) original schedule   (a) improved schedule
(register allocation failed)   (register allocation succeeded)

Fig. 6. Instruction schedule's visualizing views for ElSecond (partial)

5 Result and Analysis

We developed a new compiler ISCD_R that embeds the new register allocation techniques referred to before. ISCD_R implemented the spilling schedule and multiple repartition approaches that can be specified by command line options listed in table 1. With –auto, compiler repartitions basic block based on a heuristic approach that selects correct cut approach according to the last register allocation result.

ISCD_R is evaluated using ten benchmarks with heavy workload, including media processing, graphics processing benchmarks [3] and several IAPCM (Beijing Institute of Application Physics and Computing Mathematics) Benchmarks[7]. All benchmarks were implemented on Imagine stream processors (as shown in figure 1) in KernelC [1]

Table 1. new command options of ISCD_R

BFS	DFS	Minimum cut	Maximum cut	Equal cut	Unequal cut	Heuristic
-b	-d	-mi	-ma	-e	-ue x y	-auto

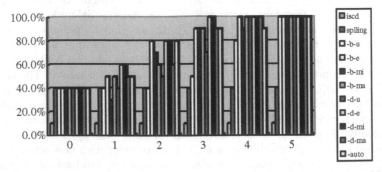

Fig. 7. Average successful ratios of various cut algorithms at different backtracking

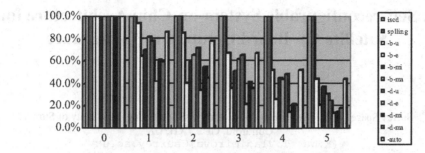

Fig. 8. Efficiency of various cut algorithms at different backtrackings

because it is the only language supported by ISCD. However, the VLIW algorithm works on basic operation. In other words, the schedule result is independent of high-level language.

Experimental result shows that the main reason, for ISCD scheduling program with heavy workload fails, is register allocation failure. ISCD_R, which is presented in this paper, introduces spilling schedule and basic block repartitioning to avoid register allocating failure. As spilling schedule has no effect on compiling efficiency, it tries to increase the LRF usage and achieve load balance between LRFs. However, spilling schedule cannot ensure that register allocation would succeed. On the contrary, basic block repartition can do it at the cost of compiling efficiency. Result of benchmarks shows that no matter what basic block repartition approach is, scheduling using ISCD_R succeeds by backtracking at most 5 times (average 2 times).

Acknowledgements. We thank Stanford CVA group for providing the simulator of Imagine and Merrimac. This research was supported by NSFC (60473080, 60573103), high performance computing creative team fund (IRT0446).

References

1. Peter Mattson, A Programming System for the Imagine Media Processor, Dept. of Electrical Engineering. Ph.D. Thesis, Stanford University.2001.
2. William J.Dally, Mattan Erez et al. Merrimac: Supercomputing with Streams, SC'03, November 15-21, 2003, Phoenix, Arizona, USA.
3. Nan Wu, Mei Wen, Haiyan Li, Li Li, Chunyuan Zhang, A stream architecture supporting multiple stream execution models, ACSAC 05 , LNCS3740, Singapore, 2005.10
4. Scott Rixner,William J. Dally, Brucek Khailany et al. Register organization for media processing. HPCA2000, pages 375-387, January 2000.
5. Preston Briggs. Register allocation via graph coloring. PhD thesis, Rice University, Houston, TX, USA, 1992.
6. Thomas H.Cormen, Charles E.Leiserson et al. Introduction to Algorithms (Second Edition), Beijing, Higher Education Press, pages 531-550 and 643-681, 2002.5.
7. Yuan Guoxing, Shao jingyun, Evaluating performance of scientific applications on several high performance processors, Beijing Institute of Application Physics and Computing Mathematics, www.ccw.com.cn, 2003.4

A Self-reconfigurable System-on-Chip Architecture for Satellite On-Board Computer Maintenance

Xiaofeng Wu and Tanya Vladimirova

Surrey Space Centre, Department of Electronic Engineering, University of Surrey,
Guildford, GU2 7XH, UK
{X.Wu, T.Vladimirova}@surrey.ac.uk

Abstract. New trends in the space industry, e.g. the development of wireless networked constellations using miniaturized satellites, have generated a pressing need for condition-based maintenance, self-repair and upgrade capabilities on-board satellites. This can be achieved by using reconfigurable hardware technologies, such as high-density Field Programmable Gate Arrays, implementing an entire on-board computer on a single chip. In this paper we present a system-on-chip architecture for on-board partial run-time reconfiguration to enable system-level functional changes on-board satellites ensuring correct operation, longer life and higher quality of service.

1 Introduction

Future space missions are envisioned as highly autonomous, intelligent and distributed multi-spacecraft missions consisting of miniaturized satellite nodes. Constellations of very small satellites can be used to implement virtual satellite missions, which are a cost-effective and flexible alternative approach to building large spacecraft. The Surrey Space Centre has a long-term research programme, codenamed ChipSat, which aims to apply advanced micro- and nano- technologies to small satellites [1]. An on-board computer is implemented in the form of a system-on-chip (SoC) device targeting the small satellite platform. The SoC design is an attempt to build a generic on-board computer (OBC), which takes advantage of high-density SRAM-based Field Programmable Gate Arrays (FPGAs). FPGAs can easily accommodate on a single chip a complex on-board computer, resulting in an efficient hardware architecture in terms of power, area and speed.

A disadvantage of SRAM-based devices is that they are vulnerable to the effects of high levels of radiation in the space environment [2]. Heavy ions from cosmic rays can easily deposit enough charge in or near an SRAM cell to cause a single-bit error, or single event upset (SEU). Because SRAM FPGAs store their logic configuration in SRAM switches, they are susceptible to configuration upsets, meaning that the routing and functionality of the circuit can be corrupted. In this paper we present a SoC architecture that utilizes partial run-time reconfiguration, which can be used to mitigate radiation effects preventing system failures in on-board electronics.

The paper is organized as follows. Section 2 reviews previous related work. Section 3 introduces the SoC architecture and software design for partial run-time

C. Jesshope and C. Egan (Eds.): ACSAC 2006, LNCS 4186, pp. 552–558, 2006.

reconfiguration. Section 4 gives a simple case study to verify the feasibility of the design. Section 5 concludes the paper.

2 Related Work

Radiation effects in SRAM FPGAs have been a topic of active investigation over the last couple of years. M. Ohlsson [3] studied the sensitivities of SRAM FPGAs to atmospheric high-energy neutrons. FPGAs were irradiated by 0-11, 14 and 100 MeV neutrons and showed a very low SEU susceptibility. P. Graham [4] classified the radiation effects in SRAM FPGAs and showed that SEUs can result in five main categories of design changes: mux select lines, programmable interconnect point states, buffer enables, LUT values, and control bit values.

M. Settler [5] introduces mitigation strategies for SRAM FPGAs. Scrubbing is the periodic readback of the FPGA's configuration memory followed by comparing of the memory content to a known good copy and writing back any corrections required. By periodically scrubbing an FPGA, configuration errors present in the FPGA can be corrected. Triple module redundancy (TMR) is an effective technique creating fault tolerant logic circuits. In TMR, the design logic is tripled and a majority voter is added at the output. Recently, Xilinx [6] have provided a design tool, XTMR that automatically implements TMR in Xilinx FPGA designs, protecting from SEUs the voting circuits. However, designs with TMR are at least three times as large as non-TMR designs, and suffer from speed degradation as well. Power consumption is also tripled along with the logic.

Some types of SRAM FPGAs are capable of partial run-time reconfiguration, which allows an FPGA to change part of its functions while the system is running. This capability can also be used to mitigate radiation effects by repairing the areas affected by soft failures. Xilinx produced two flows for partial reconfiguration: module based and difference based [7]. Module based partial reconfiguration is accomplished by dividing a design into modules. The design tool can repair, upgrade or change a module while the remaining system is running. Difference based partial reconfiguration is accomplished by making a small change to a design, and then generating a bitstream based only on the difference between the two designs. For the module based design flow, partial bitstreams can be created using the Xilinx PlanAhead tool [8], which can then be committed to FPGAs using the SelectMAP interface or the on-chip Internal Configuration Access Port (ICAP) module. For the difference based design flow, the JBits development environment [9] is widely used to create partial bitstreams, which can be committed to FPGAs via the Xilinx hardware interface (XHWIF). The OPB interface to the ICAP module permits connection of this peripheral to the MicroBlaze soft core processor [10]. J. Williams [11] developed an ICAP device driver for the uCLinux kernel, running on the MicroBlaze processor.

3 Reconfigurable SoC Design

The SoC implements an on-board computer and is targeted at the Xilinx Virtex II FPGAs. The central processing unit of the SoC is the LEON microprocessor, which is a SPARC V8 soft intellectual property (IP) core written in VHDL [12]. The SPARC architecture is a RISC architecture with typical features like large number of registers and few and simple instruction formats. However, the LEON3 IP core is more than a SPARC compatible CPU. It is also equipped with various peripherals that interconnect through two types of the AMBA bus (AHB and APB), e.g. Ethernet, SpaceWire, PCI, UART etc. The SoC is an AMBA centric design and subsystems of the OBC can be added to the LEON3 processor providing that they are AMBA interfaced. Different subsystems will be considered for specific satellite missions, for example a high-level data link controller (HDLC) interface for signal downlink and uplink, a compression core.an encryption hardware accelerator, etc..

So far we have introduced the soft IP cores of the SoC architecture, however, the Xilinx FPGAs also provide on-chip hard cores, e.g. Block SelectRAM (BRAM), multipliers. Starting from the Virtex II Xilinx have integrated an internal configuration access port into the programmable fabric, which enables a user to write software programs that modify the circuit structure and functionality at run-time for an embedded processor. The ICAP is actually a subset of the SelectMAP interface [13], which is used to configure Xilinx FPGAs. Fig. 1 shows the diagram of the SoC architecture.

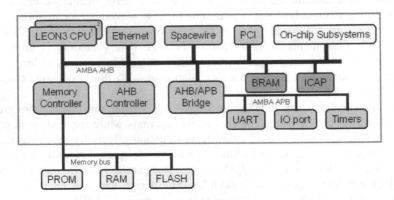

Fig. 1. The SoC architecture of the OBC

The ICAP and BRAM are connected to the LEON3 processor via the AMBA bus. Once the FPGA is initially configured, the ICAP is used as an interface to reconfigure the FPGA. The control logic for reading and writing data to the ICAP is implemented in the LEON3 processor as a software driver. The BRAM is used as a configuration cache. Because Virtex II FPGAs support reconfiguration only by frames, the BRAM must be big enough to hold one frame each time. The bitstream of each SoC component can be stored on board in a Flash memory. The bitstream of a new or upgraded SoC component can be uploaded through the satellite uplink from the ground station.

3.1 Software Design

An ICAP device driver is available in the Xilinx EDK toolkit. The driver enables an embedded microprocessor to read and write the FPGA configuration memory through the ICAP at run-time. On-chip reconfiguration is accomplished by using a read-modify-write mechanism [14]. To modify the on-chip subsystems, the ICAP first determines the configuration frames that need to be modified, and then reads each frame into the BRAM once at a time. The contents of each frame are modified before being written back to the ICAP. The current ICAP driver only supports modifying of a single frame at a time.

In the embedded microprocessors the driver is managed by a real-time operating system. For example Xilinx released a driver running in uClinux, which is ported to the MicroBlaze processor. There is an embedded Linux port to the LEON3 processor, which is called SnapGear that can be used for the OBC. The SnapGear Linux is a full source package, comprising a kernel, libraries and application code for rapid development of embedded Linux systems. The LEON port of SnapGear supports both MMU and non-MMU LEON configurations. Actually the non-MMU kernel is a uClinux port similar to the Microblaze uClinux port. In this case the original ICAP driver can be used in the LEON3 processor without significant modifications.

The device driver implements the read( ), write( ) and ioctl( ) system calls: read( ) reads a frame from the ICAP into a user memory buffer (BRAM); write( ) writes a frame from a user memory buffer to the ICAP; and ioctl( ) controls operations, like querying the status or changing operation modes. Upon system boot, the driver is automatically installed in the SnapGear, and the ICAP is registered in the Linux device subsystem, appearing as /dev/icap. This feature allows us to access the ICAP module using standard Linux system calls, such as open, read and write.

4 Technology Demonstration

In order to verify our design we demonstrate a simple example based on the LEON3 processor and a direct memory access controller (DMAC). The satellite OBC has several high data rate interface modules. For instance, the SpaceWire interface with a data rate up to 400 Mbit/s is used to connect to other on-board devices. The high-level data link controller (HDLC) interface with up to 10 Mbit/s is employed for uplink and downlink data transmission to the ground station. The DMAC handles the data transfer between the main memory and the peripherals bypassing the CPU. At the Surrey Space Centre a soft DMAC IP core was developed for the AMBA interface [15]. Fig. 2 shows the block diagram of the DMAC and its interconnection with the peripherals.

The CPU allocates a memory block and assigns it to the DMAC. Furthermore, the CPU writes the transfer mode and the peripheral device address to the DMAC registers. After configuring the DMAC there are two possibilities to trigger the data transfer process. In the first option, the CPU sends a start command to the DMAC. In the second option, the transfer will be triggered via hardware handshake between the DMAC and the peripheral device. In this case the device must be DMA-capable by providing appropriate hardware handshake signals. The minimal hardware handshake between the DMAC and the peripheral device consists of a request signal. In addition, an acknowledge signal is normally used additionally. If a peripheral device receives data from "outside" the peripheral device asserts the request signal *DREQ*. The

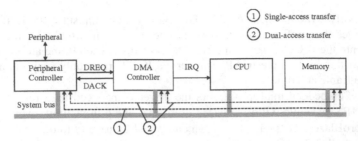

Fig. 2. Interconnection between the DMAC and the peripherals [15]

DMAC transfers the received data from the peripheral device controller to the memory and asserts the acknowledge signal *DACK*. When the transfer is completed a state bit will be set in the DMAC or the DMAC causes an interrupt.

There are two kinds of data transfer. In the single-access transfer the DMAC activates the control and address bus signals, the peripheral device puts its data on the data bus during and the memory reads the data, or the memory puts its data on the data bus and the peripheral device reads it. The second technique is called dual-access transfer. Firstly, the DMAC reads the data from a peripheral device or memory and buffers it internally. Secondly, the DMAC writes the data to memory or to a peripheral device.

4.1 Implementation Results

We first implement a partial SoC, which consists of the LEON3 processor, the ICAP, and the BRAM, into the Virtex II FPGA. Then we add the DMA controller into the partial SoC while it is running. Synplify Pro is used to produce the netlists of the partial SoC, the DMA controller, and the complete SoC that consists of both the partial SoC and the DMA controller. The resultant netlists are floorplanned using the PlanAhead tool. The reason to floorplan the complete SoC is that it provides a reference for the placing of the individual components. Hence it ensures that the dynamic circuit (i.e. the DMAC) is correctly interfaced to the static circuit (i.e. the partial SoC). Fig. 3 illustrates the design partitioning between the resultant static and dynamic circuits. Bus macros are inserted to interface signals between the static and dynamic circuits.

We download the partial SoC bitstream to the FPGA and store the DMAC bitstream *dma.bit* in the memory. At the same time the image of the SnapGear Linux is downloaded to the bootloader. After system boot the ICAP device is automatically registered as /dev/icap. We can manually reconfigure the SoC through the debugging window. The reconfiguration can be achieved simply by executing the following command:

```
$ cat dma.bit > /dev/icap
```

Now the DMAC is added to the SoC and ready to transfer data between the peripherals and the memory. In order to check whether or not the DMAC works we connect the SoC to a PC via the RS232 interface. We create a data block with arbitrary values and send the data block size and the data block to the RS232 interface.

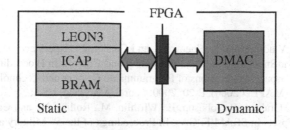

Fig. 3. Block-diagram of the design partitioning for partial reconfiguration

The LEON3 processor receives the block size from the serial interface and configures the DMAC according to this size. After initiation of the DMA transfer the UART sends a DMA request with each received byte. So the DMAC controller reads each received byte from the UART and transfers it to the main memory. Furthermore the processor calculates a check sum for all received values. The results are printed to the debugging window through the serial interface as shown in Fig. 4.

```
$ ./dmatest
I am waiting for data!
Wait for end of transfer!
The DMA controller transferred 1000 bytes from
the UART to the memory.
I am calculating check sum.
The check sum is 248.
I am waiting for data.
```

Fig. 4. Testing of the DMAC by transferring 1000 bytes from the UART to the memory

5 Conclusions

In this paper we present a system-on-chip architecture for on-board partial run-time reconfiguration to enable system-level functional changes on-board satellites ensuring correct operation, longer life and higher quality of service. Our work is focused on the hardware architecture, whereby we port an ICAP driver running in uCLinux to the LEON processor IP core. The reason for using the LEON processor core is that it is becoming more and more popular in space computing as it realizes a standard architecture, has a fault tolerant version and has already been flown successfully as part of the monitoring camera payload of the ESA Venus Express mission.

Traditional solutions to SEU mitigation, such as TMR, are very hard to realize in very small satellites, which are extremely restricted in terms of power and mass. We believe that the self-reconfigurable computing architecture proposed in this paper offers an alternative solution to the SEU problem for resource-constrained embedded applications in space and other non-benign environments.

References

1. Tiggler, H., Vladimirova, T., Zheng, D., and Gaisler, J.: Experiences Designing a System-on-a-Chip for Small Satellite Data Processing and Control. In Proceedings of the 3rd Military and Aerospace Applications of Programmable Devices and Technologies International Conference (MAPLD'2000), P-20, 2000, Laurel, Maryland, USA.
2. Caffrey, M., Graham, P., Johnson, E., Wirthlin, M., Rollins, N., and Carmichael, C.: Single-Event Upsets in SRAM FPGAs. In Proceedings of the 5th Military and Aerospace Applications of Programmable Devices and Technologies International Conference (MAPLD'2002), P8, 2002, Laurel, Maryland, USA.
3. Ohlsson, M., Dyreklev, P., Johansson, and K., Alfke, P.: Neutron Single Event Upsets in SRAM-based FPGAs. In Proceedings of IEEE Nuclear and Space Radiation Effects Conference (NSREC'1998), 1998, Newport Beach, California, USA.
4. Graham, P., Caffrey, M., Zimmerman, J., Sundararajan, P., Johnson, E., and Patterson, C.: Consequences and Categories of SRAM FPGA Configuration SEUs. In Proceedings of the 6th Military and Aerospace Applications of Programmable Devices and Technologies International Conference (MAPLD'2003), C6, 2003, Washington DC, USA.
5. Stettler, M., Caffrey, M., Graham, P., and Krone, J.: Radiation effects and mitigation strategies for modern FPGAs. In Proceedings of 10th Workshop on Electronics for LHC Experiments and Future Experiments, 2004, Boston, USA.
6. Xilinx: The First Triple Module Redundancy Development Tool for reconfigurable FPGAs. http://www.xilinx.com/esp/mil_aero/collateral/tmrtool_sellsheet_wr.pdf.
7. Xilinx: Two Flows for Partial Reconfiguration: Module Based or Difference Based. Application Note. http://www.xilinx.com/bvdocs/appnotes/xapp290.pdf.
8. Xilinx: PlanAhead 8.1 Design and Analysis Tool: Maximum Performance in Less Time. http://www.xilinx.com/publications/prod_mktg/pn0010825.pdf
9. Guccione, S., Levi, D., and Sundararajan, P.: JBits: Java Based Interface for Reconfigurable Computing. In Proceedings of the 2nd Military and Aerospace Applications of Programmable Devices and Technologies International Conference (MAPLD'1999), P-27, 1999, Laurel, Maryland, USA.
10. Xilinx: MicroBlaze Processor Reference Guide. October 2005.
11. Williams, John A. and Bergmann, Neil W. Embedded Linux as a Platform for Dynamically Self-Reconfiguring Systems-On-Chip. In Proceedings of the International Conference on Engineering of Reconfigurable Systems and Algorithms (ERSA 2004), 2004, Las Vegas, Nevada, USA.
12. Gaisler, J.: GRLIB IP Library User's Manual (Version 1.0.4). Gaisler Research, 2005.
13. Blodget, B., James-Roxby, P., Keller, E., McMillan, S., and Sundararajan, P.: A Self-reconfiguration Platform. In proceeding of 13th International Conference on Field-Programmable Logic and Applications, FPL'2003, pp. 565-574. 2003, Lisbon, Portugal.
14. Xilinx: Processor IP Reference Guide. Xilinx. February 2005.
15. M.Meier, T.Vladimirova, T.Plant, A.da Silva Curiel. DMA Controller for a Credit-Card Size Satellite Onboard Computer. In Proceedings of the 7th Military and Aerospace Applications of Programmable Devices and Technologies International Conference (MAPLD'2004), P-208, 2004, Washington, US, NASA.

Compile-Time Thread Distinguishment Algorithm on VIM-Based Architecture

Yan Xiao-Bo, Yang Xue-Jun, and Wen Pu

Shool of Computer, National University of Defense Technology,
Chang Sha, Hunan 410073, China
xbyan@tom.com

Abstract. VIM integrates vector units into memory, which exploits the low-latency and high-bandwidth memory access. On VIM-based architecture, the low temporal locality thread running on VIM processor is called Light-Weight Thread, while the low cache miss rate thread running on host processor is called Heavy-Weight Thread. The thread distinguishment can impact the system performance directly. Compared with the distinguishment at programming model level, compile-time thread distinguishment can release programmer from changing existing program. After overviewing the VIM micro-architecture and the system architecture, this paper presents an analytical model of thread distinguishment. Based on this model, we present a compile-time algorithm and evaluate it with two thread instances on the evaluation environment we develop. We find that parameters affecting the thread distinguishment are the cache miss rate, the vectorizable operation rate and the arithmetic-to-memory ratio. We believe that this algorithm is constructive to improve the performance of the VIM-based node computer.

1 Introduction

PIM (Processor-In-Memory) [1] architecture aims at the problem of memory wall [2]. It integrates a processor and a sizable memory on ONE chip which can potentially deliver high performance by enabling low-latency and high-bandwidth communication between processor and memory [3]. Now, the Embedded DRAM produced by IBM Inc. can integrate at least a 32Mb memory, whose clock frequency reaches at least 500MHZ, which is used in the SOC chip of QCDOC [4].

Vector technology can always achieve high sustained performance, such as Earth Simulator [5], while it needs the architecture support of low-latency and high-bandwidth memory access. Thus, one of the good choices is to combine vector technology with PIM technology, such as VIM [6] and VIRAM [7].

In general, the low temporal locality thread, which is relatively performed well in PIM [8], is called LWT (Light-Weight Thread) and the low cache miss rate thread is called HWT (Heavy-Weight Thread). There are two methods to distinguish these two kinds of threads.

One method is to modify the existing programming model or develop a new one. Peter M. Kogge and his partners have classified the programming models suitable for PIM architecture into the some types [9]. Another programming model used by HTMT

C. Jesshope and C. Egan (Eds.): ACSAC 2006, LNCS 4186, pp. 559–566, 2006.
© Springer-Verlag Berlin Heidelberg 2006

project [10] has also modified its syntax. The Cascade project [11] of Cay Inc develops a new programming model, Chapel [12], to support its hybrid architecture which also adopts PIM technology. The flaw of this method is that programmers have to modify or rewrite the existing programs to fit the new programming models, which would be a tremendous work.

This paper gives a compile-time method to distinguish the LWT and HWT to avoid the flaw of the method above.

The rest of the paper is organized as follows: Section 2 overviews the VIM micro-architecture and system architecture; Section 3 presents our analytical model to distinguish the LWT and HWT; Section 4 describes the evaluation environment and evaluates the algorithm by two simple threads; and Section 6 discusses related work.

2   Architecture of VIM and Entire System

VIM prototype structure consists of five main units: a 32-bit RISC core, a 32-bit vector unit with 4 Lanes (2 Lanes in earlier prototype structure [6]), a crossbar, a memory control unit and an EDRAM, and the entire system architecture, to some extent, is like Cray Cascade [11], as shown in the Fig. 1.

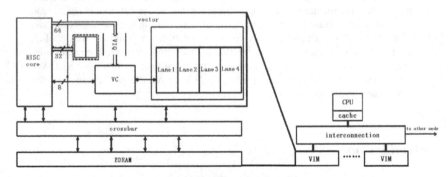

Fig. 1. VIM micro-architecture structure and a VIM-based node computer's structure

Host processor and VIM processors are distinguished by their operational parameter values as shown in Table 1. And the related parameters of a given thread are shown in Table 2.

Table 1. Parametric assumptions of hardware

Parameter	Description	Experimental Value
$T_{h.r}$	Arithmetic instruction execution time of host processor	1ns
$T_{h.m.c}$	Cache access time of host processor	2ns
$T_{h.m.m}$	Memory access time of host processor	90ns
$T_{h.m}$	Memory access average time of host processor	\
$T_{v.r}$	Arithmetic instruction execution time of VIM processor	5ns
$T_{v.m}$	Memory access time of VIM processor	30ns
N_l	Number of vector Lane in VIM processor	4
m	Number of VIM processor	\

Table 2. Parameters of a considered thread

Parameter	Description
N_r	Number of the arithmetic instruction
N_m	Number of the memory instruction
R_{rp}	Vectorizable arithmetic operation rate
R_{mp}	Vectorizable memory operation rate
$R_{r/m}$	The arithmetic-to-memory instruction ratio N_r/N_m
$Miss$	cache miss rate on host processor

3 Analytical Model of Thread Distinguishment

Whether a thread should be executed on VIM processor or host processor depends on its execution time. We let T_{VIM} denote the execution time of a thread on VIM processor and T_{host} denote the execution time of a thread on host processor. Here are the two analytical equations:

$$T_{VIM} = N_m \times (1-R_{mp}) \times T_{v.m} + N_m \times R_{mp}/N_l \times T_{v.m}/m + N_r \times (1-R_{rp}) \times T_{v.r} + N_r \times R_{rp}/N_l \times T_{v.r}/m \text{ and}$$

$$T_{host} = N_m \times T_{h.m} + N_r \times T_{h.r}, \text{ where } T_{h.m} = T_{h.m.m} \times Miss + T_{h.m.c}.$$

Therefore, the performance speedup of VIM processor relative to host processor can be computed as follow:

$$Speedup = \frac{T_{host}}{T_{VIM}} = \frac{(T_{h.m.m} \times Miss + T_{h.m.c}) + T_{h.r} \times R_{r/m}}{(1-R_{mp}) \times T_{v.m} + R_{mp}/N_l \times T_{v.m}/m + R_{r/m} \times (1-R_{rp}) \times T_{v.r} + R_{r/m} \times R_{rp}/N_l \times T_{v.r}/m}$$

The sign of (Speedup-1) is determinant:

$$sign(Speedup - 1) = sign(C_{mem} \times Miss + C_{alu} \times R_{r/m} + C_{const})$$

Let $\Delta = C_{mem} \times Miss + C_{alu} \times R_{r/m} + C_{const}$
where
$$\tag{1}$$

$$\begin{cases} C_{mem} = T_{h.m.m} \times m \\ C_{alu} = T_{h.r} \times m - [(1-R_{rp}) \times m + R_{rp}/N_l] \times T_{v.r} \\ C_{const} = T_{h.m.c} \times m - [(1-R_{mp}) \times m + R_{mp}/N_l] \times T_{v.m} \end{cases}$$

When $\Delta > 0$, $Speedup > 1$, processing the thread on VIM processor is faster than on host processor. Otherwise, processing the thread on host processor is faster than on VIM processor. The determinant parameters are $R_{r/m}$, R_{rp}, R_{mp} and $Miss$.

4 Evaluation

In this section, we develop an evaluation environment, present a compile-time algorithm based on the thread distinguishment model above and evaluate it with two thread instances on the evaluation environment.

4.1 Evaluation Environment

Two threads to be tested in our experiment are matrix plus thread and matrix multiplying thread, all matrixes used are $n \times n$ 4-byte integer.

VIMNCSim (VIM-based Node Computer's Simulator) consists of a host processor simulator and a VIM simulator. Host processor simulator implements some simple arithmetic and memory access instructions and has a 1-level cache whose parameters are shown in Table 3. VIM simulator embeds a 32Mb EDRAM and implements some simple vector instructions such as *vload, vstore, vadd, vsub, vmult, vdiv* and etc.

Table 3. Cache parameters and their experimental values

Parameter	Experimental Value
Line width	64B
Association	2-way
Cache size	128KB
Replace strategy	LRU

VIMNCFC (VIM-based Node Computer's Fortran Compiler) is a simple FORTRAN compiler for *VIMNCSim* which implements a thread distinguishment algorithm. In this algorithm, we suppose that the values of all the computer's parameters are already presented during compile time. So what we should focus on are the thread's parameters.

Miss, the cache miss rate on host processor, can be statically estimated during compile time which can be found in reference [13]. Other thread's parameters can be easily estimated. The thread distinguishment algorithm is presented in Table 4.

Table 4. Thread distinguishment algorithm

Input:	a thread in the form of nested loop
Output:	whether the thread is a LWT or a HWT

Step 1: estimate the value *Miss* of the thread statically.
Step 2: count the loop depth *Depth* and count each loop's iteration number *N[Depth]*.
Step 3: set $N_r = 0$ and $N_m = 0$.
Step 4: for each loop depth i (i is from 0 to *Depth - 1*) do the following steps:
　　Step 4.1: count NN_r, the arithmetic operation in loop i,

$$\text{Step 4.2: set } N_r = N_r + NN_r \times \prod_{j=0}^{i} N[j].$$

　　Step 4.3: count NN_m, the memory operation in loop i,

$$\text{Step 4.4: set } N_m = N_m + NN_m \times \prod_{j=0}^{i} N[j].$$

Step 5: vecorize all loops.
　Step 6: set $NV_r = 0$ and $NV_m = 0$.

Table 4. (*continued*)

Step 7: for each loop depth i (i is from 0 to *Depth - 1*) do the following steps:
Step 7.1: count NNV_r, the arithmetic non-vectoriztion operation of in loop i.

Step 7.2: set $NV_r = NV_r + NNV_r \times \prod_{j=0}^{i} N[j]$.

Step 7.3: count NNV_m, the memory non-vectoriztion operation in loop i.

Step 7.4: set $NV_m = NV_m + NNV_m \times \prod_{j=0}^{i} N[j]$.

Step 8: set $R_{rp} = 1 - \dfrac{NV_r}{N_r}$, $R_{mp} = 1 - \dfrac{NV_m}{N_m}$ and $R_{r/m} = \dfrac{N_r}{N_m}$.

Step 9: calculate Δ in Formulation (1).
Step 10: if $\Delta > 0$, this thread is a LWT, otherwise it is a HWT.

4.2 Evaluation Results

The two testing thread runs on *VIMNCSim* with both one VIM processor and more. For comparisons, they are compiled into both the executable codes on the VIM simulator and that on the host processor simulator with *VIMNCFC*.

The simulation results are shown in Table 5~ Table 8.

Table 5. results on single VIM processor computer MA = Matrix Addition, MM = Matrix Multiplication

n	Δ		Execution time($\times 10^{-4}$s)				Thread type		Correct?	
	MA	MM	MA on host	MM on host	MA on VIM	MM on VIM	MA	MM	MA	MM
10	-3.14193	-4.80465	0.06951	0.4834	0.1478	1.506	HWT	HWT	Yes	Yes
20	-2.32173	-3.83605	0.2751	3.647	0.4768	9.162	HWT	HWT	Yes	Yes
40	-2.26097	-3.66431	1.092	28.34	1.863	68.20	HWT	HWT	Yes	Yes
80	-2.2235	-3.57582	4.355	223.4	7.365	525.5	HWT	HWT	Yes	Yes
100	-2.21543	-3.55797	6.802	435.1	11.48	1019	HWT	HWT	Yes	Yes
200	-2.19872	-3.52212	27.18	3712	45.71	8024	HWT	HWT	Yes	Yes
400	-2.19008	-3.50413	108.7	31193	182.4	63696	HWT	HWT	Yes	Yes
800	-2.18569	-3.49513	434.5	249253	728.8	507585	HWT	HWT	Yes	Yes

The results above show that both the threads of matrix addition and matrix multiply should be HWTs for the major reason of low cache miss rate.

The results above show that when VIM processors are many, both the threads of matrix addition and matrix multiply should be LWTs in most situations for the major reason of parallel execution on VIM processors. When VIM processors are few, the thread of matrix multiply should be HWT for the major reason of low cache miss rate.

Table 6. results on 2 VIM processor computer MA = Matrix Addition, MM = Matrix Multiplication

n	Δ		Execution time($\times 10^{-4}$s)				Thread type		Correct?	
	MA	MM	MA on host	MM on host	MA on VIM	MM on VIM	MA	MM	MA	MM
10	0.757328	-3.4843	0.06951	0.4834	0.1023	1.111	LWT	HWT	No	Yes
20	2.719063	-1.08297	0.2751	3.647	0.2948	6.002	LWT	HWT	No	Yes
40	3.767842	0.198515	1.092	28.34	0.9528	36.60	LWT	LWT	Yes	No
80	3.862001	0.448257	4.355	223.4	3.725	272.7	LWT	LWT	Yes	No
100	3.702921	0.334631	6.802	435.1	6.021	544.6	LWT	LWT	Yes	No
200	3.923035	0.59978	27.18	3712	22.96	4074	LWT	LWT	Yes	No
400	3.94414	0.65053	108.7	31193	91.42	32096	LWT	LWT	Yes	No
800	3.954835	0.675946	434.5	249253	364.8	254785	LWT	LWT	Yes	No

Table 7. results on 4 VIM processor computer MA = Matrix Addition, MM = Matrix Multiplication

n	Δ		Execution time($\times 10^{-4}$s)				Thread type		Correct?	
	MA	MM	MA on host	MM on host	MA on VIM	MM on VIM	MA	MM	MA	MM
10	13.08233	3.093910	0.06951	0.4834	0.05675	0.7163	LWT	LWT	Yes	No
20	13.5623	5.104828	0.2751	3.647	0.2038	4.422	LWT	LWT	Yes	No
40	15.82547	7.924167	1.092	28.34	0.5888	23.96	LWT	LWT	Yes	Yes
80	16.99173	9.373327	4.355	223.4	1.9048	146.3	LWT	LWT	Yes	Yes
100	16.46043	8.963283	6.802	435.1	3.291	307.6	LWT	LWT	Yes	Yes
200	16.9346	9.549174	27.18	3712	12.04	2178	LWT	LWT	Yes	Yes
400	17.17308	9.843558	108.7	31193	45.92	16296	LWT	LWT	Yes	Yes
800	17.1966	9.902650	434.5	249253	182.8	128385	LWT	LWT	Yes	Yes

Table 8. results on 8 VIM processor computer MA = Matrix Addition, MM = Matrix Multiplication

n	Δ		Execution time($\times 10^{-4}$s)				Thread type		Correct?	
	MA	MM	MA on host	MM on host	MA on VIM	MM on VIM	MA	MM	MA	MM
10	30.69114	10.12532	0.06951	0.4834	0.05675	0.7163	LWT	LWT	Yes	No
20	39.56474	21.34302	0.2751	3.647	0.1128	2.842	LWT	LWT	Yes	Yes
40	40.32332	23.72287	1.092	28.34	0.4068	17.64	LWT	LWT	Yes	Yes
80	42.73986	26.75578	4.355	223.4	1.1768	95.76	LWT	LWT	Yes	Yes
100	42.43585	26.64232	6.802	435.1	1.926	189.1	LWT	LWT	Yes	Yes
200	43.41855	27.87132	27.18	3712	6.581	1230	LWT	LWT	Yes	Yes
400	43.91271	28.48884	108.7	31193	24.08	8712	LWT	LWT	Yes	Yes
800	44.16050	28.79834	434.5	249253	91.84	65185	LWT	LWT	Yes	Yes

Though most thread distinguishments are correct, our algorithm may distinguish the threads incorrectly in some situations, mainly because the statically estimated cache miss rates are inaccurate. In future work, we will look for more effective algorithm to statically estimate the cache miss rate.

5 Summaries and Future Work

The thread distinguishment of LWT and HWT can impact the system performance directly. Compared with the distinguishment at programming model level, compile-time thread distinguishment can release programmer from changing existing program. This paper presents a compile-time algorithm to distinguish them. Through analysis and experiments, we find that the determinant parameters are the cache miss rate, the vectorizable operation rate and the arithmetic-to-memory ratio.

The thread distinguishment algorithm may be inaccurate in an actual node computer, because it does not distinguish the execution time of different arithmetic instructions and the statically estimated cache miss rate is inaccurate too. In the future, we will aim to improve the thread distinguishment algorithm for the actual node computer.

References

1. Kogge, P.M., T. Sunaga, E. Retter, and et al. Combined DRAM and Logic Chip for Massively Parallel Applications. In Proceedings of 16th IEEE Conference on Advanced Research in VLSI, March 1995, Raleigh / NC.
2. W. Wulf and S. McKee. Hitting the memory wall: Implications and the obvious. ACM Computer Architecture News vol. 13 no. 1, March 1995.
3. J.Lee, Y.Solihin, and J.Torrellas. Automatically Mapping Code on an Intelligent Memory Architecture. In Proc. International Symposium on High-Performance Computer Architecture, January 2001, 121-132.
4. P.A. Boyle, et al. QCDOC: A 10 Teraflops Computer for Tightly-Coupled Calculations. In Proceedings of the 2004 ACM/IEEE Conference on Supercomputing (November 06 - 12, 2004). Conference on High Performance Networking and Computing. November 2004.
5. Watanabe, T. The Earth Simulator and Beyond-Technological Considerations toward the Sustained PetaFlops Machine. In Proceedings of the 13th international Conference on Parallel Architectures and Compilation Techniques (September 29 - October 03, 2004). PACT. IEEE Computer Society, Washington, DC, 149-149.
6. Yang Xue-Jun, Yan Xiao-Bo, et al. VIM: a High-Performance PIM Architecture. In Proceedings of the 13th National Conference on Information Storage Technology (NCIS2004), China. Journal of Computer Research and Development (supplement), 2004.
7. C. Kozyrakis, J. Gebis, D. Martin, S. Williams, I. Mavroidis, S. Pope, D. Jones, D. Patterson, and K. Yelick. Vector IRAM: A Media-oriented Vector Processor with Embedded DRAM. In Proc. Hot Chips XII, August 2000.
8. Upchurch, E., Sterling, T., and Brockman, J. Analysis and Modeling of Advanced PIM Architecture Design Tradeoffs. In Proceedings of the 2004 ACM/IEEE Conference on Supercomputing (November 06 - 12, 2004). Conference on High Performance Networking and Computing. November 2004.

9. P.M. Kogge, J.B. Brockman, T. Sterling, and G. Gao. Processing In Memory: Chips to Petaflops. Workshop on Mixing Logic and DRAM: Chips that Compute and Remember, 24th International Symposium on Computer Architecture, June 1997.
10. Kogge, P. M., Brockman, J. B., and Freeh, V. W. PIM Architectures to Support Petaflops Level Computation in the HTMT Machine. In Proceedings of the 1999 international Workshop on innovative Architecture (November 01 - 01, 1999). November 1999.
11. Sterling, T. In Pursuit of Petaflops - the Cray Cascade Project. In Proceedings of the 2004 Aerospace Conference, March 2004.
12. David Callahan, Bradford L. Chamberlain, Hans P. Zima. The Cascade High Productivity Language. In 9th International Workshop on High-Level Parallel Programming Models and Supportive Environments (HIPS 2004), pages 52-60. IEEE Computer Society, April 2004.
13. Calin Cascaval, David A. Padua. Estimating cache misses and locality using stack distances. In Proceedings of International Conference on Supercomputing, San Francisco, CA, June. 2003.

Designing a Coarse-Grained Reconfigurable Architecture Using Loop Self-Pipelining*

Jinhui Xu, Guiming Wu, Yong Dou, and Yazhuo Dong

School of Computer Science, National University of Defense Technology
Chang Sha, Hu Nan, P.R. of China, 410073
{jinhuixu, wuguiming, yongdou, dongyazhuo}@nudt.edu.cn

Abstract. This paper introduces LEAP(Loop Engine on Array Processor), a novel coarse-grained reconfigurable architecture which accelerates applications through Loop Self-Pipelining (LSP) technique. The LSP can provide effective execution mode for application pipelining. By mapping and distributing the expression statements of high level programming languages onto processing elements array, the LEAP can step the loop iteration automatically. The LEAP architecture has no centralized control, no centralized multi-port registers and no centralized data memory. The LEAP has the ability to exploit loop-level, instruction-level, and task-level parallelism, and it is suitable choice for stream-based application domains, such as multimedia, DSP and graphics application.

1 Introduction

In recent years, coarse-grained reconfigurable architectures have become increasingly important alternatives for accelerating applications. More and more coarse-grained reconfigurable architectures have been proposed [1,2,3,4]. Coarse-grained reconfigurable architectures become important due to their combination of the advantages of both ASICs and general processors. Compared to fine-grained reconfigurable architectures, coarse-grained reconfigurable architectures can achieve significant speedup and power saving.

Most of coarse-grained reconfigurable architectures comprise of processing elements array and interconnection mesh, which are reconfigurable for accelerating different applications. The processing elements may consist of ALUs that can implement word-level function instead of bit-level operation in fine-grained reconfigurable architectures. Coarse-grained reconfigurable architectures are far less flexible than fine-grained ones, but much more complex operations can be implemented efficiently on them.

In this paper, we propose a coarse-grained reconfigurable architecture named LEAP (Loop Engine on Array Processor), which is based on a simple technique for loop pipelining and an execution mode called FIMD (Fixed Instruction flow

---

* This research was supported by the National Science Foundation of China under contract #90307001.

C. Jesshope and C. Egan (Eds.): ACSAC 2006, LNCS 4186, pp. 567–573, 2006.

Multiple Data flow mode)[5]. The LEAP architecture is a data-driven architecture, which has 8*8 reconfigurable processing elements array and data memory that provides reconfiguration. This architecture aims to map the expression statements of high level programming languages onto processing elements and build a pipelining dataflow structure according to a static dataflow graph, and accomplishes tasks automatically and efficiently for applications. The LEAP architecture has two highlighted features: a technique provides loop self-pipelining execution, and a reconfiguration mechanism to maintain applications consistency while minimizing the impact on performance. To achieve loop self-pipelining, balancing is performed through addition of more storage (i.e., FIFOs) in each processing element.

2   Related Works

Many coarse-grained reconfigurable architectures have been proposed in recent years. Both of Morphosys [1] and REMARC [4] are typical reconfigurable architectures which consist of a RISC processor and reconfigurable arrays. They all need synchronization mechanism or global control unit to control the execution of the reconfigurable arrays. ADRES [2] is a single architecture, in which a VLIW processor is tightly coupled with a coarse-grained reconfigurable matrix. Researchers of ADRES consider that the integration of the VLIW processor and the coarse-grained reconfigurable matrix can achieve goals of improved performance, a simplified programming model and communication cost reduction. The PACT XPP architecture [3] is based on a hierarchical array and a packet-oriented communication network. The PACT XPP architecture's automatic packet-handling mechanism and its sophisticated hierarchical configuration protocols differ the PACT XPP from other coarse-grained architectures.

However, since lack of direct support for high level programming languages, performance improvement of the architectures above heavily depends on the dataflow software pipelining technique or other software pipelining approaches [6]. More or less, the use of these techniques might lead to resource problems. Our architecture may address this problem, and make compiler simpler.

3   Architecture Overview

The LEAP architecture is shown in Figure 1. It includes a processing elements array (PEA), an interface controller, a data memory array and a reconfigurable data communication network. The interface controller receives messages from the host processor, and dispatches them to the other parts. In this section, we present the main components of the LEAP architecture.

Processing elements array: Processing elements array is composed of two heterogeneous Processing elements (PEs): Computing Processing Element (cPE) and Memory Processing Element (mPE). Both cPE and mPE have their own

Fig. 1. The LEAP architecture: (a) simple diagram of the LEAP architecture; (b) data communication network

configuration cache called instruction RAM for configuration information caching, and configuration control is distributed over each PE. Before PEs running, configurations are loaded into the instruction registers. During running, the instructions in instruction registers are not changed until being reconfigured. So the interconnection of PEs creates a pipelined dataflow architecture, and data streams continuously flow through the architecture without any centralized control. The instructions on each PE are fixed when data streams flow, following the FIMD mode [6].

All of mPEs are specially designed to accomplish data loading and storing, and they drive data to flow on processing elements array (see Figure 2a). The Loop Step Engine (LSE) is connected directly with data memory, and generates the addresses for memory accessing. The LSE should synchronize with the dataflow. One mPE may fetch one word from data memory per clock cycle, and then it sends the word to two different destinations due to its two output ports. The data on the input port of an mPE, which is transferred from other PEs, can be stored into data memory by the LSE.

The cPE (see Figure 2b) contains several instruction registers which provide instructions for executing and an ALU that performs the actual computation. The ALU is able to perform common fixed-point arithmetical and logical operations, as well as some special works such as sorting, calculating maximum and sum-reduction. An operation of the ALU is performed as soon as all required data are available according to data-driven mode, and the result is immediately sent into the PEA by the two output ports. The busy signals generated in PEs control accurate data communication between PEs. When the input FIFOs of one PE are in "almost full" state, the busy signals will not allow the connected PEs to send any data. The FIFOs keep the pipelined datapath balancing.

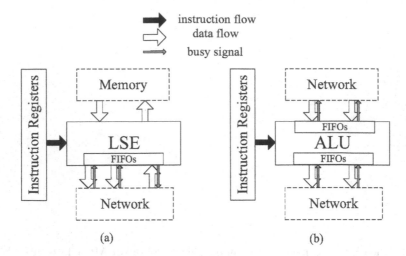

Fig. 2. Architectural model of PE: (a) architectural model of mPE; (b) architectural model of cPE

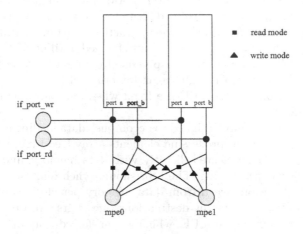

Fig. 3. Structure of a data memory pair

Data memory array: Data memory array consists of four data memory pairs in the LEAP architecture (see Figure 1a). A data memory pair contains two data memory either of which has two accessing ports that can be used in read mode or write mode. Figure 3 shows the structure of a data memory pair which can be accessed by a pair of mPEs. In Figure 3, the module mpe0 and mpe1 respectively represent the accessing port of two different mPEs, and the module if_port_wr and if_port_rd mean the write and read port by which the interface controller can access the data memory. Depending on the different configurations, one mPE can access the data memory in either read or write mode. Thus Data memory array can provide flexibility for application mapping.

4   Loop Self-Pipelining

In coarse-grained reconfigurable architectures, loop pipelining execution plays a very important role to achieve maximum throughput, which can heavily improve their performance. However, in many coarse-grained reconfigurable architectures, loop pipelining execution mostly depends on software pipelining approaches [6] but not on hardware direct support. The LEAP architecture can assure application mapping from high level programming languages to the reconfigurable architecture.

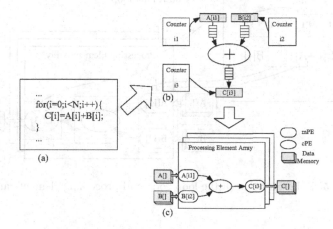

Fig. 4. Loop Self-pipelining: (a) a simple example; (b) dataflow graph mapping on the LEAP architecture; (c) operation binding

In the LEAP architecture, each individual operation in a loop body can be performed on a PE through operation binding (see Figure 4c). By operation binding, the dataflow that represents the kernel loops of an algorithm can be mapped onto the LEAP architecture, and the processing elements array, can accomplish computation tasks automatically and efficiently by utilizing data-driven principle without centralized control. This is the main idea of Loop Self-pipelining (LSP), which is similar to the software technique called self loop pipelining [6].The LSP allows efficient execution for loop pipelining, and leads to an increase in parallelism exploitation. Furthermore, it alleviates the pressure on compiler.

Figure 4 shows the procedure of Loop Self-pipelining. In Figure 4b, three counters in dataflow graph provide the index value of the FOR loop (see Figure 4a), and they are independent of each other. Three independent paths, furnishing the index value, are required for loop pipelining. There is no centralized control. The counters can drive data flowing by generating a new value when the old one has been consumed. The result of operation binding on the LEAP architecture is shown in Figure 4c. The counters are bound into mPEs, and the arithmetical operation addition is bound into cPEs. Additionally, all variables in the FOR loop are stored in their individual data memory.

The LSP technique fully utilizes the advantages of data-driven architecture. It transfers the control on loop behavior to memory operation, which manages the whole computation through the control of dataflow (see Figure 5). In Figure 5, the three mPEs act like valves, two for data-flow's flowing into, and one for flowing out. When PEs are flooded with data, throughout will be up to one result per cycle, i.e., if there are no loop-carried dependencies, a single loop iteration can be performed at one cycle no matter how many operations in this loop.

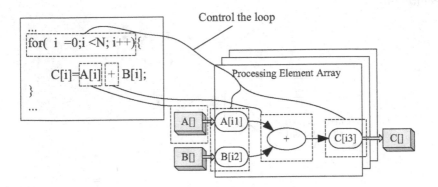

Fig. 5. Relation between the loop code and processing elements array

5   Performance Analysis

There are 56 cPEs in the LEAP architecture, and utilizing all cPEs yields a peak performance of 56 fixed point operations per cycle. Table 1 shows the performance of several algorithms by cycle-accurate Verilog simulation.

Table 1. Performance of the LEAP architecture.

Algorithm	#Cycle of Running	#PE	#Cycle of Init.	Ops/cycle	#Config mPE	cPE
FFT	5530	38	624	10	10	1
Median Filter	167001	42	1152	30	12	6
Sobel Edge Detection	166741	32	984	16	12	6

The algorithms in Table 1 are 1024 point depth first dit2 FFT, 3 ∗ 3 window median filter and 3∗3 window Sobel edge detection. Median filter and Sobel edge detection are applied to a 320 ∗ 240 image. We implemented Sobel edge detection algorithm only utilizing 50% of cPEs, and 66% for median filter algorithm at most. They utilize very few cPEs, leaving unused PEs for other algorithms running in parallel. Ops/cycle in Table 1 presents the peak performance, i.e., the number of the cPEs bound by these algorithms. In Table 1, the initial configuration takes very few cycles, e.g., only 624 cycles for FFT. Median filter and Sobel edge detection have the common features in memory accessing, and they require the same number of configuration words. Performing them take 167001 cycles and 166741 cycles respectively. The time consumed includes the cycles for data exchanging between data memory and external memory, which overrides the computation time.

6   Conclusions

This paper introduces the novel coarse-grained reconfigurable architecture named LEAP. Compared to other architectures, the LEAP architecture has simple data communication network, brief loop pipelining execution mode and flexible data memory. The feature that data can flow from up to down in mesh is suitable for stream-based application. The prototyping phase of the LEAP architecture has been implemented on an Altera FPGA EP1S80F1508C6 providing 79,040 logic elements. The host computer can communicate with the LEAP prototype through PCI bus, and testbench codes have run successfully on the prototype.

References

1. M. H. Lee, H. Singh, G. Lu, et al.. Design and Implementation of the MorphoSys Reconfigurable Computing Processor. Journal of VLSI and Signal Processing Systems for Signal, Image and Video Technology, 2000, 24: 147-164
2. B. Mei, S. Vernalde, D.Verkest, et al.. ADRES: An architecture with tightly coupled VLIW processor and coarse-grained reconfigurable matrix. Field-Programmable Logic and Applications (FPL'03), 2003. 61-70
3. V. Baumgarte, G. Ehlers, F. May, et al.. PACT XPP - A Self-Reconfigurable Data Processing Architecture. The Journal of Supercomputing, 2003, 26(2): 167-184
4. T. Miyamori and K. Olukotun. REMARC: Reconfigurable multimedia array co-processor.The ACM/SIGDA Sixth International Symposium on Field Programmable Gate Arrays(FPGA'98), 1998
5. Yong Dou and Xicheng Lu. LEAP: A Data Driven Loop Engine on Array Processor. Advanced Parallel Programming Technologies (APPT'03), 2003. 12-22
6. Joao M. P. Cardoso. Dynamic Loop Pipelining in Data-Driven Architectures. In: Proc. of the 2nd Conference on Computing Frontiers(CF'05), 2005. 106-115

Low-Power Data Cache Architecture by Address Range Reconfiguration for Multimedia Applications

Hoon-Mo Yang[1], Gi-Ho Park[2], and Shin-Dug Kim[1]

[1] Supercomputing Lab, The 3rd Engineering Building 532, Yonsei University,
120-749 134 Shinchon-Dong Seodaemun-Ku, Seoul, Korea
[2] Processor Architecture Lab. System LSI Division,
Samsung Electronics Co., LTD. Giheung, Korea
portent@parallel.yonsei.ac.kr, giho.park@samsung.com,
sdkim@yonsei.ac.kr

Abstract. Today's portable electric consumer devices tend to include more multimedia processing capabilities. This trend results increased processing resources, thus causing more power consumption. Therefore, the power-efficiency becomes important due to battery operated nature of portable devices. In this paper, we propose a reconfigurable data cache architecture, in which data allocation to a cache is constrained by address range configuration. Then we evaluate trade-off between performance and power efficiency. Comparing to the conventional cache architectures, power consumption can be reduced decently while maintaining miss rate of the proposed data cache similar to those of the conventional caches. The result shows that the reconfigurable data cache operates with 33.2%, 53.3%, and 70.4% less power when compared with direct-mapped, 2-way, and 4-way set-associative caches respectively.

Keywords: low-power, cache architecture, embedded system, multimedia application.

1 Introduction

Today's portable electric consumer devices tend to include more multimedia processing capabilities, such as encoding and decoding of digital audio, video, and still-images. As the devices are integrated with more multimedia processing capabilities, power consumption increases significantly and the power efficiency of the processing cores becomes one of the important design factors. Inside any particular processing core, it is well-known that on-chip cache consumes significant amount of power so that cache design becomes one of the main targets for power reduction usually.

In this paper, a reconfigurable data cache architecture is proposed to reduce the power consumed by data caching. For this goal, we extract the data accessing patterns of several multimedia benchmarks and utilize those characteristics to design a reconfigurable data cache architecture which distributes data accesses into a sub buffer and small direct-mapped caches. Then we evaluate its performance and power efficiency. The result shows that when the data address range is mapped carefully to

C. Jesshope and C. Egan (Eds.): ACSAC 2006, LNCS 4186, pp. 574–580, 2006.

each cache and buffer, miss rate of the reconfigurable data cache architecture is very similar to those of the conventional caches when proper sizes are given to each cache. Besides, power consumption by data caching decreases decently. When compared with direct-mapped cache, 33.2% of power consumption can be decreased, and around 55.3% and 70.4% can be decreased for 2-way and 4-way set associative caches respectively.

In Section 2, researches which cover memory system and multimedia applications are addressed as a related work. In Section 3, we propose a reconfigurable data cache architecture and describe its operation scheme. And also, we address the characteristics of memory access patterns, which are the basis for this work, within multimedia applications. Section 4 describes simulation methodology and its results are shown in Section 5. And lastly, Section 6 summarizes our work.

2 Related Work

The work in [1] performs the performance evaluation of multimedia applications for conventional memory system hierarchies and compares to SPECint95. This work shows that multimedia applications work well with conventional cache architectures and analyzes the reason. The work in [2] gives an overview of low-power techniques for mobile multimedia and internet applications. The paper classifies low-power techniques into several design-level based methodologies. Especially in the hardware architecture level, five reconfigurable hardware schemes are addressed.

There is an attempt to reduce power dissipations in memory hierarchies using special buffers. The work in [3] uses Energy-Saver Buffers(ESB) which resides between the L2 cache and main memory. ESB reduces the additional overhead incurred due to frequent resynchronization of the memory modules in a low-power state. The work in [4] presents a method that uses data buffers to smoothen request variations and to create long idleness for power management.

The work in [5] proposes hardware and software prefetching techniques for video applications to improve performance of a general purpose processor. The work in [6] performs detailed analysis on the mpeg-2 video decoder and its data usage pattern. This work evaluates the cache performance using various cache parameters and structures.

The work in [7], which is very similar to our work, proposes region-based caching. In this work, cache consists of two small caches, which are stack cache and global cache, and one main cache. The main idea of this work is filtering the stack and global data accesses out of the regular cache access so that the allocation of data is partitioned through multiple caches.

3 Reconfigurable Data Cache Architecture

To further increase the power efficiency of data cache, application-specific analysis of data access pattern should be performed and then, data cache architecture can be tailored according to the characteristics for a given system specification.

3.1 Data Access Characteristic of Multimedia Applications

Multimedia applications tend to show some common characteristics which can be summarized as the followings; (1) Data stream (audio, video, or image) goes through a predefined flow of algorithms. (2) Each data unit under processing of a certain algorithm function has the same size. (3) Data sets, such as coefficient tables required for filtering or reference block of MPEG coding, are applied to the target stream data at any consistent access rate. These can be represented as Figure 1.

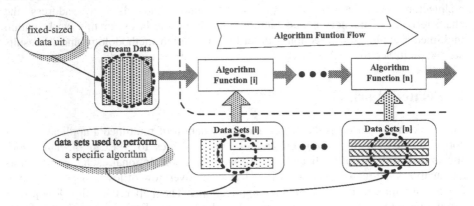

Fig. 1. Characteristics of multimedia algorithm processing flow

To observe data access characteristics of multimedia applications, we extract memory traces by executing several multimedia benchmarks. Figure 2 shows an example of mpeg2enc. We can identify that there are certain address ranges having same access characteristics within the ranges (shaded portion). Other benchmarks also show similar manner of data access pattern like mpeg2enc application.

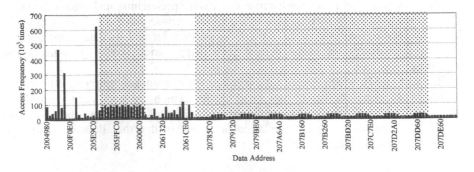

Fig. 2. Relationship between access frequencies and address ranges for mpeg2enc

3.2 Reconfigurable Data Cache Architecture and Management Policy

Our base architecture model of reconfigurable data cache consists of one sub buffer, two direct-mapped sub caches, one direct-mapped main cache, address demultiplexer, and cache select unit as presented in Figure 3. The sub buffer has four 32byte-sized entries, and each of two direct-mapped sub caches has a half size of the main cache. For example, assuming 8KB of total cache size, there are two 2KB direct-mapped sub caches, and one 4KB direct-mapped main cache.

The number and size of sub caches or buffers are not limited by the design we proposed in this paper. This can be changed depending on a target application, a given system specification, and design resource constraints. The reason why we choose one sub buffer and two sub caches is based on the access pattern extracted in Section 3.1, which shows that the address ranges having similar access characteristics can be separated into two or three ranges.

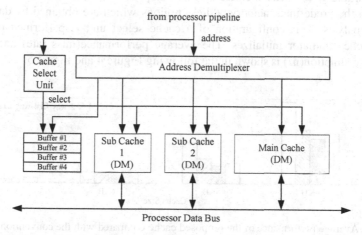

Fig. 3. Block diagram of proposing reconfigurable data cache architecture

All the caches are managed as if it is a normal cache. But the data allocation is limited by the predefined addresses which are registered in the cache select unit. Whenever there is a data access, cache select unit determines which cache to use according to the requested data address. Likewise, this scheme also applied to the sub buffer. We assume that configuring or registering addresses of the cache select unit is handled by special instructions. The processor should support these instructions so that programmer can utilize to set up the cache select unit and to load buffer data.

In this manner, the two sub caches and one sub buffer are mapped to the specified data address ranges and this kind of address mapping can be reconfigured on runtime when needed. But write-back and flush of cache data should be performed before reconfiguring the cache select unit.

4 Performance Evaluation

To perform performance evaluation, we select 6 benchmarks from mibench benchmark suite [10, 11] for image processing and audio processing. The 6 benchmarks selected are cjpeg, djpeg, lame, mad, tiff2bw, and tiffdither. And we cross-compile mpeg2enc and mpeg2dec programs [8] onto arm binary codes. Total 8 benchmarks are executed in simplescalar-arm 0.2 processor simulator [9], and then we capture addresses of the data accesses except the stack region. These data address traces are run on the cache simulator and we obtain cache performance for the different parameters. The total sizes of caches used are 4KB, 8KB, 16KB, and 32KB. And the line size of 32bytes is used for all caches.

For the power estimation of caches, we use CACTI 3.2[12, 13] model to obtain cache power parameters and apply the obtained parameters to calculate cache access power. The process technology parameter used is 0.13um. To configure reconfigurable data cache architecture, we mapped four sub buffers and two sub caches to the predefined memory address regions which are obtained by data access pattern analysis. This configuration of a cache select unit is performed only once when cache simulator initializes. The average performance(miss rate) and average power consumption(nJ) is shown in the following Figure 4 and Figure 5.

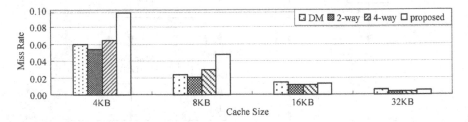

Fig. 4. Average performance of the proposed cache compared with the conventional caches

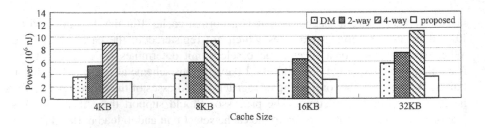

The results show that when the size of cache is either 4KB or 8KB, miss rate of proposed architecture is relatively higher than the conventional caches due to capacity misses. Therefore, effect of power reduction of the proposed cache diminishes due to frequent lower-level memory accesses. But if the size of cache becomes 16KB or 32KB, meaning that there are sufficient entries to cope with capacity miss, the miss rate goes under that of direct-mapped cache and maintains similar performance compared to 2-way or 4-way set-associative caches.

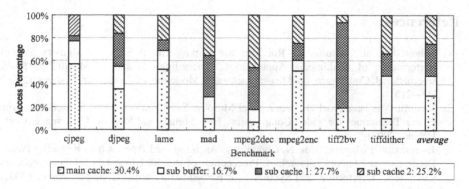

Fig. 6. Distribution effect of data accesses using reconfigurable data cache. The percentage value means the average amount of data access each cache and buffer absorbs.

The above Figure 6 presents distribution effect of data accesses. By separating data accesses into small caches and a buffer, we get reduced power consumption by accessing just one small cache or a buffer. As a result, our reconfigurable data cache consumes 33.2%, 55.3%, and 70.4% less power when compared to direct-mapped, 2-way set-associative, 4-way set-associative caches respectively. The amount of power consumption our reconfigurable data cache consumes is shown in Table 1.

Table 1. Relative amount of power the reconfigurable data cache consumes when compared to the conventional caches

Cache size	Cache architectures		
	DM	2-way	4-way
4KB	78.37%	51.63%	30.59%
8KB	59.85%	39.99%	25.12%
16KB	67.66%	48.10%	31.00%
32KB	61.21%	47.20%	31.88%
average	*66.77%*	*46.73%*	*29.65%*

5 Conclusion

In this work, a reconfigurable data cache architecture is proposed. It consists of two small direct-mapped caches and one small buffer. Before runtime, each cache and the buffer are mapped to a specific data address ranges defined by a programmer so that data accesses are distributed over small caches and buffer. Constraining data accesses to occur in one small cache or a buffer, we get reduced power consumption. The performance evaluation is performed using eight multimedia benchmarks. And we can identify that when the data address range is configured carefully to each cache and if the size of total cache becomes large to cover capacity misses, miss rates of the reconfigurable data cache becomes very similar to those of conventional caches. Furthermore, power consumption by data caching decreases decently. When compared with direct-mapped cache, 33.2% of power reduction acquired, and around 55.3% and 70.4% for 2-way and 4-way set associative caches respectively.

References

1. Sohum Sohoni, Zhiyong Xu, Rui Min and Yiming Hu: A Study of Memory System Performance of Multimedia Applications. Proceedings of the ACM SIGMETRICS International Conference on Measurement and Modeling of Computer Systems (2001) 206–215
2. Valentin Muresan, Noel O'Connor, Noel Murphy, Sean Marlow, Stephen McGrath: Low Power Techniques for Video Compression. Irish Signals and Systems Conference, Cork, Ireland (2002)
3. Jayaprakash Pisharath, Alok N. Choudhary: An Integrated Approach to Reducing Power Dissipation in Memory Hierarchies. Proceedings of the 2002 International Conference on Compilers, Architecture, and Synthesis for Embedded Systems, Grenoble, France (2002) 88-97
4. Nathaniel Pettis, Le Cai, and Yung-Hsiang Lu: Dynamic Power Management for Streaming Data. Proceedings of the 2004 International Symposium on Low Power Electronics and De-sign (2004) 62-65
5. Daniel F. Zucker, Ruby B. Lee, Michael J. Flynn: Hardware and Software Cache Prefetching Techniques for MPEG Benchmarks. IEEE Transactions of Circuits and Systems for Video Technilogy, Vol.10, No.5 (2000) 782-796
6. Peter Soderquist, Miriam Leeser: Optimizing the Data Cache Performance of a Software MPEG-2 Video Decoder. Proceedings of the fifth ACM International Conference on Multimedia, Seattle, Washington, United States (1997) 291-301
7. Hsien-Hsin S. Lee, Gary S. Tyson: Region-Based Caching: An Energy-Delay Efficient Memory Architecture for Embedded Processors. Proceedings of the 2000 International Conference on Compilers, Architecture, and Synthesis for Embedded Systems, San Jose, California, United States (2000) 120-127
8. MPEG Software Simulation Group, http://www.mpeg.org/MPEG/MSSG
9. SimpleScalar LLC, http://www.simplescalar.com
10. MiBench Version 1.0, http://www.eecs.umich.edu/mibench
11. Matthew R. Guthaus, Jeffrey S. Ringenberg, Dan Ernst, Todd M. Austin, Trevor Mudge, Richard B. Brown: MiBench: A free, commercially representative embedded benchmark suite. IEEE 4th Annual Workshop on Workload Characterization, Austin, TX,(2001)
12. Western Research Laboratory, research.compaq.com/wrl/people/jouppi/CACTI.html
13. Premkishore Shivakumar, Norman P. Jouppi: CACTI 3.0: An Integrated Cache Timing, Power, and Area Model, WRL Research Report 2001/2, Palo Alto, California, United States (2001)

Automatic Synthesis of Interface Circuits from Simplified IP Interface Protocols

ChangRyul Yun[1], YoungHwan Bae[2], HanJin Cho[2], and KyoungSon Jhang[1]

[1] Dept. of Computer Engineering, ChungNam National University, Daejeon, Korea
daedue@cnu.ac.kr, sun@cnu.ac.kr
[2] Multimedia SoC Design, ETRI, Daejeon, Korea
yhbae@etri.re.kr, hjcho@etri.re.kr

Abstract. Most approaches to interface synthesis take two interface FSMs including transactions or burst, derive a product FSM and generate an interface circuit from the product FSM. With these methods, it could be difficult and complicated to describe interface FSM of IP especially when IP has many transactions. Additionally, such descriptions may lead to a very large product FSM which results in large interface circuits. We propose a simplified interface FSM description scheme where transactions are represented based on transfers and several parameters. Since all transactions supported by IP may not be used in the system, the synthesis algorithm is designed to consider only those transactions which are involved in parameter matching. Through experiments we observed that our description scheme helps reduce the size of interface circuits and our synthesis method correctly generates the interface circuits.

1 Introduction

There are many studies on generating interface circuits from the interface protocols of intellectual properties (IP) [1, 2, 3]. One of the key problems of automatic synthesis of interface circuits revolves around how to describe the interface protocol of IP exactly and conveniently. A regular expression-based description was used to describe interface protocols [3]. But regular expression cannot convey branch conditions or multiple transactions. Timing diagram is seen as one such method to describe interface protocols of IPs [5]. But this method is not easy when it comes to representing several transactions or distinguishing among transactions.

The interface synthesis flow usually follows the steps mentioned below. The interface FSMs are derived from interface protocols described in one of aforementioned methods, and then a product FSM is built from interface FSMs of IP by the synthesis algorithm. Next, the interface circuit is generated based on the product FSM [1, 2, 5]. An interface protocol FSM consists of states and transitions. The write portion of interface protocol of AMBA AHB master is captured in Fig. 1. Only one transaction, an incremental burst of undefined length, is shown and the others are omitted with a shaded triangle as space is limited. There are 18 states and 40 transitions in FSM for the write operation of AMBA

C. Jesshope and C. Egan (Eds.): ACSAC 2006, LNCS 4186, pp. 581–587, 2006.
© Springer-Verlag Berlin Heidelberg 2006

master [2]. As we can see in the state diagram in Fig. 1, with these methods it could become difficult and complicated to describe IP interface protocols especially when IP has many transactions. Further, such descriptions may lead to a very large interface circuit generated from the product FSM. This paper proposes a simplified interface FSM description scheme where transactions are represented based on transfers and several parameters. In this way, we not only simplify the IP interface protocol description but also improve the readability and reusability of the description. Experiments show that this simplified interface protocol description scheme helps reduce the size of the generated interface circuits.

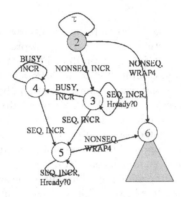

Fig. 1. The write Transaction of AMBA Master Protocol (Incremental burst of undefined length)

2   Simplified Interface Protocol Description Method

The full protocol of AMBA AHB master and OCN MNI[4] are described in the proposed scheme, called SIMPLE (a simplified interface protocol (FSM) description language), in Fig. 2. We need only three states (initial state, write state, and read state) in this case. Designers may use pseudo-variables to represent internal conditions of IP.

In the proposed method transactions are represented based on transfers and several parameters. In Fig. 2, "$transaction" on the transitions is a parameter that represents transaction type. $address, $wdata, and $rdata are parameters indicating a valid address, write data, and read data. In addition, internal variables ('count' in Fig. 2) in the description may be used for counting burst length of IP. The proposed method necessitates that the transaction parameters in interface protocol of an IP in a side have to be determined and matched or paired with those of another IP in the other side before the interface circuits are generated, and such information is described in the matching information as shown in Fig. 3.

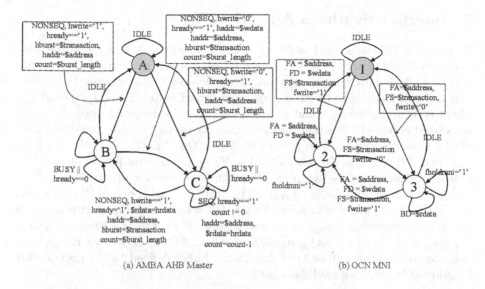

(a) AMBA AHB Master   (b) OCN MNI

Fig. 2. Protocol descriptions of AMBA master and OCN MNI in SIMPLE

The matching information includes port pairings, transaction mapping, and etc. This is generated through GUI interactions. Fig. 3 shows a part of the matching information for interface circuits between AHB and OCN MNI. Port pairing specifies the ports of the two IPs which are to be connected. For example, in Fig. 3, "FA" of OCN MNI is paired with "HADDR" of AHB. Additionally, a designer can set the size of the buffer assigned to a pair of ports. Transaction mapping specifies all transactions on both sides which are to be paired to complete the correct transfer of data. The underlined sentence in Fig. 3 represents a mapping between 4-beat burst transactions. This indicates that in order to connect two transactions, the value "011" of "HBURST (2:0)" of AHB master should be converted to the value "01" of "FS (3:2)" of OCN MNI. Matching information as shown in Fig. 3 determines the transaction-related parameters that appear in SIMPLE. The transactions not specified in matching information match single transactions of each IP. Besides, the matching information may include data on write/read signals, control signals and default value assignments on output ports.

//// Buffer Size, Signal (master), MSB, LSB, Signal (slave), MSB, LSB, $address or $wdata or $rdata
[Port Pairing] 1 , HADDR , 31 , 0 , FA , 31 , 0 , $address;
[Port Pairing] 1 , HWDATA , 31 , 0 , FD , 31 , 0 , $wdata;
//// Burst Transaction Length, Signal (master), MSB, LSB, Values, Signal (slave), MSB, LSB, Values
[Transaction Mapping] 4 , HBURST , 2 , 0 , "011" , FS , 3 , 2 , "01" ;

Fig. 3. A part of matching information for the synthesis of interface circuit between AHB master and OCN MNI

3   Interface Synthesis Algorithm

An interface FSM is defined as $P=(Q, I, O, D, V, T \in q, q_0)$, where Q is the state space and I and O are the sets of input and output control signals, D is a set of ports via which data/address are transferred, V is a set of user-defined variables, T is a set of transitions of state q, q_0 is an initial state. $T = \{ t_1: q \rightarrow (a) \ q' \}$, where t_1 is a transition, q and q' are source and destination states. 'a' is the associated action of transition. In this paper, we extract an interface FSM from SIMPLE automatically. Two protocols $PA = (Q_A, I_A, O_A, D_A, V_A, T_A \in q_A, q_{A0})$ and $PB = (Q_B, I_B, O_B, D_B, V_B, T_B \in q_B, q_{B0})$ are inputs of interface synthesis algorithm. The synthesis algorithm constructs a product FSM $PI = (Q_P, I_P, O_P, D_P, V_P, T_P \in q_P, q_{A0B0})$. The output (input) ports of PI correspond to input (output) ports of interface FSMs, D_P is determined by port pairings in matching information. q_{A0B0} is an initial state of PI. Q_P is a subset of $\{<q_A, q_B, s(a), s(w), s(r)> \mid q_A \in Q_A, q_B \in Q_B, a \in D_P, w \in D_P, r \in D_P\}$, where $s(a/w/r)$ indicates the existence (0 or 1) of data in the buffer defined by the port pairing for address/write data/read data port.

```
// Input of synthesis algorithm: FSMs(PA, PB) and Matching information
Q := null; // Q is a set of product-FSM.
PS := { [ P_AO, P_BO, s(a), s(w), s(r)] } // PS : a set of temporary states
// CurrentState := [q_AO, q_BO, s(a), s(w), s(r)] : one state of PS
while PS != null do
   Assign a state of PS to CurrentState
   Determine T_A ={t_1:q_A →(a) }, T_B ={t_2:q_B →(b) }
   // T_A ={t_1:q_A} : the set of transitions originating from q_A
   for all t_1 ∈ T_A, t_2 ∈ T_B do
   t_1':= ComputeComplement(t_1)
   // an action with all its responses complementary in transition (t_1)
   t_2':= ComputeComplement(t_2)
      if valid(t_1' ∪ t_2', s(a), s(w), s(r) ) then    /* (a) */
   ModifyCounter(s(a), s(w), s(r), t_1' ∪ t_2') /* (b) */
   NTransition := NewTransition(t_1' ∪ t_2', [q'_A, q'_B, s(a)', s(w)', s(r)'] )
   AddTransition(NTransition, CurrentState);
         if [ q'_A, q'_B, s(a)', s(w)', s(r)' ] (Q ∪ PS) then
            Add [ q'_A, q'_B, s(a)', s(w)', s(r)' ] to PS
         end if   end if
   end for
   Prune_Transition (CurrentState)
   Add CurrentState to Q and remove from PS
end while
Prune_DeadState( Q )
Generate_interface(Q, Matching_Information)
```

Fig. 4. Modified synthesis algorithm

Fig.4 displays our algorithm to generate a product FSM from interface FSMs and matching information. The synthesis algorithm presented in the paper [1] was modified in order to take the matching information into account and to prune redundant states and transitions during interface synthesis.

The meaning of *valid()* function in Fig.4 is as follows. valid(t_1' t_2' , s(a), s(w), s(r)) at (a) in Fig. 4 is defined 'true' if the sender has requested data stored in buffer or if the requested data is to be sent directly from the sender side port to the receiver side port. In the synthesis of interface circuits between IP (ip1) as a slave that sends address and data simultaneously in a transfer of a burst and IP (ip2) as a master that sends only one address followed by a number of data in a burst, *valid()* needs to be true although ip2 does not send the requested address to ip1 as long as the address buffer has the start address from ip2. The function *ModifyCounter()* function at (b) in Fig. 4 changes the number of data in each buffer as data moves in or out of the buffer. When ip1 acts as a master and ip2 acts as a slave, the addresses sent from ip1 to the address buffer are redundant except for the first start address. Therefore, the functionality of *ModifyCounter()* is changed so that the counter of the address buffer does not increase for the addresses that follow the first address. The FSM shown in Fig. 5 is a product

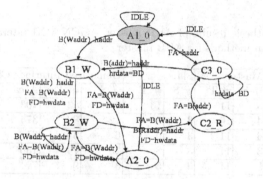

Fig. 5. The generated product FSM from AHB Master and OCN MNI

FSM derived from AHB Master in Fig 2 (a) and OCN MNI in Fig. 2 (b). We omit three wait states due to space limitation. The state name consists of a state name of master IP, a state name of slave IP, and the number of data in the corresponding buffer. The 'W' or 'R' in a state name indicates that a write or read address is stored in the address buffer. The interface circuit is generated from this product FSM.

4   Experimental Results and Summary

The proposed synthesis tool called AIG (Automatic Interface circuits Generation) has been implemented with about 16,000 lines of JAVA code. AIG takes as inputs two IP interface protocol descriptions and matching information. In the experiments to show the efficacy of the proposed interface protocol description scheme, we use AHB master interface protocols described using the previous methods (Examples 1 and 2 in Table 1) and our method (Example 3 in Table 1)

Table 1. The synthesis results of AHB master - OCN MNI interaface circuits with different description methods for AHB master

No.	AHB Master				Synthesis result			
	Description Method	Supported Transactions	# S	# T	# S	# T	area (slice)	f_{max} (MHz)
1	Previous Method [2]	Write Transactions (length: 1, 4, undefined)	3	13	6	44	60	201. 288
2	Previous Method [2]	Write/Read Transactions (length: 1, 4, undefined)	5	23	9	58	145	158. 239
3	Proposed method	All Transactions (Except for Error, Split, Abort)	3	11	9	53	103	180. 799

Table 2. The synthesis results of AHB master - OCN MNI interaface circuits with different description methods for AHB master

Master:Slave	Master		Slave		Generated Interface Circuits			
	# S	# T	# S	# T	# S	# T	Area	f_{max} (MHz)
AHB:OCN	3	11	3	13	9	53	103	180.799
OCN:AHB	4	16	3	9	12	89	374	105.430
BVCI:AHB	4	11	3	9	6	34	61	355.694
AHB:BVCI[7]	3	11	3	8	20	74	130	264.277
AHB:APB	3	11	3	5	3	9	7	581.564

to generate interface circuits between AHB master and OCN MNI. The comparison of synthesis results with different input descriptions is shown in Table 1. '# S' ('# T') in Table 1 indicates the number of states (transitions) of generated interface circuits. 'area'('f_{max}') indicates the area (the maximum frequency) of interface circuits. Please note in examples 1 and 2 in Table 1 that with previous method the more transactions are added in the description, the more states and transitions are necessary to represent such transactions. Furthermore, the descriptions supporting more transactions incur more area and make slow the maximum frequency of interface circuits. However, the interface protocol description (example 3 in Table 2) in the proposed scheme requires a very small number of states and transitions to represent all the necessary transactions by virtue of parameterization and transfer-based descriptions. Also, the description (example 3 in Table 1) using the proposed scheme results in a smaller area and faster attainment of maximum frequency of the generated interface circuit than the description (example 1, 2 in Table 1) using the previous method supporting single write, read and undefined length burst.

Considering matching information during interface synthesis, interface circuits can be generated even when it is not easy to do so with previous methods which have limitations like being unable to deal with differences in characteristics of IP interface protocols. With the proposed interface protocol description scheme, we could describe the interface protocols shown in Table 2 using only 3, 4 states. The experimental results of interface synthesis for IPs with various characteristics are displayed in Table 2. Using the synthesis of the interface circuit between AHB (mater) and OCN (MNI), we have an example of a successful generation of interface circuits between IP that sends address and data simultaneously in a burst and IP that sends a single start address followed by a number of data in a burst. To display the appropriateness of the interface synthesis method, we applied one of the generated interface circuits to a real system design. In other words, we observed that the generated interface circuits (AHB:OCN, OCN:AHB) could replace manually-designed interface circuits and work correctly on a H.264 decoder system [8].

We propose a simplified interface FSM description scheme (SIMPLE) where transactions are represented based on transfers and several parameters. The synthesis algorithm is designed to consider only transactions involved in parameter matching between two IPs to be connected. With SIMPLE, we could describe the various interface protocols only with 3, 4 states. Experiments shows that our simplified interface protocol description scheme helps reduce the size of the generated interface circuits and our synthesis method correctly generates the interface circuits.

References

1. D'silva V., Ramesh S., and Sowmya A.: Bridge Over Troubled Wrappers: Automated Interface Synthesis. Proceedings of the 17th International Conference on VLSI Design (2004)
2. D'silva V., Ramesh S, and Sowmya, A.: Synchronous Protocol Automata: A Framework for Modelling and Verification of SoC Communication Architectures. Proceedings of Design, Automation and Test in Europe Conference and Exhibition (2004)
3. Seawright, A., and Brewer, F.: Clairvoyant: A Synthesis System for Production-Based Specification. Very Large Scale Integration (VLSI) Systems, IEEE Transaction Volume 2, Issue 2 (1994)
4. Kangmin Lee, Se-Joong Lee, Hoi-Jun Yoo: SILENT: Serialized Low Energy Transmission Coding for n-Chip Interconnection Networks. Proceedings of Custom Integrated Circuits Conference, (2003)
5. Yin-Tsung Hwang and Sung-Chun Lin: Automatic Protocol Translation and Template Based Interface Synthesis for IP Reuse in SoC. Proceedings of the 2004 IEEE Asia-Pacific Conference, (2004)
6. ARM. Advanced micro-controller bus architecture specification http://www.arm.com
7. V.S.I. Alliance. http://www.vsi.org.
8. Soo Yun Hwang, Kyoung Son Jhang, June Young Chang, Han Jin Cho: An Implementation of a Flexible OCN based SoC Platform targeting H.264 Decoder, The 13th Korean Conference on Semiconductors (2006)

An Architectural Leakage Power Reduction Method for Instruction Cache in Ultra Deep Submicron Microprocessors

Chengyi Zhang, Hongwei Zhou, Minxuan Zhang, and Zuocheng Xing

College of Computer Science, National University of Defense Technology
410073, Changsha, Hunan, China
{chengyizhang, hwzhou, mxzhang, zcxing}@nudt.edu.cn

Abstract. Leakage power will exceed dynamic power in microprocessor as feature size shrinks, especially for on-chip caches. Besides developing low leakage process and circuit, how to control the leakage power in architectural level is worth to be studied. In this paper, a PDSR (Periodically Drowsy Speculatively Recover) algorithm and its extended version with adaptivity are proposed to optimize instruction cache leakage power dissipation. SPEC CPU2000 simulation results show that, with negligible performance loss, PDSR can aggressively decrease leakage power dissipation of instruction cache. Compared with other existing methods, PDSR and adaptive PDSR achieve more satisfying and more robust energy efficiency.

Keywords: Leakage Power, Drowsy cache, Periodically Drowsy Speculative Recover, Adaptive.

1 Introduction

Leakage Power of the chips is expected to increase by five times for each technology generation in the future, resulting in leakage power becoming the dominant part of chip power budget.

On-chip caches are the most leakage energy intensive components in microprocessor due to large scale transistors. State-destroying and state-preserving techniques have been proposed to reduce the leakage power of memory structures. Gated-vdd [1] is state-destroying technique, which disconnects a cell from its supply voltage or ground. Various control policies such as Cache Decay [2] have been proposed to gate cells. Accesses to the gated cells need data reloading from the lower memory level, which leads to extra dynamic energy consumption. State preserving techniques such as drowsy caches [3], put cells into low leakage mode without destroying their contents. In this mode the cells leak weakly, but still more than the gated-vdd approach. Drowsy do not entail extraneous misses but can incur performance loss. Accessing drowsy cells requires several additional cycles—to bring them back to normal state—but typically less than the latency of a decay-induced miss. DVS (Dynamic Voltage Scaling) [4] is an effective circuit to implement drowsy caches.

C. Jesshope and C. Egan (Eds.): ACSAC 2006, LNCS 4186, pp. 588–594, 2006.
© Springer-Verlag Berlin Heidelberg 2006

The key difference between drowsy caches and cache decay is that in drowsy caches the cost of being wrong is relatively small. Many papers [5,6] dedicate to controversy about which method is more effective. But this is a headachy problem, because the answer depends on many factors, such as next level cache access latency, state transition cycles, or even application behavior. Other works [6,7] attempt to combine these two techniques, resulting in more manufacturing challenges and more sophisticated control policy. In my opinion, elaborating a single technique and designing economical control policy are more practical. In this paper, we select drowsy method based on DVS as our object of optimization, because drowsy is relatively moderate in performance overhead, especially for L1 on-chip caches.

According to Flautner [3], *simple* policy—where cache lines are periodically (4k cycles) put into a low-power mode—reaches a reasonable compromise between easy implementation, power saving, and performance protection for data cache. But for more spatial and less temporal locality, L1 Icache works better with *noaccess* policy—putting only lines that were not accessed in a period into low-power mode. In this paper, an improved *simple* policy cooperating with speculatively recovering is proposed to more aggressively put I-cache lines into drowsy states without performance impact. An adaptive extension is also proposed to dynamically adjust the refresh window size for eliminating energy efficiency dithering among different workloads.

2 Methodology

Simulations in this paper are based on the *SimpleScalar* framework [8]. Our processor model closely resembles Alpha 21264 [9] (Table 1). Power estimation models are based on Princeton *Wattch* [10] and Virginia *HotLeakage* [11]. We choose 70nm technology with 0.9V supply voltage and 0.3V drowsy voltage, 5.6GHz clock speed and 80 ℃ environment temperature. The threshold voltages of N-transistor and P-transistor are 0.19V and 0.21V respectively. The benchmark suite for this study consists of a set of eight SPEC CPU2000 benchmarks: *applu*, *art*, *equake*, *mgrid*, *bzip2*, *gcc*, *mcf* and *vortex*. They are compiled for the Alpha instruction set using Compaq Alpha compiler with SPEC *peak* settings. In order to capture the most important program behaviors while at the same time accelerating simulation, we use the simulation points that were described and verified in *SimPoint* [12].

Table 1. Configuration of Simulated Processor

Processor core	
Instruction Window	80-RUU, 40-LSQ
Issue width	4
Function Unit	4-IntALU, 1-IntMULT, 2-FALU, 1-FMULT, 2-MPort
Memory Hierarchy	
L1 DCache	64KB, 4-way, 32Bblock, WB
L1 ICache	64KB, 2-way, 32B block, WB
Unified L2 Cache	1MB, 4-way, 32B block, WB, 6-cycle latency
Memory	100 cycles, 16 bus width

2.1 Metrics

IPC can be used to represent performance. Architectural leakage control polices possibly result in power overheads (P_e), which consists of four sources: dynamic power and leakage power due to extra hardware, dynamic power due to mode transitions, and dynamic power due to extra latency in accessing the drowsy lines. So *Normalizedleakagesaving* can represent the compositive effect of leakage power reduction:

$$Normalizedleakagesaving = (origleakage - newleakage - P_e) / origleakage$$

Energy efficiency is a popular metric to trade off between power and performance. *EDP* (Energy Delay Product) is an appropriate value to quantitatively represent energy efficiency. Simulation cycles can represent delay (D), then the energy efficiency optimizing ratio γ can be calculated as:

$$\gamma = EDP / EDP' = (P_d + P_s) \cdot D^2 / (P_d' + P_s') \cdot D'^2 = S^2 (P_d + P_s) / (P_d' + P_s')$$

P_d , P_s are the baseline dynamic and leakage power respectively, and P_d' , P_s' are the corresponding dynamic and leakage power after optimization. S is the speedup in Amdahl's law [13]. Assuming the average proportion between leakage power and the total power in microprocessor chip is α_1 , and the proportion between I-cache leakage power and total leakage power is α_2 , then the proportion α between I-cache leakage power and total power is $\alpha_1 \alpha_2$. Leakage power is proportional to transistor number, so α_2 can be represented by area percent of the structure. Then,

$$P = P_{s-icache} / \alpha, \quad P_s = P_{s-icache} / \alpha_2, \quad P_d = P_{s-icache} (1 - \alpha_1) / \alpha$$

Simply, we consider the extra power P_e as a part of the optimized leakage power $P_{s-icache}'$, that is $P_{s-icache}' = newleakage + P_e$. Assuming instructions committed when using leakage control policy is the same as before, the dynamic energy can be considered no change, so $P_d' = P_d \cdot S$. Architectural leakage control policies usually increase execution time, making $S \le 1$ and dynamic power reduced, but we can assume $P_d' = P_d$ conservatively. If the leakage power of I-cache is reduce to $1 / \lambda$, then

$$\gamma = \frac{P}{P_d + P_s(1 - \alpha_2) + P_{s-icache}'} \cdot S^2 = \frac{\dfrac{P_{s-icache}}{\alpha}}{P_{s-icache} \dfrac{1 - \alpha_1}{\alpha} + P_{s-icache} \dfrac{1 - \alpha_2}{\alpha_2} + \dfrac{P_{s-icache}}{\lambda}} \cdot S^2 = \frac{S^2}{1 - \alpha + \dfrac{\alpha}{\lambda}}$$

γ expresses that the improvement of energy efficiency when using architectural leakage power control policy to a structure depends on not only the power reduction ability λ and the performance impact S , but also the area proportion α_2 and leakage power importance α_1 .

3   Periodically Drowsy Speculatively Recover

For aggressive leakage power reduction, tag arrays are always drowsed together with data arrays. This results in another cycle stall for waking up all the drowsy lines in the indexed set. Longer access latency may increase total execution time and thus energy dissipation, offsetting the leakage energy saving. This negativity can be neutralized by speculatively recovering method. Researches [14] have shown that instruction access has some temporal or spatial locality, making them predictable. Cache and prefetch are all based on this observation and have been popularly equipped in modern processors. In drowsy caches, waking up latency can also be overlapped with oracle knowledge of access trace. With this approximated future knowledge, drowsy cache lines can be speculatively recovered and extra stall cycles can be partially eliminated. This would allow a more aggressive drowsy policy with negligible performance loss. Combined with traditional *simple* periodical policy, a PDSR policy is named.

Speculative recovering is somewhat different from prefetching. Recovering only raises supply voltage to normal level instead of fetching data from memory like prefetching, because the contents of drowsy lines are retained. Moreover, recovering granularity is cache set instead of block for the reason mentioned above. No matter hit or miss, waking up latency is hidden completely. PDSR can sustain inaccuracy well, because misprediction will not pollute cache except for extra transition energy.

Generally, instruction caches access cache lines sequentially except when branches are encountered. In many prefetching studies, the next-line prefetch has been shown effective for improving cache performance [15]. So a modified next-set prediction mechanism is also all right for speculatively recovering. Each access to drowsy instruction cache triggers a speculative recovering. The next set close to the indexed set by this access is pre-recovered by default. Note that all cache lines are still put into drowsy mode periodically, which is the same as traditional *simple* policy.

3.1 Comparison with Other Control Policies

Through SPEC CPU2000 simulation, we compared PDSR with other existing leakage power control policies, including *simple* policy and *noaccess* policy. A 64K bytes, 2-way set associative, 32 bytes cache line instruction cache is configured. The refresh window size is set to 4k cycles, and recover latency is set to 2 cycles. To calculate γ, α is set to 0.05, just as the setting in the last section. Normalized *IPC*, *Normalizedleakagesaving* and γ is illustrated in fig. 1, 2, and 3. From figure 1, we can see that processor performance with PDSR policy is higher than that with *simple* or *noaccess* policy, resulting from next-set speculative recovering. But due to speculative recovering, leakage power net saving with PDSR policy is a little smaller than *simple* or *noaccess* policy (see fig. 2). Considering power and performance together, the energy efficiency of PDSR policy is better than the other two policies (see fig. 3).

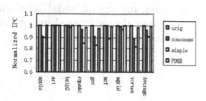

Fig. 1. Normalize IPC

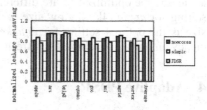

Fig. 2. Normalized leakage net saving

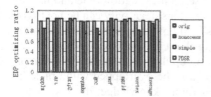

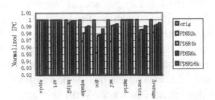

Fig. 3. Energy efficiency optimizing ratio   **Fig. 4.** Normalized IPC of different window

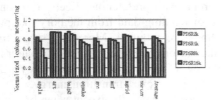

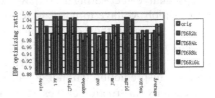

Fig. 5. Normalized leakage net saving of different window size   **Fig. 6.** EDP optimizing ratio of different window size

Note that although the average γ of PDSR is bigger than 1, two benchmarks, *gcc* and *equake* achieve deteriorated energy efficiency due to drastic performance impact. Since the access latency of Icache is crucial for pipeline throughput, leakage control policies can not increase access latency too much.

3.2 Refresh Window Size

Refresh window size will impact the effect of PDSR policy. Generally, the bigger the window size is, the higher performance is achieved (see fig. 4). On the contrary, the bigger the window size is, the less leakage power is saved (fig. 5). Longer refresh period can take advantage of instruction reuse, one recovering satisfying multiple accesses, so the number of recovering operation is reduced and wake up latency is eliminated. Smaller window size refreshes cache lines more frequently and makes the lines drowsy almost all the time, achieving higher off ratio. When considering power and performance together, PDSR with 4k and 16k windows achieve the higher average energy efficiency (see fig. 6). But for different workloads, the window sizes achieving the optimized γ are different. For example, 2k window size is the optimal setting for *applu*, 4k window size is the optimal setting for *mgrid*, and 16k window size is the optimal setting for *equake*. So, for achieving the optimized energy efficiency among all benchmarks, refresh window size must be adjustable.

4 Adaptive PDSR

PDSR can achieve satisfying average γ, but constant window size can not achieve the optimized γ among all benchmarks. Different workloads have different access pattern, even different phases in a single benchmark have different runtime behavior, resulting power and performance dithering. So making the window size adaptive will allow a finer power-performance tradeoff. We call it adaptive PDSR policy.

One way of accomplishing this is by counting the normal accesses A_n (accesses that locate in the recovered set, meaning normal accesses without extra waking up cycles) in each interval. rn is defined as the ratio between normal accesses A_n and total accesses A in the last interval. Window size (W) alters in a set of discrete values ($W \in S_w$). We still assume $\alpha = 0.05$ ($\alpha_1 = 50\%$, $\alpha_2 = 10\%$). To achieve energy efficiency improvement ($\gamma > 1$), speedup $S > 0.95^{1/2} \approx 0.975$ is necessary, and Icache off ratio $1 - f_a = 1 - 1/\lambda > (1 - S^2)/\alpha$ is also necessary. These two necessary conditions can be used to adjust W, ensuring that energy efficiency is improved at any moment. S can be approximated by rn, and Icache off ratios in each interval are gained by snooping recovering signal. The following is control flow.

```
W = min(S_w);
if (A_n/A<0.975) then
    W =W +1;  /*a bigger size in S_w is assigned */
else if (1-f_a<(1-S^2)/α) then
    W =W -1;  /*a smaller size in S_w is assigned */
```

With adaptivity, W selects the most appropriate size in S_w for current phase and current workload, eliminating power and performance dithering among different workloads and different execution phases.

Setting $S_w = \{512, 1024, 2048, 4096, 8192, 16384\}$ and wake up latency 2 cycles, we evaluate the ability of adaptive PDSR in energy efficiency balancing among benchmarks. Fig. 7 describes the track of refresh window size alteration when eight benchmarks are simulated. Note that only 100M instructions are committed. We can see that W swings in S_w until the most appropriate size is selected. Different workloads have different steady points and different convergence patterns. Fig. 8 illustrates performance of adaptive PDSR. Although it doesn't work as well as 16k PDSR, but its power saving is much more than 16k PDSR, even than 4k PDSR policy (see fig. 9). Fig. 10 describes the energy efficiency optimizing ratio of adaptive PDSR, 4k PDSR

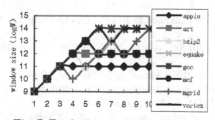

Fig. 7. Track of window size alteration

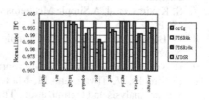

Fig. 8. Normalized IPC of APDSR

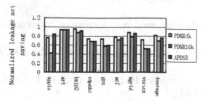

Fig. 9. Norm. leakage netsaving of APDSR

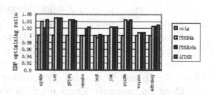

Fig. 10. EDP optimizing ratio of APDSR

and 16k PDSR policies. Obviously, with adaptive PDSR, each benchmark achieves almost the optimal energy efficiency, and the average γ is also the optimal.

5 Conclusion

We present PDSR algorithm, an improved simple policy for instruction drowsy caches with the help of next-set prediction mechanisms to speculatively recover cache lines. Simulation results show that constant window size PDSR can achieve superior energy efficiency than traditional *noaccess* and *simple* policy, but dithering among different benchmarks exists. We then propose an adaptive extension of PDSR to trade off performance and power when a wide range of applications are loaded. SPEC CPU2000 simulation results show that, with negligible performance loss, adaptive PDSR can aggressively decrease energy dissipation of Icache and achieve more robust and more satisfying energy efficiency.

Acknowledgments. This work was supported by NSFC (No. 60376018) in China.

References

1. M. D. Powell et al. Gated-Vdd: A Circuit Technique to Reduce Leakage in Deep- Submicron Cache Memories. ISLPED2000, pp.90-95.
2. S. Kaxiras, Z. Hu and M. Martonosi. Cache Decay: Exploiting Generational Behavior to Reduce Cache Leakage Power. ISCA2001, pp.240-251.
3. K. Flautner, N.S.Kim, S.Martin, D.Blaauw, and T.Mudge. Drowsy Caches: Simple Techniques for Reducing Leakage Power. ISCA2002, pp.147-157.
4. T. Pering, T. Burd and R. Brodersen. The Simulation and Evaluation of Dynamic Voltage Scaling Algorithms. ISLPED1998, pp.76-81.
5. Yingmin Li et al. State-preserving vs. Non-state-preserving Leakage Control in Caches. DATE2004.
6. Yan Meng, Timothy Sherwood and Ryan Kastner. On the Limits of Leakage Power Reduction in Caches. HPCA11, 2005
7. S. Kaxiras, et al. A Simple Mechanism to Adapt Leakage-Control Policies to Temperature. ISLPED 2005.
8. D. Burger and T. Austin. The SimpleScalar Tool Set, version 2.0. Computer Architecture News, 25(3):13-25, June 1997.
9. R. Kessler. The Alpha 21264 Microprocessor. In IEEE Micro, pp.24-36, Mar, 1999.
10. D. Brooks, V. Tiwari, and M. Martonosi. Wattch: A Framework for Architectural-level Power Analysis and Optimization. The 27th ISCA, pp.83-94, June 2000.
11. Y. Zhang, et al. Hotleakage: An Architectural, Temperature-aware Model of Subthreshold and Gate Leakage. Tech. Report CS-2003-05, University of Virginia, Mar. 2003.
12. http://www.cs.ucsd.edu/~calder/simpoint/
13. Hennessy J L and Patterson D A. Computer Architecture: A Quantitative Approach. San Francisco: Morgan Kaufmann Publish, 3rd edition, 2002
14. S. Sair, T. Sherwood, and B. Calder. Quantifying load stream behavior. In the HPCA-8, Feb. 2002.
15. J. Smith and W.-C. Hsu, Prefetching in Supercomputer Instruction Caches, Proc of Int. Conf. on Supercomputing, pp. 588- 597, Nov 1992.

An Efficient Approach to Energy Saving in Microcontrollers

Wenhong Zhao[1] and Feng Xia[2]

[1] Precision Engineering Laboratory,
Zhejiang University of Technology, Hangzhou 310014, China
wenhongzhao@gmail.com
[2] National Laboratory of Industrial Control Technology,
Zhejiang University, Hangzhou 310027, China
xia@iipc.zju.edu.cn

Abstract. Although energy saving has increasing importance for energy-limited microcontrollers, low power and high control performance are at odds with each other. This paper presents a simple yet efficient dynamic voltage scaling (DVS) scheme that targets reducing CPU energy consumption while meeting control requirements. With focus on two typical kinds of sources of workload variability, it explores a combination of time-triggered and event-triggered mechanisms. Simulations are carried out to highlight the merits of the proposed approach. It is argued that in comparison with traditional DVS scheme, it saves considerably more energy while providing comparable control performance.

Keywords: Energy saving, dynamic voltage scaling, microcontroller, control performance, workload variability.

1 Introduction

In recent years, there has been a growing use of embedded computing platforms in real-time control applications, e.g., mobile robots and automotive electronic systems, etc. An evident trend in today's embedded applications is that an increasing number of devices are battery-powered. Battery life thereby becomes a critical factor that determines the usability of the system, and must be taken into account during system design. However, the goals of achieving high performance and prolonging battery life are at odds with each other in a way that improving performance often demands higher energy consumption [1]. In the context of embedded control, the limited computing capacity further causes the problem of energy management to be much more vital for microcontrollers running on batteries. They must have low energy consumption in order to prolong battery life while providing required control performance [2-4].

One promising method to achieve tradeoffs between low power and high performance in CMOS-based embedded systems is dynamic voltage scaling (DVS) [1, 5]. The majority of existing microprocessors such as Intel's Xscale and StrongARM, AMD's K6-2+, and Transmeta's Crusoe, etc. have all supported this technique. DVS exploits the hardware characteristics of these processors to reduce

C. Jesshope and C. Egan (Eds.): ACSAC 2006, LNCS 4186, pp. 595–601, 2006.

energy consumption through dynamically changing the supply voltage and operating frequency at the same time. It has been demonstrated to be highly effective in saving energy for different types of applications, both real-time and non real-time.

In traditional microcontrollers, concurrent control tasks are usually scheduled according to their worst-case execution times (WCET). Because the actual execution time of a task is less then its WCET in most cases, budgeting for the WCET may result in excessive energy consumption even if the DVS technique is adopted [6]. Moreover, the workload of a multitasking microcontroller may vary significantly during run time. Typical reasons include, e.g., changes in either task execution times or the number of tasks. This fluctuating feature of workload makes it not so easy to develop an efficient DVS scheme for microcontrollers.

In the literature, only a few researchers have applied DVS to real-time control tasks. Lee and Kim [7] consider tradeoffs between control performance and energy consumption for the first time, and propose both static and dynamic solutions. Xia *et al.* [2] suggest the DVS-FS scheme by integrating DVS with feedback control real-time scheduling. Wang *et al.* [8] propose a static energy-aware optimization solution using evolution strategy for codesign of control and real-time scheduling. Jin *et al.* [9] has dealt with the problem of energy-aware scheduling design of control tasks. Xia and Sun [3] present the methodology of EDVS based on direct feedback scheduling. Following this methodology, we develop a cost-effective DVS approach that uses an asynchronous period adjustment mechanism in our previous work [4].

In this paper, we attack the problem of saving energy in multitasking microcontroller where the workload changes significantly over time. A DVS scheme that essentially operates in an interval-based fashion is presented. In order to properly scale the voltage of the processor, the near-future workload is predicted using a simple yet effective algorithm. Besides the time-triggered feature of our approach, we also introduce an event-triggered mechanism to cope with the workload variability due to adding or removing control loops/tasks, which may be needed during system reconfiguration. Simulation experiments are carried out to evaluate the performance of the proposed approach.

The structure of this paper is as follows. In Section 2, we describe the problem considered. Our approach is presented in Section 3. Its performance is evaluated in Section 4 by simulation experiments. Section 5 concludes this paper.

2 Problem Description

Consider a DVS-enabled microcontroller where N independent controller tasks $\{\tau_i\}$ run concurrently. Each controller task is responsible for controlling a plant. It is natural for controller tasks that they are periodic, with the deadline equal to the period. Each control task τ_i is characterized by the following parameters:

- c_i: the execution time. For various reasons, e.g., the size of sampled data to be processed by the control algorithm changes with the state of the plant, this parameter may vary during run time and is not known until the completion of task execution.
- w_i: the worst-case execution time assumed to be known.

- h_i: the period that corresponds to the sampling period of the relevant control loop. Once designed offline, the periods of all tasks will remain fixed.

For sake of simple description, we define c_i and w_i for the case where the processor operates at its full speed. Note that when the voltage is adjusted, the *actual* execution time and worst-case execution time of each task will change accordingly.

2.1 Tradeoff Between Energy and Delay

For processors built on CMOS circuits, the dominant source of energy consumption is the dynamic power dissipation. It has been found that the amount of energy consumption, E_i, for task τ_i typically increases quadratically with the supply voltage [10,11]. Therefore we have

$$E_{total} = \sum E_i = \sum (C_i \cdot R_i \cdot V_{dd}^2) \propto V_{dd}^2 \qquad (1)$$

where C_i is a constant indicating the average switched capacitance per clock cycle, R_i is the total number of cycles required for the execution of the task, and V_{dd} is the supply voltage. Employing an interval-based DVS approach, we will assign the same voltage level for all tasks within every time interval.

According to (1), reducing voltage saves energy. However, the voltage reduction increases circuit delay, D, and their relationship approximates that

$$D \propto V_{dd} / (V_{dd} - V_t)^2 \qquad (2)$$

where V_t is the threshold voltage. For control loops, a natural result of increase in circuit delay is longer control delay, which degrades control performance from the control perspective. This will be much more serious if the task schedulability is violated due to prolonged task execution times. Obviously, there is a fundamental tradeoff between saving energy and improving control performance when dynamically scaling the voltage of the microcontroller.

2.2 Workload Variability

With DVS, the degree to which the energy consumption could be reduced is highly dependent on the system workload [11]. As a consequence, workload variability affects the effectiveness of DVS, especially when the timeliness and schedulability of all tasks must be guaranteed in order to achieve required control performance. In this paper, we consider two typical kinds of sources of workload variations:

1) Varying task execution times. The execution time (parameter c_i) of each task may change over time, regardless of the voltage scaling.
2) Dynamic task activation and termination. New tasks/loops may be added, and existing tasks/loops may be removed at runtime.

In the next section, we will present an efficient DVS scheme to manage workload variability, with the primary goal of saving energy while maintaining satisfactory control performance.

3 The Proposed Approach

Assume that all CPU voltages are normalized with respect to the maximum value, and the normalized voltage, α, can be changed continuously in the range of $[\alpha_{min}, 1]$, where α_{min} is the minimum (normalized) voltage. When the voltage is set to α, the actual (worst-case) execution time of τ_i will be c_i/α (w_i/α). The switching overheads between voltage levels are neglected. Control tasks are scheduled according to the EDF algorithm. Throughout this paper, we define *workload* as the product of CPU utilization and normalized voltage.

The architecture of our approach is given in Fig. 1. Basically, the proposed DVS scheme operates in a time-triggered fashion. That is, it performs the workload prediction and voltage scaling operations at regular intervals during run time. We choose such a system-level method rather than a task-level approach mainly because of its simplicity and effectiveness. A second reason is that task-level solutions often require modification of the application program as well as support from the compiler, which cannot always be guaranteed in the context of embedded control.

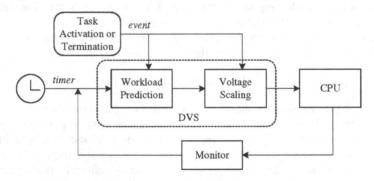

Fig. 1. Architecture of our approach

3.1 Workload Prediction

Let's consider first the workload variability caused by varying execution times only. During every invocation interval, the proposed DVS approach monitors current CPU utilization, u_k, which is the ratio of busy CPU time to the interval, T. Then the workload of current interval is calculated as $\ell_k = u_k \cdot \alpha_k$. To predict the near-future workload, several algorithms have been presented in the realm of DVS [5]. We here use a simple algorithm that has been successfully applied to job execution-time estimation for real-time control tasks [12]. The predicted workload will be:

$$\hat{\ell}_{k+1} = \lambda \hat{\ell}_k + (1-\lambda)\ell_k \tag{3}$$

where λ is a forgetting factor.

Based on the predicted workload, the DVS module will adjust the voltage such that the CPU cycles will be fully utilized in the next interval. Similar to our previous work

[4], we here set the voltage level that maximizes the CPU utilization while meeting the task schedulability constraint, i.e., $\hat{u}_{k+1} = \hat{\ell}_{k+1}/\alpha_{k+1} \leq 1$. Therefore we have

$$
\alpha_{k+1} = \begin{cases} \alpha_{min} & \hat{\ell}_{k+1} < \alpha_{min} \\ \hat{\ell}_{k+1} & \alpha_{min} \leq \hat{\ell}_{k+1} \leq 1 \\ 1 & \hat{\ell}_{k+1} > 1 \end{cases} \tag{4}
$$

3.2 Event-Triggered Mechanism

To cope with abrupt and large workload variations induced by dynamic task activation and termination, we integrate an even-triggered mechanism into the originally time-triggered DVS architecture. Each time a new control task/loop is added or an existing task/loop is removed, the DVS scheme will be triggered immediately, causing the CPU voltage to be re-assigned as follows.

In case a new control loop j is added during the time interval $[T_k, T_{k+1})$, we will first update the value of $\hat{\ell}_{k+1}$ by

$$
\hat{\ell}_{k+1} = \hat{\ell}_{k+1} + w_j / h_j . \tag{5}
$$

If several tasks are added at the same time, the above operation will be performed iteratively for every task. And then a new voltage will be determined using (4).

In case of task termination, the event-triggered mechanism operates similarly. The only difference relies on the algorithm used to update $\hat{\ell}_{k+1}$. When τ_j is removed, it becomes

$$
\hat{\ell}_{k+1} = \hat{\ell}_{k+1} - c_j / h_j \tag{6}
$$

where c_j is the recorded execution time of the latest job of task j. Note that each time a new value of $\hat{\ell}_{k+1}$ is calculated, it will be memorized temporarily for further use and the old one could be discarded.

4 Evaluation

We next conduct simulation experiments to evaluate the performance of our approach. Consider the case where four simple control loops share one variable-voltage microcontroller. The controlled plants have the same transfer function $G(s)=1000/(s^2+s)$, and each control task executes a well-designed PID control algorithm. The timing parameters (w_i, h_i) of each task are (3, 10), (2, 9), (2, 10), (2, 9) respectively, in time unit of ms. The parameter c_i of each task vary uniformly in the range $[\beta \cdot w_i, w_i]$, $0 < \beta \leq 1$. This distribution function of task execution times has been used in [13]. Other parameters are set as follows: $\alpha_{min}=0.36$, $\lambda=0.6$, $T=50ms$.

Simulations run in the following pattern. At the start, task τ_1 and τ_2 are switched on. Task τ_3 and τ_4 remain off until t = 1s. At time t = 2s, task τ_4 is removed. The whole simulation lasts 3s. Each plant experiences an input step change every 1s when active. Three methods are examined: 1) NON: the CPU always operates at full speed, 2) TRA: traditional DVS based on WCET, 3) OUR: the approach presented in Section 3. Each value reported below takes the average of 10 runs.

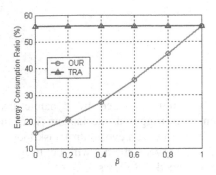

Fig. 2. Energy consumption ratio   **Fig. 3.** Control cost ratio

Energy Consumption Ratio (ECR). We define ECR as the ratio of energy consumption of TRA or OUR to that of NON. Accordingly, $ECR = \sum_{k=1}^{K} \alpha_k^2 \Big/ K$, where K is the total number of invocation. Fig. 2 shows the ECR of TRA and OUR as a function of β. It is clear that DVS is effective in energy saving, and our approach is able to save up to 40% more energy compared with traditional DVS scheme. OUR and TRA become nearly identical when $\beta=1$.

Control Cost Ratio (CCR). In simulations we record the IAE (integral Absolute Error) of each loop to assess the control performance. The CCR is defined as the ratio of the sum of all loops' IAE of TRA or OUR to that of NON. Note that the larger the control cost the worse the control performance. The simulation results are shown in Fig. 3. As we can see, the examined three schemes deliver comparable control performance, because all CCR values are quite close to one.

5 Conclusions

This paper deals with the problem of reducing energy consumption in multitasking microcontrollers. An efficient DVS scheme that features the combination of time-triggered and event-triggered mechanisms is presented. It is devoted to managing the workload variability of real-time control tasks. Simulation results show that compared with traditional DVS method, our approach is more effective in reducing energy consumption while guaranteeing comparable control performance.

Acknowledgments. This work is partially supported by Zhejiang Provincial Natural Science Foundation of China under Grant No. M503059.

References

1. P. Pillai and K.G. Shin: Real-Time Dynamic Voltage Scaling for Low Power Embedded Operating Systems, Proc. 18th ACM symposium on Operating Systems Principles, Banff, Alberta, Canada (2001) 89-102
2. Feng Xia, Xiaohua Dai, Xiaodong Wang, and Youxian Sun: Feedback Scheduling of Real-Time Control Tasks in Power-Aware Embedded Systems, Proc. 2nd Int. Conf. on Embedded Software and Systems, Xi'an, China, IEEE CS Press (2005) 513-518
3. Feng Xia and Youxian Sun: An Enhanced Dynamic Voltage Scaling Scheme for Energy-Efficient Embedded Real-Time Control Systems, Lecture Notes in Computer Science 3983 (2006) 539-548
4. Wenhong Zhao and Feng Xia: Dynamic Voltage Scaling with Asynchronous Period Adjustment for Embedded Controllers. Dynamics of Continuous, Discrete and Impulsive Systems - Series B: Applications and Algorithms, Special Issue on ICSCA'06, Watam Press (2006) 514-519
5. Mattijs Kersten: Dynamic Voltage Scaling and its Scheduling Implications, Research Seimar on Energy Awareness, University of Helsinki (2005)
6. Y. Zhu and F. Mueller: Feedback EDF Scheduling Exploiting Dynamic Voltage Scaling, Proc. IEEE Real-Time and Embedded Technology and Applications Symposium (2004) 84-93
7. H. S. Lee and B. K. Kim: Dynamic Voltage Scaling for Digital Control System Implementation, Real-Time Systems 29 (2005) 263-280
8. H. A. Wang, H. Jin, H. Wang, and G. Z. Dai: Energy-Aware Optimization Design of Digital Control Systems with Evolution Strategy, Dynamics of Continuous, Discrete and Impulsive Systems - Series B: Applications and Algorithms, Special Issue on ICSCA'06, Watam Press (2006) 1893-1898
9. Hong Jin, Danli Wang, Hong-an Wang, and Hui Wang: Energy-aware scheduling design of control tasks, The Int. Conf. on Parallel and Distributed Processing Techniques and Applications, Las Vegas, Nevada, USA (2005)
10. Woo-Cheol Kwon and Taewhan Kim: Optimal Voltage Allocation Techniques for Dynamically Variable Voltage Processors, ACM Transactions on Embedded Computing Systems 4:1 (2005) 211-230
11. A. Sinha and A. P. Chandrakasan: Energy efficient real-time scheduling, Proc. IEEE/ACM ICCAD, San Jose, California, USA (2001) 458-463
12. A. Cervin, J. Eker, B. Bernhardsson, K.-E. Årzén: Feedback-Feedforward Scheduling of Control Tasks, Real-Time Systems 23:1 (2002) 25-53
13. C. M. Krishna and Yann-Hang Lee: Voltage-Clock-Scaling Adaptive Scheduling Techniques for Low Power in Hard Real-Time Systems, IEEE Trans. on Computers 52:12 (2003) 1586-1593

Author Index

Lecture Notes in Computer Science

For information about Vols. 1–4075

please contact your bookseller or Springer

Vol. 4129: D. McGookin, S. Brewster (Eds.), Haptic and Audio Interaction Design. XII, 167 pages. 2006.

Vol. 4128: W.E. Nagel, W.V. Walter, W. Lehner (Eds.), Euro-Par 2006 Parallel Processing. XXXIII, 1221 pages. 2006.

Vol. 4127: E. Damiani, P. Liu (Eds.), Data and Applications Security XX. X, 319 pages. 2006.

Vol. 4126: P. Barahona, F. Bry, E. Franconi, N. Henze, U. Sattler, Reasoning Web. X, 269 pages. 2006.

Vol. 4124: H. de Meer, J.P. G. Sterbenz (Eds.), Self-Organizing Systems. XIV, 261 pages. 2006.

Vol. 4121: A. Biere, C.P. Gomes (Eds.), Theory and Applications of Satisfiability Testing - SAT 2006. XII, 438 pages. 2006.

Vol. 4119: C. Dony, J.L. Knudsen, A. Romanovsky, A. Tripathi (Eds.), Advanced Topics in Exception Handling Components. X, 302 pages. 2006.

Vol. 4117: C. Dwork (Ed.), Advances in Cryptology - CRYPTO 2006. XIII, 621 pages. 2006.

Vol. 4116: R. De Prisco, M. Yung (Eds.), Security and Cryptography for Networks. XI, 366 pages. 2006.

Vol. 4115: D.-S. Huang, K. Li, G.W. Irwin (Eds.), Computational Intelligence and Bioinformatics, Part III. XXI, 803 pages. 2006. (Sublibrary LNBI).

Vol. 4114: D.-S. Huang, K. Li, G.W. Irwin (Eds.), Computational Intelligence, Part II. XXVII, 1337 pages. 2006. (Sublibrary LNAI).

Vol. 4113: D.-S. Huang, K. Li, G.W. Irwin (Eds.), Intelligent Computing, Part I. XXVII, 1331 pages. 2006.

Vol. 4112: D.Z. Chen, D. T. Lee (Eds.), Computing and Combinatorics. XIV, 528 pages. 2006.

Vol. 4111: F.S. de Boer, M.M. Bonsangue, S. Graf, W.-P. de Roever (Eds.), Formal Methods for Components and Objects. VIII, 447 pages. 2006.

Vol. 4110: J. Díaz, K. Jansen, J.D.P. Rolim, U. Zwick (Eds.), Approximation, Randomization, and Combinatorial Optimization. XII, 522 pages. 2006.

Vol. 4109: D.-Y. Yeung, J.T. Kwok, A. Fred, F. Roli, D. de Ridder (Eds.), Structural, Syntactic, and Statistical Pattern Recognition. XXI, 939 pages. 2006.

Vol. 4108: J.M. Borwein, W.M. Farmer (Eds.), Mathematical Knowledge Management. VIII, 295 pages. 2006. (Sublibrary LNAI).

Vol. 4106: T.R. Roth-Berghofer, M.H. Göker, H. A. Güvenir (Eds.), Advances in Case-Based Reasoning. XIV, 566 pages. 2006. (Sublibrary LNAI).

Vol. 4105: B. Gunsel, A.K. Jain, A. M. Tekalp, B. Sankur (Eds.), Multimedia, Content Representation, Classification and Security. XIX, 804 pages. 2006.

Vol. 4104: T. Kunz, S.S. Ravi (Eds.), Ad-Hoc, Mobile, and Wireless Networks. XII, 474 pages. 2006.

Vol. 4103: J. Eder, S. Dustdar (Eds.), Business Process Management Workshops. XI, 508 pages. 2006.

Vol. 4102: S. Dustdar, J.L. Fiadeiro, A. Sheth (Eds.), Business Process Management. XV, 486 pages. 2006.

Vol. 4099: Q. Yang, G. Webb (Eds.), PRICAI 2006: Trends in Artificial Intelligence. XXVIII, 1263 pages. 2006. (Sublibrary LNAI).

Vol. 4098: F. Pfenning (Ed.), Term Rewriting and Applications. XIII, 415 pages. 2006.

Vol. 4097: X. Zhou, O. Sokolsky, L. Yan, E.-S. Jung, Z. Shao, Y. Mu, D.C. Lee, D. Kim, Y.-S. Jeong, C.-Z. Xu (Eds.), Emerging Directions in Embedded and Ubiquitous Computing. XXVII, 1034 pages. 2006.

Vol. 4096: E. Sha, S.-K. Han, C.-Z. Xu, M.H. Kim, L.T. Yang, B. Xiao (Eds.), Embedded and Ubiquitous Computing. XXIV, 1170 pages. 2006.

Vol. 4095: S. Nolfi, G. Baldassare, R. Calabretta, D. Marocco, D. Parisi, J.C. T. Hallam, O. Miglino, J.-A. Meyer (Eds.), From Animals to Animats 9. XV, 869 pages. 2006. (Sublibrary LNAI).

Vol. 4094: O. H. Ibarra, H.-C. Yen (Eds.), Implementation and Application of Automata. XIII, 291 pages. 2006.

Vol. 4093: X. Li, O.R. Zaïane, Z. Li (Eds.), Advanced Data Mining and Applications. XXI, 1110 pages. 2006. (Sublibrary LNAI).

Vol. 4092: J. Lang, F. Lin, J. Wang (Eds.), Knowledge Science, Engineering and Management. XV, 664 pages. 2006. (Sublibrary LNAI).

Vol. 4091: G.-Z. Yang, T. Jiang, D. Shen, L. Gu, J. Yang (Eds.), Medical Imaging and Augmented Reality. XIII, 399 pages. 2006.

Vol. 4090: S. Spaccapietra, K. Aberer, P. Cudré-Mauroux (Eds.), Journal on Data Semantics VI. XI, 211 pages. 2006.

Vol. 4089: W. Löwe, M. Südholt (Eds.), Software Composition. X, 339 pages. 2006.

Vol. 4088: Z.-Z. Shi, R. Sadananda (Eds.), Agent Computing and Multi-Agent Systems. XVII, 827 pages. 2006. (Sublibrary LNAI).

Vol. 4087: F. Schwenker, S. Marinai (Eds.), Artificial Neural Networks in Pattern Recognition. IX, 299 pages. 2006. (Sublibrary LNAI).

Vol. 4085: J. Misra, T. Nipkow, E. Sekerinski (Eds.), FM 2006: Formal Methods. XV, 620 pages. 2006.

Vol. 4084: M.A. Wimmer, H.J. Scholl, Å. Grönlund, K.V. Andersen (Eds.), Electronic Government. XV, 353 pages. 2006.

Vol. 4083: S. Fischer-Hübner, S. Furnell, C. Lambrinoudakis (Eds.), Trust and Privacy in Digital Business. XIII, 243 pages. 2006.

Vol. 4082: K. Bauknecht, B. Pröll, H. Werthner (Eds.), E-Commerce and Web Technologies. XIII, 243 pages. 2006.

Vol. 4081: A. M. Tjoa, J. Trujillo (Eds.), Data Warehousing and Knowledge Discovery. XVII, 578 pages. 2006.

Vol. 4080: S. Bressan, J. Küng, R. Wagner (Eds.), Database and Expert Systems Applications. XXI, 959 pages. 2006.

Vol. 4079: S. Etalle, M. Truszczyński (Eds.), Logic Programming. XIV, 474 pages. 2006.

Vol. 4077: M.-S. Kim, K. Shimada (Eds.), Geometric Modeling and Processing - GMP 2006. XVI, 696 pages. 2006.

Vol. 4076: F. Hess, S. Pauli, M. Pohst (Eds.), Algorithmic Number Theory. X, 599 pages. 2006.